Our Dramatic Heritage

VOLUME 3

Our Dramatic Heritage

VOLUME 3: *The Eighteenth Century*

Edited by Philip G. Hill

Rutherford ● Madison ● Teaneck
Fairleigh Dickinson University Press
London and Toronto: Associated University Presses

Associated University Presses
440 Forsgate Drive
Cranbury, NJ 08512

Associated University Presses
25 Sicilian Avenue
London WC1A 2QH, England

Associated University Presses
2133 Royal Windsor Drive
Unit 1
Mississauga, Ontario
Canada L5J 1K5

The paper used in this publication meets the requirements
of the American National Standard for Permanence of Paper
for Printed Library Materials Z39.48-1984.

Library of Congress Cataloging-in-Publication Data
(Revised for volume 3)

Our dramatic heritage.

Contents: v. 1. Classical drama and the early
Renaissance—v. 2. The Golden Age—v. 3. The
eighteenth century.
1. European drama.   I. Hill, Philip G. (Philip
George), 1934–   .
PN6111.087   1983   808.82   81-65294
ISBN 0-8386-3106-1 (v. 1)
ISBN 0-8386-3107-X (v. 2)
ISBN 0-8386-3266-1 (v. 3)

Printed in the United States of America

Contents

Acknowledgments

ACKNOWLEDGMENT is made to copyright holders and publishers for permission to reprint the following:

Jean de France by Ludvig Holberg. Translated by Gerald S. Argetsinger. Copyright © 1983 by Gerald S. Argetsinger. All performance rights are subject to the payment of a royalty. For permission and rights contact the translator: Gerald S. Argetsinger, 91 Saddlehorn Dr., Rochester, N.Y. 14626.

The Mistress of the Inn by Carlo Goldoni and the Preface, "The Author to the Reader." Translated by Stanley Vincent Longman. Copyright © 1984. Reprinted by permission of the translator.

Figaro's Marriage by Beaumarchais. Translated by Jacques Barzun. Copyright © 1961 by Jacques Barzun. Reprinted from *Phaedra and Figaro* by permission of Farrar, Straus and Giroux, Inc. Distributed outside the United States of America, Philippines, and Dominion of Canada by permission of the translator. Published with Robert Lowell's translation of Racine's *Phaedra* by Farrar, Straus and Cudahy (New York, 1961); reprinted separately in Eric Bentley's *The Classic Theatre* vol. 4 (New York: Doubleday, 1962).

Introduction

The eighteenth century was an age of transition in Europe. The emerging middle class, rising scientific rationalism, and waning post-Renaissance exuberance were reflected in the theater by an age of great acting, but of generally uninspired playwriting. Hence, this is a volume of exceptions, a group of plays that illustrate the few moments of true brilliance in an art form that otherwise seemed nearly moribund for almost one hundred years.

The first exception is a technical one: the English period known as the Restoration is generally considered to comprise the last forty years of the seventeenth century, but since its finest play appeared in 1700, that play can still technically be included in a volume entitled *The Eighteenth Century*. The Restoration was a truly rich theatrical period, but its abrupt decline after *The Way of the World* marked the beginning of a long period of mediocre playwriting in England.

Elsewhere in Europe, much of eighteenth-century playwriting was imitative of the works of the masters of earlier centuries, but occasional outstanding plays more than justify the time one spends looking for them. No longer is it convenient to group plays according to the country in which they were written, for increasingly the theater in one European country influenced that in another so quickly that national identity became only a secondary influence on many playwrights. The works in this volume are arranged chronologically, allowing the reader to range freely across Europe as dramatic inventiveness peaked now here, now there.

By the end of the eighteenth century, revolution was in the air—literal, violent revolution in France, as evidenced in the last play in this volume, and literary revolution elsewhere, as evidenced by the rise of romanticism, which is explored in the next volume. Thus, the eighteenth century, an age of transition, is also an age of plays that look both backward and forward—backward to Golden Age excellence that could not be fully recaptured, and forward to a series of "revolutions" in playwriting that is still in progress late in the twentieth century. The eighteenth-century plays collected here are all the more exciting for being atypical: though they may be few in number, they are theatrical masterpieces that redeem the general vapidity of their century.

Our Dramatic Heritage

VOLUME 3

The Way of the World

William Congreve

Following the great "Golden Ages" of dramatic achievement in several European countries, there was a period of cross-fertilization, a period in which the high achievements in England, Spain, and France were emulated with greater or lesser degrees of success in other countries. Perhaps it is this attempt at cultural export that most characterizes the European drama in the late seventeenth and the eighteenth centuries, for everywhere it seemed that the theatrical grass looked greener elsewhere, and that native playwrights felt a compulsion to copy what had worked so well abroad. When the monarchy was restored in England in 1660, and Charles II and his court returned from France, one of the king's first official acts was to reopen the theaters closed by decree of the Puritans since 1642. The plays that were written and produced in London during this "Restoration" period owed something to the greatness of Shakespeare and the other Elizabethans and Jacobeans, but they represented in far greater degree an attempt to transplant to British soil the theater just then flourishing in Paris, especially the comic brilliance of Molière. Restoration comedy is singularly unified stylistically, so that a great many witty, successful plays may conveniently be represented by a single example; most people would agree that there is no better example than the play that turned out to be the last high achievement of its type, William Congreve's *The Way of the World*, produced in 1700.

William Congreve was born on January 24, 1670, at Bardsey, near Leeds, Yorkshire. His father held a military commission in Ireland, and Congreve was raised there, attending Kilkenny (the Irish equivalent of Eton) and Trinity college, Dublin. Later, he studied law at the Middle Temple, London, but showed neither aptitude nor interest in that area. Even before abandoning his legal studies, he began to publish some poetry, and he quickly gained the friendship of the leading literary figures in London. In the early 1690s he wrote his first play, *The Old Bachelor*, which, after some revision by Thomas Southerne and John Dryden, opened at the Drury Lane theater in March 1693, with Thomas Betterton and Mrs. Bracegirdle heading the cast. It was exceptionally successful, and was followed within the year by *The Double-Dealer*. In 1695, Betterton opened a new theater company, choosing as his first production Congreve's *Love for Love*, a play that was in many ways his most successful; Congreve committed himself to providing Betterton with one play per year, a commitment he did not keep. In 1697, Betterton produced Congreve's one tragedy, *The Mourning Bride;* it was a great success with the audiences of its day, but is no longer favorably regarded today. In March 1700, came Congreve's masterpiece, *The Way of the World*.

But times were changing in London. The licentious manners of Charles II and his court had given way, after the short reign of James II, to the more sober posture of William and Mary of Orange. The theater that had reflected the looser moral standards of the Restoration period began to fall out of favor, and Jeremy Collier's *A Short View of the Immorality and Profaneness of the English Stage . . .* , issued in April

1698, had an influence far beyond its merits in encouraging a change in theatergoers' tastes and, consequently, in playwriting. Congreve himself wrote a reply entitled *Amendments of Mr. Collier's False and Imperfect Citations,* but came off second best from the encounter. *The Way of the World* struck many audience members of 1700 as continuing the immorality of the previous decades, and the play was not well received. Perhaps in pique, perhaps in the genuine conviction that the theater was a matter of no great consequence, Congreve never wrote another play. His other literary efforts included poetry, opera libretti, and a translation of Molière's *Monsieur de Pourceaugnac;* and he lived comfortably on government sinecures for nearly three decades. When Voltaire visited England in 1726 and sought out Congreve as the greatest living English playwright, Congreve indicated in some surprise that he preferred to be visited as a gentleman. The gentleman nevertheless was respected as the literary arbiter of his age, and was buried in Westminster Abbey following his death on January 19, 1729, from injuries received in a carriage accident.

The Way of the World is a nearly perfect expression of all that is best in Restoration comedy. Its witty language and its light, piquant spirit are obviously the products of a refined taste and a razor-sharp wit; the sobriquet "comedy of manners" was coined to designate just such a satire of the attitudes and foibles of fashionable society. Practically every line is a well-turned epigram that can be vastly amusing in the theater, but an extremely skillful acting style is required to make this technique work for the entire length of the play. *The Way of the World* has therefore occasionally been regarded as a work more successful in the study than on the stage, but a fairer assessment would be that it can excel on the stage only if actors can be engaged who are genuinely responsive to the period's unusual stylistic demands. There is much of Molière's influence in this style, and much neoclassicism in its application, but ultimately the approach is uniquely that of the Restoration comedy of manners, and nothing else will really do. The witty, elevated language is the key to this style.

The Way of the World shares with many other Restoration comedies the problems of an inordinately complicated plot. The intrigues and counterintrigues of "polite" society are themselves the point, a point which perhaps cannot be expressed through a plot that is simple, but this complexity remains a problem in the theater. Congreve compounds the problem by having all of his principal characters related to each other in ways that are important and must be kept straight, and he relies on a means of exposition that is surely the least satisfactory for most purposes: in the first act, no fewer than seven characters who do not appear are talked about at length, and what the audience learns from this conversation is vital to understanding the rest of the play. And to make matters worse, two more characters who do appear later in this act are also discussed before their entrances. The conversation is witty and the descriptive commentary is tellingly accurate, but there is a tremendous burden on the actors in this act to impress upon the audience all the information that they will need to retain. If one gets straight everything that one must remember from the first act, the plot of the rest of the play is not too difficult to follow.

Characterization in *The Way of the World* is one of the factors that lifts it above the ordinary run of Restoration comedies. The device of naming the characters in such a way as to draw attention to some of their principal qualities is at least as old as Roman drama, but too often character development has stopped at this level. Congreve has resisted the temptation to draw comic caricatures, however, and certainly has not separated his heroes from his villains in the traditional ways. Mirabell and Millamant are as attractive a pair of young lovers as exist anywhere in dramatic literature, but each is made humanly believable by both strengths and weaknesses in his or her character. Mirabell is honest enough to be a good match for Millamant and to have been trusted by Mrs. Fainall with all her property, but it is also true that he arranged the marriage between Mr. and Mrs. Fainall to cover up her feared pregnancy, with the cynical excuse that "a better man ought not to have been sacrificed to the occasion." Millamant is a charming and intelligent minx, but she is also an outrageous flirt who "love[s] to give pain." On the other hand, Fainall and Marwood, the villains of the piece, are given adequate motivations for their Machiavellian manipulations, and even such outright clowns as Lady Wishfort, Witwoud, and Sir Wilfull have sympathetic sides to their characters that prevent them from being simply fools. The truth is that one would need to search widely throughout comic dramatic literature to find so full a cast of well-developed, three-dimensional characters. They are Congreve's glory and the actors' delight.

The attitudes toward society expressed in *The Way of the World* have created a great deal of controversy. A cursory view has convinced some readers or audience members that Congreve condones sexual looseness and slack morals—the same view expressed by Jeremy Collier nearly three hundred years ago. Upon closer examination, however, it becomes clear that Congreve's view is not so simple as this. He holds much of the sexual behavior of his society up for ridicule and satire, but this is not to say that he necessarily condemns it either, as some have argued. Rather, it would seem that Congreve seeks to show his audience what is the way of the world—that there are both venal and well-intentioned people in it, and that their sexual conduct as well as their other dealings with their fellow human beings combine both admirable and not-so-admirable qualities. A consideration of moral, ethical, and practical questions is invited, but no easy, pat, moralistic answers are provided. Mirabell's behavior, for example, is neither condemned nor applauded, though it is certainly better than Fainall's. The acts of both of them are the way of the world, and the wise onlooker comes to expect both kinds. Both the philosophy and the wit of the play are epitomized in its most famous scene in which Mirabell and Millamant strike a bargain about acceptable behavior after their marriage. Their attitudes are humorous, but intensely practical, as they discuss the trivial matters that do in fact lead to the break-up of some marriages and the happy adjustment of others. Furthermore, underneath this witty practicality one senses that Millamant and Mirabell genuinely love each other, and that they are two people who can probably share a very successful marriage. They are mature and well-balanced, with a humorist's relaxed view of themselves and a good understanding of the way of the world. Congreve's several references to filthy playhouses, lewd and immoral plays, and the like are humorous references to the Collier controversy, for it is clear that even in a matter that touched him so closely Congreve had a sense of humor and could laugh at his own problems as well as those of society. This clear-eyed acceptance of the way the world works is the thematic heart of Congreve's play.

The Way of the World is widely acknowledged as the supreme example of Restoration comedy, and Congreve is generally ranked among the two or three finest writers of comedy in the English theater. The breadth of view and the eclecticism of style of Molière or Shakespeare were beyond Congreve; perhaps he did not take the writing of stage comedy seriously enough. Within the relatively narrow spectrum of the comedy of manners, however, Congreve has rarely been equaled and never excelled.

The Way of the World

Characters

Fainall, in love with Mrs. Marwood
Mirabell, in love with Mrs. Millamant
Witwoud, ⎱ *followers of Mrs. Millamant*
Petulant, ⎰
Sir Wilfull Witwoud, half-brother to
  Witwoud, and nephew to Lady Wishfort
Waitwell, servant to Mirabell

Lady Wishfort, enemy to Mirabell, for
  having falsely pretended love to her
Mrs. Millamant, a fine lady, niece to Lady
  Wishfort, and loves Mirabell
Mrs. Marwood, friend to Mr. Fainall, and
  likes Mirabell
Mrs. Fainall, daughter to Lady Wishfort,
  and wife to Fainall, formerly friend to
  Mirabell
Foible, woman to Lady Wishfort
Mincing, woman to Mrs. Millamant
Betty, waiting-maid at a Chocolate-house
Peg, maid to Lady Wishfort

Coachmen, Dancers, Footmen, and
  Attendants

SCENE: *London.*

Act 1

Scene 1

A chocolate-house. MIRABELL *and* FAINALL,
  rising from cards, BETTY *waiting.*
MIRABELL. You are a fortunate man,
  Mr. Fainall!
FAINALL. Have we done?
MIRABELL. What you please: I'll play on
  to entertain you.

FAINALL. No, I'll give you your revenge
  another time, when you are not so
  indifferent; you are thinking of
  something else now, and play too
  negligently; the coldness of a losing
  gamester lessens the pleasure of the
  winner. I'd no more play with a man
  that slighted his ill fortune than I'd
  make love to a woman who under-
  valued the loss of her reputation.
MIRABELL. You have a taste extremely
  delicate, and are for refining on your
  pleasures.
FAINALL. Prithee, why so reserved?
  Something has put you out of
  humour.
MIRABELL. Not at all: I happen to be
  grave to day, and you are gay; that's
  all.
FAINALL. Confess, Millamant and you
  quarrelled last night after I left you;
  my fair cousin has some humours
  that would tempt the patience of a
  Stoic. What, some coxcomb came in,
  and was well received by her, while
  you were by?
MIRABELL. Witwoud and Petulant; and
  what was worse, her aunt, your wife's
  mother, my evil genius: or to sum up
  all in her own name, my old Lady
  Wishfort came in.
FAINALL. O there it is then! She has a
  lasting passion for you, and with reason.—What, then my wife was there?
MIRABELL. Yes, and Mrs. Marwood, and
  three or four more, whom I never
  saw before. Seeing me, they all put
  on their grave faces, whispered one
  another; then complained aloud of
  the vapours, and after fell into a
  profound silence.
FAINALL. They had a mind to be rid of
  you.
MIRABELL. For which reason I resolved
  not to stir. At last the good old lady

broke through her painful taciturnity with an invective against long visits. I would not have understood her, but Millamant joining in the argument, I rose, and, with a constrained smile, told her, I thought nothing was so easy as to know when a visit began to be troublesome. She reddened, and I withdrew, without expecting her reply.

FAINALL. You were to blame to resent what she spoke only in compliance with her aunt.

MIRABELL. She is more mistress of herself than to be under the necessity of such a resignation.

FAINALL. What! though half her fortune depends upon her marrying with my lady's approbation?

MIRABELL. I was then in such a humour, that I should have been better pleased if she had been less discreet.

FAINALL. Now, I remember, I wonder not they were weary of you; last night was one of their cabal nights; they have 'em three times a-week, and meet by turns at one another's apartments, where they come together like the coroner's inquest, to sit upon the murdered reputations of the week. You and I are excluded; and it was once proposed that all the male sex should be excepted; but somebody moved that, to avoid scandal, there might be one man of the community; upon which motion Witwoud and Petulant were enrolled members.

MIRABELL. And who may have been the foundress of this sect? My Lady Wishfort, I warrant, who publishes her detestation of mankind; and full of the vigour of fifty-five, declares for a friend and ratafia;[1] and let posterity shift for itself, she'll breed no more.

FAINALL. The discovery of your sham addresses to her, to conceal your love to her niece, has provoked this separation; had you dissembled better, things might have continued in the state of nature.

MIRABELL. I did as much as man could, with any reasonable conscience; I proceeded to the very last act of flattery with her, and was guilty of a song in her commendation. Nay, I got a friend to put her into a lampoon, and compliment her with the imputation of an affair with a young fellow, which I carried so far, that I told her the malicious town took notice that she was grown fat of a sudden; and when she lay in of a dropsy, persuaded her she was reported to be in labour. The devil's in't, if an old woman is to be flattered further, unless a man should endeavour downright personally to debauch her; and that my virtue forbade me. But for the discovery of this amour I am indebted to your friend, or your wife's friend, Mrs. Marwood.

FAINALL. What should provoke her to be your enemy, unless she has made you advances which you have slighted? Women do not easily forgive omissions of that nature.

MIRABELL. She was always civil to me till of late.—I confess I am not one of those coxcombs who are apt to interpret a woman's good manners to her prejudice, and think that she who does not refuse 'em everything, can refuse 'em nothing.

FAINALL. You are a gallant man, Mirabell; and though you may have cruelty enough not to satisfy a lady's longing, you have too much generosity not to be tender of her honour. Yet you speak with an indifference which seems to be affected, and confesses you are conscious of a negligence.

MIRABELL. You pursue the argument with a distrust that seems to be unaffected, and confesses you are conscious of a concern for which the lady is more indebted to you than is your wife.

FAINALL. Fy, fy, friend! if you grow censorious I must leave you.—I'll look upon the gamesters in the next room.

MIRABELL. Who are they?

FAINALL. Petulant and Witwoud.—[*To* BETTY.] Bring me some chocolate. [*Exit.*]

MIRABELL. Betty, what says your clock?

BETTY. Turned of the last canonical hour, sir. [*Exit.*]

MIRABELL. How pertinently the jade an-

swers me!—[*Looking on his watch.*]—
Ha! almost one o'clock!—O, y'are
come! [*Enter* FOOTMAN.] Well, is the
grand affair over? You have been
something tedious.

FOOTMAN. Sir, there's such coupling at
Pancras,[2] that they stand behind one
another, as 'twere in a country dance.
Ours was the last couple to lead up;
and no hopes appearing of despatch;
besides, the parson growing hoarse,
we were afraid his lungs would have
failed before it came to our turn; so
we drove round to Duke's Place; and
there they were riveted in a trice.

MIRABELL. So, so, you are sure they are
married.

FOOTMAN. Married and bedded, sir; I
am witness.

MIRABELL. Have you the certificate?

FOOTMAN. Here it is, sir.

MIRABELL. Has the tailor brought Waitwell's clothes home, and the new
liveries?

FOOTMAN. Yes, sir.

MIRABELL. That's well. Do you go home
again, d'ye hear, and adjourn the
consummation till further orders.
Bid Waitwell shake his ears, and
Dame Partlet rustle up her feathers,
and meet me at one o'clock by Rosa-
mond's Pond, that I may see her
before she returns to her lady; and
as you tender your ears be secret.
[*Exit* FOOTMAN.]

Scene 2

Enter FAINALL *and* BETTY.

FAINALL. Joy of your success, Mirabell;
you look pleased.

MIRABELL. Ay; I have been engaged in a
matter of some sort of mirth, which
is not yet ripe for discovery. I am
glad this is not a cabal night. I wonder, Fainall, that you who are
married, and of consequence should
be discreet, will suffer your wife to
be of such a party.

FAINALL. Faith, I am not jealous. Besides, most who are engaged are
women and relations; and for the
men, they are of a kind too contemptible to give scandal.

MIRABELL. I am of another opinion.

The greater the coxcomb, always the
more the scandal: for a woman, who
is not a fool, can have but one reason
for associating with a man who is
one.

FAINALL. Are you jealous as often as you
see Witwoud entertained by Millamant?

MIRABELL. Of her understanding I am,
if not of her person.

FAINALL. You do her wrong; for, to give
her her due, she has wit.

MIRABELL. She has beauty enough to
make any man think so; and com-
plaiance enough not to contradict
him who shall tell her so.

FAINALL. For a passionate lover, methinks you are a man somewhat too
discerning in the failings of your mistress.

MIRABELL. And for a discerning man,
somewhat too passionate a lover; for
I like her with all her faults; nay, like
her for her faults. Her follies are so
natural, or so artful, that they become her; and those affectations
which in another woman would be
odious, serve but to make her more
agreeable. I'll tell thee, Fainall, she
once used me with that insolence,
that in revenge I took her to pieces;
sifted her, and separated her failings;
I studied 'em, and got 'em by rote.
The catalogue was so large, that I was
not without hopes one day or other
to hate her heartily: to which end I
so used myself to think of 'em, that at
length, contrary to my design and
expectation, they gave me every hour
less and less disturbance; till in a few
days it became habitual to me to
remember 'em without being dis-
pleased. They are now grown as
familiar to me as my own frailties;
and in all probability, in a little time
longer, I shall like 'em as well.

FAINALL. Marry her, marry her! be half
as well acquainted with her charms,
as you are with her defects, and my
life on't, you are your own man
again.

MIRABELL. Say you so?

FAINALL. Ay, ay, I have experience: I
have a wife, and so forth. [*Enter* MES-
SENGER.]

MESSENGER. Is one Squire Witwoud

here?

BETTY. Yes, what's your business?

MESSENGER. I have a letter for him, from his brother Sir Wilfull, which I am charged to deliver into his own hands.

BETTY. He's in the next room, friend— that way. [*Exit* MESSENGER.]

MIRABELL. What, is the chief of that noble family in town, Sir Wilful Witwoud?

FAINALL. He is expected to-day. Do you know him?

MIRABELL. I have seen him. He promises to be an extraordinary person; I think you have the honour to be related to him.

FAINALL. Yes; he is half brother to this Witwoud by a former wife, who was sister to my Lady Wishfort, my wife's mother. If you marry Millamant, you must call cousins too.

MIRABELL. I had rather be his relation than his acquaintance.

FAINALL. He comes to town in order to equip himself for travel.

MIRABELL. For travel! why, the man that I mean is above forty.

FAINALL. No matter for that; 'tis for the honour of England, that all Europe should know we have blockheads of all ages.

MIRABELL. I wonder there is not an act of parliament to save the credit of the nation, and prohibit the exportation of fools.

FAINALL. By no means; 'tis better as 'tis. 'Tis better to trade with a little loss, than to be quite eaten up with being overstocked.

MIRABELL. Pray, are the follies of this knight-errant, and those of the squire his brother, anything related?

FAINALL. Not at all: Witwoud grows by the knight, like a medlar[3] grafted on a crab.[4] One will melt in your mouth, and t'other set your teeth on edge; one is all pulp, and the other all core.

MIRABELL. So one will be rotten before he be ripe, and the other will be rotten without ever being ripe at all.

FAINALL. Sir Wilfull is an odd mixture of bashfulness and obstinacy.—But when he's drunk he's as loving as the monster in *The Tempest,* and much after the same manner. To give

t'other his due, he has something of good-nature, and does not always want wit.

MIRABELL. Not always: but as often as his memory fails him, and his commonplace of comparisons.[5] He is a fool with a good memory, and some few scraps of other folks' wit. He is one whose conversation can never be approved, yet it is now and then to be endured. He has indeed one good quality, he is not exceptious; for he so passionately affects the reputation of understanding raillery, that he will construe an affront into a jest; and call downright rudeness and ill language, satire and fire.

FAINALL. If you have a mind to finish his picture, you have an opportunity to do it at full length. Behold the original! [*Enter* WITWOUD.]

WITWOUD. Afford me your compassion, my dears! pity me, Fainall! Mirabell, pity me!

MIRABELL. I do from my soul.

FAINALL. Why, what's the matter.

WITWOUD. No letters for me, Betty?

BETTY. Did not a messenger bring you one but now, sir?

WITWOUD. Ay, but no other?

BETTY. No, sir.

WITWOUD. That's hard, that's very hard.—A messenger! a mule, a beast of burden! he has brought me a letter from the fool my brother, as heavy as a panegyric in a funeral sermon, or a copy of commendatory verses from one poet to another: and what's worse, 'tis as sure a forerunner of the author, as an epistle dedicatory.

MIRABELL. A fool, and your brother, Witwoud!

WITWOUD. Ay, ay, my half brother. My half brother he is, no nearer upon honour.

MIRABELL. Then 'tis possible he may be but half a fool.

WITWOUD. Good, good, Mirabell, *le drôle!* good, good; hang him. don't let's talk of him.—Fainall, how does your lady? Gad, I say anything in the world to get this fellow out of my head. I beg pardon that I should ask a man of pleasure, and the town, a question at once so foreign and domestic. But I talk like an old maid at a marriage; I don't know what I say: but she's the best woman in the world.

FAINALL. 'Tis well you don't know what you say, or else your commendation would go near to make me either vain or jealous.

WITWOUD. No man in town lives well with a wife but Fainall.—Your judgment, Mirabell.

MIRABELL. You had better step and ask his wife, if you would be credibly informed.

WITWOUD. Mirabell?

MIRABELL. Ay.

WITWOUD. My dear, I ask ten thousand pardons;—gad, I have forgot what I was going to say to you!

MIRABELL. I thank you heartily, heartily.

WITWOUD. No, but prithee excuse me:—my memory is such a memory.

MIRABELL. Have a care of such apologies, Witwoud; for I never knew a fool but he affected to complain, either of the spleen or his memory.

FAINALL. What have you done with Petulant?

WITWOUD. He's reckoning his money—my money it was.—I have no luck today.

FAINALL. You may allow him to win of you at play: for you are sure to be too hard for him at repartee; since you monopolise the wit that is between you, the fortune must be his of course.

MIRABELL. I don't find that Petulant confesses the superiority of wit to be your talent, Witwoud.

WITWOUD. Come, come, you are malicious now, and would breed debates.—Petulant's my friend, and a very honest fellow, and a very pretty fellow, and has a smattering—faith and troth, a pretty deal of an odd sort of a small wit: nay, I'll do him justice. I'm his friend, I won't wrong him neither.—And if he had any judgment in the world, he would not be altogether contemptible. Come, come, don't detract from the merits of my friend.

FAINALL. You don't take your friend to be over-nicely bred?

WITWOUD. No, no, hang him, the rogue has no manners at all, that I must own:—no more breeding than a bum-bailiff, that I grant you:—'tis pity, faith; the fellow has fire and life.

MIRABELL. What, courage?

WITWOUD. Hum, faith I don't know as to that, I can't say as to that—Yes, faith, in a controversy, he'll contradict anybody.

MIRABELL. Though 'twere a man whom he feared, or a woman whom he loved.

WITWOUD. Well, well, he does not always think before he speaks;—we have all our failings: you are too hard upon him, you are, faith. Let me excuse him—I can defend most of his faults, except one or two: one he has, that's the truth on't; if he were my brother, I could not acquit him:—that, indeed, I could wish were otherwise.

MIRABELL. Ay, marry, what's that, Witwoud?

WITWOUD. O pardon me!—expose the infirmities of my friend!—No, my dear, excuse me there.

FAINALL. What, I warrant he's unsincere, or 'tis some such trifle.

WITWOUD. No, no; what if he be? 'tis no matter for that, his wit will excuse that: a wit should no more be sincere, than a woman constant; one argues a decay of parts, as t'other of beauty.

MIRABELL. Maybe you think him too positive?

WITWOUD. No, no, his being positive is an incentive to argument, and keeps up conversation.

FAINALL. Too illiterate?

WITWOUD. That! that's his happiness:—his want of learning gives him the more opportunities to show his natural parts.

MIRABELL. He wants words?

WITWOUD. Ay: but I like him for that now; for his want of words gives me the pleasure very often to explain his meaning.

FAINALL. He's impudent?

WITWOUD. No, that's not it.

MIRABELL. Vain?

WITWOUD. No.

MIRABELL. What! he speaks unseasonable truths sometimes, because he has not wit enough to invent an evasion?

WITWOUD. Truths! ha! ha! no, no; since you will have it,—I mean, he never speaks truth at all,—that's all. He will lie like a chambermaid, or a woman of quality's porter. Now that is a fault. [*Enter* COACHMAN.]

COACHMAN. Is Master Petulant here, mistress?

BETTY. Yes.

COACHMAN. Three gentlewomen in a coach would speak with him.

FAINALL. O brave Petulant! three!

BETTY. I'll tell him.

COACHMAN. You must bring two dishes of chocolate and a glass of cinnamon water. [*Exeunt* BETTY *and* COACHMAN.]

WITWOUD. That should be for two fasting strumpets, and a bawd troubled with the wind. Now you may know what the three are.

MIRABELL. You are very free with your friend's acquaintance.

WITWOUD. Ay, ay, friendship without freedom is as dull as love without enjoyment, or wine without toasting. But to tell you a secret, these are trulls whom he allows coach-hire, and something more, by the week, to call on him once a day at public places.

MIRABELL. How!

WITWOUD. You shall see he won't go to 'em, because there's no more company here to take notice of him.— Why this is nothing to what he used to do:—before he found out this way, I have known him call for himself.

FAINALL. Call for himself! what dost thou mean?

WITWOUD. Mean! why he would slip you out of this chocolate-house, just when you had been talking to him— as soon as your back was turned— whip he was gone!—then trip to his lodging, clap on a hood and scarf, and a mask, slap into a hackney-coach, and drive hither to the door again in a trice, where he would send in for himself; that I mean, call for himself, wait for himself; nay, and what's more, not finding himself, sometimes leave a letter for himself.

MIRABELL. I confess this is something extraordinary.—I believe he waits for himself now, he is so long a-coming: Oh! I ask his pardon. [*Enter* PETU-

LANT *and* BETTY.]

BETTY. Sir, the coach stays. [*Exit.*]

PETULANT. Well, well;—I come.—'Sbud, a man had as good be a professed midwife, as a professed whoremaster, at this rate! to be knocked up and raised at all hours, and in all places. Pox on 'em, I won't come!—D'ye hear, tell 'em I won't come:—let 'em snivel and cry their hearts out.

FAINALL. You are very cruel, Petulant.

PETULANT. All's one, let it pass:—I have a humour to be cruel.

MIRABELL. I hope they are not persons of condition that you use at this rate.

PETULANT. Condition! condition's a dried fig, if I am not in humour!— By this hand, if they were your—a— a—your what d'ye-call-'ems themselves, they must wait or rub off, if I want appetite.

MIRABELL. What d'ye-call-'ems! what are they, Witwoud?

WITWOUD. Empresses,[6] my dear:—by your what-d'ye-call-'ems he means sultana queens.[6]

PETULANT. Ay, Roxolanas.[6]

MIRABELL. Cry you mercy!

FAINALL. Witwoud says they are—

PETULANT. What does he say th'are?

WITWOUD. I? fine ladies, I say.

PETULANT. Pass on, Witwoud.— Hark'ee, by this light his relations:— two co-heiresses his cousins, and an old aunt, who loves caterwauling better than a conventicle.

WITWOUD. Ha! ha! ha! I had a mind to see how the rogue would come off.— Ha! ha! ha! gad, I can't be angry with him, if he had said they were my mother and my sisters.

MIRABELL. No!

WITWOUD. No; the rogue's wit and readiness of invention charm me. Dear Petulant. [*Enter* BETTY.]

BETTY. They are gone, sir, in great anger. [*Exit.*]

PETULANT. Enough, let 'em trundle. Anger helps complexion, saves paint.

FAINALL. This continence is all dissembled; this is in order to have something to brag of the next time he makes court to Millamant, and swear he has abandoned the whole sex for her sake.

MIRABELL. Have you not left off your

impudent pretensions there yet? I shall cut your throat some time or other, Petulant, about that business.

PETULANT. Ay, ay, let that pass—there are other throats to be cut.

MIRABELL. Meaning mine, sir?

PETULANT. Not I—I mean nobody—I know nothing:—but there are uncles and nephews in the world—and they may be rivals—what then! all's one for that.

MIRABELL. How! hark'ee, Petulant, come hither:—explain, or I shall call your interpreter.

PETULANT. Explain! I know nothing.—Why, you have an uncle, have you not, lately come to town, and lodges by my Lady Wishfort's?

MIRABELL. True.

PETULANT. Why, that's enough—you and he are not friends; and if he should marry and have a child, you may be disinherited, ha?

MIRABELL. Where hast thou stumbled upon all this truth?

PETULANT. All's one for that; why then say I know someting.

MIRABELL. Come, thou art an honest fellow, Petulant, and shalt make love to my mistress, thou sha't, faith. What hast thou heard of my uncle?

PETULANT. I? nothing I. If throats are to be cut, let swords clash! snug's the word, I shrug and am silent.

MIRABELL. Oh, raillery, raillery! Come, I know thou art in the women's secrets.—What, you're a cabalist; I know you stayed at Millamant's last night, after I went. Was there any mention made of my uncle or me? tell me. If thou hadst but good-nature equal to thy wit, Petulant, Tony Witwoud, who is now thy competitor in fame, would show as dim by thee as a dead whiting's eye by a pearl of orient; he would no more been seen by thee, than Mercury is by the sun. Come, I'm sure thou wo't tell me.

PETULANT. If I do, will you grant me common sense then for the future?

MIRABELL. Faith, I'll do what I can for thee, and I'll pray that Heaven may grant it thee in the meantime.

PETULANT. Well, hark'ee. [MIRABELL and PETULANT talk apart.]

FAINALL. Petulant and you both will find Mirabell as warm a rival as a lover.

WITWOUD. Pshaw! pshaw! that she laughs at Petulant is plain. And for my part, but that it is almost a fashion to admire her, I should—hark'ee—to tell you a secret, but let it go no further—between friends, I shall never break my heart for her.

FAINALL. How!

WITWOUD. She's handsome; but she's a sort of an uncertain woman.

FAINALL. I thought you had died for her.

WITWOUD. Umh—no—

FAINALL. She has wit.

WITWOUD. 'Tis what she will hardly allow anybody else:—now, demme, I should hate that, if she were as handsome as Cleopatra. Mirabell is not so sure of her as he thinks for.

FAINALL. Why do you think so?

WITWOUD. We stayed pretty late there last night, and heard something of an uncle to Mirabell, who is lately come to town—and is between him and the best part of his estate. Mirabell and he are at some distance, as my Lady Wishfort has been told; and you know she hates Mirabell worse than a Quaker hates a parrot, or than a fishmonger hates a hard frost. Whether this uncle has seen Mrs. Millamant or not, I cannot say, but there were items of such a treaty being in embryo; and if it should come to life, poor Mirabell would be in some sort unfortunately fobbed, i'faith.

FAINALL. 'Tis impossible Millamant should hearken to it.

WITWOUD. Faith, my dear, I can't tell; she's a woman, and a kind of humourist.

MIRABELL. And this is the sum of what you could collect last night?

PETULANT. The quintessence. Maybe Witwoud knows more, he staid longer:—besides, they never mind him; they say anything before him.

MIRABELL. I thought you had been the greatest favourite.

PETULANT. Ay, tête-à-tête, but not in public, because I make remarks.

MIRABELL. You do?

PETULANT. Ay, ay; pox, I'm malicious,

man! Now he's soft you know; they are not in awe of him—the fellow's well-bred; he's what you call a what-d'ye-call-'em, a fine gentleman; but he's silly withal.

MIRABELL. I thank you, I know as much as my curiosity requires. Fainall, are you for the Mall?

FAINALL. Ay, I'll take a turn before dinner.

WITWOUD. Ay, we'll walk in the park; the ladies talked of being there.

MIRABELL. I thought you were obliged to watch for your brother Sir Wilfull's arrival.

WITWOUD. No, no; he comes to his aunt's, my lady Wishfort. Pox on him! I shall be troubled with him too; what shall I do with the fool?

PETULANT. Beg him for this estate, that I may beg you afterwards: and so have but one trouble with you both.

WITWOUD. O rare Petulant! thou art as quick as fire in a frosty morning; thou shalt to the Mall with us, and we'll be very severe.

PETULANT. Enough, I'm in a humour to be severe.

MIRABELL. Are you? pray then walk by yourselves: let not us be accessory to your putting the ladies out of countenance with your senseless ribaldry, which you roar out aloud as often as they pass by you; and when you have made a handsome woman blush, then you think you have been severe.

PETULANT. What, what! then let 'em either show their innocence by not understanding what they hear, or else show their discretion by not hearing what they would not be thought to understand.

MIRABELL. But hast not thou then sense enough to know that thou oughtest to be most ashamed thyself, when thou hast put another out of countenance?

PETULANT. Not I, by this hand!—I always take blushing either for a sign of guilt, or ill-breeding.

MIRABELL. I confess you ought to think so. You are in the right, that you may plead the error of your judgment in defence of your practice.
Where modesty's ill-manners, 'tis but fit

That impudence and malice pass for wit. [*Exeunt.*]

Act 2

Scene 1

St. James's Park. Enter MRS. FAINALL *and* MRS. MARWOOD.

MRS. FAINALL. Ay, ay, dear Marwood, if we will be happy, we must find the means in ourselves, and among ourselves. Men are ever in extremes; either doting or averse. While they are lovers, if they have fire and sense, their jealousies are insupportable; and when they cease to love (we ought to think at least) they loath; they look upon us with horror and distaste; they meet us like the ghosts of what we were, and as such, fly from us.

MRS. MARWOOD. True, 'tis an unhappy circumstance of life, that love should ever die before us; and that the man so often should outlive the lover. But say what you will, 'tis better to be left, than never to have been loved. To pass our youth in dull indifference, to refuse the sweets of life because they once must leave us, is as preposterous as to wish to have been born old, because we one day must be old. For my part, my youth may wear and waste, but it shall never rust in my possession.

MRS. FAINALL. Then it seems you dissemble an aversion to mankind, only in compliance to my mother's humour?

MRS. MARWOOD. Certainly. To be free; I have no taste of those insipid dry discourses, with which our sex of force must entertain themselves, apart from men. We may affect endearments to each other, profess eternal friendships, and seem to dote like lovers; but 'tis not in our natures long to persevere. Love will resume his empire in our breasts; and every heart, or soon or late, receive and re-admit him as its lawful tyrant.

MRS. FAINALL. Bless me, how have I been deceived! why you profess a libertine.

MRS. MARWOOD. You see my friendship by my freedom. Come, be sincere, acknowledge that your sentiments agree with mine.

MRS. FAINALL. Never!

MRS. MARWOOD. You hate mankind?

MRS. FAINALL. Heartily, inveterately.

MRS. MARWOOD. Your husband?

MRS. FAINALL. Most transcendently; ay, though I say it, meritoriously.

MRS. MARWOOD. Give me your hand upon it.

MRS. FAINALL. There.

MRS. MARWOOD. I join with you; what I have said has been to try you.

MRS. FAINALL. Is it possible? dost thou hate those vipers, men?

MRS. MARWOOD. I have done hating 'em, and am now come to despise 'em; the next thing I have to do, is eternally to forget 'em.

MRS. FAINALL. There spoke the spirit of an Amazon, a Penthesilea!

MRS. MARWOOD. And yet I am thinking sometimes to carry my aversion further.

MRS. FAINALL. How?

MRS. MARWOOD. Faith, by marrying; if I could but find one that loved me very well, and would be thoroughly sensible of ill usage, I think I should do myself the violence of undergoing the ceremony.

MRS. FAINALL. You would not make him a cuckold?

MRS. MARWOOD. No; but I'd make him believe I did, and that's as bad.

MRS. FAINALL. Why, had not you as good do it?

MRS. MARWOOD. Oh! if he should ever discover it, he would then know the worst, and be out of his pain; but I would have him ever to continue upon the rack of fear and jealousy.

MRS. FAINALL. Ingenious mischief! would thou wert married to Mirabell.

MRS. MARWOOD. Would I were!

MRS. FAINALL. You change colour.

MRS. MARWOOD. Because I hate him.

MRS. FAINALL. So do I; but I can hear him named. But what reason have you to hate him in particular?

MRS. MARWOOD. I never loved him; he is, and always was, insufferably proud.

MRS. FAINALL. By the reason you give for your aversion, one would think it dissembled; for you have laid a fault to his charge, of which his enemies must acquit him.

MRS. MARWOOD. Oh then, it seems, you are one of his favourable enemies! Methinks you look a little pale, and now you flush again.

MRS. FAINALL. Do I? I think I am a little sick o' the sudden.

MRS. MARWOOD. What ails you?

MRS. FAINALL. My husband. Don't you see him? He turned short upon me unawares, and has almost overcome me. [*Enter* FAINALL *and* MIRABELL.]

MRS. MARWOOD. Ha! ha! ha! he comes opportunely for you.

MRS. FAINALL. For you, for he has brought Mirabell with him.

FAINALL. My dear!

MRS FAINALL. My soul!

FAINALL. You don't look well to-day, child.

MRS. FAINALL. D'ye think so?

MIRABELL. He is the only man that does, madam.

MRS. FAINALL. The only man that would tell me so at least; and the only man from whom I could hear it without mortification.

FAINALL. O my dear, I am satisfied of your tenderness; I know you cannot resent anything from me; especially what is an effect of my concern.

MRS. FAINALL. Mr. Mirabell, my mother interrupted you in a pleasant relation last night; I would fain hear it out.

MIRABELL. The persons concerned in that affair have yet a tolerable reputation.—I am afraid Mr. Fainall will be censorious.

MRS. FAINALL. He has a humour more prevailing than his curiosity, and will willingly dispense with the hearing of one scandalous story, to avoid giving an occasion to make another by being seen to walk with his wife. This way, Mr. Mirabell, and I dare promise you will oblige us both. [*Exeunt* MRS. FAINALL *and* MIRABELL.]

FAINALL. Excellent creature! Well, sure if I should live to be rid of my wife, I should be a miserable man.

MRS. MARWOOD. Ay!

FAINALL. For having only that one hope, to accomplishment of it, of consequence, must put an end to all my hopes; and what a wretch is he who must survive his hopes! Nothing remains when that day comes, but to sit down and weep like Alexander, when he wanted other worlds to conquer.

MRS. MARWOOD. Will you not follow 'em?

FAINALL. Faith, I think not.

MRS. MARWOOD. Pray let us; I have a reason.

FAINALL. You are not jealous?

MRS. MARWOOD. Of whom?

FAINALL. Of Mirabell.

MRS. MARWOOD. If I am, is it inconsistent with my love to you that I am tender of your honour?

FAINALL. You would intimate, then, as if there were a fellow-feeling between my wife and him.

MRS. MARWOOD. I think she does not hate him to that degree she would be thought.

FAINALL. But he, I fear, is too insensible.

MRS. MARWOOD. It may be you are deceived.

FAINALL. It may be so. I do now begin to apprehend it.

MRS. MARWOOD. What?

FAINALL. That I have been deceived, madam, and you are false.

MRS. MARWOOD. That I am false! what mean you?

FAINALL. To let you know I see through all your little arts.—Come, you both love him; and both have equally dissembled your aversion. Your mutual jealousies of one another have made you clash till you have both struck fire. I have seen the warm confession reddening on your checks, and sparkling from your eyes.

MRS. MARWOOD. You do me wrong.

FAINALL. I do not. 'Twas for my ease to oversee and wilfully neglect the gross advances made him by my wife; that by permitting her to be engaged, I might continue unsuspected in my pleasures; and take you oftener to my arms in full security. But could you think, because the nodding husband would not wake, that e'er the watchful lover slept?

MRS. MARWOOD. And wherewithal can you reproach me?

FAINALL. With infidelity, with loving another, with love of Mirabell.

MRS. MARWOOD. 'Tis false! I challenge you to show an instance that can confirm your groundless accusation. I hate him.

FAINALL. And wherefore do you hate him? he is insensible, and your resentment follows his neglect. An instance! the injuries you have done him are a proof: your interposing in his love. What cause had you to make discoveries of his pretended passion? to undeceive the credulous aunt, and be the officious obstacle of his match with Millamant?

MRS. MARWOOD. My obligations to my lady urged me; I had professed a friendship to her; and could not see her easy nature so abused by that dissembler.

FAINALL. What, was it conscience then? Professed a friendship! O the pious friendships of the female sex!

MRS. MARWOOD. More tender, more sincere, and more enduring, than all the vain and empty vows of men, whether professing love to us, or mutual faith to one another.

FAINALL. Ha! ha! ha! you are my wife's friend too.

MRS. MARWOOD. Shame and ingratitude! do you reproach me? you, you upbraid me? Have I been false to her, through strict fidelity to you, and sacrificed my friendship to keep my love inviolate? And have you the baseness to charge me with the guilt, unmindful of the merit? To you it should be meritorious, that I have been vicious: and do you reflect that guilt upon me, which should lie buried in your bosom?

FAINALL. You misinterpret my reproof. I meant but to remind you of the slight account you once could make of strictest ties, when set in competition with your love to me.

MRS. MARWOOD. 'Tis false, you urged it

with deliberate malice! 'twas spoken in scorn, and I never will forgive it.

FAINALL. Your guilt, not your resentment, begets your rage. If yet you loved, you could forgive a jealousy: but you are stung to find you are discovered.

MRS. MARWOOD. It shall be all discovered. You too shall be discovered; be sure you shall. I can but be exposed.—If I do it myself I shall prevent your baseness.

FAINALL. Why, what will you do?

MRS. MARWOOD. Disclose it to your wife; own what has passed between us.

FAINALL. Frenzy!

MRS. MARWOOD. By all my wrongs I'll do't!—I'll publish to the world the injuries you have done me, both in my fame and fortune! With both I trusted you, you bankrupt in honour, as indigent of wealth.

FAINALL. Your fame I have preserved: your fortune has been bestowed as the prodigality of your love would have it, in pleasures which we both have shared. Yet, had not you been false, I had ere this repaid it—'tis true—had you permitted Mirabell with Millamant to have stolen their marriage, my lady had been incensed beyond all means of reconcilement: Millamant had forfeited the moiety of her fortune; which then would have descended to my wife;—and wherefore did I marry, but to make lawful prize of a rich widow's wealth, and squander it on love and you?

MRS. MARWOOD. Deceit and frivolous pretence!

FAINALL. Death, am I not married? What's pretence? Am I not imprisoned, fettered? Have I not a wife? nay a wife that was a widow, a young widow, a handsome widow, and would be again a widow, but that I have a heart of proof, and something of a constitution to bustle through the ways of wedlock and this world! Will you yet be reconciled to truth and me?

MRS. MARWOOD. Impossible. Truth and you are inconsistent: I hate you, and shall for ever.

FAINALL. For loving you?

MRS. MARWOOD. I loathe the name of love after such usage; and next to the guilt with which you would asperse me, I scorn you most. Farewell!

FAINALL. Nay, we must not part thus.

MRS. MARWOOD. Let me go.

FAINALL. Come, I'm sorry.

MRS. MARWOOD. I care not—let me go—break my hands, do—I'd leave 'em to get loose.

FAINALL. I would not hurt you for the world. Have I no other hold to keep you here?

MRS. MARWOOD. Well, I have deserved it all.

FAINALL. You know I love you.

MRS. MARWOOD. Poor dissembling!—O that—well, it is not yet—

FAINALL. What? what is it not? what is it not yet? It is not yet too late—

MRS. MARWOOD. No, it is not yet too late;—I have that comfort.

FAINALL. It is, to love another.

MRS. MARWOOD. But not to loathe, detest, abhor mankind, myself, and the whole treacherous world.

FAINALL. Nay, this is extravagance.— Come, I ask your pardon—no tears— I was to blame, I could not love you and be easy in my doubts. Pray forbear—I believe you; I'm convinced I've done you wrong; and any way, every way will make amends. I'll hate my wife yet more, damn her! I'll part with her, rob her of all she's worth, and we'll retire somewhere, anywhere, to another world. I'll marry thee—be pacified.—'Sdeath, they come, hide your face, your tears;— you have a mask, wear it a moment.[7] This way, this way—be persuaded. [*Exeunt.*]

Scene 2

Enter MIRABELL *and* MRS. FAINALL.

MRS. FAINALL. They are here yet.

MIRABELL. They are turning into the other walk.

MRS. FAINALL. While I only hated my husband, I could bear to see him; but since I have despised him, he's too offensive.

MIRABELL. O you should hate with prudence.

MRS. FAINALL. Yes, for I have loved with

indiscretion.

MIRABELL. You should have just so much disgust for your husband, as may be sufficient to make you relish your lover.

MRS. FAINALL. You have been the cause that I have loved without bounds, and would you set limits to that aversion of which you have been the occasion? why did you make me marry this man?

MIRABELL. Why do we daily commit disagreeable and dangerous actions? to save that idol, reputation. If the familiarities of our loves had produced that consequence of which you were apprehensive, where could you have fixed a father's name with credit, but on a husband? I knew Fainall to be a man lavish of his morals, an interested and professing friend, a false and a designing lover; yet one whose wit and outward fair behaviour have gained a reputation with the town enough to make that woman stand excused who has suffered herself to be won by his addresses. A better man ought not to have been sacrificed to the occasion; a worse had not answered to the purpose. When you are weary of him you know your remedy.

MRS. FAINALL. I ought to stand in some degree of credit with you, Mirabell.

MIRABELL. In justice to you, I have made you privy to my whole design, and put it in your power to ruin or advance my fortune.

MRS. FAINALL. Whom have you instructed to represent your pretended uncle?

MIRABELL. Waitwell, my servant.

MRS. FAINALL. He is an humble servant to Foible my mother's woman, and may win her to your interest.

MIRABELL. Care is taken for that—she is won and worn by this time. They were married this morning.

MRS. FAINALL. Who?

MIRABELL. Waitwell and Foible. I would not tempt my servant to betray me by trusting him too far. If your mother, in hopes to ruin me, should consent to marry my pretended uncle, he might, like Mosca in *The Fox*,[8] stand upon terms; so I made him sure beforehand.

MRS. FAINALL. So if my poor mother is caught in a contract, you will discover the imposture betimes; and release her by producing a certificate of her gallant's former marriage?

MIRABELL. Yes, upon condition that she consent to my marriage with her niece, and surrender the moiety of her fortune in her possession.

MRS. FAINALL. She talked last night of endeavouring at a match between Millamant and your uncle.

MIRABELL. That was by Foible's direction, and my instruction, that she might seem to carry it more privately.

MRS. FAINALL. Well, I have an opinion of your success; for I believe my lady will do anything to get a husband; and when she has this, which you have provided for her, I suppose she will submit to anything to get rid of him.

MIRABELL. Yes, I think the good lady would marry anything that resembled a man, though 'twere no more than what a butler could pinch out of a napkin.

MRS. FAINALL. Female frailty! we must all come to it, if we live to be old, and feel the craving of a false appetite when the true is decayed.

MIRABELL. An old woman's appetite is depraved like that of a girl—'tis the green sickness of a second childhood; and, like the faint offer of a latter spring, serves but to usher in the fall, and withers in an affected bloom.

MRS. FAINALL. Here's your mistress. [*Enter* MRS. MILLAMANT, WITWOUD, *and* MINCING.]

MIRABELL Here she comes, i'faith, full sail, with her fan spread and her streamers out, and a shoal of fools for tenders; ha, no, I cry her mercy!

MRS. FAINALL. I see but one poor empty sculler; and he tows her woman after him.

MIRABELL. [*To* MRS. MILLAMANT.] You seem to be unattended, madam—you used to have the *beau monde* throng after you; and a flock of gay fine perukes hovering round you.

WITWOUD. Like moths about a candle.—I had like to have lost my comparison for want of breath.

MRS. MILLAMANT. O I have denied my-self airs to-day, I have walked as fast through the crowd.

WITWOUD. As a favourite just disgraced; and with as few followers.

MRS. MILLAMANT. Dear Mr. Witwoud, truce with your similitudes; for I'm as sick of 'em—

WITWOUD. As a physician of a good air.—I cannot help it, madam, though 'tis against myself.

MRS. MILLAMANT. Yet, again! Mincing, stand between me and his wit.

WITWOUD. Do, Mrs. Mincing, like a screen before a great fire.—I confess I do blaze to-day, I am too bright.

MRS. FAINALL. But, dear Millamant, why were you so long?

MRS. MILLAMANT. Long! Lord, have I not made violent haste; I have asked every living thing I met for you; I have inquired after you, as after a new fashion.

WITWOUD. Madam, truce with your si-militudes.—No, you met her husband, and did not ask him for her.

MRS. MILLAMANT. By your leave, Wit-woud, that were like inquiring after an old fashion, to ask a husband for his wife.

WITWOUD. Hum, a hit! a hit! a palpable hit! I confess it.

MRS. FAINALL. You were dressed before I came abroad.

MRS. MILLAMANT. Ay, that's true.—O but then I had—Mincing, what had I? why was I so long?

MINCING. O mem, your la'ship stayed to peruse a packet of letters.

MRS. MILLAMANT. O ay, letters—I had letters—I am persecuted with let-ters—I hate letters—Nobody knows how to write letters, and yet one has 'em, one does not know why. They serve one to pin up one's hair.

WITWOUD. Is that the way? Pray, madam, do you pin up your hair with all your letters? I find I must keep copies.

MRS. MILLAMANT. Only with those in verse, Mr. Witwoud, I never pin up my hair with prose.—I think I tried once, Mincing.

MINCING. O mem, I shall never forget it.

MRS. MILLAMANT. Ay, poor Mincing tift and tift all the morning.

MINCING. Till I had the cramp in my fingers, I'll vow, mem: and all to no purpose. But when your la'ship pins it up with poetry, it sits so pleasant the next day as anything, and is so pure and so crips.

WITWOUD. Indeed, so crips?

MINCING. You're such a critic, Mr. Wit-woud.

MRS. MILLAMANT. Mirabell, did you take exceptions last night? O ay, and went away.—Now I think on't I'm angry—no, now I think on't I'm pleased—for I believe I gave you some pain.

MIRABELL. Does that please you?

MRS. MILLAMANT. Infinitely; I love to give pain.

MIRABELL. You would affect a cruelty which is not in your nature; your true vanity is in the power of pleas-ing.

MRS. MILLAMANT. Oh I ask you pardon for that—one's cruelty is one's power; and when one parts with one's cru-elty, one parts with one's power; and when one has parted with that, I fancy one's old and ugly.

MIRABELL. Ay, ay, suffer your cruelty to ruin the object of your power, to destroy your lover—and then how vain, how lost a thing you'll be! Nay, 'tis true: you are no longer hand-some when you've lost your lover; your beauty dies upon the instant; for beauty is the lover's gift; 'tis he bestows your charms—your glass is all a cheat. The ugly and the old, whom the looking-glass mortifies, yet after commendation can be flattered by it, and discover beauties in it; for that reflects our praises, rather than your face.

MRS. MILLAMANT. O the vanity of these men!—Fainall, d'ye hear him? If they did not commend us, we were not handsome! Now you must know they could not commend one, if one was not handsome. Beauty the lover's gift!—Lord, what is a lover, that it can give? Why, one makes lovers as fast as one pleases, and they live as long as one pleases, and they die as soon as one pleases; and then, if one pleases, one makes more.

WITWOUD. Very pretty. Why, you make no more of making of lovers, madam, than of making so many card-matches.

MRS. MILLAMANT. One no more owes one's beauty to a lover, than one's wit to an echo. They can but reflect what we look and say; vain empty things if we are silent or unseen, and want a being.

MIRABELL. Yet to those two vain empty things you owe the two greatest pleasures of your life.

MRS. MILLAMANT. How so?

MIRABELL. To your lover you owe the pleasure of hearing yourselves praised; and to an echo the pleasure of hearing yourselves talk.

WITWOUD. But I know a lady that loves talking so incessantly, she won't give an echo fair play; she has that everlasting rotation of tongue, that an echo must wait till she dies, before it can catch her last words.

MRS. MILLAMANT. O fiction!—Fainall, let us leave these men.

MIRABELL. [*Aside to* MRS. FAINALL.] Draw off Witwoud.

MRS. FAINALL. Immediately.—I have a word or two for Mr. Witwoud. [*Exeunt* MRS. FAINALL *and* WITWOUD.]

MIRABELL. I would beg a little private audience too.—You had the tyranny to deny me last night; though you knew I came to impart a secret to you that concerned my love.

MRS. MILLAMANT. You saw I was engaged.

MIRABELL. Unkind! You had the leisure to entertain a herd of fools; things who visit you from their excessive idleness; bestowing on your easiness that time which is the incumbrance of their lives. How can you find delight in such society? It is impossible they should admire you, they are not capable: or if they were, it should be to you as a mortification; for sure to please a fool is some degree of folly.

MRS. MILLAMANT. I please myself:—besides, sometimes to converse with fools is for my health.

MIRABELL. Your health! is there a worse disease than the conversation of fools?

MRS. MILLAMANT. Yes, the vapours; fools are physic for it, next to asafœtida.

MIRABELL. You are not in a course of fools?

MRS. MILLAMANT. Mirabell, if you persist in this offensive freedom, you'll displease me.—I think I must resolve, after all, not to have you:—we shan't agree.

MIRABELL. Not in our physic, it may be.

MRS. MILLAMANT. And yet our distemper, in all likelihood, will be the same; for we shall be sick of one another. I shan't endure to be reprimanded nor instructed: 'tis so dull to act always by advice, and so tedious to be told of one's faults—I can't bear it. Well, I won't have you, Mirabell—I'm resolved—I think—you may go.—Ha! ha! ha! what would you give, that you could help loving me?

MIRABELL. I would give something that you did not know I could not help it.

MRS. MILLAMANT. Come, don't look grave then. Well, what do you say to me?

MIRABELL. I say that a man may as soon make a friend by his wit, or a fortune by his honesty, as win a woman by plain-dealing and sincerity.

MRS. MILLAMANT. Sententious Mirabell!—Prithee, don't look with that violent and inflexible wise face, like Solomon at the dividing of the child in an old tapestry hanging.

MIRABELL. You are merry, madam, but I would persuade you for a moment to be serious.

MRS. MILLAMANT. What, with that face? no, if you keep your countenance, 'tis impossible I should hold mine. Well, after all, there is something very moving in a love-sick face. Ha! ha! ha!—well, I won't laugh, don't be peevish—Heigho! now I'll be melancholy, as melancholy as a watch-light. Well, Mirabell, if ever you will win me woo me now.—Nay, if you are so tedious, fare you well;—I see they are walking away.

MIRABELL. Can you not find in the variety of your disposition one moment—

MRS. MILLAMANT. To hear you tell me Foible's married, and your plot like to speed;—no.

MIRABELL. But how came you to know it?

MRS. MILLAMANT. Without the help of the devil, you can't imagine; unless she should tell me herself. Which of the two it may have been I will leave you to consider; and when you have done thinking of that, think of me. [*Exit.*]

MIRABELL. I have something more.— Gone!—Think of you? to think of a whirlwind, though't were in a whirlwind, were a case of more steady contemplation; a very tranquillity of mind and mansion. A fellow that lives in a windmill, has not a more whimsical dwelling than the heart of a man that is lodged in a woman. There is no point of the compass to which they cannot turn, and by which they are not turned; and by one as well as another; for motion, not method, is their occupation. To know this, and yet continue to be in love, is to be made wise from the dictates of reason, and yet persevere to play the fool by the force of instinct.—Oh, here come my pair of turtles!⁹—What, billing so sweetly! is not Valentine's day over with you yet? [*Enter* WAITWELL *and* FOIBLE.] Sirrah, Waitwell, why sure you think you were married for your own recreation, and not for my conveniency.

WAITWELL. Your pardon, sir. With submission, we have indeed been solacing in lawful delights; but still with an eye to business, sir. I have instructed her as well as I could. If she can take your directions as readily as my instructions, sir, your affairs are in a prosperous way.

MIRABELL. Give you joy, Mrs. Foible.

FOIBLE. O las, sir, I'm so ashamed!—I'm afraid my lady has been in a thousand inquietudes for me. But I protest, sir, I made as much haste as I could.

WAITWELL. That she did indeed, sir. It was my fault that she did not make more.

MIRABELL. That I believe.

FOIBLE. But I told my lady as you instructed me, sir, that I had a prospect of seeing Sir Rowland your uncle; and that I would put her ladyship's picture in my pocket to show him; which I'll be sure to say has made him so enamoured of her beauty, that he burns with impatience to lie at her ladyship's feet, and worship the original.

MIRABELL. Excellent Foible! matrimony has made you eloquent in love.

WAITWELL. I think she has profited, sir, I think so.

FOIBLE. You have seen Madam Millamant, sir?

MIRABELL. Yes.

FOIBLE. I told her, sir, because I did not know that you might find an opportunity; she had so much company last night.

MIRABELL. Your diligence will merit more—in the mean time—[*Gives money.*]

FOIBLE. O dear sir, your humble servant!

WAITWELL. Spouse.

MIRABELL. Stand off, sir, not a penny!— Go on and prosper, Foible:—the lease shall be made good, and the farm stocked, if we succeed.

FOIBLE. I don't question your generosity, sir: and you need not doubt of success. If you have no more commands, sir, I'll be gone; I'm sure my lady is at her toilet, and can't dress till I come.—O dear, I'm sure that [*Looking out.*] was Mrs. Marwood that went by in a mask! If she has seen me with you I'm sure she'll tell my lady. I'll make haste home and prevent her. Your servant, sir.—B'w'y,¹⁰ Waitwell. [*Exit.*]

WAITWELL. Sir Rowland, if you please.— The jade's so pert upon her preferment she forgets herself.

MIRABELL. Come, sir, will you endeavour to forget yourself, and transform into Sir Rowland?

WAITWELL. Why, sir, it will be impossible I should remember myself.—Married, knighted, and attended all in one day! 'tis enough to make any man forget himself. The difficulty will be how to recover my acquaintance and familiarity with my former self, and fall from my transformation to a reformation into Waitwell. Nay, I shan't be quite the same Waitwell neither; for now, I remember me, I'm married, and can't be my own man again.

Ay there's my grief; that's the sad change of life,
To lose my title, and yet keep my wife. [*Exeunt.*]

Act 3

Scene 1

A room in LADY WISHFORT's *house.* LADY WISHFORT *at her toilet,* PEG *waiting.*

LADY WISHFORT. Merciful! no news of Foible yet?

PEG. No, madam.

LADY WISHFORT. I have no more patience.—If I have not fretted myself till I am pale again, there's no veracity in me! Fetch me the red—the red, do you hear, sweetheart?—An arrant ash-colour, so I am a person! Look you how this wench stirs! Why dost thou not fetch me a little red? didst thou not hear me, Mopus?

PEG. The red ratafia does your ladyship mean, or the cherry-brandy?

LADY WISHFORT. Ratafia, fool! no, fool. Not the ratafia, fool—grant me patience!—I mean the Spanish paper,[11] idiot—complexion, darling. Paint, paint, paint, dost thou understand that, changeling, dangling thy hands like bobbins before thee? Why dost thou not stir, puppet? thou wooden thing upon wires!

PEG. Lord, madam, your ladyship is so impatient!—I cannot come at the paint, madam; Mrs. Foible has locked it up, and carried the key with her.

LADY WISHFORT. A pox take you both!—fetch me the cherry-brandy then. [*Exit* PEG.] I'm as pale and as faint, I look like Mrs. Qualmsick, the

curate's wife, that's always breeding.—Wench, come, come, wench, what art thou doing? sipping, tasting?—Save thee, dost thou not know the bottle? [*Re-enter* PEG *with a bottle and china cup.*]

PEG. Madam, I was looking for a cup.

LADY WISHFORT. A cup, save thee! and what a cup hast thou brought!—Dost thou take me for a fairy, to drink out of an acorn? Why didst thou not bring thy thimble? Hast thou ne'er a brass thimble clinking in thy pocket with a bit of nutmeg?—I warrant thee. Come, fill, fill!—So—again.— [*Knocking at the door.*]—See who that is.—Set down the bottle first—here, here, under the table.—What, wouldst thou go with the bottle in thy hand, like a tapster? As I am a person, this wench has lived in an inn upon the road, before she came to me, like Maritornes the Asturian in *Don Quixote!*—No Foible yet?

PEG. No, madam; Mrs. Marwood.

LADY WISHFORT. Oh, Marwood; let her come in.—Come in, good Marwood. [*Enter* MRS. MARWOOD.]

MRS. MARWOOD. I'm surprised to find your ladyship in dishabille at this time of day.

LADY WISHFORT. Foible's a lost thing; has been abroad since morning, and never heard of since.

MRS. MARWOOD. I saw her but now, as I came masked through the park, in conference with Mirabell.

LADY WISHFORT. With Mirabell!—You call my blood into my face, with mentioning that traitor. She durst not have the confidence! I sent her to negotiate an affair, in which, if I'm detected, I'm undone. If that wheedling villain has wrought upon Foible to detect me, I'm ruined. O my dear friend, I'm a wretch of wretches if I'm detected.

MRS. MARWOOD. O madam, you cannot suspect Mrs. Foible's integrity!

LADY WISHFORT. Oh, he carries poison in his tongue that would corrupt integrity itself! If she has given him an opportunity, she has as good as put her integrity into his hands. Ah, dear Marwood, what's integrity to an opportunity?—Hark! I hear her!—dear friend, retire into my closet, that I may examine her with more freedom.—You'll pardon me, dear friend; I can make bold with you.—There are books over the chimney.—Quarles and Prynne, and "The Short View of the Stage,"[12] with Bunyan's works, to entertain you.—[*To* PEG.]—Go, you thing, and send her in. [*Exeunt* MRS. MARWOOD *and* PEG.] [*Enter* FOIBLE.]

LADY WISHFORT. O Foible, where hast thou been? what hast thou been doing?

FOIBLE. Madam, I have seen the party.

LADY WISHFORT. But what hast thou done?

FOIBLE. Nay, 'tis your ladyship has done, and are to do; I have only promised. But a man so enamoured—so transported!—Well, here it is, all that is left; all that is not kissed away.—Well, if worshipping of pictures be a sin—poor Sir Rowland, I say.

LADY WISHFORT. The miniature has been counted like;—but hast thou not betrayed me, Foible? hast thou not detected me to that faithless Mirabell?—What hadst thou to do with him in the park? Answer me, has he got nothing out of thee?

FOIBLE. [*Aside.*] So the devil has been beforehand with me. What shall I say?—[*Aloud.*]—Alas, madam, could I help it, if I met that confident thing? was I in fault? If you had heard how he used me, and all upon your ladyship's account, I'm sure you would not suspect my fidelity. Nay, if that had been the worst, I could have borne; but he had a fling at your ladyship too; and then I could not hold; but i'faith I gave him his own.

LADY WISHFORT. Me? what did the filthy fellow say?

FOIBLE. O madam! 'tis a shame to say what he said—with his taunts and his fleers, tossing up his nose. Humph! (says he) what, you are a hatching some plot (says he), you are so early abroad, or catering[13] (says he), ferreting some disbanded officer, I warrant.—Half-pay is but thin subsistence (says he);—well, what pension does your lady propose? Let me see (says he), what, she must come down pretty deep now, she's superannuated (says he) and—

LADY WISHFORT. Odds my life, I'll have him, I'll have him murdered! I'll have him poisoned! Where does he eat?—I'll marry a drawer[14] to have him poisoned in his wine. I'll send for Robin from Locket's[15] immediately.

FOIBLE. Poison him! poisoning's too good for him. Starve him, madam, starve him; marry Sir Rowland, and get him disinherited. Oh you would bless yourself to hear what he said!

LADY WISHFORT. A villain! superannuated!

FOIBLE. Humph (says he), I hear you are laying designs against me too (says he), and Mrs. Millamant is to marry my uncle (he does not suspect a word of your ladyship); but (says he) I'll fit you for that. I warrant you (says he) I'll hamper you for that (says he); you and your old frippery too (says he); I'll handle you—

LADY WISHFORT. Audacious villain! handle me; would he durst!—Frippery! old frippery! was there ever such a foul-mouthed fellow? I'll be married to-morrow, I'll be contracted to-night.

FOIBLE. The sooner the better, madam.

LADY WISHFORT. Will Sir Rowland be here, sayest thou? when, Foible?

FOIBLE. Incontinently, madam. No new sheriff's wife expects the return of her husband after knighthood with that impatience in which Sir Rowland burns for the dear hour of kissing your ladyship's hand after dinner.

LADY WISHFORT. Frippery! superannuated frippery! I'll frippery the villain; I'll reduce him to frippery and rags! a tatterdemalion! I hope to see him hung with tatters, like a Long Lane penthouse[16] or a gibbet thief. A slander-mouthed railer! I warrant the spendthrift prodigal's in debt as much as the million lottery, or the whole court upon a birthday.[17] I'll spoil his credit with his tailor. Yes, he shall have my niece with her fortune, he shall.

FOIBLE. He! I hope to see him lodge in Ludgate first, and angle into Blackfriars for brass farthings with an old mitten.[18]

LADY WISHFORT. Ay, dear Foible; thank thee for that, dear Foible. He has put me out of all patience. I shall never recompose my features to receive Sir Rowland with any economy of face. This wretch has fretted me that I am absolutely decayed. Look, Foible.

FOIBLE. Your ladyship has frowned a little too rashly, indeed, madam. There are some cracks discernible in the white varnish.

LADY WISHFORT. Let me see the glass.—Cracks, sayest thou?—why, I am errantly flayed—I look like an old peeled wall. Thou must repair me, Foible, before Sir Rowland comes, or I shall never keep up to my picture.

FOIBLE. I warrant you, madam, a little art once made your picture like you; and now a little of the same art must make you like your picture. Your picture must sit for you, madam.

LADY WISHFORT. But art thou sure Sir Rowland will not fail to come? or will he not fail when he does come? Will he be importunate, Foible, and push? For if he should not be importunate, I shall never break decorums:—I shall die with confusion, if I am forced to advance.—Oh no, I can never advance!—I shall swoon if he should expect advances. No, I hope Sir Rowland is better bred than to put a lady to the necessity of breaking her forms. I won't be too coy, neither.—I won't give him despair—but a little disdain is not amiss; a little scorn is alluring.

FOIBLE. A little scorn becomes your ladyship.

LADY WISHFORT. Yes, but tenderness becomes me best—a sort of dyingness—you see that picture has a sort of a—ha, Foible! a swimmingness in the eye—yes, I'll look so—my niece affects it; but she wants features. Is Sir Rowland handsome? Let my toilet be removed—I'll dress above. I'll receive Sir Rowland here. Is he handsome? Don't answer me. I won't know: I'll be surprised, I'll be taken by surprise.

FOIBLE. By storm, madam, Sir Rowland's a brisk man.

LADY WISHFORT. Is he! O then he'll importune, if he's a brisk man. I shall save decorums if Sir Rowland importunes. I have a mortal terror at the apprehension of offending against decorums. O, I'm glad he's a brisk man. Let my things be removed, good Foible. [*Exit.*] [*Enter* MRS. FAINALL.]

MRS. FAINALL. O Foible, I have been in a fright, lest I should come too late! That devil Marwood saw you in the park with Mirabell, and I'm afraid will discover it to my lady.

FOIBLE. Discover what, madam!

MRS. FAINALL. Nay, nay, put not on that strange face, I am privy to the whole design, and know that Waitwell, to whom thou wert this morning married, is to personate Mirabell's uncle, and as such, winning my lady, to involve her in those difficulties from which Mirabell only must release her, by his making his conditions to have my cousin and her fortune left to her own disposal.

FOIBLE. O dear madam, I beg your pardon. It was not my confidence in your ladyship that was deficient; but I thought the former good correspondence between your ladyship and Mr. Mirabell might have hindered his communicating this secret.

MRS. FAINALL. Dear Foible, forget that.

FOIBLE. O dear madam, Mr. Mirabell is such a sweet, winning gentleman—but your ladyship is the pattern of generosity.—Sweet lady, to be so good! Mr. Mirabell cannot choose but be grateful. I find your ladyship has his heart still. Now, madam, I can safely tell your ladyship our success; Mrs. Marwood had told my lady; but I warrant I managed myself; I turned it all for the better. I told my lady that Mr. Mirabell railed at her; I laid horrid things to his charge, I'll vow; and my lady is so incensed that she'll be contracted to Sir Rowland to-night, she says; I warrant I worked her up, that he may have her for asking for, as they say of a Welsh maidenhead.

MRS. FAINALL. O rare Foible!

FOIBLE. I beg your ladyship to acquaint Mr. Mirabell of his success. I would be seen as little as possible to speak to him:—besides, I believe Madam Marwood watches me.—She has a month's mind;[19] but I know Mr. Mirabell can't abide her.—John!—[Calls.] remove my lady's toilet.—Madam, your servant: my lady is so impatient, I fear she'll come for me if I stay.

MRS. FAINALL. I'll go with you up the back stairs, lest I should meet her. [Exeunt.]

Scene 2

LADY WISHFORT's closet.

MRS. MARWOOD. Indeed, Mrs. Engine, is it thus with you? are you become a go-between of this importance? yes, I shall watch you. Why this wench is the passe-partout, a very master-key to everybody's strong-box. My friend Fainall, have you carried it so swimmingly? I thought there was something in it; but it seems 'tis over with you. Your loathing is not from a want of appetite, then, but from a surfeit. Else you could never be so cool to fall from a principal to be an assistant; to procure for him! a pattern of generosity that, I confess. Well, Mr. Fainall, you have met with your match.—O man, man! woman, woman! the devil's an ass: if I were a painter, I would draw him like an idiot, a driveller with a bib and bells: man should have his head and horns, and woman the rest of him. Poor simple fiend!—"Madam Marwood has a month's mind, but he can't abide her."—'Twere better for him you had not been his confessor in that affair, without you could have kept his counsel closer. I shall not prove another pattern of generosity: he has not obliged me to that with those excesses of himself! and now I'll have none of him. Here comes the good lady, panting ripe; with a heart full of hope, and a head full of care, like any chemist upon the day of projection.[20] [Enter LADY WISHFORT.]

LADY WISHFORT. O dear, Marwood, what shall I say for this rude forgetfulness?—but my dear friend is all goodness.

MRS. MARWOOD. No apologies, dear madam, I have been very well entertained.

LADY WISHFORT. As I'm a person, I am in a very chaos to think I should so forget myself:—but I have such an olio of affairs, really I know not what to do.—Foible!—[Calls.] I expect my nephew, Sir Wilfull, every moment too.—Why, Foible!—He means to travel for improvement.

MRS. MARWOOD. Methinks Sir Wilfull should rather think of marrying than travelling at his years. I hear he is turned of forty.

LADY WISHFORT. O he's in less danger of being spoiled by his travels—I am against my nephew's marrying too young. It will be time enough when he comes back, and has acquired discretion to choose for himself.

MRS. MARWOOD. Methinks Mrs. Millamant and he would make a very fit match. He may travel afterwards. 'Tis a thing very usual with young gentlemen.

LADY WISHFORT. I promise you I have thought on't—and since 'tis your judgment, I'll think on't again. I assure you I will; I value your judgment extremely. On my word, I'll propose it. [Enter FOIBLE.]

LADY WISHFORT. Come, come, Foible—I had forgot my nephew will be here before dinner:—I must make haste.

FOIBLE. Mr. Witwoud and Mr. Petulant are come to dine with your ladyship.

LADY WISHFORT. O dear, I can't appear till I'm dressed.—Dear Marwood, shall I be free with you again, and beg you to entertain 'em? I'll make all imaginable haste. Dear friend, excuse me. [Exeunt.]

Scene 3

A room in LADY WISHFORT's house. Enter MRS. MARWOOD, MRS. MILLAMANT, and MINCING.

MRS. MILLAMANT. Sure never anything was so unbred as that odious man!— Marwood, your servant.

MRS. MARWOOD. You have a colour; what's the matter?

MRS. MILLAMANT. That horrid fellow, Petulant, has provoked me into a

flame:—I have broken my fan.—
Mincing, lend me yours; is not all the
powder out of my hair?

MRS. MARWOOD. No. What has he done?

MRS. MILLAMANT. Nay, he has done
nothing; he has only talked—nay, he
has said nothing neither; but he has
contradicted everything that has
been said. For my part, I thought
Witwoud and he would have quarrelled.

MINCING. I vow, mem, I thought once
they would have fit.

MRS. MILLAMANT. Well, 'tis a lamentable
thing, I swear, that one has not the
liberty of choosing one's acquaintance as one does one's clothes.

MRS. MARWOOD. If we had that liberty,
we should be as weary of one set of
acquaintance, though never so good,
as we are of one suit though never so
fine. A fool and a doily stuff would
now and then find days of grace, and
be worn for variety.

MRS. MILLAMANT. I could consent to
wear 'em, if they would wear alike;
but fools never wear out—they are
such *drap de Berri*[21] things! without
one could give 'em to one's chambermaid after a day or two.

MRS. MARWOOD. 'Twere better so indeed. Or what think you of the
playhouse? A fine gay glossy fool
should be given there, like a new
masking habit, after the masquerade
is over, and we have done with the
disguise. For a fool's visit is always a
disguise; and never admitted by a
woman of wit, but to blind her affair
with a lover of sense. If you would
but appear barefaced now, and own
Mirabell, you might as easily put off
Petulant and Witwoud as your hood
and scarf. And indeed, 'tis time, for
the town has found it; the secret is
grown too big for the pretence. 'Tis
like Mrs. Primly's great belly; she
may lace it down before, but it bur-
nishes on her hips. Indeed,
Millamant, you can no more conceal
it, than my Lady Strammel can her
face; that goodly face, which in defiance of her Rhenish wine tea, will
not be comprehended in a mask.

MRS. MILLAMANT. I'll take my death,
Marwood, you are more censorious
than a decayed beauty, or a discarded
toast.—Mincing, tell the men they
may come up.—My aunt is not dressing here; their folly is less provoking
than your malice. [*Exit* MINCING.]
The town has found it! what has it
found? That Mirabell loves me is no
more a secret, than it is a secret that
you discovered it to my aunt, or than
the reason why you discovered it is a
secret.

MRS. MARWOOD. You are nettled.

MRS. MILLAMANT. You're mistaken.
Ridiculous!

MRS. MARWOOD. Indeed, my dear, you'll
tear another fan, if you don't miti-
gate those violent airs.

MRS. MILLAMANT. O silly! ha! ha! ha! I
could laugh immoderately. Poor Mirabell! his constancy to me has quite
destroyed his complaisance for all
the world beside. I swear, I never
enjoined it him to be so coy—If I had
the vanity to think he would obey
me, I would command him to show
more gallantry—'tis hardly well-bred
to be so particular on one hand, and
so insensible on the other. But I
despair to prevail, and so let him
follow his own way. Ha! ha! ha! pardon me, dear creature, I must laugh,
ha! ha! ha! though I grant you 'tis a
little barbarous, ha! ha! ha!

MRS. MARWOOD. What pity 'tis so much
fine raillery, and delivered with so
significant gesture, should be so un-
happily directed to miscarry!

MRS. MILLAMANT. Ha! dear creature, I
ask your pardon—I swear I did not
mind you.

MRS. MARWOOD. Mr. Mirabell and you
both may think it a thing impossible,
when I shall tell him by telling you—

MRS. MILLAMANT. O dear, what? for it is
the same thing if I hear it—ha! ha!
ha!

MRS. MARWOOD. That I detest him, hate
him, madam.

MRS. MILLAMANT. O madam, why so do
I—and yet the creature loves me, ha!
ha! ha! how can one forbear laughing to think of it.—I am a sibyl if I
am not amazed to think what he can
see in me. I'll take my death, I think
you are handsomer—and within a
year or two as young—if you could

but stay for me, I should overtake you—but that cannot be.—Well, that thought makes me melancholic.— Now, I'll be sad.

MRS. MARWOOD. Your merry note may be changed sooner than you think.

MRS. MILLAMANT. D'ye say so? Then I'm resolved I'll have a song to keep up my spirits. [*Re-enter* MINCING.]

MINCING. The gentlemen stay but to comb, madam, and will wait on you.

MRS. MILLAMANT. Desire Mrs. ——— that is in the next room to sing the song I would have learned yesterday.—You shall hear it, madam—not that there's any great matter in it— but 'tis agreeable to my humour.

SONG.

Love's but the frailty of the mind,
    When 'tis not with ambition joined;
A sickly flame, which, if not fed,
    expires,
And feeding, wastes in self-consuming fires.

'Tis not to wound a wanton boy
Or amorous youth, that gives the joy;
But 'tis the glory to have pierced a swain,
For whom inferior beauties sighed in vain.

Then I alone the conquest prize,
    When I insult a rival's eyes:
If there's delight in love, 'tis when I see
That heart, which others bleed for, bleed for me.
    [*Enter* PETULANT *and* WITWOUD.]

MRS. MILLAMANT. Is your animosity composed, gentlemen?

WITWOUD. Raillery, raillery, madam; we have no animosity—we hit off a little wit now and then, but no animosity.—The falling-out of wits is like the falling-out of lovers:—we agree in the main, like treble and bass.—Ha, Petulant?

PETULANT. Ay, in the main—but when I have a humour to contradict—

WITWOUD. Ay, when he has a humour to contradict, then I contradict too. What, I know my cue. Then we contradict one another like two battledores;[22] for contradictions beget one another like Jews.

PETULANT. If he says black's black—if I have a humour to say 'tis blue—let that pass—all's one for that. If I have a humour to prove it, it must be granted.

WITWOUD. Not positively must—but it may—it may.

PETULANT. Yes, it positively must, upon proof positive.

WITWOUD. Ay, upon proof positive it must; but upon proof presumptive it only may.—That's a logical distinction now, madam.

MRS. MARWOOD. I perceive your debates are of importance, and very learnedly handled.

PETULANT. Importance is one thing, and learning's another, but a debate's a debate, that I assert.

WITWOUD. Petulant's an enemy to learning; he relies altogether on his parts.

PETULANT. No, I'm no enemy to learning; it hurts not me.

MRS. MARWOOD. That's a sign indeed it's no enemy to you.

PETULANT. No, no, it's no enemy to anybody but them that have it.

MRS. MILLAMANT. Well, an illiterate man's my aversion: I wonder at the impudence of any illiterate man to offer to make love.

WITWOUD. That I confess I wonder at too.

MRS. MILLAMANT. Ah! to marry an ignorant that can hardly read or write!

PETULANT. Why should a man be any further from being married, though he can't read, than he is from being hanged? The ordinary's[23] paid for setting the psalm, and the parish-priest for reading the ceremony. And for the rest which is to follow in both cases, a man may do it without book—so all's one for that.

MRS. MILLAMANT. D'ye hear the creature?—Lord, here's company, I'll be gone. [*Exit. Enter* SIR WILFULL WITWOUD *in a riding dress, followed by* FOOTMAN.]

WITWOUD. In the name of Bartlemew and his fair, what have we here?

MRS. MARWOOD. 'Tis your brother, I fancy. Don't you know him?

WITWOUD. Not I.—Yes, I think it is he—

I've almost forgot him; I have not seen him since the Revolution.

FOOTMAN. [*To* SIR WILFULL.] Sir, my lady's dressing. Here's company; if you please to walk in, in the meantime.

SIR WILFULL. Dressing! what, it's but morning here, I warrant, with you in London; we should count it towards afternoon in our parts, down in Shropshire.—Why then, belike, my aunt han't dined yet, ha, friend?

FOOTMAN. Your aunt, sir?

SIR WILFULL. My aunt, sir! yes, my aunt, sir, and your lady, sir; your lady is my aunt, sir.—Why, what dost thou not know me, friend? why then send somebody hither that does. How long hast thou lived with thy lady, fellow, ha?

FOOTMAN. A week, sir; longer than anybody in the house, except my lady's woman.

SIR WILFULL. Why then belike thou dost not know thy lady, if thou seest her, ha, friend?

FOOTMAN. Why, truly, sir, I cannot safely swear to her face in a morning, before she is dressed. 'Tis like I may give a shrewd guess at her by this time.

SIR WILFULL. Well, prithee try what thou canst do; if thou canst not guess, inquire her out, dost hear, fellow? and tell her, her nephew, Sir Wilfull Witwoud, is in the house.

FOOTMAN. I shall, sir.

SIR WILFULL. Hold ye, hear me, friend; a word with you in your ear; prithee who are these gallants?

FOOTMAN. Really, sir, I can't tell; here come so many here, 'tis hard to know 'em all. [*Exit.*]

SIR WILFULL. Oons, this fellow knows less than a starling; I don't think a' knows his own name.

MRS. MARWOOD. Mr. Witwoud, your brother is not behindhand in forgetfulness—I fancy he has forgot you too.

WITWOUD. I hope so—the devil take him that remembers first, I say.

SIR WILFULL. Save you, gentlemen and lady!

MRS. MARWOOD. For shame, Mr. Witwoud; why don't you speak to

him?—And you, sir.

WITWOUD. Petulant, speak.

PETULANT. And you, sir.

SIR WILFULL. No offence, I hope. [*Salutes* MRS. MARWOOD.]

MRS. MARWOOD. No sure, sir.

WITWOUD. This is a vile dog, I see that already. No offence! ha! ha! ha! To him; to him, Petulant, smoke him.

PETULANT. It seems as if you had come a journey, sir; hem, hem. [*Surveying him round.*]

SIR WILFULL. Very likely, sir, that it may seem so.

PETULANT. No offence, I hope, sir.

WITWOUD. Smoke the boots, the boots; Petulant, the boots: ha! ha! ha!

SIR WILFULL. May be not, sir; thereafter, as 'tis meant, sir.

PETULANT. Sir, I presume upon the information of your boots.

SIR WILFULL. Why, 'tis like you may, sir: if you are not satisfied with the information of my boots, sir, if you will step to the stable, you may inquire further of my horse, sir.

PETULANT. Your horse, sir! your horse is an ass, sir!

SIR WILFULL. Do you speak by way of offence, sir?

MRS. MARWOOD. The gentleman's merry, that's all sir.—[*Aside.*] S'life, we shall have a quarrel betwixt an horse and an ass before they find one another out.—[*Aloud.*] You must not take anything amiss from your friends, sir. You are among your friends here, though it may be you don't know it.—If I am not mistaken, you are Sir Wilfull Witwoud.

SIR WILFULL. Right, lady; I am Sir Wilfull Witwoud, so I write myself; no offence to anybody, I hope; and nephew to the Lady Wishfort of this mansion.

MRS. MARWOOD. Don't you know this gentleman, sir?

SIR WILFULL. Hum! what, sure 'tis not—yea by'r Lady, but 'tis—s'heart, I know not whether 'tis or no—yea, but 'tis, by the Wrekin.[24] Brother Anthony! what Tony, i'faith! what, dost thou not know me? By'r Lady, nor I thee, thou art so becravated, and so beperiwigged.—S'heart, why dost not speak? art thou overjoyed!

WITWOUD. Odso, brother, is it you? your servant, brother.

SIR WILFULL. Your servant! why yours, sir. Your servant again—s'heart, and your friend and servant to that—and a—and a—flap-dragon for your service, sir! and a hare's foot and a hare's scut[25] for your service, sir! an you be so cold and so courtly.

WITWOUD. No offence, I hope, brother.

SIR WILFULL. S'heart, sir, but there is, and much offence!—A pox, is this your inns o' court breeding, not to know your friends and your relations, your elders and your betters?

WITWOUD. Why, brother Wilfull of Salop, you may be as short as a Shrewsbury cake, if you please. But I tell you 'tis not modish to know relations in town: you think you're in the country, where great lubberly brothers slabber and kiss one another when they meet, like a call of serjeants[26]—'tis not the fashion here; 'tis not indeed, dear brother.

SIR WILFULL. The fashion's a fool; and you're a fop, dear brother. S'heart, I've suspected this—by'r Lady, I conjectured you were a fop, since you began to change the style of your letters, and write on a scrap of paper gilt round the edges, no bigger than a *subpœna*. I might expect this when you left off, "Honoured brother;" and "hoping you are in good health," and so forth—to begin with a "Rat me, knight, I'm so sick of a last night's debauch"—'ods heart, and then tell a familiar tale of a cock and a bull, and a whore and a bottle, and so conclude.—You could write news before you were out of your time,[27] when you lived with honest Pimple Nose the attorney of Furnival's Inn— you could entreat to be remembered then to your friends round the Wrekin. We could have gazettes, then, and Dawks's Letter, and the Weekly Bill,[28] till of late days.

PETULANT. S'life, Witwoud, were you ever an attorney's clerk? of the family of the Furnival? Ha! ha! ha!

WITWOUD. Ay, ay, but that was but for a while: not long, not long. Pshaw! I was not in my own power then;—an orphan, and this fellow was my guardian; ay, ay, I was glad to consent to that, man, to come to London: he had the disposal of me then. If I had not agreed to that, I might have been bound 'prentice to a felt-maker in Shrewsbury; this fellow would have bound me to a maker of felts.

SIR WILFULL. S'heart, and better than to be bound to a maker of fops; where, I suppose, you have served your time; and now you may set up for yourself.

MRS. MARWOOD. You intend to travel, sir, as I'm informed.

SIR WILFULL. Belike I may, madam. I may chance to sail upon the salt seas, if my mind hold.

PETULANT. And the wind serve.

SIR WILFULL. Serve or not serve, I shan't ask licence of you, sir; nor the weathercock your companion: I direct my discourse to the lady, sir.— 'Tis like my aunt may have told you, madam—yes, I have settled my concerns, I may say now, and am minded to see foreign parts. If an how that the peace holds, whereby that is, taxes abate.

MRS. MARWOOD. I thought you had designed for France at all adventures.

SIR WILFULL. I can't tell that; 'tis like I may, and 'tis like I may not. I am somewhat dainty in making a resolution—because when I make it I keep it. I don't stand shill I, shall I, then; if I say't, I'll do't; but I have thoughts to tarry a small matter in town, to learn somewhat of your lingo first, before I cross the seas. I'd gladly have a spice of your French as they say, whereby to hold discourse in foreign countries.

MRS. MARWOOD. Here's an academy in town for that use.

SIR WILFULL. There is? 'Tis like there may.

MRS. MARWOOD. No doubt you will return very much improved.

WITWOUD. Yes, refined, like a Dutch skipper from a whale fishing. [*Enter* LADY WISHFORT *and* FAINALL.]

LADY WISHFORT. Nephew, you are welcome.

SIR WILFULL. Aunt, your servant.

FAINALL. Sir Wilfull, your most faithful

servant.

SIR WILFULL. Cousin Fainall, give me your hand.

LADY WISHFORT. Cousin Witwoud, your servant; Mr. Petulant, your servant—nephew, you are welcome again. Will you drink anything after your journey, nephew; before you eat? dinner's almost ready.

SIR WILFULL. I'm very well, I thank you, aunt—however, I thank you for your courteous offer. S'heart I was afraid you would have been in the fashion too, and have remembered to have forgot your relations. Here's your cousin Tony, belike, I mayn't call him brother for fear of offence.

LADY WISHFORT. O, he's a railleur, nephew—my cousin's a wit: and your great wits always rally their best friends to choose. When you have been abroad, nephew, you'll understand raillery better. [FAINALL *and* MRS. MARWOOD *talk apart.*]

SIR WILFULL. Why then let him hold his tongue in the meantime; and rail when that day comes. [*Enter* MINCING.]

MINCING. Mem, I am come to acquaint your la'ship that dinner is impatient.

SIR WILFULL. Impatient! why then belike it won't stay till I pull off my boots.—Sweetheart, can you help me to a pair of slippers?—My man's with his horses, I warrant.

LADY WISHFORT. Fy, fy, nephew! you would not pull off your boots here?—Go down into the hall—dinner shall stay for you.—My nephew's a little unbred, you'll pardon him, madam.—Gentlemen, will you walk?—Marwood—

MRS. MARWOOD. I'll follow you, madam—before Sir Wilfull is ready. [*Exeunt all but* MRS. MARWOOD *and* FAINALL.]

FAINALL. Why then, Foible's a bawd, an arrant, rank, match-making bawd: and I, it seems, am a husband, a rank husband; and my wife a very arrant, rank wife—all in the way of the world. 'Sdeath, to be a cuckold by anticipation, a cuckold in embryo! sure I was born with budding antlers, like a young satyr, or a citizen's child. 'Sdeath! to be out-witted—to be out-jilted—out-matrimony'd!—If I had kept my speed like a stag, 'twere somewhat,—but to crawl after, with my horns, like a snail, and be outstripped by my wife—'tis scurvy wedlock.

MRS. MARWOOD. Then shake it off; you have often wished for an opportunity to part—and now you have it. But first prevent their plot—the half of Millamant's fortune is too considerable to be parted with, to a foe, to Mirabell.

FAINALL. Damn him! that had been mine—had you not made that fond discovery—that had been forfeited, had they been married. My wife had added lustre to my horns by that increase of fortune; I could have worn 'em tipped with gold, though my forehead had been furnished like a deputy-lieutenant's hall.

MRS. MARWOOD. They may prove a cop of maintenance to you still, if you can away with your wife.[29] And she's no worse than when you had her—I dare swear she had given up her game before she was married.

FAINALL. Hum! that may be.

MRS. MARWOOD. You married her to keep you; and if you can contrive to have her keep you better than you expected, why should you not keep her longer than you intended.

FAINALL. The means, the means.

MRS. MARWOOD. Discover to my lady your wife's conduct; threaten to part with her!—my lady loves her, and will come to any composition to save her reputation. Take the opportunity of breaking it, just upon the discovery of this imposture. My lady will be enraged beyond bounds, and sacrifice niece, and fortune, and all, at that conjuncture. And let me alone to keep her warm; if she should flag in her part, I will not fail to prompt her.

FAINALL. Faith, this has an appearance.

MRS. MARWOOD. I'm sorry I hinted to my lady to endeavour a match between Millamant and Sir Wilfull: that may be an obstacle.

FAINALL. Oh, for that matter, leave me to manage him: I'll disable him for that; he will drink like a Dane; after dinner, I'll set his hand in.

MRS. MARWOOD. Well, how do you stand affected towards your lady?

FAINALL. Why, faith, I'm thinking of it.—Let me see—I am married already, so that's over:—my wife has played the jade with me—well, that's over too:—I never loved her, or if I had, why that would have been over too by this time:—jealous of her I cannot be, for I am certain; so there's an end of jealousy:—weary of her I am, and shall be—no, there's no end of that—no, no, that were too much to hope. Thus far concerning my repose; now for my reputation. As to my own, I married not for it, so that's out of the question;—and as to my part in my wife's—why, she had parted with her's before; so bringing none to me, she can take none from me; 'tis against all rule of play, that I should lose to one who has not wherewithal to stake.

MRS. MARWOOD. Besides, you forget, marriage is honourable.

FAINALL. Hum, faith, and that's well thought on; marriage is honourable as you say; and if so, wherefore should cuckoldom be a discredit, being derived from so honourable a root?

MRS. MARWOOD. Nay, I know not; if the root be honourable, why not the branches?

FAINALL. So, so, why this point's clear—well, how do we proceed?

MRS. MARWOOD. I will contrive a letter which shall be delivered to my lady at the time when that rascal who is to act Sir Rowland is with her. It shall come as from an unknown hand—for the less I appear to know of the truth, the better I can play the incendiary. Besides, I would not have Foible provoked if I could help it—because you know she knows some passages—nay, I expect all will come out—but let the mine be sprung first, and then I care not if I am discovered.

FAINALL. If the worst comes to the worst—I'll turn my wife to grass—I have already a deed of settlement of the best part of her estate; which I wheedled out of her; and that you

shall partake at least.

MRS. MARWOOD. I hope you are convinced that I hate Mirabell now; you'll be no more jealous?

FAINALL. Jealous! no—by this kiss—let husbands be jealous; but let the lover still believe; or if he doubt, let it be only to endear his pleasure, and prepare the joy that follows, when he proves his mistress true. But let husbands' doubts convert to endless jealousy; or if they have belief, let it corrupt to superstition and blind credulity. I am single, and will herd no more with 'em. True, I wear the badge, but I'll disown the order. And since I take my leave of 'em, I care not if I leave 'em a common motto to their common crest:—

All husbands must or pain or shame
    endure;
The wise too jealous are, fools too
    secure. [*Exeunt.*]

Act 4

Scene 1

A room in LADY WISHFORT's *house. Enter* LADY WISHFORT *and* FOIBLE.

LADY WISHFORT. Is Sir Rowland coming, sayest thou, Foible? and are things in order?

FOIBLE. Yes, madam, I have put wax lights in the sconces, and placed the footmen in a row in the hall, in their best liveries, with the coachman and postillion to fill up the equipage.

LADY WISHFORT. Have you pulvilled[30] the coachman and postillion, that they may not stink of the stable when Sir Rowland comes by?

FOIBLE. Yes, madam.

LADY WISHFORT. And are the dancers and the music ready, that he may be entertained in all points with correspondence to his passion?

FOIBLE. All is ready, madam.

LADY WISHFORT. And—well—and how

do I look, Foible?

FOIBLE. Most killing well, madam.

LADY WISHFORT. Well, and how shall I receive him? in what figure shall I give his heart the first impression? there is a great deal in the first impression. Shall I sit?—no, I won't sit—I'll walk—ay, I'll walk from the door upon his entrance; and then turn full upon him—no, that will be too sudden. I'll lie—ay, I'll lie down—I'll receive him in my little dressing-room, there's a couch—yes, yes, I'll give the first impression on a couch.—I won't lie neither, but loll and lean upon one elbow: with one foot a little dangling off, jogging in a thoughtful way—yes—and then as soon as he appears, start, ay, start and be surprised, and rise to meet him in a pretty disorder—yes—O, nothing is more alluring than a levee from a couch, in some confusion:—it shows the foot to advantage, and furnishes with blushes, and recomposing airs beyond comparison. Hark! there's a coach.

FOIBLE. 'Tis he, madam.

LADY WISHFORT. O dear!—Has my nephew made his addesses to Millamant? I ordered him.

FOIBLE. Sir Wilfull is set in to drinking, madam, in the parlour.

LADY WISHFORT. Odds my life, I'll send him to her. Call her down, Foible; bring her hither. I'll send him as I go—when they are together, then come to me, Foible, that I may not be too long alone with Sir Rowland. [*Exit. Enter* MRS. MILLAMANT *and* MRS. FAINALL.]

FOIBLE. Madam, I stayed here, to tell your ladyship that Mr. Mirabell has waited this half hour for an opportunity to talk with you: though my lady's orders were to leave you and Sir Wilfull together. Shall I tell Mr. Mirabell that you are at leisure?

MRS. MILLAMANT. No,—what would the dear man have? I am thoughtful, and would amuse myself—bid him come another time.

"There never yet was woman made
Nor shall but to be cursed."
[*Repeating, and walking about.*]

That's hard.

MRS. FAINALL. You are very fond of Sir John Suckling to-day, Millamant, and the poets.

MRS. MILLAMANT. He? Ay, and filthy verses—so I am.

FOIBLE. Sir Wilfull is coming, madam. Shall I send Mr. Mirabell away?

MRS. MILLAMANT. Ay, if you please, Foible, send him away—or send him hither—just as you will, dear Foible.—I think I'll see him—shall I? ay, let the wretch come. [*Exit* FOIBLE.]

"Thyrsis, a youth of the inspirèd train."
[*Repeating.*]

Dear Fainall, entertain Sir Wilfull—thou hast philosophy to undergo a fool, thou art married and hast patience—I would confer with my own thoughts.

MRS. FAINALL. I am obliged to you, that you would make me your proxy in this affair; but I have business of my own. [*Enter* SIR WILFULL.]

MRS. FAINALL. O Sir Wilfull, you are come at the critical instant. There's your mistress up to the ears in love and contemplation; pursue your point now or never.

SIR WILFULL. Yes; my aunt will have it so—I would gladly have been encouraged with a bottle or two, because I'm somewhat wary at first before I am acquainted.—[*This while* MILLAMANT *walks about repeating to herself.*]—But I hope, after a time, I shall break my mind—that is, upon further acquaintance—so for the present, cousin, I'll take my leave—if so be you'll be so kind to make my excuse, I'll return to my company—

MRS. FAINALL. O fy, Sir Wilfull! what, you must not be daunted.

SIR WILFULL. Daunted! no, that's not it, it is not so much for that—for if so be that I set on't, I'll do't. But only for the present, 'tis sufficient till further acquaintance, that's all—your servant.

MRS. FAINALL. Nay, I'll swear you shall never lose so favourable an opportunity, if I can help it. I'll leave you together, and lock the door. [*Exit.*]

SIR WILFULL. Nay, nay, cousin—I have

forgot my gloves—what d'ye do?—
S'heart, a'has locked the door indeed,
I think—nay, Cousin Fainall, open
the door—pshaw, what a vixen trick
is this?—Nay, now a 'has seen me
too.—Cousin, I made bold to pass
through as it were—I think this
door's enchanted!

MRS. MILLAMANT. [*Repeating.*]

"I prithee spare me, gentle boy,
Press me no more for that slight toy."

SIR WILFULL. Anan? Cousin, your servant.

MRS. MILLAMANT. [*Repeating.*]

"That foolish trifle of a heart."

Sir Wilfull!

SIR WILFULL. Yes—your servant. No
offence, I hope, cousin.

MRS. MILLAMANT. [*Repeating.*]

"I swear it will not do its part,
Though thou dost thine, employest
thy power and art."

Natural, easy Suckling!

SIR WILFULL. Anan? Suckling! no such
suckling neither, cousin, nor stripling: I thank Heaven, I'm no minor.

MRS. MILLAMANT. Ah, rustic, ruder than
Gothic!

SIR WILFULL. Well, well, I shall understand your lingo one of these days,
cousin; in the meanwhile I must answer in plain English.

MRS. MILLAMANT. Have you any business with me, Sir Wilfull?

SIR WILFULL. Not at present, cousin—
yes I make bold to see, to come and
know if that how you were disposed
to fetch a walk this evening, if so be
that I might not be troublesome, I
would have sought a walk with you.

MRS. MILLAMANT. A walk! what then?

SIR WILFULL. Nay, nothing—only for
the walk's sake, that's all.

MRS. MILLAMANT. I nauseate walking;
'tis a country diversion; I loathe the
country, and everything that relates
to it.

SIR WILFULL. Indeed! ha! look ye, look
ye, you do? Nay, 'tis like you may—
here are choice of pastimes here in
town, as plays and the like; that must
be confessed indeed.

MRS. MILLAMANT. *Ah l'étourdi!* I hate the
town too.

SIR WILFULL. Dear heart, that's much—
ha! that you should hate 'em both!
ha! 'tis like you may; there are some
can't relish the town, and others can't
away with the country—'tis like you
may be one of those, cousin.

MRS. MILLAMANT. Ha! ha! ha! yes, 'tis
like I may.—You have nothing further to say to me?

SIR WILFULL. Not at present, cousin.—
'Tis like when I have an opportunity
to be more private—I may break my
mind in some measure—I conjecture
you partly guess—however, that's as
time shall try—but spare to speak
and spare to speed, as they say.

MRS. MILLAMANT. If it is of no great
importance, Sir Wilfull, you will
oblige me to leave me; I have just
now a little business—

SIR WILFULL. Enough, enough, cousin:
yes, yes, all a case—when you're disposed: now's as well as another time;
and another time as well as now. All's
one for that—yes, yes, if your concerns call you, there's no haste; it will
keep cold, as they say.—Cousin, your
servant—I think this door's locked.

MRS. MILLAMANT. You may go this way,
sir.

SIR WILFULL. Your servant; then with
your leave I'll return to my company.
[*Exit.*]

MRS. MILLAMANT. Ay, ay; ha! ha! ha!

"Like Phœbus sung the no less amorous boy."

[*Enter* MIRABELL.]

MIRABELL.

"Like Daphne she, as lovely and as
coy."

Do you lock yourself up from me, to
make my search more curious? or is
this pretty artifice contrived to sig-
nify that here the chase must end,
and my pursuits be crowned? For
you can fly no further.

MRS. MILLAMANT. Vanity! no—I'll fly,
and be followed to the last moment.
Though I am upon the very verge of
matrimony, I expect you should solicit me as much as if I were wavering
at the grate of a monastery, with one
foot over the threshold. I'll be solic-

ited to the very last, nay, and afterwards.

MIRABELL. What, after the last?

MRS. MILLAMANT. Oh, I should think I was poor and had nothing to bestow, if I were reduced to an inglorious ease, and freed from the agreeable fatigues of solicitation.

MIRABELL. But do not you know, that when favours are conferred upon instant and tedious solicitation, that they diminish in their value, and that both the giver loses the grace, and the receiver lessens his pleasure?

MRS. MILLAMANT. It may be in things of common application; but never sure in love. Oh, I hate a lover that can dare to think he draws a moment's air, independent of the bounty of his mistress. There is not so impudent a thing in nature, as the saucy look of an assured man, confident of success. The pedantic arrogance of a very husband has not so pragmatical an air. Ah! I'll never marry, unless I am first made sure of my will and pleasure.

MIRABELL. Would you have 'em both before marriage? or will you be contented with the first now, and stay for the other till after grace?

MRS. MILLAMANT. Ah! don't be impertinent.—My dear liberty, shall I leave thee! my faithful solitude, my darling contemplation, must I bid you then adieu? Ay-h adieu—my morning thoughts, agreeable wakings, indolent slumbers, all ye *douceurs, ye sommeils du matin, adieu?*— I can't do't, 'tis more than impossible— positively, Mirabell, I'll lie abed in a morning as long as I please.

MIRABELL. Then I'll get up in a morning as early as I please.

MRS. MILLAMANT. Ah! idle creature, get up when you will—and d'ye hear, I won't be called names after I'm married; positively I won't be called names.

MIRABELL. Names!

MRS. MILLAMANT. Ay, as wife, spouse, my dear, joy, jewel, love, sweetheart, and the rest of that nauseous cant, in which men and their wives are so fulsomely familiar—I shall never bear that—good Mirabell, don't let us

be familiar or fond, nor kiss before folks, like my Lady Fadler and Sir Francis: nor go to Hyde Park together the first Sunday in a new chariot, to provoke eyes and whispers, and then never to be seen there together again; as if we were proud of one another the first week, and ashamed of one another ever after. Let us never visit together, nor go to a play together; but let us be very strange and well-bred: let us be as strange as if we had been married a great while; and as well-bred as if we were not married at all.

MIRABELL. Have you any more conditions to offer? Hitherto your demands are pretty reasonable.

MRS. MILLAMANT. Trifles!—As liberty to pay and receive visits to and from whom I please; to write and receive letters, without interrogatories or wry faces on your part; to wear what I please; and choose conversation with regard only to my own taste; to have no obligation upon me to converse with wits that I don't like, because they are your acquaintance: or to be intimate with fools, because they may be your relations. Come to dinner when I please; dine in my dressing-room when I'm out of humour, without giving a reason. To have my closet inviolate; to be sole empress of my tea-table, which you must never presume to approach without first asking leave. And lastly, wherever I am, you shall always knock at the door before you come in. These articles subscribed, if I continue to endure you a little longer, I may by degrees dwindle into a wife.

MIRABELL. Your bill of fare is something advanced in this latter account.— Well, have I liberty to offer conditions—that when you are dwindled into a wife, I may not be beyond measure enlarged into a husband?

MRS. MILLAMANT. You have free leave; propose your utmost, speak and spare not.

MIRABELL. I thank you.—*Imprimis* then, I covenant, that your acquaintance be general; that you admit no sworn confidant, or intimate of your own sex; no she friend to screen her affairs under your countenance, and tempt you to make trial of a mutual secrecy. No decoy duck to wheedle you a fop-scrambling to the play in a mask—then bring you home in a pretended fright, when you think you shall be found out—and rail at me for missing the play, and disappointing the frolic which you had to pick me up, and prove my constancy.

MRS. MILLAMANT. Detestable *imprimis!* I go to the play in a mask!

MIRABELL. *Item,* I article, that you continue, to like your own face, as long as I shall: and while it passes current with me, that you endeavour not to new-coin it. To which end, together with all vizards for the day, I prohibit all masks for the night, made of oiled-skins, and I know not what—hogs' bones, hares' gall, pig-water, and the marrow of a roasted cat. In short, I forbid all commerce with the gentlewoman in what d'ye call it court. *Item,* I shut my doors against all bawds with baskets, and pennyworths of muslin, china, fans, atlases, etc.—*Item,* when you shall be breeding—

MRS. MILLAMANT. Ah! name it not.

MIRABELL. Which may be presumed with a blessing on our endeavours.

MRS. MILLAMANT. Odious endeavours!

MIRABELL. I denounce against all strait lacing, squeezing for a shape, till you mould my boy's head like a sugar-loaf, and instead of a man child, make me father to a crooked billet. Lastly, to the dominion of the tea-table I submit—but with proviso, that you exceed not in your province; but restrain yourself to native and simple tea-table drinks, as tea, chocolate, and coffee: as likewise to genuine and authorised tea-table talk—such as mending fashions, spoiling reputations, railing at absent friends, and so forth—but that on no account you encroach upon the men's prerogative, and presume to drink healths, or toast fellows; for prevention of which I banish all foreign forces, all auxiliaries to the tea-table, as orange-brandy, all aniseed, cinnamon, citron, and Barbadoes waters, together with ratafia, and the most noble spirit of clary[31]—but for cowslip wine, poppy water, and all dormitives, those I allow.—These provisos admitted, in other things I may prove a tractable and complying husband.

MRS. MILLAMANT. O horrid provisos! filthy strong-waters! I toast fellows! odious men! I hate your odious provisos.

MIRABELL. Then we are agreed! shall I kiss your hand upon the contract? And here comes one to be a witness to the sealing of the deed. [*Enter* MRS. FAINALL.]

MRS. MILLAMANT. Fainall, what shall I do? shall I have him? I think I must have him.

MRS. FAINALL. Ay, ay, take him, take him, what should you do?

MRS. MILLAMANT. Well then—I'll take my death I'm in a horrid fright—Fainall, I shall never say it—well—I think—I'll endure you.

MRS. FAINALL. Fy! fy! have him, have him, and tell him so in plain terms: for I am sure you have a mind to him.

MRS. MILLAMANT. Are you? I think I have—and the horrid man looks as if he thought so too—well, you ridiculous thing you, I'll have you—I won't be kissed, nor I won't be thanked—here kiss my hand though.—So, hold your tongue now, don't say a word.

MRS. FAINALL. Mirabell, there's a necessity for your obedience;—you have neither time to talk nor stay. My mother is coming; and in my conscience if she should see you, would fall into fits, and maybe not recover time enough to return to Sir Rowland, who, as Foible tells me, is in a fair way to succeed. Therefore spare your ecstasies for another occasion, and slip down the back stairs, where Foible waits to consult you.

MRS. MILLAMANT. Ay, go, go. In the meantime I suppose you have said something to please me.

MIRABELL. I am all obedience. [*Exit.*]

MRS. FAINALL. Yonder Sir Wilfull's drunk, and so noisy that my mother has been forced to leave Sir Rowland to appease him; but he answers her

only with singing and drinking—
what they may have done by this time
I know not; but Petulant and he were
upon quarrelling as I came by.

MRS. MILLAMANT. Well, if Mirabell
should not make a good husband, I
am a lost thing,—for I find I love
him violently.

MRS. FAINALL. So it seems; for you mind
not what's said to you.—If you doubt
him, you had best take up with Sir
Wilfull.

MRS. MILLAMANT. How can you name
that superannuated lubber? foh! [*Enter* WITWOUD.]

MRS. FAINALL. So, is the fray made up,
that you have left 'em?

WITWOUD. Left 'em? I could stay no
longer—I have laughed like ten
christenings—I am tipsy with laughing—if I had stayed any longer I
should have burst,—I must have
been let out and pieced in the sides
like an unsized camlet.—Yes, yes, the
fray is composed; my lady came in
like a *noli prosequi,* and stopped the
proceedings.

MRS. MILLAMANT. What was the dispute?

WITWOUD. That's the jest; there was no
dispute. They could neither of 'em
speak for rage, and so fell a sputter-
ing at one another like two roasting
apples. [*Enter* PETULANT, *drunk.*]

WITWOUD. Now, Petulant, all's over, all's
well. Gad, my head begins to whim it
about—why dost thou not speak?
thou art both as drunk and as mute
as a fish.

PETULANT. Look you, Mrs. Millamant—
if you can love me, dear nymph—say
it—and that's the conclusion—pass
on, or pass off—that's all.

WITWOUD. Thou hast uttered volumes,
folios, in less than *decimo sexto,*[32] my
dear Lacedemonian.[33] Sirrah, Petulant, thou art an epitomiser of words.

PETULANT. Witwoud—you are an anni-
hilator of sense.

WITWOUD. Thou art a retailer of
phrases; and dost deal in remnants
of remnants, like a maker of pin-
cushions—thou art in truth
(metaphorically speaking) a speaker
of shorthand.

PETULANT. Thou art (without figure)
just one half of an ass, and Baldwin[34]

yonder, thy half-brother, is the
rest.—A Gemini of asses split would
make just four of you.

WITWOUD. Thou dost bite, my dear
mustard-seed; kiss me for that.

PETULANT. Stand off!—I'll kiss no more
males—I have kissed your twin
yonder in a humour of reconciliation, till he [*Hiccups.*] rises upon my
stomach like a radish.

MRS. MILLAMANT. Eh! filthy creature!
what was the quarrel?

PETULANT. There was no quarrel—
there might have been a quarrel.

WITWOUD. If there had been words
enow between 'em to have expressed
provocation, they had gone together
by the ears like a pair of castanets.

PETULANT. You were the quarrel.

MRS. MILLAMANT. Me!

PETULANT. If I have a humour to quarrel, I can make less matters conclude
premises.—If you are not handsome,
what then, if I have a humour to
prove it? If I shall have my reward,
say so; if not, fight for your face the
next time yourself—I'll go sleep.

WITWOUD. Do, wrap thyself up like a
wood-louse, and dream revenge—
and hear me, if thou canst learn to
write by to-morrow morning, pen me
a challenge.—I'll carry it for thee.

PETULANT. Carry your mistress's
monkey a spider!—Go flea dogs, and
read romances!—I'll go to bed to my
maid. [*Exit.*]

MRS. FAINALL. He's horridly drunk.—
How came you all in this pickle?

WITWOUD. A plot! a plot! to get rid of
the night—your husband's advice;
but he sneaked off.

Scene 2

The dining-room in LADY WISHFORT'*s
house. Enter* SIR WILFULL *drunk,* LADY
WISHFORT, WITWOUD, MRS. MILLA-
MANT, *and* MRS. FAINALL.

LADY WISHFORT. Out upon't, out
upon't! At years of discretion, and
comport yourself at this rantipole
rate!

SIR WILFULL. No offence, aunt.

LADY WISHFORT. Offence! as I'm a person, I'm ashamed of you—foh! how

you stink of wine! D'ye think my niece will ever endure such a borachio! you're an absolute borachio.[35]

SIR WILFULL. Borachio?

LADY WISHFORT. At a time when you should commence an amour, and put your best foot foremost—

SIR WILFULL. S'heart, an you grudge me your liquor, make a bill—give me more drink, and take my purse— [Sings.]

"Prithee fill me the glass,
   Till it laugh in my face,
With ale that is potent and mellow;
   He that whines for a lass,
   Is an ignorant ass,
For a bumper has not its fellow."

But if you would have me marry my cousin—say the word, and I'll do't— Wilfull will do't, that's the word— Wilfull will do't, that's my crest—my motto I have forgot.

LADY WISHFORT. My nephew's a little overtaken, cousin—but 'tis with drinking your health.—O' my word you are obliged to him.

SIR WILFULL. In vino veritas, aunt.—If I drunk your health to-day, cousin—I am a borachio. But if you have a mind to be married, say the word, and send for the piper; Willful will do't. If not, dust it away, and let's have t'other round.—Tony!—Odds heart, where's Tony!—Tony's an honest fellow; but he spits after a bumper, and that's a fault.— [Sings.]

"We'll drink, and we'll never ha'
   done, boys,
   Put the glass then around with the
   sun, boys,
Let Apollo's example invite us;
   For he's drunk every night,
   And that makes him so bright,
That he's able next morning to light
us."

The sun's a good pimple,[36] an honest soaker; he has a cellar at your Antipodes.[37] If I travel, aunt, I touch at your Antipodes.—Your Antipodes are a good, rascally sort of topsy-turvy fellows: if I had a bumper, I'd stand upon my head and drink a health to 'em.—A match or no match,

cousin with the hard name?—Aunt, Wilfull will do't. If she has her maid-enhead, let her look to't; if she has not, let her keep her own counsel in the meantime, and cry out at the nine months' end.

MRS. MILLAMANT. Your pardon, madam, I can stay no longer—Sir Wilfull grows very powerful. Eh! how he smells! I shall be overcome, if I stay.—Come, cousin. [Exeunt MRS. MILLAMANT and MRS. FAINALL.]

LADY WISHFORT. Smells! he would poison a tallow-chandler and his family! Beastly creature, I know not what to do with him!—Travel, quotha! ay, travel, travel, get thee gone, get thee gone, get thee but far enough, to the Saracens, or the Tartars, or the Turks!—for thou art not fit to live in a Christian commonwealth, thou beastly Pagan!

SIR WILFULL. Turks, no; no Turks, aunt: your Turks are infidels, and believe not in the grape. Your Mahometan, your Mussulman, is a dry stinkard— no offence, aunt. My map says that your Turk is not so honest a man as your Christian. I cannot find by the map that your Mufti is orthodox— whereby it is a plain case, that orthodox is a hard word, aunt, and [Hiccups.] Greek for claret.—[Sings.]

"To drink is a Christian diversion,
Unknown to the Turk or the Persian:
   Let Mahometan fools
   Live by heathenish rules,
And be damned over tea-cups and
   coffee.
   But let British lads sing,
   Crown a health to the king,
And a fig for your sultan and sophy!"

Ah Tony! [Enter FOIBLE, who whispers to LADY WISHFORT.]

LADY WISHFORT. [Aside to FOIBLE.]—Sir Rowland impatient? Good lack! what shall I do with this beastly tumbril?— [Aloud.] Go lie down and sleep, you sot!—or, as I'm a person, I'll have you bastinadoed with broomsticks.— Call up the wenches.

SIR WILFULL. Ahey! wenches, where are the wenches?

LADY WISHFORT. Dear Cousin Witwoud, get him away, and you will bind me to you inviolably. I have an affair of moment that invades me with some precipitation—you will oblige me to all futurity.

WITWOUD. Come, knight.—Pox on him, I don't know what to say to him.—Will you go to a cock-match?

SIR WILFULL. With a wench, Tony! Is she a shakebag, sirrah? Let me bite your cheek for that.

WITWOUD. Horrible! he has a breath like a bag-pipe!—Ay, ay; come, will you march, my Salopian?

SIR WILFULL. Lead on, little Tony—I'll follow thee, my Anthony, my Tantony, sirrah, thou shalt be my Tantony, and I'll be thy pig. [*Sings.*]

"And a fig for your sultan and sophy."
[*Exeunt* SIR WILFULL *and* WITWOUD.]

LADY WISHFORT. This will never do. It will never make a match—at least before he has been abroad. [*Enter* WAITWELL, *disguised as* SIR ROWLAND.]

LADY WISHFORT. Dear Sir Rowland, I am confounded with confusion at the retrospection of my own rudeness!—I have more pardons to ask than the pope distributes in the year of jubilee. But I hope, where there is likely to be so near an alliance, we may unbend the severity of decorums, and dispense with a little ceremony.

WAITWELL. My impatience, madam, is the effect of my transport; and till I have the possession of your adorable person, I am tantalised on the rack; and do but hang, madam, on the tenter of expectation.

LADY WISHFORT. You have an excess of gallantry, Sir Rowland, and press things to a conclusion with a most prevailing vehemence.—But a day or two for decency of marriage—

WAITWELL. For decency of funeral, madam! The delay will break my heart—or, if that should fail, I shall be poisoned. My nephew will get an inkling of my designs, and poison me—and I would willingly starve him before I die—I would gladly go out of the world with that satisfaction.—That would be some comfort to me, if I could but live so long as to be revenged on that unnatural viper!

LADY WISHFORT. Is he so unnatural, say you? Truly I would contribute much both to the saving of your life, and the accomplishment of your revenge.—Not that I respect myself, though he has been a perfidious wretch to me.

WAITWELL. Perfidious to you!

LADY WISHFORT. O Sir Rowland, the hours that he has died away at my feet, the tears that he has shed, the oaths that he has sworn, the palpitations that he has felt, the trances and the tremblings, the ardours and the ecstacies, the kneelings and the risings, the heart-heavings and the hand-gripings, the pangs and the pathetic regards of his protesting eyes!—Oh, no memory can register!

WAITWELL. What, my rival! is the rebel my rival?—a' dies.

LADY WISHFORT. No, don't kill him at once, Sir Rowland, starve him gradually, inch by inch.

WAITWELL. I'll do't. In three weeks he shall be barefoot; in a month out at knees with begging an alms.—He shall starve upward and upward, till he has nothing living but his head, and then go out in a stink like a candle's end upon a save-all.[38]

LADY WISHFORT. Well, Sir Rowland, you have the way—you are no novice in the labyrinth of love—you have the clue.—But as I am a person, Sir Rowland, you must not attribute my yielding to any sinister appetite, or indigestion of widowhood; nor impute my complacency to any lethargy of continence—I hope you do not think me prone to any iteration of nuptials—

WAITWELL. Far be it from me—

LADY WISHFORT. If you do, I protest I must recede—or think that I have made a prostitution of decorums; but in the vehemence of compassion, and to save the life of a person of so much importance—

WAITWELL. I esteem it so.

LADY WISHFORT. Or else you wrong my condescension.

WAITWELL. I do not, I do not!

LADY WISHFORT. Indeed you do.

WAITWELL. I do not, fair shrine of virtue!

LADY WISHFORT. If you think the least scruple of carnality was an ingredient—

WAITWELL. Dear madam, no. You are all camphor[39] and frankincense, all chastity and odour.

LADY WISHFORT. Or that—[Enter FOIBLE.]

FOIBLE. Madam, the dancers are ready; and there's one with a letter, who must deliver it into your own hands.

LADY WISHFORT. Sir Rowland, will you give me leave? Think favourably, judge candidly, and conclude you have found a person who would suffer racks in honours' cause, dear Sir Rowland, and will wait on you incessantly. [Exit.]

WAITWELL. Fy, fy!—What a slavery have I undergone! Spouse, hast thou any cordial; I want spirits.

FOIBLE. What a washy rogue art thou, to pant thus for a quarter of an hour's lying and swearing to a fine lady!

WAITWELL. Oh, she is the antidote to desire! Spouse, thou wilt fare the worse for't—I shall have no appetite to iteration of nuptials this eight-and-forty hours.—By this hand I'd rather be a chairman in the dog-days—than act Sir Rowland till this time to-morrow! [Re-enter LADY WISHFORT, with a letter.]

LADY WISHFORT. Call in the dancers.— Sir Rowland, we'll sit, if you please, and see the entertainment. [A dance.] Now, with your permission, Sir Rowland, I will peruse my letter.—I would open it in your presence, because I would not make you uneasy. If it should make you uneasy, I would burn it.—Speak, if it does— but you may see the superscription is like a woman's hand.

FOIBLE. [Aside to WAITWELL.] By Heaven! Mrs. Marwood's, I know it.—My heart aches—get it from her.

WAITWELL. A woman's hand! no, madam, that's no woman's hand, I see that already. That's somebody whose throat must be cut.

LADY WISHFORT. Nay, Sir Rowland, since you give me a proof of your passion by your jealousy, I promise you I'll make a return, by a frank communication.—You shall see it—

we'll open it together—look you here.—[Reads.]—"Madam, though unknown to you"—Look you there, 'tis from nobody that I know—"I have that honour for your character, that I think myself obliged to let you know you are abused. He who pretends to be Sir Rowland, is a cheat and a rascal."—Oh Heavens! what's this?

FOIBLE. [Aside.] Unfortunate! all's ruined!

WAITWELL. How, how, let me see, let me see!—[Reads] "A rascal, and disguised and suborned for that imposture,"— O villany! O villany!—"by the contrivance of—"

LADY WISHFORT. I shall faint, I shall die, oh!

FOIBLE. [Aside to WAITWELL.] Say 'tis your nephew's hand—quickly, his plot, swear it, swear it!

WAITWELL. Here's a villain! madam, don't you perceive it, don't you see it?

LADY WISHFORT. Too well, too well! I have seen too much.

WAITWELL. I told you at first I knew the hand.—A woman's hand! The rascal writes a sort of a large hand; your Roman hand—I saw there was a throat to be cut presently. If he were my son, as he is my nephew, I'd pistol him!

FOIBLE. O treachery!—But are you sure, Sir Rowland, it is his writing?

WAITWELL. Sure! am I here? do I live? do I love this pearl of India? I have twenty letters in my pocket from him in the same character.

LADY WISHFORT. How!

FOIBLE. O what luck it is, Sir Rowland, that you were present at this juncture!—This was the business that brought Mr. Mirabell disguised to Madam Millamant this afternoon. I thought something was contriving, when he stole by me and would have hid his face.

LADY WISHFORT. How, how!—I heard the villain was in the house indeed; and now I remember, my niece went away abruptly, when Sir Wilfull was to have made his addresses.

FOIBLE. Then, then, madam, Mr. Mirabell waited for her in her chamber!

but I would not tell your ladyship to
discompose you when you were to
receive Sir Rowland.

WAITWELL. Enough, his date is short.

FOIBLE. No, good Sir Rowland, don't
incur the law.

WAITWELL. Law! I care not for law. I
can but die, and 'tis in a good
cause.—My lady shall be satisfied of
my truth and innocence, thought it
cost me my life.

LADY WISHFORT. No, dear Sir Rowland,
don't fight; if you should be killed I
must never show my face; or
hanged—O, consider my reputation,
Sir Rowland!—No, you shan't fight—
I'll go in and examine my niece; I'll
make her confess. I conjure you, Sir
Rowland, by all your love, not to
fight.

WAITWELL. I am charmed, madam, I
obey. But some proof you must let
me give you; I'll go for a black box,
which contains the writings of my
whole estate, and deliver them into
your hands.

LADY WISHFORT. Ay, dear Sir Rowland,
that will be some comfort, bring the
black box.

WAITWELL. And may I presume to
bring a contract to be signed this
night? may I hope so far?

LADY WISHFORT. Bring what you will;
but come alive, pray come alive. Oh,
this is a happy discovery!

WAITWELL. Dead or alive I'll come—and
married we will be in spite of treachery; ay, and get an heir that shall
defeat the last remaining glimpse of
hope in my abandoned nephew.
Come, my buxom widow:—

Ere long you shall substantial proofs
   receive,
That I'm an errant knight—

FOIBLE. [*Aside.*] Or errant knave. [*Exeunt.*]

Act 5

Scene 1

A room in LADY WISHFORT's *house. Enter*
LADY WISHFORT *and* FOIBLE.

LADY WISHFORT. Out of my house, out
of my house, thou viper! thou ser-
pent, that I have fostered! thou
bosom traitress, that I raised from
nothing!—Begone! begone! begone!—go! go!—That I took from
washing of old gauze and weaving of
dead hair,[40] with a bleak blue nose
over a chafing-dish of starved embers, and dining behind a traverse
rag, in a shop no bigger than a bird-
cage!—Go! go! starve again, do, do!

FOIBLE. Dear Madam, I'll beg pardon
on my knees.

LADY WISHFORT. Away! out! out!—Go,
set up for yourself again!—Do, drive
a trade, do, with your three-pen-
nyworth of small ware, flaunting
upon a packthread, under a brandy-
seller's bulk, or against a dead wall by
a ballad-monger! Go, hang out an
old Frisoneer gorget,[41] with a yard of
yellow colberteen[42] again. Do; an old
gnawed mask, two rows of pins, and
a child's fiddle; a glass necklace with
the beads broken, and a quilted
nightcap with one ear. Go, go, drive
a trade!—These were your com-
modities, you treacherous trull! this
was the merchandise you dealt in
when I took you into my house,
placed you next myself, and made
you governante of my whole family!
You have forgot this, have you, now
you have feathered your nest?

FOIBLE. No, no, dear madam. Do but
hear me, have but a moment's patience, I'll confess all. Mr. Mirabell

seduced me; I am not the first that he has wheedled with his dissembling tongue; your ladyship's own wisdom has been deluded by him; then how should I, a poor ignorant, defend myself? O madam, if you knew but what he promised me, and how he assured me your ladyship should come to no damage!—Or else the wealth of the Indies should not have bribed me to conspire against so good, so sweet, so kind a lady as you have been to me.

LADY WISHFORT. No damage! What, to betray me, and marry me to a cast[43] servingman! to make me a receptacle, an hospital for a decayed pimp! No damage! O thou frontless impudence, more than a big-bellied actress!

FOIBLE. Pray, do but hear me, madam; he could not marry your ladyship, madam.—No, indeed, his marriage was to have been void in law, for he was married to me first, to secure your ladyship. He could not have bedded your ladyship; for if he had consummated with your ladyship, he must have run the risk of the law, and been put upon his clergy.[44]— Yes, indeed, I inquired of the law in that case before I would meddle or make.

LADY WISHFORT. What then, I have been your property, have I? I have been convenient to you, it seems!—While you were catering for Mirabell, I have been broker for you! What, have you made a passive bawd of me?—This exceeds all precedent; I am brought to fine uses, to become a botcher of second-hand marriages between Abigails and Andrews!—I'll couple you!—Yes, I'll baste you together, you and your Philanderer! I'll Duke's Place[45] you, as I am a person! Your turtle is in custody already: you shall coo in the same cage, if there be a constable or warrant in the parish. [Exit.]

FOIBLE. Oh that ever I was born! Oh that I was ever married!—A bride!— ay, I shall be a Bridewell[46] bride.— Oh! [Enter MRS. FAINALL.]

MRS. FAINALL. Poor Foible, what's the matter?

FOIBLE. O madam, my lady's gone for a constable. I shall be had to a justice, and put to Bridewell to beat hemp. Poor Waitwell's gone to prison already.

MRS. FAINALL. Have a good heart, Foible; Mirabell's gone to give security for him. This is all Marwood's and my husband's doing.

FOIBLE. Yes, yes; I know it, madam: she was in my lady's closet, and overheard all that you said to me before dinner. She sent the letter to my lady; and that missing effect, Mr. Fainall laid this plot to arrest Waitwell, when he pretended to go for the papers; and in the meantime Mrs. Marwood declared all to my lady.

MRS. FAINALL. Was there no mention made of me in the letter? My mother does not suspect my being in the confederacy? I fancy Marwood has not told her, though she has told my husband.

FOIBLE. Yes, madam; but my lady did not see that part; we stifled the letter before she read so far,—Has that mischievous devil told Mr. Fainall of your ladyship then?

MRS. FAINALL. Ay, all's out—my affair with Mirabell—everything discovered. This is the last day of our living together, that's my comfort.

FOIBLE. Indeed, madam; and so 'tis a comfort if you knew all;—he has been even with your ladyship, which I could have told you long enough since, but I love to keep peace and quietness by my goodwill. I had rather bring friends together, than set 'em at distance: but Mrs. Marwood and he are nearer related than ever their parents thought for.

MRS. FAINALL. Sayest thou so, Foible? canst thou prove this?

FOIBLE. I can take my oath of it, madam; so can Mrs. Mincing. We have had many a fair word from Madam Marwood, to conceal something that passed in our chamber one evening when you were at Hyde Park; and we were thought to have gone a-walking, but we went up unawares;—though we were sworn to secrecy too. Madam Marwood took a book and swore us upon it, but it was but a book of poems. So long as it was not a Bible oath, we may break it with a safe conscience.

MRS. FAINALL. This discovery is the most opportune thing I could wish.—Now, Mincing! [*Enter* MINCING.]

MINCING. My lady would speak with Mrs. Foible, mem. Mr. Mirabell is with her; he has set your spouse at liberty, Mrs. Foible, and would have you hide yourself in my lady's closet till my old lady's anger is abated. Oh, my old lady is in a perilous passion at something Mr. Fainall has said; he swears, and my old lady cries. There's a fearful hurricane, I vow. He says, mem, how that he'll have my lady's fortune made over to him, or he'll be divorced.

MRS. FAINALL. Does your lady or Mirabell know that?

MINCING. Yes, mem; they have sent me to see if Sir Wilfull be sober, and to bring him to them. My lady is resolved to have him, I think, rather than lose such a vast sum as six thousand pounds.—O come, Mrs. Foible, I hear my old lady.

MRS. FAINALL. Foible, you must tell Mincing that she must prepare to vouch when I call her.

FOIBLE. Yes, yes, madam.

MINCING. O yes, mem, I'll vouch anything for your ladyship's service, be what it will.

Scene 2

Another room in LADY WISHFORT'*s house. Enter* MRS. FAINALL, LADY WISHFORT, *and* MRS. MARWOOD.

LADY WISHFORT. O my dear friend, how can I enumerate the benefits that I have received from your goodness! To you I owe the timely discovery of the false vows of Mirabell; to you I owe the detection of the impostor Sir Rowland. And now you are become an intercessor with my son-in-law, to save the honour of my house, and compound for the frailties of my daughter. Well, friend, you are enough to reconcile me to the bad world, or else I would retire to deserts and solitudes, and feed harmless sheep by groves and purling streams. Dear Marwood, let us leave the world, and retire by ourselves and be shepherdesses.

MRS. MARWOOD. Let us first despatch the affair in hand, madam. We shall have leisure to think of retirement afterwards. Here is one who is concerned in the treaty.

LADY WISHFORT. Oh daughter, daughter! is it possible thou shouldst be my child, bone of my bone, and flesh of my flesh, and, as I may say, another me, and yet transgress the most minute particle of severe virtue? Is it possible you should lean aside to iniquity, who have been cast in the direct mold of virtue? I have not only been a mold but a pattern for you, and a model for you, after you were brought into the world.

MRS. FAINALL. I don't understand your ladyship.

LADY WISHFORT. Not understand! Why, have you not been naught? have you not been sophisticated? Not understand! here I am ruined to compound for your caprices and your cuckoldoms. I must pawn my plate and my jewels, and ruin my niece, and all little enough—

MRS. FAINALL. I am wronged and abused, and so are you. 'Tis a false accusation, as false as hell, as false as your friend there, ay, or your friend's friend, my false husband.

MRS. MARWOOD. My friend, Mrs. Fainall! your husband my friend! what do you mean?

MRS. FAINALL. I know what I mean, madam, and so do you; and so shall the world at a time convenient.

MRS. MARWOOD. I am sorry to see you so passionate, madam. More temper would look more like innocence. But I have done. I am sorry my zeal to serve your ladyship and family should admit of misconstruction, or make me liable to affronts. You will pardon me, madam, if I meddle no more with an affair in which I am not personally concerned.

LADY WISHFORT. O dear friend, I am so ashamed that you should meet with such returns!—[*to* MRS. FAINALL.] You ought to ask pardon on your knees, ungrateful creature! she deserves more from you than all your life can accomplish.—[*To* MRS. MARWOOD.] Oh, don't leave me destitute in this perplexity!—no, stick to me, my good genius.

MRS. FAINALL. I tell you, madam, you are abused.—Stick to you! ay, like a leech, to suck your best blood—she'll drop off when she's full. Madam, you shan't pawn a bodkin, nor part with a brass counter, in composition for me. I defy 'em all. Let 'em prove their aspersions; I know my own innocence, and dare stand a trial. [*Exit.*]

LADY WISHFORT. Why, if she should be innocent, if she should be wronged after all, ha?—I don't know what to think;—and I promise you her education has been unexceptionable—I may say it; for I chiefly made it my own care to initiate her very infancy in the rudiments of virtue, and to impress upon her tender years a young odium and aversion to the very sight of men:—ay, friend, she would ha' shrieked if she had but seen a man, till she was in her teens. As I am a person 'tis true;—she was never suffered to play with a male child, though but in coats; nay, her very babies[47] were of the feminine gender. Oh, she never looked a man in the face but her own father, or the chaplain, and him we made a shift to put upon her for a woman, by the help of his long garments, and his sleek face, till she was going in her fifteen.

MRS. MARWOOD. 'Twas much she should be deceived so long.

LADY WISHFORT. I warrant you, or she would never have borne to have been catechised by him; and have heard his long lectures against singing and dancing, and such debaucheries; and going to filthy plays, and profane music-meetings, where the lewd trebles squeak nothing but bawdy, and the basses roar blasphemy. Oh, she would have swooned at the sight or name of an obscene play-book!—and can I think, after all this, that my daughter can be naught? What, a whore? and thought it excommunica-

tion to set her foot within the door of a playhouse! O dear friend, I can't believe it, no, no! as she says, let him prove it, let him prove it.

MRS. MARWOOD. Prove it, madam! What, and have your name prostituted in a public court! yours and your daughter's reputation worried at the bar by a pack of bawling lawyers! To be ushered in with an O yes of scandal; and have your case opened by an old fumbling lecher in a quoif[48] like a man-midwife; to bring your daughter's infamy to light; to be a theme for legal punsters and quibblers by the statute; and become a jest against a rule of court, where there is no precedent for a jest in any record—not even in Doomsday Book; to discompose the gravity of the bench, and provoke naughty interrogatories in more naughty law Latin; while the good judge, tickled with the proceeding, simpers under a grey beard, and fidgets off and on his cushion as if he had swallowed cantharides,[49] or sat upon cow-itch!—

LADY WISHFORT. Oh, 'tis very hard!

MRS. MARWOOD. And then to have my young revellers of the Temple take notes, like 'prentices at a conventicle; and after talk it over again in commons, or before drawers in an eating-house.

LADY WISHFORT. Worse and worse!

MRS. MARWOOD. Nay, this is nothing; if it would end here 'twere well. But it must, after this, be consigned by the short-hand writers to the public press; and from thence be transferred to the hands, nay into the throats and lungs of hawkers, with voices more licentious than the loud flounder-man's: and this you must hear till you are stunned; nay, you must hear nothing else for some days.

LADY WISHFORT. Oh, 'tis insupportable! No, no, dear friend, make it up, make it up; ay, ay, I'll compound. I'll give up all, myself and my all, my niece and her all—anything, everything for composition.

MRS. MARWOOD. Nay, madam, I advise nothing, I only lay before you, as a friend, the inconveniences which perhaps you have overseen. Here comes Mr. Fainall; if he will be satisfied to huddle up all in silence, I shall be glad. You must think I would rather congratulate than condole with you. [*Enter* FAINALL.]

LADY WISHFORT. Ay, ay, I do not doubt it, dear Marwood; no, no, I do not doubt it.

FAINALL. Well, madam; I have suffered myself to be overcome by the importunity of this lady your friend; and am content you shall enjoy your own proper estate during life, on condition you oblige yourself never to marry, under such penalty as I think convenient.

LADY WISHFORT. Never to marry!

FAINALL. No more Sir Rowlands;—the next imposture may not be so timely detected.

MRS. MARWOOD. That condition, I dare answer, my lady will consent to without difficulty; she had already but too much experienced the perfidiousness of men.—Besides, madam, when we retire to our pastoral solitude we shall bid adieu to all other thoughts.

LADY WISHFORT. Ay, that's true; but in case of necessity, as of health, or some such emergency—

FAINALL. Oh, if you are prescribed marriage, you shall be considered; I will only reserve to myself the power to choose for you. If your physic be wholesome, it matters not who is your apothecary. Next, my wife shall settle on me the remainder of her fortune, not made over already; and for her maintenance depend entirely on my discretion.

LADY WISHFORT. This is most inhumanly savage; exceeding the barbarity of a Muscovite husband.

FAINALL. I learned it from his Czarish majesty's retinue, in a winter evening's conference over brandy and pepper, amongst other secrets of matrimony and policy, as they are at present practised in the northern hemisphere. But this must be agreed unto, and that positively. Lastly, I will be endowed, in right of my wife, with that six thousand pounds, which is the moiety of Mrs. Millamant's fortune in your possession; and which she has forfeited (as will appear by the last will and testament of your deceased husband, Sir Jonathan Wishfort) by her disobedience in contracting herself against your consent or knowledge; and by refusing the offered match with Sir Wilfull Witwoud, which you, like a careful aunt, had provided for her.

LADY WISHFORT. My nephew was *non compos*, and could not make his addresses.

FAINALL. I come to make demands—I'll hear no objections.

LADY WISHFORT. You will grant me time to consider?

FAINALL. Yes, while the instrument is drawing, to which you must set your hand till more sufficient deeds can be perfected: which I will take care shall be done with all possible speed. In the meantime I'll go for the said instrument, and till my return you may balance this matter in your own discretion. [*Exit.*]

LADY WISHFORT. This insolence is beyond all precedent, all parallel; must I be subject to this merciless villain?

MRS. MARWOOD. 'Tis severe indeed, madam, that you should smart for your daughter's wantonness.

LADY WISHFORT. 'Twas against my consent that she married this barbarian, but she would have him, though her year[50] was not out.—Ah! her first husband, my son Languish, would not have carried it thus. Well, that was my choice, this is hers: she is matched now with a witness.—I shall be mad!—Dear friend, is there no comfort for me? must I live to be confiscated at this rebelrate?—Here come two more of my Egyptian plagues too. [*Enter* MRS. MILLAMANT, *and* SIR WILFULL WITWOUD.]

SIR WILFULL. Aunt, your servant.

LADY WISHFORT. Out, caterpillar, call not me aunt! I know thee not!

SIR WILFULL. I confess I have been a little in disguise, as they say.—S'heart! and I'm sorry for't. What would you have? I hope I have committed no offence, aunt—and if I did I am willing to make satisfaction; and what can a man say fairer? If I have broke anything I'll pay for't, an it cost a pound. And so let that content for what's past, and make no more words. For what's to come, to pleasure you I'm willing to marry my cousin. So pray let's all be friends, she and I are agreed upon the matter before a witness.

LADY WISHFORT. How's this, dear niece? have I any comfort? can this be true?

MRS. MILLAMANT. I am content to be a sacrifice to your repose, madam; and to convince you that I had no hand in the plot, as you were misinformed, I have laid my commands on Mirabell to come in person, and be a witness that I give my hand to this flower of knighthood: and for the contract that passed between Mirabell and me, I have obliged him to make a resignation of it in your ladyship's presence;—he is without, and waits your leave for admittance.

LADY WISHFORT. Well, I'll swear I am something revived at this testimony of your obedience; but I cannot admit that traitor.—I fear I cannot fortify myself to support his appearance. He is as terrible to me as a gorgon; if I see him I fear I shall turn to stone, and petrify incessantly.

MRS. MILLAMANT. If you disoblige him, he may resent your refusal, and insist upon the contract still. Then 'tis the last time he will be offensive to you.

LADY WISHFORT. Are you sure it will be the last time?—If I were sure of that—shall I never see him again?

MRS. MILLAMANT. Sir Wilfull, you and he are to travel together, are you not?

SIR WILFULL. S'heart, the gentleman's a civil gentleman, aunt, let him come in; why, we are sworn brothers and fellow-travellers.—We are to be Pylades and Orestes, he and I.—He is to be my interpreter in foreign parts. He has been over-seas once already; and with proviso that I marry my cousin, will cross 'em once again, only to bear me company.— S'heart, I'll call him in,—an I set on't once, he shall come in; and see who'll hinder him. [*Goes to the door and hems.*]

MRS. MARWOOD. This is precious fool-

ing, if it would pass; but I'll know the bottom of it.

LADY WISHFORT. O dear Marwood, you are not going.

MRS. MARWOOD. Not far, madam; I'll return immediately. [*Exit. Enter* MIRABELL]

SIR WILFULL. Look up, man, I'll stand by you; 'sbud an she do frown, she can't kill you;—besides—harkee, she dare not frown desperately, because her face is none of her own. S'heart, an she should, her forehead would wrinkle like the coat of a cream-cheese; but mum for that, fellow-traveller.

MIRABELL. If a deep sense of the many injuries I have offered to so good a lady, with a sincere remorse, and a hearty contrition, can but obtain the least glance of compassion, I am too happy.—Ah, madam, there was a time!—but let it be forgotten—I confess I have deservedly forfeited the high place I once held of sighing at your feet. Nay, kill me not, by turning from me in disdain.—I come not to plead for favour;—nay, not for pardon; I am a suppliant only for pity—I am going where I never shall behold you more—

SIR WILFULL. How, fellow-traveller! you shall go by yourself then.

MIRABELL. Let me be pitied first, and afterwards forgotten.—I ask no more.

SIR WILFULL. By'r lady, a very reasonable request, and will cost you nothing, aunt! Come, come, forgive and forget, aunt; why you must, an you are a Christian.

MIRABELL. Consider, madam, in reality, you could not receive much prejudice; it was an innocent device; though I confess it had a face of guiltiness,—it was at most an artifice which love contrived;—and errors which love produces have ever been accounted venial. At least think it is punishment enough, that I have lost what in my heart I hold most dear, that to your cruel indignation I have offered up this beauty, and with her my peace and quiet; nay, all my hopes of future comfort.

SIR WILFULL. An he does not move me,

would I may never be o' the quorum!—an it were not as good a deed as to drink, to give her to him again, I would I might never take shipping!—Aunt, if you don't forgive quickly, I shall melt, I can tell you that. My contract went no farther than a little mouth-glue, and that's hardly dry;—one doleful sigh more from my fellow-traveller, and 'tis dissolved.

LADY WISHFORT. Well, nephew, upon your account—Ah, he has a false insinuating tongue!—Well, sir, I will stifle my just resentment at my nephew's request.—I will endeavour what I can to forget,—but on proviso that you resign the contract with my niece immediately.

MIRABELL. It is in writing, and with papers of concern; but I have sent my servant for it, and will deliver it to you, with all acknowledgments for your transcendent goodness.

LADY WISHFORT. [*Aside.*] Oh, he has witchcraft in his eyes and tongue!—When I did not see him, I could have bribed a villain to his assassination; but his appearance rakes the embers which have so long lain smothered in my breast.

Scene 3

Enter FAINALL, *and* MRS. MARWOOD.

FAINALL. Your date of deliberation, madam, is expired. Here is the instrument; are you prepared to sign?

LADY WISHFORT. If I were prepared, I am not impowered. My niece exerts a lawful claim, having matched herself by my direction to Sir Wilfull.

FAINALL. That sham is too gross to pass on me—though 'tis imposed on you, madam.

MRS. MILLAMANT. Sir, I have given my consent.

MIRABELL. And, sir, I have resigned my pretensions.

SIR WILFULL. And, sir, I assert my right; and will maintain it in defiance of you, sir, and of your instrument. S'heart, an you talk of an instrument, sir, I have an old fox by my thigh that shall hack your instrument of

ram vellum to shreds, sir!—it shall not be sufficient for a mittimus or a tailor's measure. Therefore withdraw your instrument, sir, or by'r lady, I shall draw mine.

LADY WISHFORT. Hold, nephew, hold!

MRS. MILLAMANT. Good Sir Wilfull, respite your valour.

FAINALL. Indeed! Are you provided of your guard, with your single beef-eater there? but I'm prepared for you, and insist upon my first proposal. You shall submit your own estate to my management, and absolutely make over my wife's to my sole use, as pursuant to the purport and tenor of this other covenant.—I suppose, madam, your consent is not requisite in this case; nor, Mr. Mirabell, your resignation; nor, Sir Wilfull, your right.—You may draw your fox if you please, sir, and make a bear-garden flourish somewhere else; for here it will not avail. This, my Lady Wishfort, must be subscribed, or your darling daughter's turned adrift, like a leaky hulk, to sink or swim, as she and the current of this lewd town can agree.

LADY WISHFORT. Is there no means, no remedy to stop my ruin? Ungrateful wretch! dost thou not owe thy being, thy subsistence, to my daughter's fortune?

FAINALL. I'll answer you when I have the rest of it in my possession.

MIRABELL. But that you would not accept of a remedy from my hands—I own I have not deserved you should owe any obligation to me; or else perhaps I could advise—

LADY WISHFORT. O what? what? to save me and my child from ruin, from want, I'll forgive all that's past; nay, I'll consent to anything to come, to be delivered from this tyranny.

MIRABELL. Ay, madam; but that is too late, my reward is intercepted. You have disposed of her who only could have made me a compensation for all my services; but be it as it may, I am resolved I'll serve you! you shall not be wronged in this savage manner.

LADY WISHFORT. How! dear Mr. Mirabell, can you be so generous at last! But it is not possible. Harkee, I'll break my nephew's match; you shall have my niece yet, and all her fortune, if you can but save me from this imminent danger.

MIRABELL. Will you? I'll take you at your word. I ask no more. I must have leave for two criminals to appear.

LADY WISHFORT. Ay, ay, anybody, anybody!

MIRABELL. Foible is one, and a penitent. [*Enter* MRS. FAINALL, FOIBLE, *and* MINCING.]

MRS. MARWOOD. O my shame! [MIRABELL *and* LADY WISHFORT *go to* MRS. FAINALL *and* FOIBLE. *To* FAINALL.] These corrupt things are brought hither to expose me.

FAINALL. If it must all come out, why let 'em know it; 'tis but the way of the world. That shall not urge me to relinquish or abate one title of my terms; no, I will insist the more.

FOIBLE. Yes, indeed, madam, I'll take my Bible oath of it.

MINCING. And so will I, mem.

LADY WISHFORT. O Marwood, Marwood, art thou false? my friend deceive me! hast thou been a wicked accomplice with that proligate man?

MRS. MARWOOD. Have you so much ingratitude and injustice to give credit against your friend, to the aspersions of two such mercenary trulls?

MINCING. Mercenary, mem? I scorn your words. 'Tis true we found you and Mr. Fainall in the blue garret; by the same token, you swore us to secrecy upon Messalina's poems. Mercenary! No, if we would have been mercenary, we should have held our tongues; you would have bribed us sufficiently.

FAINALL. Go, you are an insignificant thing!—Well, what are you the better for this; is this Mr. Mirabell's expedient? I'll be put off no longer.—You thing, that was a wife, shall smart for this! I will not leave thee therewithall to hide thy shame; your body shall be naked as your reputation.

MRS. FAINALL. I despise you, and defy your malice—you have aspersed me wrongfully—I have proved your falsehood—go you and your treacherous—I will not name it, but starve together—perish!

FAINALL. Not while you are worth a groat, indeed, my dear.—Madam, I'll be fooled no longer.

LADY WISHFORT. Ah, Mr. Mirabell, this is small comfort, the detection of this affair.

MIRABELL. Oh, in good time—your leave for the other offender and penitent to appear, madam. [*Enter* WAITWELL *with a box of writings.*]

LADY WISHFORT. O Sir Rowland!—Well, rascal!

WAITWELL. What your ladyship pleases. I have brought the black box at last, madam.

MIRABELL. Give it me.—Madam, you remember your promise.

LADY WISHFORT. Ay, dear sir.

MIRABELL. Where are the gentlemen?

WAITWELL. At hand, sir, rubbing their eyes—just risen from sleep.

FAINALL. 'Sdeath, what's this to me? I'll not wait your private concerns. [*Enter* PETULANT *and* WITWOUD.]

PETULANT. How now? What's the matter? whose hand's out?

WITWOUD. Heyday! what, are you all got together, like players at the end of the last act?

MIRABELL. You may remember, gentlemen, I once requested your hands as witnesses to a certain parchment.

WITWOUD. Ay, I do, my hand I remember—Petulant set his mark.

MIRABELL. You wrong him, his name is fairly written, as shall appear.—You do not remember, gentlemen, anything of what that parchment contains?— [*Undoing the box.*]

WITWOUD. No.

PETULANT. Not I; I writ, I read nothing.

MIRABELL. Very well, now you shall know.—Madam, your promise.

LADY WISHFORT. Ay, ay, sir, upon my honour.

MIRABELL. Mr. Fainall, it is now time that you should know, that your lady, while she was at her own disposal, and before you had by your insinuations wheedled her out of a pretended settlement of the greatest part of her fortune—

FAINALL. Sir! pretended!

MIRABELL. Yes, sir. I say that this lady while a widow, having it seems received some cautions respecting your inconstancy and tyranny of temper, which from her own partial opinion and fondness of you she could never have suspected—she did, I say, by the wholesome advice of friends, and of sages learned in the laws of this land, deliver this same as her act and deed to me in trust, and to the uses within mentioned. You may read if you please—[*Holding out the parchment.*] though perhaps what is written on the back may serve your occasions.

FAINALL. Very likely, sir. What's here?—Damnation! [*Reads.*] "A deed of conveyance of the whole estate real of Arabella Lanquish, widow, in trust to Edward Mirabell."—Confusion!

MIRABELL. Even so, sir; 'tis the Way of the World, sir, of the widows of the world. I suppose this deed may bear an elder date than what you have obtained from your lady.

FAINALL. Perfidious fiend! then thus I'll be revenged. [*Offers to run at* MRS. FAINALL.]

SIR WILFULL. Hold, sir! now you may make your bear-garden flourish somewhere else, sir.

FAINALL. Mirabell, you shall hear of this, sir, be sure you shall.—Let me pass, oaf! [*Exit.*]

MRS. FAINALL. Madam, you seem to stifle your resentment; you had better give it vent.

MRS. MARWOOD. Yes, it shall have vent—and to your confusion; or I'll perish in the attempt. [*Exit.*]

LADY WISHFORT. O daughter, daughter! 'tis plain thou hast inherited thy mother's prudence.

MRS. FAINALL. Thank Mr. Mirabell, a cautious friend, to whose advice all is owing.

LADY WISHFORT. Well, Mr. Mirabell, you have kept your promise—and I must perform mine.—First, I pardon, for your sake, Sir Rowland there, and Foible; the next thing is to break the matter to my nephew—and how to do that—

MIRABELL. For that, madam, give yourself no trouble; let me have your consent. Sir Wilfull is my friend; he has had compassion upon lovers, and generously engaged a volunteer in this action, for our service; and now designs to prosecute his travels.

SIR WILFULL. S'heart, aunt, I have no mind to marry. My cousin's a fine lady, and the gentleman loves her, and she loves him, and they deserve one another; my resolution is to see foreign parts—I have set on't—and when I'm set on't I must do't. And if these two gentlemen would travel too, I think they may be spared.

PETULANT. For my part, I say little—I think things are best off or on.

WITWOUD. I'gad, I understand nothing of the matter; I'm in a maze yet, like a dog in a dancing-school.

LADY WISHFORT. Well, sir, take her, and with her all the joy I can give you.

MRS. MILLAMANT. Why does not the man take me? would you have me give myself to you over again?

MIRABELL. Ay, and over and over again; [*Kisses her hand.*] I would have you as often as possibly I can. Well, Heaven grant I love you not too well, that's all my fear.

SIR WILFULL. S'heart, you'll have time enough to toy after you're married; or if you will toy now, let us have a dance in the meantime, that we who are not lovers may have some other employment besides looking on.

MIRABELL. With all my heart, dear Sir Wilfull. What shall we do for music?

FOIBLE. O sir, some that were provided for Sir Rowland's entertainment are yet within call. [*A dance.*]

LADY WISHFORT. As I am a person, I can hold out no longer;—I have wasted my spirits so to-day already, that I am ready to sink under the fatigue; and I cannot but have some fears upon me yet, that my son Fainall will pursue some desperate course.

MIRABELL. Madam, disquiet not yourself on that account; to my knowledge his circumstances are such he must of course comply. For my part, I will contribute all that in me lies to a reunion; in the meantime, madam,—[*To* MRS. FAINALL.] let me before these witnesses restore to you this deed of trust; it may be a means, well-managed, to make you live easily together.

From hence let those be warned, who
    mean to wed;
Lest mutual falsehood stain the
    bridal bed;
For each deceiver to his cost may
    find,
That marriage-frauds too oft are
    paid in kind.

[*Exeunt omnes.*]

1. A kind of liqueur.
2. St. Pancras was a church much used for quick marriages, as was Duke's Place.
3. A bitter apple eaten only when partly decayed.
4. A crabapple, very sour.
5. Notebook of similes.
6. Slang terms for prostitutes.
7. Fashionable ladies frequently wore masks in public.
8. Ben Jonson's *Volpone.*
9. Turtledoves.
10. Abbreviated form of "God be with you."
11. A red cosmetic.
12. See p. 13 above. The other works cited are deeply moralistic.
13. Pimping.
14. Bartender.
15. A popular tavern.
16. A used clothing shop in Long Lane, where many such shops were located.
17. On the occasion of the king's birthday, the whole court customarily bought new clothes.
18. At Ludgate, a debtors' prison located in Blackfriars, the inmates begged for coins by lowering mittens from their cell windows.
19. Desire (for Mirabell).
20. Alchemist at the culmination of his work.
21. A long-wearing woolen cloth.
22. Wooden paddles used in a game like badminton.
23. Prison chaplain.
24. A hill in Shropshire.
25. Tail.
26. A group of lawyers admitted simultaneously to the bar.
27. Apprenticeship.
28. Newspapers.
29. Your horns may prove to be a protective cap to you still, if you can endure your wife.
30. Powdered.
31. All alcoholic drinks.
32. A very small book.
33. A Spartan, noted for saying very little.
34. The ass in *Reynard the Fox.*
35. Drunkard.
36. Drinking companion.
37. That point diametrically at the opposite side of the earth; thus, in legend, the people who, in such a land, stand on their heads.
38. A pan designed to let a candle burn to its very end.
39. Supposed to produce impotence.
40. Working in a wig maker's shop.
41. A kerchief worn over the bosom.
42. Lace.
43. Discharged.
44. Forced to claim benefit of clergy (by proving his literacy) in order to escape hanging.
45. See note 2 above.
46. A women's prison.
47. Dolls.
48. Lawyer's cap.
49. A preparation of powdered, dried Spanish flies, supposed to be an aphrodisiac.
50. Of mourning.

Jean de France

Ludvig Holberg

The eighteenth century was an era of greatly increased international communication in Europe, and the development of new ideas in drama in one country rather quickly led to the spread of those ideas to other countries. The Scandinavian countries had previously developed little or no drama of their own beyond medieval farces and miracle plays, being content with occasional productions of French or German works. Thus it fell to Ludvig Holberg, one of the early cosmopolitan Europeans, to become the "Molière of the North" and the "founder of Danish literature," as he established almost single-handedly a theater of real excellence in Copenhagen and a group of plays that quickly ranked him as the leading European playwright of his day.

Holberg was born in Bergen, Norway, on December 3, 1684, the last of twelve children in his family. Both his parents died when Ludvig was very young, and he was raised by an uncle who provided, within his limited means, for the boy's education in Bergen. Ludvig's insatiable thirst for knowledge brought him to the University of Copenhagen in 1702, and from there he departed on a series of extended journeys about Europe that completed both a practical and a classical education. He spent two years at Oxford, for example (1706–8), reading voraciously, and traveled on foot throughout France, Italy, and Germany, returning at intervals to Copenhagen. Only in 1717 did he settle down at last to a professorship at the University of Copenhagen, thus achieving both financial security and scholarly respectability.

Educated Danes at this time were fluent in several languages and regarded Danish as somewhat vulgar. It was popularly said that a gentleman "wrote Latin to his friends, talked French to the ladies, called his dogs in German and only used Danish to swear at his servants." French comedies were performed at court for the royal family and their guests, and occasional performances were given for the public as well. When the king developed a new interest in German opera and released his French players, two of them, Étienne Capion and René Montaigu, decided to remain in Copenhagen; they obtained a patent from the king to produce French plays. When their Little Grønnegade Theater opened in January 1722, they encountered financial difficulties, and soon hit upon the idea of performing in Danish. In the meantime, Ludvig Holberg had published several nondramatic works, including a poetic satire that provoked both laughter and outrage, and the French actors approached Holberg to write native Danish comedies. His first, *The Political Tinker,* opened on September 25, 1722, and it was followed by four more (including *Jean de France*) before the end of the year. In continuing creative fervor, Holberg wrote a total of twenty-seven plays before the theater closed for lack of money early in 1727.

As an established scholar at the University of Copenhagen, Holberg turned his attention to other matters. A royal subsidy was obtained to reopen the theater, but by this time Holberg's interests lay elsewhere. Fire destroyed most of Copenhagen in October 1728, and before the economy recovered from that blow, a new king, who found the theater immoral, succeeded to the throne. The production of plays ceased until after the death of Christian VI in 1746. Shortly thereafter, the theater was reopened and Holberg was appointed director, but he was then too old for the arduous labors involved. He soon resigned, but nevertheless wrote six new plays; these failed to measure up to the quality of the brilliant work of his earlier years. Holberg died in Copenhagen on January 28, 1754, having never married. His sole heir was an academy for noblemen at Sorø, which Holberg endowed to encourage Danish study—but with the stipulation that students had to study for three years either at Sorø or in Copenhagen before they could travel abroad. Holberg's literary legacy was far greater; not only did he establish Danish drama, but he created a whole library of Danish literature and scholarly writing that shaped the entire development of Danish letters. He was one of the foremost authors of Europe, and remains a subject of study for every Danish school child.

Holberg shared with his countrymen a great admiration for French literature, and frankly admits to modeling at least some of his plays on the work of Molière. The influence of the commedia dell'arte is strong in much of his work also, as is his debt to English drama and especially to the Jonsonian theory of humours. This derivative quality, perhaps inevitable in an author trying to establish a new literature where there previously was none, is especially evident when his work is read in translation; one is constantly reminded that Molière did a similar thing better. On the other hand, Holberg's unique ability to capture in his characters the essence of the Danish peasant and middle classes lifts his work far above mere imitation. *Jean de France* evidences each of these qualities: its structure is derived largely from Molière, but its characters are uniquely and eternally Danish.

The plot of *Jean de France* is perhaps its most obviously derivative characteristic. Like that of Molière's *The Misanthrope,* it consists largely of introducing a central character whose idiosyncracy dominates his behavior, then subjecting that character to a series of humiliations until he is finally driven away in disgust. The potential for tragedy lurks very near the surface of such a plot (both Jean and Alceste ruin their lives and destroy their own chances of happiness), but the absurdity of the protagonist's behavior is sufficient to insure the audience's continued laughter. As in many Molière plays, the forward momentum of *Jean de France* depends heavily on the machinations of a pair of clever servants, who seek to insure that their nubile young mistress is not forced to marry an unsuitable mate. As in nearly all of Molière's plays, plot is not of great importance anyway in the final assessment of the play's theatrical effectiveness, but rather is a simple and yet effective framework upon which to hang some excitingly developed comic characters.

There is a sense in which the characters in *Jean de France* may be said to be derivative also. Obviously the tradition of the clever servants who can manipulate their masters at will goes far back through Molière and the commedia dell'arte at least to Roman comedy. The curmudgeonly old father, the young lovers, and the duped parents are all equally ancient traditions from which Holberg borrows shamelessly as he creates a Danish theater. Yet it is also the case that each of these characters is given uniquely Danish qualities that make them well-rounded human beings distinct from even the finest characters created by other playwrights. Jeronimus and Elsebet are not Orgon and Marianne, Marthe is far from Dorine, Frands and Magdelone are unlike anyone Molière created at all. Working directly from the characteristics of the actors whom he knew would play his roles, Holberg fashioned each as a Dane, reflecting life in and about eighteenth-century Copenhagen as surely as Shakespeare's characters live in and around Elizabethan London. Especially are the servants and the other lowlife characters drawn with swift, sure strokes that make of each an individual who lives as a fresh creation.

Indeed, this realism in his drama, more than a century before realism became a significant movement in Europe, is one of Holberg's more remarkable characteristics. Simply and unpretentiously, he portrays real people in real situations; though they are heightened by comic exaggeration, they rarely spin off in farcical extravaganza as Molière's characters often do. What Holberg loses thereby in comic exuberance he regains in true-to-life identification with the concerns of the people, an approach to bourgeois theater that the realists were to exploit so effectively in the nineteenth century. Nowhere is this realism more apparent than in Holberg's language; perhaps because he was using the Danish idiom of the common people anyway, with conscious intent to create a literature in that idiom, Holberg catches not only the words of the common people, but the very rhythms of their lives.

Thematically, Holberg's plays are not notably successful. He makes trenchant use of satire, and many of his contemporaries were outraged by the attacks on their own dignity that they perceived in Holberg's works, but this all seems remarkably gentle from a modern perspective. When Holberg does want to raise thought-provoking issues, he tends to stop his play and lecture about them, as when Jeronimus lectures in *Jean de France*'s first scene, for example, on the disadvantages of sending a son abroad for an education. There is little that is profound in such an approach, and *Jean de France* succeeds, as do most of Holberg's plays, on the level of pure comic entertainment more than on that of instruction or enlightenment.

That Holberg's plays are relatively little known in English is a significant loss to the English-speaking theater. *Erasmus Montanus* (1722), regarded by some as Holberg's greatest play, is a skillful parody on academic life as perceived by a young scholar newly initiated into the glories of Latin disputation; it is made more difficult for modern audiences by the necessity that one understand Latin. *Jeppe of the Hill* (1722) is a loosely structured work about a peasant who falls into a drunken sleep on a dung-heap and awakens as lord of a manor; the lovable rogue Jeppe is one of the truly great comic characters in all dramatic literature. *The Political Tinker* (1722) concerns the delusions of grandeur of a tinker who, fond of espousing political opinions, is fooled into believing that he has been elected burgomaster. In *The Fussy Man* (1723), a befuddled old father who imagines himself terribly busy over nothing is tricked into marrying his daughter to a man she loves despite the father's intention to wed her to a bookkeeper who will aid him in his business (the similarity to Molière's *The Imaginary Invalid* is more than accidental). Even these brief plot summaries of some of Holberg's major works reveal both his essential theatrical comicality and the derivative nature of his plots. They do not fully reflect the strength of Holberg's local color. Holberg remains today a towering figure in Danish literature, but too little known and produced in the English-speaking world.

Jean de France
or
Hans Frandsen

Translated by Gerald S. Argetsinger

Characters
Jeronimus, a citizen
Elsebet, his daughter
Espen, his servant
Marthe, his maid
Antonius, Elsebet's sweetheart
Frands Hansen, Jeronimus's neighbor
Magdelone Hansen, his wife
Hans Frandsen/Jean de France, their son
Peer/Pierre, Jean's servant
Arv, Frands's outdoor servant
An Actor
A Boy

Act 1

Scene 1

Enter JERONIMUS *and* FRANDS.
JERONIMUS. Good morning, Frands. What are you doing up so early?
FRANDS. I had business at Gammeltorv.
JERONIMUS. What's new in the market place?
FRANDS. Not much. They were hauling some man off to jail.
JERONIMUS. That's nothing new. Why were they jailing him?
FRANDS. He couldn't pay his debts.
JERONIMUS. That's nothing new either.
FRANDS. It seems he took a long trip abroad and ran up an enormous stack of bills.
JERONIMUS. Still nothing new! If I may

say so, dear neighbor, look at your own predicament. Your son . . . I won't say any more. I just hope I'm wrong. His fate affects me as much as it does you. After all, I promised him my daughter, Elsebet. But you wouldn't listen to me. He had to have his way. He wants to travel, he gets to travel, even though he's only a nineteen-year-old child!
FRANDS. May I remind you, Jeronimus, he turned twenty last January.
JERONIMUS. I can remember when he was born. It was the same time my sweet Birthe died. But that doesn't matter. Even if he is twenty years old, its foolish to let him go running off to foreign countries.
FRANDS. I won't argue about whether or not it's safe. You know that most young men in this country go abroad at his age.
JERONIMUS. You're absolutely right, dear neighbor. And they end up just like that scoundrel you saw in the market place—ready to be hanged for his debt. Why shouldn't your son hang as well as another?
FRANDS. That will never happen. Before he left he assured me of his honorable intentions.
JERONIMUS. Don't they all! I don't know how he's living in Paris, but I know one thing: I don't like his letters! He calls my daughter Elsebet, "Isabelle." He calls himself "Jean," and he calls me "Jerome"! He can call himself what he pleases. He can name himself "Fairfax" or "Rover" if he wants, as long as he calls my daughter and

me by our Christian names!

FRANDS. My dear neighbor, that's the custom! Young men do that to show off that they're learning a foreign language.

JERONIMUS. I don't doubt that it's the custom. I merely ask, is it a good custom? If a Frenchman named "Jean" visited this country and changed his name to "Hans" when he returned home, wouldn't his countrymen think he was crazy? It's a wonderful thing to learn a foreign language, but after we've mastered our own. It's a wonderful thing to visit foreign countries, but after we've gathered some years and maturity, after we've earned enough capital to live on our interest; or to learn a profession we can't learn here at home. But nowadays it's become the right of poor middle-class children to go on such trips. They plunge their families into debt just to learn a language, which for a few rixdalers they can learn from a tutor at home! Most of them get spoiled and learn nothing but dishonesty and immorality which they bring back to infect the homeland. They forget the good that our schools taught them. I can name at least a dozen young men who studied for the ministry. They even preached and earned great respect in Our Lady's Church and the Round Church, which has an educated congregation. Those same boys, following the custom, traveled abroad and, following the custom, threw away their Christianity for the Catechism! They threw away their money and brought back all sorts of strange political ideas. They walk around with their *Bonjure* and *Comment vous portez-vous*, starving themselves sick until they fall to melancholy and drunkeness! The parents see their children corrupted and themselves destroyed. Go on and laugh at me, dear neighbor, but it's true! If you saw all the money our children waste abroad you'd know why our country is so poor and powerless! Your son has already spent more than 1,500 rixdalers in

France. You say it's taught him to speak French, but you haven't said anything about how much Latin he's forgotten. The first things he's learned are foolishness and madness! I can see that in the letters he's sent me. What the devil am I going to do with a letter written in French? First I have to pay postage; next I have to give Jan Baptist a bottle of wine to translate it into German; and then I can hardly understand it!

FRANDS. It's no good arguing about it. We can't change what's already happened. Besides, it's not my fault. My wife insisted on it.

JERONIMUS. For shame! You should never put the blame on your wife! When you blame your wife you're merely blaming yourself. It's just as ridiculous for a man to say, "I'm ruined, but it's not my fault; that's what my wife wanted."

FRANDS. My heart, neighbor! You are so pessimistic! I'm not ruined yet, thank heaven. My son's coming home, so you can just be still. He left Paris four weeks ago. Let that be the end of it.

JERONIMUS. End of it! Ha ha ha! End of it? You'll learn neighbor, you'll learn! Our Danish youth aren't like the youth in Holland. Remember Herr Kalf's son out in Serdam? He traveled abroad a few years ago impersonating a prince, acting like royalty with his whole court! When he came home his family had to dispose of their horses, carriages, coachmen, servants—their entire estate—and put on peasants' clothes again. Maybe our cavalier, our loafer, will do the same. Sure, sure! Just try to give your son ale and bread for breakfast, like before, and see if he doesn't say, "I became accustomed to chocolate in Holland." Try to give him good Danish wheat or barley porridge and see if he doesn't cringe and the next night dine with a French chef! If they only brought home one nation's madness it might be all right. But they come home intertwining all of the absurdities from England, Germany, France, and Italy! I won't shut up, neighbor, because that's just how our young cavaliers act when they come home. In the morning they want their tea or chocolate, "Like I had in Holland"; in the afternoon, their coffee, "Like I had in England"; in the evening they want to play cards with their mistress, "Like I did in France"! When they go on an errand they want a lackey with them, "Like I had in Germany." Before they go to church they ask whether or not there's music, "Like there was in Italy." They think everything that's foreign is stylish and smart, even when they're being hauled off to jail because they can't pay their bills!

FRANDS. Now, now, Jeronimus. It can't be as bad as you think. Hasn't it been a long time since you got a letter from my son?

JERONIMUS. It must have been about four weeks.

FRANDS. He'd already left Paris four weeks ago.

JERONIMUS. That's possible. His last letter was postmarked from Rouen—or should I say "Ruin"? Isn't that somewhere in France?

FRANDS. Yes. From there he was going to sail home.

JERONIMUS. Rouen sounds like a name for a horse. But here comes your servant, Arv, on the run. I wonder what he wants.

Scene 2

Enter ARV.

ARV. I swear I'd give a daler to have my master at home. Hans Frandsen has arrived and no one can understand a word he says! He no sooner walked in when he asked, "Where is *mon pear?*" I couldn't believe my ears! Where the hell can I find a ripe pear in the month of May? I answered, "There aren't any in this country this time of year." Hans was bewildered by my answer and looks as though he'd never seen a Danish orchard. Then he asked about his *tray share mare.* I told him he could find a mare either at Ulfeld's Place or at the Halland Pond, because that's where

horses are kept. Then he called me a dog's name, *Garsong,* and other names I'm ashamed to mention.

FRANDS. What news, Arv?

ARV. A whole sackful.

FRANDS. Good or bad?

ARV. Both good and bad. Hans Frandsen has come home from the West Indies, but . . .

FRANDS. The West Indies?

ARV. He must have come from the West Indies—he's gone crazy! Or, maybe he's pregnant. After all, the first thing he craved was a ripe pear.

FRANDS. Otherwise, how does he look? I mean, how is he dressed?

ARV. He looks very strange. I don't know if you've seen a gilded cavalier, but that's how he looks. He has on a red coat and a hat on his head that's wider than six of mine. It's just as wide as the one that clown, Hans Wurst,[1] wore at the fair. Let me put it this way, he doesn't have to tell jokes to make us laugh. When he walks out in public he's a laughing stock! Now I have to run and deliver this letter for him.

FRANDS. Who's the letter for?

ARV. Some one named "Moens."

FRANDS. Let me see that letter. *"A Mons. Monsieur de Pedersen, Auditeur de la primiere Classe, in Copenhague."* This must be for his good friend Herr Professor Pedersen. You'd have run around for a long time looking for a man named "Moens." Where is my son?

ARV. He'll be here in a moment. Right now he's in the Green Room adjusting his wig for the play. I have to run! [*Exit.*]

Scene 3

Enter JEAN.

JEAN. La la la la la la. I can't quite remember the *bougre de pagrad* that *Monsieur Blondis* recently taught me. Excuse me, it's a *grand malleur. Mais voilà mon père et mon père*-in-law; *bon matin, Messieurs! comment vive ma chère Isabelle?*

JERONIMUS. Listen to me, Hans Frandsen! I was born on Christian-

Bernikov Street, as was my father. There has never been an *Isabelle* or *Fidelle* in our house. My name is Jeronimus Christophersen and my daughter's Elsebet, as God is my witness.

JEAN. It's all the same, *mon cher papa*-in-law. Elsebet is *Isabelle* or *Belle. Belle* does have more *panache.*

JERONIMUS. Anyone who calls my daughter "Bell" will have me to contend with! That's a dog's name! If you can't call us by our Christian names you'll have to find new in-laws. I'm an old-fashioned, honorable citizen and I don't like all of these new fads. You'd better listen to me instead of your highfaluten *parlez-vous.*

JEAN. *Pardonnez-moi, mon cher papa*-in-law, one never says, "new fads," *c'est ne pas bon Parisian, c'est Bas-breton, pardi.* La la la la. That's the latest *minuet, composé par le Sieur Blondis. Pardi,* that is an *habile homme, le plus grand Dantze-maitre en Europe.* Isn't it *"Dantze-maître"* in Danish, too? I completely lost my Danish in Paris.

JERONIMUS. It's a shame that you didn't forget every letter because neither the Danes nor the French can understand you! If you'd stayed in Paris another fortnight I suppose you'd have forgotten your name!

JEAN. *Non ma foi,* I'll never forget anything so simple; my name is *Jean de France, non pardi, non.*

FRANDS. "Jean de France Nong Paradise Nong?" Is that French for Hans Frandsen? Neighbor, that language must be more formal than ours!

JERONIMUS. Instead of asking me such trivia, don't you think it would be better if you rapped your son alongside the head!

JEAN. *Messieurs! je demande pardon,* I must go, we *Parisiens* don't spend too much time in one place. La la la la la la. I think I'll wander down to *à la Greve. Adieu* for now. [*Exit.*]

Scene 4

JERONIMUS. Goodbye neighbor, I pray you'll forgive me for being so pre-sumptuous as to speak to you. I hear your son will be a baron, therefore my daughter and I are unworthy of your company.

FRANDS. My heart, Jeronimus. Don't be so hasty. Have patience for two weeks. I hope by then this madness will have passed. You remember that Herman Frandsen's son was just like that. Remember how he killed everyone with his French jibberish? He was so caught up in it that he wouldn't even bed a girl if she wasn't French. He'd rather have eaten broth cooked over a fire by a French cook than Denmark's best meat soup. He even called the highest officials "monsieur," just because it was French, no matter how many enemies he made. Rather than step inside a Danish church he traveled all the way to Aabenraa for those French Calvinist meetings. But no more. Now when that man is in a rage he burns every French book he can find, including Bibles. He fights with men because he thinks they look French, even when they're Danish-born Christians! I hope in just a little time my son will become like him. But he must have something to do. I think I'll put him to work in my office. Then he'll have more to do all day than sing "la la la" and dance a "Fiol de Spain."

JERONIMUS. All right. One thing you can't say is I'm unreasonable. I'll be patient for two weeks. If he improves I'll see that he and my daughter are quickly married and that he gets a respectable job. But, neighbor, you don't want him to be around your office boys! It will only make trouble.

FRANDS. On the other hand, it just might be good. I'll see you later.

JERONIMUS. Goodbye. [*Exit.*]

Scene 5

Enter MAGDELONE.

MAGDELONE. Oh my dear husband! Have you seen Hans Frandsen?

FRANDS. All too much of him, God knows.

MAGDELONE. You always complained

that we did too much for our son.

FRANDS. That's true.

MAGDELONE. Well now we can be happy for him!

FRANDS. That's the truth! We can laugh ourselves to death when we look at him!

MAGDELONE. He's such a sweet boy.

FRANDS. Do tell!

MAGDELONE. Just think, how well he's learned to speak French in such a short time.

FRANDS. Incredible.

MAGDELONE. I hardly recognized him when I saw him!

FRANDS. Me neither.

MAGDELONE. He's so alive!

FRANDS. Isn't he.

MAGDELONE. And so polite.

FRANDS. Terribly.

MAGDELONE. France can completely change a man.

FRANDS. That's for damned sure.

MAGDELONE. He called me *Mardamme.*

FRANDS. Did he?

MAGDELONE. He said it's too common to say, "Mother."

FRANDS. That might be.

MAGDELONE. But he called his sweetheart *"Mattress."* I thought that was odd.

FRANDS. How so?

MAGDELONE. Maybe it has another use in France.

FRANDS. Could be.

MAGDELONE. Thank heaven he doesn't mind being seen with his old-fashioned parents.

FRANDS. That's true.

MAGDELONE. Then why are you crying, dear husband? It must be because he's so happy. [*Aside.*] That man thinks more of his children than he lets on. [*To Frands.*] I've also cried for joy.

FRANDS. And I for sorrow!

MAGDELONE Sorrow?

FRANDS. Yes! For sorrow! Can't an honorable man cry when he sees his son transformed into a phony French fool?

MAGDELONE. What did you say, dumbox? Is my son a fool?

FRANDS. Yes! Captain of all fools!

MAGDELONE. Why must I be plagued with such a boorish husband who can't even recognize quality? My only joy in the world is that sweet boy, who my husband doesn't appreciate. Wild beasts love their offspring. Even Turks and heathens love their children! You alone hate your son, whom cultured foreigners adore. I shouldn't brag about my own son, but I don't believe there's a more refined boy in Denmark than Hans Frandsen. If only you had common sense you could see it!

FRANDS. Just where in him is this culture?

MAGDELONE. It is in him because he is cultured.

FRANDS. I don't see any culture in him worth 1,500 rixdalers!

MAGDELONE. All you talk about is money. You say nothing of what he's learned.

FRANDS. I see that he learned to dance a *Fiol de Spain,* to sing a lot of love poems, and to destroy his own language. I don't think he can speak either Danish or French!

MAGDELONE. I have nothing more to say to that crass man. I swear I won't share my bed with you for one more night!

FRANDS. Stay, dear wife, while I tell you something.

MAGDELONE. Not one more word.

FRANDS. Good God! What a temper!

MAGDELONE. Let me go!

FRANDS. No, Magdelone, I didn't mean any harm.

MAGDELONE. No more talk. I *will* go.

FRANDS. Stay, Little Sweetheart, and you'll hear what you want to hear.

MAGDELONE. Slanderer!

FRANDS. My sugar.

MAGDELONE. Gossip!

FRANDS. Ducky.

MAGDELONE. Let me go!

FRANDS. Little syrup cake.

MAGDELONE. Away!

FRANDS. Buttercup.

MAGDELONE. I won't listen!

FRANDS. My daffodil.

MAGDELONE. Nothing!

FRANDS. My heart's joy.

MAGDELONE. Go sleep with the devil!

FRANDS. My perfumed posy.

MAGDELONE. Go to hell!

FRANDS. My dearest wife. Don't be so

mad at your little husband.
MAGDELONE. No sweet talk.
FRANDS. At your own little Frands.
MAGDELONE. Away! You deceiving snake!
FRANDS. I was only joking, sweetheart. Did you think I was serious?
MAGDELONE. Didn't you mean it?
FRANDS. Honest. Don't you think I can see how cultured my own son has become? I said those things to joke a little with you. Believe me, I cried of utter joy. [*Aside.*] Oh God, to have peace at home it's better to give up both my own and my son's welfare!
MAGDELONE. Since you were only joking, sweet husband, I'm all right again. Oh! Here he comes!

Scene 6

JEAN *enters singing a French verse.*
MAGDELONE. Just look at him and see if we don't have reason to love our son.
FRANDS. You're right about that, Magdelone.
MAGDELONE. My heart, son! You mustn't stay away from your mama so long. I can't stand to be without you for a second.
JEAN. What does Madam think of this *Contretemps* that I learned just before I left Paris? [*He does a little dance step.*] I don't believe, *pardi,* anyone can do it in this country. I can even do it in several *façons;* for example, first [*He does a slight variation.*] and second like this. [*He does another slight variation.*]
MAGDELONE. Isn't that a marvelous Capriol, Frands?
JEAN. It is not a "Capriol," Madam! It is a *Contretemps!*
MAGDELONE. I don't understand, dear son, you must forgive me. In the old days I learned a plain, simple minuet, but nothing more.
JEAN. Can Madam still dance?
MAGDELONE. Yes . . . maybe.
JEAN. Then let us dance a minuet together, so you can see the steps I know.
MAGDELONE. I'm afraid it would be an odd minuet. I'm too old to dance.
JEAN. Don't be ridiculous! *La tour seulement!*

MAGDELONE. No, my dearest son. I pray you, excuse me.
JEAN. *Ah pardi, je m'en mocque. La tour seulement!*
FRANDS. [*Aside.*] I couldn't be more pleased if you gave me ten rixdalers. I don't care if he makes her dance in front of the royal palace! After all, she encouraged him.
MAGDELONE. My heart, son! Don't embarrass me!
JEAN. No, *sans façon!* It doesn't become you to beg. *La tour seulement!*
FRANDS. [*Aside.*] It's beautiful!
MAGDELONE. My feet are too stiff for dancing.
JEAN. *Pardi! mardi! peste! diantre! tête bleue!* Now I'm mad! Can't you just do this for me! *La tour seulement!*
MAGDELONE. If you promise not to be angry, I'll do what I can.
FRANDS. [*Aside.*] Ha ha ha!
JEAN. Papa, you must sing a minuet.
FRANDS. What? Me, sing?
JEAN. And be sure you keep the right beat while you're doing it!
FRANDS. I'm upset enough already. You'd better sing for yourself.
JEAN. *No, pardi c'est impossible,* how can I sing and dance *dans le même temps?*
MAGDELONE. If I can do our son the favor of dancing, you can certainly sing for him!
FRANDS. You don't seem to think I'm serious, wife. I won't make a fool of myself! I'm too old for that.
JEAN. *Tête bleue! j'enrage!*
MAGDELONE. My dear son! Don't be so angry! You'd better believe he'll sing, even if it drives him crazy!
JEAN. *Ach pardi, chantez donc.*
MAGDELONE. You are the most annoying man in the whole world!
JEAN. *Diable m'emporte, si . . .* [*Crying,* FRANDS *begins to sing the Watchmen's Song, while* JEAN *and* MAGDELONE *dance.*]
JEAN. That isn't a minuet, papa. Don't you know a minuet?
FRANDS. This is the only song I know.
MAGDELONE. Then sing it! It doesn't matter if its an old song! [FRANDS *sings and whistles as they turn away, dancing very absurdly. Intermittently* JEAN *yells,* "La cadance, mon père! La cadance!" *At the end of the dance he*

exits.]

FRANDS. [*Aside.*] Woe is me that I should have brought such a son into the world. I'd better get some advice before my entire house becomes a laughing stock! [*Exeunt.*]

don't you ask Espen and me to put our heads together? You know that nothing is impossible when the two of us scheme! Give us a little time to think about it. In the meantime, don't worry. [*Exit* ANTONIUS *and* ELSEBET.]

Act 2

Scene 1

Enter ANTONIUS, ELSEBET, MARTHE, *and* ESPEN.

ANTONIUS. Elsebet, my dearest love! My heart is breaking because my rival has returned from Paris.

ELSEBET. How do you think my heart feels? I'm the one who is supposed to marry Hans Frandsen, the most abominable man in the whole world! I hated him even before he went to France. He's so conceited and repulsive. I knew he'd go crazy if he traveled abroad.

ANTONIUS. Would you actually marry such a man?

ELSEBET. Not if I have my way, sweet Antonius. But you know my father. He's hard-headed as flint. What he says, goes—even if it ruins his own home.

ANTONIUS. I promise as long as I live I won't let that happen.

ELSEBET. How do you intend to stop it?

ANTONIUS. I say it; therefore it is so. Before I allowed my eyes to see such a thing, I would kill myself.

ELSEBET. And I promise you, you passionate man, that if you kill yourself, with that same sword I will also end my days. But let's not do that! Instead we must find someone who can save us from this predicament. Neither our parents nor anything in the world shall destroy the pact that has joined our hearts together.

ANTONIUS. Now I am satisfied.

MARTHE. You love-crazed fools! Instead of standing there groaning, why

Scene 2

MARTHE. Espen, you're a conniving rascal, what can we do to help Elsebet?

ESPEN. You're right. I am so clever!

MARTHE. Any scheme will do. It doesn't have to be bad enough to get you hanged. But if you aren't hanged for this, they'll get you for something else soon enough.

ESPEN. I don't think I'll be hanged too soon. At least not if I believe the gypsy who read my palm the other day.

MARTHE. What did she say?

ESPEN. She told me that I wouldn't be hanged until you'd been whipped and jailed for at least three years.

MARTHE. Rubbish! The old prophets are dead and the new ones don't work.

ESPEN. That's what you think. That hag was so old she didn't have a tooth in her mouth. You couldn't understand a word because she mumbled.

MARTHE. Then how could she tell you that I'd be jailed? Liars have to have good memories!

ESPEN. She explained everything with gestures.

MARTHE. Such talk! Let's get to work. We're losing valuable time.

ESPEN. I'm not in the mood to scheme just now, Mammeselle.

MARTHE. Shame on you, snake! I'll show you who's in the mood! If you won't help me I'll find someone else. If I felt like it I could arrange for ten carriages with gentlemen's lackeys to serve me. Now, I believe our work is to come up with some intrigue.

ESPEN. You made yourself clear. [*They pace back and forth.*]

MARTHE. Have you thought of anything, Espen?

ESPEN. Yes. I figured out a way to weasle money out of old man Jeronimus.

MARTHE. You dunce! That's so passé!
You probably stole the idea from a
French comedy. I have a plan that
will work. Let's call back the lovers
and see what they think of it. Hey!
Paris and Helen! Come in and listen
to this.

Scene 3

Enter ELSEBET *and* ANTONIUS.

ELSEBET. Here we are. What have you
come up with?

MARTHE. We counselors have agreed
that since society is of the opinion
that it is a terrible sin to rebel against
your parents, it would be best for
you to dismiss this love from your
mind and marry the man to whom
you have been promised.

ELSEBET. You must be joking!

MARTHE. Yes, I am joking. But I have
learned that you can't reason with
parents in these matters. They arrange marriages for their own
interests, so they can align themselves
with families who can help them.
They often sacrifice their children's
welfare for such arrangements.
Young people, on the other hand,
don't think about such things. They
want to marry for happiness, or love
just for love's sake. Do you concur
with me, Herr Colleague?

ESPEN. Yes, that's the way it is.

MARTHE. If I was a lawyer assessing
your case it would be the same as if I
was a judge with a fool at his side—
I'd always have two *vota*.

ESPEN. Do you understand Latin, Marthe?

MARTHE. As much as you.

ESPEN. Do you know what this means:
Mulier taceat in Ecclesia?

MARTHE. No, I don't.

ESPEN. In Danish we say it this way: that
sows, like you, had better stick to
their spinning wheels and not trouble themselves with matters that the
Lord created men, like me, to resolve.

MARTHE. Watch your mouth, Espen!
The time will come when society will
consider brains more important than
sex and ability greater than name!

When our intellects are weighed I
shall be elevated to the position of
magistrate and you won't be any
higher than a pancake!

ESPEN. Let's stop wasting time bickering
and get to the heart of the matter!

MARTHE. Let Espen talk. He has some
wise counsel for you.

ESPEN. Stop preaching, Marthe. Tell us
what you've planned to help these
poor lovers.

MARTHE. First, you will admit you're a
dummy.

ESPEN. Like hell I will.

ELSEBET. Sweet Espen, for my sake,
can't you admit you're a dummy?

ESPEN. All right! I'm a dummy! Are you
satisfied?

MARTHE. Whether you mean it or not,
it's true. He meditated almost a half-
hour like he was preparing a sermon,
but all he came up with was a worn-
out comic device. On the other hand,
here's my plan: You've heard that
Hans Frandsen is so caught up in
anything French, that if it were Parisian to walk around in broad daylight
without pants, he'd do it! Now, remember I worked for a French chef
for three years? Well I learned
enough French for everyday conversation. I'll masquerade as a French
lady who has just come here from
Paris because I love Hans Frandsen.
What happens after that only time
will tell. Just follow my lead. Espen
will be my valet.

ELSEBET. We'd better get you dressed
for the part, then!

ANTONIUS. Hurry, sweetheart! You
dress Marthe and I'll take care of
Espen.

ESPEN. You must no longer call me
Espen. Refer to me as Herr Valet.

ANTONIUS. Then go, Herr Valet! [*Exit*
ELSEBET, MARTHE, *and* ESPEN.]

Scene 4

Enter ARV.

ARV. Ha ha ha ha ha ha!

ANTONIUS. Isn't that Arv, Frands
Hansen's servant?

ARV. Ha ha ha ha ha! The devil's made
them all crazy!

ANTONIUS. What's so funny, Arv?

ARV. Oh, Monsieur Antonius, I'm ready to die laughing!

ANTONIUS. What could possibly make you laugh like that?

ARV. I was walking down the street and saw the most absurd dance!

ANTONIUS. Who was dancing?

ARV. Hans Frandsen was dancing with his mother while his father sang for them!

ANTONIUS. No! What talk!

ARV. I swear it's true! I didn't know Magdelone could dance so shamelessly. She wiggled her rump like this. I wish I could draw a picture of the whole scene. All the while Hans danced he yelled, "*Lacka Dance! My pear, Lacka Dance!*" What that means only the devil knows. I could see that poor old Frands was singing against his will—he sang, cried, and swore all at the same time!

ANTONIUS. Who could have forced him to sing against his will?

ARV. Everyone in that house dances to Hans Frandsen's tune. He rules over his mother and she rules Frands.

ANTONIUS. That boy must be crazy.

ARV. I think he suffered a hard blow to the head in France. He calls me *Garsong*, a dog's name. I swear if he calls me *Garsong* once more I'll answer, "Listen, Twinkle Toes, I can prove by the parish records that I was christened Arv Andersen." But what can I say when his mother lets him call her *Mare*? That's much worse. And when Jeronimus finds out what he calls his daughter, he'll thrash him!

ANTONIUS. What does he call her?

ARV. I'm afraid you'll tell someone else.

ANTONIUS. I swear I won't.

ARV. He calls her his *Mattress!* It's true enough that a wife is sort of a blanket in bed, but it's not right for Hans to call Elsebet either his blanket or his mattress. They aren't even married! I've got to run. [*Exit.*]

Scene 5

Enter ELSEBET.

ELSEBET. It's terrible for parents to let themselves be dominated by a mad child.

ANTONIUS. My dearest Elsebet. The madder he gets, the better it is for us. The worst news I could hear is that he's improving.

ELSEBET. My dear Antonius! Our happiness lies in the hands of Espen and Marthe. My father has a kind of absurd honor; even though he sees misery, he won't break his promise. He says it's not for the sake of the individual, but for the family.

ANTONIUS. But what if their scheme fails and Jeronimus won't go back on his word? What will you do then?

ELSEBET. Antonius! Stop plaguing me with your foolish questions! I already declared myself once. But here comes my father. Run away as fast as you can. [*Exit* ANTONIUS.]

Scene 6

Enter JERONIMUS.

JERONIMUS. My little buttercup! Don't you have more to do than stand in the doorway watching young men stroll by? I'm not like Frands Hansen. I'm not going to be as lax as he is with his children. If I had a son like Hans Frandsen, I'd twist his head on straight!

ELSEBET. My dear Father, if you can see how revolting he is, why will you force me to marry him?

JERONIMUS. Will you argue, too? Will you ask why I do things? It should be enough for you that I want it. At the least we'll become related to a fine family. That's worth everything! Frands Hansen is not only honest, but is quite well-to-do. Besides that, I've given my promise and I will not break it.

ELSEBET. But, Papa . . .

JERONIMUS. "Papa! Papa?" Are you going to speak French, too? Don't you dare call me Papa again! What else do you have to say?

ELSEBET. Just this, Frands Hansen is a wonderful man. But it's not him I have to marry; it's his son. And his son is revolting! I've already heard a dozen crazy stories about him since he came home.

JERONIMUS. [*Aside.*] Notice how she's trying to weasel news out of me. [*Aloud.*]Get inside to your embroidery! "I've already heard a dozen stories!" Do you believe everything you hear? I'll tell you one thing, Elsebet, you're going to be married next week. I'm a man who's strong enough to keep both you and Hans Frandsen in control! Now get inside! [*Exeunt.*]

Act 3

Scene 1

Enter JEAN *and* PIERRE.
JEAN. Pierre!
PIERRE. *Que voulez vous?*
JEAN. *Fripon! maraut! coquin! bougre! badaud! fainéant! que la peste t'étouffe, que le Diable t'emporte, t'enlève, t'abîme, que le diantre.*
PIERRE. What are you swearing at me for?
JEAN. How could you have lived with me *dans* Paris for fifteen weeks and not learned, *comment* to answer your lord when he calls you? You should say: *Monsieur! mais non pas: Que voulez-vous?*
PIERRE. Such a minor thing! Not worth so much swearing!
JEAN. That's true. But it isn't so much to curse at you. I need to practice my French. Last month I received a list of forty new curses from my *Maître de langue.* I can't practice them without you.
PIERRE. You can practice your curses on yourself! Just say *me* instead of *te.* Then no one is offended.
JEAN. Oh, Pierre. I wish we were back in Paris again. *Dieu donne, que nous étions dans Paris* again. Damn! I can't remember the French word for "again."
PIERRE. It's *"aussi."*
JEAN. That's right, *"aussi."* Feel free to correct me whenever I make a mistake. Don't you wish we were in Paris *aussi?*
PIERRE. Oh, sure! Anywhere we can be hungry, thirsty, and freeze is the place for me.
JEAN. Oh! *bougre! crasseux! gourmand!* You speak as if you were born *à la Place Maubere* or *à la Pont neuf, comme un crocheteur, un décrotteur des souliers, un porteur d'eau.*
PIERRE. Monsieur talks like *un fou, un bête un* Fool, *un sot, un bouffon,* as if you were born *dans un* madhouse or in a theater!
JEAN. What did you say, *bourreau?*
PIERRE. You shouldn't get so upset, Monsieur, I was just practicing my French.
JEAN. Of course. *Ecoutez,* Pierre.
PIERRE. Monsieur!
JEAN. I can't stand to see all these Danish faces.
PIERRE. Mademoiselle Isabelle has a pretty face.
JEAN. It's pretty enough, but it's so Danish; *c'est une visage à la Danois, à la Copenhague, pardi.* But I could get used to her face if she didn't speak Danish.
PIERRE. Has Monsieur talked with her since he's come home?
JEAN. *Ouis pardi si fait,* but do you know what she said?
PIERRE. *Non pardi non fait.*
JEAN. She said, "Welcome home again, Hans!" Oh! When I think about it my stomach leaps to my throat! If she were a French woman she would have said, *"Je suis ravi de vous voir, mon cher m'aime Jean de France!"*
PIERRE. *Ouis pardi si fait.* The French language really is picturesque, even though they don't mean anything by it.
JEAN. *Mademoiselle Isabelle parle comme une blanchisseuse dans Paris.*
PIERRE. *Ouis pardi si fait.*
JEAN. *Comme une fripière.*
PIERRE. *Ouis pardi si fait.*
JEAN. *Comme une femme, qui clame: Renet, renet! dans les rues.*
PIERRE. *Ouis pardi si fait.*
JEAN. *Comme une femme, qui va avec un âne dans la rue et clame: Lait, lait!*
PIERRE. *Ouis pardi si fait.*

JEAN. Pierre, we'll practice our French and not say one word of Danish.

PIERRE. *Ouis pardi si fait.* What we can't say in French we'll explain by gestures and grimaces. Then we'll even look like we were born in France!

JEAN. Pierre.

PIERRE. Monsieur.

JEAN. I'm going to eat dinner *chez Pêche.*

PIERRE. Wouldn't you rather eat at Master Jacob's? You get a lot better food there for a lot less.

JEAN. At Master Jacob's? The name alone proves he's a bad cook! If there weren't a French chef in the city I'd starve to death.

PIERRE. That's true, the food does taste good when it's French, since they give you so little of it. Nothing piques the appetite more than being served a tiny portion.

JEAN. Do you know of any other French chef?

PIERRE. *Ouis Monsieur! si fait pardi,* there's another named Cabo.

JEAN. Which of them speaks the better French?

PIERRE. They both speak about the same. It's nice to listen to both of them. When they do their best they throw in a few Spanish words, and that's very beautiful. But who is that strange servant? I wonder where he's going.

Scene 2

Enter ESPEN.

ESPEN. I was told he lives somewhere around here. There are two people, I can ask them. *Avec Permission, Monsieurs!* Do you know any of the people around here?

JEAN. Yes, I know myself, *moi-même.*

ESPEN. There are a lot of people who know themselves. But I don't think there are four people in this city who could say it! Isn't there a Danish Monsieur who lives around here, named Jean de France?

JEAN. *Je m'appelle Jean de France à votre très humble service.*

PIERRE. I'll translate his answer to Danish. "My name is Hans Frandsen, at your service." You'll excuse me for having to explain my master's words. He can still understand Danish, but he has difficulty expressing himself. He has just returned from living fifteen weeks in Paris, where he didn't hear a single Danish word.

ESPEN. Wow! Fifteen weeks! You certainly have my respect. I've been in the service of the French lady, Madame la Flèche, for only two days and already when I speak Danish I find a French word or two in my mouth. If his name is Monsieur Jean de France, he's the man I'm looking for. Aren't you the man who just came back from Paris?

JEAN. *Ouis, Monsieur.*

ESPEN. The one who lived there for fifteen weeks?

JEAN. *Ouis, Monsieur!*

ESPEN. The one who lived in the Quarter of the city—what's it called— it's right on the tip of my tongue.

JEAN. *Faubourg St. Germain.*

ESPEN. That's the one! And on the street that's so crooked.

JEAN. No, the street is very straight.

ESPEN. Yes, it's straight enough, but when you reach its end you do have to turn onto another street. I think that's what my lady said. The street's name is . . .

JEAN. *La rue de Seine.*

ESPEN. Yes, that's the street! The gentleman is supposed to have a servant—a very talented and good-looking man named Pierre.

PIERRE. *À votre très humble service.*

ESPEN. I see that I've found the right man. I have a humble compliment to deliver to Monsieur from Madame la Flèche.

JEAN. Is it possible? And how is the charming lady?

ESPEN. She said that she had the honor of meeting you in Paris and that she came to Denmark because of you.

JEAN. *Ah la charmante Dame!* I spent many wonderful hours with her in Paris!

PIERRE. Monsieur, you've never met the woman.

JEAN. *Taisez-vous, bougre!* Don't you know it's *à la française* to answer that

way? If I admitted I didn't know her
he'd take me for a native Dane. You'll
never learn to act refined. I should
say that I respect Madame la Flèche
above all others. *Pardi, est-il possibel*
that Madame la Flèche came to Denmark on my account? I would gladly
travel to India, or even further—to
Africa—just to kiss her beautiful
hand. How long ago did she leave
Paris?

ESPEN. Twelve days.

JEAN. Oh, *est-il possibel?* Just twelve
days! May I have the *bonheur* to kiss
her hand, and the honor to speak
with her?

ESPEN. Nothing would please her more.
That's why she sent me to find you.

JEAN. Oh, Monsieur! Please arrange our
meeting and, here, accept these
ducats as a sign of friendship.

ESPEN. My lady, Madame la Flèche, is
one of the wealthiest women in
France, so I am not in need of your
gift. But so you don't think me aloof,
I will accept it. On the other hand, I
hope Monsieur is not above accept-
ing this small gift from my lady—a
portrait painted by Monsieur Cabbage Banàl, France's greatest
miniature artist. Just before she left
Paris it became the highest fashion
for a cavalier to wear one of these
around his neck in honor of his lady.
My lady hopes that Monsieur will
wear this around his neck for her.

JEAN. I shall quickly *dans votre presence*
hang it around my neck. May I be so
bold and *impudent* to take the *Liberté*
to ask, just how can Madame la
Flèche speak with you? I mean, after
all, you don't understand French.

ESPEN. Madame la Flèche can travel
anywhere in the world! She, of
course speaks Parisien, her mother
tongue, but also German, Italian,
Dutch, Polandish, Prussian, and a lot
of Danish that she picked up along
the way.

JEAN. It's a great *complaisance*, that such
a distinguished lady would take the
trouble to learn such a low language.
Since you were born in Denmark,
does she speak Danish to you?

ESPEN. No, Monsieur! I was not born in
Denmark! Only my enemies say that.
I was born more than fifty miles
south of Randers, where we are considered a branch of the Holy Roman
Empire. So I'm Roman, not Danish! I
humbly request Monsieur to explain
that to everyone he knows.

JEAN. It would be a shame to do otherwise. After all, it's evident by your
manières and accent that you're not
Danish. Tell me, where might I have
the good fortune of seeing Madame
la Flèche?

ESPEN. Anywhere you like. Or at three
o'clock right here.

JEAN. Then I will *présentement* take the
opportunity to kiss her *belles mains*.

ESPEN. I'm sure she'll love that!

JEAN. *Je me recommende.* [*Exit* ESPEN.]

Scene 3

JEAN. Pierre.

PIERRE. Monsieur!

JEAN. What do you think of this portrait?

PIERRE. If you didn't know it was a
miniature, you'd think it was a picture cut out of a book and pasted
onto a piece of wood.

JEAN. *C'est pourtant fait per le Sieur Cabbage Banàl, le plus grand* painter *en
Europa.*

PIERRE. Just how does Monsieur know
that?

JEAN. Didn't you hear Monsieur say it
with his own mouth? Don't you think
he knows? I'll tell you one thing, men
who were born in the Holy Roman
Empire are no dummies! Oh, no!
Here come those two old philistines
again. I was so happy in France; but
here you can't have an elegant conversation with anyone! All they talk
about is the weather and their families.

Scene 4

Enter JERONIMUS *and* FRANDS.

JERONIMUS. You'd better believe it,
Frands, anyone who invests in only
coffee, tea, and tobacco can amass
several kegs of gold a year. That

money can be saved for your old age.

FRANDS. It takes a lot of gold to fill a keg.

JERONIMUS. Not true, neighbor, not true! The average household doesn't spend 100 rixdalers a year. Now that's just one account, if we add in several others you'll quickly understand what I mean. For example, just the other day, to be stylish, I went into a Coffee House. It cost me a small fortune for just a few cups of coffee. You can believe I won't go back there soon.

FRANDS. True, it has been expensive. But now the prices are beginning to go down.

JERONIMUS. That's not true in Tea Houses. I've noticed that here in Copenhagen, once prices are raised they stay high even when the wholesale price drops.

FRANDS. That's the truth, Jeronimus. But remember that we also have to eat. What's the use of having money if you don't use it?

JERONIMUS. Can you get a good, natural taste from water and burnt beans? Try to give coffee without sugar to a baby. He spits it out! Maybe some people, like your son, Hans Frandsen, think it tastes heavenly. But I say, such idiots have forced themselves to go against nature, merely because coffee is fashionable and because it's foreign. Later they think it tastes good by force of habit.

FRANDS. Look, there's my son now.

JERONIMUS. Yes, it's him. I'm not afraid to set the record straight. I'll tell him to his face. What the hell is that trinket hanging around his neck?

FRANDS. Maybe it's the style in Paris.

JERONIMUS. I don't give a damn if it's fashionable. Only a fool walks around dressed differently than all his countrymen.

FRANDS. Listen to me, son. What is that little saint-thing hanging around your neck? Everyone is going to think you're either crazy or Catholic.

JEAN. Pierre!

PIERRE. Monsieur.

JEAN. *Pierre! expliquez cela pour ce vieux homme; je vais, vous me trouverez après de Monsieur Pêche.* [*Exit.*]

Scene 5

FRANDS. Peer! Why did my son run off so abruptly?

PIERRE. He had something to do and asked me to make his excuses.

FRANDS. What kind of pendant was that around his neck?

PIERRE. That is a miniature portrait that he brought back from France.

FRANDS. It's the style to wear those in France?

PIERRE. Good heavens, yes! Anyone in France who doesn't wear one is labeled a bumpkin and can never amount to anything!

FRANDS. But the workmanship was so shoddy. I think I could do better.

PIERRE. Be careful what you say, Monsieur, you could get into a lot of trouble! That portrait was executed by Monsieur Cabbage Banàl, the greatest living artist in all of Paris!

JERONIMUS. I'll bet I can find that in an old chronicle at home. I could see that it was only a picture clipped out of a book. Neighbor, your son is a fool! And you're not much better. Much as I favored this engagement, I won't sell out my only daughter to the likes of him. And you, scoundrel, if you want to stay healthy, tell us who drove him to this madness!

PIERRE. I give you my word that I don't know where he got that picture. But I swear under the portrait are the words, *Monsieur Cabbage Banàl fecit.*

FRANDS. Shame on you, Peer, for being so coarse!

JERONIMUS. Give me your cane, neighbor! When your master asks who beat you, just say, "Jeronimus faked it!" [PIERRE *runs out crying.*]

Scene 6

JERONIMUS. Listen, neighbor, I hope we can continue our friendship even though I've cancelled the engagement.

FRANDS. You promised to be patient for two weeks to see if my son would come to his senses. If you break down so quickly there'll be such gossip in this city! For the sake of our friendship, be patient for that long.

JERONIMUS. All right. Two weeks will pass quickly. But I'm convinced he'll only get worse.

FRANDS. I ask for nothing more than the two weeks.

JERONIMUS. I can wait that long.

FRANDS. Goodbye! If I don't get home for dinner my wife will come after me!

JERONIMUS. *Prosit Mahlzeit!* [*Exeunt.*]

Act 4

Scene 1

Enter ANTONIUS, ELSEBET, MARTHE, *and* ESPEN.

ANTONIUS. How's everything going, Marthe?

MARTHE. Fine! But you've come at a terrible time! Hans Frandsen's on his way here. He hasn't even seen me yet, but he's as beguiled as a rat. What an ass! I made a pendant by pasting an old picture on a piece of wood. I told him it was French and he's actually wearing it!

ELSEBET. What idiocy! How can he do this to himself?

MARTHE. He believes I'm a French lady, newly arrived from Paris. I can make him do anything!

ANTONIUS. What's the point of debasing him?

MARTHE. When I'm finished, Jeronimus would rather see his daughter married to a chimney sweep than to Hans Frandsen. I don't know how it will work out for you and Elsebet. Right now I feel like the author of a comedy—while he's writing he has no idea how everthing will work out. Oh! I see him coming! Quick, get out of sight! [*Exit* ANTONIUS *and* ELSEBET.]

Scene 2

Enter JEAN.

MARTHE. *A cette heure il doit venir;* war das nicht um drei Uhr, *Monsieur d'Espang!* dasz is promised zu kommen?

JEAN. [*Kneeling, he takes her hand.*] *Ach charmante Madame! souffrez que j'adore vous, souffrez, que je baise votres beaux mains.*

MARTHE. [*Motions him to rise.*] *Levez-vous, Monsieur! c'est trop de humblesses pour un gentil-homme comme vous.*

JEAN. *Ah Madame! est-il possibel*, that I have the honor, *le plaisir, contentement et* meet you in this country?

MARTHE. May I practice my Danish? I have come to see *vous, mais je ne croyais pas, que vous étiez si changé.* Your clothes are so *antique bourgeois.* Ha ha ha!

JEAN. *Pourquoi* do you laugh, *charmante Princesse?*

MARTHE. *Rien, Monsieur de France!* It's nothing. Merely the joy of seeing *vous, c'est toujours une plaisir de vous voir.*

JEAN. *Je vous rend grace, Madame!* What do you think of our little country?

MARTHE. *Oh bon, Monsieur!* The Danes are such a good people. They are just ignorant of Parisian manners.

JEAN. *Ouis pardi si fait, Madame.* How true! *Dieu donne, que j'étais dans Paris* again. Have you brought any other new styles from Paris?

MARTHE. *Ouis Monsieur!* Here is the latest tune:

Frère Jacque, Frère Jacque
Dormez-vous, Dormez-vous
Sonnes les matines, Sonnes les matines
Din din dong, din din dong.

JEAN. I have never heard such a beautiful tune! Ah, Paris, Paris!

MARTHE. Why do you weep, *Monseigneur?*

JEAN. *Ah Madame! on veut me marier dans cette pays.*

MARTHE. *Marier?*

JEAN. *Ouis Madame.*

MARTHE. Marriage?

JEAN. *Ouis c'est veritable.* I have been engaged to a girl named [*He grimaces.*] "Elsebet."

MARTHE. What a vulgar name! *Parlezvous tout de bon, Monsieur? ah est-il possible?* [*She swoons;* ESPEN *rushes to her.*]

ESPEN. You can see how much Madame loves you Monsieur! It sickens her to learn that you will be married in this country.

JEAN. If Madame dies, I'll kill myself. Monsieur Valet! Inform Elsebet that I would rather die than marry her. [*Kneeling.*] *Ah belle Princesse! êtes-vous malade?*

MARTHE. It has passed, Monsieur! *Levez-vous.* [ESPEN *whispers in her ear; she looks very pleased.*]

Scene 3

ARV *enters and sits on the floor with a large piece of chalk and draws the dance he saw.*

ARV. This is how they looked when they danced—twisted like a pretzel! Here is Hans Frandsen—and there goes his mother. No. I have to draw her again. I didn't make her rump wide enough. This is where his father stood crying. [*He stands up to examine his work. All the while, the others have watched, pointed, and whispered.*] Ha ha ha! That's so lifelike! Everyone will know who it is and what they're doing! Oh! There are people over there! Isn't that Marthe talking to Hans Frandsen? Hey, Marthe! Where the devil did you get that costume? It's too early! Halloween isn't for months!

JEAN. [*He raps* ARV *alongside the head.*] You snake! How dare you speak to such a fine French lady?

ARV. Excuse me, Monsieur Hans! I thought it was Jeronimus's servant, Marthe!

MARTHE. *Ah, Monsieur! faites le sortir!* Get him away! I am afraid of madmen!

JEAN. Get out, snake! Before I smash your head! [ARV *runs out.* MARTHE *begins to examine* JEAN's *clothes. She whispers to* ESPEN *and they laugh. She*

looks at JEAN's *legs, whispers again to* ESPEN *and they laugh again.*]

JEAN. *Pourquoi riez-vous, belle Madame?*

MARTHE. I must leave now. *Monsieur d'Espang, mon valet de chambre,* will explain. *Excusez. Adieu!* [*Exit.*]

Scene 4

JEAN. *Monsieur le valet de chambre, Monsieur d'Espang!* Why did your lady treat me with such contempt? What did she whisper to you?

ESPEN. If I'd only known earlier I could have prepared you! But it should be easy to correct. Madame la Flèche said that even though she has great respect for your character, she despises the way you are dressed.

JEAN. Have the styles changed since I left Paris? On my way home I stayed for three weeks in Rouen.

ESPEN. Yes, Monsieur, you've discovered the problem. Madame le Flèche says that no Parisian cavalier has buttoned his coat like that in weeks! Coats are buttoned in the back now. It may seem a little uncomfortable, but you get used to it. All of the gentlemen have their servants button their coats up the back for them.

JEAN. *Ah malheureaux que je suis!*

ESPEN. It's easy to change. I'll help you.

JEAN. *Vous me faites un grand plaisir, pardi.*

ESPEN. [*Buttons* JEAN's *coat up his back.*] Now don't you look different!

JEAN. Are there any other changes I should make?

ESPEN. Yes. Fortunately they're all easy to make. According to Madame la Flèche, all of the elegant men in Paris smear their mouths with snuff.

JEAN. I can do that! My snuff box is right here. I assure you, I'm never the last one to accept the new styles! Just before I left Paris I heard that several new styles were expected, but my papa was so anxious to have me home I could not wait for them. *Je vous prie, Monsieur de Valet,* please make my apologies to Madame la Flèche—these styles weren't in vogue when I left Paris, *non pardi non.* I have too great a respect for Parisian styles to neglect them.

ESPEN. The whole world must admit that Paris is the birthplace of fashion. All civilized men accept Parisian fashions sooner or later. If Parisians decided to walk the streets without their pants, all of the world would soon do likewise.

JEAN. I know I would. In the beginning everyone would laugh, but within a year they would all follow suit. But, *Monsieur de Valet,* are there any changes with wigs, shoes, hats, or stockings?

ESPEN. No, Madame says that your hat and wig are all right. But, your jabot must hang down your back.

JEAN. Oh, yes! [*Changes it.*] That is stylish! Paris invents more wonderful fashions in one week than the rest of the world does in a year! Why wouldn't Madame tell me herself?

ESPEN. You know French ladies! They're much too polite to point out faults in a friend. They simply smile and let others guess what they mean. But now everything is perfect. It will be a pleasure for her to visit you again at your home in one hour. I will personally have the honor of presenting you. But first I must complete my errands.

JEAN. Oh, thank you, Monsieur d'Espang!

ESPEN. *Votre Serviteur!* But *à-propos,* I have forgotten one little thing. When Monsieur yawns do not cover your mouth with your hand. That is very old-fashioned and is not done by the best citizens in Paris.

JEAN. *Ouis da.*

ESPEN. Your servant! [*Exit.*]

Scene 5

JEAN. [*Dances and sings.*] La la la la la la la. [*Looks himself over.*] La la la la la. I usually think new styles are strange at first, but these are wonderful! It's very comfortable and becoming. La la la la la. *Mon Père* and mon *Père*-in-law will adopt them whether they like it or not. I refuse to live with an old-

fashioned family. I'm sure I can convince my papa to put aside his old common clothing, but I'll probably have to force my papa-in-law. He still dresses the way his grandpapa did. You see, it's not enough for me to be elegant. I will not allow my family to embarrass me in front of my friends. Pierre! Pierre, where are you? [*Enter* PIERRE.]

PIERRE. Oh, ow, Monsieur! If you don't have pity on me I will not remain in your service.

JEAN. What happened?

PIERRE. Monsieur Jeronimus beat me so hard I can barely walk.

JEAN. *Pourquoi donc?*

PIERRE. Because you wear a portrait around your neck.

JEAN. *Pardi!* I'll teach him that he can't beat a gentleman's servant! How dare he beat you!

PIERRE. Monsieur, excuse me, but Monsieur has his coat on backwards. Your mind must be on your marriage. Hold still while I fix it.

JEAN. You idiot! *sot! bouffon! Maraut!* Can't you see that this is the latest Parisian style? Madame la Flèche mocked me because I buttoned my coat like—a Dane.

PIERRE. I never saw that style in Paris.

JEAN. It changed while we were in Rouen.

PIERRE. In that case, I'd better change my coat.

JEAN. No you don't! This style is only for gentlemen.

PIERRE. So the rest of the world must suffer. When *Monsieur's papa*-in-law sees it he's going to be furious.

JEAN. He must not only tolerate it, I'll insist that he adopt it!

PIERRE. That will never happen.

JEAN. He *will!*

PIERRE. How?

JEAN. If I must, I'll use physical force. Madame la Flèche may laugh at the rest of Denmark, but I will not tolerate her laughing at my family.

PIERRE. Since you've made up your mind, I'll help you like a good servant. I just wish we had him now, while I still ache from the beatings he gave me. But look! Here he comes! *Ma foi fort a propos!*

Scene 6

Enter JERONIMUS.

JERONIMUS. Two weeks will pass quickly. That's no problem. I think I'll wait an extra day so no one can accuse me of breaking my promise. But the boy won't change. He won't change, I'd bet my life on it. Oh, there he is. I'd like to talk to him alone—while his loving father isn't around. Hans Frandsen, I want to talk to you, seriously, once and for all. What the hell are you doing? Are you afraid people won't remember that you're crazy? Must you advertise it by your absurd clothing? You have your coat on backwards! What kind of man changes his back into a belly? Dimwit! Oh, I pity poor old Frands Hansen, to have such a demented son! [JEAN *and* PIERRE *laugh.*] Yes! You should laugh now, and everytime you realize what a fop, what a dunce, what a madman you are.

JEAN. [*Laughing.*] A-propos, mon cher Papa-in-law. Wasn't the coat you're wearing made years ago for some old celebration?

JERONIMUS. You clown! You fool! Wasn't your backwards coat made for Halloween or April Fool's? Ha ha ha!

JEAN. *Mon cher Papa*-in-law, forgive me for laughing at your incredibly old-fashioned coat; but it can easily be corrected. All you have to do is button it up the back and you'll get by. This is how all the chic men dress in Paris.

JERONIMUS. I'm the one who's crazy to stand here talking to a madman!

JEAN. *Annendez, mon cher papa*-in-law, but you're not leaving here until you reverse your coat like mine. Madame la Flèche, who has just arrived from France, told me it's the highest fashion in Paris?

JERONIMUS. [*Beating him.*] You snake! How dare you lay a hand on a honest citizen? I don't care if it's for Madam la Pig, or Madame la Cabbage, or Madame la Sausage, or Madame la Lard!

JEAN. Pierre! Grab hold of the stubborn old knave! I, *ma foi*, will not have bumpkins for in-laws! Take it off!

PIERRE. Hurry, Monsieur!

JERONIMUS. Help! Thieves! Robbers!

JEAN. When old men behave like children they must be treated like children.

JERONIMUS. Help! Help! Thieves!

PIERRE. Be quiet! It's for your own good. After it's done you'll thank me, just like a patient who doesn't want his tooth pulled. After it's over he thanks the doctor and kisses his hands.

JERONIMUS. Get away! Help!

JEAN. Be quiet, *mon cher papa*-in-law! Now you look *pardi* like an ambassador. Now your entire family must be converted. I'll take my mama-in-law and Mademoiselle Isabelle to Madame la Flèche so they can be taught the most fashionable Parisian mode for women.

PIERRE. Monsieur, shouldn't we change his jabot, too?

JEAN. *Ouis pardi si fait.* [*He turns the jabot while* PIERRE *holds him.*]

JERONIMUS. Ah . . . Ah . . . Help!

Scene 7

ANTONIUS *runs on with his rapier drawn.*

ANTONIUS. Thieves! Highwaymen! I'll teach you to attack an honorable old man! [JEAN *and* PIERRE *run away.*] My dear Herr Jeronimus. It grieves me to see you being treated so roughly. Look what they've done to you. Don't worry, Herr Jeronimus, I'll revenge you, even at the risk of my own life!

JERONIMUS. My dear young man! You've saved my life, my honor! I'd rather die than have anyone see me like this. It would be a privilege for me to repay your kindness. Perhaps God needs my help and wanted to test me.

ANTONIUS. Herr Jeronimus, I believe that heaven is smiling on me. It has prepared the way for me to declare that of which I have not dared speak. You have, m'lord, a daughter?

JERONIMUS. Yes. What of it?

ANTONIUS. I dare not speak more. Surely you can guess my intent?

JERONIMUS. I can guess what he wants. He probably loves my daughter. But

I can't say that, I don't know who he is. First I must ask, who are your parents?

ANTONIUS. I am the son of Jesper Lorentzen of Snare Street. My father is well known by the good people of Copenhagen.

JERONIMUS. He *is* well known! If this is Jesper Lorentzen's son, he has a noble father and one of the grandest homes in the city. He and I used to travel together in the old days, both to the Keiler and Viborg market places. It would be a great pleasure and honor to have you in our family. But first, your father must meet my daughter.

ANTONIUS. If you don't object, I'd like to begin calling myself your son-in-law immediately. Over the years I haven't just fallen in love with Elsebet, I've also won her heart. But neither of us dared say anything because of her engagement to Hans Frandsen. His return worries me just as much as your daughter, but we don't know what to do.

JERONIMUS. If there are no more obstacles, that engagement is easily broken. Here's my hand on it. No one shall have my daughter but you. Here comes Elsebet now; how convenient!

Scene 8

Enter ELSEBET.

JERONIMUS. Elsebet! Do you know this man?

ELSEBET. No, I don't think so, Papa.

JERONIMUS. Oh yes you do. See how she blushes. There, there—relax, don't cry my child. I know everything. Come here, give him your hand. You're going to be his bride!

ELSEBET. My dear Papa! Why do you tease me? You've already promised me to Hans Frandsen.

JERONIMUS. That's all in the past. Right now I promise to see Hans Frandsen in court! I'll make him pay for the humiliation he caused me. Your fiancé saw everything. He'll help me. Go on, give him your hand. Look how cute she is, as though she's never seen him before. Come, let's go home together. I'll have my revenge on Hans Frandsen before the sun goes down! [*Exeunt.*]

Act 5

Scene 1

Enter JEAN *and* PIERRE.

JEAN. *Pardi, est-il possibel?* How barbaric!

PIERRE. Monsieur! It's our necks if we don't hide! Jeronimus is combing the city for you; and I hear your father is just as angry.

JEAN. It's terrible to live in a country where people are so quick to condemn. I thought my papa and papa-in-law would dance for joy when they saw me.

PIERRE. I thought so, too.

JEAN. Total strangers accept me more than my own parents.

PIERRE. Remember the old proverb: "A poet is without honor in his own country."

JEAN. I don't have to brag about my own elegance. The fact that one of the most stylish women in Paris came here because of me proves it!

PIERRE. That's true, Monsieur, all the way from Paris! If she'd been some hottentot, cossack, coarse, uncouth woman; or if she came from Bog Island, Iceland, or Greenland, they might think that she rarely saw an elegant man. So she must dote on you. She came all the way from Paris, where everyone is stylish; where lowly servants read the newspaper, dance the minuet, and speak perfect French—the three requisites of gentility. Notwithstanding the fact that Monsieur is stylish, the whole world must acknowledge that you have the distinction of spending, in just a few short weeks, 1,500 rixdalers in the most fashionable city in Europe! For that alone, all good people should esteem you.

JEAN. *Ouis pardi si fait.*

PIERRE. Even guttersnipes must admit that Monsieur has lived the elegant life in Paris.

JEAN. *Si fait.*

PIERRE. Not as a rogue.

JEAN. *Vous avez raison.*

PIERRE. Not as a snake.

JEAN. *Si fait.*

PIERRE. Not as a pig.

JEAN. *Cela s' entend.*

PIERRE. Not as a mountain goat.

JEAN. *Non pardi non.*

PIERRE. Not as a lazy ass.

JEAN. *Non si fait non.*

PIERRE. Not as a lap dog.

JEAN. *Peste,* you can stop with the titles, I know what you mean.

PIERRE. Monsieur, I just want to say that any honorable man who knows how much money you spent in Paris, in so short a time, must rationally conclude that you are a fine companion. You must have learned something for all that money! Therefore, he would gladly give you his daughter.

JEAN. That's just it, Pierre. You can see what poor judgment my parents have.

PIERRE. How can common Danish girls esteem you, Monsieur? Instead of valuing your qualities, they heap insults upon you.

JEAN. What do they say about me?

PIERRE. I'm embarrassed to repeat it. But since I was almost whipped for your sake . . .

JEAN. *Ah dites hardiessement*—you know that we Parisians never take such talk seriously.

PIERRE. Many call you "Hans Lowlips," because you constantly kiss the hands of *every* woman.

JEAN. Those idiots! That's one of the most stylish qualities a *galant homme* can have.

PIERRE. Some are more base and call you "Hans Salami, Hans Dunderhead, Hans Monkey, Hans Swindler, Hans Stocking-peeker, Hans Caperer, Hans Rump-wiggler, Hans Stuck-up, Hans Cavorter, Hans . . ."

JEAN. All right, that's enough! I don't feel like hearing any more.

PIERRE. "Hans *Petit-maître,* Hans Dancer, Hans French-killer, Hans . . ."

JEAN. Stop it! That's enough!

PIERRE. "Hans Loonybird, Hans Strutter, Hans Harlequin . . ."

JEAN. If you don't shut up I'll split your head in two! *Je t'écraserai ton tête.*

PIERRE. Well you said you wanted to hear it. Oh, here comes Arv again.

Scene 2

Enter ARV.

ARV. I wouldn't be in Hans Frandsen's shoes right now if you paid me. Jeronimus swore that he won't go to bed until he has that scoundrel in the "Bar House," or jail, as we call it. It's unforgivable to treat an old man that way—especially one who's paid taxes for so many years. Remember how he changed his clothes like this? I'll switch my coat. [*Reverses his coat.*] Don't I look like a fool? [*Laughs.*] That's just how Jeronimus looked. I wouldn't walk down the street like that if you paid me two shillings! People would try to lock me up in the madhouse. [*He puts his coat on right, again.*] Magdelone is sitting at home crying as though she were beaten. But that's all right. She deserves it. When Frands refused to send Hans more money while he was in Paris, she sold her best dresses to finance his foolishness.

JEAN. How is everything at home?

ARV. [*Scratches behind his ear.*] Well enough, Monsewer.

JEAN. Why do you scratch like that? Something isn't right! Tell me, what *is* the situation at home?

ARV. Good enough, Monsewer. Thanks for asking, but . . . farewell! I have to go.

JEAN. What do you mean by that? If you don't tell me what's happening, by *ma foi,* I'll beat you!

ARV. Everything is fine as a nightmare. But there's some hell fire, too.

JEAN. Speak freely, Arv, and I'll give you a *Livre.*

ARV. I don't like liver, *Monsewer;* when it's served I give mine to the dog.

But, if *Monsewer* could give me the price of a beer . . .

JEAN. Here's two marks. That's what I meant.

ARV. *Gramarcis, Monsewer!*

JEAN. What a dumb animal he is! He doesn't even recognize a *Livre de France.*

ARV. I'll just warn *Monsewer* that he'd better get his boots greased. Jeronimus has ordered the Watchmen and the King's Guard to arrest you. Your father has washed his hands of you and swears that you'll sit shackled in a hole for a year!

PIERRE. Do they want to lock me up, too?

ARV. You don't have anything to worry about, Peer. They'll slap your wrists and let you go. [*Noise offstage.*]

JEAN. What's that racket out there!

ACTOR. [*Offstage.*] I'll teach that rogue to run off without paying!

JEAN. *Peste*, what shall I do? That man's got me by the neck! He won 100 rixdalers from me gambling; but I ran away when he turned his back. I don't have any money!

ACTOR. [*Offstage.*] He's either going to pay me or fight me!

PIERRE. Oh! M'lord! Nature calls! I have to run for a minute, but I'll be right back!

JEAN. You traitor! The minute you see I'm in trouble you run off.

PIERRE. Oh, my stomach! My stomach! I must have drunk too quickly in the pub—what a misfortune! [*He runs and hides.*]

ACTOR. [*Offstage.*] I'll teach him what it means to gamble with an honest man.

JEAN. My dear Arv! Can't you hide me? I'll reward you as though you were an honorable man!

ARV. I have some fabric here, if *Monsieur* will let me wrap him in it.

JEAN. It doesn't matter, Arv. Just hide me! [*He wraps* JEAN *in the cloth like a sack and sits on it.*]

Scene 3

Enter ACTOR.

ACTOR. I swear I won't go to bed tonight until I catch him! It's not so much for the money, but for the principle. Others might try to escape from their gambling debts. [JEAN *shakes under the cover.*]

ARV. [*Hitting him.*] Stop shaking!

ACTOR. Who are you talking to, friend?

ARV. I'm talking to my sack.

ACTOR. Your sack? What's in your sack?

ARV. [*Stutters from fright.*] I swear I don't have anything in it but lard.

ACTOR. It's not possible to sit on a sack of lard.

ARV. You're right! It's candles.

ACTOR. Candles? That's even more absurd.

ARV. Right again. It's, uh, lace!

ACTOR. Then it must be one hell of a lot of lace. But lace isn't that solid. It must be stolen goods!

ARV. No! It's green peas!

ACTOR. You're a thief, all right! Let me see what's in the bag.

ARV. I swear it isn't Hans Frandsen, *Monsewer!* You have my word! How could he fit in a sack?

ACTOR. Ha ha ha. I daresay, I've just found my money. See here *Monsieur* Frandsen, are you there? I love this. You have two choices: either hand over the money, or fight.

JEAN. *Monsieur! je n'ai point d'argent.*

ACTOR. I don't understand French; we'll do our fighting in Danish! Come out of there and fight—or pay me.

JEAN. I'll give you my I.O.U.

ACTOR. No deal! Ready cash—or fight.

ARV. I hate to have to leave . . . [*He runs out.*]

JEAN. *Monsieur*, have patience! I'll get you the money.

ACTOR. All I want is you—out of that sack!

JEAN. Here, take my watch!

ACTOR. That's good. That covers about 40 rixdalers. Now hand over your coat, vest, and hat. Then I'll be satisfied.

JEAN. I know you don't want to leave me here naked.

ACTOR. [*Draws his rapier.*] All of it! Your clothes or a thrashing! [JEAN *throws his coat, vest, hat and wig to the* ACTOR.]

ACTOR. *Monsieur, votre très humble serviteur.* I thank you for a well paid debt. [*Exits laughing.*]

PIERRE. [*Coming out of hiding.*] Oh, *Monsieur!* What terrible thing has happened? You're naked as a baby!

JEAN. You know that babies aren't born with pants, shoes, and stockings! You swine! I should flog you! How could you abandon your master?

PIERRE. I truly wish I could have stayed and ended up looking as glorious as you! But I faint at the sight of a naked blade.

JEAN. Let's find Madame la Flèche. She'll protect us. Do you know where she lives?

PIERRE. How should I know that?

JEAN. What crass and coarse people surround us! Oh, Paris! Paris! I wish we were there again. But here comes Madame la Flèche's *valet de chambre*, *Monsieur d'Espang*.

Scene 4

Enter ESPEN.

ESPEN. I've looked everywhere for *Monsieur* Jean de France, but he's nowhere to be found. I asked at his father's house, at . . . But it's him— and his servant! *Monsieur!* Madame la Flèche asked me to convey her deepest respect and to deliver a letter as she sailed.

JEAN. Madame la Flèche has sailed?

ESPEN. Yes, about half an hour ago.

JEAN. Why didn't you go with her?

ESPEN. She no longer had need of my services.

JEAN. She sailed alone?

ESPEN. Yes. Well, such as ladies travel alone. She took at least four lackeys with her. I was only hired for her stay in Copenhagen. Here's the letter she asked me to deliver.

JEAN. [*Reads it.*] Pierre?

PIERRE. *Monsieur?*

JEAN. We're off the hook; high in the air!

PIERRE. We're going to be hanged?

JEAN. Madame la Flèche writes that she heard of my dilemma and decided to leave this barbaric country. But, I will be able to find her in Hamburg with Monsieur Gobere. She'll take me with her to Paris where she'll support me as a gentleman! We must depart

at once! *Allons, depêchons.* I'm ready as soon as we can hire a coach. I'll write a quick farewell to my Papa. *Adieu, mon cher Monsieur d'Espang!* Thank you for everything! [*Exit* JEAN *and* PIERRE.]

Scene 5

ESPEN. Marthe! You can come out now! The fool has gone! [*Enter* MARTHE.]

MARTHE. I told you it would work. You have to admit, Espen, I've got style.

ESPEN. I admit it, little wench. When luck is with you great things can be accomplished by small means. So far as I could see, you didn't use witchcraft. You thought only of making Hans Frandsen more French and more mad than he already was. But you can't take the credit for Antonius's good fortune; he just happened to be in the right place in the right time. Sometimes a plan is laid for great results; and sometimes for devious ends. But when luck, or the lack of it, is applied, it can result in greatness being considered nothing; and deviousness as wisdom. That's what happens when the world cares about the end and not the means.

MARTHE. That doesn't mean anything. I operate like a great general: when they win a battle they are hailed as great, understanding men. Even if you examine everything closely, it contributes to the victory and honor. No matter how the battle is fought, the means are seen through the end. Most people operate by dumb luck.

ESPEN. Marthe, you speak like an angel. You're so wise you could write books. But if people read them they'd go crazy!

MARTHE. I knew you'd say that.

ESPEN. I thought so.

MARTHE. How did you know?

ESPEN. Because when you cook for us, our supper is either under-cooked or over-salted. I like smart women, but I prefer them as wives or maids!

MARTHE. Such talk! Now be still, here come the two old men.

Scene 6

Enter JERONIMUS *and* FRANDS.

JERONIMUS. I can't forget it! You only hurt yourself by making excuses for your son.

FRANDS. I'm not making excuses for him any more. I don't think I'll ever see him again. I'm only thinking of myself. If you reject him it reflects on the entire family. [A BOY *enters.*]

FRANDS Go away boy! What are you doing here?

BOY. Your son instructed me to deliver this letter to his father.

FRANDS. [*Reading the letter.*] Madame la Flèche, a respected French lady, has found me too good for Denmark and has invited me to live with her in Paris. Since I am accustomed to the foreign manners and gallantry, and cannot therefore tolerate backward people, such as those in my family, I have decided to join her. I will never return to Copenhagen. If you write me, address the letter *à la Madame la Flèche, Dame très célèbre et très renommée dans la France.* The letter must be written in French. I have decided that within a few short months I will no longer understand one word of Danish. The letter must be addressed: *A Monsieur Monsieur Jean de France, gentilhomme et grand favorit de la Madame la Flèche, Courtisane tres renommée, dans la Cour de France.* If I am not addressed properly I will return the letter unopened. *Je suis le Votre. Jean de France, gentil-homme Parisien. Copenhague,* the eighteenth *Majus*—

JERONIMUS. Do you still acknowledge him as your son? Am I free to give my daughter to whomever I wish?

FRANDS. Yes.

JERONIMUS. In that case, I announce her engagement to Jesper Lorentzen's son, Antonius.

FRANDS. He's a wonderful man. Congratulations.

JERONIMUS. Will you come to their wedding and not sulk?

FRANDS. Of course. I've already wiped my son from my mind.

JERONIMUS. You'll be glad you did.

FRANDS. The thing that hurts, neighbor, is to be severed from such an honorable man as yourself. I had longed for our families to be joined through marriage.

JERONIMUS. Neighbor! Isn't your daughter Lisbet grown?

FRANDS. Yes she is.

JERONIMUS. So is my son, Jochum. Can't there be a new engagement?

FRANDS. That would be wonderful! If you're sure . . .

JERONIMUS. You have my hand that he'll be her husband. I've noticed that he likes her already.

I think, dear friend, that it remains
   Hereafter very sure;
Our sons are made to marry Danes
   Before exotic tours.
Your son's madness illustrates
   The example that we feared.
Why venture out to foreign states
   Before one grows a beard?
Foreign lands keep their youth pure,
   At home where they belong,
But Danish youth who go on tour
   Think their upbringing wrong.
In kingly style they wine and dine;
   Begin to sow wild oats;
Learn gallantries and monkeyshines,
   While wearing foreign coats.
If they must travel far from home
   While in their youthful days,
Then off to Jutland let them roam
   To keep their Danish ways.
The moral of this little play
   The author does in mirth write:
In Scandinavia let us stay,
   And love our Danish birthright.

                  [*Exeunt.*]

1. Hanswurst was a clown character popular throughout Germany and portrayed by many different actors. A Hanswurst played in Copenhagen early in 1722.

The Beggar's Opera

John Gay

After the excellence of comic playwriting that characterized the Restoration period (roughly from 1660 to 1700), English drama descended to the maudlin during most of the eighteenth century. It was an age of sentimentality and of appeal to bourgeois taste in all its less attractive aspects. The vast majority of even the very successful plays produced in England during the eighteenth century are now of interest only to the most dedicated scholars, but happily there are a few exceptions that managed to rise above the general mediocrity. *The Beggar's Opera* is such an exception.

Its author, John Gay, was born on June 30, 1685, in Barnstaple, Devonshire. After a routine education and a short period of apprenticeship to a silk merchant, Gay joined the literary scene in London, where he quickly made friends among the important figures of the day. He published some poetry and gained a reputation as a satirist, albeit an honest and gentle one as compared with the commanding satirist of the age, Jonathan Swift. Gay tried his hand at playwriting with *The What d'ye Call It* (1715) and *Three Hours after Marriage* (1717), but neither enjoyed any notable success. When *The Beggar's Opera* opened at John Rich's theater on January 29, 1728, however, it reportedly made "Gay rich and Rich gay."

The time was ripe for a work like *The Beggar's Opera*. Italian opera was very much in fashion, and despite the derision heaped upon it in some quarters, and several earlier attempts to parody the form, *The Beggar's Opera* was the first genuinely successful parody. Indeed, it was so successful that opera was virtually driven from the stage for a time, while numerous other parodies and imitations were attempted—none with the success enjoyed by Gay. Furthermore, by portraying crooks and beggars as no different in principle from businessmen and politicians, Gay was criticizing and satirizing the administration of Sir Robert Walpole (in power as England's first prime minister from 1721 to 1742), a scandalous but no longer life-endangering enterprise. Walpole is said to have been in the audience on opening night, and, as the public eagerly watched to see how he would take it, to have called out "Encore." The play ran for an unprecedented sixty-two performances, and Gay quickly followed up this success with a sequel entitled *Polly*, in which Macheath has become a buccaneer in the West Indies. Walpole arranged to have performances forbidden, however, and Gay achieved even more fame and fortune. He raised a subscription for *Polly* to be published; the printed book sold at incredible rates, and Gay became the darling of the political opposition. *Polly* was never actually performed until 1777, long after Gay's death, and it has been infrequently produced since.

Except for the posthumously produced *Achilles* (1733), Gay did not write again for the stage. His poetry brought him a high reputation in the eighteenth century, and his wealth from *The Beggar's Opera* and *Polly*, though not lavish, was enough to sustain him for the rest of his life. He died in London on December 4, 1732, and was buried in a place of honor in Westminster Abbey.

In his ballad opera, Gay created virtually a new form of theater that may indirectly be said to be the ancestor of modern musical comedy. The "airs" he used throughout were popular tunes of his day, at least one of which is still widely familiar as "Greensleeves." The music, although not written specifically for the play, was well selected and makes a pleasant enough score for modern production as well. Gay's lyrics are effective but unpretentious poetry that serve the play very well. The spoof of other musical theater forms is still effective, and the political satire, although no longer as scandalous as it was to Walpole and his associates, still communicates with a modern audience accustomed to the venality of human institutions. Although there no longer seems anything very remarkable about its form, the play opened up new possibilities in theater in the eighteenth century that have only been fully explored in the twentieth. Indeed, Bertolt Brecht in 1928 reworked the script as *The Threepenny Opera,* adding new lyrics and engaging Kurt Weill to provide the score, and created a major twentieth-century masterpiece.

There is no need to linger over detailed analysis of *The Beggar's Opera.* It is a good theater piece and delightful fun, but requires no special explanations to make its meanings clear. Its plot combines the romantic highwayman with a look at the seamy underworld, a love story with political satire—in short, those sure-fire elements certain to hold an audience's attention in the theater. The parodied *deus ex machina* ending (retained by Brecht in *The Threepenny Opera*) is so outrageous as to be funny for its own sake—a device that Molière had used effectively in *Tartuffe.* Characterization and language effectively satirize the lush sentimentality of the tearful comedy that pleased the public but outraged the critics in eighteenth-century London, highlighting the ridiculousness of that lachrymose genre. Thematically, the play can scarcely be said to hit very hard, at least as compared with the works of some of the great satirists, but what the play says is so welcome to most audiences that it finds ready acceptance. It smacks of truth, and is deeply (if perversely) comforting, to be told that the power structures of society are actually peopled with crooks, even if the full truth is rarely that simple.

Although *The Beggar's Opera* stands out in the eighteenth century simply by contrast with the general quality of other British drama, that fact should not be allowed to conceal the intrinsic merit of the work. If it is not among the great works of theatrical art of all time, it is nevertheless a fine and effective piece of theater that pleases audiences today nearly as well (if for somewhat different reasons) as it pleased those of 1728. Furthermore, Gay's significant steps in the development of musical drama may be even more fully appreciated today in the light of the extraordinary twentieth-century success of that genre. *The Beggar's Opera* well merits careful attention and study.

The Beggar's Opera

Characters

Peachum
Lockit
Macheath
Filch
Jemmy Twitcher
Crook-finger'd Jack
Wat Dreary
Robin of Bagshot } *Macheath's gang*
Nimming Ned
Harry Padington
Mat of the Mint
Ben Budge
Beggar
Player
Constables, Drawer, Jailer, etc.
Mrs. Peachum
Polly Peachum
Lucy Lockit
Diana Trapes
Mrs. Coaxer
Dolly Trull
Mrs. Vixen
Betty Doxy } *women of the town*
Jenny Diver
Mrs. Slammekin
Suky Tawdry
Molly Brazen

Introduction

Enter BEGGAR *and* PLAYER.

BEGGAR. If Poverty be a Title to Poetry, I am sure No-body can dispute mine. I own myself of the Company of Beggars; and I make one at their Weekly Festivals at St. Giles. I have a small Yearly Salary for my Catches, and am welcome to a Dinner there whenever I please, which is more than most Poets can say.

PLAYER. As we live by the Muses, 'tis but Gratitude in us to encourage Poetical Merit where-ever we find it. The Muses, contrary to all other Ladies, pay no Distinction to Dress, and never partially mistake the Pertness of Embroidery for Wit, nor the Modesty of Want for Dullness. Be the Author who he will, we push his Play as far as it will go. So (though you are in Want) I wish you Success heartily.

BEGGAR. This Piece I own was originally writ for the celebrating the Marriage of James Chanter and Moll Lay, two most excellent Ballad-Singers. I have introduc'd the Similes that are in all your celebrated Operas: the Swallow, the Moth, the Bee, the Ship, the Flower, &c. Besides, I have a Prison Scene which the Ladies always reckon charmingly pathetick. As to the Parts, I have observ'd such a nice Impartiality to our two Ladies, that it is impossible for either of them to take Offence. I hope I may be forgiven, that I have not made my Opera throughout unnatural, like those in vogue; for I have no Recitative: Excepting this, as I have consented to have neither Prologue nor Epilogue, it must be allow'd an Opera in all its forms. The Piece indeed hath been heretofore frequently represented by our selves in our great Room at St. Giles's, so that I cannot too often acknowledge your Charity in bringing it now on the Stage.

PLAYER. But I see 'tis time for us to withdraw; the Actors are preparing to begin. Play away the Overture. [*Exeunt.*]

Act 1

Scene 1

PEACHUM's *house.*
PEACHUM. [*Sitting at a table with a large book of accounts before him.*]

AIR 1. An old Woman cloathed in Gray, &c.

Through all the Employments of Life
 Each Neighbour abuses his Brother;
Whore and Rogue they call Husband and Wife:
All Professions be-rogue one another.
The Priest calls the Lawyer a Cheat,
 The Lawyer be-knaves the Divine;
And the Statesman, because he's so great,
 Thinks his Trade as honest as mine.

A Lawyer is an honest Employment, so is mine. Like me too he acts in a double Capacity, both against Rogues and for 'em; for 'tis but fitting that we should protect and encourage Cheats, since we live by them.

Scene 2

Enter FILCH.
FILCH. Sir, Black Moll hath sent word her Tryal comes on in the Afternoon, and she hopes you will order Matters so as to bring her off.
PEACHUM. Why, she may plead her Belly[1] at worst; to my Knowledge she hath taken care of that Security. But as the Wench is very active and industrious, you may satisfy her that I'll soften the Evidence.
FILCH. Tom Gagg, Sir, is found guilty.
PEACHUM. A lazy Dog! When I took him the time before, I told him what he would come to if he did not mend his Hand. This is Death without Reprieve. I may venture to Book him. [*Writes.*] For Tom Gagg, forty Pounds. Let Betty Sly know that I'll save her from Transportation, for I can get more by her staying in England.
FILCH. Betty hath brought more Goods into our Lock to-year[2] than any five

of the Gang; and in truth, 'tis a pity to lose so good a Customer.
PEACHUM. If none of the Gang take her off, she may, in the common course of Business, live a Twelve-month longer. I love to let Women scape. A good Sportsman always lets the Hen Partridges fly, because the breed of the Game depends upon them. Besides, here the Law allows us no Reward; there is nothing to be got by the Death of Women—except our Wives.
FILCH. Without dispute, she is a fine Woman! 'Twas to her I was oblig'd for my Education, and (to say a bold Word) she hath train'd up more young Fellows to the Business than the Gamingtable.
PEACHUM. Truly, Filch, thy Observation is right. We and the Surgeons are more beholden to Women than all the Professions besides.

AIR 2. The bonny grey-ey'd Morn, &c.

FILCH. *'Tis Woman that seduces all Mankind,*
 By her we first were taught the wheedling Arts:
Her very Eyes can cheat; when most she's kind,
 She tricks us of our Money with our Hearts.
For her, like Wolves by night we roam for Prey,
 And practise ev'ry Fraud to bribe her Charms;
For Suits of Love, like Law, are won by Pay,
 And Beauty must be fee'd into our Arms.

PEACHUM. But make haste to Newgate, Boy, and let my Friends know what I intend; for I love to make them easy one way or other.
FILCH. When a Gentleman is long kept in suspence, Penitence may break his Spirit ever after. Besides, Certainty gives a Man a good Air upon his Tryal, and makes him risque another without Fear or Scruple. But I'll away, for 'tis a Pleasure to be the Messenger of Comfort to Friends in Affliction. [*Exit.*]

Scene 3

PEACHUM. But 'tis now high time to look about me for a decent Execution against next Sessions. I hate a lazy Rogue, by whom one can get nothing 'til he is hang'd. A Register of the Gang, [*Reading.*] Crooked-finger'd Jack. A Year and a half in the Service; Let me see how much the Stock owes to his Industry; one, two, three, four, five Gold Watches, and seven Silver ones. A mighty clean-handed Fellow! Sixteen Snuff-boxes, five of them of true Gold. Six dozen of Handkerchiefs, four silver-hilted Swords, half a dozen of Shirts, three Tye-Perriwigs, and a Piece of Broad Cloth. Considering these are only the Fruits of his leisure Hours, I don't know a prettier Fellow, for no Man alive hath a more engaging Presence of Mind upon the Road. Wat Dreary, alias Brown Will, an irregular Dog, who hath an underhand way of disposing of his Goods. I'll try him only for a Sessions or two longer upon his good Behaviour. Harry Padington, a poor petty-larceny Rascal, without the least Genius; that Fellow, though he were to live these six Months, will never come to the Gallows with any Credit. Slippery Sam; he goes off the next Sessions, for the Villain hath the Impudence to have views of following his Trade as a Taylor, which he calls an honest Employment. Mat of the Mint; listed not above a Month ago, a promising sturdy Fellow, and diligent in his way; somewhat too bold and hasty, and may raise good Contributions on the Publick, if he does not cut himself short by Murder. Tom Tipple, a guzzling soaking Sot, who is always too drunk to stand himself, or to make others stand. A Cart is absolutely necessary for him. Robin of Bagshot, alias Gorgon, alias Bluff Bob, alias Carbuncle, alias Bob Booty.

Scene 4

Enter MRS. PEACHUM.
MRS. PEACHUM. What of Bob Booty, Husband? I hope nothing bad hath betided him. You know, my Dear, he's a favourite Customer of mine. 'Twas he made me a Present of this Ring.
PEACHUM. I have set his Name down in the Black-List, that's all, my Dear; he spends his Life among Women, and as soon as his Money is gone, one or other of the Ladies will hang him for the Reward, and there's forty Pound lost to us for-ever.
MRS. PEACHUM. You know, my Dear, I never meddle in matters of Death; I always leave those Affairs to you. Women indeed are bitter bad Judges in these cases, for they are so partial to the Brave that they think every Man handsome who is going to the Camp or the Gallows.

AIR 3. Cold and Raw, &c.

If any Wench Venus's Girdle wear,
Though she be never so ugly;
Lillys and Roses will quickly appear,
And her Face look wond'rous smuggly.
Beneath the left Ear so fit but a Cord,
(A Rope so charming a Zone is!)
The Youth in his Cart hath the Air of a
Lord,
And we cry, There dies an Adonis!

But really, Husband, you should not be too hard-hearted, for you never had a finer, braver set of Men than at present. We have not had a Murder among them all, these seven Months. And truly, my Dear, that is a great Blessing.
PEACHUM. What a dickens is the Woman always a whimpring about Murder for? No Gentleman is ever look'd upon the worse for killing a Man in his own Defence; and if Business cannot be carried on without it, what would you have a Gentleman do?
MRS. PEACHUM. If I am in the wrong, my Dear, you must excuse me, for No-body can help the Frailty of an over-scrupulous Conscience.
PEACHUM. Murder is as fashionable a Crime as a Man can be guilty of. How many fine Gentlemen have we in Newgate every Year, purely upon that Article! If they have wherewithal to persuade the Jury to bring it in

Manslaughter, what are they the worse for it? So, my Dear, have done upon this Subject. Was Captain Macheath here this Morning, for the Bank-notes he left with you last Week?

MRS. PEACHUM. Yes, my Dear; and though the Bank hath stopt Payment, he was so cheerful and so agreeable! Sure there is not a finer Gentleman upon the Road than the Captain! If he comes from Bagshot at any reasonable Hour he hath promis'd to make one this Evening with Polly and me, and Bob Booty, at a Party of Quadrille. Pray, my Dear, is the Captain rich?

PEACHUM. The Captain keeps too good Company ever to grow rich. Marybone[3] and the Chocolate-houses are his undoing. The Man that proposes to get Money by Play should have the Education of a fine Gentleman, and be train'd up to it from his Youth.

MRS. PEACHUM. Really, I am sorry upon Polly's Account the Captain hath not more Discretion. What business hath he to keep Company with Lords and Gentlemen? he should leave them to prey upon one another.

PEACHUM. Upon Polly's Account! What, a Plague, does the Woman mean?— Upon Polly's Account!

MRS. PEACHUM. Captain Macheath is very fond of the Girl.

PEACHUM. And what then?

MRS. PEACHUM. If I have any Skill in the Ways of Women, I am sure Polly thinks him a very pretty Man.

PEACHUM. And what then? You would not be so mad to have the Wench marry him! Gamesters and Highwaymen are generally very good to their Whores, but they are very Devils to their Wives.

MRS. PEACHUM. But if Polly should be in love, how should we help her, or how can she help herself? Poor Girl, I am in the utmost Concern about her.

AIR 4. Why is your faithful Slave disdain'd? &c.

If Love the Virgin's Heart invade,
How, like a Moth, the simple Maid
  Still plays about the Flame!
If soon she be not made a Wife,

Her Honour's sing'd, and then for Life,
  She's—what I dare not name.

PEACHUM. Look ye, Wife. A handsome Wench in our way of Business is as profitable as at the Bar of a Temple Coffee-house, who looks upon it as her livelihood to grant every Liberty but one. You see I would indulge the Girl as far as prudently we can. In any thing, but Marriage! After that, my Dear, how shall we be safe? Are we not then in her Husband's Power? For a Husband hath the absolute Power over all a Wife's Secrets but her own. If the Girl had the Discretion of a Court Lady, who can have a dozen young Fellows at her Ear without complying with one, I should not matter it; but Polly is Tinder, and a Spark will at once set her on a Flame. Married! If the Wench does not know her own Profit, sure she knows her own Pleasure better than to make herself a Property! My Daughter to me should be, like a Court Lady to a Minister of State, a Key to the whole Gang. Married! If the Affair is not already done, I'll terrify her from it, by the Example of our Neighbours.

MRS. PEACHUM. May-hap, my Dear, you may injure the Girl. She loves to imitate the fine Ladies, and she may only allow the Captain Liberties in the View of Interest.

PEACHUM. But 'tis your Duty, my Dear, to warn the Girl against her Ruin, and to instruct her how to make the most of her Beauty. I'll go to her this moment, and sift her. In the mean time, Wife, rip out the Coronets and Marks of these dozen of Cambric Handkerchiefs, for I can dispose of them this Afternoon to a Chap in the City. [*Exit.*]

Scene 5

MRS. PEACHUM. Never was a Man more out of the way in an Argument than my Husband! Why must our Polly, forsooth, differ from her Sex, and love only her Husband? And why must Polly's Marriage, contrary to all Observation, make her the less followed by other Men? All Men are

Thieves in Love, and like a Woman the better for being another's Property.

AIR 5. Of all the simple Things we do, &c.

A Maid is like the golden Oar,
Which hath Guineas intrinsical in't,
Whose Worth is never known, before
It is try'd and imprest in the Mint.

A Wife's like a Guinea in Gold,
Stampt with the Name of her Spouse;
Now here, now there; is bought, or is
sold;
And is current in every House.

Scene 6

Enter FILCH.

MRS. PEACHUM. Come hither, Filch. I am as fond of this Child, as though my Mind misgave me he were my own. He hath as fine a Hand at picking a Pocket as a Woman, and is as nimble-finger'd as a Juggler. If an unlucky Session does not cut the Rope of thy Life, I pronounce, Boy, thou wilt be a great Man in History. Where was your Post last Night, my Boy?

FILCH. I ply'd at the Opera, Madam; and considering 'twas neither dark nor rainy, so that there was no great Hurry in getting Chairs and Coaches, made a tolerable hand on't. These seven Handkerchiefs, Madam.

MRS. PEACHUM. Colour'd ones, I see. They are of sure Sale from our Warehouse at Redress among the Seamen.

FILCH. And this Snuff-box.

MRS. PEACHUM. Set in Gold! A pretty Encouragement this to a young Beginner.

FILCH. I had a fair tug at a charming Gold Watch. Pox take the Taylors for making the Fobs so deep and narrow! It stuck by the way, and I was forc'd to make my Escape under a Coach. Really, Madam, I fear I shall be cut off in the Flower of my Youth, so that every now and then (since I was pumpt) I have thoughts of taking up and going to Sea.

MRS. PEACHUM. You should go to Hockley in the Hole, and to Marybone, Child, to learn Valour. These are the Schools that have bred so many brave Men. I thought, Boy, by this time, thou hadst lost Fear as well as Shame. Poor Lad! how little does he know as yet of the Old-Bailey! For the first Fact I'll insure thee from being hang'd; and going to Sea, Filch, will come time enough upon a Sentence of Transportation. But now, since you have nothing better to do, ev'n go to your Book, and learn your Catechism; for really a Man makes but an ill Figure in the Ordinary's Paper, who cannot give a satisfactory Answer to his Questions. But, hark you, my Lad. Don't tell me a Lye; for you know I hate a Lyar. Do you know of any thing that hath past between Captain Macheath and our Polly?

FILCH. I beg you, Madam, don't ask me; for I must either tell a Lye to you or to Miss Polly; for I promis'd her I would not tell.

MRS. PEACHUM. But when the Honour of our Family is concern'd—

FILCH. I shall lead a sad Life with Miss Polly, if ever she come to know that I told you. Besides, I would not willingly forfeit my own Honour by betraying any body.

MRS. PEACHUM. Yonder comes my Husband and Polly. Come, Filch, you shall go with me into my own Room, and tell me the whole Story. I'll give thee a most delicious Glass of a Cordial that I keep for my own drinking. [*Exeunt.*]

Scene 7

Enter PEACHUM *and* POLLY.

POLLY. I know as well as any of the fine Ladies how to make the most of my self and of my Man too. A Woman knows how to be mercenary, though she hath never been in a Court or at an Assembly. We have it in our Natures, Papa. If I allow Captain Macheath some trifling Liberties, I have this Watch and other visible Marks of his Favour to show for it. A

Girl who cannot grant some Things, and refuse what is most material, will make but a poor hand of her Beauty, and soon be thrown upon the Common.

AIR 6. What shall I do to show how much I love her, &c.

Virgins are like the fair Flower in its Lustre,
Which in the Garden enamels the Ground;
Near it the Bees in Play flutter and cluster,
And gaudy Butterflies frolick around.
But, when once pluck'd, 'tis no longer alluring,
To Covent-Garden⁴ 'tis sent, (as yet sweet,)
There fades, and shrinks, and grows past all enduring,
Rots, stinks, and dies, and is trod under feet.

PEACHUM. You know, Polly, I am not against your toying and trifling with a Customer in the way of Business, or to get out a Secret, or so. But if I find out that you have play'd the fool and are married, you Jade you, I'll cut your Throat, Hussy. Now you know my Mind.

Scene 8

Enter MRS. PEACHUM.

AIR 7. Oh London is a fine Town
MRS. PEACHUM. [*In a very great Passion.*]

Our Polly is a sad Slut! nor heeds what we taught her.
I wonder any Man alive will ever rear a Daughter!
For she must have both Hoods and Gowns, and Hoops to swell her Pride.
With Scarfs and Stays, and Gloves and Lace; and she will have Men beside;
And when she's drest with Care and Cost, all-tempting, fine and gay,
As Men should serve a Cowcumber, she flings herself away.
Our Polly is a sad Slut, &c.

You Baggage! you Hussy! you inconsiderate Jade! had you been hang'd, it would not have vex'd me, for that

might have been your Misfortune; but to do such a mad thing by Choice! The Wench is married, Husband.

PEACHUM. Married! The Captain is a bold man, and will risque any thing for Money; to be sure he believes her a Fortune. Do you think your Mother and I should have liv'd comfortably so long together, if ever we had been married? Baggage!

MRS. PEACHUM. I knew she was always a proud Slut; and now the Wench hath play'd the Fool and married, because forsooth she should do like the Gentry. Can you support the expence of a Husband, Hussy, in gaming, drinking and whoring? have you Money enough to carry on the daily Quarrels of Man and Wife about who shall squander most? There are not many Husbands and Wifes, who can bear the Charges of plaguing one another in a handsome way. If you must be married, could you introduce nobody into our Family but a Highwayman? Why, thou foolish Jade, thou wilt be as ill-us'd, and as much neglected, as if thou hadst married a Lord!

PEACHUM. Let not your Anger, my Dear, break through the Rules of Decency, for the Captain looks upon himself in the Military Capacity, as a Gentleman by his Profession. Besides what he hath already, I know he is in a fair way of getting, or of dying; and both these ways, let me tell you, are most excellent Chances for a Wife. Tell me, Hussy, are you ruin'd or no?

MRS. PEACHUM. With Polly's Fortune, she might very well have gone off to a Person of Distinction. Yes, that you might, you pouting Slut!

PEACHUM. What, is the Wench dumb? Speak, or I'll make you plead by squeezing out an Answer from you. Are you really bound Wife to him, or are you only upon liking? [*Pinches her.*]

POLLY. Oh! [*Screaming.*]

MRS. PEACHUM. How the Mother is to be pitied who hath handsome Daughters! Locks, Bolts, Bars, and Lectures of Morality are nothing to them:

They break through them all. They have as much Pleasure in cheating a Father and Mother, as in cheating at Cards.

PEACHUM. Why, Polly, I shall soon know if you are married, by Macheath's keeping from our House.

AIR 8. Grim King of the Ghosts, &c.

POLLY. *Can Love be controul'd by Advice?*
Will Cupid our Mothers obey?
Though my Heart were as frozen as Ice,
    At his Flame 'twould have melted away.

When he kist me so closely he prest,
    'Twas so sweet that I must have comply'd:
So I thought it both safest and best
    To marry, for fear you should chide.

MRS. PEACHUM. Then all the Hopes of our Family are gone for ever and ever!

PEACHUM. And Macheath may hang his Father and Mother-in-Law, in hope to get into their Daughter's Fortune.

POLLY. I did not marry him (as 'tis the Fashion) cooly and deliberately for Honour or Money. But, I love him.

MRS. PEACHUM. Love him! worse and worse! I thought the Girl had been better bred. Oh Husband, Husband! her Folly makes me mad! my Head swims! I'm distracted! I can't support myself—Oh! [*Faints.*]

PEACHUM. See, Wench, to what a Condition you have reduc'd your poor Mother! a Glass of Cordial, this instant. How the poor Woman takes it to Heart! [POLLY *goes out, and returns with it.*]
Ah, Hussy, now this is the only Comfort your Mother has left!

POLLY. Give her another Glass, Sir; my Mama drinks double the Quantity whenever she is out of Order. This, you see, fetches her.

MRS. PEACHUM. The Girl shows such a Readiness, and so much Concern, that I could almost find in my Heart to forgive her.

AIR 9. O Jenny, O Jenny, where hast thou been

O Polly, you might have toy'd and kist.
By keeping Men off, you keep them on.

POLLY. *But he so teaz'd me,*
    And he so pleas'd me,
What I did, you must have done.

MRS. PEACHUM. Not with a Highwayman.—You sorry Slut!

PEACHUM. A Word with you, Wife. 'Tis no new thing for a Wench to take Man without consent of Parents. You know 'tis the Frailty of Woman, my Dear.

MRS. PEACHUM. Yes, indeed, the Sex is frail. But the first time a Woman is frail, she should be somewhat nice methinks, for then or never is the time to make her Fortune. After that, she hath nothing to do but to guard herself from being found out, and she may do what she pleases.

PEACHUM. Make your self a little easy; I have a Thought shall soon set all Matters again to rights. Why so melancholy, Polly? since what is done cannot be undone, we must all endeavour to make the best of it.

MRS. PEACHUM. Well, Polly; as far as one Woman can forgive another, I forgive thee.—Your Father is too fond of you, Hussy.

POLLY. Then all my Sorrows are at an end.

MRS. PEACHUM. A mighty likely Speech in troth, for a Wench who is just married!

AIR 10. Thomas, I cannot, &c.

POLLY. *I like a Ship in Storms, was tost;*
Yet afraid to put in to Land;
For seiz'd in the Port the Vessel's lost,
Whose Treasure is contreband.
    The Waves are laid,
    My Duty's paid.
O Joy beyond Expression!
    Thus, safe a-shore,
    I ask no more,
My All is in my Possession.

PEACHUM. I hear Customers in t'other Room; Go, talk with 'em, Polly; but come to us again, as soon as they are gone.—But, heark ye, Child, if 'tis the Gentleman who was here Yesterday about the Repeating-Watch; say, you believe we can't get Intelligence of it, till to-morrow. For I lent it to Suky Straddle, to make a Figure with it to-night at a Tavern in Drury-Lane. If t'other Gentleman calls for the Silver-hilted Sword; you know Bee-tle-brow'd Jemmy hath it on, and he doth not come from Tunbridge till Tuesday Night; so that it cannot be had till then. [*Exit* POLLY.]

Scene 9

PEACHUM. Dear Wife, be a little paci-fied. Don't let your Passion run away with your Senses. Polly, I grant you, hath done a rash thing.

MRS. PEACHUM. If she had had only an Intrigue with the Fellow, why the very best Families have excus'd and huddled up a Frailty of that sort. 'Tis Marriage, Husband, that makes it a blemish.

PEACHUM. But Money, Wife, is the true Fuller's Earth for Reputations, there is not a Spot or a Stain but what it can take out. A rich Rogue now-a-days is fit Company for any Gen-tleman; and the World, my Dear, hath not such a Contempt for Rogu-ery as you imagine. I tell you, Wife, I can make this Match turn to our Advantage.

MRS. PEACHUM. I am very sensible, Hus-band, that Captain Macheath is worth Money, but I am in doubt whether he hath not two or three Wives already, and then if he should dye in a Ses-sion or two, Polly's Dower would come into Dispute.

PEACHUM. That, indeed, is a Point which ought to be consider'd.

AIR 11. A Soldier and a Sailor

A Fox may steal your Hens, Sir,
A Whore your Health and Pence, Sir,
Your Daughter rob your Chest, Sir,
Your Wife may steal your Rest, Sir,
  A Thief your goods and Plate.
But this is all but picking;
With Rest, Pence, Chest and Chicken,
It ever was decreed, Sir,
If Lawyer's Hand is fee'd, Sir,
  He steals your whole Estate.

The Lawyers are bitter Enemies to those in our Way. They don't care that any Body should get a Clan-destine Livelihood but themselves.

Scene 10

Enter POLLY.

POLLY. 'Twas only Nimming Ned. He brought in a Damask Window-Cur-tain, a Hoop-Petticoat, a Pair of Silver Candlesticks, a Perriwig, and one Silk Stocking, from the Fire that hap-pen'd last Night.

PEACHUM. There is not a Fellow that is cleverer in his way, and saves more Goods out of the Fire than Ned. But now, Polly, to your Affair; for Matters must not be left as they are. You are married then, it seems?

POLLY. Yes, Sir.

PEACHUM. And how do you propose to live, Child?

POLLY. Like other Women, Sir, upon the Industry of my Husband.

MRS. PEACHUM. What, is the Wench turn'd Fool? A Highwayman's Wife, like a Soldier's, hath as little of his Pay, as of his Company.

PEACHUM. And had not you the com-mon Views of a Gentlewoman in your Marriage, Polly?

POLLY. I don't know what you mean, Sir.

PEACHUM. Of a Jointure,[5] and of being a Widow.

POLLY. But I love him, Sir: how then could I have Thoughts of parting with him?

PEACHUM. Parting with him! Why, that is the whole Scheme and Intention of all Marriage Articles. The comfort-able Estate of Widow-hood is the only hope that keeps up a Wife's Spirits. Where is the Woman who would scruple to be a Wife, if she had it in her Power to be a widow whenever she pleas'd? If you have any Views of this sort, Polly, I shall think the Match not so very unreasonable.

POLLY. How I dread to hear your Ad-vice! Yet I must beg you to explain yourself.

PEACHUM. Secure what he hath got, have him peach'd[6] the next Sessions, and then at once you are made a rich Widow.

POLLY. What, murder the Man I love! The Blood runs cold at my Heart with the very Thought of it.

PEACHUM. Fye, Polly! What hath

Murder to do in the Affair? Since the thing sooner or later must happen, I dare say, the Captain himself would like that we should get the Reward for his Death sooner than a Stranger. Why, Polly, the Captain knows, that as 'tis his Employment to rob, so 'tis ours to take Robbers; every Man in his Business. So that there is no Malice in the Case.

MRS. PEACHUM. Ay, Husband, now you have nick'd the Matter. To have him peach'd is the only thing could ever make me forgive her.

AIR 12. Now ponder well, ye Parents dear

POLLY. *Oh, ponder well! be not severe;*
So save a wretched Wife!
For on the Rope that hangs my Dear
Depends poor Polly's Life.

MRS. PEACHUM. But your Duty to your Parents, Hussy, obliges you to hang him. What would many a Wife give for such an Opportunity!

POLLY. What is a Jointure, what is Widow-hood to me? I know my Heart. I cannot survive him.

AIR 13. *Le printemps rappelle aux armes*

The Turtle thus with plaintive crying,
Her Lover dying,
The Turtle thus with plaintive crying,
Laments her Dove.
Down she drops quite spent with sighing,
Pair'd in Death, as pair'd in Love.

Thus, Sir, it will happen to your poor Polly.

MRS. PEACHUM. What, is the Fool in love in earnest then? I hate thee for being particular: Why, Wench, thou art a Shame to thy very Sex.

POLLY. But hear me, Mother.—If you ever lov'd—

MRS. PEACHUM. Those cursed Playbooks she reads have been her Ruin. One Word more, Hussy, and I shall knock your Brains out, if you have any.

PEACHUM. Keep out of the way, Polly, for fear of Mischief, and consider of what is propos'd to you.

MRS. PEACHUM. Away, Hussy. Hang your Husband, and be dutiful. [POLLY *exits, but remains to eavesdrop.*]

Scene 11

MRS. PEACHUM. The Thing, Husband, must and shall be done. For the sake of Intelligence we must take other Measures, and have him peach'd the next Session without her Consent. If she will not know her Duty, we know ours.

PEACHUM. But really, my Dear, it grieves one's Heart to take off a great Man. When I consider his Personal Bravery, his fine Stratagem, how much we have already got by him, and how much more we may get, methinks I can't find in my Heart to have a Hand in his Death. I wish you could have made Polly undertake it.

MRS. PEACHUM. But in a Case of Necessity—our own Lives are in danger.

PEACHUM. Then, indeed, we must comply with the Customs of the World, and make Gratitude give way to Interest.—He shall be taken off.

MRS. PEACHUM. I'll undertake to manage Polly.

PEACHUM. And I'll prepare Matters for the Old-Baily. [*Exeunt.*]

Scene 12

POLLY. Now I'm a Wretch, indeed.— Methinks I see him already in the Cart, sweeter and more lovely than the Nosegay in his Hand!—I hear the Crowd extolling his Resolution and Intrepidity!—What Vollies of Sighs are sent from the Windows of Holborn, that so comely a Youth should be brought to disgrace!—I see him at the Tree! The whole Circle are in Tears!—even Butchers weep!—Jack Ketch himself hesitates to perform his Duty, and would be glad to lose his Fee, by a Reprieve. What then will become of Polly!—As yet I may inform him of their Design, and aid him in his Escape.—It shall be so.—But then he flies, absents himself, and I bar my self from his dear, dear Conversation! That too will distract me.—If he keep out of the way, my Papa and Mama may in time relent, and we may be happy.— If he stays, he is hang'd, and then he is lost for ever!—He intended to lye conceal'd in my Room, 'till the Dusk of the Evening: If they are abroad, I'll this Instant let him out, lest some Accident should prevent him. [*Exit, and returns with* MACHEATH.]

Scene 13

AIR 14. Pretty Parrot, say—

MACHEATH. *Pretty Polly say,*
When I was away,
Did your Fancy never stray
To some newer Lover?
POLLY. *Without Disguise,*
Heaving Sighs,
Doating Eyes,
My constant Heart discover.
Fondly let me loll!
MACHEATH. *O pretty, pretty Poll.*

POLLY. And are *you* as fond as ever, my Dear?

MACHEATH. Suspect my Honour, my Courage, suspect any thing but my Love.—May my Pistols miss Fire, and my Mare slip her Shoulder while I am pursu'd, if I ever forsake thee!

POLLY. Nay, my Dear, I have no Reason to doubt you, for I find in the Romance you lent me, none of the great Heroes were ever false in Love.

AIR 15. Pray, Fair One, be kind—

MACHEATH. *My Heart was so free,*
It rov'd like the Bee,
'Till Polly my Passion requited;
I sipt each Flower,
I chang'd ev'ry Hour,
But here ev'ry Flower is United.

POLLY. Were you sentenc'd to Transportation, sure, my Dear, you could not leave me behind you—could you?

MACHEATH. Is there any Power, any Force that could tear me from thee? You might sooner tear a Pension out of the Hands of a Courtier, a Fee from a Lawyer, a pretty Woman from a Looking-glass, or any Woman from Quadrille.—But to tear me from thee is impossible!

AIR 16. Over the Hills and far away

Were I laid on Greenland's Coast
And in my Arms embrac'd my Lass;

Warm amidst eternal Frost,
Too soon the Half Year's Night would
pass.
POLLY. *Were I sold on Indian Soil,*
Soon as the burning Day was clos'd,
I could mock the sultry Toil,
When on my Charmer's Breast repos'd.
MACHEATH. *And I would love you all*
the Day,
POLLY. *Every Night would kiss and*
play,
MACHEATH. *If with me you'd fondly*
stray
POLLY. *Over the Hills and far away.*

POLLY. Yes, I would go with thee. But oh!—how shall I speak it? I must be torn from thee. We must part.

MACHEATH. How! Part!

POLLY. We must, we must.—My Papa and Mama are set against thy Life. They now, even now are in Search after thee. They are preparing Evidence against thee. Thy Life depends upon a Moment.

AIR 17. Gin thou wert mine awn thing—

O what Pain it is to part!
Can I leave thee, can I leave thee?
O what Pain it is to part!
Can thy Polly ever leave thee?
But lest Death my Love should thwart,
And bring thee to the fatal Cart,
Thus I tear thee from my bleeding Heart!
Fly hence, and let me leave thee.

One Kiss and then—one Kiss—begone—farewell.

MACHEATH. My Hand, my Heart, my Dear, is so rivited to thine, that I cannot unloose my Hold.

POLLY. But my Papa may intercept thee, and then I should lose the very glimmering of Hope. A few Weeks, perhaps, may reconcile us all. Shall thy Polly hear from thee?

MACHEATH. Must I then go?

POLLY. And will not Absence change your Love?

MACHEATH. If you doubt it, let me stay—and be hang'd.

POLLY. O how I fear! how I tremble!—Go—but when Safety will give you leave, you will be sure to see me again; for 'till then Polly is wretched.

AIR 18. O the Broom, &c.

[*Parting, and looking back at each other with fondness; he at one Door, she at the other.*]

MACHEATH. *The Miser thus a Shilling sees,*
Which he's oblig'd to pay,
With Sighs resigns it by degrees,
And fears 'tis gone for aye.
POLLY. *The Boy, thus, when his Sparrow's flown,*
The Bird in Silence eyes;
But soon as out of Sight 'tis gone,
Whines, whimpers, sobs and cries.

[*Exeunt.*]

Act 2

Scene 1

A Tavern near Newgate. JEMMY TWITCHER, CROOK-FINGER'D JACK, WAT DREARY, ROBIN OF BAGSHOT, NIMMING NED, HENRY PADINGTON, MATT OF THE MINT, BEN BUDGE, *and the rest of the* GANG, *at the Table, with Wine, Brandy and Tobacco.*

BEN. But pr'ythee, Matt, what is become of thy Brother Tom? I have not seen him since my Return from Transportation.

MATT. Poor Brother Tom had an Accident this time Twelve-month, and so clever a made Fellow he was, that I could not save him from those fleaing Rascals the Surgeons; and now, poor Man, he is among the Otamys[7] at Surgeon's Hall.

BEN. So it seems, his Time was come.

JEMMY. But the present Time is ours, and no Body alive hath more. Why are the Laws levell'd at us? are we more dishonest than the rest of Mankind? What we win, Gentlemen, is our own by the Law of Arms, and the Right of Conquest.

JACK. Where shall we find such another Set of practical Philosophers, who to a Man are above the Fear of Death?

WAT. Sound Men, and true!

ROBIN. Of try'd Courage, and indefatigable Industry!

NED. Who is there here that would not dye for his Friend?

HARRY. Who is there here that would betray him for his Interest?

MATT. Show me a Gang of Courtiers that can say as much.

BEN. We are for a just Partition of the World, for every Man hath a Right to enjoy Life.

MATT. We retrench the Superfluities of Mankind. The World is avaricious, and I hate Avarice. A covetous fellow, like a Jackdaw, steals what he was never made to enjoy, for the sake of hiding it. These are the Robbers of Mankind, for Money was made for the Free-hearted and Generous, and where is the injury of taking from another, what he hath not the Heart to make use of?

JEMMY. Our several Stations for the Day are fixt. Good luck attend us all. Fill the Glasses.

AIR 1. Fill ev'ry Glass, &c.

MATT. *Fill ev'ry Glass, for wine inspires us,*
And fires us
With Courage, Love and Joy.
Women and Wine should Life employ
Is there ought else on Earth desirous?
CHORUS. *Fill ev'ry Glass, &c.*

Scene 2

Enter MACHEATH.

MACHEATH. Gentlemen, well met. My Heart hath been with you this Hour; but an unexpected Affair hath detain'd me. No Ceremony, I beg you.

MATT. We were just breaking up to go upon Duty. Am I to have the Honour of taking the Air with you, Sir, this Evening upon the Heath? I drink a Dram now and then with the Stage-Coachmen in the way of Friendship and Intelligence; and I know that about this Time there will be Passengers upon the Western Road, who are worth speaking with.

MACHEATH. I was to have been of that Party—but—

MATT. But what, Sir?

MACHEATH. Is there any man who suspects my Courage?

MATT. We have all been witnesses of it.

MACHEATH. My Honour and Truth to the Gang?

MATT. I'll be answerable for it.

MACHEATH. In the Division of our Booty, have I ever shown the least Marks of Avarice or Injustice?

MATT. By these Questions something seems to have ruffled you. Are any of us suspected?

MACHEATH. I have a fixt Confidence, Gentlemen, in you all, as Men of Honour, and as such I value and respect you. Peachum is a Man that is useful to us.

MATT. Is he about to play us any foul Play? I'll shoot him through the Head.

MACHEATH. I beg you, Gentlemen, act with Conduct and Discretion. A Pistol is your last resort.

MATT. He knows nothing of this Meeting.

MACHEATH. Business cannot go on without him. He is a Man who knows the World, and is a necessary Agent to us. We have had a slight Difference, and till it is accommodated I shall be oblig'd to keep out of his way. Any private Dispute of mine shall be of no ill consequence to my Friends. You must continue to act under his Direction, for the moment we break loose from him, our Gang is ruin'd.

MATT. As a Bawd to a Whore, I grant you, he is to us of great Convenience.

MACHEATH. Make him believe I have quitted the Gang, which I can never do but with Life. At our private Quarters I will continue to meet you. A Week or so will probably reconcile us.

MATT. Your Instructions shall be observ'd. 'Tis now high time for us to repair to our several Duties; so till the Evening at our Quarters in Moor-fields we bid you farewell.

MACHEATH. I shall wish my self with you. Success attend you. [*Sits down melancholy at the Table.*]

AIR 2 March in Rinaldo, with Drums and Trumpets

MATT. *Let us take the Road.*
Hark! I hear the sound of Coaches!
The hour of Attack approaches,
  To your Arms, brave Boys, and load.
  See the Ball I hold!
Let the Chymists toil like Asses,
Our fire their fire surpasses.
  And turns all our Lead to Gold.

[*The* GANG, *rang'd in the Front of the Stage, load their Pistols, and stick them under their Girdles; then go off singing the first Part in Chorus.*]

Scene 3

MACHEATH. What a Fool is a fond Wench! Polly is most confoundedly bit.—I love the Sex. And a Man who loves Money, might as well be contented with one Guinea, as I with one Woman. The Town perhaps hath been as much oblig'd to me, for recruiting it with free-hearted Ladies, as to any Recruiting Officer in the Army. If it were not for us and the other Gentlemen of the Sword, Drury-Lane would be uninhabited.

AIR 3. Would you have a Young Virgin, &c.

If the Heart of a Man is deprest with Cares,
The Mist is dispell'd when a Woman appears;
Like the Notes of a Fiddle, she sweetly, sweetly
Raises the Spirits, and charms our Ears.
Roses and Lillies her Cheeks disclose,
But her ripe Lips are more sweet than those.
    Press her,
    Caress her
    With Blisses,
    Her Kisses
Dissolve us in Pleasure, and soft Repose.

I must have Women. There is nothing unbends the Mind like them. Money is not so strong a Cordial for the Time, Drawer. [*Enter* DRAWER.] Is the Potter gone for all the Ladies, according to my directions?

DRAWER. I expect him back every Minute. But you know, Sir, you sent him as far as Hockey in the Hole, for three of the Ladies, for one in Vinegar Yard, and for the rest of them somewhere about Lewkner's Lane. Sure some of them are below, for I hear the Barr Bell. As they come I will show them up. Coming, coming.

Scene 4

Enter MRS. COAXER, DOLLY TRULL, MRS. VIXEN, BETTY DOXY, JENNY DIVER, MRS. SLAMMEKIN, SUKY TAWDRY, *and* MOLLY BRAZEN.

MACHEATH. Dear Mrs. Coaxer, you are welcome. You look charmingly to-day. I hope you don't want the Repairs of Quality, and lay on Paint.—Dolly Trull! kiss me, you Slut; are you as amorous as ever, Hussy? You are always so taken up with stealing Hearts, that you don't allow yourself Time to steal anything else.—Ah Dolly, thou wilt ever be a Coquette!—Mrs. Vixen, I'm yours, I always lov'd a Woman of Wit and Spirit; they make charming Mistresses, but plaguy Wives.—Betty Doxy! Come hither, Hussy. Do you drink as hard as ever? You had better stick to good Wholesome Beer; for in troth, Betty, Strong-Waters will in time ruin your Constitution. You should leave those to your Betters.—What! and my pretty Jenny Diver too! As prim and demure as ever! There is not any Prude, though ever so high bred, hath a more sanctify'd Look, with a more mischievous Heart. Ah! thou art a dear artful Hypocrite.—Mrs. Slammekin! as careless and genteel as ever! all you fine Ladies, who know your own Beauty, affect an Undress.—But see, here's Suky Tawdry come to contradict what I was saying. Every thing she gets one way she lays out upon her Back. Why Suky, you must keep at least a dozen Tallymen. Molly Brazen! [*She kisses him.*] That's well done. I love a free-hearted Wench. Thou hast a most agreeable Assurance, Girl, and art as willing as a Turtle.—But hark! I hear musick. The Harper is at the Door. If Musick be the Food of Love, play on. E'er

you seat your selves, Ladies, what think you of a Dance? Come in. [*Enter* HARPER.] Play the French Tune, that Mrs. Slammekin was so fond of. [*A Dance à la ronde in the French Manner; near the End of it this Song and Chorus.*]

AIR 4. Cotillon

Youth's the Season made for Joys,
    Love is then our Duty,
She alone who that employs,
    Well deserves her Beauty.
        Let's be gay,
        While we may,
    Beauty's a Flower, despis'd in decay.
Youth's the Season, &c.

Let us drink and sport to-day,
    Ours is not to-morrow.
Love with Youth flies swift away,
    Age is nought but Sorrow.
        Dance and sing.
        Time's on the Wing,
Life never knows the return of Spring.
    CHORUS. *Let us drink, &c.*

MACHEATH. Now, pray Ladies, take your Places. Here Fellow [*Pays the* HARPER.], Bid the Drawer bring us more Wine. [*Exit* HARPER.] If any of the Ladies chuse Ginn, I hope they will be so free to call for it.

JENNY DIVER. You look as if you meant me. Wine is strong enough for me. Indeed, Sir, I never drink Strong-Waters, but when I have the Cholic.

MACHEATH. Just the Excuse of the fine Ladies! Why, a Lady of Quality is never without the Cholic. I hope, Mrs. Coaxer, you have had good Success of late in your Visits among the Mercers.

MRS. COAXER. We have so many Interlopers—Yet with Industry, one may still have a little Picking. I carried a silver flower'd Lutestring, and a Piece of black Padesoy to Mr. Peachum's Lock but last Week.

MRS. VIXEN. There's Molly Brazen hath the Ogle of a Rattle-Snake. She riveted a Linnen-draper's Eye so fast upon her, that she was nick'd of three Pieces of Cambric before he could look off.

MOLLY BRAZEN. Oh dear Madam!—But sure nothing can come up to your handling of Laces! And then you have such a sweet deluding Tongue! To cheat a Man is nothing; but the Woman must have fine Parts indeed who cheats a Woman!

MRS. VIXEN. Lace, Madam, lyes in a small Compass, and is of easy Conveyance. But you are apt, Madam, to think too well of your Friends.

MRS. COAXER. If any Woman hath more Art than another, to be sure, 'tis Jenny Diver. Though her Fellow be never so agreeable, she can pick his Pocket as cooly, as if Money were her only Pleasure. Now that is a Command of Passions uncommon in a Woman!

JENNY DIVER. I never go to the Tavern with a Man, but in the View of Business. I have other Hours, and other sort of Men for my Pleasure. But had I your Address, Madam—

MACHEATH. Have done with your Compliments, Ladies; and drink about: You are not so fond of me, Jenny, as you use to be.

JENNY DIVER. 'Tis not convenient, Sir, to show my Fondness among so many Rivals. 'Tis your own Choice, and not the warmth of my Inclination that will determine you.

AIR 5. All in a misty Morning, &c.

Before the Barn-door crowing,
The Cock by Hens attended,
His Eyes around him throwing,
Stands for a while suspended.
Then One he singles from the Crew,
And cheers the happy Hen;
With how do you do, and how do you do.
And how do you do again.

MACHEATH. Ah Jenny! thou art a dear Slut.

DOLLY TRULL. Pray, Madam, were you ever in keeping?

SUKY TAWDRY. I hope, Madam, I ha'n been so long upon the Town, but I have met with some good Fortune as well as my Neighbours.

DOLLY TRULL. Pardon me, Madam, I meant no harm by the Question; 'twas only in the way of Conversation.

SUKY TAWDRY. Indeed, Madam, if I had not been a Fool, I might have liv'd

very handsomely with my last Friend. But upon his missing five Guineas, he turn'd me off. Now I never suspected he had counted them.

MRS. SLAMMEKIN. Who do you look upon, Madam, as your best sort of Keepers?

DOLLY TRULL. That, Madam, is thereafter as they be.

MRS. SLAMMEKIN. I, Madam, was once kept by a Jew; and bating their Religion, to Women they are a good sort of People.

SUKY TAWDRY. Now for my part, I own I like an old Fellow: for we always make them pay for what they can't do.

MRS. VIXEN. A spruce Prentice, let me tell you, Ladies, is no ill thing, they bleed freely. I have sent at least two or three dozen of them in my time to the Plantations.

JENNY DIVER. But to be sure, Sir, with so much good Fortune as you have had upon the Road, you must be grown immensely rich.

MACHEATH. The Road, indeed, hath done me justice, but the Gaming-Table hath been my ruin.

AIR 6. When once I lay with another Man's Wife, &c.

JENNY DIVER. *The Gamesters and*
Lawyers are Jugglers alike,
If they meddle your All is in danger.
Like Gypsies, if once they can finger a
Souse,
Your Pockets they pick, and they pilfer
your House,
And give your Estate to a Stranger.

These are the Tools of a Man of Honour. Cards and Dice are only fit for cowardly Cheats, who prey upon their Friends. [*She takes up his Pistol.* TAWDRY *takes up the other.*]

SUKY TAWDRY. This, Sir, is fitter for your Hand. Besides your Loss of Money, 'tis a Loss to the Ladies. Gaming takes you off from Women. How fond could I be of you! but before Company, 'tis ill-bred.

MACHEATH. Wanton Hussies!

JENNY DIVER. I must and will have a Kiss to give my Wine a zest. [*They take him about the Neck, and make Signs to*

PEACHUM *and* CONSTABLES, *who rush in upon him.*]

Scene 5

PEACHUM. I seize you, Sir, as my Prisoner.

MACHEATH. Was this well done, Jenny?—Women are Decoy Ducks; who can trust them! Beasts, Jades, Jilts, Harpies, Furies, Whores!

PEACHUM. Your Case, Mr. Macheath, is not particular. The greatest Heroes have been ruin'd by Women. But, to do them justice, I must own they are a pretty sort of Creatures, if we could trust them. You must now, Sir, take your leave of the Ladies, and if they have a Mind to make you a Visit, they will be sure to find you at home. The Gentleman, Ladies, lodges in Newgate. Constables, wait upon the Captain to his Lodgings.

AIR 7. When first I said Siege to my Chloris, &c.

MACHEATH. *At the Tree I shall suffer with pleasure,*
At the Tree I shall suffer with pleasure,
Let me go where I will,
In all kinds of Ill,
I shall find no such Furies as these are.

PEACHUM. Ladies, I'll take care the Reckoning shall be discharg'd. [*Exit* MACHEATH, *guarded with* PEACHUM *and* CONSTABLES.]

Scene 6

The WOMEN *remain*

MRS. VIXEN. Look ye, Mrs. Jenny, though Mr. Peachum may have made a private Bargain with you and Suky Tawdry for betraying the Captain, as we were all assisting, we ought all to share alike.

MRS. COAXER. I think Mr. Peachum, after so long an acquaintance, might have trusted me as well as Jenny Diver.

MRS. SLAMMEKIN. I am sure at least three Men of his hanging, and in a Year's time too (if he did me justice) should be set down to my account.

DOLLY TRULL. Mrs. Slammekin, that is not fair. For you know one of them was taken in Bed with me.

JENNY DIVER. As far as a Bowl of Punch or a Treat, I believe Mrs. Suky will join with me.—As for any thing else, Ladies, you cannot in conscience expect it.

MRS. SLAMMEKIN. Dear Madam—

DOLLY TRULL. I would not for the World—

MRS. SLAMMEKIN. 'Tis impossible for me—

DOLLY TRULL. As I hope to be sav'd, Madam—

MRS. SLAMMEKIN. Nay, then I must stay here all Night—

DOLLY TRULL. Since you command me. [*Exeunt with great Ceremony.*]

Scene 7

Newgate. Enter LOCKIT, TURNKEYS, MACHEATH, CONSTABLES.

LOCKIT. Noble Captain, you are welcome. You have not been a Lodger of mine this Year and half. You know the custom, Sir. Garnish,[8] Captain, Garnish. Hand me down those Fetters there.

MACHEATH. Those, Mr. Lockit, seem to be the heaviest of the whole set. With your leave, I should like the further pair better.

LOCKIT. Look ye, Captain, we know what is fittest for our Prisoners. When a Gentleman uses me with Civility, I always do the best I can to please him.—Hand them down I say.—We have them of all Prices, from one Guinea to ten, and 'tis fitting every Gentleman should please himself.

MACHEATH. I understand you, Sir. [*Gives Money.*] The Fees here are so many, and so exorbitant, that few Fortunes can bear the Expence of getting off handsomly, or of dying like a Gentleman.

LOCKIT. Those, I see, will fit the Captain better.—Take down the further Pair. Do but examine them, Sir.—Never was better work.—How genteely they are made!—They will fit as easy as a Glove, and the nicest Man in England might not be asham'd to wear them. [*He puts on the Chains.*] If I had the best Gentleman in the Land in my Custody I could not equip him more handsomely. And so, Sir—I now leave you to your private Meditations.

Scene 8

Exeunt all but MACHEATH.

AIR 8. Courtiers, Courtiers think it no harm, &c.

Man may escape from Rope and Gun
Nay, some have out-liv'd the Doctor's Pill;
Who takes a Woman must be undone,
    That Basilisk is sure to kill.
The Fly that sips Treacle is lost in the
    Sweets,
So he that tastes Woman, Woman,
    Woman,
He that tastes Woman, Ruin meets.

To what a woeful plight have I brought my self! Here must I (all day long, 'till I am hang'd) be confin'd to hear the Reproaches of a Wench who lays her Ruin at my Door.—I am in the Custody of her Father, and to be sure if he knows of the matter, I shall have a fine time on't betwixt this and my Execution.—But I promis'd the Wench Marriage.—What signifies a Promise to a Woman? Does not Man in Marriage itself promise a hundred things that he never means to perform? Do all we can, Women will believe us; for they look upon a Promise as an Excuse for following their own Inclinations.—But here comes Lucy, and I cannot get from her.—Wou'd I were deaf!

Scene 9

Enter LUCY.

LUCY. You base Man you,—how can you look me in the Face after what hath past between us?—See here, perfidious Wretch, how I am forc'd to bear about the load of Infamy you have laid upon me.—O Macheath! thou hast robb'd me of my Quiet—to

see thee tortur'd would give me pleasure.

AIR 9. A lovely Lass to a Friar came, &c.

Thus when a good Huswife sees a Rat
    In her Trap in the Morning taken,
With pleasure her Heart goes pit a pat,
    In Revenge for her loss of Bacon.
        Then she throws him
        To the Dog or Cat,
To be worried, crush'd and shaken.

MACHEATH. Have you no Bowels, no Tenderness, my dear Lucy, to see a Husband in these Circumstances?
LUCY. A Husband!
MACHEATH. In ev'ry respect but the form, and that, my Dear, may be said over us at any time.—Friends should not insist upon Ceremonies. From a Man of honour, his Word is as good as his Bond.
LUCY. 'Tis the pleasure of all you fine Men to insult the Women you have ruin'd.

AIR 10. 'Twas when the Sea was roaring, &c.

How cruel are the Traytors,
    Who lye and swear in jest,
To cheat unguarded Creatures
    Of Virtue, Fame, and Rest!
Whoever steals a Shilling,
    Through shame the Guilt conceals:
In Love the perjur'd Villain
    With Boasts the Theft reveals.

MACHEATH. The very first opportunity, my Dear, (have but patience) you shall be my Wife in whatever manner you please.
LUCY. Insinuating Monster! And so you think I know nothing of the Affair of Miss Polly Peachum.—I could tear thy Eyes out!
MACHEATH. Sure Lucy, you can't be such a Fool as to be jealous of Polly!
LUCY. Are you not married to her, you Brute, you?
MACHEATH. Married! Very good. The Wench gives it out only to vex thee, and to ruin me in thy good Opinion. 'Tis true, I go to the House; I chat with the Girl, I kiss her, I say a thousand things to her (as all Gen-

tlemen do) that mean nothing, to divert my self; and now the silly Jade hath set it about that I am married to her, to let me know what she would be at. Indeed, my dear Lucy, these violent Passions may be of ill consequence to a Woman in your condition.

LUCY. Come, come, Captain, for all your Assurance, you know that Miss Polly hath put it out of your power to do me the Justice you promis'd me.

MACHEATH. A jealous Woman believes ev'ry thing her Passion suggests. To convince you of my Sincerity, if we can find the Ordinary, I shall have no scruples of making you my Wife; and I know the consequence of having two at a time.

LUCY. That you are only to be hang'd, and so get rid of them both.

MACHEATH. I am ready, my dear Lucy, to give you satisfaction—if you think there is any in Marriage.—What can a Man of Honour say more?

LUCY. So then it seems, you are not married to Miss Polly.

MACHEATH. You know, Lucy, the Girl is prodigiously conceited. No Man can say a civil thing to her, but (like other fine Ladies) her Vanity makes her think he's her own for ever and ever.

AIR 11. The Sun had loos'd his weary Teams, &c.

The first time at the Looking-glass
The Mother sets her Daughter,
The Image strikes the smiling Lass
With Self-love ever after.
Each time she looks, she, fonder grown,
Thinks ev'ry Charm grows stronger.
But alas, vain Maid, all Eyes but your own
Can see you are not younger.

When Women consider their own Beauties, they are all alike unreasonable in their demands; for they expect their Lovers should like them as long as they like themselves.

LUCY. Yonder is my Father—perhaps this way we may light upon the Ordinary, who shall try if you will be as good as your Word.—For I long to be made an honest Woman.

Scene 10

Enter PEACHUM *and* LOCKIT *with an Account-Book.*

LOCKIT. In this last Affair, Brother Peachum, we are agreed. You have consented to go halves in Macheath.

PEACHUM. We shall never fall out about an Execution.—But as to that Article, pray how stands our last Year's account?

LOCKIT. If you will run your Eye over it, you'll find 'tis fair and clearly stated.

PEACHUM. This long Arrear of the Government is very hard upon us! Can it be expected that we should hang our Acquaintance for nothing, when our Betters will hardly save theirs without being paid for it? Unless the People in employment pay better, I promise them for the future, I shall let other Rogues live besides their own.

LOCKIT. Perhaps, Brother, they are afraid these matters may be carried too far. We are treated too by them with Contempt, as if our Profession were not reputable.

PEACHUM. In one respect indeed, our Employment may be reckon'd dishonest, because, like Great Statesmen, we encourage those who betray Their Friends.

LOCKIT. Such Language, Brother, any where else, might turn to your prejudice. Learn to be more guarded, I beg you.

AIR 12. How happy are we, &c.

When you censure the Age,
Be cautious and sage.
Lest the Courtiers offended should be:
If you mention Vice or Bribe,
'Tis so pat to all the Tribe;
Each crys—That was levell'd at me.

PEACHUM. Here's poor Ned Clincher's Name, I see. Sure, Brother Lockit, there was a little unfair proceeding in Ned's case: for he told me in the Condemn'd Hold, that for Value receiv'd, you had promis'd him a Session or two longer without Molestation.

LOCKIT. Mr. Peachum—This is the first

time my Honour was ever call'd in Question.

PEACHUM. Business is at an end—if once we act dishonourably.

LOCKIT. Who accuses me?

PEACHUM. You are warm, Brother.

LOCKIT. He that attacks my Honour, attacks my Livelyhood.—And this Usage—Sir—is not to be born.

PEACHUM. Since you provoke me to speak—I must tell you too, that Mrs. Coaxer charges you with defrauding her of her Information-Money, for the apprehending of curl-pated Hugh. Indeed, indeed, Brother, we must punctually pay our Spies, or we shall have no Information.

LOCKIT. Is this Language to me, Sirrah—who have sav'd you from the Gallows, Sirrah! [*Collaring each other.*]

PEACHUM. If I am hang'd, it shall be for ridding the World of an arrant Rascal.

LOCKIT. This Hand shall do the office of the Halter you deserve, and throttle you—you Dog!—

PEACHUM. Brother, Brother—We are both in the Wrong—We shall be both Losers in the Dispute—for you know we have it in our Power to hang each other. You should not be so passionate.

LOCKIT. Nor you so provoking.

PEACHUM. 'Tis our mutual Interest; 'tis for the Interest of the World we should agree. If I said any thing, Brother, to the Prejudice of your Character, I ask pardon.

LOCKIT. Brother Peachum—I can forgive as well as resent.—Give me your Hand. Suspicion does not become a Friend.

PEACHUM. I only meant to give you occasion to justifie yourself: But I must now step home, for I expect the Gentleman about this Snuff-box, that Filch nimm'd two Nights ago in the Park. I appointed him at this hour. [*Exit.*]

Scene 11

Enter LUCY.

LOCKIT. Whence come you, Hussy?

LUCY. My Tears might answer that Question.

LOCKIT. You have then been whimpering and fondling, like a Spaniel, over the Fellow that hath abus'd you.

LUCY. One can't help Love; one can't cure it. 'Tis not in my Power to obey you, and hate him.

LOCKIT. Learn to bear your Husband's Death like a reasonable Woman. 'Tis not the fashion, now-a-days, so much as to affect Sorrow upon these Occasions. No Woman would ever marry, if she had not the Chance of Mortality for a Release. Act like a Woman of Spirit, Hussy, and thank your Father for what he is doing.

AIR 13. Of a noble Race was Shenkin

LUCY. *Is then his Fate decreed, Sir?*
Such a Man can I think of quitting?
When first we met, so moves me yet,
O see how my Heart is splitting!

LOCKIT. Look ye, Lucy—There is no saving him.—So, I think you must ev'n do like other Widows—Buy your self Weeds, and be cheerful.

AIR 14

You'll think e'er many Days ensue
    This Sentence not severe;
I hang your Husband, Child, 'tis true,
    But with him hang your Care.
    Twang dang dillo dee.

Like a good Wife, go moan over your dying Husband. That, Child, is your Duty—Consider, Girl, you can't have the Man and the Money too—so make yourself as easy as you can, by getting all you can from him. [*Exit.*]

Scene 12

MACHEATH *in cell; enter* LUCY.

LUCY. Though the Ordinary was out of the way to-day I hope, my Dear, you will, upon the first opportunity, quiet my Scruples—Oh Sir!—my Father's hard Heart is not to be soften'd, and I am in the utmost Despair.

MACHEATH. But if I could raise a small Sum—Would not twenty Guineas, think you, move him?—Of all the

Arguments in the way of Business, the Perquisite is the most prevailing.—Your Father's Perquisites for the Escape of Prisoners must amount to a considerable Sum in the Year. Money well tim'd, and properly apply'd, will do any thing.

AIR 15. London Ladies

If you at an Office solicit your Due,
*   And would not have Matters neglected;*
You must quicken the Clerk with the per-
*   quisite too,*
*   To do what his Duty directed.*
Or would you the Frowns of a Lady
*   prevent,*
*   She too has this palpable Failing*
The Perquisite softens her into Consent;
*   That Reason with all is prevailing.*

LUCY. What Love or Money can do shall be done: for all my Comfort depends upon your Safety.

Scene 13

Enter POLLY.

POLLY. Where is my dear Husband?— Was a Rope ever intended for this Neck!—O let me throw my Arms about it, and throttle thee with Love!—Why dost thou turn away from me?—'Tis thy Polly—'Tis thy Wife.

MACHEATH. Was ever such an unfortunate Rascal as I am!

LUCY. Was there ever such another Villain!

POLLY. O Macheath! was it for this we parted? Taken! Imprison'd! Try'd! Hang'd!—cruel Reflection! I'll stay with thee 'till Death—no Force shall tear thy dear Wife from thee now.— What means my Love?—Not one kind Word! not one kind Look! think what thy Polly suffers to see thee in this Condition.

AIR 16. All in the Downs, &c.

Thus when the Swallow, seeking Prey,
*   Within the Sash is closely pent,*
His Comfort, with bemoaning Lay,
*   Without sits pining for th' Event.*
Her chatt'ring Lovers all around her
*   skim;*

She heeds them not (poor Bird!), her
*   Soul's with him.*

MACHEATH. I must disown her. [*Aside.*] The Wench is distracted.

LUCY. Am I then bilk'd of my Virtue? Can I have no Reparation? Sure Men were born to lye, and Women to believe them! O Villain! Villain!

POLLY. Am I not thy Wife?—Thy Neglect of me, thy Aversion to me too severely proves it.—Look on me.— Tell me, am I not thy Wife?

LUCY. Perfidious Wretch!

POLLY. Barbarous Husband!

LUCY. Hadst thou been hang'd five Months ago, I had been happy.

POLLY. And I too—If you had been kind to me 'till Death, it would not have vex'd me. And that's no very unreasonable Request, (though from a Wife) to a Man who hath not above seven or eight Days to live.

LUCY. Art thou then married to another? Hast thou two Wives, Monster?

MACHEATH. If Women's Tongues can cease for an Answer—hear me.

LUCY. I won't.—Flesh and Blood can't bear my Usage.

POLLY. Shall I not claim my own? Justice bids me speak.

AIR 17. Have you heard of a frolicksome Ditty, &c.

MACHEATH. *How happy could I be*
*   with either,*
Were t'other dear Charmer away!
But while you thus teaze me together,
To neither a Word will I say;
*   But tol de rol, &c.*

POLLY. Sure, my Dear, there ought to be some Preference shown to a Wife! At least she may claim the Appearance of it. He must be distracted with his Misfortunes, or he could not use me thus!

LUCY. O Villain, Villain! thou hast deceiv'd me—I could even inform against thee with Pleasure. Not a Prude wishes more heartily to have Facts against her intimate Acquaintance, than I now wish to have Facts against thee. I would have her Satisfaction, and they should all out.

AIR 18. Irish Trot

POLLY. *I'm bubbled.*
LUCY. *I'm bubbled.*
POLLY. *Oh how I am troubled!*
LUCY. *Bambouzled, and bit!*
POLLY. *My Distresses are doubled.*
LUCY. *When you come to the Tree, should
the Hangman refuse, These Fingers,
with Pleasure, could fasten the Noose.*
POLLY. *I'm bubbled, &c.*

MACHEATH. Be pacified, my dear
Lucy—This is all a Fetch[9] of Polly's,
to make me desperate with you in
case I get off. If I am hang'd, she
would fain have the Credit of being
thought my Widow—Really, Polly,
this is no time for a Dispute of this
sort; for whenever you are talking of
Marriage, I am thinking of Hanging.
POLLY. And hast thou the Heart to persist in disowning me?
MACHEATH. And hast thou the Heart to
persist in persuading me that I am
married? Why Polly, dost thou seek
to aggravate my Misfortunes?
LUCY. Really, Miss Peachum, you but
expose yourself. Besides, 'tis barbarous in you to worry a Gentleman in
his Circumstances.

AIR 19

POLLY. *Cease your Funning;
Force or Cunning
Never shall my Heart trapan.[10]
All these Sallies
Are but Malice
To seduce my constant Man.
'Tis most certain,
By their flirting
Women oft' have Envy shown;
Pleas'd, to ruin
Others wooing;
Never happy in their own!*

POLLY. Decency, Madam, methinks
might teach you to behave yourself
with some Reserve with the Husband, while his Wife is present.
MACHEATH. But seriously, Polly, this is
carrying the Joke a little too far.
LUCY. If you are determin'd, Madam, to
raise a Disturbance in the Prison, I
shall be oblig'd to send for the Turn-
key to show you the Door. I am sorry,
Madam, you force me to be so ill-
bred.

POLLY. Give me leave to tell you,
Madam: These forward Airs don't
become you in the least, Madam.
And my Duty, Madam, obliges me to
stay with my Husband, Madam.

AIR 20. Good-morrow, Gossip Joan

LUCY. *Why how now, Madam Flirt?
If you thus must chatter;
And are for flinging Dirt,
Let's try for best can spatter;
Madam Flirt!*
POLLY. *Why how now, saucy Jade;
Sure the Wench is Tipsy*
[To him.] *How can you see me made
The Scoff of such a Gipsy?*
[To her.] *Saucy Jade!*

Scene 14

Enter PEACHUM.
PEACHUM. Where's my Wench? Ah
Hussy! Hussy!—Come you home,
you Slut; and when your Fellow is
hang'd, hang yourself, to make your
Family some amends.
POLLY. Dear, dear Father, do not tear
me from him—I must speak; I have
more to say to him—Oh! twist thy
Fetters about me, that he may not
haul me from thee!
PEACHUM. Sure all Women are alike! If
ever they commit the Folly, they are
sure to commit another by exposing
themselves—Away—Not a Word
more—You are my Prisoner now,
Hussy.

AIR 21. Irish Howl

[*Holding MACHEATH, PEACHUM pulling
her.*]

POLLY. *No Power on Earth can e'er
divide,
The Knot that Sacred Love hath ty'd.
When Parents draw against our Mind,
The True-love's Knot they faster bind.
Oh, oh ray, oh Amborah—oh, oh, &c.*
[*Exit PEACHUM and POLLY.*]

Scene 15

MACHEATH. I am naturally compassionate, Wife; so that I could not use the

Wench as she deserv'd; which made you at first suspect there was something in what she said.

LUCY. Indeed, my Dear, I was strangely puzzled.

MACHEATH. If that had been the Case, her Father would never have brought me into this Circumstance—No, Lucy,—I had rather dye than be false to thee.

LUCY. How happy am I, if you say this from your Heart! For I love thee so, that I could sooner bear to see thee hang'd than in the Arms of another.

MACHEATH. But couldst thou bear to see me hang'd?

LUCY. O Macheath, I can never live to see that Day.

MACHEATH. You see, Lucy, in the Account of Love you are in my debt, and you must now be convinc'd that I rather chuse to die than be another's.—Make me, if possible, love thee more, and let me owe my Life to thee—If you refuse to assist me, Peachum and your Father will immediately put me beyond all means of Escape.

LUCY. My father, I know, hath been drinking hard with the Prisoners: and I fancy he is now taking his Nap in his own Room—if I can procure the Keys, shall I go off with thee, my Dear?

MACHEATH. If we are together, 'twill be impossible, to lye conceal'd. As soon as the Search begins to be a little cool, I will send to thee—'Till then my Heart is thy Prisoner.

LUCY. Come then, my dear Husband—owe thy Life to me—and though you love me not—be grateful—But that Polly runs in my Head strangely.

MACHEATH. A Moment of time may make us unhappy for-ever.

AIR 22. The Lass of Patie's Mill, &c.

LUCY. *I like the Fox shall grieve,*
Whose Mate hath left her side,
Whom Hounds, from Morn to Eve,
Chase o'er the Country wide.

Where can my Lover hide?
Where cheat the weary Pack?
If Love be not his Guide,
He never will come back!

[*Exeunt.*]

Act 3

Scene 1
Newgate

Enter LOCKIT *and* LUCY.

LOCKIT. To be sure, Wench, you must have been aiding and abetting to help him to this Escape.

LUCY. Sir, here hath been Peachum and his Daughter Polly, and to be sure they know the Ways of Newgate as well as if they had been born and bred in the Place all their Lives. Why must all your Suspicion light upon me?

LOCKIT. Lucy, Lucy, I will have none of these shuffling Answers.

LUCY. Well then—If I know any Thing of him I wish I may be burnt!

LOCKIT. Keep your Temper, Lucy, or I shall pronounce you guilty.

LUCY. Keep yours, Sir,—I do wish I may be burnt. I do—And what can I say more to convince you?

LOCKIT. Did he tip handsomely?—How much did he come down with? Come Hussy, don't cheat your Father; and I shall not be angry with you—Perhaps, you have made a better Bargain with him than I could have done—How much, my good Girl?

LUCY. You know, Sir, I am fond of him, and would have given Money to have kept him with me.

LOCKIT. Ah Lucy! thy Education might have put thee more upon thy Guard; for a Girl in the Bar of an Alehouse is always besieg'd.

LUCY. Dear Sir, mention not my Education—for 'twas to that I owe my Ruin.

AIR 1. If Love's a sweet Passion, &c.

When young at the Bar you first taught
me to score,
And bid me be free of my Lips, and no
more;
I was kiss'd by the Parson, the Squire, and
the Sot.
When the Guest was departed; the Kiss
was forgot.
But his Kiss was so sweet, and so closely
he prest,

That I languish'd and pin'd till I granted the rest.

If you can forgive me, Sir, I will make a fair Confession, for to be sure he hath been a most barbarous Villain to me.

LOCKIT. And so you have let him escape, Hussy—Have you?

LUCY. When a Woman loves, a kind Look, a tender Word can persuade her to any thing—And I could ask no other Bribe.

LOCKIT. Thou wilt always be a vulgar Slut, Lucy.—If you would not be look'd upon as a Fool, you should never do any thing but upon the Foot of Interest. Those that act otherwise are their own Bubbles.

LUCY. But Love, Sir, is a Misfortune that may happen to the most discreet Woman, and in Love we are all Fools alike.—Not withstanding all he swore, I am now fully convinc'd that Polly Peachum is actually his Wife.— Did I let him escape, (Fool that I was!) to go to her?—Polly will wheedle herself into his Money, and then Peachum will hang him, and cheat us both.

LOCKIT. So I am to be ruin'd, because forsooth, you must be in Love!—a very pretty Excuse!

LUCY. I could murder that impudent happy Strumpet:—I gave him his Life, and that Creature enjoys the Sweets of it.—Ungrateful Macheath!

AIR 2. South-Sea Ballad

My Love is all Madness and Folly,
Alone I lye,
Toss, tumble, and cry,
What a happy Creature is Polly!
Was e'er such a Wretch as I!
With Rage I redden like Scarlet,
That my dear inconstant Varlet,
Stark blind to my Charms,
Is lost in the Arms
Of that Jilt, that inveigling Harlot!
Stark blind to my Charms,
Is lost in the Arms
Of that Jilt, that inveigling Harlot!
This, this my Resentment alarms.

LOCKIT. And so, after all this Mischief, I must stay here to be entertain'd with your catterwauling, Mistress Puss!— Out of my sight, wanton Strumpet! you shall fast and fortify yourself into Reason, with now and then a little handsome Discipline to bring you to your Senses.—Go. [*She exits.*]

Scene 2

LOCKIT. Peachum then intends to outwit me in this Affair; but I'll be even with him—The Dog is leaky in his Liquor, so I'll ply him that way, get the Secret from him, and turn this Affair to my own Advantage.—Lions, Wolves, and Vulturs don't live together in Herds, Droves or Flocks.— Of all Animals of Prey, Man is the only sociable one. Every one of us preys upon his Neighbour, and yet we herd together.—Peachum is my Companion, my Friend—According to the Customs of the World, indeed, he may quote thousands of Precedents to cheating me—And shall not I make use of the Privilege of Friendship to make him a Return?

AIR 3. Packington's Pound

Thus Gamesters united in Friendship are
found,
Though they know that their Industry all
is a Cheat;
They flock to their Prey at the Dice-Box's
Sound,
And join to promote one another's Deceit.
But if by mishap
They fail of a Chap,
To keep in their Hands, they each other
entrap.
Like Pikes, lank with Hunger, who miss
of their Ends,
They bite their Companions, and prey on
their Friends.

Now, Peachum, you and I, like honest Tradesmen, are to have a fair Tryal which of us two can over-reach the other.—Lucy. [*Enter* LUCY.] Are there any of Peachum's People's now in the House?

LUCY. Filch, Sir, is drinking a Quartern of Strong-Waters in the next Room with Black Moll.

LOCKIT. Bid him come to me.

Scene 3

Exit LUCY, *enter* FILCH.

LOCKIT. Why, Boy, thou lookest as if thou wert half starv'd; like a shotten Herring.[11]

FILCH. One had need have the Constitution of a Horse to go through the Business.—Since the favourite Child-getter was disabled by a Mis-hap, I have pick'd up a little Money by helping the Ladies to a Pregnancy against their being call'd down to Sentence.—But if a Man cannot get an honest Livelyhood any easier way, I am sure, 'tis what I can't undertake for another Session.

LOCKIT. Truly, if that great Man should tip off, 'twould be an irreparable Loss. The Vigour and Prowess of a Knight Errant never sav'd half the Ladies in Distress that he hath done.—But, Boy, can'st thou tell me where thy Master is to be found?

FILCH. At his Lock,[12] Sir, at the Crooked Billet.

LOCKIT. Very well.—I have nothing more with you. [*Exit* FILCH.] I'll go to him there, for I have many important Affairs to settle with him; and in the way of those Transactions, I'll artfully get into his Secret.—So that Macheath shall not remain a Day longer out of my Clutches. [*Exit.*]

Scene 4
A Gaming-House.

Enter MACHEATH *in a fine tarnish'd Coat,* BEN BUDGE, MATT OF THE MINT.

MACHEATH. I am sorry, Gentlemen, the Road was so barren of Money. When my Friends are in Difficulties, I am always glad that my Fortune can be serviceable to them. [*Gives them Money.*] You see, Gentlemen, I am not a mere Court Friend, who professes every thing and will do nothing.

AIR 4. Lillibullero

The Modes of the Court so common are grown,
That a true Friend can hardly be met;
Friendship for Interest is but a Loan,
Which they let out for what they can get.
'Tis true, you find
Some Friends so kind,
Who will give you good Counsel themselves to defend.
In sorrowful Ditty,
They promise, they pity,
But shift you for Money, from Friend to Friend.

But we, Gentlemen, have still Honour enough to break through the Corruptions of the World.—And while I can serve you, you may command me.

BEN. It grieves my Heart that so generous a Man should be involv'd in such Difficulties, as oblige him to live with such ill Company, and herd with Gamesters.

MATT. See the Partiality of Mankind!—One Man may steal a Horse, better than another look over a Hedge—Of all Mechanics, of all servile Handy-crafts-men, a Gamester is the vilest. But yet, as many of the Quality are of the Profession, he is admitted amongst the politest Company. I wonder we are not more respected.

MACHEATH. There will be deep Play to-night at Marybone, and consequently Money may be pick'd up upon the Road. Meet me there, and I'll give you the Hint who is worth Setting.

MATT. The Fellow with a brown Coat with a narrow Gold Binding, I am told, is never without Money.

MACHEATH. What do you mean, Matt?—Sure you will not think of meddling with him!—He's a good honest kind of a Fellow, and one of us.

BEN. To be sure, Sir, we will put our selves under your Direction.

MACHEATH. Have an Eye upon the Money-Lenders.—A Rouleau,[13] or two, would prove a pretty sort of an Expedition. I hate Extortion.

MATT. Those Rouleaus are very pretty Things.—I hate your Bank Bills.—There is such a Hazard in putting them off.

MACHEATH. There is a certain Man of Distinction, who in his Time hath nick'd me out of a great deal of the Ready. He is in my Cash, Ben;—I'll point him out to you this Evening, and you shall draw upon him for the Debt.—The Company are met; I hear the Dice-box in the other Room. So, Gentlemen, your Servant. You'll meet me at the Marybone. [*Exeunt.*]

Scene 5

PEACHUM'*s Lock. A Table with Wine, Brandy, Pipes and Tobacco. Enter* PEA-CHUM *and* LOCKIT.

LOCKIT. The Coronation Account, Brother Peachum, is of so intricate a Nature, that I believe it will never be settled.

PEACHUM. It consists indeed of a great Variety of Articles.—It was worth to our People, in Fees of different Kinds, above ten Installments.—This is part of the Account, Brother, that lies open before us.

LOCKIT. A Lady's Tail of rich Brocade—that, I see, is dispos'd of.

PEACHUM. To Mrs. Diana Trapes, the Tally-woman, and she will make a good Hand on't in Shoes and Slippers, to trick out young Ladies, upon their going into Keeping.—

LOCKIT. But I don't see any Article of the Jewels.

PEACHUM. Those are so well known, that they must be sent abroad—You'll find them enter'd under the Article of Exportation.—As for the Snuff-Boxes, Watches, Swords, &c.—I thought it best to enter them under their several Heads.

LOCKIT. Seven and twenty Women's Pockets compleat; with the several things therein contain'd; all Seal'd, Number'd, and enter'd.

PEACHUM. But, Brother, it is impossible for us now to enter upon this Affair.—We should have the whole Day before us.—Besides, the Account of the last Half Year's Plate is in a Book by itself, which lies at the other Office.

LOCKIT. Bring us then more Liquor.—To-day shall be for Pleasure—To-morrow for Business.—Ah Brother, those Daughters of ours are two flippery Hussies—Keep a watchful Eye

upon Polly, and Macheath in a Day or two shall be our own again.

AIR 5. Down in the North Country, &c.

LOCKIT. *What Gudgeons*[14] *are we Men!*
Ev'ry Woman's easy Prey.
Though we have felt the Hook, agen
 We bite and they betray.
The Bird that hath been trapt,
 When he hears his calling Mate,
To her he flies, again he's clapt
 Within the wiry Grate.

PEACHUM. But what signifies catching the Bird, if your Daughter Lucy will set open the Door of the Cage?

LOCKIT. If Men were answerable for the Follies and Frailties of their Wives and Daughters, no Friends could keep a good Correspondence together for two Days.—This is unkind of you, Brother; for among good Friends, what they say or do goes for nothing. [*Enter a* SERVANT.]

SERVANT. Sir, here's Mrs. Diana Trapes wants to speak with you.

PEACHUM. Shall we admit her, Brother Lockit?

LOCKIT. By all means—She's a good Customer, and a fine-spoken Woman—And a Woman who drinks and talks so freely, will enliven the Conversation.

PEACHUM. Desire her to walk in. [*Exit* SERVANT.]

Scene 6

Enter MRS. TRAPES.

PEACHUM. Dear Mrs. Dye, your Servant—One may know by your Kiss, that your Ginn is excellent.

TRAPES. I was always very curious in my Liquors.

LOCKIT. There is no perfum'd Breath like it—I have been long acquainted with the Flavour of those Lips—Han't I, Mrs. Dye?

TRAPES. Fill it up.—I take as large Draughts of Liquor, as I did of Love.—I hate a Flincher in either.

AIR 6. A Shepherd kept Sheep, &c.

In the Days of my Youth I could bill like a

Dove, fa, la, la, &c.
Like a Sparrow at all times was ready for
Love, fa, la, la &c.
The Life of all Mortals in Kissing should
pass,
Lip to Lip while we're young—then the
Lip to the Glass, fa, &c.

But now, Mr. Peachum, to our Business.—If you have Blacks of any
kind, brought in of late, Mantoes—
Velvet Scarfs—Petticoats—Let it be
what it will—I am your Chap—for all
my Ladies are very fond of Mourning.

PEACHUM. Why, look ye, Mrs. Dye—you
deal so hard with us, that we can
afford to give the Gentlemen, who
venture their Lives for the Goods,
little or nothing.

TRAPES. The hard Times oblige me to
go very near in my Dealing.—To be
sure of late Years I have been a great
Sufferer by the Parliament.—Three
thousand Pounds would hardly make
me amends.—The Act for destroying
the Mint,[15] was a severe Cut upon
our Business—'Till then, if a Customer stept out of the way—we knew
where to have her—No doubt you
know Mrs. Coaxer—there's a Wench
now ('till to-day) with a good Suit of
Cloaths of mine upon her Back, and
I could never set Eyes upon her for
three Months together.—Since the
Act too against Imprisonment for
small Sums, my Loss there too hath
been very considerable, and it must
be so, when a Lady can borrow a
handsome Petticoat, or a clean Gown,
and I not have the least Hank upon
her! And, o' my conscience, now-a-
days most Ladies take a Delight in
cheating, when they can do it with
Safety.

PEACHUM. Madam, you had a handsome Gold Watch of us t'other Day
for seven Guineas.—Considering we
must have our Profit—To a Gentleman upon the Road, a Gold Watch
will be scarce worth the taking.

TRAPES. Consider, Mr. Peachum, that
Watch was remarkable, and not of
very safe Sale.—If you have any black
Velvet Scarfs—they are a handsome
Winter-wear; and take with most

Gentlemen who deal with my Customers.—'Tis I that put the Ladies
upon a good Foot. 'Tis not Youth or
Beauty that fixes their Price. The
Gentlemen always pay according to
their Dress, from half a Crown to
two Guineas; and yet those Hussies
make nothing of bilking of me.—
Then, too, allowing for Accidents.—I
have eleven fine customers now
down under the Surgeon's Hands,—
what with Fees and other Expences,
there are great Goings-out, and no
Comings-in, and not a Farthing to
pay for at least a Month's cloathing.—
We run great Risques—great Risques
indeed.

PEACHUM. As I remember, you said
something just now of Mrs. Coaxer.

TRAPES. Yes, Sir.—To be sure I stript
her of a Suit of my own Cloaths
about two hours ago; and have left
her as she should be, in her Shift,
with a Lover of hers at my House.
She call'd him up Stairs, as he was
going to Marybone in a Hackney
Coach.—And I hope, for her own
sake and mine, she will persuade the
Captain to redeem her, for the Captain is very generous to the Ladies.

LOCKIT. What Captain?

TRAPES. He thought I did not know
him—An intimate Acquaintance of
yours, Mr. Peachum—Only Captain
Macheath—as fine as a Lord.

PEACHUM. To-morrow, dear Mrs. Dye,
you shall set your own Price upon
any of the Goods you like—We have
at least half a dozen Velvet Scarfs,
and all at your service. Will you give
me leave to make you a Present of
this Suit of Night-cloaths for your
own wearing?—But are you sure it is
Captain Macheath?

TRAPES. Though he thinks I have forgot him, no Body knows him better.
I have taken a great deal of the
Captain's Money in my Time at second-hand, for he always lov'd to have
his Ladies well drest.

PEACHUM. Mr. Lockit and I have a little
business with the Captain;—You understand me—and we will satisfye
you for Mrs. Coaxer's Debt.

LOCKIT. Depend upon it—we will deal
like Men of Honour.

TRAPES. I don't enquire after your Affairs—so whatever happens, I wash my hand on't.—It hath always been my Maxim, that one Friend should assist another—But if you please—I'll take one of the Scarfs home with me. 'Tis always good to have something in Hand. [*Exeunt.*]

Scene 7

Newgate. Enter LUCY.

LUCY. Jealously, Rage, Love and Fear are at once tearing me to pieces. How I am weather-beaten and shatter'd with distresses!

> AIR 7. One Evening, having lost my Way, &c.

> *I'm like a Skiff on the Ocean tost,*
>> *Now high, now low, with each Billow born*
> *With her Rudder broke, and her Anchor lost,*
>> *Deserted and all forlorn.*
> *While thus I lye rolling and tossing all Night,*
> *That Polly lyes sporting on Seas of Delight!*
>> *Revenge, Revenge, Revenge,*
> *Shall appease my restless Sprite.*

I have the Rats-bane ready.—I run no Risque; for I can lay her Death upon the Ginn, and so many dye of that naturally that I shall never be call'd in Question.—But say, I were to be hang'd—I never could be hang'd for any thing that would give me greater Comfort, than the poysoning that Slut. [*Enter* FILCH.]

FILCH. Madam, here's our Miss Polly come to wait upon you.

LUCY. Show her in.

Scene 8

Exit FILCH, *enter* POLLY.

LUCY. Dear Madam, your Servant.—I hope you will pardon my Passion, when I was so happy to see you last.—I was so overrun with the Spleen, that I was perfectly out of my self. And really when one hath the Spleen, every thing is to be excus'd by a Friend.

> AIR 8. Now Roger, I'll tell thee, because thou'rt my Son

> *When a Wife's in her Pout*
> *(As she's sometimes, no doubt;)*
>> *The good Husband as meek as a Lamb,*
>> *Her Vapours to still,*
>> *First grants her her Will,*
> *And the quieting Draught is a Dram.*
> *Poor Man! And the quieting Draught is a Dram.*

—I wish all our Quarrels might have so comfortable a Reconciliation.

POLLY. I have no Excuse for my own Behaviour, Madam, but my Misfortunes.—And really, Madam, I suffer too upon your Account.

LUCY. But, Miss Polly—in the way of Friendship, will you give me leave to propose a Glass of Cordial to you?

POLLY. Strong-Waters are apt to give me the Head-ache—I hope, Madam, you will excuse me.

LUCY. Not the greatest Lady in the Land could have better in her Closet, for her own private drinking.—You seem mighty low in Spirits, my Dear.

POLLY. I am sorry, Madam, my Health will not allow me to accept of your Offer.—I should not have left you in the rude Manner I did when we met last, Madam, had not my Papa haul'd me away so unexpectedly—I was indeed somewhat provok'd, and perhaps might use some Expressions that were disrespectful.—But really, Madam, the Captain treated me with so much Contempt and Cruelty, that I deserv'd your Pity, rather than your Resentment.

LUCY. But since his Escape, no doubt all Matters are made up again.—Ah Polly! Polly! 'tis I am the unhappy Wife; and he loves you as if you were only his Mistress.

POLLY. Sure, Madam, you cannot think me so happy as to be the Object of your Jealousy.—A Man is always afraid of a Woman who loves him too well—so that I must expect to be neglected and avoided.

LUCY. Then our Cases, my dear Polly, are exactly alike. Both of us indeed have been too fond.

AIR 9. O Bessy Bell

POLLY. *A Curse attends that Woman's Love,*
  Who always would be pleasing.
LUCY. *The Pertness of the billing Dove,*
  Like tickling, is but teazing.
POLLY. *What then in Love can Woman do?*
LUCY. *If we grow fond, they shun us.*
POLLY. *And when we fly them, they pursue.*
LUCY. *But leave us when they've won us.*

LUCY. Love is so very whimsical in both Sexes, that it is impossible to be lasting.—But my Heart is particular, and contradicts my own Observation.
POLLY. But really, Mistress Lucy, by his last Behaviour, I think I ought to envy you.—When I was forc'd from him, he did not shew the least Tenderness.—But perhaps, he hath a Heart not capable of it.

AIR 10. Would Fate to me Belinda give—

Among the Men, Coquets we find,
Who Court by turns all Woman-kind;
And we grant all their Hearts desir'd,
When they are flatter'd, and admir'd.

The Coquets of both Sexes are Self-lovers, and that is a Love no other whatever can dispossess. I fear, my dear Lucy, our Husband is one of those.
LUCY. Away with these melancholy Reflections,—indeed, my dear Polly, we are both of us a Cup too low.—Let me prevail upon you, to accept of my Offer.

AIR 11. Come, sweet Lass, &c.

Come, sweet Lass,
Let's banish Sorrow
'Till To-morrow;
Come, sweet Lass,
Let's take a chirping Glass.

Wine can clear
The Vapours of Despair;
And make us light as Air;
Then drink, and banish Care.

I can't bear, Child, to see you in such low Spirits.—And I must persuade you to what I know will do you good. [*Aside, as she exits.*] I shall now soon be even with the hypocritical Strumpet.

Scene 9

POLLY. All this wheedling of Lucy cannot be for nothing.—At this time too! when I know she hates me!—The Dissembling of a Woman is always the Fore-runner of Mischief.—By pouring Strong-Waters down my Throat, she thinks to pump some Secrets out of me.—I'll be upon my Guard, and won't taste a Drop of her Liquor, I'm resolv'd.

Scene 10

Re-enter LUCY, *with Strong-Waters.*
LUCY. Come, Miss Polly.
POLLY. Indeed, Child, you have given yourself trouble to no purpose.—You must, my Dear, excuse me.
LUCY. Really, Miss Polly, you are so squeamishly affected about taking a Cup of Strong-Waters as a Lady before Company. I vow, Polly, I shall take it monstrously ill if you refuse me.—Brandy and Men (though Women love them never so well) are always taken by us with some Reluctance—unless 'tis in private.
POLLY. I protest, Madam, it goes against me.—What do I see! Macheath again in Custody!—Now every glimm'ring of Happiness is lost. [*Drops the Glass of Liquor on the Ground.*]
LUCY. [*Aside.*] Since things are thus, I'm glad the Wench hath escap'd: for by this Event, 'tis plain, she was not happy enough to deserve to be poison'd.

Scene 11

Enter LOCKIT, MACHEATH, PEACHUM.
LOCKIT. Set your Heart to rest, Captain.—You have neither the Chance of Love or Money for another Escape,—for you are order'd to be

call'd down upon your Tryal immediately.

POLLY. Away, Hussies!—This is not a
time for a Man to be hamper'd with
his Wives.—You see, the Gentleman
is in Chains already.

LUCY. O Husband, Husband, my heart
long'd to see thee; but to see thee
thus distracts me!

POLLY. Will not my dear Husband look
upon his Polly? Why hadst thou not
flown to me for Protection? with me
thou hadst been safe.

AIR 12. The last time I went o'er the
Moor

POLLY. *Hither, dear Husband, turn your
Eyes.*
LUCY. *Bestow one Glance to cheer me.*
POLLY. *Think with that Look, thy Polly
dyes.*
LUCY. *O shun me not—but hear me.*
POLLY. *'Tis Polly sues.*
LUCY. *'Tis Lucy speaks.*
POLLY. *Is thus true Love requited?*
LUCY. *My Heart is bursting.*
POLLY. *Mine too breaks.*
LUCY. *Must I*
POLLY. *Must I be slighted?*

MACHEATH. What would you have me
say, Ladies?—You see, this Affair will
soon be at an end, without my dis-
obliging either of you.

PEACHUM. But the settling this Point,
Captain, might prevent a Law-suit
between your two Widows.

AIR 13. Tom Tinker's my true Love

MACHEATH. *Which way shall I turn
me?—How can I decide?*
*Wives, the Day of our Death, are as fond
as a Bride.*
*One Wife is too much for most Husbands
to bear,*
*But two at a time there's no Mortal can
bear.*
*This way, and that way, and which way I
will,*
*What would comfort the one, t'other Wife
would take ill.*

POLLY. But if his own Misfortunes have
made him insensible to mine—A Father sure will be more
compassionate.—Dear, dear Sir, sink
the material Evidence, and bring him

off at his Tryal—Polly upon her
Knees begs it of you.

AIR 14. I am a poor Shepherd
undone

When my Hero in Court appears,
And stands arraign'd for his Life;
Then think of poor Polly's Tears;
For Ah! Poor Polly's his Wife.
Like the Sailor he holds up his Hand,
Distrest on the dashing Wave.
To die a dry Death at Land,
Is as bad as a watry Grave.
And alas, poor Polly!
Alack, and well-a-day!
Before I was in Love,
Oh! every Month was May.

LUCY. If Peachum's Heart is harden'd,
sure you, Sir, will have more Compassion on a Daughter.—I know the
Evidence is in your Power.—How
then can you be a Tyrant to me?
[*Kneeling.*]

AIR 15. Ianth the lovely, &c.

*When he holds up his Hand arraign'd for
his Life,*
*O think of your Daughter, and think I'm
his Wife!*
*What are Cannons, or Bombs, or clashing
of Swords?*
*For Death is more certain by Witnesses
Words.*
*Then nail up their Lips; that dread
Thunder allay;*
*And each Month of my Life will hereafter
be May.*

LOCKIT. Macheath's time is come,
Lucy.—We know our own Affairs,
therefore let us have no more Whimpering or Whining.

PEACHUM. Set your Heart at rest,
Polly.—Your Husband is to dye to-
day.—Therefore, if you are not already provided, 'tis high time to look
about for another. There's Comfort
for you, you Slut.

LOCKIT. We are ready, Sir, to conduct
you to the Old-Baily.

AIR 16. Bonny Dundee

MACHEATH. *The Charge is prepar'd;*
The Lawyers are met,
The Judges all rang'd (a
terrible Show!)

*I go, undismay'd.—For
Death is a Debt,
A Debt on demand.—So,
take what I owe.
Then farewell, my Love—
Dear Charmers, adieu.
Contented I die—'Tis the
better for you.
Here ends all Dispute the
rest of our Lives.
For this way at once I please
all my Wives.*

Now, Gentlemen, I am ready to attend you. [*Exit* LOCKIT, MACHEATH, PEA-CHUM; *enter* FILCH.]

Scene 12

POLLY. Follow them, Filch, to the Court. And when the Tryal is over, bring me a particular Account of his Be-haviour, and of everything that happen'd.—You'll find me here with Miss Lucy. [*Exit* FILCH.] But why is all this Musick?
LUCY. The Prisoners, whose Tryals are put off till next Session, are diverting themselves.
POLLY. Sure there is nothing so charm-ing as Musick! I'm fond of it to distraction!—But alas!—now, all Mirth seems an Insult upon my Af-fliction.—Let us retire, my dear Lucy, and indulge our Sorrows.—The noisy Crew, you see, are coming upon us. [*Exeunt; A Dance of Prisoners in Chains, &c.*]

Scene 13

The Condemn'd Hold. MACHEATH *in a melancholy Posture.*

AIR 17. Happy Groves

*O cruel, cruel, cruel Case!
Must I suffer this Disgrace?*

AIR 18. Of all the Girls that are so smart

*Of all the Friends in time of Grief,
When threatning Death looks grimmer,
Not one so sure can bring Relief,
As this best Friend, a Brimmer.*
[*Drinks.*]

AIR 19. Britons

Since I must swing,—I scorn, I scorn to wince or whine.
[*Rises.*]

AIR 20. Chevy Chase

*Bus not again my Spirits sink;
I'll raise them high with Wine.*
[*Drinks a Glass of Wine.*]

AIR 21. To old Sir Simon the King

*But Valour the stronger grows,
The stronger Liquor we're drinking.
And how can we feel our Woes,
When we've lost the Trouble of Thinking?*
[*Drinks.*]

AIR 22. Joy to great Cæsar

*If thus—A Man can die
Much bolder with Brandy.*
[*Pours out a Bumper of Brandy.*]

AIR 23. There was an old Woman

*So I drink off this Bumper.—And now I
can stand the Test.
And my Comrades shall see, that I die as
brave as the Best.*
[*Drinks.*]

AIR 24. Did you ever hear of a gallant Sailor

*But can I leave my pretty Hussies,
Without one Tear, or tender Sigh?*

AIR 25. Why are mine Eyes still flowing

*Their Eyes, their Lips, their Busses
Recall my Love.—Ah must I die!*

AIR 26. Green Sleeves

*Since Laws were made for ev'ry Degree,
To curb Vice in others, as well as me,
I wonder we han't better Company,
    Upon Tyburn Tree!
But Gold from Law can take out the
    Sting;
And if rich Men like us were to swing,
'Twou'd thin the Land, such Numbers
    to string
    Upon Tyburn Tree!*
[*Enter* JAILER.]

JAILER. Some friends of yours, Captain, desire to be admitted.—I leave you together. [*Exit.*]

Scene 14

Enter BEN BUDGE, MATT OF THE MINT.

MACHEATH. For my having broke Prison, you see, Gentlemen, I am order'd immediate Execution.—The Sheriff's Officers, I believe, are now at the Door.—That Jemmy Twitcher should peach me, I own surpriz'd me!—'Tis a plain Proof that the World is all alike, and that even our Gang can no more trust one another than other People. Therefore, I beg you, Gentlemen, look well to yourselves, for in all probability you may live some Months longer.

MATT. We are heartily sorry, Captain, for your Misfortune.—But 'tis what we must all come to.

MACHEATH. Peachum and Lockit, you know, are infamous Scoundrels. Their Lives are as much in your Power, as yours are in theirs.—Remember your dying Friend!—'Tis my last Request.—Bring those Villains to the Gallows before you, and I am satisfied.

MATT. We'll do't. [*Enter* JAILER.]

JAILER. Miss Polly and Miss Lucy intreat a Word with you.

MACHEATH. Gentlemen, Adieu. [*Exit all but* MACHEATH.]

Scene 15

Enter, LUCY, POLLY.

MACHEATH. My dear Lucy—My dear Polly—Whatsoever hath past between us is now at an end.—If you are fond of marrying again, the best Advice I can give you, is to Ship yourselves off for the West-Indies, where you'll have a fair chance of getting a Husband a-piece; or by good Luck, two or three, as you like best.

POLLY. How can I support this Sight!

LUCY. There is nothing moves one so much as a great Man in Distress.

AIR 27. All you that must take a leap, &c.

LUCY. *Would I might be hang'd!*
POLLY. *And I would so too!*
LUCY. *To be hang'd with you.*

POLLY. *My Dear, with you.*
MACHEATH. *O Leave me to Thought! I fear! I doubt! I tremble! I droop!—See, my Courage is out.*
[*Turns up the empty Bottle.*]

POLLY. *No token of Love?*
MACHEATH. *See my Courage is out.*
[*Turns up the empty Pot.*]

LUCY. *No token of Love?*
POLLY. *Adieu.*
LUCY. *Farewell.*
MACHEATH. *But hark! I hear the Toll of the Bell.*
CHORUS. *Tol de rol lol, &c.*
[*Enter* JAILER.]

JAILER. Four Women more, Captain, with a Child a-piece! See, here they come. [*Enter* WOMEN *and* CHILDREN.]

MACHEATH. What—four Wives more!—This is too much.—Here—tell the Sheriff's Officers I am ready. [*Exit* MACHEATH *guarded.*]

Scene 16

Enter PLAYER *and* BEGGAR.

PLAYER. But honest Friend, I hope you don't intend that Macheath shall be really executed.

BEGGAR. Most certainly, sir.—To make the Piece perfect, I was for doing strict poetical Justice.—Macheath is to be hang'd; and for the other Personages of the Drama, the Audience must have suppos'd they were all either hang'd or transported.

PLAYER. Why then, Friend, this is a down-right deep Tragedy. The Catastrophe is manifestly wrong, for an Opera must end happily.

BEGGAR. Your Objection, Sir, is very just; and is easily remov'd. For you must allow, that in this kind of Drama, 'tis no matter how absurdly things are brought about.—So—you Rabble there—run and cry a Reprieve—let the Prisoner be brought back to his Wives in Triumph.

PLAYER. All this we must do, to comply with the Taste of the Town.

BEGGAR. Through the whole Piece you may observe such a similitude of Manners in high and low Life, that it

is difficult to determine whether (in
the fashionable Vices) the fine Gentlemen imitate the Gentlemen of the
Road, or the Gentlemen of the Road
the fine Gentlemen.—Had the Play
remain'd, as I at first intended, it
would have carried a most excellent
Moral. 'Twould have shown that the
lower Sort of People have their Vices
in a degree as well as the Rich: And
that they are punish'd for them.

Scene 17

Enter to them, MACHEATH *with* RABBLE,
&c.

MACHEATH. So, it seems, I am not left to
my Choice, but must have a Wife at
last.—Look ye, my Dears, we will
have no Controversie now. Let us
give this Day to Mirth, and I am sure
she who thinks herself my Wife will
testifie her Joy by a Dance.

ALL. Come, a Dance—a Dance.

MACHEATH. Ladies, I hope you will give
me leave to present a Partner to each
of you. And (if I may without Offence) for this time, I take Polly for
mine.—[*To* POLLY.] And for Life, you
Slut,—for we were really marry'd.—
As for the rest—But at present keep
your own Secret.

A DANCE

AIR 28. Lumps of Pudding, &c.

Thus I stand like the Turk, *with his
  Doxies around;*
*From all Sides their Glances his Passion
  confound;*
*For black, brown, and fair, his Incons-
  tancy burns,*
*And the different Beauties subdue him by
  turns:*
*Each calls forth her Charms, to provoke
  his Desires:*
*Though willing to all, with but one he
  retires.*
*But think of this Maxim, and put off your
  Sorrow,*
*The Wretch of To-day, may be happy To-
  morrow.*

CHORUS. *But think of this Maxim, &c.*

1. Pregnant women were exempt from hanging.
2. This year.
3. A gambling establishment in London.
4. The flower market, and also the site of a
well-known theater competing with the one in
which *The Beggar's Opera* was produced.
5. An arrangement whereby a husband's
property is settled upon his widow after his death.
6. Impeached; indicted.
7. Anatomies.
8. Give me a bribe.
9. Trick.
10. Trick.
11. One that has recently spawned.
12. Hideout.
13. A roll of coins.
14. Persons easily tricked.
15. Where debtors were safe from arrest.

Act 1

AIR 11

AIR 12

AIR 13

AIR 14

AIR 15

Act 2

End of the second Act

Act 3

AIR 7

AIR 8

AIR 9

AIR 10

AIR 11

AIR 12

AIR 21

AIR 22

AIR 23

AIR 24

AIR 25

AIR 26

AIR 27

AIR 28

The Mistress of the Inn

Carlo Goldoni

"Papa Goldoni," the father of the Italian theater, was born in Venice on February 25, 1707. Carlo Goldoni was the son of a doctor and was himself trained as a lawyer, but spent his early years vascillating between a "respectable" legal career and his love of the theater. The commedia dell'arte, though by this time greatly reduced in quality from the brilliance it had enjoyed for some 150 years, still toured Italy and was the principal form of popular theater; Goldoni early toured with such a company, writing scenarios and acting minor roles, but his familiarity with dramatic literature from elsewhere in Europe, especially the plays of Molière, convinced him that a more literary drama was needed in Italy. One of his early efforts to write dialogue for the actors who were accustomed to improvising proved to work well for that company, and eventually Goldoni was lured from the practice of law in Pisa to become company playwright for the commedia dell'arte company then in residence at the Teatro San'Angelo in Venice. At the age of forty, Goldoni finally abandoned a legal career altogether and devoted himself full-time to writing for the theater.

For fourteen years, from 1748 to 1762, Goldoni's output of scripts was prodigious. He once committed himself to write fifteen plays in a single year, then not only lived up to his commitment but wrote an extra one for good measure. One of his finest plays, *The Superior Residence* (1760), was written in three days and nights. Almost all of the best work for which Goldoni is remembered was written during this extraordinarily prolific period in Venice. Having attempted a few tragedies with little success, and finding that he could successfully write dialogue for the commedia dell'arte actors, Goldoni devoted himself to nothing less than revolutionizing the Italian theater. The stock characters, the *lazzi,* and the healthy ribaldry of the earlier commedia had degenerated into platitudinous repetition and vulgarity; Goldoni built upon the genuine skill of the actors to create new characters, based on the old ones but now without masks—both figuratively and literally. With the traditional stage masks stripped away, characters became more human and believable, and Goldoni had a fine ear for reproducing the Venetian dialect that he heard about him. His characters used everyday speech, avoiding the bombast and rhetoric that had become associated with the commedia. Goldoni created plays peopled by the bourgeois and servant classes of Venice and of Italy, occasionally introducing aristocrats primarily for the purpose of ridiculing them. These characters, extraordinarily realistic by the standards of his day, were employed in facile plots growing out of daily life, yet were left ample opportunity for comic business and laugh-provoking dialogue still highly reminiscent of the commedia at its best.

Almost as though he were a part of one of his own dramatic plots, Goldoni soon encountered enemies. Led by the critic and sometime playwright Carlo Gozzi, a movement got under way to bring back the traditional commedia and to discredit Goldoni's work. For a time, the movement was successful, and Gozzi's plays, though

130

in some ways less truly representative of commedia than Goldoni's, temporarily became the rage. Today Gozzi is virtually unknown, but Goldoni, partly in discouragement over this setback, left Venice for Paris in 1762, where he had been invited by King Louis XV to write plays for the troupe of Italian comedians in residence there. He never returned to Venice.

Goldoni wrote many plays in French, became personal tutor to the king's children, and was awarded a lifetime pension. Past his seventy-fifth birthday, Goldoni retired from playwriting and devoted himself to his *Memoires,* but with the French Revolution he suddenly found his pension cut off and himself in dire poverty. His last few years were a period of want and deprivation; the National Assembly voted to reinstate his pension on February 7, 1793, only to learn that Goldoni had died on the previous day. The Assembly voted his widow a smaller pension and a benefit performance by the Comédie-Française, for Goldoni had favorably portrayed the common people and parodied the aristocracy many years before the earliest French revolutionary had done so.

Goldoni has been credited with writing as many as 200 or 300 plays; it is difficult to set an accurate figure because many he wrote in French were adaptations of those written earlier in Italian. It is reasonably accurate to say that he wrote about 150 comedies, 10 tragedies, and 83 other theatrical works. Almost inevitably, so large a number of plays must include a good many that are second rate. Actually, Goldoni's theatrical facility was not matched with an incisive world view, and he is known as the greatest of Italian playwrights largely because the competition is not keen. Some have proclaimed Goldoni the Molière of the south, but although he admired Molière greatly and would have liked to equal him in talent, he did not. Still, a few of Goldoni's plays survive the vicissitudes of translation to make excellent theater in any language; besides *The Mistress of the Inn, The Boors* (1760) is a clever twist on the gulled old man who intends to marry off his daughter without her consent (the wives gang up to control the outcome); *The Fan* (1763) is a light-hearted portrayal of the complications resulting from a lady's accidental loss of her fan; *The Servant of Two Masters* (1745) is a widely known *tour de force* for the actor playing a servant who desperately, but wittily, serves two masters simultaneously. Because in general Goldoni does not dig deeply into characterization (having depended heavily on actors whose basic characterizations had been sharpened and set in the commedia dell'arte), but instead depends chiefly on facile plots and witty language (especially the Venetian dialect) for his success, his plays are extraordinarily difficult to translate. Few scholars are satisfied with the quality of his work that is available to the English-speaking public.

La Locandiera, which has variously been translated as *The Mistress of the Inn, Mirandolina,* and *Mine Hostess,* was first performed at the Teatro San'Angelo in Venice on December 26, 1752. It is reported that the company's leading lady was ill and that Goldoni created the role of Mirandolina for the soubrette who usually played servant girls. The leading lady was insanely jealous, the story continues, of the tremendous success that Mirandolina instantly achieved. Goldoni regularly showed more skill at creating good female roles than he did at male ones, and it is the marvelous starring role of Mirandolina that has made this play so popular in revivals. Eleanora Duse fascinated Europe with it again in the late nineteenth century, and Eva LeGallienne delighted the United States in the role in the 1920s. Some translations, and many performances in Italy and elsewhere, omit the scenes involving the two actresses, cutting these two characters from the play altogether. But while this undoubtedly streamlines the play, it also loses the character contrast with Mirandolina (who is also acting) that Goldoni evidently intended. The fresh, new translation printed here is unabridged, yet delightfully captures Goldoni's facile theatricality and vernacular wit.

The plot of *The Mistress of the Inn* is, in outline, the simple old one of a thousand comedies before it. No sooner is the Squire identified as a woman-hater than the audience can expect that he will soon be converted by Mirandolina, the woman who always gets her man. Through an interesting combination of plot and character development, however, this play does not turn out quite so predictably: the Squire falls in love with Mirandolina, all right, but is humiliated and sent away in disgrace for his temerity, while Mirandolina loses some of her attractiveness when, around the beginning of act 3, she is gradually revealed as a heartless manipulator. The ending of the play is ambiguous, for the script does not make it altogether clear whether Mirandolina is genuinely chastened by a situation that has gotten somewhat out of her control or whether, by marrying Fabrizio, she is simply manipulating him as cleverly as she has always manipulated him before. The actress interpreting the role has a number of interesting choices open to her.

If Mirandolina is a brilliant new development of the traditional clever maidservant, the Marquis is a totally new twist on Pantalone. The gulled old miser is now a fop; elevated to the aristocracy, he takes on the supercilious pride of his class without any of the geuine nobility. The Marquis is an extremely strong comic role for a character actor. The Squire is an interesting reversal of the Capitano, who traditionally was a great womanizer and a braggart warrior; here, by the very act of resisting feminine charms, he becomes peculiarly susceptible to them and manifestly ready to be made a fool of. Probably in no other play does Goldoni so effectively create universal characters translatable to other times and languages.

Although Goldoni aspired to bring the standards of Molière to the Italian theater, he is more interesting now for the transitional role he played in bringing commedia dell'arte virtues into the literary drama. Historically, the fact is that Goldoni was chiefly responsible for revolutionizing the Italian theater; it was certainly not his fault if later Italian writers did not rise to the heights toward which Goldoni pointed them. With minimal thematic content, and linguistic brilliance often based on untranslatable vagaries of the Venetian dialect, Goldoni's international success rests almost entirely on facile plots and characters adapted from the commedia. He achieved remarkable mastery in turning these commedia figures, who by his time had become reduced to a nearly mechanical collection of theatrical tricks, into living human beings. For the most part, their commedia ancestry is now of more interest than their humanity, but occasionally, as in *The Mistress of the Inn*, a happy combination of these factors creates genuinely lively theater. With a good cast, the play is sheer delight.

The Mistress of the Inn
(La Locandiera)

Translated by Stanley Vincent Longman

Author's Note to His Reader

Among all the plays I have composed so far, I would almost say that this is the most moral, the most useful and the most instructive. This will certainly seem paradoxical to anyone who considers only the character of the Mistress of the Inn, perhaps a more enticing, more dangerous woman than any I have ever before drawn. One should, however, consider the character and the fate of the Squire, for in him we find a vivid example of that conceit that can undo a man and a lesson that teaches us to avert the danger and to avoid joining the fallen.

Mirandolina makes us see how men fall in love. She worms her way into the good graces of our woman-hater by indulging in his very own way of thinking, praising the things that please him and stirring him up in his prejudices even by condemning women herself. Doing this, she rises above his former aversion against her. She then begins to please him with little favors, showing a studied kindness, meanwhile seeming to be far from wanting to obligate him in any way. She visits him, she serves him at table, she speaks humbly and respectfully, and as she senses his rudeness diminish, she takes on more ardor. She speaks in broken phrases, she makes eyes at him, and without his quite realizing it, she deals him mortal wounds. The poor man knows the danger and he wants to flee it, but with a couple of tears she cuts him off and with a calculated swoon she brings him down, lays him out and humiliates him. It seems impossible that a man could become enamored in a matter of a few hours, especially a man of his stamp, a man who hates women, who refuses to deal with them, but it is for just this reason that he is prone to succumb. Despising women without knowing them keeps him from recognizing their wiles and from knowing on what they base their hope of triumph. So, while he thinks his general aversion to women is enough to defend himself, he is actually exposing his bare breast to the arrows of his adversary.

I myself worried about getting him to the point of falling in love by the end of the play, and yet, conducted step by step by nature herself, he satisfied my wishes by being done in at the end of the second act.

Indeed, I was not quite sure what to do with the third until it occurred to me that such enticing women are wont to treat their lovers harshly once caught, and I determined to show an example of this barbarousness through the abusive disdain with which she might make fun of her miserable victim. Such a spectacle of enslavement might serve to strike horror in those wretches who could fall into it; certainly it can render properly hateful the type of insidious siren capable of inflicting this pain. Does not the ironing scene, in which the Mistress of the Inn mocks the suffering Squire, arouse indignation against such a woman? First she moves a man to love and then she insults him! Oh, what a fine example to hold up to the eyes of the young! Would to God I had had such an example early enough to have saved me from the scornful laughter of a certain cruel mistress of an inn! Oh, how many scenes were provided by my very own misfortunes! . . . But this is not the place to confess my past follies nor to repent my weaknesses. It is enough that

133

some people be grateful for the lesson I offer. I can include among them those honest women who will rejoice to see their scheming sisters exposed, for they dishonor their sex. Meanwhile the seductresses will blush when they see me, and even if the more brazen among them curse me when we meet, I shall remain unruffled.

I must alert you, dear reader, to a small change I have made in this play. Fabrizio, the servant of the inn, spoke in Venetian in the original production. He did so because the actor was used to speaking as Brighella. Since then, I converted the character into a Tuscan, for it is unseemly to introduce foreign speech into a play without good reason. I draw attention to this because I do not know how Bettinelli will print the play; he may avail himself of this, my own copy, with all its proper corrections, but the scruples that have guided him in printing my other pieces as I actually wrote them are such that he may ignore even this convenience.

Characters

The Marquis of Forlipopoli ⎱ *guests of the inn*
The Count of Albafiorita ⎰
Fabrizio, servant in the inn
The Squire of Ripafratta, guest
Mirandolina, mistress of the inn
Servant to the Squire
Ortensia ⎱ *actresses, guests of the inn*
Dejanira ⎰
Servant to the Count

SCENE: *The play is set in various rooms in Mirandolina's inn, in the city of Florence, in the mid-eighteenth century.*

Act 1

Scene 1

A room in the inn. The MARQUIS OF FOR-LIPOPOLI *and the* COUNT OF ALBAFIORITA *are discovered engaged in intense conversation.*

MARQUIS. Need I remind you that between yourself and myself there are differences?

COUNT. Oh? And what might they be?

MARQUIS. Surely you don't count yourself my equal.

COUNT. Why not? My money will go as far as yours. In this inn, maybe a little farther.

MARQUIS. You must have noticed that the mistress of the inn extends spe-cial courtesies to me, which is only natural.

COUNT. What's so natural about it?

MARQUIS. I am the Marquis of For-lipopoli.

COUNT. And I am the Count of Al-bafiorita.

MARQUIS. You're a Count all right. You got the title when you *bought* a county.

COUNT. Yes, about the time you sold off your property.

MARQUIS. Enough! The fact remains, I am what I am. I command respect.

COUNT. Who's treating you with dis-respect?

MARQUIS. Umph!

COUNT. My dear Marquis, you get your-self all puffed up and take great liberties in what you say . . .

MARQUIS. I am in this inn for one rea-son only. I am in love with its mistress. It's a simple fact and every-one knows it. What's more, I insist everyone respect a young woman who pleases me so.

COUNT. Ah, that's a good one! You de-mand I respect her, but no one is to love her. Why do you suppose *I* am in Florence? *And* in this particular inn?

MARQUIS. All right, fine. But you won't get far, I can tell you that.

COUNT. I won't and you will?

MARQUIS. I will and you won't. I am what I am. Mirandolina can use my influence.

COUNT. My money talks louder than your "influence." What's more, I make my money talk very day.

MARQUIS. Always dropping a florin here and a ducat there. For my part, I do not boast about what I do.

COUNT. You don't boast because you can't. We all know you do nothing.

MARQUIS. No one knows what I do.

COUNT. Yes, my dear Marquis, we all know. The servants talk. We hear about your unpaid bills.

MARQUIS. You must be referring to that fellow, Fabrizio. I don't like him. What's worse, the mistress seems taken with him.

COUNT. Well now, think about it. Six months ago her father died, leaving her to run this inn by herself. She might well consider marriage. In fact, I've promised her a wedding present of three hundred florins.

MARQUIS. Should she marry, I as her patron will undertake to . . . Never mind. I know what I will do.

COUNT. Come on now: let's settle this as friends and share and share alike. We'll *each* give her three hundred florins.

MARQUIS. [*Stepping away from him.*] What I do, I shall do on my own account. And without boasting about it. I am what I am. [*He turns and calls into the wing.*] Hullo! Anyone there?

COUNT. [*Aside.*] Poor fellow. So proud. And he hasn't a cent to his name. [*Enter* FABRIZIO.]

FABRIZIO. [*He crosses in front of the* MARQUIS, *then turns back to him.*] Was it you who called, sir?

MARQUIS. Whom are you calling "sir"? Where'd you learn your manners?

FABRIZIO. Forgive me.

COUNT. [*On the other side of* FABRIZIO.] Tell me. How is our dear mistress of the inn this morning?

FABRIZIO. She is well, your Lordship.

COUNT. She has arisen?

FABRIZIO. Yes, your Lordship.

MARQUIS. Ass!

FABRIZIO. Excuse me, your Lordship?

MARQUIS. What is this "lordship" business?

FABRIZIO. It's what I call you and the other gentleman.

MARQUIS. Between him and myself there are differences.

COUNT. [*Taking* FABRIZIO *aside.*] Do you hear that?

FABRIZIO. [*Sotto voce to the* COUNT.] He's right, there are differences. I notice them every time a bill's to be paid.

MARQUIS. [*Loudly.*] Tell the mistress to come here. I wish to speak with her.

FABRIZIO. Yes, Excellency. [*He starts out.*] Did I get it right that time?

MARQUIS. Of course. You've known it for three months now, but you're too impertinent to use it.

FABRIZIO. As you wish, Excellency.

COUNT. [*Summoning* FABRIZIO *back.*] Would you like to test these differences between the Marquis and me?

MARQUIS. What's this about?

COUNT. Hold on. [FABRIZIO *crosses back to the* COUNT.] Now, here is a florin. Have him give you another one.

FABRIZIO. [*Bowing to the* COUNT.] Many thanks, your Lordship. [*He turns to the* MARQUIS.] Excellency . . .

MARQUIS. I don't throw money around like a madman. Get out of here.

FABRIZIO. [*To the* COUNT.] Your Lordship, may Heaven bless you. Excellency. [*He excuses himself, and passes in front of the* MARQUIS. *Before leaving, he says aside:*] Poor fellow. When you leave home, money will carry you a lot farther than your grand titles. [*Exit.*]

MARQUIS. You may think you can outdo me with all your money, but when all is said and done, it's rank that talks.

COUNT. Rank can't buy a thing.

MARQUIS. Money can't buy respect. Spend it till you're blue in the face, you won't change Mirandolina's opinion of you,

COUNT. You'd do well to put some money in your pocket, sir.

MARQUIS. Patronage and influence, that's the ticket. To be in the position to do a person a favor.

COUNT. To be in a position to make a person a gift or a loan.

MARQUIS. One must command respect.

COUNT. Easily done if you have money.

MARQUIS. You don't know what you're talking about.

COUNT. It's you who are muddle-headed.

MARQUIS. Who are you calling muddle-headed?

COUNT. You, my dear Marquis.

MARQUIS. I'd advise you to keep a civil tongue. [*The* SQUIRE OF RIPAFRATTA *enters from his room.*]

SQUIRE. Here, here, my friends. Why all this noise? Is there something wrong between you?

COUNT. We are arguing a fine point.

MARQUIS. The Count here denies the merit of nobility.

COUNT. On the contrary, I merely say that it takes money to satisfy one's whims.

SQUIRE. Oh, really, my dear Marquis . . .

MARQUIS. Come, come, let's talk about something else.

SQUIRE. How did you two ever get into such a row?

COUNT. For the most laughable of reasons.

MARQUIS. This is no laughing matter.

COUNT. The Marquis is in love with the mistress of the inn. I love her even more. He thinks she'll requite his love out of respect for his rank, while I hope for the same thing as repayment for my gifts. You see how laughable it is.

MARQUIS. You have to understand what pains I have taken to exert my influence on her behalf.

COUNT. [*To the* SQUIRE.] You see, while he protects, I lavish gifts on her. Ha, ha, ha. [*He finds he's laughing alone.*]

SQUIRE. What?! You've let a woman do this to you? Nothing could be less worthy of dispute. A woman! A woman! I would never let a woman be the cause of a falling out with a friend. I never loved one, never admired one, and never gave one a second thought. A weakness for women is simply intolerable.

MARQUIS. Ah, but you overlook the special charms of Mirandolina.

COUNT. Quite so. This time I agree with the Marquis.

MARQUIS. Of course. Since I love her, she must be quite extraordinary.

SQUIRE. You make me laugh. Extraordinary? An innkeeper's daughter?

MARQUIS. She has a way about her that is enchanting.

COUNT. A way of talking, a way of dressing, that reflects sheer good taste.

SQUIRE. A way of this, a way of that! What nonsense! I've been in this inn for three days, and in all that time she's made no impression on me whatsoever.

COUNT. Ah, well, look again.

SQUIRE. You're both mad. I've seen her a dozen times. She's like any other woman.

MARQUIS. She is not. She has that certain, very special *je ne sais quoi.*

SQUIRE. Oh, Lord!

MARQUIS. I assure you, sir, I have known women in the finest society, and never, never, I tell you, have I met one who combines with such grace the qualities of engaging charm and polite decorum.

COUNT. Egad, I'm used to dealing with women, I am. I know their defects and weaknesses, and I know how to get my way. But in this case, despite my long courtship and expense, I haven't managed to touch even her little finger.

SQUIRE. She's leading you both around by the nose, you blockheads. How can you be taken in by these wiles? Women! To hell with 'em all!

COUNT. Haven't you ever been in love?

SQUIRE. Never. And I never shall be. Some have tried their damnedest to entrap me, but I've escaped every snare.

MARQUIS. But you are the last of the family. Surely you want a son to carry on the name?

SQUIRE. That does bother me, but then I remind myself that to have a son I'd need a wife, and I put it right out of my mind.

COUNT. What'll you do with your money?

SQUIRE. Spend it.

MARQUIS. Wonderful! Count us in on it, all right?

COUNT. And none of it is to go to women?

SQUIRE. None. Not one of them will live off me, I can tell you.

COUNT. Ah, here is our dear mistress of the inn. Look at her. She's adorable!

SQUIRE. Ha! I would rather have a good hunting dog.

MARQUIS. If you don't admire her, so much the better for us.

SQUIRE. Egad. I'd leave her to you fools even if she were more beautiful than Venus herself. [*Enter* MIRANDOLINA.]

MIRANDOLINA. My respects, gentlemen. Which of you wished to see me?

MARQUIS. It was I, but not here.

MIRANDOLINA. Where would you like to see me, Excellency?

MARQUIS. In my room.

MIRANDOLINA. In your room? If you need something, call a servant.

MARQUIS. [*Aside to the* SQUIRE.] Notice that sense of decorum.

SQUIRE. [*To the* MARQUIS.] Looks like impertinence to me.

COUNT. Dear Mirandolina, I shall speak to you here in public rather than inconvenience you. Take a look at these earrings. Do you like them?

MIRANDOLINA. They're beautiful.

COUNT. They're diamonds, you know.

MIRANDOLINA. Yes.

COUNT. They're yours.

SQUIRE. [*Aside to the* COUNT.] You realize that you are throwing them away.

MIRANDOLINA. Why would you want to give me these earrings?

MARQUIS. Such a fine gift! She already has some twice as beautiful.

COUNT. These are mounted, you see, in the latest fashion. Please take them with my love.

SQUIRE. Oh, God, what a fool!

MIRANDOLINA. No, really, sir . . .

COUNT. If you don't take them, I'll be offended.

MIRANDOLINA. I don't know what to say. . . . I do wish to maintain the good will of my guests. So, not to offend our good friend the Count, I'll take them.

SQUIRE. Oh, the hussy!

COUNT. [*To the* SQUIRE.] Pray, sir, notice her ready wit.

SQUIRE. Oh, indeed! Ready to eat you up. She takes your diamonds without so much as a thank you.

MARQUIS. Really, my dear Count, you've outdone yourself, making such a presentation in public, out of sheer vanity. Mirandolina, I must confer with you in private. Remember, I am a gentleman.

MIRANDOLINA. [*Aside.*] Oh, and a skinflint! Can't get anything out of *him.* [*Aloud.*] If you gentlemen require nothing further of me, I shall retire.

SQUIRE. [*With condescension.*] Look here, Mistress! The linen you've given me simply won't suit. If you have nothing else, I shall have to provide for myself.

MIRANDOLINA. My good sir, you shall have better, although you might have asked more courteously.

SQUIRE. You take my money. You want compliments thrown into the bargain?

COUNT. [*To* MIRANDOLINA.] Try to forgive him. He is a woman-hater on principle.

SQUIRE. I have no need of her forgiveness.

MIRANDOLINA. Why, the poor women! What have they done to you to make you so cold and cruel?

SQUIRE. Let's leave it at that. I have no wish to enter into this further. Just change the linen in my room. In fact, I'll send my servant for it. Gentlemen, farewell. [*He leaves.*]

MIRANDOLINA. What a rude man! I've never seen the like.

COUNT. Dearest Mirandolina, not everyone is sensitive to your great merits.

MIRANDOLINA. I tell you, I'm so fed up with his behavior, I shall send him packing at once.

MARQUIS. You do that. And if he resists, just tell me, and I'll have him out of here in a jot. Just make use of my influence.

COUNT. And any money you may lose by his departure, I'll make up to you. [*Aside to* MIRANDOLINA.] Listen, the same goes for the Marquis if you send him packing.

MIRANDOLINA. Thank you, gentlemen. But I am fully capable of telling a guest when he isn't wanted. As for the matter of income, I never have trouble filling a room once it's empty. [*Enter* FABRIZIO.]

FABRIZIO. [*To the* COUNT.] Your Lordship, someone is asking for you.

COUNT. Do you know who it is?

FABRIZIO. I believe it is a jeweler. [*Sotto voce to* MIRANDOLINA.] Have a care, Mirandolina, these men can be bad company. [*He leaves.*]

COUNT. Ah, yes. He's come to show me some jewelry. Mirandolina, those earrings need good company.

MIRANDOLINA. No, please, Count . . .

COUNT. You fully deserve it and the money means nothing to me. Let me go look at this new piece of jewelry. Good-bye, Mirandolina. My respects, Marquis. [*He leaves.*]

MARQUIS. [*Aside.*] Damn him and his money!

MIRANDOLINA. The Count puts himself to too much trouble.

MARQUIS. I know his type. They have some money which they spend recklessly out of sheer arrogance. I've seen such behavior before, out in the world.

MIRANDOLINA. Oh, I know the way of the world.

MARQUIS. They think a woman of your sort can be bought with a few expensive trinkets.

MIRANDOLINA. Well, now, gifts don't exactly turn my stomach.

MARQUIS. I would never consider insulting you by obligating you through a few gifts.

MIRANDOLINA. I can believe that.

MARQUIS. I have never done so and never shall.

MIRANDOLINA. I do believe you.

MARQUIS. But, if there is ever anything I can do for you, you have only to ask.

MIRANDOLINA. I should need to know *what* you can do first.

MARQUIS. Why anything at all. Try me.

MIRANDOLINA. Give me some indication what I could ask.

MARQUIS. By Jove, what an astonishingly exquisite woman you are!

MIRANDOLINA. You are too kind, Excellency.

MARQUIS. Oh, oh! I could say such foolish things now. I could even renounce my noble station.

MIRANDOLINA. Why, sir?

MARQUIS. Sometimes, I even wish I were merely a Count like that fellow.

MIRANDOLINA. Because of his money, perhaps?

MARQUIS. No! Confound his money. Because then . . . I might marry you. [*Exit.*]

MIRANDOLINA. [*Alone.*] Uh, what's that he said? His excellency the miserly Marquis would marry me? Well, my dear fellow, besides your exalted rank, there's another little impediment to our marriage. *I* wouldn't want any part of it. Always so much smoke and so little real fire. Think how many husbands I'd have now if I'd married every one that said he loved me! They arrive at the inn, ogle me, declare their undying love, and propose marriage. Ha! But then there's this Squire who's as rude as a bear: he's the first one ever to lodge here who took no pleasure conversing with me. A woman-hater, is he? Well, perhaps he has only just now met a woman who knew how to handle him. Here's one can match wits with him. Those who've been running after me are becoming annoying. Nobility matters little to me and I can take riches or leave them alone. What I really enjoy is being fussed over, longed for and adored. That is my weakness, and the weakness of nearly every woman. As for marriage, forget it! I don't need anyone. I live honestly and I enjoy my freedom. I like making fun of these ardent love-sick caricatures, but more than that I'd enjoy using my skills to conquer and shatter a cruel heart hardened against us women. We are, after all, the finest of all Mother Nature's creations. [*Enter* FABRIZIO.]

FABRIZIO. Uh . . . ma'am?

MIRANDOLINA. What is it?

FABRIZIO. That guest in the middle room is screaming about the sheets. He says they're common and he doesn't want them.

MIRANDOLINA. I know, I know. So he told me and I'll give him others.

FABRIZIO. Very well. Come give them to me to take to him.

MIRANDOLINA. You go on. I'll take them myself.

FABRIZIO. You?

MIRANDOLINA. Yes, me.

FABRIZIO. You seem very concerned about this guest.

MIRANDOLINA. I'm concerned about all of them. And none of this concerns you!

FABRIZIO. [*Aside.*] So it seems. She likes toying with me. It's hopeless.

MIRANDOLINA. [*Aside.*] Poor fool! He's taken with me, too. I'll have to keep his hopes alive because he serves me so faithfully.

FABRIZIO. It has always been customary for me to wait upon the guests.

MIRANDOLINA. You're a little coarse with them.

FABRIZIO. And you a little too gentle.

MIRANDOLINA. I don't need advice. I know what I'm doing.

FABRIZIO. Fine. Then, get yourself another servant.

MIRANDOLINA. Why, Fabrizio, are you angry with me?

FABRIZIO. Have you forgotten what your father said to us before he died?

MIRANDOLINA. No. And when I decide to marry, I'll recall what he said.

FABRIZIO. Perhaps I'm sensitive, but there are certain things that are hard for me to take. You treat me now this way, now that way.

MIRANDOLINA. What do you take me for? A fickle woman? A flirt? A madwoman? I'm surprised at you. What use have I for all the guests who come and go here? If I treat them well, I do so only in the interests of business. I have no use for gifts. As for love, I shall need no more than one, and he is always hereabout. I know who deserves me and who suits me. And when the time comes that I should marry . . . I'll remember my father. Whoever serves me well won't complain about me. I'm not ungrateful. I recognize it . . . even if I am not myself fully recognized. That's enough, Fabrizio. Try to understand me, if you can. [*She exits.*]

FABRIZIO. He'd be a smart fellow who could understand her. She says she's not a flirt, but she does like to do things her way. Well, let's just close an eye and let things take their course. After all, the guests, they come and go, but I . . . am "always hereabout." Ah, yes. Think of that, Fabrizio. [*Exit.*]

Scene 2

The SQUIRE's *room.*

SERVANT. Your Lordship, this letter has just arrived for you.

SQUIRE. Bring me my cup of chocolate. [*The* SERVANT *leaves. The* SQUIRE *opens the letter and reads.*]

SQUIRE. "Siena, January 1st, 1753." Who is this who's writing? [*He looks at the back.*] Ah, Orazio Taccagni. Let's see what he has to say. "Dearest friend, out of friendship to you I hasten to inform you that you must return home. Count Manna has died . . ." Ah, poor fellow. "He leaves behind a young marriageable daughter, heiress to one hundred and fifty thousand ducats. Your friends would all like this fortune to fall to you and they are busy making arrangements on your behalf." They needn't trouble themselves for me. In fact, I'd as soon hear nothing of it at all. They ought to know, especially this friend here, that I can't stand having women underfoot. [*He tears up the letter.*] What's a hundred and fifty thousand ducats to me? So long as I am alone, I can get by on much less. And if I were married, even a great deal more wouldn't suffice. A wife! I'd rather have the pox. [*Enter the* MARQUIS.]

MARQUIS. Dear friend, might I spend a few moments with you?

SQUIRE. You do me an honor.

MARQUIS. [*Settling himself.*] At least you and I can talk in confidence. That ass of a Count, however, isn't worthy of joining us.

SQUIRE. Dear Marquis, forgive me, but I must insist that you respect others if you wish to be respected yourself.

MARQUIS. Ah, well, you know me. I'm always obliging to everyone, but that man I simply cannot abide.

SQUIRE. Because he's your rival in love. Come, sir, shame. A gentleman of your standing to fall in love with an innkeeper's daughter! A sensible man like you!

MARQUIS. Oh, my dear sir, she has simply bewitched me.

SQUIRE. Stuff and nonsense! Witchcraft? It amounts to nothing but wily tricks and a lot of flattery. Do you ever see me bewitched? No. And do you know why? Because I steer clear of them. Anyone who does as I do is free of danger.

MARQUIS. You may be right, or then again you might be wrong. Anyway, what is disturbing me just at the moment is something else. It's the steward of my estates.

SQUIRE. Has he done you a bad turn?

MARQUIS. [Nodding gravely.] He has broken his word. [The SERVANT enters with a cup of chocolate.]

SQUIRE. I am sorry . . . [To the SERVANT.] Bring another one quickly.

SERVANT. I'm terribly sorry, Lordship, but there's no more in the house.

SQUIRE. Well, then send out for some. [To the MARQUIS.] If you please . . . [The MARQUIS seizes the cup, and without a nod begins to drink and discourse.]

MARQUIS. This steward of mine, you see . . .

SQUIRE. [Aside.] And I shall go without.

MARQUIS. . . . promised to send me by mail . . . [He drinks.] . . . twenty florins . . . [Drinks.]

SQUIRE. [Aside.] Ah, here it comes.

MARQUIS. And he has not sent them . . . [Drinks.]

SQUIRE. He'll send them another time.

MARQUIS. The point is . . . The point is . . . [He finishes the chocolate.] Here you are. [He hands the cup back to the SQUIRE.] The point is that I find myself in great difficulty and I simply don't know what to do.

SQUIRE. Ah well, a week more or less . . .

MARQUIS. But you, sir, as a gentleman, know the importance of keeping one's word. Here I am in a financial embarrassment, and, well, confound it all, I'm at my wits' end.

SQUIRE. I'm so sorry to see you so unhappy. [Aside.] Oh, for a way out of this!

MARQUIS. Would it cause you any great difficulty to do me a favor?

SQUIRE. My dear Marquis, if I could, I would, with all my heart. If I had the money, I would've given you some at once. But I too am waiting.

MARQUIS. You wouldn't have me believe that you are without funds?

SQUIRE. [He pulls some coins from his purse.] Have a look. This is all I have. There can't be more than two florins there.

MARQUIS. [Examining the coins carefully.] There's a gold florin there.

SQUIRE. My last one.

MARQUIS. Loan it to me, and meanwhile I'll see . . .

SQUIRE. But then what will I . . . ?

MARQUIS. What are you afraid of? I'll pay you back.

SQUIRE. You wear me out . . . Here, take it.

MARQUIS. [He takes the coin.] Listen, I have a pressing engagement . . . my friend. Much obliged. See you at dinner. [He is gone.]

SQUIRE. [Alone.] The good Marquis wanted to fleece me out of twenty florins, but then he's content with one. As for me, I don't mind losing one, and should he fail to pay it back, perhaps I won't be hearing from him any more. What really annoys me is that he's drunk up my chocolate. What arrogance! But then, "I am what I am!" My gentle nobleman! [Enter MIRANDOLINA with new linen, somewhat shyly.]

MIRANDOLINA. May I come in, your Lordship?

SQUIRE. [Harshly.] What do you want?

MIRANDOLINA. [She comes in one or two more steps.] Here is some better linen.

SQUIRE. [Indicates the little table.] Fine. Put it there.

MIRANDOLINA. I pray you condescend to see if it is to your taste.

SQUIRE. What's the material?

MIRANDOLINA. [She comes in a little further.] The sheets are of the finest French linen.

SQUIRE. French?

MIRANDOLINA. Yes, sir, the finest. Have a look.

SQUIRE. I did not ask for that, merely for a better quality than I had.

MIRANDOLINA. This linen I put aside for persons of genuine merit, persons who recognize its worth. Just now, I wouldn't give it to anyone but you, your Lordship.

SQUIRE. "Just for me." The usual flattery.

MIRANDOLINA. Look at the tablecloth.

SQUIRE. Oh, this is that Flemish material that loses its shape when washed. For heaven's sake, let's not soil it on my account.

MIRANDOLINA. You see, I have the napkins to match. In the case of a gentleman of your quality, I don't bother my head about these little trifles.

SQUIRE. [*Aside.*] She is certainly most obliging.

MIRANDOLINA. [*Aside.*] What a sour, surly face he has!

SQUIRE. [*Pulling himself together.*] Give the linen to my servant, or simply leave it there. There's no need to put yourself out.

MIRANDOLINA. Oh, I am never put out serving gentlemen of such worth.

SQUIRE. Fine, fine. That'll be all. [*Aside.*] She's fawning over me. Women! They're all alike.

MIRANDOLINA. I'll just put the linen back here in the alcove.

SQUIRE. [*Gravely.*] Wherever you like.

MIRANDOLINA. [*Aside.*] Oh, he's a hard nut to crack. I'm afraid I'm not getting anywhere. [*She is gone.*]

SQUIRE. [*Aside.*] That's how fools are taken in: they start listening to this sort of flattery and end up believing it and adoring the woman who utters it. [MIRANDOLINA *returns.*]

MIRANDOLINA. Sir, what would you like for dinner?

SQUIRE. Why, I'll eat whatever there is.

MIRANDOLINA. Still, I'd like to know your taste. If there is something you especially like, please feel free to say so.

SQUIRE. Should I wish to order something, I will say so to the waiter.

MIRANDOLINA. But men don't care about these details as we women do. Please, if you particularly like some dish or a sauce, do tell me.

SQUIRE. I thank you. You may succeed in wrapping the Count and the Marquis around your little finger this way, but not me.

MIRANDOLINA. Oh, yes, what a pair of spineless dolts. They no sooner arrive in the inn than they claim to be hopelessly in love with the landlady. I have better things to do than listen to their chatter. I humor them just in the interests of business. Still, I must say, when they begin falling all over themselves with their cloying flatteries, I'm hard-pressed not to laugh.

SQUIRE. Brava! I like your frankness.

MIRANDOLINA. I'm always frank. It's my only good quality.

SQUIRE. Is that so? You mean, you don't lead those two on just a bit?

MIRANDOLINA. I? Lead them on? Heaven forbid! Just ask them if I have ever given them a sign of affection or encouragement. I don't abuse them, of course, because it wouldn't be in my best interest, but I've come close. I can't stand these effeminate peacocks, just as I can't stand women who are forever chasing after men. Look here: I'm not a little girl and I'm no great beauty. But I've put some years behind me and had my chances and I still have no wish to marry. I like my freedom too much.

SQUIRE. Oh, freedom, yes! It's a great treasure.

MIRANDOLINA. And yet so many lose it foolishly.

SQUIRE. I know what to do. I keep my distance.

MIRANDOLINA. Your Lordship has a wife?

SQUIRE. Saints preserve me, no. I dislike women.

MIRANDOLINA. Brava! Keep it that way. Because women, sir . . . That's enough. Far be it from me to speak ill of them.

SQUIRE. You are the first woman I've heard speak this way.

MIRANDOLINA. Well, I'll go ahead and say it. When you run an inn, as I do, you see and hear a lot. I can understand why any man would be wary of women, I can tell you.

SQUIRE. [*Aside.*] What a strange woman this is!

MIRANDOLINA. [*She makes to leave.*] With your Lordship's permission.

SQUIRE. Must you leave?

MIRANDOLINA. I don't want to impose.

SQUIRE. Oh, no, not at all. I am pleased . . . or amused to chat with you.

MIRANDOLINA. There, you see how it is, sir. I do this with others. I stay and talk a bit, I am cheerful and I tell a few jokes to amuse them, and all at once they become . . . Well, you understand: they start leering at me.

SQUIRE. That happens simply because you have a pleasant manner.

MIRANDOLINA. [*Curtsying.*] You are too kind, you Lordship.

SQUIRE. And so they fall for you.

MIRANDOLINA. What absurd weakness! To fall in love all of a sudden.

SQUIRE. I could never understand such a thing.

MIRANDOLINA. Ah, what strength! How manly!

SQUIRE. Such weakness is a human disgrace.

MIRANDOLINA. That's the way for a man to talk. Your lordship, give me your hand.

SQUIRE. Whatever for?

MIRANDOLINA. Because it would be such an honor. You see, mine is clean.

SQUIRE. Oh. All right.

MIRANDOLINA. [*She shakes his hand.*] This is the first time I've had the honor of taking the hand of a man who truly has a man's mind.

SQUIRE. Stop. That's enough.

MIRANDOLINA. There you are. If I had taken the hand of one of those peacocks, he'd have thought I was enamored, infatuated with him. He would have gone into a faint. I wouldn't allow either of them the slightest liberty with me for all the world's gold. Oh, how pleasant it is to be able to converse openly and honestly, without sentiment, or malice, or foolishness. Please, your Lordship, forgive my impertinence. If I can serve you in any way, you need only ask, and I'll oblige more willingly than I have ever done for anyone else.

SQUIRE. Why treat me so specially?

MIRANDOLINA. Because, beyond your merit and station, I feel I can deal with you freely without your taking advantage of my attentions. You would treat me as a servant and so won't abuse me with protestations of love or ridiculous declarations.

SQUIRE. [*Aside.*] How the devil she manages this attitude I don't understand.

MIRANDOLINA. [*Aside.*] Little by little the beast is tamed.

SQUIRE. Well, then, if you've other business, don't let me keep you.

MIRANDOLINA. Yes sir. I must go tend to the business of the inn. That is my love, and my life. Should you wish anything, I will send one of the servants.

SQUIRE. Very good. . . . Should you come yourself from time to time, I would be pleased to see you.

MIRANDOLINA. I have a policy not to go to the guests' rooms, but in your case I would do so sometimes.

SQUIRE. Why in my case?

MIRANDOLINA. Because, your Lordship, I like you.

SQUIRE. You like me?

MIRANDOLINA. I like you because you aren't effeminate and because you aren't the type to fall in love. [*Aside.*] I'll eat my hat if he isn't in love by tomorrow! [*She exits.*]

SQUIRE. [*Alone.*] Hey, now. I know what I'm doing. I keep my distance. That one could make me lose my resolve more readily than the others. She has a certain quality . . . an ease in speaking, a truthfulness. . . . altogether uncommon. But I won't let that weaken me. But for a little amusement, I might well pass some time with her. But to fall in love? No! To lose my freedom? Not a chance. What fools they are who fall in love! [*He exits.*]

Scene 3

Another room in the inn. FABRIZIO *is showing the room to two ladies,* ORTENSIA *and* DEJANIRA.

FABRIZIO. I assure your Ladyships, you will be well served here. Please look at this other room. It could serve as the bedroom and this as the dining room or parlor, or whatever you please.

ORTENSIA. Very good, very good. Are you the innkeeper or a servant?

FABRIZIO. A servant, at your Ladyships' command.

DEJANIRA. [*To* ORTENSIA, *laughing.*] He

calls us ladyships.

ORTENSIA. Let's play along. My good man.

FABRIZIO. Your Ladyship?

ORTENSIA. Tell the innkeeper to come here. We'd like to speak with him about the arrangements.

FABRIZIO. I shall tell her. [*Aside.*] What the devil are these ladies? Why do they travel alone? To judge by their manner and clothes, they appear to be noblewomen. [FABRIZIO *exits.*]

DEJANIRA. He thinks we're noble-women.

ORTENSIA. That's fine. That way he'll treat us better.

DEJANIRA. But they'll make us pay more.

ORTENSIA. Just let me take care of the bill. I've been around.

DEJANIRA. I wouldn't want these titles to get us into trouble.

ORTENSIA. Deary, you haven't much gumption. Two actresses used to playing countesses, marchionesses, and princesses on stage shouldn't balk at doing it in an inn.

DEJANIRA. When the other actors get here, we'll be found out.

ORTENSIA. They can't reach Florence today. Coming upriver by boat from Pisa takes at least three days.

DEJANIRA. How beastly! Traveling by river boat.

ORTENSIA. That's what comes of lacking the legal tender. At least we came by coach, eh?

DEJANIRA. It was a good thing we did that extra performance.

ORTENSIA. Yes, but it wouldn't have gotten us anywhere if I hadn't stayed by the door to collect. [*Enter* FABRIZIO.]

FABRIZIO. The landlady will be here directly to serve you.

ORTENSIA. Very good.

FABRIZIO. And I beg you give me your orders. I've served other noble-women and I would be honored to give all my attention to your Ladyships.

ORTENSIA. Should I require anything, I shall employ your services.

DEJANIRA. [*Aside.*] Ortensia does these parts well.

FABRIZIO. [*Taking out an inkstand and a register.*] Thank you. In the mean-time, may I humbly request your Ladyships' names for the register?

DEJANIRA. [*Aside.*] Now we're in for it.

ORTENSIA. Why must I give my name?

FABRIZIO. We innkeepers are required to report the name, birthplace, province, and rank of each of our guests. If we don't, we're through.

DEJANIRA. [*Softly to* ORTENSIA.] Oh, dear, that's it for the titles.

ORTENSIA. Many must give fictitious names, do they not?

FABRIZIO. As to that, madam, I cannot say. We simply put down the names given and don't look any farther.

ORTENSIA. Write down: Baroness Ortensia del Poggio Palermitana.

FABRIZIO. [*Aside, as he writes.*] Ah, hot Sicilian blood. [*To* DEJANIRA.] And you, your Ladyship?

DEJANIRA. Who? Me? . . . [*To* ORTENSIA.] What do I say?

ORTENSIA. Oh, come, come, Countess Dejanira, give him your name.

FABRIZIO. Please.

DEJANIRA. You didn't hear it?

FABRIZIO. [*Writing.*] Her Ladyship the Countess Dejanira . . . Of what?

DEJANIRA. Of?

ORTENSIA. Of course: "dal Sole." She's Roman.

FABRIZIO. Very well. That's all I need. Please pardon the inconvenience. Now, the landlady will be here directly. [*Aside.*] I hope I can bring off some good business here. At least I shouldn't lack for good tips. [*Exit.*]

DEJANIRA. [*The two women make fun of one another.*] Your most humble servant, Baroness.

ORTENSIA. Countess, I salute you.

DEJANIRA. What stroke of fortune has afforded me the singularly happy opportunity to offer you my most profound respects?

ORTENSIA. From the well of your heart, only torrents of grace could ever flow. [MIRANDOLINA *enters and observes this game.*]

DEJANIRA. Madam, you flatter me.

ORTENSIA. Your considerable merit, dear Countess, deserves even better.

MIRANDOLINA. [*Aside.*] Oh, what ceremonious ladies!

DEJANIRA. [*Having tried to stifle her giggles, she bursts forth.*] Oh, ho, ho.

ORTENSIA. [*Sotto voce.*] Shut up! The landlady's here.

MIRANDOLINA. I curtsy before such great ladies.

ORTENSIA. Good morning, young woman.

DEJANIRA. My most humble respects to you as mistress of this inn. [*She curtsies elaborately.*]

ORTENSIA. [*Signaling to* DEJANIRA *that she has overdone it.*] Easy!

MIRANDOLINA. Permit me to kiss your hand.

ORTENSIA. [*Extending her hand.*] You are most obliging.

[DEJANIRA *again stifles herself.*]

MIRANDOLINA. And yours, too, your Ladyship.

DEJANIRA. Oh, please don't bother . . .

ORTENSIA. Come, come, accept the courtesies of this young woman. Give her your hand.

MIRANDOLINA. I beg of you.

DEJANIRA. Here, then. [*She turns aside and snorts.*]

MIRANDOLINA. Are you laughing, your Ladyship? What is it?

ORTENSIA. Oh, the dear Countess. She's laughing at a little absurdity I uttered a while ago.

MIRANDOLINA. [*Aside.*] These are noble-women?

ORTENSIA. Now, we should like to discuss our arrangements.

MIRANDOLINA. Are you all alone? Is there no one, no gentlemen, no servants, with you?

ORTENSIA. My husband, the Baron . . .

DEJANIRA. [*Bursting into laughter.*] Oh, ho, ho, ho.

MIRANDOLINA. Madam, what is it?

ORTENSIA. Here now, what are you laughing about?

DEJANIRA. Your husband, the Baron . . . ho, ho, ho . . . whom we can scarcely bear, ha!

ORTENSIA. Well, yes, he is a jolly sort of gentleman, always telling jokes that have us all laughing. At any rate, he should arrive even ahead of Count Orazio, the Countess's husband.

DEJANIRA. [*Trying to bring herself under control.*] Oh, uhm, uhm.

MIRANDOLINA. Does the Count also make her laugh?

ORTENSIA. Come, come, Countess, do control yourself.

MIRANDOLINA. My dear ladies, please do me a favor. We're perfectly alone and no one can hear us. Now, about these titles, Countess, Baroness . . .

ORTENSIA. You doubt them?

MIRANDOLINA. Forgive me, your Ladyship. Don't get excited; it'll make the Countess laugh again.

DEJANIRA. That's it. What's the use?!

ORTENSIA. [*Threatening.*] Countess, Countess!

MIRANDOLINA. I believe I know what she's trying to say.

DEJANIRA. [*Suddenly dignified.*] If you fathom that, you have my undying esteem.

MIRANDOLINA. You were trying to say, what's the use of pretending any longer. Isn't that right?

DEJANIRA. Oh, you know who we are?

ORTENSIA. What an actress! She cannot even keep up her part.

DEJANIRA. Offstage, I don't know how to pretend.

MIRANDOLINA. Brava, Baroness. I like your spirit and your blunt good humor.

ORTENSIA. Oh, I do like a little fun now and then.

MIRANDOLINA. Oh, I am so fond of people with spirit. Please, make your-selves comfortable here. Make yourselves at home. Still, I must ask, if some persons of rank should show up, please give up this apartment. I'll give you comfortable rooms.

DEJANIRA. Yes, yes, of course.

ORTENSIA. When I spend the money, I expect to be served as a lady. I shall retain these quarters.

MIRANDOLINA. Come on, madam Bar-oness, be good . . . [*Seeing the* MARQUIS.] Oh! Here comes a gen-tleman who is staying in the inn. Whenever he sees a woman, the hunting horn is sounded.

ORTENSIA. Is he rich?

MIRANDOLINA. I don't know his business affairs. [*Enter the* MARQUIS.]

MARQUIS. Ahem. May I?

ORTENSIA. Sir, we are yours to com-mand.

MARQUIS. I am at your service, ladies.

DEJANIRA. Your most humble servant.

ORTENSIA. Please accept our deepest respect.

MARQUIS. [*To* MIRANDOLINA.] Are they guests here?

MIRANDOLINA. Yes, Excellency. They are doing my inn that honor.

ORTENSIA. [*Aside.*] Ooo! "Excellency!" That's capital.

DEJANIRA. [*Aside.*] She's already claiming him for herself.

MARQUIS. [*To* MIRANDOLINA.] And who are these ladies?

MIRANDOLINA. Ah! This is the Baroness Ortensia del Poggio Palermitana, and this the Countess Dejanira dal Sole.

MARQUIS. Oh, ladies of high station.

ORTENSIA. And who are you, sir?

MARQUIS. I am the Marquis of Forlipopoli.

DEJANIRA. [*Aside.*] I see the mistress of the inn is keeping our little joke running.

ORTENSIA. What an honor to meet a gentleman of such prominence.

MARQUIS. If I can be of service to you in any way, you have only to ask. I am delighted that you are lodging here. You'll find the mistress a lady of infinite grace.

MIRANDOLINA. The gentleman is altogether too kind. He honors me with his protection.

MARQUIS. Indeed I do. I protect her and all who come into this inn. Should my influence be of use to you in any matter, do let me know.

ORTENSIA. Should the occasion arise, I shall take advantage of your kindness.

MARQUIS. And you, too, Countess.

DEJANIRA. I should count myself happy to be enrolled among your humble servants.

MIRANDOLINA. [*To* ORTENSIA.] That has to be a line out of a play.

ORTENSIA. [*To* MIRANDOLINA.] Yes. And its cue was, "And you, too, Countess." [*The* MARQUIS *takes out of his pocket a beautiful silk handkerchief and makes great show of it as he prepares to mop his brow.*]

MIRANDOLINA. What a magnificent handkerchief, Marquis.

MARQUIS. Ah! What do you think of it? Isn't it beautiful? Shows good taste, doesn't it?

MIRANDOLINA. Most assuredly—exquisite taste.

MARQUIS. [*To* ORTENSIA.] Have you ever seen one more beautiful?

ORTENSIA. It is superb. I've never seen its like. [*Aside.*] Should he give it to me, I'd take it.

MARQUIS. [*To* DEJANIRA.] It comes from London.

DEJANIRA. I like it very much.

MARQUIS. I do have good taste, don't I?

DEJANIRA. [*Aside.*] But he doesn't seem about to give it away!

MARQUIS. I'm sorry the Count does not know how to spend money. He throws it away and never gets anything of truly good taste.

MIRANDOLINA. The Marquis recognizes, knows, distinguishes, and understands these things.

MARQUIS. [*Folding the handkerchief with great care.*] It must be folded gently or you'll ruin it. This material must be cared for. Here. [*He presents it to* MIRANDOLINA.]

MIRANDOLINA. You want me to take it to your room?

MARQUIS. No. Take it to yours.

MIRANDOLINA. Why to mine?

MARQUIS. Because . . . I'm giving it to you.

MIRANDOLINA. Oh, Excellency, forgive me . . .

MARQUIS. No matter. It's yours . . .

MIRANDOLINA. But I couldn't.

MARQUIS. Here now. Don't make me angry.

MIRANDOLINA. Well, as your Excellency knows, I never wish to upset anyone. So to keep you from getting angry, I'll take it.

DEJANIRA. [*To* ORTENSIA.] Now that was a nice piece of business.

ORTENSIA. [*To* DEJANIRA.] They're not bad actors themselves.

MARQUIS. [*To* ORTENSIA.] Ah, what do you say to that? Here I have given an exquisite handkerchief to the mistress of the inn.

ORTENSIA. You are most generous.

MARQUIS. Just so.

MIRANDOLINA. [*Aside.*] This is the first gift he's ever made to me. How do you suppose he came by this handkerchief?

DEJANIRA. Marquis, can one find those handkerchiefs in Florence? I should like to have one.

MARQUIS. It would be difficult to find one like it, but we shall see.

MIRANDOLINA. [*Aside.*] Oh, well done, Countess.

ORTENSIA. Since, Marquis, you know the city so well, be so good as to send me a good cobbler. I need some shoes.

MARQUIS. Why, yes. I'll send you mine.

MIRANDOLINA. [*Aside.*] Ah, they're all over him, and yet he hasn't a penny to his name.

ORTENSIA. Dear Marquis, do us the goodness to share our company awhile.

DEJANIRA. Won't you dine with us?

MARQUIS. Most willingly. [*Aside to* MIRANDOLINA.] Now, Mirandolina, don't be jealous. I'm all yours, and you know it.

MIRANDOLINA. [*To the* MARQUIS.] Rest easy. I'm pleased to have you enjoy yourself.

ORTENSIA. You shall be our dinner companion.

DEJANIRA. We know no one here but you.

MARQUIS. Oh, my dear ladies! I put myself heartily at your disposal. [*Enter the* COUNT.]

COUNT. Mirandolina, I have been looking for you.

MIRANDOLINA. Here I am with these ladies.

COUNT. Oh, pardon me, ladies. My regards.

ORTENSIA. Your most devoted. [*Aside to* DEJANIRA.] This one's a fatter cat than the other.

DEJANIRA. [*To* ORTENSIA.] But I'm not much of a golddigger.

MARQUIS. [*Aside to* MIRANDOLINA.] Say, show the Count the handkerchief.

MIRANDOLINA. [*Showing it to the* COUNT.] Count, look at the beautiful gift the Marquis has given me.

COUNT. Well, I'm delighted. Well done, Marquis.

MARQUIS. Ah, it's nothing. A mere bagatelle. Come, come, put it away. I'd rather you didn't mention it. People don't need to know what I do.

MIRANDOLINA. [*Aside.*] Show it, but don't mention it. Pride gallops ahead of poverty.

COUNT. [*to* MIRANDOLINA.] With these ladies' permission, I should like a word with you.

ORTENSIA. Be our guest.

MARQUIS. [*To* MIRANDOLINA.] In your pocket, that handkerchief will get all creased.

MIRANDOLINA. I'll wrap it in cotton wool so it won't be damaged.

COUNT. You see this little piece of jewelry made of diamonds?

MIRANDOLINA. It's very beautiful.

COUNT. It's to accompany those earrings I gave you. [ORTENSIA *and* DEJANIRA *watch this closely and converse quietly.*]

MIRANDOLINA. It's even more beautiful.

MARQUIS. Damn this Count, his diamonds, and his money. May the devil take him.

COUNT. Now, since you have the companions, I give you this jewelry.

MIRANDOLINA. I simply cannot take it.

COUNT. Don't make me upset with you.

MIRANDOLINA. Oh, I never upset people. Isn't this jewel elegant?

MARQUIS. Of its kind, the handkerchief is in better taste.

COUNT. But what a difference in kind!

MARQUIS. Oh, fine, fine! Here you are boasting publicly of your extravagance!

COUNT. I know, while you give your gifts in secret.

MIRANDOLINA. [*Aside.*] While two dogs scrap over a bone, a third makes off with it!

MARQUIS. And so, my good ladies, we shall sup together.

ORTENSIA. Please, this other gentlemen, who is he?

COUNT. I am the Count of Albafiorita, at your service.

DEJANIRA. Gracious me! That's an illustrious family. I know them.

COUNT. Your servant.

ORTENSIA. Are you staying here?

COUNT. Yes, madam.

DEJANIRA. Will you be staying long?

COUNT. I believe so.

MARQUIS. Dear ladies, you must be tired of standing so long. Would you wish me to wait upon you in your room?

ORTENSIA. [*Impatiently.*] Most obliged. [*To the* COUNT.] Pray, where are you from, Count?

COUNT. I am Neapolitan.

ORTENSIA. Ah! We are nearly com-
patriots. I am from Palermo.

DEJANIRA. And I Roman. But I have
been to Naples. I would be delighted
to have the opportunity to converse
with a Neapolitan gentleman.

COUNT. I should be pleased to oblige.
Are you two alone?

ORTENSIA. We are. We'll explain later.

COUNT. Mirandolina.

MIRANDOLINA. Yes sir.

COUNT. Make a table ready for three in
my room. [*To* ORTENSIA *and* DE-
JANIRA.] Would you do me the
honor?

ORTENSIA. We are pleased to accept
your courtesy.

MARQUIS. But . . . but these ladies invited me.

COUNT. It is entirely their choice, but
there is room for no more than three
at my table.

MARQUIS. I should like to see . . .

ORTENSIA. Come, come, my dear
Count. We shall enjoy the Marquis's
company another time. [*Exit.*]

DEJANIRA. Oh, and Marquis, should you
find another handkerchief, do let me
know. [*Exit.*]

MARQUIS. Count, you'll pay for this.

COUNT. What are you complaining
about?

MARQUIS. I am what I am, and I am not
to be treated this way. So! She wants
a handkerchief? She'll never have it.
Mirandolina, guard it closely. Such
handkerchiefs are hard to come by.
You can find diamonds, but not
handkerchiefs of that sort. [*Exit.*]

MIRANDOLINA. [*Aside.*] Poor fellow, he's
out of his mind.

COUNT. Dearest Mirandolina, does it
displease you that I entertain these
two ladies?

MIRANDOLINA. Not at all.

COUNT. I'm doing it for you, to increase
your business in the inn. You know,
nevertheless, that I am completely
yours: my heart and my riches. They
are all at your disposal, my dear.
[*Exit.*]

MIRANDOLINA. [*Alone.*] All his riches and
all his gifts will never make me love
him, nor could I love the Marquis
with all his ridiculous protection. Of
course, if I had to choose between

them, I'd take the one who spends
the more, but I don't have to choose.
Besides, at the moment I'm busy
making the Squire fall for me, and
that'll give me more pleasure than a
jewel twice this size. I don't know if I
can do it with the style of these two
grand actresses, but we'll see. While
the Count and the Marquis are distracted with those two, I am free to
deal with the Squire. Could he possibly not yield? Could he resist a
woman who now has the time to
practice all her skills? If he runs
away, he might avoid it, but if he
stays and listens, sooner or later, he'll
fall in spite of himself. [*Exit.*]

Act 2

Scene 1

The SQUIRE'*s room, with a table laid for
dinner. The* SQUIRE *is pacing back and
forth reading a book.* FABRIZIO *places a
bowl of soup on the table and addresses
the* SQUIRE'S SERVANT.

FABRIZIO. Tell your master, if it pleases
him, the soup is served.

SERVANT. You could tell him yourself.

FABRIZIO. He is so peculiar a fellow I'd
rather not talk to him.

SERVANT. He's not a bad sort. True, he
can't stand women, but he is quite
pleasant among men.

FABRIZIO. Can't stand women? Why, the
poor fool! He doesn't know what he's
missing. [*Exit.*]

SERVANT. Your Lordship, if you please,
dinner is served.

SQUIRE. [*He puts down his book and takes
his place at the table. As he begins to eat,
he speaks.*] We seem to be eating earlier than usual.

SERVANT. [*Standing behind the* SQUIRE, *a
napkin over his arm.*] You have been
served ahead of all the others. The
Count kicked up a fuss about it, but
the mistress still wishes your Lord-

ship's table to be laid first.

SQUIRE. I am most obliged for her consideration.

SERVANT. She is a very able woman, your Lordship. In all my travels, I've never met a more gracious mistress of an inn.

SQUIRE. [*Turning his head.*] You like her, eh?

SERVANT. Except for my loyalty to you as my master, I should like to be a waiter in her inn.

SQUIRE. [*Giving the* SERVANT *his bowl and the* SERVANT *replaces it with a clean plate.*] Poor fool! What do you want her to do with you, after all?

SERVANT. With a woman like that, she'd only have to call and I'd come running like her puppy dog. [*He goes for another plate.*]

SQUIRE. Ye gods, she bewitches them all! It'd be funny if she managed to charm even me. Well then, tomorrow I'm off to Livorno. Meanwhile, she may give it her best shot, but she'll find my aversion to women intractable.

SERVANT. [*Returning with some boiled meat and another plate.*] The mistress says that if you do not care for the chicken, she'll be happy to provide quail.

SQUIRE. I like it all. What's this?

SERVANT. Oh, she wants to know if your Lordship likes this sauce, which she made herself.

SQUIRE. Always out to please me. [*He tastes it.*] Ummm. Delicious. Tell her so and give her my thanks.

SERVANT. I will, your Lordship.

SQUIRE. Right now!

SERVANT. Now? [*Aside, as he goes.*] Amazing! He sends a compliment to a woman!

SQUIRE. This is exquisite. I've never tasted better. [*He goes on eating.*] Certainly, if she does things this well, she'll never lack for guests. A good table, laid with fine linen . . . And one cannot deny she is very kind, but what I most admire is her sincerity. What a rare thing. Why can't I stand women? [*He tastes the sauce again.*] Umm. Because they are all liars, pretenders, flatterers. But his one . . . [*He tastes again.*]

SERVANT. [*Returning.*] She thanks your Lordship for appreciating her humble efforts.

SQUIRE. Well done, my man.

SERVANT. She is now making you another dish, but I don't know what it is.

SQUIRE. She is making it?

SERVANT. Yes, sir.

SQUIRE. [*He considers this a moment.*] Give me something to drink.

SERVANT. At once. [*He goes.*]

SQUIRE. Hm. Well then, I'll have to match her generosity. She is much too kind. I'll pay her double, treat her well, and then be on my way. [*The* SERVANT *returns with wine and pours it.*] Has the Count been served?

SERVANT. Yes, your Lordship, just now. Today, he is entertaining two ladies.

SQUIRE. Really? Who?

SERVANT. They've just arrived at the inn a few hours ago. I don't know who they are.

SQUIRE. Did the Count know them?

SERVANT. I don't think so, but as soon as he saw them, he invited them to dinner.

SQUIRE. Ha, no self-control! As soon as he sees them, he is after them, though heaven knows who they may be. They're women, however, and that's enough for me. The Count is bound to ruin himself. Tell me, is the Marquis at the table?

SERVANT. He went out and hasn't been seen since.

SQUIRE. [*Indicating a plate he wants changed.*] Here.

SERVANT. As you please.

SQUIRE. At table with two ladies! What fine company! The airs they'd put on would destroy my appetite. [*Enter* MIRANDOLINA, *a plate in her hand.*]

MIRANDOLINA. May I?

SQUIRE. Are you there?

SERVANT. Yes, sir, at your service.

SQUIRE. Relieve the mistress of that dish.

MIRANDOLINA. No, no, forgive me, but let me have the honor of placing it on your table personally.

SQUIRE. This is not something you should be doing.

MIRANDOLINA. Oh, sir, what am I? One of your fine ladies? No, I'm simply the servant of those who are good enough to stay at my inn.

SQUIRE. [*To himself.*] My, what humility!

MIRANDOLINA. Naturally, I could easily wait table for all my guests, but for certain reasons, I choose not to, if you catch my meaning. But in your case, I can do so openly, without scruples.

SQUIRE. And I thank you. Tell me, what is this dish?

MIRANDOLINA. It is a ragout I made myself.

SQUIRE. Ah, well then, if you yourself made it, it will be very good.

MIRANDOLINA. You are too kind, sir. I don't know how to do anything well, but I wish that I could, if only to please so fine a gentleman as yourself.

SQUIRE. [*To himself.*] Tomorrow, I must get to Livorno. [*To* MIRANDOLINA.] If you have other things to do, don't let me keep you.

MIRANDOLINA. Not at all, sir. The house is well staffed, and I would like to know how you like that dish.

SQUIRE. Certainly. Let me taste it. [*He does so.*] Ah, that's good, delicious. What a taste! I cannot guess what's in it.

MIRANDOLINA. Ah, I have my secrets. These hands know a thing or two.

SQUIRE. [*Venting his frustration on his* SERVANT.] Give me some wine!

MIRANDOLINA. You'll want a good wine with this dish.

SQUIRE. Bring the Burgundy

MIRANDOLINA. Wonderful! Burgundy is just right. In fact, I think there's no better table wine.

SQUIRE. Your judgment is discriminating in everything.

MIRANDOLINA. It rarely leads me astray.

SQUIRE. Well, this time it has.

MIRANDOLINA. How so, sir?

SQUIRE. You seem to think I deserve special attention.

MIRANDOLINA. [*Heaving a sigh.*] Oh, sir . . .

SQUIRE. [*Becoming testy.*] What's the matter? What are you sighing for?

MIRANDOLINA. Well, it's just that I try to give everyone some special attention, but no one seems grateful.

SQUIRE. [*Calm again.*] I won't be ungrateful.

MIRANDOLINA. I'm not trying to win your favor, understand. I am simply doing my duty.

SQUIRE. No, now, I understand perfectly. I'm not such an oaf as you may think. You won't have any cause to complain about me. [*He pours wine.*]

MIRANDOLINA. Oh, sir, please don't think that I meant . . .

SQUIRE. To your health.

MIRANDOLINA. Much obliged, but you do me too much honor.

SQUIRE. Ah, this wine is delicious.

MIRANDOLINA. I adore Burgundy.

SQUIRE. Be my guest.

MIRANDOLINA. Oh, no, thank you.

SQUIRE. Have you dined?

MIRANDOLINA. Yes, your Lordship.

SQUIRE. How about a little glass?

MIRANDOLINA. I don't deserve such courtesies.

SQUIRE. Really, it's my pleasure.

MIRANDOLINA. I don't know what to say. Well . . . I will accept your kindness.

SQUIRE. [*To his* SERVANT.] Bring us a glass.

MIRANDOLINA. No, no. Let me take this one. [*She takes the* SQUIRE'*s glass.*]

SQUIRE. No, no! I've been drinking out of that one.

MIRANDOLINA. [*Laughing.*] Here's to your dashing good looks! [*She drinks as the* SERVANT *places another glass on a saucer. The* SQUIRE *pours wine into it.*]

SQUIRE. [*To himself.*] Oh, she's cunning!

MIRANDOLINA. It's been some time since I ate. I may get tipsy.

SQUIRE. Oh, I doubt it.

MIRANDOLINA. Perhaps just a morsel of bread.

SQUIRE. Why, of course. Here you are. [*He hands her a piece of bread. She stands there holding the glass in one hand, the bread in the other, looking very ill at ease.*]

SQUIRE. Perhaps you would feel more comfortable sitting down?

MIRANDOLINA. Oh. I'm not worthy, sir.

SQUIRE. Oh, come, come. We're alone here. [*To his* SERVANT.] Bring her a chair.

SERVANT. [*Aside, as he goes.*] He must be ill; I've never seen him like this.

MIRANDOLINA. I'd be in for it if the Count or the Marquis knew about this!

SQUIRE. Oh? Why?

MIRANDOLINA. Over and over they've asked me to sit down and eat or drink with them, and I've always refused. [*The* SERVANT *returns with a chair.*]

SQUIRE. Forget them. Please sit down.

MIRANDOLINA. Just to please you. [*She does, and immediately dunks her bread in the wine.*]

SQUIRE. [*To his* SERVANT.] Listen. Don't tell anyone that the mistress joined me at table.

SERVANT. Whatever you say. [*He shakes his head in disbelief, as soon as the* SQUIRE *has looked away.*]

MIRANDOLINA. To the health of all who are good to the Squire!

SQUIRE. My thanks, gracious hostess.

MIRANDOLINA. Of course, that toast doesn't include women.

SQUIRE. Why not?

MIRANDOLINA. Because, I know you can't stand them.

SQUIRE. True, I never was able to.

MIRANDOLINA. Right. Keep it that way.

SQUIRE. [*He glances over at the* SERVANT.] Look, I wouldn't want . . .

MIRANDOLINA. Yes?

SQUIRE. Listen. [*He whispers in her ear.*] I wouldn't want you to get me to thinking differently.

MIRANDOLINA. I, sir? How in the world could I do that?

SQUIRE. [*Glancing at the* SERVANT *again.*] Get out of here!

SERVANT. May I bring you something else?

SQUIRE. Oh . . . Have them cook me two eggs, and when they're ready, bring them here.

SERVANT. How would you like the eggs cooked, sir?

SQUIRE. Any way you like, you dolt! Now, get going!

SERVANT. [*Aside, as he goes.*] Ah, he's getting angry. I think I get it.

SQUIRE. Mirandolina, you are a very attractive young lady.

MIRANDOLINA. Oh, sir, now you're pulling my leg.

SQUIRE. No, now seriously, I want you to listen to me. I'm going to tell you the truth, the complete truth, and, I assure you, it will make you proud.

MIRANDOLINA. I'm all ears.

SQUIRE. You are the first woman I have met in this whole world whose conversation I could abide. And I abide yours with pleasure.

MIRANDOLINA. Well, I will tell you the truth, sir. It's not that I'm anything special. It's just that there are such things as kindred spirits in the world. Such a feeling of sympathy, such warmth, happens sometimes between people who don't even know one another. And for myself, I admit that I have feelings for you I have never had for anyone else.

SQUIRE. I worry that you're going to take away my peace of mind.

MIRANDOLINA. Come, come, sir. You're a sensible man. Now, act like one and don't give in to weakness as others do. Indeed, if I thought you'd do that, I would never came here again. Because, you see, I sense certain feelings within that I never felt before, but I won't let myself fall for a man, much less one who hates women. After all, he might just be making fun of me, talking to me in a special way just to tempt me. . . . Might I have just a little more Burgundy?

SQUIRE. Ah, I see . . . I see . . . [*He takes her glass and pours wine into it.*]

MIRANDOLINA. [*Aside.*] He's about to topple.

SQUIRE. [*Handing her her glass.*] Here. [*From off stage, the sounds of the* MARQUIS *calling for the* SQUIRE *are heard.*]

MIRANDOLINA. Thank you so much. [*She is about to drink.*] Won't you have some?

SQUIRE. What? Oh, yes, I will. [*He pours himself some more saying aside.*] I might as well get drunk and let one devil chase out the other.

MIRANDOLINA. [*Putting on the charm.*] My dear sir.

SQUIRE. What?

MIRANDOLINA. Clink! [*She holds up her glass.*] Here's to good friends!

SQUIRE. [*Tenderly.*] Good friends! [*They clink.*]

MIRANDOLINA. [*A new toast.*] And to those who love one another . . . without malice! Clink!

SQUIRE. [*He clinks.*] Cheers. [*Enter the* MARQUIS.]

MARQUIS. I'm here as well. Whom are we toasting?

SQUIRE. [*Angry.*] What is it, Marquis?

MARQUIS. Easy, my friend. I called, you know, but no one answered.

MIRANDOLINA. [*Rising.*] With your permission . . .

SQUIRE. [*To Mirandolina.*] Stay there! [*To the* MARQUIS.] I would never take such a liberty with you, sir.

MARQUIS. Please do forgive me. After all, we're friends, right? I thought you were alone, but I'm delighted to see you here with our adorable little hostess. Ah! What do you say? Isn't she a gem, eh?

MIRANDOLINA. Sir, I was here to serve the Squire. I began to feel a little faint, and this gentleman came to my aid with a little glass of Burgundy.

MARQUIS. Oh. Is that Burgundy?

SQUIRE. Yes.

MARQUIS: The real thing?

SQUIRE. That's what I paid for.

MARQUIS. I know all about these things. Just let me try it once and I can tell you if it is or not.

SQUIRE. Hullo! Are you there? [*Enter the* SERVANT, *carrying a platter of eggs.*]

SQUIRE. Bring the Marquis a little glass.

MARQUIS. Not too little. After all, Burgundy is not liqueur. To judge it, I'll need a fair amount.

SERVANT. [*Attempting to put the eggs down on the table.*] Here are your eggs.

SQUIRE. I don't want them.

MARQUIS. What are they?

SQUIRE. They seem to be scrambled eggs.

MARQUIS. Oh. I don't care for eggs. [*The* SERVANT *takes them away.*]

MIRANDOLINA. Your Excellency, with the Squire's permission, have a taste of this ragout which I made myself.

MARQUIS. Oh, really? Hmmm! A chair! [*The* SERVANT *places a chair for him and sets his wine glass in a saucer.*] A fork!

SQUIRE. Oh, get him a full place setting. [*The* SERVANT *leaves.*]

MIRANDOLINA. Sir, I'm feeling better now. I'll just be on my way.

MARQUIS. Oh, please stay a while.

MIRANDOLINA. But, Excellency, I have things to do. And, the Squire here . . .

MARQUIS. Is it all right with you if she

stays?

SQUIRE. What do you want with her?

MARQUIS. I'd like her to taste a little glass of Cyprus wine, unlike any wine you've ever had on this earth. I'd like Mirandolina's opinion of it.

SQUIRE. [*To* MIRANDOLINA.] Well, then, do stay if it makes the Marquis happy.

MIRANDOLINA. I'm sure the Marquis will excuse me.

MARQUIS. Don't you want to taste it?

MIRANDOLINA. Perhaps another time, Excellency.

SQUIRE. Come, come. Stay with us.

MIRANDOLINA. Is that an order?

SQUIRE. I'm telling you to stay.

MIRANDOLINA. I obey. [*She sits down again.*]

SQUIRE. [*To himself.*] She does it just for me!

MARQUIS. [*He is already digging into the ragout.*] Ummm. Oh, what a dish! What an aroma! [*He tastes again.*] What flavor! This is an extraordinary ragout.

SQUIRE. [*Quietly to* MIRANDOLINA.] The Marquis may get jealous if you sit so close to me. [*The two converse quietly while the* MARQUIS *wolfs down his food.*]

MIRANDOLINA. I don't care one way or the other how he feels.

SQUIRE. Are you yourself an enemy of men?

MIRANDOLINA. Just as you're an enemy of women.

SQUIRE. Those enemies are just now getting the best of me.

MIRANDOLINA. How so?

SQUIRE. Ah, you cunning little wench, you! You know very well what I mean . . .

MARQUIS. Hey, old fellow! To your health! [*He swallows a great gulp of Burgundy.*]

SQUIRE. Well? What do you think of it?

MARQUIS. Forgive me, but it's not worth much. You should try my Cyprus wine.

SQUIRE. Well, where is this Cyprus wine of yours?

MARQUIS. Here it is. I brought it with me. I want us to enjoy it together. Ah, this is something else! [*He pulls a tiny flask from his pocket.*] Here it is! Bring some little glasses. [*The* SER-

VANT *leaves.*]

MIRANDOLINA: [*Eying the little flask.*] I see you don't want anyone to get drunk on this wine.

MARQUIS. This? Ah, this wine you drink by sips, you see, like a cordial. Drop by drop. [*The* SERVANT *returns with three small glasses. The* MARQUIS *immediately puts his hand over the open mouth of his flask.*] Oh, those are too big. Don't you have any smaller?

SQUIRE. Bring the liqueur glasses. [*The* SERVANT *leaves again.*]

MIRANDOLINA. I think it may do simply to whiff it.

MARQUIS. [*Who is indeed whiffing it.*] Oh, lovely! Such a soothing aroma! [*The* SERVANT *returns with three liqueur glasses on a tray. The* MARQUIS *pours slowly a very little bit into each tiny glass. He hands one to the* SQUIRE, *one to* MIRANDOLINA, *and takes one for himself. He then carefully re-corks the flask. He sips delicately.*] Ah, what nectar! What ambrosia! It's simply distilled manna from heaven!

SQUIRE. [*Softly to* MIRANDOLINA.] What do you think of this hogwash?

MIRANDOLINA. [*To the* SQUIRE.] I'd say it's something like dishwater.

MARQUIS. [*To the* SQUIRE.] Well, what do you think?

SQUIRE. Good. Delicious.

MARQUIS. Ah, yes! Do you like it, Mirandolina?

MIRANDOLINA. I'm not one to lie, sir. I don't like it. I think it's awful, and I could never bring myself to say otherwise. I admire anyone who can pretend, but one who does in one matter is apt to do so in another.

SQUIRE. [*Aside.*] That seems aimed at me.

MARQUIS. Mirandolina, you just don't know anything about these kinds of wine. I'm sorry for you. You do know and appreciate good handkerchiefs, such as the one I gave you, but you don't know Cyprus wines. [*He tips his glass up and empties it.*]

MIRANDOLINA. [*Softly to the* SQUIRE.] Listen to him boast.

SQUIRE. [*To her.*] I would never do so.

MIRANDOLINA. No. Your boast is in despising women.

SQUIRE. And yours in conquering men.

MIRANDOLINA. [*Again putting on the charm.*] Not all of them, no.

SQUIRE. [*With some feeling.*] Yes, all of them!

MARQUIS. [*To the* SERVANT.] Hey, bring us three clean glasses. [*The* SERVANT *brings them on another tray.*]

MIRANDOLINA. No more for me.

MARQUIS. Don't worry, it's not for you. [*He carefully pours out a bit of Cyprus wine in the three glasses.*] Young man, with your master's permission, please tell the Count of Albafiorita, loudly so everyone can hear, that I would like him to have a taste of my Cyprus wine.

SERVANT. As you please. [*Aside as he goes.*] He won't get drunk on it, that's for sure.

SQUIRE. Marquis, you are so generous.

MARQUIS. I? Oh, yes. Just ask Mirandolina here.

MIRANDOLINA. That's right.

MARQUIS. Has the Squire seen the handerchief?

MIRANDOLINA. Not yet.

MARQUIS. [*To the* SQUIRE.] You will. [*He puts the flask away with a little wine still left in it.*] This bit of balm I'll keep for later this evening.

MIRANDOLINA. Don't let it go to your head, Excellency.

MARQUIS. You know what goes to my head?

MIRANDOLINA. What?

MARQUIS. The limpid beauty of your eyes.

MIRANDOLINA. Is that so?

MARQUIS. My dear sir, I am desperately in love.

SQUIRE. I'm very sorry.

MARQUIS. Ah, if ever you had been in love with a woman, you would sympathize.

SQUIRE. Yes, I do.

MARQUIS. And I'm jealous as the green-eyed monster. I don't mind her being here with you, because I know how you feel, but let her near anyone else, and you couldn't pay me enough to suffer it.

SQUIRE. [*Aside.*] This fellow is beginning to annoy me. [*The* SERVANT *enters with a bottle on a tray.*]

SERVANT. The Count thanks your Excellency and sends you this bottle of

Canary Islands wine.

MARQUIS. Oh, he wants to put his Canary wine up against my Cyprus wine? Let's have a look, the upstart. [*He takes the bottle and sniffs it.*] It's hogwash. I can tell by the smell.

SQUIRE. You ought to taste it first.

MARQUIS. I will not. This is one of his impertinent gestures. He's always trying to outdo me. He wants to eclipse me, provoke me, make me do something silly. Well, I've had it with him. I swear to heaven, Mirandolina, if you don't drive him out of here, something awful's going to happen. Something just awful. I am what I am, and I won't suffer insults like him. I won't! [*He storms out taking the Canary wine with him.*]

SQUIRE. The poor Marquis is going mad.

MIRANDOLINA. Well, he didn't forget to take the bottle with him, you notice.

SQUIRE. No, I tell you, he is going mad. And it's you who've driven him to it.

MIRANDOLINA. Really! Am I the sort of woman to drive men mad?

SQUIRE. [*Seeming troubled.*] Yes, you are.

MIRANDOLINA. [*She rises.*] Sir, please excuse me.

SQUIRE. Stay there.

MIRANDOLINA. I'm sorry. But I do not drive anyone mad.

SQUIRE. Listen to me. [*He stands, but remains at the table.*]

MIRANDOLINA. Pardon me.

SQUIRE. Stay where you are, I tell you.

MIRANDOLINA. [*Turning toward him, proudly.*] What do you want from me?

SQUIRE. [*Suddenly he becomes bewildered.*] Nothing . . . Let's have another glass of Burgundy.

MIRANDOLINA. All right, but hurry it up. I've got to be going.

SQUIRE. Sit down.

MIRANDOLINA. No. On our feet.

SQUIRE. Here you are. [*Gently he gives her her glass.*]

MIRANDOLINA. I'll make a toast, then I'll be on my way. It's a toast my grandmother taught me:

Here's to love and here's to wine,
That they may both cheer impart!
One comes in by mouth to the mind,

The other by eye to the heart.
While I drink, these eyes of mine
Bring me into the depths of thine.
                              [*She exits.*]

SQUIRE: [*He has been listening raptly, eyes closed.*] Beautiful! Come here a moment. Why she's gone, the little devil, and left a thousand other devils to torment me.

SERVANT. Shall I put the fruit on the table now, sir?

SQUIRE. And the devil take you, too.

SERVANT: Yes, sir. [*He leaves.*]

SQUIRE. [*Alone.*] Hmmm. "These eyes of mine . . . into the depths of thine?" What an intriguing toast that was! Ah, you little rogue, I know what you're up to. You're trying to wear me down, force me to give in. But oh, she does it charmingly. The devil take it, but I'll be putty in her hands. I've got to get out of here. I've got to leave for Livorno, to-morrow—no, now. I must not see her ever again. May she never cross my path! Oh, damnable women! I'll never set foot in the same room with a woman again. Never! [*Exit.*]

Scene 2

The COUNT's *room. The* COUNT *is engaged in conversation with* ORTENSIA *and* DEJANIRA.

COUNT. The Marquis of Forlipopoli is a queer duck. He's a born nobleman, you can't deny that, but between his father and himself, they've frittered away the whole estate, so that now he has scarcely enough to live on. And still he goes on playing the gallant.

ORTENSIA. He'd like to be generous, but just can't.

DEJANIRA. Whenever he gives a little token away, he wants the whole world to know it.

COUNT. He'd be a great character for one of your comedies, don't you think?

ORTENSIA. Just wait until the rest of our company arrives. When we get on stage, we'll have at it.

DEJANIRA. We have some actors just made for the job.

COUNT. But if you really want to make good sport with him, shouldn't you go right on pretending to be fine ladies?

ORTENSIA. I'll do it all right, but Dejanira here is always dropping her mask.

DEJANIRA. I get to laughing the minute some blockhead takes me for a lady.

COUNT. You did well to take me into your confidence, because now I can do something on your behalf.

ORTENSIA. Oh, nice! The Count has become our patron.

DEJANIRA. As we're friends, his protection extends to the both of us.

COUNT. I must tell you, in all sincerity, that I will help you in every way I can, but I do have a certain involvement that will prevent me from frequenting your quarters.

ORTENSIA. Ah, the good Count has a little affair going, eh?

COUNT. Yes. Confidentially, it's the mistress of this inn.

ORTENSIA. Fantastic! Now, there's a grand lady for you! I'm amazed you'd be taken with the landlady.

DEJANIRA. You'd do better getting involved with an actress.

COUNT. That I wouldn't consider. You actresses are here one minute, gone the next.

ORTENSIA. That's all the better, don't you see? That way affairs can't drag on and on, and men can avoid their own ruin.

COUNT. All that is neither here nor there. I am involved. I love her and I don't want to turn her against me.

DEJANIRA. What's she got that's so good?

COUNT. Oh, a great deal.

ORTENSIA. Why, Dejanira, she's all lovely and rosy, don't you know? [*She mimes making up her face.*]

COUNT. She has a beautiful soul.

DEJANIRA. Oh, just try pitting her soul against one of ours!

COUNT. That's enough! At any rate, Mirandolina pleases me and if you desire my friendship, you'll speak well of her. Otherwise, we may as well suppose that we never met.

ORTENSIA. I'm perfectly willing to say that she's a Venus.

DEJANIRA. Right. She has a soul and she speaks well.

COUNT. Now, that's more like it.

ORTENSIA. Oh, we can serve it up with the best of them.

COUNT. [*Glancing into the wings.*] Did you notice who just went through that room?

ORTENSIA. I saw him.

COUNT. That's another one who would make a great stage character.

ORTENSIA. What type's he?

COUNT. A misogynist.

DEJANIRA. A what?

COUNT. Can't stand women.

DEJANIRA. Oh. He probably had some bad experience with one.

COUNT. Certainly not. He's never been in love. He won't deal with women at all. He despises them, even Mirandolina.

ORTENSIA. Poor fellow. I bet I could change his mind.

DEJANIRA. Oh, I'd like a crack at him.

COUNT. Listen, dear ladies. Just for the fun of it, see if you can't bring him to his knees. You succeed and I'll donate a fine gift worthy of my station.

ORTENSIA. I don't need to be paid. If I do it, I'll do it for the sheer sport of it all.

DEJANIRA. We're perfectly happy for the Count to be good to us, but we'll do this for our own enjoyment.

COUNT. Well, I doubt you can get anywhere with him.

ORTENSIA. Why, the Count has too little regard for us.

DEJANIRA. We may not have the charm of Mirandolina, but we do know a thing or two.

COUNT. Shall I call him in here?

ORTENSIA. Just as you please.

COUNT. Hullo! Anyone there? [*Enter the* COUNT's SERVANT.]

COUNT. Ask the Squire of Ripafratta to do us the honor of joining us here. I must speak with him.

SERVANT. But he's not in his room.

COUNT. I just saw him going toward the kitchen. You'll find him.

SERVANT. Right away, sir. [*He leaves.*]

COUNT. [*Aside as he watches him go.*] Why ever would he be going to the kitchen? I suppose he's going to berate Mirandolina for something.

ORTENSIA. My dear Count, I asked the

Marquis to send his shoemaker to me, but I'm afraid he'll never show up.

COUNT. Don't give it another thought. I'll take care of it.

DEJANIRA. And he promised me a handkerchief, but does he bring it?

COUNT. We'll find some handkerchiefs.

DEJANIRA. The fact is, I really needed one.

COUNT. [*Offering her his silken one.*] If this one pleases you, it is yours. It's clean.

DEJANIRA. Why, thank you. You're so kind.

COUNT. Ah, here's the Squire. You'd best play your roles as ladies, just to inspire a little civility in him. Step back a bit. If he sees you, he'll walk right out.

ORTENSIA. What's his name?

COUNT. The Squire of Ripafratta. Tuscan, you know.

DEJANIRA. Is he married?

COUNT. He can't stand women.

ORTENSIA. [*Stepping back.*] Is he rich?

COUNT. Oh, yes.

DEJANIRA. [*Also stepping back.*] And generous?

COUNT. That, too.

DEJANIRA. All right!

ORTENSIA. Just give us a little time. [*They have retired. The* SQUIRE *enters.*]

SQUIRE. Did you call for me, Count?

COUNT. Yes, sorry to bother you.

SQUIRE. How can I serve you?

COUNT. These two ladies need your help. [*He gestures toward them and they step forward.*]

SQUIRE. Please excuse me. I haven't time to talk.

ORTENSIA. Sir, we don't want to trouble you.

DEJANIRA. Favor us with just a few words, your Lordship.

SQUIRE. Ladies, you must pardon me, but I have pressing business . . .

ORTENSIA. We'll hurry. Just let us say two words.

DEJANIRA. Two little words, and that's it, sir.

SQUIRE. [*Aside.*] Damn the count!

COUNT. Dear friend, these two ladies, the Baroness Ortensia del Poggio Palermitana and the Countess Dejanira dal Sole, need your help. It is only

civil to listen to their request.

SQUIRE. [*Screwing up his face.*] How can I be of service to you, ladies?

ORTENSIA. You are Tuscan, are you not, your Lordship?

SQUIRE. Yes, madam.

DEJANIRA. So then, you have friends here in Florence?

SQUIRE. Friends and relatives.

DEJANIRA. Well, then, know, sir . . . [*To* ORTENSIA.] Dear friend, you begin . . .

ORTENSIA. Well, sir, I'll tell you. You know how it is sometimes . . . that . . .

SQUIRE. Oh, please, I beg you. I have pressing business.

COUNT. Ah, of course. It's my presence that embarrasses you. Please do forgive me. Feel free to confide in the Squire. I'll discreetly absent myself.

SQUIRE. No, please, friend. Don't go . . .

COUNT. I see it as my duty. I am your most humble servant, ladies. [*He leaves. The* SQUIRE *makes a move to go, too.*]

ORTENSIA. Sir, please. Let us sit down.

SQUIRE. I'd rather not.

DEJANIRA. My! So rude with ladies!

SQUIRE. Please, tell me what you want.

ORTENSIA. We are in need of your help, your protection, your kindness.

SQUIRE. What's happened to you?

DEJANIRA. Our husbands have abandoned us.

SQUIRE. [*Becoming angry.*] What? Abandoned? Two ladies abandoned? Who are these husbands of yours?

DEJANIRA. [*To* ORTENSIA, *aside.*] What'll I do now?

ORTENSIA. [*To* DEJANIRA, *aside.*] He's in such a rage, I don't know myself.

SQUIRE. [*He turns to go.*] Ladies, my respects.

ORTENSIA. What!? This is how you would treat us?

DEJANIRA. You a Squire and a gentleman?

SQUIRE. I'm very sorry, but I happen to like my peace of mind. And here I find two ladies abandoned by their husbands, and that can only mean trouble. I don't wish to get involved. I prefer to keep to myself. Dear ladies, don't expect advice or help from me.

ORTENSIA. Well, then, enough of this. Let's not play games with our dear Squire.

DEJANIRA. Yes. Let's talk openly and frankly.

SQUIRE. Now what?

ORTENSIA. We are not ladies.

SQUIRE. Oh?

DEJANIRA. The Count wanted to play a little joke on you.

SQUIRE. Well, you've had your little joke. [*He makes to go.*] My respects . . .

ORTENSIA. Wait a moment.

SQUIRE. What *do* you want?

DEJANIRA. Do give us the pleasure of your charming conversation.

SQUIRE. I have things to do. I simply cannot stay.

ORTENSIA. We aren't trying to get anything out of you.

DEJANIRA. And we certainly won't relieve you of your reputation.

ORTENSIA. We know you cannot stand women.

SQUIRE. That's fine, then. [*He starts out again.*] My respects . . .

ORTENSIA. Just listen a minute. We are women such as could scarcely arouse your suspicions.

SQUIRE. Who are you?

ORTENSIA. You tell him, Dejanira.

DEJANIRA. You could tell him just as well.

SQUIRE. Oh, come on, say it.

ORTENSIA. We're actresses.

SQUIRE. Actresses?! Well, then, talk away all you like. I'm not afraid of your sort, knowing the work you do.

ORTENSIA. What do you mean?

SQUIRE. Why, I know you are always pretending, on stage and off. Knowing that, I feel perfectly safe.

DEJANIRA. I hate to tell you this, but I don't know how to pretend offstage.

SQUIRE. Oh? And what's your name? Mrs. Candid?

DEJANIRA. I am . . .

SQUIRE. [*To* ORTENSIA.] And you? What's yours? Mistress Fleece?

ORTENSIA. Dear Squire . . .

SQUIRE. Ah, how you delight in fleecing people, plucking out of them whatever you can!

ORTENSIA. I am not . . .

SQUIRE. [*To* DEJANIRA.] Tell me, do you upstage your juvenile lead, eh?

DEJANIRA. I don't know what . . .

SQUIRE. See, I can talk your langugage.

ORTENSIA. Oh, dear Squire! [*She moves toward him and tries to take him by the arm.*]

SQUIRE. Ah, ah! I'll counter that cross! [*He steps in front of her.*]

ORTENSIA. Oh, for heavens' sakes. He's turning into a stage ham. Certainly he's no gentleman.

SQUIRE. Stage ham, eh? No gentleman, you say. Well, let me tell you, you're a pair of impudent hussies.

DEJANIRA. You would say that to me?

ORTENSIA. To a lady?

SQUIRE. [*To* ORTENSIA.] Oh, what a fine painted face!

ORTENSIA. You ass! [*She leaves.*]

SQUIRE. [*To* DEJANIRA.] And what a splendid wig!

DEJANIRA. Damn him! [*She leaves.*]

SQUIRE. [*Alone.*] There! That's done it! What did they think they were doing? Seducing me? Ha! The fools! Now they'll run to the Count and tell him the whole scene. Well, let them. If they were indeed ladies, I would have been satisfied simply to get out of here, but since they weren't, I enjoyed the chance to abuse them. Oh, I'm good at it! Somehow, though, I haven't been able to do it to Mirandolina. With her I feel altogether differently. I admit it: she has charmed me! And yet, don't forget: she *is* a woman. Yes. And for that very reason, I cannot trust her. I have to get out of here. I've got to leave tomorrow. Just a minute: if I wait until tomorrow, I'll have to sleep in this house tonight. And what's to prevent Mirandolina from ruining me in that time? [*He ponders this.*] Yes! Be a man! Be resolute and decisive! That's the ticket! [*Enter the Servant.*]

SERVANT. Sir?

SQUIRE. What do you want?

SERVANT. The Marquis wishes to speak with you in your room.

SQUIRE. What does that lunatic want with me? He won't get another penny out of me, I can tell you that. Let him cool his heels, and when he gets tired of waiting, maybe he'll go away. Look, go to the desk clerk and have him prepare my bill.

SERVANT. The bill? [*He starts to leave.*] Very good, sir.

SQUIRE. And listen: make sure my trunks are packed and ready to go in two hours' time.

SERVANT. It seems we're leaving.

SQUIRE. Right. Bring me my hat and my sword, without letting on to the Marquis.

SERVANT. Suppose he sees me packing the trunks?

SQUIRE. Tell him whatever you like. Understand? [SERVANT *leaves.*]

SQUIRE. And yet I must admit I feel badly about leaving, somehow. Well, all the worse for me if I stay, I can tell that. The sooner I'm gone, the better. Yes, you women, I'll go right on finding ways to abuse you, for you do us men great harm, even when you love us. [*Enter* FABRIZIO.]

FABRIZIO. Is it true that you want your bill, sir?

SQUIRE. Did you bring it?

FABRIZIO. The mistress is preparing it now.

SQUIRE. She makes up the bills?

FABRIZIO. Oh, yes. She's done it even back in the days when her father was still alive. She writes and adds figures better than any store clerk, I tell you.

SQUIRE. [*Aside.*] What a singular woman!

FABRIZIO. But, sir, must you go away so soon?

SQUIRE. Yes, on business.

FABRIZIO. The bill, you understand, won't include the gratuities.

SQUIRE. Just bring it. I know how to settle up.

FABRIZIO. You want me to bring the bill here?

SQUIRE. Yes, here. I'm not going to my room just now.

FABRIZIO. Very wise. That bore, the Marquis, is waiting for you there. Poor little fellow! He's in love with the mistress of the inn, you know, but he can whine and pant all he likes, she's going to be my wife.

SQUIRE. [*Suddenly angry.*] The bill!

FABRIZIO. I'll bring it at once. [*Exit.*]

SQUIRE. [*Alone.*] Everyone falls in love with Mirandolina! Is it any surprise then that I too am just a little inflamed? But I'm leaving, I'll rise above this . . . What's this? [*Looking off.*] Mirandolina coming with a paper in her hand? What's she want with me? Is that the bill? What am I going to do? I'm going to have to weather this last assault—in two hours I'll be out of here. [MIRANDOLINA *enters, the bill in her hand.*]

MIRANDOLINA. [*Sadly.*] Sir . . . [*She hangs back.*]

SQUIRE. What is it, Mirandolina?

MIRANDOLINA. Excuse me.

SQUIRE. Come forward.

MIRANDOLINA. You wanted your bill. I've brought it.

SQUIRE. Let me have it.

MIRANDOLINA. Here. [*She hands him the bill, drying her eye with the edge of her apron.*]

SQUIRE. What's the matter? Are you crying?

MIRANDOLINA. Oh, it's nothing, sir. I've gotten some smoke in my eye.

SQUIRE. Smoke? Oh, well . . . Never mind. How much is the bill? [*He reads it.*] One florin? In four days, with such generous service, I only owe one florin?

MIRANDOLINA. That's your bill.

SQUIRE. What about the two special dishes you prepared? Aren't they on the bill?

MIRANDOLINA. Forgive me, but what I give I don't put on the bill.

SQUIRE. You gave those to me?

MIRANDOLINA. Excuse the liberty. Accept them as a . . . [*She covers her face, seeming to cry.*]

SQUIRE. Hey there, what is it?

MIRANDOLINA. I don't know if it's the smoke or if something else has gotten in my eye.

SQUIRE. I hope you haven't done it cooking those two dishes for me.

MIRANDOLINA. If it were that, I could easily bear it. [*She seems to hold back the tears.*] Gladly.

SQUIRE. [*Aside.*] Oh, I've got to get out of here! [*Aloud.*] Hey, come now. Here are two ducats. Take them and enjoy them for my sake . . . [*He becomes bewildered.*] And . . . please, have pity on me. [MIRANDOLINA *does not answer, but seems to faint, dropping into a chair.*]

SQUIRE. Mirandolina! Oh, dear! Oh my! She's fainted. Could she be in love with me? So soon? And why not? Aren't I in love with her? Dear Mirandolina! Imagine me saying "dear" to a woman! She fainted for me! [*He kneels beside her.*] Oh, how beautiful you are. If only I could bring her around. [*He's on his feet again.*] But how? I'm not used to being around women. I don't have any smelling salts or whatever. Hullo! Is anyone there? [*Into the wings.*] Anyone! . . . Oh, I'll go myself. Poor, dear girl. [*He leaves.*]

MIRANDOLINA. [*She opens one eye, the other one, smiles, and sits up.*] Well, he's done for. We women have our ways, but when a man is really obstinate, the *coup de grâce* is always a good faint. Here he comes again. [*She goes back into her faint.*]

SQUIRE. [*Entering with a vase of water.*] Here I am, here I am. She still hasn't recovered? Ah, surely she's in love! Sprinkle a little water on her face, that'll bring her back. [*He does so, and she begins to move.*] Courage, dearest. I'm here. I won't leave you. [*Enter the* SERVANT *with the* SQUIRE'*s hat and sword.*]

SERVANT. Here's your hat and your sword, sir.

SQUIRE. Get out of here!

SERVANT. Your trunks are . . .

SQUIRE. Damn you. Get out!

SERVANT. Why, Mirandolina . . .

SQUIRE. Out, or I'll knock you on the head. [*He threatens him with the vase. The* SERVANT *leaves.*] You still haven't revived, dear? Oh, your forehead is damp. Come, dear Mirandolina, courage, open your eyes. Talk to me! [*Enter the* MARQUIS *and the* COUNT.]

MARQUIS. My dear Squire.

COUNT. Dear fellow.

SQUIRE. [*Aside, in a rage.*] Oh, damn them!

MARQUIS. [*He sees* MIRANDOLINA.] Why, Mirandolina!

MIRANDOLINA. [*Sitting up.*] Oh, dear me.

MARQUIS. There! I've brought her around.

COUNT. [*To the* SQUIRE.] Well, sir, I am glad for you.

MARQUIS. Yes, well done, considering you're a man who can't stand the sight of women.

SQUIRE. You're both impertinent.

COUNT. It seems you've capitulated, old boy.

SQUIRE. Go to hell, both of you! [*He throws the vase to the ground, breaking it, and storms out.*]

COUNT. Well! The Squire has gone mad.

MARQUIS. I want satisfaction for this affront. [*They leave.*]

MIRANDOLINA. [*Left alone, she stands, and addresses the audience.*] Well, the task is done. Poor fellow. His heart's afire, in flames and ashes. Now, all I have left to do is to make my triumph public to the honor of our sex and the shame of all men. [*Exit.*]

Act 3

MIRANDOLINA'*s own room in the inn, a room with three doors. Linen has been set out on a small table to be ironed.*

MIRANDOLINA. Now that's enough fun for awhile. I've got to get back to work. This linen's got to be ironed before it's completely dry. Oh, Fabrizio?

FABRIZIO. [*He enters.*] Ma'am?

MIRANDOLINA. Do me a favor and bring me the hot iron.

FABRIZIO. [*Morosely as he turns to go.*] Yes, ma'am.

MIRANDOLINA. I'm sorry if I'm bothering you.

FABRIZIO. Not at all, ma'am. So long as I eat your bread, I must obey.

MIRANDOLINA. Wait a minute. There's no "must obey" between you and me. You don't have to do anything for me, but I know you do things willingly . . . and I . . . Well, that's enough for now.

FABRIZIO. For you I'd move heaven and earth, but I see now there's no use in it.

MIRANDOLINA. No use? Why? Am I an ingrate?

FABRIZIO. You've taken a shine to men "of quality."

MIRANDOLINA. Don't be silly. If only I

could tell you the whole story. Anyway, get on with you: bring me that iron.

FABRIZIO. But I tell you, I saw with my own eyes . . .

MIRANDOLINA. That's enough idle chatter. Bring me the iron.

FABRIZIO. [*Going.*] All right! I'm going, but pretty soon I'll be going for good.

MIRANDOLINA. [*She seems to be talking to herself, but she makes sure she's heard.*] Men! The more you love them the worse off you are.

FABRIZIO. [*At the door, with a certain tenderness.*] What was that?

MIRANDOLINA. Get on with you. Are you going to bring me that iron or not?

FABRIZIO. Sure, I'm going to get it. [*Aside.*] I don't know what to make of her. She gives me the come-on one minute and the cold shoulder the next. I don't get it. [*Exit.*]

MIRANDOLINA. [*Alone.*] Poor silly fellow! He just can't help but serve me. Oh, I like making men do as I please! Why, I've got that Squire, who was such a woman-hater, to the point where he'd do any little foolishness I desired. [*The* SQUIRE's *servant enters.*]

SERVANT. Mistress Mirandolina?

MIRANDOLINA. Yes, what is it, friend?

SERVANT. My master sends his respects and wishes to know how you are.

MIRANDOLINA. Tell him I'm just fine.

SERVANT. [*Holding out a golden flask.*] He says for you to take a sip of these spirits of Melissa. It's good for you.

MIRANDOLINA. [*She takes the flask and examines it.*] Is this flask made of gold?

SERVANT. Why, yes. I know it for a fact.

MIRANDOLINA. Why didn't he give me these spirits when I had that awful fainting spell?

SERVANT. Because he didn't have them then.

MIRANDOLINA. Oh? And how did he get them?

SERVANT. [*Winking at her.*] I'll tell you, confidentially, you understand? He sent me to bring in a goldsmith, and he bought the flask—paid twelve florins for it. And then he sent me to the apothecary for the spirits.

MIRANDOLINA. [*Laughing.*] Ha, ha, ha!

SERVANT. You laugh at that?

MIRANDOLINA. I'm laughing because he sends me the medicine after I'm cured.

SERVANT. It'll do for another time.

MIRANDOLINA. All right, then. I'll take a sip as a preventive. [*She does, then hands back the flask.*] There. Tell him thanks.

SERVANT. Oh, the flask is yours.

MIRANDOLINA. Mine!?

SERVANT. Yes. My master bought it just for you.

MIRANDOLINA. Just for me?

SERVANT. Yes, for you, but don't let on what I told you.

MIRANDOLINA. Take him back his flask and my thanks.

SERVANT. Come on.

MIRANDOLINA. I mean it. I don't want it.

SERVANT. You want to insult him?

MIRANDOLINA. I don't wish to discuss it. Just take it back.

SERVANT. Well, if I must, I must. [*Aside.*] What a woman! She can refuse twelve florins. Pure gold! I've never met a woman like her in my life. [*Exit.*]

MIRANDOLINA. [*Alone.*] Ah, he's skewered, roasted, and done to a turn! And I did it to him. Not out of any selfish motive. I won't get anything out of it for myself. All I want is his confession that women have power, power that they don't necessarily use selfishly.

FABRIZIO. [*Entering with the iron in his hand.*] Here's your iron.

MIRANDOLINA. Is it good and hot?

FABRIZIO. Yes, ma'am, it's hot. And I'm pretty burned myself.

MIRANDOLINA. Oh? What's happened?

FABRIZIO. That servant tells me that the Squire is sending you messages and gifts.

MIRANDOLINA. That's right. He sent me a golden flask and I sent it back.

FABRIZIO. You did?

MIRANDOLINA. Sure. Ask the servant yourself.

FABRIZIO. Why?

MIRANDOLINA. Because, Fabrizio . . . so that he can't say . . . Come on, let's not talk about it.

FABRIZIO. Mirandolina, please, have a

heart.

MIRANDOLINA. Come on, now, let me iron.

FABRIZIO. I'm not stopping you.

MIRANDOLINA. Look, go heat up the other iron, and when it's hot, bring it here.

FABRIZIO. Yes, yes, I'll go, but believe me when I say . . .

MIRANDOLINA. Don't say it. You'll make me angry.

FABRIZIO. All right, I'll be still. [*Aside.*] What a scatterbrain, but I love her anyway. [*Exit.*]

MIRANDOLINA. [*Alone.*] How about that? Now I win favor with Fabrizio by refusing the Squire's golden flask. Obviously, I know how to do, how to live and how to take advantage of things, all with good grace, finesse, and just a little nonchalance. In cleverness, never let it be said that I've done my sex wrong. [*She goes back to ironing.*]

SQUIRE. [*He enters, observes* MIRAN-DOLINA, *steps back and says aside:*] There she is. I didn't want to come here, but the devil pushed me.

MIRANDOLINA. [*Watching him out of the corner of her eye.*] Ah, he's here!

SQUIRE. Mirandolina?

MIRANDOLINA. Oh! Squire! Your humble servant. [*She resumes ironing.*]

SQUIRE. How are you.

MIRANDOLINA. Very well, and at your service. [*Still ironing.*]

SQUIRE. I have cause for complaint.

MIRANDOLINA. With me, sir? [*She peers at him.*]

SQUIRE. Yes, with you. You refused the little flask I sent.

MIRANDOLINA. What did you want me to do with it? [*Still ironing.*]

SQUIRE. Keep it for when you might need it.

MIRANDOLINA. Thank goodness, I am not given to fainting. It has never happened to me before today, and never will again. (*Still ironing.*)

SQUIRE. Dearest Mirandolina . . . I would be distressed if I were the cause of it.

MANDOLINA. I'm afraid you were.

SQUIRE. Was I? Really? [*He is moved.*]

MIRANDOLINA. You had me drink that diabolical Burgundy. It wasn't good for me. [*Now she is ironing furiously.*]

SQUIRE. Really? Can it be? [*Mortified.*]

MIRANDOLINA. It surely can be. What's more I'll never set foot in your room again.

SQUIRE. I understand you. You won't come to my room again? Ah, yes, I get it. Yes, I do. [*Amorously.*] But meanwhile, dearest, come to me. You won't regret it.

MIRANDOLINA. This iron isn't hot enough any more. [*She calls into the wings.*] Hey, Fabrizio? If that other iron is hot now, bring it here.

SQUIRE. Be so good as to take this little flask.

MIRANDOLINA. [*Disdainfully, as she returns to her ironing.*] Really, Squire, I do not take gifts.

SQUIRE. You have taken them from the Count of Albafiorita.

MIRANDOLINA. I had to, so he wouldn't get angry.

SQUIRE. But you're willing to make *me* angry?

MIRANDOLINA. What's it matter if a woman angers you? You already can't stand them.

SQUIRE. Oh, Mirandolina, I can no longer say that.

MIRANDOLINA. [*Still ironing.*] Is your Lordship affected by the phases of the moon?

SQUIRE. My change of heart is not lunacy! It's not the moon, but your beauty and charm that has worked this miracle.

MIRANDOLINA. [*Laughing as she irons.*] Ha, ha, ha!

SQUIRE. You're laughing?

MIRANDOLINA. Why, you make a joke and of course I laugh.

SQUIRE. You little rogue! You think I'm making a joke? Come, come. Take the flask.

MIRANDOLINA. [*She goes right on ironing.*] No thanks.

SQUIRE. Take it! Or you'll make me angry.

MIRANDOLINA. [*She calls loudly into the wings.*] Fabrizio, the iron!

SQUIRE. Are you going to take it or not? [*He is beginning to get angry.*]

MIRANDOLINA. Ah, temper, temper! [*She takes it and throws it disdainfully into the clothes hamper.*]

SQUIRE. You toss it away so easily?

MIRANDOLINA. [*Crossing to the wings.*] Fabrizio!

FABRIZIO. [*Entering with the iron.*] Here I am.

MIRANDOLINA. [*Taking the iron.*] Is it hot?

FABRIZIO. [*Aloof, restraining his jealousy.*] Yes, ma'am.

MIRANDOLINA. [*To* FABRIZIO, *tenderly.*] What's the matter? You seem upset.

FABRIZIO. Nothing, Mistress. It's nothing.

MIRANDOLINA. Are you sick?

FABRIZIO. Give me the other iron if you'd like me to put it in the fire.

MIRANDOLINA. Really, I'm afraid you may be coming down with something.

SQUIRE. Come on, give him the iron so he can get out of here.

MIRANDOLINA. I think a lot of him, you know. He is my faithful servant.

SQUIRE. [*To himself.*] I can't take much more of this!

MIRANDOLINA. [*Giving* FABRIZIO *the iron.*] Here, dear. Warm it up.

FABRIZIO. [*Tenderly.*] Yes, ma'am.

MIRANDOLINA. [*Shooing him out.*] Go on. Hurry.

FABRIZIO. [*Aside, leaving.*]What a life! I can't stand it any more. [*Exit.*]

SQUIRE. How considerate you are of this servant!

MIRANDOLINA. And what do you mean by that?

SQUIRE. One would think you were in love with him.

MIRANDOLINA. Me? In love with a servant? Why, you flatter me, sir. I haven't such bad taste as to waste my time so. [*She is ironing again.*]

SQUIRE. You deserve the love of a king.

MIRANDOLINA. The King of Spades or the King of Hearts?

SQUIRE. Please, let's talk seriously, Mirandolina.

MIRANDOLINA. Go ahead. I'm listening. [*Although, of course, she is still ironing.*]

SQUIRE. Couldn't you stop ironing for a little?

MIRANDOLINA. Oh, forgive me, but I have to have this linen ready for tomorrow.

SQUIRE. This linen is more important than I?

MIRANDOLINA. Certainly. [*Still ironing.*]

SQUIRE. You mean that?

MIRANDOLINA. Of course. I have a use for this linen, but I can't get anything out of you.

SQUIRE. On the contrary, you can use me any way you like.

MIRANDOLINA. You? You, who can't stand the sight of a woman?

SQUIRE. Don't torment me any more. You've had your revenge. I admire you and any women like you, if there are any. I admire you, I love you, and I ask your pity.

MIRANDOLINA. Very good, sir. I'll tell them all. [*Ironing in a hurry, she drops a cuff.*]

SQUIRE. [*He picks the cuff up and gives it to her.*] Believe me . . .

MIRANDOLINA. Please, don't trouble yourself.

SQUIRE. You deserve to be served.

MIRANDOLINA. [*Laughing loudly.*] Ha, ha, ha!

SQUIRE. You laugh at that?

MIRANDOLINA. I'm laughing because you're making fun of me.

SQUIRE. Mirandolina, I warn you, I can't stand much more of this.

MIRANDOLINA. What's the matter? Are you ill?

SQUIRE. Yes, I'm feeling faint.

MIRANDOLINA. Here, have some spirits of Melissa. [*She tosses him the flask.*]

SQUIRE. Don't be so cruel. I tell you, I love you, I swear it. [*He tries to take her hand and manages only to burn himself.*] Ow!

MIRANDOLINA. I'm sorry. I didn't do it on purpose.

SQUIRE. Never mind. It's nothing. You've dealt me a much deeper wound already.

MIRANDOLINA. Really? Where, sir?

SQUIRE. In the heart.

MIRANDOLINA. [*She laughs again and goes to call into the wings.*] Fabrizio!

SQUIRE. Oh, please, don't call him back in here.

MIRANDOLINA. But I need the other iron.

SQUIRE. Wait a minute . . . [*Aside.*] What am I doing? . . . [*Aloud.*] I'll call my servant.

MIRANDOLINA. [*She tries to call again.*] Hey, Fabrizio!

SQUIRE. I swear to God, if that guy comes in here, I'll split his skull.

MIRANDOLINA. That's a fine how-do-you-do. I can't even make use of my own servants now?

SQUIRE. Well, call another one, not him. I can't stand him.

MIRANDOLINA. I think you're out of bounds now, Squire. [*She stands away from the table, holding the iron in her hand.*]

SQUIRE. [*Alarmed.*] Oh, please, forgive me. I'm beside myself.

MIRANDOLINA. I will go into the kitchen. Then you'll be fine.

SQUIRE. No, dear, don't go!

MIRANDOLINA. [*She begins to pace about.*] This is a fine business, I must say.

SQUIRE. [*Following her.*] Have pity!

MIRANDOLINA. I can't call whomever I please?

SQUIRE. I admit it. He makes me jealous.

MIRANDOLINA. [*Aside, as she paces and he follows.*] He comes along behind like a little puppy dog.

SQUIRE. This is the first time I've known what love might be.

MIRANDOLINA. This is the first time anyone has ever ordered me about.

SQUIRE. I didn't mean to order you about, please understand. [*Still following.*]

MIRANDOLINA. [*She suddenly turns on him angrily.*] What do you want from me?

SQUIRE. Love, compassion, pity.

MIRANDOLINA. This morning you couldn't stand women and now you're asking for love and pity? You expect me to take this seriously? Hah! It's not possible. I don't believe a word of it. [*Then, aside, as she leaves.*] Choke on that, fellow, or learn to despise women again. [*Exit.*]

SQUIRE. [*Alone.*] Oh, damn the moment I first set eyes on her! I've fallen into the trap and there's no getting out now. [*Enter the* MARQUIS.]

MARQUIS. Sir, you have insulted me. You threw a vase at me.

SQUIRE. I'm sorry. It was an accident.

MARQUIS. I am surprised at you.

SQUIRE. At any rate, the vase didn't hit you.

MARQUIS. A drop of water did, and it stained my coat.

SQUIRE. I repeat, I'm sorry.

MARQUIS. It was an impertinence.

SQUIRE. I did not do it on purpose. Now, for the third time, I am sorry.

MARQUIS. I want satisfaction.

SQUIRE. If that is what you want, fine. I'm not afraid of you.

MARQUIS. [*Changing tone.*] You see, I worry that the spot won't go away. That's what made me so angry.

SQUIRE. After a gentleman has asked your pardon, what more do you want?

MARQUIS. Oh, well, if you did not do it deliberately, let's forget it.

SQUIRE. I swear, I am fully prepared to give you satisfaction.

MARQUIS. Come, come, not another word.

SQUIRE. You ill-bred snob!

MARQUIS. Well, I like that! I manage to put my anger away and you go and haul yours out!

SQUIRE. Fact is, you caught me in a bad mood.

MARQUIS. Ah! That's too bad, but I know what the trouble is.

SQUIRE. Look here, I don't stick my nose into your business.

MARQUIS. Sir Lady-Hater, it looks as though you've taken the plunge, eh?

SQUIRE. Me?

MARQUIS. Why, yes, you've fallen in love . . .

SQUIRE. You go to hell!

MARQUIS. Why try to hide it?

SQUIRE. Leave me alone or I swear to God you'll live to regret it. [*Exit.*]

MARQUIS. [*Alone.*] He's in love and he's ashamed of it. Doesn't want anyone to know about it. I suppose it could be that he's afraid of being my rival. I'm really upset about this spot. How can I get it out? The maids usually have some sort of powder to take out stains. [*He looks about the table and the clothes hamper.*] Say, this is a nice flask! Is it gold? [*He examines it closely.*] No, it must be pinchbeck or some other imitation. Otherwise, they wouldn't have thrown it in with the laundry. Now, if there's some turpentine in here, it'll be good for taking out the stain. [*He opens the flask, sniffs it and then tastes it.*] It's spirits of Melissa. Well, that may do. I'll try it. [*Enter

DEJANIRA.]

DEJANIRA. Why, dear Marquis, what are you doing here all alone? Won't you ever do us the honor of a visit?

MARQUIS. Oh, Countess, I was just coming to pay my respects.

DEJANIRA. What were you doing?

MARQUIS. I'll tell you: I'm a great lover of cleanliness and I wanted to remove this little stain.

DEJANIRA. With what?

MARQUIS. With these spirits of Melissa.

DEJANIRA. I'm sorry to tell you this, but spirits of Melissa won't work. In fact, that will simply make a bigger stain.

MARQUIS. Well, then, what should I do?

DEJANIRA. I have a secret for removing stains.

MARQUIS. Oh, please teach it to me.

DEJANIRA. Certainly. I'll bet you a florin that I can remove that spot so well that you could never tell where it was.

MARQUIS. A whole florin?

DEJANIRA. Why yes. Is it too much?

MARQUIS. I'd just as soon try the spirits of Melissa.

DEJANIRA. May I? Is it any good?

MARQUIS. Delicious. Taste it. [*He offers her the flask.*]

DEJANIRA. [*Tasting.*] Hmm. I know how to make better spirits.

MARQUIS. You know how to make spirits?

DEJANIRA. Yes, sir. I dabble in everything.

MARQUIS. That's wonderful, little lady. I like that.

DEJANIRA. Is this flask made of gold?

MARQUIS. What do you think? Of course it is. [*Aside.*] She can't tell gold from pinchbeck.

DEJANIRA. Is it yours, sir?

MARQUIS. It's mine, and if you like, it's yours.

DEJANIRA. I am most obliged. You're very kind. [*She puts it away.*]

MARQUIS. Ha, now I know you're joking.

DEJANIRA. How's that? Didn't you offer it to me?

MARQUIS. It's not worthy of you. It's a mere bagatelle. You deserve something much finer.

DEJANIRA. You amaze me, dear Marquis. You are too kind. I thank you.

MARQUIS. Well, confidentially, it's not gold at all. It's pinchbeck.

DEJANIRA. So much the better. I admire it all the more. After all, anything that comes from your hands is precious.

MARQUIS. Now, now, that's enough. I don't know what to say. [*Aside.*] Oh dear, I'll have to pay Mirandolina for that thing. What's it worth? A half-florin maybe?

DEJANIRA. The good Marquis is a generous gentleman.

MARQUIS. I'm ashamed to give away such a trifle. I wish that flask really were gold.

DEJANIRA. Truly, it looks like gold. [*She takes it out to examine it again.*] It would fool anyone.

MARQUIS. Anyone not familiar with gold, yes, but a connoisseur recognizes the imitation at once.

DEJANIRA. To judge by the weight, too, I'd say it was gold.

MARQUIS. And yet it's not.

DEJANIRA. I'm going to show it to my friend.

MARQUIS. Listen, dear Countess. Don't show it to Mirandolina. She's a bit of a gossip, if you know what I mean.

DEJANIRA. I do indeed. I'll show it only to Ortensia.

MARQUIS. The Baroness?

DEJANIRA. Right. The Baroness. [*She exits, laughing.*]

MARQUIS. [*Alone.*] I suppose she's laughing because she thinks her charm relieved me of a golden flask. So much the better that it isn't gold. I may have to put this to rights. When Mirandolina wants her little bottle, I'll pay for it—just as soon as I can.

SERVANT. [*He enters and begins to search the table.*] Where the devil has that flask got to?

MARQUIS. What are you looking for, my good man?

SERVANT. I'm looking for a little flask of spirits of Melissa. Mistress Mirandolina wants it. She said she left it here, but I don't see it.

MARQUIS. A flask made out of pinchbeck?

SERVANT. No sir. It was gold.

MARQUIS. Gold?

SERVANT. Yes, gold. I saw the money

change hands myself: twelve florins it was. [*He goes on searching.*]

MARQUIS. [*Aside.*] Oh, poor me! [*Aloud.*] But why would a gold flask be left here abouts?

SERVANT. She says she forgot it here, but I can't find it.

MARQUIS. I just can't believe it was real gold.

SERVANT. Well, it was. Perhaps your Excellency has seen it?

MARQUIS. I? I haven't seen a thing.

SERVANT. I give up. I'll tell her I can't find it. So much the worse for her. She ought to have put it in her pocket. [*Exit.*]

MARQUIS. [*Alone.*] Oh, poor Marquis of Forlipopoli! Now he's gone and done it! Gave away a golden flask worth twelve florins, and what's worse gave it away as pinchbeck, and worse still it wasn't his to give. Now what am I going to do? If I take it back from the Countess, I'll cut a ridiculous figure with her. If Mirandolina should discover that I had it, my honor's at stake. As I am a gentleman, I'll have to pay for it. But how? I haven't the money. [*Enter the* COUNT.]

COUNT. Ah, my dear Marquis. What do you say to the great news?

MARQUIS. What great news is that?

COUNT. Why the ill-mannered Squire, that woman-hater, is in love with Mirandolina!

MARQUIS. I'm glad. He should recognize that woman's good qualities in spite of himself. And he should know that only someone worthy could infatuate me. May he suffer pains and agonies as punishment for his impertinence.

COUNT. Suppose Mirandolina encourages him?

MARQUIS. Oh, that can't be. She couldn't make such a mistake. She knows what I am. She knows what I've done for her.

COUNT. I've done a sight more than you have, but we're both washed up. She is definitely cultivating the Squire of Ripafratta, doing him little favors she's never done for you or me. That's how it is with women. The more you do for them, the less you're repaid. They'll make fun of

anyone who adores them and run after those who despise them.

MARQUIS. If I thought that . . . no, no, it can't be!

COUNT. Why can't it?

MARQUIS. You would put the Squire on a par with me?

COUNT. You yourself saw her sit at his table. That's something she has never done with either of us. And how about the special linen? Why is he always the first one served here? And those special dishes she prepares for him herself? I tell you, the servants have noticed. Poor Fabrizio is fuming with jealousy. And what about that fainting spell? Whether she fainted or merely pretended to, wasn't that a sign of love?

MARQUIS. Why, you're right. He gets fresh, new linen, while my napkin's full of holes. He gets a ragout especially prepared by her, while I get tough beef and rice soup. Why, it's an insult to my rank and station.

COUNT. What about me, who spent so much money on her?

MARQUIS. And what about me, who constantly gave her gifts? Why, I even gave her some of my precious Cyprus wine. The Squire never gave her a fraction of what we gave her.

COUNT. You may be sure he gave her gifts, too.

MARQUIS. Is that so? What did he ever give her?

COUNT. A golden flask of spirits of Melissa.

MARQUIS. [*To himself.*] Oh, no! A golden flask! [*Aloud.*] How do you know?

COUNT. His servant told me.

MARQUIS. [*Aside.*] Worse and worse. Now I'm in for it with the Squire.

COUNT. I see now that she's an ingrate. I'm absolutely set on leaving her. I shall leave this unworthy inn this very day.

MARQUIS. You are right to do so. Go.

COUNT. And as you are a gentleman of reputation, you're obliged to leave with me.

MARQUIS. But . . . where should I go?

COUNT. Don't worry about that. I'll find us lodging.

MARQUIS. This place you have in mind . . . Will it perhaps . . . ?

COUNT. We'll go to the house of one of my friends. It won't cost us a thing.

MARQUIS. [*After a brief pause.*] Fine! You are such a friend, I simply cannot refuse you.

COUNT. Let's go. We'll be revenged on this ungrateful wench.

MARQUIS. Yes, let's. [*Aside.*] But what about that little flask? I am a gentlemen, after all, incapable of a base act.

COUNT. Let's get out of here, dear Marquis, and don't look back. Do me that favor. Now if there's any way I can be of help to you, just let me know.

MARQUIS. Well, confidentially, no one must know this, my steward is late in sending me my receipts, you see . . .

COUNT. You owe something?

MARQUIS. Yes, twelve florins.

COUNT. Twelve florins? You must not have paid for weeks.

MARQUIS. I'm afraid so, and I owe twelve florins. I can't leave without paying. If you would be so good . . .

COUNT. Of course. Here you are: twelve florins. [*He takes them out of his purse.*]

MARQUIS. Wait. Now I think about it, it's thirteen. Thirteen florins. [*Aside.*] I've got to give a florin back to the Squire.

COUNT. Twelve, thirteen, it's all the same to me. Here you are.

MARQUIS. I'll pay you back as soon as possible.

COUNT. Whenever you like. Money means nothing to me. Why, to be revenged on that woman, I'd willingly spend a thousand florins.

MARQUIS. Such ingratitude. To treat me this way after all I've spent on her.

COUNT. Oh, I'd like to bring this inn to ruin. In fact, I've already sent away those two actresses.

MARQUIS. What actresses?

COUNT. You know: Ortensia and Dejanira.

MARQUIS. What? They aren't ladies?

COUNT. Why, no. They're actresses. Their fellow players arrived and the jig was up.

MARQUIS. [*Aside.*] Oh, my little flask! [*Aloud.*] Where are they staying now?

COUNT. In a house near the theater.

MARQUIS. [*Aside as he leaves.*] I'll go get my flask back. [*Exit.*]

COUNT. [*Alone.*] I'm beginning to get my revenge on her. Now, as to the Squire, who played a role in order to betray me, I'll even that score as well. [*Exit.*] [MIRANDOLINA *rushes in by another door.*]

MIRANDOLINA. Oh, wretched me! I've gotten myself into an awful mess. If the Squire comes in here, I'll be in a fix. I think the devil's gotten into him and the next thing I know the devil will tempt him into this room. I'll lock the door. [*She does.*] I'm beginning to regret starting all this. It was amusing at first to get this proud woman-hater to run after me; but now he's like a satyr in a rage. I find my reputation in danger, perhaps my very life. I'm going to have to come up with something quick. I'm all on my own. I don't have anyone to come to my defense. The only one who might is that good man Fabrizio. Perhaps if I promised to marry him? But promises, promises . . . he'll get tired of hearing them. I really ought to marry him. That way I could protect my business and my reputation without sacrificing my freedom. [*There is a beating at the door.*]

MIRANDOLINA. Oh! Listen to that. [*She approaches the door.*] Who can it be?

SQUIRE. [*Outside the door.*] Mirandolina.

MIRANDOLINA. Ah, speak of the devil!

SQUIRE. Open up, Mirandolina.

MIRANDOLINA. Please go to your room and wait for me there. I'll be with you presently.

SQUIRE. Why don't you open up?

MIRANDOLINA. Some new guests are arriving. Please be good and go away. When I've finished with them I'll attend to you.

SQUIRE. All right, I'm going. But if you don't come, you'll be sorry. [*He leaves.*]

MIRANDOLINA. "If you don't come, you'll be sorry." Ha! I'd be sorry if I went. Things are going from bad to worse. I've got to do something. Has he really gone? [*She peers through the keyhole.*] He has. He's waiting for me in his room, but that's one place I'm not going. [*She goes to another door and calls.*] Fabrizio? Wouldn't it be a fine kettle of fish if he chose this moment to get even with me? Oh, but he wouldn't do that. I mean, I have certain little ways to win them over even if they're made of stone. [*She goes to the third door.*] Fabrizio! [*Enter* FABRIZIO *by the second door.*]

FABRIZIO. You called?

MIRANDOLINA. Oh! Come here, I want to tell you something.

FABRIZIO. I'm here.

MIRANDOLINA. Then listen: the Squire of Ripafratta tells me that he's in love with me.

FABRIZIO. I'm aware of that.

MIRANDOLINA. You are? That's funny. I hadn't noticed.

FABRIZIO. Oh, you dear innocent! You didn't notice? Didn't you see the faces he made while you were ironing? Couldn't you sense the jealousy he had for me?

MIRANDOLINA. I work without ulterior motives, so I don't notice them in others. But just now he was saying things to me that actually made me blush.

FABRIZIO. That sort of thing is bound to happen to you because you're young and alone, without father or mother. You'd be free of it if you were married.

MIRANDOLINA. Oh, my yes! You're right. I've been thinking of getting married.

FABRIZIO. Remember your father.

MIRANDOLINA. Yes, I do. [*There is a knock at the door.*]

MIRANDOLINA. Someone's knocking.

FABRIZIO. [*Addressing the door.*] Who is it?

SQUIRE. [*Outside.*] Open up!

MIRANDOLINA. It's the Squire.

FABRIZIO. [*Next to the door.*] What do you want?

MIRANDOLINA. Don't open it until I leave.

FABRIZIO. What are you afraid of?

MIRANDOLINA. I'm afraid for my honor.

FABRIZIO. Just leave this to me. [*She exits.*]

SQUIRE. Open this door, or I swear to God . . .

FABRIZIO. What is it you wish, sir? Why all this shouting? This is a respectable inn.

SQUIRE. Open this door! [*He is heard trying to force it.*]

FABRIZIO. Ye gods! This could get bad. [*He goes to the middle door and calls.*] Hullo, are there any servants there? [*Pause.*] No one? [*Enter the* COUNT *and the* MARQUIS, *remaining just inside the door.*]

COUNT. What's the matter?

MARQUIS. What is all this noise?

FABRIZIO. [*Softly to the two noblemen.*] Gentlemen, please, it's the Squire there. He's trying to knock the door down.

SQUIRE. Open or I'll beat the door in.

MARQUIS. [*To the* COUNT.] Sounds as though he's gone mad. We'd better get out of here.

COUNT. [*To* FABRIZIO.] It just so happens I'd like a chat with him.

FABRIZIO. All right, I'll open it, but I beg you . . .

COUNT. Never fear. We're both here.

MARQUIS. [*To himself.*] If it starts looking ugly, I'm beating it. [FABRIZIO *opens the door and the* SQUIRE *storms in. He stops and looks around wildly.*]

SQUIRE. All right. Where is she?

FABRIZIO. Whom are you looking for, sir?

SQUIRE. Mirandolina! Where is she?

FABRIZIO. I don't know.

MARQUIS. [*Aside.*] What a relief! He's after Mirandolina, not me.

SQUIRE. The wretch. Wait till I find her. [*He starts for the opposite door and comes face to face with the* COUNT *and the* MARQUIS.]

COUNT. You seem to be angry with someone.

MARQUIS. Now you know, surely, that we're your friends.

SQUIRE. [*Aside.*] Oh, damn! Somehow I've got to hide this weakness of mine.

FABRIZIO. Sir, what is it you wish from the mistress?

SQUIRE. I don't have to account to you. I expect my orders to be obeyed. That's what I pay my good money for, and I swear to Heaven, she's going to answer for this.

FABRIZIO. Your good money buys you open and honest service, your Lordship, but you have no legitimate claims, forgive me, on this respectable woman . . .

SQUIRE. What are you talking about?

You have nothing to do with this. I know what I ordered from her.

FABRIZIO. You ordered her to come to your room.

SQUIRE. Get out of here, you scoundrel, or I'll split your head open.

FABRIZIO. Why, sir, you surprise me . . .

MARQUIS. Shut up.

COUNT. [*To* FABRIZIO.] Go away.

SQUIRE. Get the hell out of here.

FABRIZIO. [*Getting angry.*] Now, wait just a minute, sir . . .

MARQUIS. Out!

COUNT. Out! [*They chase him out.*]

FABRIZIO. [*Aside as he goes.*] Now I'm ready to make trouble for someone myself.

SQUIRE. The nerve! Making me wait in my room!

MARQUIS. [*Sotto voce to the* COUNT.] What the devil's wrong with him?

COUNT. Can't you tell? He is in love with Mirandolina.

SQUIRE. [*Aside.*] So, she dallies with Fabrizio and talks marriage, eh?

COUNT. [*Aside.*] Now's my chance for revenge. [*Aloud.*] My dear Squire, it seems scarcely right to make fun of other people's weaknesses when you have so fragile a heart as yours.

SQUIRE. What are you talking about?

COUNT. I'm well aware what your little tantrum's all about.

SQUIRE. [*Whipping around to the* MARQUIS.] Do you know what he's talking about?

MARQUIS. Oh, no, not I, my friend.

COUNT. I am talking about you. You pretend you can't stand women while you rob me of my Mirandolina.

SQUIRE. [*Again turning on the* MARQUIS.] Me?

MARQUIS. I'm not saying a word.

COUNT. Quit turning to him. Are you so ashamed you can't look me in the face?

SQUIRE. I am only ashamed to have listened to you this long without telling you that you are a liar.

COUNT. Now I'm a liar, am I?

MARQUIS. Oh dear, things are going from bad to worse.

SQUIRE. On what grounds can you say. . . ? [*He again turns to the* MARQUIS.] He's raving, you know that?

MARQUIS. Leave me out of this.

COUNT. It is you who are a liar, sir!

MARQUIS. [*Trying to leave.*] I'll just be going.

SQUIRE. [*Putting his hand firmly on his shoulder.*] Stay where you are!

COUNT. I demand satisfaction.

SQUIRE. You shall have it. [*To the* MARQUIS.] Give me your sword.

MARQUIS. Come, come, gentlemen. Please calm down, both of you. My dear Count, why should you care if the Squire here is in love with Mirandolina?

SQUIRE. What? Whoever says that is lying!

MARQUIS. Lying, you say? That lie isn't mine, you know. I'm not the one who says it.

SQUIRE. Who does, then?

COUNT. I say it. And I'll say it again: you're in love with Mirandolina! I'm not afraid of you.

SQUIRE. Grrr. [*To the* MARQUIS.] Give me that sword!

MARQUIS. No, I tell you.

SQUIRE. So you're against me, too, eh?

MARQUIS. I'm not against anyone, I swear.

COUNT. Your behavior, sir, is not that of a gentleman.

SQUIRE. Damn! [*He snatches the* MARQUIS's *sword, which comes away scabbard and all.*]

MARQUIS. Have a little respect.

SQUIRE. If you're offended, I'll give you satisfaction, too.

MARQUIS. Come, sir, you've got yourself too worked up. [*Then to himself, regretfully.*] Oh dear, I'm so sorry . . .

COUNT. [*Taking his guard.*] I demand satisfaction.

SQUIRE. I'm for you. [*He yanks at the sword, but it appears stuck in the scabbard.*]

MARQUIS. About that sword . . .

SQUIRE. Damn! [*He yanks harder.*]

MARQUIS. That's not how you do it . . .

COUNT. I'm losing patience.

SQUIRE. [*One last big yank.*] Ah, there it is! [*He sees that there is only half a blade.*] What is this?

MARQUIS. You broke my sword.

SQUIRE. Where's the rest of it? There's nothing in the scabbard.

MARQUIS. Oh, that's right. I forgot. I broke it in my last duel.

SQUIRE. [*To the* COUNT.] Let me go get a sword.

COUNT. I swear to heaven I'm not letting you out of this.

SQUIRE. Who wants out? I'll stand up to you even with this half blade.

MARQUIS. Rest assured, that's good Spanish steel there.

COUNT. Enough bravado. Show your stuff.

SQUIRE. [*Advancing.*] For you, a half blade'll do just fine.

COUNT. *En garde!* [*Enter* MIRANDOLINA *and* FABRIZIO.]

FABRIZIO. Stop, stop, gentlemen!

MIRANDOLINA. Stop this nonsense.

SQUIRE. [*Seeing her.*] Oh, damn her!

MIRANDOLINA. The very idea, fighting with swords in my inn.

MARQUIS. Ah, but it's all on your account.

MIRANDOLINA. My account? [*Turning to the* COUNT.] Is that so?

COUNT. That fellow there [*Indicating the* SQUIRE.], he's in love with you.

SQUIRE. In love? That's a lie!

MIRANDOLINA. You say the Squire is in love with me? No, Count, you're mistaken. I can assure you of that.

COUNT. Not only that, but the two of you have an understanding . . .

MARQUIS. Oh, one knows, one sees . . .

SQUIRE. [*Turning on him.*] *What* does one know? *What* does one see?

MARQUIS. [*Frightened.*] I mean, when something is so, one knows it, you see, and when it isn't so, one doesn't see it.

MIRANDOLINA. The Squire denies that he loves me, and he mortifies me, he humiliates me, and he makes me see how constant and true he is and how weak I am. I confess that if I had succeeded in making him fall for me, I would have accomplished the eighth wonder of the world. But one could never hope to weaken a man who so firmly despises all women. Gentlemen, I am a plain and open woman, and when the truth must be said, I say it. Yes, I did try to make the Squire fall in love with me, but I failed. [*She turns to the* SQUIRE.] Isn't that so, sir? I tried and tried, but I failed. I got nowhere.

SQUIRE. [*Aside.*] What am I supposed to say?

COUNT. [*To* MIRANDOLINA.] There, you see what you do to him?

MARQUIS. He can't bring himself to say no.

SQUIRE. [*Turning on the* MARQUIS.] You don't know what the hell you're talking about.

MARQUIS. Why does everyone have it in for me?

MIRANDOLINA. Oh, the Squire is not one to fall in love. He knows women's wiles, he knows all their tricks. He's not taken in by their sweet words, their tears, or their fainting spells. He laughs them all off.

SQUIRE. So, the tears and the faints are all put on?

MIRANDOLINA. What? Don't you know that? You're kidding!

SQUIRE. I swear to God, such pretense deserves a dagger in the heart!

MIRANDOLINA. Dear Squire, don't let yourself get angry just because these gentlemen say you're in love.

COUNT. He certainly is, and he simply cannot hide it.

MARQUIS. One sees it . . . there, about the eyes.

SQUIRE. [*Turning on the* MARQUIS.] The hell you do!

MARQUIS. There you go again.

MIRANDOLINA. No, no, he's not in love, gentlemen. I am sure of it and I can prove it.

SQUIRE. [*Aside.*] Oh, I can't stand it any more. [*Aloud.*] Count, at another time you'll find me ready for you, equipped with another sword. [*He throws the* MARQUIS's *half-blade sword to the ground.*]

MARQUIS. Hey, careful! Hilts like that cost money.

MIRANDOLINA. Hold on, Squire, your honor is at stake here. We have to disabuse these gentlemen of the notion that you are in love.

SQUIRE. I don't care what they think.

MIRANDOLINA. Oh, yes, you do. Stay just a moment.

SQUIRE. [*Aside.*] What does she have up her sleeve this time?

MIRANDOLINA. Gentlemen, jealousy is the surest sign of love. A lover cannot endure the thought that his beloved belongs to someone else. But the Squire here can stand it. You'll see . . .

SQUIRE. What? Who?

MIRANDOLINA. I belong to the man my father chose as my husband.

FABRIZIO. You mean me?

MIRANDOLINA. Yes, dearest Fabrizio, you. In the presence of these gentlemen, I wish to give you my hand.

SQUIRE. [*Aside.*] That fellow?! Oh no, I can't bear it!

COUNT. [*Aside*] Ah well, if she'll marry Fabrizio, she can't be in love with the Squire. [*Aloud.*] Yes, and when you marry, I promise you both a wedding present of three hundred ducats.

MARQUIS. Dear Mirandolina, a bird in hand is worth two in the bush. Marry right now and I'll give you twelve florins.

MIRANDOLINA. Gentlemen, I thank you, but I don't need any dowry. I am a simple woman without the grace or spirit to inspire love in men of quality or high station. But Fabrizio here loves me, and in your presence I take him as my husband.

SQUIRE. Yes, damn you. Marry whoever you like! You deceived me, and I know that you're relishing my humiliation. You enjoy putting my tolerance to the test. Smile if you like, but what I'd like is to drive a dagger into your heart, tear it out, and display it as a warning to all women who act like you. Let me out of your sight. Damn your flattery, your tears, and your tricks. You made me pay for it dearly, but you did one thing for me: you taught me it's not enough to despise women. One must flee them and stay forever clear of them, as I do now. [*He storms out.*]

COUNT. Now tell me he's not in love.

MARQUIS. Right! Next time he tells me a lie, I'll challenge him to a duel. [*He holds up his half-blade sword.*]

MIRANDOLINA. Hush, gentlemen, that's enough. He is gone, and if he doesn't come back and all this can pass away, I'll consider myself lucky. I managed to make the poor fellow fall for me

and I'm sorry. I see now that I was playing with fire, and I want nothing to do with it ever again. Dear Fabrizio, come here. Give me your hand.

FABRIZIO. Oh, no. Not so fast, ma'am.

MIRANDOLINA. "Not so fast"? "Ma'am?" What are you talking about?

FABRIZIO. Well, I'm not so sure about this.

MIRANDOLINA. Not so sure? What is this? Come on, give me your hand!

FABRIZIO. You enjoy making "men of quality" fall in love with you, do you? And still you think I'd like to marry you?

MIRANDOLINA. Come on, don't start acting crazy now. It was a joke, a whim, a caprice. I was being silly, I know, but that's no call for you to back out.

FABRIZIO. Well, I think we need to lay down some provisos.

MIRANDOLINA. Please, Fabrizio. I was behaving like a little girl with no one to keep me in line. When we're married, I know what I'll do.

FABRIZIO. What will you do? [*Enter the* SQUIRE'S SERVANT.]

SERVANT. Mistress, I've come to pay my respects before leaving.

MIRANDOLINA. You are going away?

SERVANT. Yes. My master is going to order the coach and have the horses harnessed. He's waiting for me with our baggage and we're off to Livorno.

MIRANDOLINA. I'm sorry if I have done anything to . . .

SERVANT. I can't stay, madam. Goodbye. My thanks and my respects to you. [*Exit.*]

MIRANDOLINA. I'm so glad he's gone. What a relief! Still I feel badly. I'm sure he left feeling miserable, and it's my fault. I'll never do such a thing again.

COUNT. Dear Mirandolina, no matter if you're married or single, I am devoted to you.

MARQUIS. You know you can always count on my protection.

MIRANDOLINA. Gentlemen, now that I am getting married . . . [*She glances at* FABRIZIO *but gets no response.*] I no longer have any need for gifts, protection, or suitors. Up to now I've been amusing myself, but I've behaved badly and I've risked too much. But no more of that. This is my husband.

FABRIZIO. Now wait a minute.

MIRANDOLINA. What now?! What's the matter with you?

FABRIZIO. I'd like to draw up a contract first.

MIRANDOLINA. What contract? You want a contract? Here's a contract: either you give me your hand or you go back to your own home town.

FABRIZIO. I'll give you my hand . . . but then . . .

MIRANDOLINA. But then, yes, my dear, I'll be all yours, heart and soul. Don't doubt me. I love you and I always will.

FABRIZIO. [*Laughing, he gives her his hand.*] There you are. I couldn't do otherwise.

MIRANDOLINA. [*Aside.*] Ah, now that's settled at last.

COUNT. Mirandolina, you are simply an extraordinary woman. You have the uncanny ability to lead men wherever you want.

MARQUIS. Your manner is most obliging.

MIRANDOLINA. If I can still expect favors from you gentlemen, I'd like to ask one last one.

COUNT. You have only to ask.

MARQUIS. Please.

FABRIZIO. [*Aside.*] What's this going to be?

MIRANDOLINA. Please do me the infinite goodness of finding lodging elsewhere.

FABRIZIO. [*Aside.*] Ah, beautiful! Now I see she really does love me.

COUNT. Yes, I understand and I offer my compliments. I'll be on my way, but rest assured that wherever I may be, you will always have my admiration and respect.

MARQUIS. Tell me. Have you by any chance lost a little golden flask?

MIRANDOLINA. Why yes, I have.

MARQUIS. [*He hands it to her.*] Here it is. I found it and I restore it to you. Now to please you, I will be leaving, but know that any time you may need it, you may count on my protection and influence.

MIRANDOLINA. Gentlemen, your words I shall always hold dear, within the limits of propriety, of course. Since I am changing my state, I shall also change my ways. [*She turns toward the audience.*] And may you gentlemen profit by what you have seen tonight to steel your hearts against the wiles of women. Should you ever feel that you are falling in love and wonder if you should yield, think back to these tricks and that wily mistress of the inn.

She Stoops to Conquer

Oliver Goldsmith

In England, the general dreariness of eighteenth-century drama was broken in the 1770s by the appearance of the stage works of two important writers, both of whom made significant contributions in other branches of literature and letters as well. The first of these was Oliver Goldsmith, an Irishman who rose from poverty and obscurity to join the literary taste-makers and style-setters of London. His essays, novels, poems, and other works were greatly admired in his own time and widely read in later generations; one of his two plays has taken a permanent place among the comic masterpieces of the British stage.

Goldsmith was born on November 10, probably in either 1730 or 1731, in the village of Pallas in County Galway, Ireland. Described as "an ugly, undersized, pock-marked oaf of a boy," Oliver grew up as something of a ne'er-do-well who was continually getting into scrapes with his impoverished family or his stern and dictatorial schoolmasters. Graduating in 1750 from Trinity College, Dublin, after having once dropped out, Goldsmith entered upon an extended period of drifting. He got as far as the seaport of Cork with the intention of emigrating to America, but missed his ship and thought better of the whole idea. He made plans to study law, but gambled away the money given him for the purpose; he did study medicine at Edinburgh and Leiden, but did not enter into practice. From 1754 to 1756, inspired by the example of Holberg, he made an extended tour on foot through Europe, earning his living at odd jobs as he went and carrying little with him but his flute.

Arriving back in London in 1756, Goldsmith worked for the next several years in a number of capacities, and began a series of literary endeavors, mostly hack work and pot-boilers at first. Still gripped by wanderlust, he almost shipped out to India in 1758 as a doctor; but his essays, which began to appear in 1759, finally set the pattern of his life. The fifteen years that remained to him were entirely devoted to literature.

By 1764, Goldsmith was already an intimate of the leading literary figures of London, most notably of Dr. Samuel Johnson, the arbiter of the age. Goldsmith joined with Johnson, Sir Joshua Reynolds, Edmund Burke, and others to form The Club, a group that met weekly for dinner and discussion and that dominated literary London. Variously regarded as an "idiot," an "inspired idiot," a "fool," a "man of genius," "impudent," and the "most beloved of English writers," Goldsmith was continually in debt and died an extravagant pauper on April 4, 1774, of a kidney ailment.

As a literary man attracted to the theater, rather than a dedicated playwright, Goldsmith wrote only two plays. *The Good-Natur'd Man* was produced in 1768 by George Colman, manager of the Convent Garden, after being rejected by David Garrick at the Drury Lane. Garrick produced a fashionable comedy entitled *False Delicacy* at the same time, and its sentimentality swamped Goldsmith's effort; he

171

withdrew from the theater for nearly five years. *The Good-Natur'd Man* is not a particularly good play, but it is a great deal better than the sentimental trivia then in fashion, and it has been revived occasionally even to the present day. Goldsmith's second play, *She Stoops to Conquer,* was offered first to Colman, then to Garrick, then finally to Colman again, who reluctantly produced it upon the urging of Dr. Johnson. Despite the serious misgivings of both the manager and the actors, the play opened at Covent Garden on March 15, 1773, with Dr. Johnson in the audience to lead the applause. No claque was needed, for *She Stoops to Conquer* was an immediate hit with the audience and has remained one of the most popular staples of the British theater ever since.

Mistaken identity as a basis for comedy is at least as old as Menander. *She Stoops to Conquer* is built entirely around a single such misunderstanding, in this case a deliberate deception instigated by Tony Lumpkin as a prank on his stepfather. Credibility is somewhat strained by the extraordinary failure of any party to the misunderstanding either to see through it or to mention any of the many facts that one might let fall while stopping at an inn—details that would reveal the mistake. This lack of credibility is gradually mitigated as more and more people are let in on the secret and, for their several reasons, agree to continue to deceive poor Marlow. Thus, act 1 is taken up almost entirely with exposition and with setting up the trick, and the remaining acts explore with great comic dexterity the ramifications resulting from it. Only at the end of act 5 is Marlow fully undeceived, and that abruptly ends the play. Structurally, then, the play is about as simple as any can be; the extreme complexity that had characterized the plots of Restoration high comedies has been utterly reversed in Goldsmith's middle-class comedy; instead of the intricacy of detail that is sometimes needed to create a sense of comic confusion, Goldsmith offers simple dramatic irony. The audience's enjoyment of the mix-ups is in no way impaired, and their ready understanding of the plot is a great aid to stage production.

Another aspect of great importance in the stage success of the play is its extraordinarily well-balanced cast. All seven of its major characters are well-written roles that provide excellent opportunities for actors. No single role dominates the play, but all are vital to its success and all are extremely well-drawn comic caricatures. As the instigator of not only the central trick, but also several of the devices by which it is embellished, Tony Lumpkin is an interesting, but not unbelievable, contrast of loutish slow-wittedness and clever conniving. His high-spirited knavery endears him to audiences and provides reasonable motivation for some of the more fanciful turns of the plot. His mother, foolish and greedy and yet as roguishly high-spirited as her son, is as fine a female character role as is to be found anywhere in English drama. Mr. Hardcastle is also a merry old soul, quick to see and appreciate a joke even when he has been a victim of it, and refreshingly willing to marry his daughter only to a man of whom she will approve. He might, indeed, be the genial host of a good country inn. Hastings and Miss Neville are deeply in love but are something more than the traditional young lovers, for the practical business of money and property as well as of moral concern for others clearly motivates a great many of their actions. Even the minor roles of Sir Charles Marlow, Stingo, Diggory, and the other servants are developed sufficiently to hold the interest of both the audience and the actor.

Without totally dominating the show, Marlow and Kate Hardcastle are clearly its comic highlights. Marlow's split personality is not altogether credible in the reading, but a good actor can combine his shyness with well-bred women and his forwardness with others in the most compelling fashion. Marlow overcompensates when he is at ease, boasting of a readiness with women that he does not in fact possess, but he is fundamentally so honest and appealing a young man that Kate falls promptly in love with him. Kate, on the other hand, is something of a minx, enjoying hugely the deception she works on Marlow and deliberately torturing him with his uneasiness when his mistake is revealed. Still, she carefully avoids pushing the joke so far as to cause irreversible damage, but rather uses Marlow's embarrassment to break through his natural shyness, thus winning his love and confirming her own. The scenes between these two are undeniably the best in the play, owing first to Marlow's exaggeratedly acute discomfort in the presence of a well-bred lady and later to Kate's impersonation of a barmaid and Marlow's self-assured playfulness with her in that guise.

Thematically the play has little to say, but there is a pervading geniality of spirit and an honesty of human relationships and human pleasures that characterize much of Goldsmith's writing and that almost constitute a thematic statement in themselves. Especially when contrasted with the tedious sentimentalism in fashion in England during much of this period, Goldsmith's plays speak tellingly of simpler truths. Goldsmith fought vigorously (and with some success) against this sentimentalism, noting sarcastically in the preface to *The Good-Natur'd Man* that "the French comedy is now become so very elevated and sentimental, that it has not only banished humor and Molière from the stage, but it has banished all spectators too."

Eschewing the poetry and elevated language of an earlier day, Goldsmith writes prose that, although entirely believable in the mouths of middle-class people, is nevertheless felicitously phrased and possesses charm and a good sense of style. The frequent use of asides seems somewhat tedious in the twentieth century, but was so common a device as to be completely unremarkable in the eighteenth. These asides remind one that, despite the move toward middle-class characters, situations, and sentiments, the eighteenth century theater remained essentially presentational in acting and scenic style and hence ultimately in writing style as well. Genuinely representational theater was still more than a half-century away.

It is unfortunate that Oliver Goldsmith's life ended so early that he had no opportunity to write further for the stage. In just two plays he sharpened his art to a degree that produced one in a handful of works, outside those of Shakespeare, that is regularly revived with unflagging success on the British stage. *She Stoops to Conquer* is a deceptively simple but compellingly good play.

She Stoops to Conquer
or
The Mistakes of a Night

Characters
Sir Charles Marlow
Young Marlow, his son
Hardcastle
Hastings
Tony Lumpkin
Diggory
Stingo, landlord of the inn
Mrs. Hardcastle
Miss Kate Hardcastle
Miss Constance Neville
Pimple, maid to Kate Hardcastle
Servants and country fellows

Act 1

A chamber in an old-fashioned house. Enter
MRS. HARDCASTLE *and* MR. HARDCAS-
TLE.

MRS. HARDCASTLE. I vow, Mr. Hardcastle, you're very particular. Is there a
creature in the whole country, but
ourselves, that does not take a trip to
town now and then, to rub off the
rust a little? There's the two Miss
Hoggs, and our neighbour, Mrs.
Grigsby, go to take a month's polish-
ing every winter.

HARDCASTLE. Ay, and bring back vanity
and affectation to last them the whole
year. I wonder why London cannot
keep its own fools at home. In my
time, the follies of the town crept
slowly among us, but now they travel
faster than a stage-coach. Its fopperies come down, not only as inside
passengers, but in the very basket.[1]

MRS. HARDCASTLE. Ay, *your* times were

fine times, indeed; you have been
telling us of *them* for many a long
year. Here we live in an old rumbling
mansion, that looks for all the world
like an inn, but that we never see
company. Our best visitors are old
Mrs. Oddfish, the curate's wife, and
little Cripplegate, the lame dancing-
master: And all our entertainment
your old stories of Prince Eugene
and the Duke of Marlborough. I hate
such old-fashioned trumpery.

HARDCASTLE. And I love it. I love every
thing that's old: old friends, old
times, old manners, old books, old
wine; and, I believe, Dorothy [*Taking
her hand.*], you'll own I have been
pretty fond of an old wife.

MRS. HARDCASTLE. Lord, Mr. Hardcastle, you're for ever at your Dorothy's
and your old wife's. You may be a
Darby, but I'll be no Joan, I promise
you. I'm not so old as you'd make
me, by more than one good year.
Add twenty to twenty, and make
money of that.

HARDCASTLE. Let me see; twenty added
to twenty, makes just fifty and seven.

MRS. HARDCASTLE. It's false, Mr. Hardcastle: I was but twenty when I was
brought to bed of Tony, that I had by
Mr. Lumpkin, my first husband; and
he's not come to years of discretion
yet.

HARDCASTLE. Nor ever will, I dare answer for him. Ay, you have taught
him finely!

MRS. HARDCASTLE. No matter, Tony
Lumpkin has a good fortune. My son
is not to live by his learning. I don't
think a boy wants much learning to
spend fifteen hundred a year.

HARDCASTLE. Learning, quotha! A mere composition of tricks and mischief.

MRS. HARDCASTLE. Humour, my dear: nothing but humour. Come, Mr. Hardcastle, you must allow the boy a little humour.

HARDCASTLE. I'd sooner allow him an horse-pond. If burning the footmen's shoes, frighting the maids, and worrying the kittens, be humour, he has it. It was but yesterday he fastened my wig to the back of my chair, and when I went to make a bow, I popped my bald head in Mrs. Frizzle's face.

MRS. HARDCASTLE. And am I to blame? The poor boy was always too sickly to do any good. A school would be his death. When he comes to be a little stronger, who knows what a year or two's Latin may do for him?

HARDCASTLE. Latin for him! A cat and fiddle. No, no, the ale-house and the stable are the only schools he'll ever go to.

MRS. HARDCASTLE. Well, we must not snub the poor boy now, for I believe we shan't have him long among us. Any body that looks in his face may see he's consumptive.

HARDCASTLE. Ay, if growing too fat be one of the symptoms.

MRS. HARDCASTLE. He coughs sometimes.

HARDCASTLE. Yes, when his liquor goes the wrong way.

MRS. HARDCASTLE. I'm actually afraid of his lungs.

HARDCASTLE. And truly, so am I; for he sometimes whoops like a speaking trumpet—[TONY *hallooing behind the scenes.*]—O, there he goes—A very consumptive figure, truly. [*Enter* TONY, *crossing the stage.*]

MRS. HARDCASTLE. Tony, where are you going, my charmer? Won't you give papa and I a little of your company, lovee?

TONY. I'm in haste, mother, I cannot stay.

MRS. HARDCASTLE. You shan't venture out this raw evening, my dear: You look most shockingly.

TONY. I can't stay, I tell you. *The Three Pigeons* expects me down every moment. There's some fun going forward.

HARDCASTLE. Ay; the ale-house, the old place: I thought so.

MRS. HARDCASTLE. A low, paltry set of fellows.

TONY. Not so low neither. There's Dick Muggins the exciseman, Jack Slang the horse doctor, Little Aminadab that grinds the music box, and Tom Twist that spins the pewter platter.

MRS. HARDCASTLE. Pray, my dear, disappoint them for one night at least.

TONY. As for disappointing *them,* I should not so much mind; but I can't abide to disappoint *myself.*

MRS. HARDCASTLE. [*Detaining him.*] You shan't go.

TONY. I will, I tell you.

MRS. HARDCASTLE. I say you shan't.

TONY. We'll see which is strongest, you or I. [*Exit, hauling her out.*]

HARDCASTLE. [*Alone.*] Ay, there goes a pair that only spoil each other. But is not the whole age in a combination to drive sense and discretion out of doors? There's my pretty darling, Kate; the fashions of the times have almost infected her too. By living a year or two in town, she is as fond of gauze, and French frippery, as the best of them. [*Enter* MISS HARDCASTLE.]

HARDCASTLE. Blessings on my pretty innocence! Dressed out as usual, my Kate. Goodness! What a quantity of superfluous silk hast thou got about thee, girl! I could never teach the fools of this age, that the indigent world could be clothed out of the trimmings of the vain.

MISS HARDCASTLE. You know our agreement, Sir. You allow me the morning to receive and pay visits, and to dress in my own manner; and in the evening, I put on my housewife's dress to please you.

HARDCASTLE. Well, remember, I insist on the terms of our agreement; and, by the bye, I believe I shall have occasion to try your obedience this very evening.

MISS HARDCASTLE. I protest, Sir, I don't comprehend your meaning.

HARDCASTLE. Then, to be plain with you, Kate, I expect the young gentleman I have chosen to be your husband from town this very day. I have his father's letter, in which he informs me his son is set out, and that he intends to follow himself shortly after.

MISS HARDCASTLE. Indeed! I wish I had known something of this before. Bless me, how shall I behave? It's a thousand to one I shan't like him; our meeting will be so formal, and so like a thing of business, that I shall find no room for friendship or esteem.

HARDCASTLE. Depend upon it, child, I'll never control your choice; but Mr. Marlow, whom I have pitched upon, is the son of my old friend, Sir Charles Marlow, of whom you have heard me talk so often. The young gentleman has been bred a scholar, and is designed for an employment in the service of his country. I am told he's a man of an excellent understanding.

MISS HARDCASTLE. Is he?

HARDCASTLE. Very generous.

MISS HARDCASTLE. I believe I shall like him.

HARDCASTLE. Young and brave.

MISS HARDCASTLE. I'm sure I shall like him.

HARDCASTLE. And very handsome.

MISS HARDCASTLE. My dear papa, say no more [*Kissing his hand.*], he's mine, I'll have him.

HARDCASTLE. And to crown all, Kate, he's one of the most bashful and reserved young fellows in all the world.

MISS HARDCASTLE. Eh! you have frozen me to death again. That word *reserved* has undone all the rest of his accomplishments. A reserved lover, it is said, always makes a suspicious husband.

HARDCASTLE. On the contrary, modesty seldom resides in a breast that is not enriched with nobler virtues. It was the very feature in his character that first struck me.

MISS HARDCASTLE. He must have more striking features to catch me, I promise you. However, if he be so young, so handsome, and so every thing, as you mention, I believe he'll do still. I think I'll have him.

HARDCASTLE. Ay, Kate, but there is still an obstacle. It's more than an even wager, he may not have *you*.

MISS HARDCASTLE. My dear Papa, why will you mortify one so?—Well, if he refuses, instead of breaking my heart at his indifference, I'll only break my glass for its flattery, set my cap to some newer fashion, and look out for some less difficult admirer.

HARDCASTLE. Bravely resolved! In the mean time I'll go prepare the servants for his reception; as we seldom see company, they want as much training as a company of recruits, the first day's muster.[*Exit.*]

MISS HARDCASTLE. [*Alone.*] Lud, this news of Papa's, puts me all in a flutter. Young, handsome; these he put last; but I put them foremost. Sensible, good-natured; I like all that. But then reserved, and sheepish, that's much against him. Yet, can't he be cured of his timidity, by being taught to be proud of his wife? Yes, and can't I—But I vow I'm disposing of the husband, before I have secured the lover. [*Enter* MISS NEVILLE.]

MISS HARDCASTLE. I'm glad you're come, Neville, my dear. Tell me, Constance, how do I look this evening? Is there any thing whimsical about me? Is it one of my well looking days, child? Am I in face to day?

MISS NEVILLE. Perfectly, my dear. Yet now I look again—bless me!—sure no accident has happened among the canary birds or the gold-fishes. Has your brother or the cat been meddling? Or has the last novel been too moving?

MISS HARDCASTLE. No; nothing of all this. I have been threatened—I can scarce get it out—I have been threatened with a lover.

MISS NEVILLE. And his name—

MISS HARDCASTLE. Is Marlow.

MISS NEVILLE. Indeed!

MISS HARDCASTLE. The son of Sir Charles Marlow.

MISS NEVILLE. As I live, the most intimate friend of Mr. Hastings, *my* admirer. They are never asunder. I believe you must have seen him when we lived in town.

MISS HARDCASTLE. Never.

MISS NEVILLE. He's a very singular character, I assure you. Among women of reputation and virtue, he is the modestest man alive; but his acquaintance give him a very different character among creatures of another stamp: you understand me.

MISS HARDCASTLE. An odd character, indeed. I shall never be able to manage him. What shall I do? Pshaw, think no more of him, but trust to occurrences for success. But how goes on your own affair, my dear? has my mother been courting you for my brother Tony, as usual?

MISS NEVILLE. I have just come from one of our agreeable *tête-à-têtes*. She has been saying a hundred tender things, and setting off her pretty monster as the very pink of perfection.

MISS HARDCASTLE. And her partiality is such, that she actually thinks him so. A fortune like yours is no small temptation. Besides, as she has the sole management of it, I'm not surprised to see her unwilling to let it go out of the family.

MISS NEVILLE. A fortune like mine, which chiefly consists in jewels, is no such mighty temptation. But at any rate, if my dear Hastings be but constant, I make no doubt to be too hard for her at last. However, I let her suppose that I am in love with her son, and she never once dreams that my affections are fixed upon another.

MISS HARDCASTLE. My good brother holds out stoutly. I could almost love him for hating you so.

MISS NEVILLE. It is a good natured creature at bottom, and I'm sure would wish to see me married to any body but himself. But my aunt's bell rings for our afternoon's walk round the improvements. *Allons.* Courage is necessary, as our affairs are critical.

MISS HARDCASTLE. Would it were bed time and all were well.[2] [*Exeunt.*]

An ale-house room. Several shabby fellows, with punch and tobacco. TONY *at the head of the table, a little higher than the rest: A mallet in his hand.*

OMNES. Hurrea, hurrea, hurrea, bravo!

FIRST FELLOW. Now, gentlemen, silence for a song. The 'Squire is going to knock himself down for a song.

OMNES. Ay, a song, a song.

TONY. Then I'll sing you, gentlemen, a song I made upon this ale-house, *The Three Pigeons.*

SONG

Let school-masters puzzle their brain,
  With grammar, and nonsense, and learning;
Good liquor, I stoutly maintain,
  Gives genus a better discerning.
Let them brag of their Heathenish Gods,
  Their Lethes, their Styxes, and Stygians;
Their Quis, and their Quæs, and their Quods,
  They're all but a parcel of Pigeons.
    Toroddle, toroddle, toroll!

When Methodist preachers come down,
  A preaching that drinking is sinful,
I'll wager the rascals a crown,
  They always preach best with a skinful.
But when you come down with your pence,
  For a slice of their scurvy religion,
I'll leave it to all men of sense,
  But you, my good friend, are the pigeon.
    Toroddle, toroddle, toroll!

Then come, put the jorum[3] about,
  And let us be merry and clever,
Our hearts and our liquors are stout,
  Here's the Three Jolly Pigeons for ever.
Let some cry up woodcock or hare,
  Your bustards, your ducks, and your widgeons;
But of all the birds in the air,
  Here's a health to the Three Jolly Pigeons.
    Toroddle, toroddle, toroll!

OMNES. Bravo, bravo.

FIRST FELLOW. The 'Squire has got spunk in him.

SECOND FELLOW. I loves to hear him sing, bekeays he never gives us nothing that's *low.*

THIRD FELLOW. O damn any thing that's *low,* I cannot bear it.

FOURTH FELLOW. The genteel thing is the genteel thing at any time. If so be that a gentleman bees in a concatenation accordingly.

THIRD FELLOW. I like the maxum of it,

Master Muggins. What, tho' I am obligated to dance a bear, a man may be a gentleman for all that. May this be my poison if my bear ever dances but to the very genteelest of tunes. *Water Parted,* or the minuet in *Ariadne.*

SECOND FELLOW. What a pity it is the 'Squire is not come to his own. It would be well for all the publicans within ten miles round of him.

TONY. Ecod, and so it would, Master Slang. I'd then shew what it was to keep choice of company.

SECOND FELLOW. O, he takes after his own father for that. To be sure old 'Squire Lumpkin was the finest gentleman I ever set my eyes on. For winding the straight horn, or beating a thicket for a hare, or a wench, he never had his fellow. It was a saying in the place, that he kept the best horses, dogs and girls in the whole country.

TONY. Ecod, and when I'm of age I'll be no bastard, I promise you. I have been thinking of Bett Bouncer and the miller's grey mare to begin with. But come, my boys, drink about and be merry, for you pay no reckoning. Well, Stingo, what's the matter? [*Enter* LANDLORD.]

LANDLORD. There be two gentlemen in a post-chaise at the door. They have lost their way upo' the forest; and they are talking something about Mr. Hardcastle.

TONY. As sure as can be, one of them must be the gentleman that's coming down to court my sister. Do they seem to be Londoners?

LANDLORD. I believe they may. They look woundily like Frenchmen.

TONY. Then desire them to step this way, and I'll set them right in a twinkling. [*Exit* LANDLORD.] Gentlemen, as they mayn't be good enough company for you, step down for a moment, and I'll be with you in the squeezing of a lemon. [*Exeunt* MOB.]

TONY. [*Alone.*] Father-in-law has been calling me whelp, and hound, this half-year. Now if I pleased, I could be so revenged upon the old grumbletonian. But then I'm afraid— afraid of what? I shall soon be worth fifteen hundred a year, and let him frighten me out of that if he can. [*Enter* LANDLORD, *conducting* MARLOW *and* HASTINGS.]

MARLOW. What a tedious, uncomfortable day have we had of it! We were told it was but forty miles across the country, and we have come above threescore.

HASTINGS. And all, Marlow, from that unaccountable reserve of yours, that would not let us enquire more frequently on the way.

MARLOW. I own, Hastings, I am unwilling to lay myself under an obligation to every one I meet; and often, stand the chance of an unmannerly answer.

HASTINGS. At present, however, we are not likely to receive any answer.

TONY. No offence, gentlemen. But I'm told you have been enquiring for one Mr. Hardcastle, in these parts. Do you know what part of the country you are in?

HASTINGS. Not in the least, Sir, but should thank you for information.

TONY. Nor the way you came?

HASTINGS. No, Sir; but if you can inform us—

TONY. Why, gentlemen, if you know neither the road you are going, nor where you are, nor the road you came, the first thing I have to inform you is, that—You have lost your way.

MARLOW. We wanted no ghost to tell us that.[4]

TONY. Pray, gentlemen, may I be so bold as to ask the place from whence you came?

MARLOW. That's not necessary towards directing us where we are to go.

TONY. No offence; but question for question is all fair, you know. Pray, gentlemen, is not this same Hardcastle a cross-grain'd, old-fashion'd, whimsical fellow, with an ugly face, a daughter, and a pretty son?

HASTINGS. We have not seen the gentleman, but he has the family you mention.

TONY. The daughter, a tall trapesing, trolloping, talkative maypole—The son, a pretty, well-bred, agreeable youth, that every body is fond of.

MARLOW. Our information differs in

this. The daughter is said to be well-bred and beautiful; the son, an awkward booby, reared up, and spoiled at his mother's apron-string.

TONY. He-he-hem—Then, gentlemen, all I have to tell you is that you won't reach Mr. Hardcastle's house this night, I believe.

HASTINGS. Unfortunate!

TONY. It's a damn'd long, dark, boggy, dirty, dangerous way. Stingo, tell the gentlemen the way to Mr. Hardcastle's [*Winking upon the* LANDLORD.]; Mr. Hardcastle's, of Quagmire Marsh, you understand me.

LANDLORD. Master Hardcastle's! Lack-a-daisy, my masters, you're come a deadly deal wrong! When you came to the bottom of the hill, you should have cross'd down Squash Lane.

MARLOW. Cross down Squash Lane!

LANDLORD. Then you were to keep straight forward, 'till you came to four roads.

MARLOW. Come to where four roads meet!

TONY. Ay; but you must be sure to take only one of them.

MARLOW. O, Sir, you're facetious.

TONY. Then keeping to the right, you are to go side-ways till you come upon Crack-skull Common: there you must look sharp for the track of the wheel, and go forward, 'till you come to farmer Murrain's barn. Coming to the farmer's barn, you are to turn to the right, and then to the left, and then to the right about again, till you find out the old mill—

MARLOW. Zounds, man! we could as soon find out the longitude.[5]

HASTINGS. What's to be done, Marlow?

MARLOW. This house promises but a poor reception; though perhaps the Landlord can accommodate us.

LANDLORD. Alack, master, we have but one spare bed in the whole house.

TONY. And to my knowledge, that's taken up by three lodgers already. [*After a pause, in which the rest seem disconcerted.*] I have hit it. Don't you think, Stingo, our landlady could accommodate the gentlemen by the fire-side, with—three chairs and a bolster?

HASTINGS. I hate sleeping by the fireside.

MARLOW. And I detest your three chairs and a bolster.

TONY. You do, do you?—then let me see—what—if you go on a mile further to the Buck's Head; the old Buck's Head on the hill, one of the best inns in the whole country?

HASTINGS. O ho! so we have escaped an adventure for this night, however.

LANDLORD. [*Apart to* TONY.] Sure, you be'nt sending them to your father's as an inn, be you?

TONY. Mum, you fool you. Let *them* find that out. [*To them.*] You have only to keep on straight forward, till you come to a large old house by the road side. You'll see a pair of large horns over the door. That's the sign. Drive up the yard, and call stoutly about you.

HASTINGS. Sir, we are obliged to you. The servants can't miss the way?

TONY. No no: But I tell you though, the landlord is rich, and going to leave off business; so he wants to be thought a Gentleman, saving your presence, he! he! he! He'll be for giving you his company, and, ecod, if you mind him, he'll persuade you that his mother was an alderman, and his aunt a justice of peace.

LANDLORD. A troublesome old blade, to be sure; but a keeps as good wines and beds as any in the whole country.

MARLOW. Well, if he supplies us with these, we shall want no further connexion. We are to turn to the right, did you say?

TONY. No, no; straight forward. I'll just step myself, and shew you a piece of the way. [*To the* LANDLORD.] Mum.

LANDLORD. Ah, bless your heart, for a sweet, pleasant—damn'd mischievous son of a whore. [*Exeunt.*]

Act 2

An old-fashioned house. Enter HARDCASTLE, *followed by three or four awkward* SERVANTS.

HARDCASTLE. Well, I hope you're perfect in the table exercise I have been teaching you these three days. You all know your posts and your places, and can shew that you have been used to good company, without ever stirring from home.

OMNES. Ay, ay.

HARDCASTLE. When company comes, you are not to pop out and stare, and then run in again, like frighted rabbits in a warren.

OMNES. No, no.

HARDCASTLE. You, Diggory, whom I have taken from the barn, are to make a shew at the side-table; and you, Roger, whom I have advanced from the plough, are to place yourself behind *my* chair. But you're not to stand so, with your hands in your pockets. Take your hands from your pockets, Roger; and from your head, you blockhead you. See how Diggory carries his hands. They're a little too stiff indeed, but that's no great matter.

DIGGORY. Ay, mind how I hold them. I learned to hold my hands this way, when I was upon drill for the militia. And so being upon drill—

HARDCASTLE. You must not be so talkative, Diggory. You must be all attention to the guests. You must hear us talk, and not think of talking; you must see us drink, and not think of drinking; you must see us eat, and not think of eating.

DIGGORY. By the laws, your worship, that's perfectly unpossible. Whenever Diggory sees yeating going forward, ecod, he's always wishing for a mouthful himself.

HARDCASTLE. Blockhead! Is not a belly-full in the kitchen as good as a belly-full in the parlour? Stay your stomach with that reflection.

DIGGORY. Ecod, I thank your worship, I'll make a shift to stay my stomach with a slice of cold beef in the pantry.

HARDCASTLE. Diggory, you are too talkative. Then, if I happen to say a good thing, or tell a good story at table, you must not all burst out a-laughing, as if you made part of the company.

DIGGORY. Then, ecod, your worship must not tell the story of Ould Grouse in the gun-room: I can't help laughing at that— he! he! he!—for the soul of me. We have laughed at that these twenty years—ha! ha! ha

HARDCASTLE. Ha! ha! ha! The story is a good one. Well, honest Diggory, you may laugh at that—but still remember to be attentive. Suppose one of the company should call for a glass of wine, how will you behave? A glass of wine, Sir, if you please. [*To* DIGGORY.]—Eh, why don't you move?

DIGGORY. Ecod, your worship, I never have courage till I see the eatables and drinkables brought upo' the table, and then I'm as bold as a lion.

HARDCASTLE. What, will no body move?

FIRST SERVANT. I'm not to leave this place.

SECOND SERVANT. I'm sure it's no place of mine.

THIRD SERVANT. Not mine, for sartain.

DIGGORY. Wauns,[6] and I'm sure it canna be mine.

HARDCASTLE. You numbskulls! and so while, like your betters, you are quarrelling for places, the guests must be starved. O you dunces! I find I must begin all over again.—But don't I hear a coach drive into the yard? To your posts, you blockheads. I'll go in the mean time and give my old friend's son a hearty reception at the gate. [*Exit* HARDCASTLE.]

DIGGORY. By the elevens, my place is gone quite out of my head.

ROGER. I know that my place is to be every where.

FIRST SERVANT. Where the devil is mine?

SECOND SERVANT. My place is to be no where at all; and so I'ze go about my business. [*Exeunt* SERVANTS, *running about as if frighted, different ways. Enter* SERVANT *with candles, shewing in* MARLOW *and* HASTINGS.]

SERVANT. Welcome, gentlemen, very welcome. This way.

HASTINGS. After the disappointments of the day, welcome once more, Charles, to the comforts of a clean room and a good fire. Upon my word, a very well-looking house; antique, but creditable.

MARLOW. The usual fate of a large mansion. Having first ruined the master by good housekeeping, it at last comes to levy contributions as an inn.

HASTINGS. As you say, we passengers are to be taxed to pay all these fineries. I have often seen a good sideboard, or a marble chimney-piece, tho' not actually put in the bill, enflame a reckoning confoundedly.

MARLOW. Travellers, George, must pay in all places. The only difference is, that in good inns, you pay dearly for luxuries; in bad inns, you are fleeced and starved.

HASTINGS. You have lived pretty much among them. In truth, I have been often surprised, that you who have seen so much of the world, with your natural good sense, and your many opportunities, could never yet acquire a requisite share of assurance.

MARLOW. The Englishman's malady. But tell me, George, where could I have learned that assurance you talk of? My life has been chiefly spent in a college, or an inn, in seclusion from that lovely part of the creation that chiefly teach men confidence. I don't know that I was ever familiarly acquainted with a single modest woman—except my mother—But among females of another class, you know—

HASTINGS. Ay, among them you are impudent enough of all conscience.

MARLOW. They are of *us*, you know.

HASTINGS. But in the company of women of reputation I never saw such an idiot, such a trembler; you look for all the world as if you wanted an opportunity of stealing out of the room.

MARLOW. Why, man, that's because I *do* want to steal out of the room. Faith, I have often formed a resolution to break the ice, and rattle away at any rate. But I don't know how, a single glance from a pair of fine eyes has totally overset my resolution. An impudent fellow may counterfeit modesty, but I'll be hanged if a modest man can ever counterfeit impudence.

HASTINGS. If you could but say half the fine things to them that I have heard you lavish upon the barmaid of an inn, or even a college bed maker—

MARLOW. Why, George, I can't say fine things to them. They freeze, they petrify me. They may talk of a comet, or a burning mountain, or some such bagatelle. But to me, a modest woman, dressed out in all her finery, is the most tremendous object of the whole creation.

HASTINGS. Ha! ha! ha! At this rate, man, how can you ever expect to marry!

MARLOW. Never, unless, as among kings and princes, my bride were to be courted by proxy. If, indeed, like an Eastern bridegroom, one were to be introduced to a wife he never saw before, it might be endured. But to go through all the terrors of a formal courtship, together with the episode of aunts, grandmothers and cousins, and at last to blurt out the broad staring question of, madam, will you marry me? No, no, that's a strain much above me, I assure you.

HASTINGS. I pity you. But how do you intend behaving to the lady you are come down to visit at the request of your father?

MARLOW. As I behave to all other ladies. Bow very low. Answer yes, or no, to all her demands—But for the rest, I don't think I shall venture to look in her face, till I see my father's again.

HASTINGS. I'm surprised that one who is so warm a friend can be so cool a lover.

MARLOW. To be explicit, my dear Hastings, my chief inducement down was to be instrumental in forwarding your happiness, not my own. Miss Neville loves you, the family don't know you, as my friend you are sure of a reception, and let honour do the rest.

HASTINGS. My dear Marlow! But I'll suppress the emotion. Were I a wretch, meanly seeking to carry off a fortune, you should be the last man in the world I would apply to for assistance. But Miss Neville's person is all I ask, and that is mine, both from her deceased father's consent, and her own inclination.

MARLOW. Happy man! You have talents and art to captivate any woman. I'm doom'd to adore the sex, and yet to converse with the only part of it I despise. This stammer in my address, and this awkward prepossessing visage of mine, can never permit me to soar above the reach of a milliner's 'prentice, or one of the dutchesses of Drury Lane.[7] Pshaw! this fellow here to interrupt us. [*Enter* HARDCASTLE.]

HARDCASTLE. Gentlemen, once more you are heartily welcome. Which is Mr. Marlow? Sir, you're heartily welcome. It's not my way, you see, to receive my friends with my back to the fire. I like to give them a hearty reception in the old style, at my gate. I like to see their horses and trunks taken care of.

MARLOW. [*Aside.*] He has got our names from the servants already. [*To him.*] We approve your caution and hospitality, Sir. [*To* HASTINGS.] I have been thinking, George, of changing our travelling dresses in the morning. I am grown confoundedly ashamed of mine.

HARDCASTLE. I beg, Mr. Marlow, you'll use no ceremony in this house.

HASTINGS. I fancy, Charles, you're right: the first blow is half the battle. I intend opening the campaign with the white and gold.

HARDCASTLE. Mr. Marlow—Mr. Hastings—gentlemen—pray be under no constraint in this house. This is Liberty Hall, gentlemen. You may do just as you please here.

MARLOW. Yet, George, if we open the campaign too fiercely at first, we may want ammunition before it is over. I think to reserve the embroidery to secure a retreat.

HARDCASTLE. Your talking of a retreat, Mr. Marlow, puts me in mind of the Duke of Marlborough, when we went to besiege Denain. He first summoned the garrison—

MARLOW. Don't you think the *ventre dor* waistcoat will do with the plain brown?

HARDCASTLE. He first summoned the garrison, which might consist of about five thousand men—

HASTINGS. I think not: brown and yellow mix but very poorly.

HARDCASTLE. I say, gentlemen, as I was telling you, he summoned the garrison, which might consist of about five thousand men—

MARLOW. The girls like finery.

HARDCASTLE. Which might consist of about five thousand men, well appointed with stores, ammunition, and other implements of war. "Now," says the Duke of Marlborough, to George Brooks, that stood next to him—You must have heard of George Brooks; "I'll pawn my Dukedom," says he, "but I take that garrison without spilling a drop of blood." So—

MARLOW. What, my good friend, if you give us a glass of punch in the meantime; it would help us to carry on the siege with vigour.

HARDCASTLE. Punch, Sir! [*Aside.*] This is the most unaccountable kind of modesty I ever met with.

MARLOW. Yes, Sir, punch. A glass of warm punch, after our journey, will be comfortable. This is Liberty Hall, you know.

HARDCASTLE. Here's cup, Sir.

MARLOW. [*Aside*] So this fellow, in his Liberty Hall, will only let us have just what he pleases.

HARDCASTLE. [*Taking the cup.*] I hope you'll find it to your mind. I have prepared it with my own hands, and I believe you'll own the ingredients are tolerable. Will you be so good as to pledge me, Sir? Here, Mr. Marlow, here is to our better acquaintance. [*Drinks.*]

MARLOW. [*Aside.*] A very impudent fellow this! but he's a character, and I'll humour him a little. Sir, my service to you. [*Drinks.*]

HASTINGS. [*Aside.*] I see this fellow wants to give us his company, and forgets that he's an innkeeper, before he has learned to be a gentleman.

MARLOW. From the excellence of your cup, my old friend, I suppose you have a good deal of business in this part of the country. Warm work, now and then, at elections, I suppose?

HARDCASTLE. No, Sir, I have long given that work over. Since our betters have hit upon the expedient of electing each other, there's no business *for us that sell ale.*[8]

HASTINGS. So, then you have no turn for politics, I find.

HARDCASTLE. Not in the least. There was a time, indeed, I fretted myself about the mistakes of government, like other people; but finding myself every day grow more angry, and the government growing no better, I left it to mend itself. Since that, I no more trouble my head about Heyder Ally, or Ally Cawn,[9] than about Ally Croaker.[10] Sir, my service to you.

HASTINGS. So that with eating above stairs, and drinking below, with receiving your friends within, and amusing them without, you lead a good, pleasant, bustling life of it.

HARDCASTLE. I do stir about a great deal, that's certain. Half the differences of the parish are adjusted in this very parlour.

MARLOW. [*After drinking.*] And you have an argument in your cup, old gentleman, better than any in Westminster Hall.

HARDCASTLE. Ay, young gentleman, that, and a little philosophy.

MARLOW. [*Aside.*] Well, this is the first time I ever heard of an innkeeper's philosophy.

HASTINGS. So then, like an experienced general, you attack them on every quarter. If you find their reason manageable, you attack it with your philosophy; if you find they have no reason, you attack them with this. Here's your health, my philosopher. [*Drinks.*]

HARDCASTLE. Good, very good, thank you; ha! ha! Your Generalship puts me mind of Prince Eugene, when he fought the Turks at the battle of Belgrade. You shall hear—

MARLOW. Instead of the battle of Belgrade, I believe it's almost time to talk about supper. What has your philosophy got in the house for supper?

HARDCASTLE. For supper, Sir! [*Aside.*] Was ever such a request to a man in his own house!

MARLOW. Yes, Sir, supper, Sir; I begin to feel an appetite. I shall make devilish work tonight in the larder, I promise you.

HARDCASTLE. [*Aside.*] Such a brazen dog sure never my eyes beheld. [*To him.*] Why really, Sir, as for supper I can't well tell. My Dorothy, and the cook maid, settle these things between them. I leave these kind of things entirely to them.

MARLOW. You do, do you?

HARDCASTLE. Entirely. By-the-bye, I believe they are in actual consultation upon what's for supper this moment in the kitchen.

MARLOW. Then I beg they'll admit *me* as one of their privy council. It's a way I have got. When I travel, I always choose to regulate my own supper. Let the cook be called. No offence, I hope, Sir.

HARDCASTLE. O, no, Sir, none in the least; yet I don't know how: our Bridget, the cook maid, is not very communicative upon these occasions. Should we send for her, she might scold us all out of the house.

HASTINGS. Let's see your list of the larder then. I ask it as a favour. I always match my appetite to my bill of fare.

MARLOW. [*To* HARDCASTLE, *who looks at them with surprise.*] Sir, he's very right, and it's my way too.

HARDCASTLE. Sir, you have a right to command here. Here, Roger, bring us the bill of fare for tonight's supper. I believe it's drawn out. Your manner, Mr. Hastings, puts me in mind of my uncle, Colonel Wallop. It was a saying of his, that no man was sure of his supper till he had eaten it.

HASTINGS. [*Aside.*] All upon the high ropes! His uncle a Colonel! We shall soon hear of his mother being a justice of peace. But let's hear the bill of fare.

MARLOW. [*Perusing.*] What's here? For the first course; for the second course; for the dessert. The devil, Sir, do you think we have brought down the whole Joiners Company, or the Corporation of Bedford, to eat up such a supper? Two or three little things, clean and comfortable, will do.

HASTINGS. But, let's hear it.

MARLOW. [*Reading.*] For the first course, at the top, a pig, and prune sauce.

HASTINGS. Damn your pig, I say.

MARLOW. And damn your prune sauce, say I.

HARDCASTLE. And yet, gentlemen, to men that are hungry, pig, with prune sauce, is very good eating.

MARLOW. At the bottom, a calve's tongue and brains.

HASTINGS. Let your brains be knock'd out, my good Sir; I don't like them.

MARLOW. Or you may clap them on a plate by themselves. I do.

HARDCASTLE. [*Aside.*] Their impudence confounds me. [*To them.*] Gentlemen, you are my guests; make what alterations you please. Is there any thing else you wish to retrench or alter, gentlemen?

MARLOW. Item: A pork pie, a boiled rabbit and sausages, a florentine, a shaking pudding, and a dish of tiff-taff-taffety cream!

HASTINGS. Confound your made dishes, I shall be as much at a loss in this house as at a green and yellow dinner at the French Ambassador's table. I'm for plain eating.

HARDCASTLE. I'm sorry, gentlemen, that I have nothing you like, but if there be any thing you have a particular fancy to—

MARLOW. Why, really, Sir, your bill of fare is so exquisite, that any one part of it is full as good as another. Send us what you please. So much for supper. And now to see that our beds are air'd, and properly taken care of.

HARDCASTLE. I entreat you'll leave all that to me. You shall not stir a step.

MARLOW. Leave that to you! I protest, Sir, you must excuse me, I always look to these things myself.

HARDCASTLE. I must insist, Sir, you'll make yourself easy on that head.

MARLOW. You see I'm resolved on it. [*Aside.*] A very troublesome fellow this, as ever I met with.

HARDCASTLE. Well, Sir, I'm resolved at least to attend you. [*Aside.*] This may be modern modesty, but I never saw anything look so like old-fashioned impudence. [*Exeunt* MARLOW *and* HARDCASTLE.]

HASTINGS. [*Alone.*] So I find this fellow's civilities begin to grow troublesome. But who can be angry at those assiduities which are meant to please

him? Ha! what do I see? Miss Neville, by all that's happy! [*Enter* MISS NEVILLE.]

MISS NEVILLE. My dear Hastings! To what unexpected good fortune, to what accident am I to ascribe this happy meeting?

HASTINGS. Rather let me ask the same question, as I could never have hoped to meet my dearest Constance at an inn.

MISS NEVILLE. An inn! sure you mistake! my aunt, my guardian, lives here. What could induce you to think this house an inn?

HASTINGS. My friend Mr. Marlow, with whom I came down, and I, have been sent here as to an inn, I assure you. A young fellow whom we accidentally met at a house hard by directed us hither.

MISS NEVILLE. Certainly it must be one of my hopeful cousin's tricks, of whom you have heard me talk so often, ha! ha! ha! ha!

HASTINGS. He whom your aunt intends for you? He of whom I have such just apprehensions?

MISS NEVILLE. You have nothing to fear from him, I assure you. You'd adore him if you knew how heartily he despises me. My aunt knows it too, and has undertaken to court me for him, and actually begins to think she has made a conquest.

HASTINGS. Thou dear dissembler! You must know, my Constance, I have just seized this happy opportunity of my friend's visit here to get admittance into the family. The horses that carried us down are now fatigued with their journey, but they'll soon be refreshed; and then, if my dearest girl will trust in her faithful Hastings, we shall soon be landed in France, where even among slaves the laws of marriage are respected.

MISS NEVILLE. I have often told you, that though ready to obey you, I yet should leave my little fortune behind with reluctance. The greatest part of it was left me by my uncle, the India Director, and chiefly consists in jewels. I have been for some time persuading my aunt to let me wear them. I fancy I'm very near succeeding. The instant they are put into my possession you shall find me ready to make them and myself yours.

HASTINGS. Perish the baubles! Your person is all I desire. In the meantime, my friend Marlow must not be let into his mistake. I know the strange reserve of his temper is such, that if abruptly informed of it, he would instantly quit the house before our plan was ripe for execution.

MISS NEVILLE. But how shall we keep him in the deception? Miss Hardcastle is just returned from walking; what if we still continue to deceive him?—This, this way— [*They confer. Enter* MARLOW]

MARLOW. The assiduities of these good people tease me beyond bearing. My host seems to think it ill manners to leave me alone, and so he claps not only himself but his old-fashioned wife on my back. They talk of coming to sup with us too; and then, I suppose, we are to run the gauntlet thro' all the rest of the family.—What have we got here!—

HASTINGS. My dear Charles! Let me congratulate you!—The most fortunate accident!—Who do you think is just alighted?

MARLOW. Cannot guess.

HASTINGS. Our mistresses, boy, Miss Hardcastle and Miss Neville. Give me leave to introduce Miss Constance Neville to your acquaintance. Happening to dine in the neighbourhood, they called, on their return, to take fresh horses, here. Miss Hardcastle has just stepped into the next room, and will be back in an instant. Wasn't it lucky? eh!

MARLOW. [*Aside.*] I have just been mortified enough of all conscience, and here comes something to complete my embarrassment.

HASTINGS. Well! but wasn't it the most fortunate thing in the world?

MARLOW. Oh! yes. Very fortunate—a most joyful encounter—But our dresses, George, you know, are in disorder—What if we should postpone the happiness 'till tomorrow?—Tomorrow at her own house—It will be every bit as convenient—And rather more respectful—Tomor-

row let it be. [*Offering to go.*]

MISS NEVILLE. By no means, Sir. Your ceremony will displease her. The disorder of your dress will shew the ardour of your impatience. Besides, she knows you are in the house, and will permit you to see her.

MARLOW. O! the devil! how shall I support it? Hem! hem! Hastings, you must not go. You are to assist me, you know. I shall be confoundedly ridiculous. Yet, hang it! I'll take courage. Hem!

HASTINGS. Pshaw, man! it's but the first plunge, and all's over. She's but a woman, you know.

MARLOW. And of all women, she that I dread most to encounter! [*Enter* MISS HARDCASTLE *as returned from walking, a Bonnet,*[11] &c.]

HASTINGS. [*Introducing him.*] Miss Hardcastle, Mr. Marlow; I'm proud of bringing two persons of such merit together, that only want to know, to esteem each other.

MISS HARDCASTLE. [*Aside.*] Now, for meeting my modest gentleman with a demure face, and quite in his own manner. [*After a pause, in which he appears very uneasy and disconcerted.*] I'm glad of your safe arrival, Sir— I'm told you had some accidents by the way.

MARLOW. Only a few, madam. Yes, we had some. Yes, Madam, a good many accidents, but should be sorry— Madam—or rather glad of any accidents—that are so agreeably concluded. Hem!

HASTINGS. [*To him.*] You never spoke better in your whole life. Keep it up, and I'll insure you the victory.

MISS HARDCASTLE. I'm afraid you flatter, Sir. You that have seen so much of the finest company can find little entertainment in an obscure corner of the country.

MARLOW. [*Gathering courage.*] I have lived, indeed, in the world, Madam; but I have kept very little company. I have been but an observer upon life, Madam, while others were enjoying it.

MISS NEVILLE. But that, I am told, is the way to enjoy it at last.

HASTINGS. [*To him.*] Cicero never spoke

better. Once more, and you are confirm'd in assurance for ever.

MARLOW. [*To him.*] Hem! Stand by me
then, and when I'm down, throw in a
word or two to set me up again.

MISS HARDCASTLE. An observer, like
you, upon life, were, I fear, dis-
agreeably employed, since you must
have had much more to censure than
to approve.

MARLOW. Pardon me, Madam. I was
always willing to be amused. The
folly of most people is rather an object of mirth than uneasiness.

HASTINGS. [*To him.*] Bravo, bravo. Never
spoke so well in your whole life. Well!
Miss Hardcastle, I see that you and
Mr. Marlow are going to be very
good company. I believe our being
here will but embarrass the interview.

MARLOW. Not in the least, Mr. Hastings.
We like your company of all things.
[*To him.*] Zounds! George, sure you
won't go? How can you leave us?

HASTINGS. Our presence will but spoil
conversation, so we'll retire to the
next room. [*To him.*] You don't consider, man, that we are to manage a
little tête-à-tête of our own. [*Exeunt.*]

MISS HARDCASTLE. [*After a pause.*] But
you have not been wholly an observer, I presume, Sir: The ladies I
should hope have employed some
part of your addresses.

MARLOW. [*Relapsing into timidity.*] Pardon
me, Madam, 1—I—I—as yet have
studied—only—to—deserve them.

MISS HARDCASTLE. And that, some say, is
the very worst way to obtain them.

MARLOW. Perhaps so, madam. But I love
to converse only with the more grave
and sensible part of the sex.—But
I'm afraid I grow tiresome.

MISS HARDCASTLE. Not at all, Sir; there
is nothing I like so much as grave
conversation myself; I could hear it
for ever. Indeed I have often been
surprised how a man of *sentiment*
could ever admire those light, airy
pleasures, where nothing reaches the
heart.

MARLOW. It's—a disease—of the mind,
Madam. In the variety of tastes there
must be some who, wanting a relish—for—um—a—um.

MISS HARDCASTLE. I understand you,

Sir. There must be some, who, wanting a relish for refined pleasures,
pretend to despise what they are incapable of tasting.

MARLOW. My meaning, Madam, but infinitely better expressed. And I can't
help observing—a—

MISS HARDCASTLE. [*Aside.*] Who could
ever suppose this fellow impudent
upon some occasions. [*To him.*] You
were going to observe, Sir—

MARLOW. I was observing, Madam—I
protest, Madam, I forget what I was
going to observe.

MISS HARDCASTLE. [*Aside.*] I vow and so
do I. [*To him.*] You were observing,
Sir, that in this age of hypocrisy—
something about hyprocrisy, Sir.

MARLOW. Yes, Madam. In this age of
hypocrisy there are few who upon
strict enquiry do not—a—a—a—

MISS HARDCASTLE. I understand you
perfectly, sir.

MARLOW. [*Aside.*] Egad! and that's more
than I do myself.

MISS HARDCASTLE. You mean that in this
hypocritical age there are few that do
not condemn in public what they
practise in private, and think they
pay every debt to virtue when they
praise it.

MARLOW. True, Madam; those who have
most virtue in their mouths, have
least of it in their bosoms. But I'm
sure I tire you, Madam.

MISS HARDCASTLE. Not in the least, Sir;
there's something so agreeable and
spirited in your manner, such life
and force—pray, Sir go on.

MARLOW. Yes, Madam. I was saying—
that there are some occasions—when
a total want of courage, Madam, de-
stroys all the—and puts us—upon
a—a—a—

MISS HARDCASTLE. I agree with you entirely: a want of courage upon some
occasions assumes the appearance of
ignorance, and betrays us when we
most want to excel. I beg you'll proceed.

MARLOW. Yes, Madam. Morally speaking, Madam—But I see Miss Neville
expecting us in the next room. I
would not intrude for the world.

MISS HARDCASTLE. I protest, Sir, I never
was more agreeably entertained in all

my life. Pray go on.

MARLOW. Yes, Madam. I was—But she beckons us to join her. Madam, shall I do myself the honour to attend you?

MISS HARDCASTLE. Well then, I'll follow.

MARLOW. [*Aside.*] This pretty smooth dialogue has done for me. [*Exit.*]

MISS HARDCASTLE. [*Alone.*] Ha! ha! ha! Was there ever such a sober, sentimental interview? I'm certain he scarce look'd in my face the whole time. Yet the fellow, but for his unaccountable bashfulness, is pretty well too. He has good sense, but then so buried in his fears, that it fatigues one more than ignorance. If I could teach him a little confidence, it would be doing somebody that I know of a piece of service. But who is that somebody?—that, faith, is a question I can scarce answer. [*Exit. Enter* TONY *and* MISS NEVILLE, *followed by* MRS. HARDCASTLE *and* HASTINGS.]

TONY. What do you follow me for, Cousin Con? I wonder you're not ashamed to be so very engaging.

MISS CONSTANCE NEVILLE. I hope, Cousin, one may speak to one's own relations, and not be to blame.

TONY. Ay, but I know what sort of a relation you want to make me though; but it won't do. I tell you, Cousin Con, it won't do, so I beg you'll keep your distance. I want no nearer relationship. [*She follows coqueting him to the back scene.*]

MRS. HARDCASTLE. Well! I vow, Mr. Hastings, you are very entertaining. There's nothing in the world I love to talk of so much as London, and the fashions, though I was never there myself.

HASTINGS. Never there! You amaze me! From your air and manner, I concluded you had been bred all your life either at Ranelagh, St. James's, or Tower Wharf.[12]

MRS. HARDCASTLE. O! Sir, you're only pleased to say so. We country persons can have no manner at all. I'm in love with the town, and that serves to raise me above some of our neighbouring rustics; but who can have a manner, that has never seen the Pantheon, the Grotto Gardens, the Borough, and such places where the nobility chiefly resort? All I can do, is to enjoy London at second-hand. I take care to know every tête-à-tête from the *Scandalous Magazine,* and have all the fashions, as they come out, in a letter from the two Miss Rickets of Crooked-lane.[13] Pray how do you like this head,[14] Mr. Hastings?

HASTINGS. Extremely elegant and *dégagée,* upon my word, Madam. Your Friseur is a Frenchman, I suppose?

MRS. HARDCASTLE. I protest, I dressed it myself from a print in the *Ladies Memorandum Book* for the last year.

HASTINGS. Indeed. Such a head in a side-box, at the Playhouse, would draw as many gazers as my Lady May'ress at a City Ball.

MRS. HARDCASTLE. I vow, since inoculation began, there is no such thing to be seen as a plain woman,[15] one must dress a little particular or one may escape in the crowd.

HASTINGS. But that can never be your case Madam, in any dress. [*Bowing.*]

MRS. HARDCASTLE. Yet, what signifies *my* dressing when I have such a piece of antiquity by my side as Mr. Hardcastle: all I can say will never argue down a single button from his clothes. I have often wanted him to throw off his great flaxen wig, and where he was bald, to plaster it over like my Lord Pately, with powder.

HASTINGS. You are right, Madam; for, as among the ladies, there are none ugly, so among the men there are none old.

MRS. HARDCASTLE. But what do you think his answer was? Why, with his usual Gothic vivacity, he said I only wanted him to throw off his wig to convert it into a tête for my own wearing.

HASTINGS. Intolerable! At your age you may wear what you please, and it must become you.

MRS. HARDCASTLE. Pray, Mr. Hastings, what do you take to be the most fashionable age about town?

HASTINGS. Some time ago, forty was all the mode; but I'm told the ladies intend to bring up fifty for the ensuing winter.

MRS. HARDCASTLE. Seriously? Then I shall be too young for the fashion.

HASTINGS. No lady begins now to put on jewels 'till she's past forty. For instance, Miss there, in a polite circle, would be considered as a child, as a mere maker of samplers.

MRS. HARDCASTLE. And yet Mrs. Niece thinks herself as much a woman, and is as fond of jewels as the oldest of us all.

HASTINGS. Your niece, is she? And that young gentlemen,—a brother of yours, I should presume?

MRS. HARDCASTLE. My son, Sir. They are contracted to each other. Observe their little sports. They fall in and out ten times a day, as if they were man and wife already. [*To them.*] Well, Tony, child, what soft things are saying to your Cousin Constance this evening?

TONY. I have been saying no soft things; but that it's very hard to be followed about so. Ecod! I've not a place in the house now that's left to myself but the stable.

MRS. HARDCASTLE. Never mind him, Con, my dear. He's in another story behind your back.

MISS NEVILLE. There's something generous in my cousin's manner. He falls out before faces to be forgiven in private.

TONY. That's a damned confounded—crack.

MRS. HARDCASTLE. Ah! he's a sly one. Don't you think they're like each other about the mouth, Mr. Hastings? The Blenkinsop mouth to a T. They're of a size too. Back to back, my pretties, that Mr. Hastings may see you. Come Tony.

TONY. You had as good not make me, I tell you. [*Measuring.*]

MISS NEVILLE. O lud! he has almost cracked my head.

MRS. HARDCASTLE. O the monster! For shame, Tony. You a man, and behave so!

TONY. If I'm a man, let me have my fortune. Ecod! I'll not be made a fool of no longer.

MRS. HARDCASTLE. Is this, ungrateful boy, all that I'm to get for the pains I have taken in your education? I that

have rock'd you in your cradle, and fed that pretty mouth with a spoon! Did not I work that waistcoat to make you genteel? Did not I prescribe for you every day, and weep while the receipt was operating?

TONY. Ecod! you had reason to weep, for you have been dosing me ever since I was born. I have gone through every receipt in *The Complete Huswife*[16] ten times over; and you have thoughts of coursing me through *Quincy*[16] next spring. But, Ecod! I tell you, I'll not be made a fool of no longer.

MRS. HARDCASTLE. Wasn't it all for your good, viper? Wasn't it all for your good?

TONY. I wish you'd let me and my good alone then. Snubbing this way when I'm in spirits. If I'm to have any good, let it come of itself; not to keep dinging it, dinging it into one so.

MRS. HARDCASTLE. That's false; I never see you when you're in spirits. No, Tony, you then go to the ale-house or kennel. I'm never to be delighted with your agreeable, wild notes, unfeeling monster!

TONY. Ecod! Mamma, your own notes are the wildest of the two.

MRS. HARDCASTLE. Was ever the like? But I see he wants to break my heart, I see he does.

HASTINGS. Dear Madam, permit me to lecture the young gentleman a little. I'm certain I can persuade him to his duty.

MRS. HARDCASTLE. Well! I must retire. Come, Constance, my love. You see, Mr. Hastings, the wretchedness of my situation: Was ever poor woman so plagued with a dear, sweet, pretty, provoking, undutiful boy. [*Exeunt* MRS. HARDCASTLE *and* MISS NEVILLE.]

TONY. [*Singing.*] *There was a young man riding by, and fain would have his will. Rang do didlo dee.* Don't mind her. Let her cry. It's the comfort of her heart. I have seen her and sister cry over a book for an hour together, and they said, they liked the book the better the more it made them cry.

HASTINGS. Then you're no friend to the ladies, I find, my pretty young gentleman?

TONY. That's as I find 'um.

HASTINGS. Not to her of your mother's choosing, I dare answer? And yet she appears to me a pretty, well-tempered girl.

TONY. That's because you don't know her as well as I. Ecod! I know every inch about her; and there's not a more bitter, cantankerous toad in all Christendom.

HASTINGS. [*Aside.*] Pretty encouragement this for a lover!

TONY. I have seen her since the height of that. She has as many tricks as a hare in a thicket, or a colt the first day's breaking.

HASTINGS. To me she appears sensible and silent!

TONY. Ay, before company. But when she's with her playmates, she's as loud as a hog in a gate.

HASTINGS. But there is a meek modesty about her that charms me.

TONY. Yes, but curb her never so little, she kicks up, and you're flung in a ditch.

HASTINGS. Well, but you must allow her a little beauty.—Yes, you must allow her some beauty.

TONY. Bandbox! She's all a made up thing, mun. Ah! could you but see Bet Bouncer of these parts, you might then talk of beauty. Ecod, she has two eyes as black as sloes, and cheeks as broad and red as a pulpit cushion. She'd make two of she.

HASTINGS. Well, what say you to a friend that would take this bitter bargain off your hands?

TONY. Anon.

HASTINGS. Would you thank him that would take Miss Neville and leave you to happiness and your dear Betsy?

TONY. Ay; but where is there such a friend, for who would take *her*?

HASTINGS. I am he. If you but assist me, I'll engage to whip her off to France, and you shall never hear more of her.

TONY. Assist you! Ecod, I will, to the last drop of my blood. I'll clap a pair of horses to your chaise that shall trundle you off in a twinkling, and may be get you a part of her fortune beside, in jewels, that you little dream of.

HASTINGS. My dear 'Squire, this looks like a lad of spirit.

TONY. Come along then, and you shall see more of my spirit before you have done with me. [*Singing.*]

We are the boys
That fears no noise
Where the thundering cannons roar.
[*Exeunt.*]

Act 3

Enter HARDCASTLE, *alone.*

HARDCASTLE. What could my old friend Sir Charles mean by recommending his son as the modestest young man in town? To me he appears the most impudent piece of brass that ever spoke with a tongue. He has taken posession of the easy chair by the fire-side already. He took off his boots in the parlour, and desired me to see them taken care of. I'm desirous to know how his impudence affects my daughter.—She will certainly be shocked at it. [*Enter* MISS HARDCASTLE, *plainly dressed.*]

HARDCASTLE. Well, my Kate, I see you have changed your dress as I bid you; and yet, I believe, there was no great occasion.

MISS HARDCASTLE. I find such a pleasure, Sir, in obeying your commands, that I take care to observe them without ever debating their propriety.

HARDCASTLE. And yet, Kate, I sometimes give you some cause, particularly when I recommended my *modest* gentleman to you as a lover today.

MISS HARDCASTLE. You taught me to expect something extraordinary, and I find the original exceeds the description.

HARDCASTLE. I was never so surprised in my life! He has quite confounded all my faculties!

MISS HARDCASTLE. I never saw any thing like it: And a man of the world too!

HARDCASTLE. Ay, he learned it all

abroad,—what a fool was I, to think a young man could learn modesty by travelling. He might as soon learn wit at a masquerade.

MISS HARDCASTLE. It seems all natural to him.

HARDCASTLE. A good deal assisted by bad company and a French dancing-master.

MISS HARDCASTLE. Sure, you mistake, papa! a French dancing-master could never have taught him that timid look,—that awkward address,—that bashful manner—

HARDCASTLE. Whose look? whose manner? child!

MISS HARDCASTLE. Mr. Marlow's: his *mauvaise honte*,[17] his timidity struck me at the first sight.

HARDCASTLE. Then your first sight deceived you; for I think him one of the most brazen first sights that ever astonished my senses.

MISS HARDCASTLE. Sure, Sir, you rally! I never saw any one so modest.

HARDCASTLE. And can you be serious! I never saw such a bouncing, swaggering puppy since I was born. Bully Dawson was but a fool to him.

MISS HARDCASTLE. Surprising! He met me with a respectful bow, a stammering voice, and a look fixed on the ground.

HARDCASTLE. He met me with a loud voice, a lordly air, and a familiarity that made my blood freeze again.

MISS HARDCASTLE. He treated me with diffidence and respect; censured the manners of the age; admired the prudence of girls that never laughed; tired me with apologies for being tiresome; then left the room with a bow, and, "madam, I would not for the world detain you."

HARDCASTLE. He spoke to me as if he knew me all his life before. Asked twenty questions, and never waited for an answer. Interrupted my best remarks with some silly pun, and when I was in my best story of the Duke of Marlborough and Prince Eugene, he asked if I had not a good hand at making punch. Yes, Kate, he ask'd your father if he was a maker of punch!

MISS HARDCASTLE. One of us must certainly be mistaken.

HARDCASTLE. If he be what he has shewn himself, I'm determined he shall never have my consent.

MISS HARDCASTLE. And if he be the sullen thing I take him, he shall never have mine.

HARDCASTLE. In one thing then we are agreed—to reject him.

MISS HARDCASTLE. Yes. But upon conditions. For if you should find him less impudent, and I more presuming; if you find him more respectful, and I more importunate—I don't know—the fellow is well enough for a man—Certainly we don't meet many such at a horse race in the country.

HARDCASTLE. If we should find him so—But that's impossible. The first appearance has done my business. I'm seldom deceived in that.

MISS HARDCASTLE. And yet there may be many good qualities under that first appearance.

HARDCASTLE. Ay, when a girl finds a fellow's outside to her taste, she then sets about guessing the rest of his furniture. With her, a smooth face stands for good sense, and a genteel figure for every virtue.

MISS HARDCASTLE. I hope, Sir, a conversation begun with a compliment to my good sense won't end with a sneer at my understanding?

HARDCASTLE. Pardon me, Kate. But if young Mr. Brazen can find the art of reconciling contradictions, he may please us both, perhaps.

MISS HARDCASTLE. And as one of us must be mistaken, what if we go to make further discoveries?

HARDCASTLE. Agreed. But depend on't I'm in the right.

MISS HARDCASTLE. And depend on't I'm not much in the wrong. [*Exeunt. Enter* TONY, *running in with a casket.*]

TONY. Ecod! I have got them. Here they are. My Cousin Con's necklaces, bobs and all. My mother shan't cheat the poor souls out of their fortune neither. O! my genius, is that you? [*Enter* HASTINGS.]

HASTINGS. My dear friend, how have you managed with your mother? I hope you have amused her with pretending love for your cousin, and that you are willing to be reconciled at last? Our horses will be refreshed in a short time, and we shall soon be ready to set off.

TONY. And here's something to bear your charges by the way. [*Giving the casket.*] Your sweetheart's jewels. Keep them, and hang those, I say, that would rob you of one of them.

HASTINGS. But how have you procured them from your mother?

TONY. Ask me no questions, and I'll tell you no fibs. I procured them by the rule of thumb. If I had not a key to every drawer in mother's bureau, how could I go to the ale-house so often as I do? An honest man may rob himself of his own at any time.

HASTINGS. Thousands do it every day. But to be plain with you; Miss Neville is endeavouring to procure them from her aunt this very instant. If she succeeds, it will be the most delicate way at least of obtaining them.

TONY. Well, keep them, till you know how it will be. But I know how it will be well enough; she'd as soon part with the only sound tooth in her head.

HASTINGS. But I dread the effects of her resentment, when she finds she has lost them.

TONY. Never you mind her resentment, leave *me* to manage that. I don't value her resentment the bounce of a cracker. Zounds! here they are. Morrice. Prance. [*Exit* HASTINGS. *Enter* MRS. HARDCASTLE, MISS NEVILLE.]

MRS. HARDCASTLE. Indeed, Constance, you amaze me. Such a girl as you want jewels? It will be time enough for jewels, my dear, twenty years hence, when your beauty begins to want repairs.

MISS NEVILLE. But what will repair beauty at forty, will certainly improve it at twenty, Madam.

MRS. HARDCASTLE. Yours, my dear, can admit of none. That natural blush is beyond a thousand ornaments. Besides, child, jewels are quite out at present. Don't you see half the ladies of our acquaintance, my Lady Killday-light, and Mrs. Crump, and the rest of them, carry their jewels to town, and bring nothing but Paste and Marcasites[18] back?

MISS NEVILLE. But who knows, Madam, but somebody that shall be nameless would like me best with all my little finery about me?

MRS. HARDCASTLE. Consult your glass, my dear, and then see, if with such a pair of eyes, you want any better sparklers. What do you think, Tony, my dear, does your Cousin Con want any jewels, in your eyes, to set off her beauty?

TONY. That's as thereafter may be.

MISS NEVILLE. My dear aunt, if you knew how it would oblige me.

MRS. HARDCASTLE. A parcel of old-fashioned rose and table-cut things. They would make you look like the court of King Solomon at a puppet-shew. Besides, I believe I can't readily come at them. They may be missing, for aught I know to the contrary.

TONY. [*Apart to* MRS. HARDCASTLE.] Then why don't you tell her so at once, as she's so longing for them. Tell her they're lost. It's the only way to quiet her. Say they're lost, and call me to bear witness.

MRS. HARDCASTLE. [*Apart to* TONY.] You know, my dear, I'm only keeping them for you. So if I say they're gone, you'll bear me witness, will you? He! he! he!

TONY. Never fear me. Ecod! I'll say I saw them taken out with my own eyes.

MISS NEVILLE. I desire them but for a day, Madam. Just to be permitted to shew them as relicks, and then they may be lock'd up again.

MRS. HARDCASTLE. To be plain with you, my dear Constance, if I could find them, you should have them. They're missing, I assure you. Lost, for aught I know; but we must have patience wherever they are.

MISS NEVILLE. I'll not believe it; this is but a shallow pretence to deny me. I know they're too valuable to be so slightly kept, and as you are to answer for the loss.

MRS. HARDCASTLE. Don't be alarm'd, Constance. If they be lost, I must restore an equivalent. But my son knows they are missing, and not to be found.

TONY. That I can bear witness to. They are missing, and not to be found, I'll take my oath on't.

MRS. HARDCASTLE. You must learn resignation, my dear; for tho' we lose our fortune, yet we should not lose our patience. See me, how calm I am.

MISS NEVILLE. Ay, people are generally calm at the misfortunes of others.

MRS. HARDCASTLE. Now, I wonder a girl of your good sense should waste a thought upon such trumpery. We shall soon find them; and, in the meantime, you shall make use of my garnets till your jewels be found.

MISS NEVILLE. I detest garnets.

MRS. HARDCASTLE. The most becoming things in the world to set off a clear complexion. You have often seen how well they look upon me. You *shall* have them. [*Exit.*]

MISS NEVILLE. I dislike them of all things. You shan't stir.—Was ever any thing so provoking—to mislay my own jewels, and force me to wear her trumpery.

TONY. Don't be a fool. If she gives you the garnets, take what you can get. The jewels are your own already. I have stolen them out of her bureau, and she does not know it. Fly to your spark, he'll tell you more of the matter. Leave me to manage *her.*

MISS NEVILLE. My dear cousin.

TONY. Vanish. She's here, and has missed them already. [*Exit* MISS NEVILLE.] Zounds! how she fidgets and spits about like a Catharine wheel.[19] [*Enter* MRS. HARDCASTLE.]

MRS. HARDCASTLE. Confusion! thieves! robbers! We are cheated, plundered, broke open, undone.

TONY. What's the matter, what's the matter, mamma? I hope nothing has happened to any of the good family!

MRS. HARDCASTLE. We are robbed. My bureau has been broke open, the jewels taken out, and I'm undone.

TONY. Oh! is that all? Ha! ha! ha! By the laws, I never saw it better acted in my life. Ecod, I thought you was ruin'd in earnest, ha, ha, ha.

MRS. HARDCASTLE. Why, boy, I *am* ruin'd in earnest. My bureau has been broke open, and all taken away.

TONY. Stick to that; ha, ha, ha! stick to that. I'll bear witness, you know, call me to bear witness.

MRS. HARDCASTLE. I tell you, Tony, by all that's precious, the jewels are gone, and I shall be ruin'd for ever.

TONY. Sure I know they're gone, and I am to say so.

MRS. HARDCASTLE. My dearest Tony, but hear me. They're gone, I say.

TONY. By the laws, mamma, you make me for to laugh, ha! ha! I know who took them well enough, ha! ha! ha!

MRS. HARDCASTLE. Was there ever such a blockhead, that can't tell the difference between jest and earnest. I tell you I'm not in jest, booby.

TONY. That's right, that's right: You must be in a bitter passion, and then nobody will suspect either of us. I'll bear witness that they are gone.

MRS. HARDCASTLE. Was there ever such a cross-grain'd brute, that won't hear me! Can you bear witness that you're no better than a fool? Was ever poor woman so beset with fools on one hand, and thieves on the other?

TONY. I can bear witness to that.

MRS. HARDCASTLE. Bear witness again, you blockhead you, and I'll turn you out of the room directly. My poor niece, what will become of *her!* Do you laugh, you unfeeling brute, as if you enjoyed my distress?

TONY. I can bear witness to that.

MRS. HARDCASTLE. Do you insult me, monster? I'll teach you to vex your mother, I will.

TONY. I can bear witness to that. [*He runs off, she follows him. Enter* MISS HARDCASTLE *and* MAID.]

MISS HARDCASTLE. What an unaccountable creature is that brother of mine, to send them to the house as an inn, ha! ha! I don't wonder at his impudence.

MAID. But what is more, Madam, the young gentleman as you passed by in your present dress, ask'd me if you were the barmaid? He mistook you for the barmaid, Madam.

MISS HARDCASTLE. Did he? Then as I live, I'm resolved to keep up the delusion. Tell me, Pimple, how do you like my present dress? Don't you think I look something like *Cherry* in the *Beaux' Stratagem?*[20]

MAID. It's the dress, Madam, that every lady wears in the country, but when she visits, or receives company.

MISS HARDCASTLE. And are you sure he does not remember my face or person?

MAID. Certain of it.

MISS HARDCASTLE. I vow, I thought so; for though we spoke for some time together, yet his fears were such, that he never once looked up during the interview. Indeed, if he had, my bonnet would have kept him from seeing me.

MAID. But what do you hope from keeping him in his mistake?

MISS HARDCASTLE. In the first place, I shall be *seen,* and that is no small advantage to a girl who brings her face to market. Then I shall perhaps make an acquaintance, and that's no small victory gained over one who never addresses any but the wildest of her sex. But my chief aim is to take my gentleman off his guard, and, like an invisible champion of romance, examine the giant's force before I offer to combat.

MAID. But are you sure you can act your part, and disguise your voice, so that he may mistake that, as he has already mistaken your person?

MISS HARDCASTLE. Never fear me. I think I have got the true bar-cant.—Did your honour call?—Attend the Lion there.—Pipes and tobacco for the Angel.—The Lamb[21] has been outrageous this half hour.

MAID. It will do, madam. But he's here. [*Exit* MAID. *Enter* MARLOW.]

MARLOW. What a bawling in every part of the house. I have scarce a moment's repose. If I go to the best room, there I find my host and his story. If I fly to the gallery,[22] there we have my hostess with her curtsy down to the ground. I have at last got a moment to myself, and now for recollection. [*Walks and muses.*]

MISS HARDCASTLE. Did you call, Sir? Did your honour call?

MARLOW. [*Musing.*] As for Miss Hardcastle, she's too grave and sentimental for me.

MISS HARDCASTLE. Did your honour call? [*She still places herself before him, he turning away.*]

MARLOW. No, child. [*Musing.*] Besides, from the glimpse I had of her, I think she squints.

MISS HARDCASTLE. I'm sure, Sir, I heard the bell ring.

MARLOW. No, no. [*Musing.*] I have pleased my father, however, by coming down, and I'll tomorrow please myself by returning. [*Taking out his tablets, and perusing.*]

MISS HARDCASTLE. Perhaps the other gentleman called, Sir?

MARLOW. I tell you, no.

MISS HARDCASTLE. I should be glad to know, Sir. We have such a parcel of servants.

MARLOW. No, no, I tell you. [*Looks full in her face.*] Yes, child, I think I did call. I wanted—I wanted—I vow, child, you are vastly handsome.

MISS HARDCASTLE. O la, Sir, you'll make one asham'd.

MARLOW. Never saw a more sprightly, malicious eye. Yes, yes, my dear, I did call. Have you got any of your—a—what d'ye call it in the house?

MISS HARDCASTLE. No, Sir, we have been out of that these ten days.

MARLOW. One may call in this house, I find, to very little purpose. Suppose I should call for a taste, just by way of trial, of the nectar of your lips; perhaps I might be disappointed in that too.

MISS HARDCASTLE. Nectar! nectar! That's a liquor there's no call for in these parts. French, I suppose. We keep no French wines here, Sir.

MARLOW. Of true English growth, I assure you.

MISS HARDCASTLE. Then it's odd I should not know it. We brew all sorts of wines in this house, and I have lived here these eighteen years.

MARLOW. Eighteen years! Why one would think, child, you kept the bar before you were born. How old are you?

MISS HARDCASTLE. O! Sir, I must not tell my age. They say women and music should never be dated.

MARLOW. To guess at this distance, you can't be much above forty. [*Approaching.*] Yet nearer, I don't think so much. [*Approaching.*] By coming close to some women, they look younger still; but when we come very close indeed—[*Attemping to kiss her.*]

MISS HARDCASTLE. Pray, Sir, keep your distance. One would think you wanted to know one's age as they do horses, by mark of mouth.

MARLOW. I protest, child, you use me extremely ill. If you keep me at this distance, how is it possible you and I can be ever acquainted?

MISS HARDCASTLE. And who wants to be acquainted with you? I want no such acquaintance, not I. I'm sure you did not treat Miss Hardcastle that was here awhile ago in this obstropalous manner. I'll warrant me, before her you look'd dash'd, and kept bowing to the ground, and talk'd, for all the world, as if you was before a justice of peace.

MARLOW. [*Aside.*] Egad! she has hit it, sure enough. [*To her.*] In awe of her, child? Ha! ha! ha! A mere, awkward, squinting thing, no, no! I find you don't know me. I laugh'd, and rallied her a little; but I was unwilling to be too severe. No, I could not be too severe, curse me!

MISS HARDCASTLE. O! then, Sir, you are a favourite, I find, among the ladies?

MARLOW. Yes, my dear, a great favourite. And yet, hang me, I don't see what they find in me to follow. At the Ladies Club in town, I'm called their agreeable Rattle. Rattle, child, is not my real name, but one I'm known by. My name is Solomons. Mr. Solomons, my dear, at your service. [*Offering to salute her.*]

MISS HARDCASTLE. Hold, Sir; you are introducing me to your club, not to yourself. And you're so great a favourite there, you say?

MARLOW. Yes, my dear. There's Mrs. Mantrap, Lady Betty Blackleg, the Countess of Sligo, Mrs. Langhorns, old Miss Biddy Buckskin, and your humble servant, keep up the spirit of the place.

MISS HARDCASTLE. Then it's a very merry place, I suppose?

MARLOW. Yes, as merry as cards, suppers, wine, and old women can make us.

MISS HARDCASTLE. And their agreeable Rattle, ha! ha! ha!

MARLOW. [*Aside.*] Egad! I don't quite like this chit. She looks knowing, methinks. You laugh, child!

MISS HARDCASTLE. I can't but laugh to think what time they all have for minding their work or their family.

MARLOW. [*Aside.*] All's well; she don't laugh at me. [*To her.*] Do *you* ever work, child?

MISS HARDCASTLE. Ay, sure. There's not a screen or a quilt in the whole house but what can bear witness to that.

MARLOW. Odso! Then you must shew me your embroidery. I embroider and draw patterns myself a little. If you want a judge of your work you must apply to me. [*Seizing her hand.*]

MISS HARDCASTLE. Ay, but the colours don't look well by candlelight. You shall see all in the morning. [*Struggling.*]

MARLOW. And why not now, my angel? Such beauty fires beyond the power of resistance—Pshaw! the father here! My old luck: I never nick'd seven that I did not throw ames ace[23] three times following. [*Exit* MARLOW. *Enter* HARDCASTLE, *who stands in surprise.*]

HARDCASTLE. So, madam. So I find *this* is your *modest* lover. This is your humble admirer that kept his eyes fixed on the ground, and only ador'd at humble distance. Kate, Kate, art thou not asham'd to deceive your father so?

MISS HARDCASTLE. Never trust me, dear papa, but he's still the modest man I first took him for; you'll be convinced of it as well as I.

HARDCASTLE. By the hand of my body, I believe his impudence is infectious! Didn't I see him seize your hand? Didn't I see him haul you about like a milk-maid? and now you talk of his respect and his modesty, forsooth!

MISS HARDCASTLE. But if I shortly convince you of his modesty, that he has only the faults that will pass off with time, and the virtues that will improve with age, I hope you'll forgive him.

HARDCASTLE. The girl would actually make one run mad! I tell you I'll not be convinced. I am convinced. He has scarcely been three hours in the house, and he has already encroached on all my prerogatives. You may like his impudence, and call it modesty. But my son-in-law, madam, must have very different qualifications.

MISS HARDCASTLE. Sir, I ask but this night to convince you.

HARDCASTLE. You shall not have half the time, for I have thoughts of turning him out this very hour.

MISS HARDCASTLE. Give me that hour then, and I hope to satisfy you.

HARDCASTLE. Well, an hour let it be then. But I'll have no trifling with your father. All fair and open, do you mind me?

MISS HARDCASTLE. I hope, Sir, you have ever found that I considered your commands as my pride; for your kindness is such, that my duty as yet has been inclination. [*Exeunt.*]

Act 4

Enter HASTINGS *and* MISS NEVILLE.

HASTINGS. You surprise me! Sir Charles Marlow expected here this night? Where have you had your information?

MISS NEVILLE. You may depend upon it. I just saw his letter to Mr. Hardcastle, in which he tells him he intends setting out a few hours after his son.

HASTINGS. Then, my Constance, all must be completed before he arrives. He knows me; and should he find me here, would discover my name, and perhaps my designs, to the rest of the family.

MISS NEVILLE. The jewels, I hope, are safe.

HASTINGS. Yes, yes. I have sent them to Marlow, who keeps the keys of our baggage. In the meantime, I'll go to prepare matters for our elopement. I have had the Squire's promise of a fresh pair of horses; and, if I should not see him again, will write him further directions.

MISS NEVILLE. Well! success attend you. In the meantime, I'll go amuse my aunt with the old pretence of a violent passion for my cousin. [*Exeunt. Enter* MARLOW, *followed by a* SERVANT.]

MARLOW. I wonder what Hastings could mean by sending me so valuable a thing as a casket to keep for him, when he knows the only place I have is the seat of a post-coach at an Inndoor. Have you deposited the casket with the landlady, as I ordered you? Have you put it into her own hands?

SERVANT. Yes, your honour.

MARLOW. She said she'd keep it safe, did she?

SERVANT. Yes, she said she'd keep it safe enough; she ask'd me how I came by it? and she said she had a great mind to make me give an account of myself. [*Exit* SERVANT.]

MARLOW. Ha! ha! ha! They're safe, however. What an unaccountable set of beings have we got amongst! This little barmaid, though, runs in my head most strangely, and drives out the absurdities of all the rest of the family. She's mine, she must be mine, or I'm greatly mistaken. [*Enter* HASTINGS.]

HASTINGS. Bless me! I quite forgot to tell her that I intended to prepare at the bottom of the garden. Marlow here, and in spirits too!

MARLOW. Give me joy, George! Crown me, shadow me with laurels! Well, George, after all, we modest fellows don't want for success among the women.

HASTINGS. Some women you mean. But what success has your honour's modesty been crowned with now, that it grows so insolent upon us?

MARLOW. Didn't you see the tempting, brisk, lovely little thing that runs about the house with a bunch of keys to its girdle?

HASTINGS. Well! and what then?

MARLOW. She's mine, you rogue you. Such fire, such motion, such eyes, such lips—but, egad! she would not let me kiss them though.

HASTINGS. But are you so sure, so very sure of her?

MARLOW. Why man, she talk'd of shewing me her work abovestairs, and I am to improve the pattern.

HASTINGS. But how can *you*, Charles, go about to rob a woman of her honour?

MARLOW. Pshaw! pshaw! we all know the honour of the barmaid of an inn. I don't intend to *rob* her, take my word for it; there's nothing in this house, I shan't honestly *pay* for.

HASTINGS. I believe the girl has virtue.

MARLOW. And if she has, I should be the last man in the world that would attempt to corrupt it.

HASTINGS. You have taken care, I hope, of the casket I sent you to lock up? It's in safety?

MARLOW. Yes, yes. It's safe enough. I have taken care of it. But how could you think the seat of a post-coach at an Inn-door a place of safety? Ah! numbskull! I have taken better precautions for you than you did for yourself.—I have—

HASTINGS. What!

MARLOW. I have sent it to the landlady to keep for you.

HASTINGS. To the landlady!

MARLOW. The landlady.

HASTINGS. You did!

MARLOW. I did. She's to be answerable for its forth-coming, you know.

HASTINGS. Yes, she'll bring it forth, with a witness.

MARLOW. Wasn't I right? I believe you'll allow that I acted prudently upon this occasion?

HASTINGS. [*Aside.*] He must not see my uneasiness.

MARLOW. You seem a little disconcerted though, methinks. Sure nothing has happened?

HASTINGS. No, nothing. Never was in better spirits in all my life. And so you left it with the landlady, who, no doubt, very readily undertook the charge?

MARLOW. Rather too readily. For she not only kept the casket; but, thro' her great precaution, was going to keep the messenger too. Ha! ha! ha!

HASTINGS. He! he! he! They're safe, however.

MARLOW. As a guinea in a miser's purse.

HASTINGS. [*Aside.*] So now all hopes of fortune are at an end, and we must set off without it. [*To him.*] Well,

Charles, I'll leave you to your meditations on the pretty barmaid, and, he! he! he! may you be as successful for yourself as you have been for me! [*Exit.*]

MARLOW. Thank ye, George! I ask no more. Ha! ha! ha! [*Enter* HARDCASTLE.]

HARDCASTLE. I no longer know my own house. It's turned all topsey-turvey. His servants have got drunk already. I'll bear it no longer, and yet, from my respect for his father, I'll be calm. [*To him.*] Mr. Marlow, your servant. I'm your very humble servant. [*Bowing low.*]

MARLOW. Sir, your humble servant. [*Aside.*] What's to be the wonder now?

HARDCASTLE. I believe, Sir, you must be sensible, Sir, that no man alive ought to be more welcome than your father's son, Sir. I hope you think so?

MARLOW. I do from my soul, Sir. I don't want much entreaty. I generally make my father's son welcome wherever he goes.

HARDCASTLE. I believe you do, from my soul, Sir. But tho' I say nothing to your own conduct, that of your servants is insufferable. Their manner of drinking is setting a very bad example in this house, I assure you.

MARLOW. I protest, my very good Sir, that's no fault of mine. If they don't drink as they ought, *they* are to blame. I ordered them not to spare the cellar. I did, I assure you. [*To the side scene.*] Here, let one of my servants come up. [*To him.*] My positive directions were, that as I did not drink myself, they should make up for my deficiencies below.

HARDCASTLE. Then they had your orders for what they do! I'm satisfied!

MARLOW. They had, I assure you. You shall hear from one of themselves. [*Enter* SERVANT *drunk.*]

MARLOW. You, Jeremy! Come forward, Sirrah! What were my orders? Were you not told to drink freely, and call for what you thought fit, for the good of the house?

HARDCASTLE. [*Aside.*] I begin to lose my patience.

JEREMY. Please your honour, liberty and Fleet Street for ever! Tho' I'm but a servant, I'm as good as another man. I'll drink for no man before supper, Sir, dammy! Good liquor will set upon a good supper, but a good supper will not sit upon—*hiccup*—upon my conscience, Sir. [*Exit* JEREMY.]

MARLOW. You see, my old friend, the fellow is as drunk as he can possibly be. I don't know what you'd have more, unless you'd have the poor devil soused in a beer-barrel.

HARDCASTLE. Zounds! He'll drive me distracted if I contain myself any longer. Mr. Marlow. Sir; I have submitted to your insolence for more than four hours, and I see no likelihood of its coming to an end. I'm now resolved to be master here, Sir, and I desire that you and your drunken pack may leave my house directly.

MARLOW. Leave your house!—Sure you jest, my good friend! What, when I'm doing what I can to please you!

HARDCASTLE. I tell you, Sir, you don't please me; so I desire you'll leave my house.

MARLOW. Sure you cannot be serious? At this time o'night, and such a night. You only mean to banter me?

HARDCASTLE. I tell you, Sir, I'm serious; and, now that my passions are roused, I say this house is mine, Sir; this house is mine, and I command you to leave it directly.

MARLOW. Ha! ha! ha! A puddle in a storm. I shan't stir a step, I assure you. [*In a serious tone.*] This, your house, fellow! It's my house. This is my house. Mine, while I choose to stay. What right have you to bid me leave this house, Sir? I never met with such impudence, curse me, never in my whole life before.

HARDCASTLE. Nor I, confound me if ever I did. To come to my house, to call for what he likes, to turn me out of my own chair, to insult the family, to order his servants to get drunk, and then to tell me *This house is mine, Sir*. By all that's impudent, it makes me laugh. Ha! ha! ha! Pray, Sir [*Bantering.*], as you take the house, what think you of taking the rest of the furniture? There's a pair of silver

candlesticks, and there's a fire-screen, and here's a pair of brazen nosed bellows, perhaps you may take a fancy to them?

MARLOW. Bring me your bill, Sir, bring me your bill, and let's make no more words about it.

HARDCASTLE. There are a set of prints too. What think you of the *Rake's Progress* for your own apartment?

MARLOW. Bring me your bill, I say; and I'll leave you and your infernal house directly.

HARDCASTLE. Then there's a mahogany table, that you may see your own face in.

MARLOW. My bill, I say.

HARDCASTLE. I had forgot the great chair, for your own particular slumbers, after a hearty meal.

MARLOW. Zounds! bring me my bill, I say, and let's hear no more on't.

HARDCASTLE. Young man, young man, from your father's letter to me, I was taught to expect a well-bred, modest man, as a visitor here, but now I find him no better than a coxcomb and a bully; but he will be down here presently, and shall hear more of it. [*Exit.*]

MARLOW. How's this! Sure I have not mistaken the house? Every thing looks like an inn. The servants cry, Coming. The attendance is awkward; the barmaid, too, to attend us. But she's here, and will further inform me. Whither so fast, child? A word with you. [*Enter* MISS HARDCASTLE.]

MISS HARDCASTLE. Let it be short then. I'm in a hurry. [*Aside.*] I believe he begins to find out his mistake, but it's too soon quite to undeceive him.

MARLOW. Pray, child, answer me, one question. What are you, and what may your business in this house be?

MISS HARDCASTLE. A relation of the family, Sir.

MARLOW. What! A poor relation?

MISS HARDCASTLE. Yes, Sir. A poor relation appointed to keep the keys, and to see that the guests want nothing in my power to give them.

MARLOW. That is, you act as the barmaid of this inn.

MISS HARDCASTLE. O Law—What brought that in your head? One of the best families in the county keep an inn! Ha, ha, ha, old Mr. Hardcastle's house an inn?

MARLOW. Mr. Hardcastle's house? Is this house Mr. Hardcastle's house, child?

MISS HARDCASTLE. Ay, sure. Whose else should it be?

MARLOW. So then all's out, and I have been damnably imposed on. O, confound my stupid head, I shall be laugh'd all over the whole town. I shall be stuck up in caricature in all the print-shops. The Dullissimo Maccaroni.[24] To mistake this house of all others for an inn, and my father's old friend for an innkeeper. What a swaggering puppy must he take me for. What a silly puppy do I find myself. There again, may I be hang'd, my dear, but I mistook you for the barmaid.

MISS HARDCASTLE. Dear me! dear me! I'm sure there's nothing in my *behaviour* to put me upon a level with one of that stamp.

MARLOW. Nothing, my dear, nothing. But I was in for a list of blunders, and could not help making you a subscriber. My stupidity saw every thing the wrong way. I mistook your assiduity for assurance, and your simplicity for allurement. But its over—This house I no more shew *my* face in.

MISS HARDCASTLE. I hope, Sir, I have done nothing to disoblige you. I'm sure I should be sorry to affront any gentleman who has been so polite, and said so many civil things to me. I'm sure I should be sorry [*Pretending to cry.*] if he left the family upon my account. I'm sure I should be sorry people said any thing amiss, since I have no fortune but my character.

MARLOW. [*Aside.*] By heaven, she weeps. This is the first mark of tenderness I ever had from a modest woman, and it touches me. [*To her.*] Excuse me, my lovely girl, you are the only part of the family I leave with reluctance. But to be plain with you, the difference of our birth, fortune and education, make an honourable connexion impossible; and I can never harbour a thought of seducing simplicity that trusted in my honour, or bringing ruin upon one, whose only fault was being too lovely.

MISS HARDCASTLE. [*Aside.*] Generous man! I now begin to admire him. [*To him.*] But I'm sure my family is as good as Miss Hardcastle's, and though I'm poor, that's no great misfortune to a contented mind, and, until this moment, I never thought that it was bad to want fortune.

MARLOW. And why now, my pretty simplicity?

MISS HARDCASTLE. Because it puts me at a distance from one, that if I had a thousand pound I would give it all to.

MARLOW. [*Aside.*] This simplicity bewitches me, so that if I stay I'm undone. I must make one bold effort, and leave her. [*To her.*] Your partiality in my favour, my dear, touches me most sensibly, and were I to live for myself alone, I could easily fix my choice. But I owe too much to the opinion of the world, too much to the authority of a father, so that— I can scarcely speak it—it affects me. Farewell. [*Exit.*]

MISS HARDCASTLE. I never knew half his merit till now. He shall not go, if I have power or art to detain him. I'll still preserve the character in which I stoop'd to conquer, but will undeceive my papa, who, perhaps, may laugh him out of his resolution. [*Exit. Enter* TONY, MISS NEVILLE.]

TONY. Ay, you may steal for yourselves the next time. I have done my duty. She has got the jewels again, that's a sure thing; but she believes it was all a mistake of the servants.

MISS HARDCASTLE. But, my dear cousin, sure you won't forsake us in this distress. If she in the least suspects that I am going off, I shall certainly be locked up, or sent to my Aunt Pedigree's which is ten times worse.

TONY. To be sure, aunts of all kinds are damn'd bad things. But what can I do? I have got you a pair of horses that will fly like Whistlejacket, and I'm sure you can't say but I have courted you nicely before her face. Here she comes; we must court a bit or two more, for fear she should suspect us. [*They retire, and seem to fondle. Enter* MRS. HARDCASTLE.]

MRS. HARDCASTLE. Well, I was greatly fluttered, to be sure. But my son tells me it was all a mistake of the servants. I shan't be easy, however, till they are fairly married, and then let her keep her own fortune. But what do I see! Fondling together, as I'm alive. I never saw Tony so sprightly before. Ah! have I caught you, my pretty doves? What, billing, exchanging stolen glances, and broken murmurs. Ah!

TONY. As for murmurs, mother, we grumble a little now and then, to be sure. But there's no love lost between us.

MRS. HARDCASTLE. A mere sprinkling, Tony, upon the flame, only to make it burn brighter.

MISS NEVILLE. Cousin Tony promises to give us more of his company at home. Indeed, he shan't leave us any more. It won't leave us, Cousin Tony, will it?

TONY. O! it's a pretty creature. No, I'd sooner leave my horse in a pond, than leave you when you smile upon one so. Your laugh makes you so becoming.

MISS NEVILLE. Agreeable cousin! Who can help admiring that natural humour, that pleasant, broad, red, thoughtless [*Patting his cheek.*], ah! it's a bold face.

MRS. HARDCASTLE. Pretty innocence!

TONY. I'm sure I always lov'd Cousin Con's hazel eyes, and her pretty long fingers, that she twists this way and that, over the haspicholls,[25] like a parcel of bobbins.

MRS. HARDCASTLE. Ah, he would charm the bird from the tree. I was never so happy before. My boy takes after his father, poor Mr. Lumpkin, exactly. The jewels, my dear Con, shall be yours incontinently. You shall have them. Isn't he a sweet boy, my dear? You shall be married tomorrow, and we'll put off the rest of his education, like Dr. Drowsy's sermons, to a fitter opportunity. [*Enter* DIGGORY.]

DIGGORY. Where's the 'Squire? I have got a letter for your worship.

TONY. Give it to my mamma. She reads all my letters first.

DIGGORY. I had orders to deliver it into your own hands.

TONY. Who does it come from?

DIGGORY. Your worship mun ask that o' the letter itself. [*Exit* DIGGORY.]

TONY. I could wish to know, tho'. [*Turning the letter, and gazing on it.*]

MISS NEVILLE. [*Aside.*] Undone, undone. A letter to him from Hastings. I know the hand. If my aunt sees it, we are ruined forever. I'll keep her employ'd a little if I can. [*To* MRS. HARDCASTLE.] But I have not told you, Madam, of my cousin's smart answer just now to Mr. Marlow. We so laugh'd—You must know, Madam—this way a little, for he must not hear us. [*They confer.*]

TONY. [*Still gazing.*] A damn'd cramp piece of penmanship, as ever I saw in my life. I can read your print-hand very well. But here there are such handles, and shanks, and dashes, that one can scarce tell the head from the tail. *To Anthony Lumpkin, Esquire.* It's very odd, I can read the outside of my letters, where my own name is, well enough. But when I come to open it, it's all—buzz. That's hard, very hard; for the inside of the letter is always the cream of the correspondence.

MRS. HARDCASTLE. Ha! ha! ha! Very well, very well. And so my son was too hard for the philosopher.

MISS NEVILLE. Yes, Madam; but you must hear the rest, Madam. A little more this way, or he may hear us. You'll hear how he puzzled him again.

MRS. HARDCASTLE. He seems strangely puzzled now himself, methinks.

TONY. [*Still gazing.*] A damn'd up and down hand, as if it was disguised in liquor. [*Reading.*] *Dear Sir.* Ay, that's that. Then there's an *M,* and a *T,* and an *S,* but whether the next be an *izzard* or an *R,* confound me, I cannot tell.

MRS. HARDCASTLE. What's that, my dear? Can I give you any assistance?

MISS NEVILLE. Pray, aunt, let me read it. No body reads a cramp hand better than I. [*Twitching the letter from her.*] do you know who it is from?

TONY. Can't tell, except from Dick Ginger the feeder.

MISS NEVILLE. Ay, so it is. [*Pretending to read.*] Dear 'Squire, Hoping that you're in health, as I am at this present. The gentlemen of the Shakebag club has cut the gentlemen of Goosegreen quite out of feather.[26] The odds—um—odd battle—um—long fighting—um, here, here, it's all about cocks, and fighting; it's of no consequence; here, put it up, put it up. [*Thrusting the crumpled letter upon him.*]

TONY. But I tell you, Miss, it's of all the consequence in the world. I would not lose the rest of it for a guinea. Here, mother, do you make it out. Of no consequence! [*Giving* MRS. HARDCASTLE *the letter.*]

MRS. HARDCASTLE. How's this! [*Reads.*] "Dear 'Squire, I'm now waiting for Miss Neville, with a post-chaise and pair, at the bottom of the garden, but I find my horses yet unable to perform the journey. I expect you'll assist us with a pair of fresh horses, as you promised. Dispatch is necessary, as the *hag*, (ay, the hag) your mother, will otherwise suspect us. Yours, Hastings." Grant me patience. I shall run distracted. My rage chokes me.

MISS NEVILLE. I hope, Madam, you'll suspend your resentment for a few moments, and not impute to me any impertinence, or sinister design that belongs to another.

MRS. HARDCASTLE. [*Curtsying very low.*] Fine spoken, Madam; you are most miraculously polite and engaging, and quite the very pink of curtesy and circumspection, Madam. [*Changing her tone.*] And you, you great ill-fashioned oaf, with scarce sense enough to keep your mouth shut. Were you too join'd against me? But I'll defeat all your plots in a moment. As for you, Madam, since you have got a pair of fresh horses ready, it would be cruel to disappoint them. So, if you please, instead of running away with your spark, prepare, this very moment, to run off with *me*. Your old Aunt Pedigree will keep you secure, I'll warrant me. You too, Sir, may mount your horse, and guard us

upon the way. Here, Thomas, Roger, Diggory! I'll shew you, that I wish you better than you do yourselves. [*Exit.*]

MISS NEVILLE. So now I'm completely ruined.

TONY. Ay, that's a sure thing.

MISS NEVILLE. What better could be expected from being connected with such a stupid fool, and after all the nods and signs I made him.

TONY. By the laws, Miss, it was your own cleverness, and not my stupidity, that did your business. You were so nice and so busy with your Shakebags and Goose-greens, that I thought you could never be making believe. [*Enter* HASTINGS.]

HASTINGS. So, Sir, I find by my servant, that you have shewn my letter, and betray'd us. Was this well done, young gentleman?

TONY. Here's another. Ask Miss there who betray'd you. Ecod, it was her doing, not mine. [*Enter* MARLOW.]

MARLOW. So I have been finely used here among you. Rendered contemptible, driven into ill manners, despised, insulted, laugh'd at.

TONY. Here's another. We shall have old Bedlam[27] broke loose presently.

MISS NEVILLE. And there, Sir, is the gentleman to whom we all owe every obligation.

MARLOW. What can I say to him, a mere boy, an idiot, whose ignorance and age are a protection.

HASTINGS. A poor contemptible booby, that would but disgrace correction.

MISS NEVILLE. Yet with cunning and malice enough to make himself merry with all our embarrassments.

HASTINGS. An insensible cub.

MARLOW. Replete with tricks and mischief.

TONY. Baw! damme, but I'll fight you both one after the other,—with baskets.[28]

MARLOW. As for him, he's below resentment. But your conduct, Mr. Hastings, requires an explanation. You knew of my mistakes, yet would not undeceive me.

HASTINGS. Tortured as I am with my own disappointments, is this a time for explanations? It is not friendly,

Mr. Marlow.

MARLOW. But, Sir—

MISS NEVILLE. Mr. Marlow, we never kept on your mistake, till it was too late to undeceive you. Be pacified. [*Enter* SERVANT.]

SERVANT. My mistress desires you'll get ready immediately, Madam. The horses are putting to. Your hat and things are in the next room. We are to go thirty miles before morning. [*Exit* SERVANT.]

MISS NEVILLE. Well, well; I'll come presently.

MARLOW. [*To* HASTINGS.] Was it well done, Sir, to assist in rendering me ridiculous? To hand me out for the scorn of all my acquaintance? Depend upon it, Sir, I shall expect an explanation.

HASTINGS. Was it well done, Sir, if you're upon that subject, to deliver what I entrusted to yourself, to the care of another, Sir?

MISS NEVILLE. Mr. Hastings. Mr. Marlow. Why will you increase my distress by this groundless dispute? I implore, I entreat you—[*Enter* SERVANT.]

SERVANT. Your cloak, Madam. My mistress is impatient.

MISS NEVILLE. I come. [*Exit* SERVANT.] Pray be pacified. If I leave you thus, I shall die with apprehension. [*Enter* SERVANT.]

SERVANT. Your fan, muff, and gloves, Madam. The horses are waiting.

MISS NEVILLE. O, Mr. Marlow! if you knew what a scene of constraint and ill-nature lies before me, I'm sure it would convert your resentment into pity.

MARLOW. I'm so distracted with a variety of passions, that I don't know what I do. Forgive me, Madam. George, forgive me. You know my hasty temper, and should not exasperate it.

HASTINGS. The torture of my situation is my only excuse.

MISS NEVILLE. Well, my dear Hastings, if you have that esteem for me that I think, that I am sure you have, your constancy for three years will but increase the happiness of our future connexion. If—

MRS. HARDCASTLE. [*Within.*] Miss Ne-

ville. Constance, why Constance, I say.

MISS NEVILLE. I'm coming. Well, constancy. Remember, constancy is the word. [*Exit.*]

HASTINGS. My heart! How can I support this? To be so near happiness, and such happiness.

MARLOW. [*To* TONY.] You see now, young gentleman, the effects of your folly. What might be amusement to you, is here disappointment, and even distress.

TONY. [*From a reverie.*] Ecod, I have hit it. It's here. Your hands. Yours and yours, my poor Sulky. My boots there, ho! Meet me two hours hence at the bottom of the garden; and if you don't find Tony Lumpkin a more good-natur'd fellow than you thought for, I'll give you leave to take my best horse, and Bet Bouncer into the bargain. Come along. My boots, ho! [*Exeunt.*]

Act 5

Enter HASTINGS *and* SERVANT.

HASTINGS. You saw the old lady and Miss Neville drive off, you say?

SERVANT. Yes, your honour. They went off in a post coach, and the young 'Squire went on horseback. They're thirty miles off by this time.

HASTINGS. Then all my hopes are over.

SERVANT. Yes, Sir. Old Sir Charles is arrived. He and the old gentleman of the house have been laughing at Mr. Marlow's mistake this half hour. They are coming this way.

HASTINGS. Then I must not be seen. So now to my fruitless appointment at the bottom of the garden. This is about the time. [*Exit. Enter* SIR CHARLES *and* HARDCASTLE.]

HARDCASTLE. Ha! ha! ha! The peremptory tone in which he sent forth his sublime commands.

SIR CHARLES. And the reserve with which I suppose he treated all your advances.

HARDCASTLE. And yet he might have seen something in me above a common innkeeper, too.

SIR CHARLES. Yes, Dick, but he mistook you for an uncommon innkeeper, ha! ha! ha!

HARDCASTLE. Well, I'm in too good spirits to think of any thing but joy. Yes, my dear friend, this union of our families will make our personal friendships hereditary; and tho' my daughter's fortune is but small—

SIR CHARLES. Why, Dick, will you talk of fortune to *me*. My son is possessed of more than a competence already, and I can want nothing but a good and virtuous girl to share his happiness and increase it. If they like each other as you say they do—

HARDCASTLE. *If,* man. I tell you they *do* like each other. My daughter as good as told me so.

SIR CHARLES. But girls are apt to flatter themselves, you know.

HARDCASTLE. I saw him grasp her hand in the warmest manner myself; and here he comes to put you out of your *ifs,* I warrant him. [*Enter* MARLOW.]

MARLOW. I come Sir, once more, to ask pardon for my strange conduct. I can scarce reflect on my insolence without confusion.

HARDCASTLE. Tut, boy, a trifle. You take it too gravely. An hour or two's laughing with my daughter will set all to rights again. She'll never like you the worse for it.

MARLOW. Sir, I shall be always proud of her approbation.

HARDCASTLE. Approbation is but a cold word, Mr. Marlow; if I am not deceived, you have something more than approbation thereabouts. You take me.

MARLOW. Really, sir, I have not that happiness.

HARDCASTLE. Come, boy, I'm an old fellow, and know what's what, as well as you that are younger. I know what has passed between you; but mum.

MARLOW. Sure, Sir, nothing has passed between us but the most profound respect on my side, and the most distant reserve on hers. You don't think, Sir, that my impudence has been passed upon all the rest of the family?

HARDCASTLE. Impudence! No, I don't say that—Not quite impudence— Though girls like to be play'd with, and rumpled a little, too, sometimes. But she has told no tales, I assure you.

MARLOW. I never gave her the slightest cause.

HARDCASTLE. Well, well, I like modesty in its place well enough. But this is over-acting, young gentleman. You may be open. Your father and I will like you the better for it.

MARLOW. May I die, Sir, if I ever—

HARDCASTLE. I tell you, she don't dislike you; and as I'm sure you like her—

MARLOW. Dear Sir—I protest, Sir—

HARDCASTLE. I see no reason why you should not be joined as fast as the parson can tie you.

MARLOW. But hear me, Sir—

HARDCASTLE. Your father approves the match, I admire it, every moment's delay will be doing mischief, so—

MARLOW. But why won't you hear me? By all that's just and true, I never gave Miss Hardcastle the slightest mark of my attachment or even the most distant hint to suspect me of affection. We had but one interview, and that was formal, modest and uninteresting.

HARDCASTLE. [*Aside.*] This fellow's formal, modest impudence is beyond bearing.

SIR CHARLES. And you never grasp'd her hand, or made any protestations!

MARLOW. As heaven is my witness, I came down in obedience to your commands. I saw the lady without emotion, and parted without reluctance. I hope you'll exact no further proofs of my duty, nor prevent me from leaving a house in which I suffer so many mortifications. [*Exit.*]

SIR CHARLES. I'm astonish'd at the air of sincerity with which he parted.

HARDCASTLE. And I'm astonish'd at the deliberate intrepidity of his assurance.

SIR CHARLES. I dare pledge my life and honour upon his truth.

HARDCASTLE. Here comes my daughter, and I would stake my happiness upon her veracity. [*Enter* MISS HARD-

CASTLE.]

HARDCASTLE. Kate, come hither, child. Answer us sincerely, and without reserve; has Mr. Marlow made you any professions of love and affection?

MISS HARDCASTLE. The question is very abrupt, Sir! But since you require unreserved sincerity, I think he has.

HARDCASTLE. [*To* SIR CHARLES.] You see.

SIR CHARLES. And pray, Madam, have you and my son had more than one interview?

MISS HARDCASTLE. Yes, Sir, several.

HARDCASTLE. [*To* SIR CHARLES.] You see.

SIR CHARLES. But did he profess any attachment?

MISS HARDCASTLE. A lasting one.

SIR CHARLES. Did he talk of love?

MISS HARDCASTLE. Much, Sir.

SIR CHARLES. Amazing! And all this formally?

MISS HARDCASTLE. Formally.

HARDCASTLE. Now, my friend, I hope you are satisfied.

SIR CHARLES. And how did he behave, Madam?

MISS HARDCASTLE. As most professed admirers do. Said some civil things of my face, talked much of his want of merit, and the greatness of mine; mentioned his heart, gave a short tragedy speech, and ended with pretended rapture.

SIR CHARLES. Now I'm perfectly convinced, indeed. I know his conversation among women to be modest and submissive. This forward, canting, ranting manner by no means describes him, and I am confident, he never sat for the picture.

MISS HARDCASTLE. Then what, Sir, if I should convince you to your face of my sincerity? If you and my papa, in about half an hour, will place yourselves behind that screen, you shall hear him declare his passion to me in person.

SIR CHARLES. Agreed. And if I find him what you describe, all my happiness in him must have an end. [*Exit.*]

MISS HARDCASTLE. And if you don't find him what I describe—I fear my happiness must never have a beginning. [*Exeunt. Scene changes to the back of the garden. Enter* HASTINGS.]

HASTINGS. What an idiot am I, to wait here for a fellow, who probably takes delight in mortifying me. He never intended to be punctual, and I'll wait no longer. What do I see! It is he, and perhaps with news of my Constance. [*Enter* TONY, *booted and spattered.*]

HASTINGS. My honest 'Squire! I now find you a man of your word. This looks like friendship.

TONY. Ay, I'm your friend, and the best friend you have in the world, if you knew but all. This riding by night, by the bye, is cursedly tiresome. It has shook me worse than the basket of a stage-coach.

HASTINGS. But how? Where did you leave your fellow travellers? Are they in safety? Are they housed?

TONY. Five and twenty miles in two hours and a half is no such bad driving. The poor beasts have smoked for it: Rabbet me, but I'd rather ride forty miles after a fox, then ten miles with such *varment.*[29]

HASTINGS. Well, but where have you left the ladies? I die with impatience.

TONY. Left them? Why, where should I leave them, but where I found them?

HASTINGS. This is a riddle.

TONY. Riddle me this then. What's that goes round the house, and round the house, and never touches the house?

HASTINGS. I'm still astray.

TONY. Why that's it, mon. I have led them astray. By jingo, there's not a pond or slough within five miles of the place but they can tell the taste of.

HASTINGS. Ha, ha, ha, I understand; you look them in a round, while they supposed themselves going forward. And so you have at last brought them home again.

TONY. You shall hear. I first took them down Feather-bed Lane, where we stuck fast in the mud. I then rattled them crack over the stones of Up-and-down Hill—I then introduc'd them to the gibbet on Heavy-tree Heath, and from that, with a circumbendibus, I fairly lodged them in the horse-pond at the bottom of the garden.

HASTINGS. But no accident, I hope.

TONY. No, no. Only mother is confoundedly frightened. She thinks herself forty miles off. She's sick of the journey, and the cattle can scarce crawl. So if your own horses be ready, you may whip off with Cousin, and I'll be bound that no soul here can budge a foot to follow you.

HASTINGS. My dear friend, how can I be grateful?

TONY. Ay, now its dear friend, noble 'Squire. Just now, it was all idiot, cub, and run me through the guts. Damn *your* way of fighting, I say. After we take a knock in this part of the country, we kiss and be friends. But if you had run me through the guts, then I should be dead, and you might go kiss the hangman.

HASTINGS. The rebuke is just. But I must hasten to relieve Miss Neville; if you keep the old lady employed, I promise to take care of the young one. [*Exit* HASTINGS.]

TONY. Never fear me. Here she comes. Vanish. She's got from the pond, and draggled up to the waist like a mermaid. [*Enter* MRS. HARDCASTLE.]

MRS. HARDCASTLE. Oh, Tony, I'm killed. Shook. Battered to death. I shall never survive it. That last jolt that laid us against the quickset hedge has done my business.

TONY. Alack, mama, it was all your own fault. You would be for running away by night, without knowing one inch of the way.

MRS. HARDCASTLE. I wish we were at home again. I never met so many accidents in so short a journey. Drench'd in the mud, overturn'd in a ditch, stuck fast in a slough, jolted to a jelly, and at last to lose our way. Whereabouts do you think we are, Tony?

TONY. By my guess we should be upon Crackskull Common, about forty miles from home.

MRS. HARDCASTLE. O lud! O lud! the most notorious spot in all the country. We only want a robbery to make a complete night on't.

TONY. Don't be afraid, mama, don't be afraid. Two of the five that kept here are hanged, and the other three may not find us. Don't be afraid. Is that a man that's galloping behind us? No;

it's only a tree. Don't be afraid.

MRS. HARDCASTLE. The fright will certainly kill me.

TONY. Do you see any thing like a black hat moving behind the thicket?

MRS. HARDCASTLE. O death!

TONY. No, it's only a cow. Don't be afraid, mama; don't be afraid.

MRS. HARDCASTLE. As I'm alive, Tony, I see a man coming towards us. Ah! I'm sure on't. If he perceives us, we are undone.

TONY. [*Aside.*] Father-in-law, by all that's unlucky, come to take one of his night walks. [*To her.*]Ah, it's a highwayman, with pistols as long as my arm. A damn'd ill-looking fellow.

MRS. HARDCASTLE. Good heaven defend us! He approaches.

TONY. Do you hide yourself in that thicket, and leave me to manage him. If there be any danger, I'll cough, and cry hem. When I cough be sure to keep close. [MRS. HARDCASTLE *hides behind a tree in the back scene. Enter* HARDCASTLE.]

HARDCASTLE. I'm mistaken, or I heard voices of people in want of help. Oh, Tony, is that you? I did not expect you so soon back. Are your mother and her charge in safety?

TONY. Very safe, Sir, at my Aunt Pedigree's. Hem.

MRS. HARDCASTLE. [*From behind.*] Ah death! I find there's danger.

HARDCASTLE. Forty miles in three hours; sure, that's too much, my youngster.

TONY. Stout horses and willing minds make short journeys as they say. Hem.

MRS. HARDCASTLE. [*From behind.*] Sure he'll do the dear boy no harm.

HARDCASTLE. But I heard a voice here; I should be glad to know from whence it came?

TONY. It was I, Sir, talking to myself, Sir. I was saying that forty miles in four hours was very good going. Hem. As to be sure it was. Hem. I have got a sort of cold by being out in the air. We'll go in, if you please. Hem.

HARDCASTLE. But if you talk'd to yourself, you did not answer yourself. I am certain I heard two voices, and am resolved [*Raising his voice.*] to find the other out.

MRS. HARDCASTLE. [*From behind.*] Oh! he's coming to find me out. Oh!

TONY. What need you go, Sir, if I tell you? Hem. I'll lay down my life for the truth—hem—I'll tell you all, Sir. [*Detaining him.*]

HARDCASTLE. I tell you, I will not be detained. I insist on seeing. It's in vain to expect I'll believe you.

MRS. HARDCASTLE. [*Running forward from behind.*] O lud, he'll murder my poor boy, my darling. Here, good gentleman, whet your rage upon me. Take my money, my life, but spare that young gentleman, spare my child, if you have any mercy!

HARDCASTLE. My wife! as I'm a Christian. From whence can she come, or what does she mean?

MRS. HARDCASTLE. [*Kneeling.*] Take compassion on us, good Mr. Highwayman. Take our money, our watches, all we have, but spare our lives. We will never bring you to justice, indeed we won't, good Mr. Highwayman.

HARDCASTLE. I believe the woman's out of her senses. What, Dorothy, don't you know *me?*

MRS. HARDCASTLE. Mr. Hardcastle, as I'm alive! My fears blinded me. But who, my dear, could have expected to meet you here, in this frightful place, so far from home. What has brought you to follow us?

HARDCASTLE. Sure, Dorothy, you have not lost your wits. So far from home, when you are within forty yards of your own door. [*To him.*] This is one of your old tricks, you graceless rogue you. [*To her.*] Don't you know the gate, and the mulberry-tree; and don't you remember the horse-pond, my dear?

MRS. HARDCASTLE. Yes, I shall remember the horse-pond as long as I live; I have caught my death in it. [*To* TONY.] And is it to you, you graceless varlet, I owe all this? I'll teach you to abuse your mother, I will.

TONY. Ecod, mother, all the parish says you have spoil'd me, and so you may take the fruits on't.

MRS. HARDCASTLE. I'll spoil you, I will.

[*Follows him off the stage. Exit.*]

HARDCASTLE. There's morality, however, in his reply. [*Exit. Enter* HASTINGS *and* MISS NEVILLE.]

HASTINGS. My dear Constance, why will you deliberate thus? If we delay a moment, all is lost for ever. Pluck up a little resolution, and we shall soon be out of the reach of her malignity.

MISS NEVILLE. I find it impossible. My spirits are so sunk with the agitations I have suffered, that I am unable to face any new danger. Two or three years patience will at last crown us with happiness.

HASTINGS. Such a tedious delay is worse than inconstancy. Let us fly, my charmer. Let us date our happiness from this very moment. Perish fortune. Love and content will increase what we possess beyond a monarch's revenue. Let me prevail.

MISS NEVILLE. No, Mr. Hastings; no. Prudence once more comes to my relief, and I will obey its dictates. In the moment of passion, fortune may be despised, but it ever produces a lasting repentance. I'm resolved to apply to Mr. Hardcastle's compassion and justice for redress.

HASTINGS. But tho' he had the will, he has not the power to relieve you.

MISS NEVILLE. But he has influence, and upon that I am resolved to rely.

HASTINGS. I have no hopes. But since you persist, I must reluctantly obey you. [*Exeunt. Scene changes to inside the house. Enter* SIR CHARLES *and* MISS HARDCASTLE.]

SIR CHARLES. What a situation am I in. If what you say appears, I shall then find a guilty son. If what he says be true, I shall then lose one that, of all others, I most wish'd for a daughter.

MISS HARDCASTLE. I am proud of your approbation, and to shew I merit it, if you place yourselves as I directed, you shall hear his explicit declaration. But he comes.

SIR CHARLES. I'll to your father, and keep him to the appointment. [*Exit* SIR CHARLES. *Enter* MARLOW.]

MARLOW. Tho' prepar'd for setting out, I come once more to take leave, nor did I, till this moment, know the pain I feel in the separation.

MISS HARDCASTLE. [*In her own natural manner.*] I believe these sufferings cannot be very great, Sir, which you can so easily remove. A day or two longer, perhaps, might lessen your uneasiness, by shewing the little value of what you now think proper to regret.

MARLOW. [*Aside.*] This girl every moment improves upon me. [*To her.*] It must not be, Madam. I have already trifled too long with my heart. My very pride begins to submit to my passion. The disparity of education and fortune, the anger of a parent, and the contempt of my equals, begin to lose their weight; and nothing can restore me to myself, but this painful effort of resolution.

MISS HARDCASTLE. Then go, Sir. I'll urge nothing more to detain you. Tho' my family be as good as hers you came down to visit, and my education, I hope, not inferior, what are these advantages without equal affluence? I must remain contented with the slight approbation of imputed merit; I must have only the mockery of your addresses, while all your serious aims are fix'd on fortune. [*Enter* HARDCASTLE *and* SIR CHARLES *from behind.*]

SIR CHARLES. Here, behind this screen.

HARDCASTLE. Ay, ay, make no noise. I'll engage my Kate covers him with confusion at last.

MARLOW. By heavens, Madam, fortune was ever my smallest consideration. Your beauty at first caught my eye; for who could see that without emotion? But every moment that I converse with you steals in some new grace, heightens the picture, and gives it stronger expression. What at first seem'd rustic plainness, now appears refin'd simplicity. What seem'd forward assurance, now strikes me as the result of courageous innocence, and conscious virtue.

SIR CHARLES. What can it mean! He amazes me!

HARDCASTLE. I told you how it would be. Hush!

MARLOW. I am now determined to stay, Madam, and I have too good an opinion of my father's discernment, when he sees you, to doubt his approbation.

MISS HARDCASTLE. No, Mr. Marlow, I will not, cannot detain you. Do you think I could suffer a connexion, in which there is the smallest room for repentance? Do you think I would take the mean advantage of a transient passion, to load you with confusion? Do you think I could ever relish that happiness, which was acquired by lessening your's?

MARLOW. By all that's good, I can have no happiness but what's in your power to grant me. Nor shall I ever feel repentance, but in not having seen your merits before. I will stay, even contrary to your wishes; and tho' you should persist to shun me, I will make my respectful assiduities atone for the levity of my past conduct.

MISS HARDCASTLE. Sir, I must entreat you'll desist. As our acquaintance began, so let it end, in indifference. I might have given an hour or two to levity; but seriously, Mr. Marlow, do you think I could ever submit to a connexion, where *I* must appear mercenary, and *you* imprudent? Do you think I could ever catch at the confident addresses of a secure admirer?

MARLOW. [*Kneeling.*] Does this look like security? Does this look like confidence? No, Madam, every moment that shews me your merit, only serves to increase my diffidence and confusion. Here let me continue—

SIR CHARLES. I can hold it no longer. Charles, Charles, how hast thou deceived me! Is this your indifference, your uninteresting conversation!

HARDCASTLE. Your cold contempt; your formal interview! What have you to say now?

MARLOW. That I'm all amazement! What can it mean!

HARDCASTLE. It means that you can say and unsay things at pleasure. That you can address a lady in private, and deny it in public; that you have one story for us, and another for my daughter.

MARLOW. Daughter!—this lady your daughter!

HARDCASTLE. Yes, Sir, my only daughter. My Kate, whose else should she be?

MARLOW. Oh, the devil!

MISS HARDCASTLE. Yes, Sir, that very identical tall, squinting lady you were pleased to take me for. [*Curtsying.*] She that you addressed as the mild, modest, sentimental man of gravity, and the bold, forward, agreeable Rattle of the Ladies Club; ha, ha, ha.

MARLOW. Zounds, there's no bearing this; it's worse than death.

MISS HARDCASTLE. In which of your characters, Sir, will you give us leave to address you? As the faltering gentleman, with looks on the ground, that speaks just to be heard, and hates hypocrisy; or the loud, confident creature, that keeps it up with Mrs. Mantrap, and old Miss Biddy Buckskin, till three in the morning; ha, ha, ha!

MARLOW. O, curse on my noisy head. I never attempted to be impudent yet, that I was not taken down. I must be gone.

HARDCASTLE. By the hand of my body, but you shall not. I see it was all a mistake, and I am rejoiced to find it. You shall not, Sir, I tell you. I know she'll forgive you. Won't you forgive him, Kate? We'll all forgive you. Take courage, man. [*They retire, she tormenting him, to the back scene. Enter* MRS. HARDCASTLE, TONY.]

MRS. HARDCASTLE. So, so, they're gone off. Let them go, I care not.

HARDCASTLE. Who gone?

MRS. HARDCASTLE. My dutiful niece and her gentleman, Mr. Hastings, from Town. He who came down with our modest visitor here.

SIR CHARLES. Who, my honest George Hastings? As worthy a fellow as lives, and the girl could not have made a more prudent choice.

HARDCASTLE. Then, by the hand of my body, I'm proud of the connexion.

MRS. HARDCASTLE. Well, if he has taken away the lady, he has not taken her fortune; that remains in this family to console us for her loss.

HARDCASTLE. Sure, Dorothy, you would not be so mercenary?

MRS. HARDCASTLE. Ay, that's my affair, not your's.

HARDCASTLE. But you know if your son, when of age, refuses to marry his cousin, her whole fortune is then at her own disposal.

MRS. HARDCASTLE. Ay, but he's not of age, and she has not thought proper to wait for his refusal. [*Enter* HASTINGS *and* MISS NEVILLE.]

MRS. HARDCASTLE. [*Aside.*] What! returned so soon? I begin not to like it.

HASTINGS. [*To* HARDCASTLE.] For my late attempt to fly off with your niece, let my present confusion be my punishment. We are now come back, to appeal from your justice to your humanity. By her father's consent, I first paid her my addresses, and our passions were first founded in duty.

MISS NEVILLE. Since his death, I have been obliged to stoop to dissimulation to avoid oppression. In an hour of levity, I was ready even to give up my fortune to secure my choice. But I'm now recover'd from the delusion, and hope from your tenderness what is denied me from a nearer connexion.

MRS. HARDCASTLE. Pshaw, pshaw, this is all but the whining end of a modern novel.

HARDCASTLE. Be it what it will, I'm glad they're come back to reclaim their due. Come hither. Tony boy. Do you refuse this lady's hand whom I now offer you?

TONY. What signifies my refusing? You know I can't refuse her till I'm of age, father.

HARDCASTLE. While I thought concealing your age, boy, was likely to conduce to your improvement, I concurred with your mother's desire to keep it secret. But since I find she turns it to a wrong use, I must now declare, you have been of age these three months.

TONY. Of age! Am I of age, father?

HARDCASTLE. Above three months.

TONY. Then you'll see the first use I'll make of my liberty. [*Taking* MISS NEVILLE's *hand.*] Witness all men by these presents, that I, Anthony Lumpkin, Esquire, of Blank place, refuse you, Constantia Neville, spinster, of no place at all, for my true and lawful wife. So Constance Neville may marry whom she pleases, and Tony Lumpkin is his own man again!

SIR CHARLES. O brave 'Squire!

HASTINGS. My worthy friend!

MRS. HARDCASTLE. My undutiful offspring!

MARLOW. Joy, my dear George, I give you joy sincerely. And could I prevail upon my little tyrant here to be less arbitrary, I should be the happiest man alive, if you would return me the favour.

HASTINGS. [To MISS HARDCASTLE.] Come, Madam, you are now driven to the very last scene of all your contrivances. I know you like him, I'm sure he loves you, and you must and shall have him.

HARDCASTLE. [Joining their hands.] And I say so too. And Mr. Marlow, if she makes as good a wife as she has a daughter, I don't believe you'll ever repent your bargain. So now to supper; tomorrow we shall gather all the poor of the parish about us, and the Mistakes of the Night shall be crowned with a merry morning; so boy, take her; and as you have been mistaken in the mistress, my wish is, that you may never be mistaken in the wife.

1. At the top of the coach, in the back.
2. Cf. *1 Henry IV*, 5.1.126.
3. Drinking bowl.
4. Cf. *Hamlet*, 1.5.125.
5. At the time the play was written, an impossible task.
6. Wounds, an oath on Christ's wounds.
7. Prostitutes.
8. A popular expression commenting on the political situation, since voters were often bribed with free ale.
9. Indian rulers.
10. A popular Irish song.
11. The bonnets then in fashion almost totally concealed the face.
12. Locations in London, the last of which was not at all fashionable.
13. Who distributed newsletters regarding high fashion.
14. Hair style.
15. I.e., all women are now attractive because none are disfigured by smallpox.
16. Popular books of home remedies.
17. Embarrassment.
18. Fool's gold.
19. A spinning firework.
20. A play by George Farquhar (1707).
21. Typical names of rooms in a pub.
22. The second story walkway around the innyard.
23. "Snake eyes," double ones on the dice.
24. Fop.
25. Harpsichord.
26. The supposed letter contains a number of terms from cock fighting.
27. Bethlehem Hospital, an insane asylum.
28. Swords with basketlike guards.
29. Objectionable or troublesome persons.

The School for Scandal

Richard B. Sheridan

After Goldsmith, the other great writer whose plays illuminated the otherwise benighted eighteenth-century London stage was Richard Brinsley Sheridan. Like his older colleague, Sheridan had many other interests and thus did not devote his full energies to playwriting, but his plays represent a high level of achievement by any standards, and *The School for Scandal* is widely accepted as the best English comedy after those of Shakespeare. In fact, only Shakespeare's plays have been more regularly and frequently produced than this one, both in London and throughout the English-speaking world.

Sheridan was the third son of Thomas Sheridan, a successful actor and elocution teacher, and his wife Frances, a writer of some note whose best play, *The Discovery*, was produced by David Garrick at Drury Lane in 1763. Richard was born in Dublin; the exact date is unknown, but he was baptized on November 4, 1751. Although his family was Irish, they moved to London while Richard was a child, and he never returned to Ireland; he was educated in London and later at Harrow. He moved to Bath in 1770, where he met and married Elizabeth Ann Linely after a tempestuous courtship, an elopement to France, and two duels. She was a fine singer, and her father was a composer and conductor who later collaborated in both business and artistic ventures with Sheridan.

It was perhaps natural that Sheridan, after his marriage, turned to the theater for a livelihood. His first play, *The Rivals*, opened in London on January 17, 1775, and, after some rewriting, was a major hit. It revolves around a young man who, in disguise, wins a young woman's heart and then finds that their guardians have planned their marriage. A number of the characters are excellent comic portraits, and Mrs. Malaprop, who regularly and hilariously misuses the English language, has now given it her name as a common noun expressing that particular solecism. *The Rivals* is still regularly revived and enjoyed. Later in the same year, Sheridan wrote a short farce entitled *St. Patrick's Day*, and a ballad opera called *The Duenna*, which enjoyed an even longer initial run than had John Gay's *The Beggar's Opera*. The next year, Sheridan entered a partnership to purchase the Drury Lane theater, which he then managed until its destruction by fire in 1809.

On May 8, 1777, Sheridan opened *The School for Scandal* in his theater. Its success was immediate, and Sheridan's fame and fortune seemed secure. In 1779, he staged *The Critic* as a comic afterpiece to *Hamlet*, and from time to time he rewrote the plays of others, but Sheridan never wrote another original full-length play. Even his interest in the management of his theater waned as he entered Parliament in 1780 at the age of twenty-eight. He served for the next thirty-two years, rising to several cabinet posts and distinguishing himself as an orator. His speeches during his management of the impeachment of Warren Hastings marked the high point of his political influence. Hastings's acquittal and Sheridan's failure to attain the leadership of the Whig party were signal defeats, and he was finally outmaneuvered and lost his parliamentary seat in 1812. Beset by financial woes resulting from this loss and the Drury Lane fire, Sheridan died amid bailiffs and creditors on July 7, 1816, in London.

Sheridan openly admired the Restoration playwrights, especially William Congreve, and Congreve's influence can be clearly seen in Sheridan's work. Still, it would be a mistake to see *The School for Scandal* as a Restoration comedy out of its time or Sheridan as a latter-day Congreve. Congreve's verbal wit is the very essence of his characters, and Millamant or Mirabell is clearly a more intriguing human being than Charles Surface or Maria precisely because of the multifaceted insight into human behavior that their verbal wit affords. On the other hand, Sheridan was a master of stagecraft, whose characters not only are reasonably witty, but also partake in stage action that creates outstanding theater. Whereas *The Way of the World* gains its principal effectiveness from its language, and thus may be more appreciated in the study than on the stage, *The School for Scandal* depends primarily on staged action, and must be seen (or at least imagined) on the stage to be appreciated fully. What makes the screen scene, for example, justly famous is not only the marvelous image of Lady Teazle suddenly revealed to the delight of Charles and the distress of Joseph and Sir Peter, but also the superb way that this carefully engineered bit of stage business resolves some of the major questions of the plot. The building dramatic irony as the audience knows of Lady Teazle's presence and anticipates Charles's discomfort explodes in a magnificently theatrical moment in which the audience sees and grasps the full significance of the revelation simultaneously with the characters involved. This is not only masterful plotting, it is using the very essence of the theatrical to carry the play. Congreve was a greater literary figure than Sheridan, and *The Way of the World* succeeds despite its theatrical shortcomings, but Sheridan was the better theatrical craftsman. Shakespeare, achieving supreme mastery in both respects, was the greatest playwright of them all.

Sheridan constructed *The School for Scandal* out of the drafts of two earlier plays on which he had been working, one concerning the marital difficulties of the Teazles and the other portraying the scandal and backbiting of a rumor-mongering society. He has integrated those two story lines brilliantly but not completely in the present work so that the Teazle story is the play's central action but the rumor mongers provide so effective a background that they sometimes become the chief comic interest of the play. The entire first scene, for example, provides a modicum of expository material regarding the Teazles, but is primarily entertaining because the characters introduced, though secondary to the main plot for the most part, are so comically interesting. Although Charles and Maria are the nearest approach to the traditional young lovers in the play, and thus of some interest to the outcome of the plot, Charles is not even introduced until act 3, scene 3. The effective way in which Sheridan has built to Charles's entrance, however, makes him the more engaging when he does appear. Still another sense in which the structure of this play clearly grows out of the theatrical environment for which it was written is its dependence on wing-and-drop scene shifts. The distracting quality that results from frequent scene shifts in some plays is not in evidence here, for one scene flows neatly into the next by the simple expedient of sliding one set aside to reveal the next. Thus, changes of scene, which could be debilitating, are here an enhancing factor that lend an increased sense of movement and urgency to the play's rhythm.

Although *The School for Scandal* may be categorized as a comedy of manners, the society whose manners it reflects is clearly a different one from that of the Restoration period. The eighteenth century was an age of sentimental comedy, the function of which was to praise virtue rather than to ridicule vice. Whereas Restoration comedy (along with the great comedy of Aristophanes, Molière, and others) portrayed the folly of mankind in such a way as to provoke appreciative laughter, sentimental comedy instructed its audiences in virtuous behavior both by sententious maxims and by rewarding at the end those "good" characters who deserved it.

Thus, the brittle dialogue and sometimes angry satire that offended some in the seventeenth century are largely replaced in the eighteenth with a more balanced play world in which virtue is rewarded and vice punished. In mediocre plays, this obvious simplicity is wearing, and *The School for Scandal* does not altogether escape it. Thus, Charles's refusal to sell his uncle's portrait convinces Sir Oliver of his essential goodness, and Charles similarly expiates years of profligacy by his generous impulses toward Mr. Stanley. Snake, Lady Sneerwell, Joseph, and all the rumor mongers must suffer defeat in the last act. Happily, however, Sheridan has managed to meet these demands of his society without allowing sentimentalism to dominate his play, for he finds theatrical strokes that hold an audience's interest without focusing undue attention on the moralistic issues underneath. Hence, Sir Oliver's disguise and the portrait auction are vastly more interesting than Sir Oliver's exact reason for supporting Charles; Charles's profligacy is portrayed as love of life and good times, in as merry a party scene and drinking song as may be found anywhere in dramatic literature; Snake and the others, though defeated, are each given a superb exit that comically mitigates any audience tendency to hiss the villains and cheer the heroes. Of course Joseph Surface's hypocritical sentiments serve as satire on the public's appreciation of the sentiments expressed in a great many plays, but in a more fundamental way *The School for Scandal* is still an expression of the sentiment-cloyed era from which it emerged.

The structural features of *The School for Scandal* discussed above are among the play's most interesting elements. Its characters, though very effective caricatures, are of no great note as three-dimensional dramatic portraits. The old husband and the young wife were regularly done better by Molière; Charles and Joseph Surface are too utterly opposite to be fully believable; Sir Oliver, Maria, Moses, and the others merely perform plot functions. Snake, Lady Sneerwell, Mrs. Candour, Sir Benjamin Backbite, and Crabtree are hilarious sketches that make their satirical point most effectively, but they lose credibility as soon as they attempt to take on other human dimensions. Lady Sneerwell's love for Charles, for example, is advanced to meet a plot need but is totally without foundation in the character of either. Thematically, the play has little to say that is not obvious, and its use of language shows the deterioration of elegance that has been nearly uninterrupted in English drama from the Restoration to today.

The School for Scandal is a work with a rather curious history. It has been attacked by literary critics for the faults discussed here and many more, yet it has continued to hold the stage as has no other English play save those of Shakespeare. Some critics even find its stage success a fault in itself, as though theatrical art were somehow a shade less respectable than the other arts. It is finally as a theatrical work, however, that the play is brilliant, and one only regrets that Sheridan, only twenty-five years old when he wrote it, did not continue to develop this brilliance into other masterpieces for the stage. Clearly, his was an extraordinary talent.

The School for Scandal

Characters
Sir Peter Teazle
Sir Oliver Surface
Sir Harry Bumper
Sir Benjamin Backbite
Joseph Surface
Charles Surface
Careless
Snake
Crabtree
Rowley
Moses
Trip
Lady Teazle
Lady Sneerwell
Mrs. Candour
Maria
Gentlemen, Maid, Servants

Act 1

Scene 1

LADY SNEERWELL's *dressing-room.* LADY SNEERWELL *discovered at her toilet;* SNAKE *drinking chocolate.*

LADY SNEERWELL. The paragraphs, you say, Mr. Snake, were all inserted?

SNAKE. They were, madam; and, as I copied them myself in a feigned hand, there can be no suspicion whence they came.

LADY SNEERWELL. Did you circulate the report of Lady Brittle's intrigue with Captain Boastall?

SNAKE. That's in as fine a train as your ladyship could wish. In the common course of things, I think it must reach Mrs. Clackitt's ears within four-and-twenty hours; and then, you know, the business is as good as done.

LADY SNEERWELL. Why, truly, Mrs. Clackitt has a very pretty talent, and a great deal of industry.

SNAKE. True, madam, and has been tolerably successful in her day. To my knowledge, she has been the cause of six matches being broken off, and three sons being disinherited; of four forced elopements, and as many close confinements; nine separate maintenances, and two divorces. Nay, I have more than once traced her causing a tête-à-tête in the "Town and Country Magazine," when the parties, perhaps, had never seen each other's face before in the course of their lives.

LADY SNEERWELL. She certainly has talents, but her manner is gross.

SNAKE. 'Tis very true. She generally designs well, has a free tongue and a bold invention; but her colouring is too dark, and her outlines often extravagant. She wants that delicacy of tint, and mellowness of sneer, which distinguish your ladyship's scandal.

LADY SNEERWELL. You are partial, Snake.

SNAKE. Not in the least; everybody allows that Lady Sneerwell can do more with a word or look than many can with the most laboured detail, even when they happen to have a little truth on their side to support it.

LADY SNEERWELL. Yes, my dear Snake; and I am no hypocrite to deny the satisfaction I reap from the success of my efforts. Wounded myself, in the early part of my life, by the envenomed tongue of slander, I confess I have since known no pleasure equal to the reducing others to the level of my own injured reputation.

SNAKE. Nothing can be more natural. But, Lady Sneerwell, there is one affair in which you have lately employed me, wherein, I confess, I am at a loss to guess your motives.

LADY SNEERWELL. I conceive you mean with respect to my neighbour, Sir Peter Teazle, and his family?

SNAKE. I do. Here are two young men, to whom Sir Peter has acted as a kind of guardian since their father's death; the eldest possessing the most amiable character, and universally well spoken of—the youngest, the most dissipated and extravagant young fellow in the kingdom, without friends or character: the former an avowed admirer of your ladyship, and apparently your favourite; the latter attached to Maria, Sir Peter's ward, and confessedly beloved by her. Now, on the face of these circumstances, it is utterly unaccountable to me, why you, the widow of a city knight, with a good jointure, should not close with the passion of a man of such character and expectations as Mr. Surface; and more so why you should be so uncommonly earnest to destroy the mutual attachment subsisting between his brother Charles and Maria.

LADY SNEERWELL. Then, at once to unravel this mystery, I must inform you that love has no share whatever in the intercourse between Mr. Surface and me.

SNAKE. No!

LADY SNEERWELL. His real attachment is to Maria or her fortune; but, finding in his brother a favored rival, he has been obliged to mask his pretensions, and profit by my assistance.

SNAKE. Yet still I am more puzzled why you should interest yourself in his success.

LADY SNEERWELL. Heavens! how dull you are! Cannot you surmise the weakness which I hitherto, through shame, have concealed even from you? Must I confess that Charles— that libertine, that extravagant, that bankrupt in fortune and reputation—that he it is for whom I am thus anxious and malicious, and to gain whom I would sacrifice everything?

SNAKE. Now, indeed, your conduct appears consistent; but how came you and Mr. Surface so confidential?

LADY SNEERWELL. For our mutual interest. I have found him out a long time since. I know him to be artful, selfish, and malicious—in short, a sentimental knave; while with Sir Peter, and indeed with all his acquaintance, he passes for a youthful miracle of prudence, good sense, and benevolence.

SNAKE. Yes; yet Sir Peter vows he has not his equal in England; and, above all, he praises him as a man of sentiment.

LADY SNEERWELL. True; and with the assistance of his sentiment and hypocrisy he has brought Sir Peter entirely into his interest with regard to Maria; while poor Charles has no friend in the house—though, I fear, he has a powerful one in Maria's heart, against whom we must direct our schemes. [*Enter* SERVANT.]

SERVANT. Mr. Surface.

LADY SNEERWELL. Show him up.—[*Exit* SERVANT.] He generally calls about this time. I don't wonder at people giving him to me for a lover. [*Enter* JOSEPH SURFACE.]

JOSEPH. My dear Lady Sneerwell, how do you do to-day? Mr. Snake, your most obedient.

LADY SNEERWELL. Snake has just been rallying me on our mutual attachment; but I have informed him of our real views. You know how useful he has been to us; and, believe me, the confidence is not ill-placed.

JOSEPH. Madam, it is impossible for me to suspect a man of Mr. Snake's sensibility and discernment.

LADY SNEERWELL. Well, well, no compliments now; but tell me when you saw your mistress, Maria—or, what is more material to me, your brother.

JOSEPH. I have not seen either since I left you; but I can inform you that they never meet. Some of your stories have taken a good effect on Maria.

LADY SNEERWELL. Ah, my dear Snake! the merit of this belongs to you. But do your brother's distresses increase?

JOSEPH. Every hour. I am told he has had another execution in the house yesterday. In short, his dissipation and extravagance exceed anything I have ever heard of.

LADY SNEERWELL. Poor Charles!

JOSEPH. True, madam; notwithstanding his vices, one can't help feeling for him. Poor Charles! I'm sure I wish it were in my power to be of any essential service to him; for the man who does not share in the distresses of a brother, even though merited by his own misconduct, deserves—

LADY SNEERWELL. O Lud! you are going to be moral, and forget that you are among friends.

JOSEPH. Egad, that's true! I'll keep that sentiment till I see Sir Peter. However, it is certainly a charity to rescue Maria from such a libertine, who, if he is to be reclaimed, can be so only by a person of your ladyship's superior accomplishments and understanding.

SNAKE. I believe, Lady Sneerwell, here's company coming; I'll go and copy the letter I mentioned to you. Mr. Surface, your most obedient.

JOSEPH. Sir, your very devoted.—[*Exit* SNAKE.] Lady Sneerwell, I am very sorry you have put any farther confidence in that fellow.

LADY SNEERWELL. Why so?

JOSEPH. I have lately detected him in frequent conference with old Rowley, who was formerly my father's steward, and has never, you know, been a friend of mine.

LADY SNEERWELL. And do you think he would betray us?

JOSEPH. Nothing more likely: take my word for't, Lady Sneerwell, that fellow hasn't virtue enough to be faithful even to his own villany. Ah, Maria! [*Enter* MARIA.]

LADY SNEERWELL. Maria, my dear, how do you do? What's the matter?

MARIA. Oh! there's that disagreeable lover of mine, Sir Benjamin Backbite, has just called at my guardian's, with his odious uncle, Crabtree; so I slipped out, and ran hither to avoid them.

LADY SNEERWELL. Is that all?

JOSEPH. If my brother Charles had been of the party, madam, perhaps you would not have been so much alarmed.

LADY SNEERWELL. Nay, now you are severe; for I dare swear the truth of the matter is, Maria heard you were here. But, my dear, what has Sir Benjamin done, that you should avoid him so?

MARIA. Oh, he had done nothing—but 'tis for what he has said: his conversation is a perpetual libel on all his acquaintance.

JOSEPH. Ay, and the worst of it is, there is no advantage in not knowing him; for he'll abuse a stranger just as soon as his best friend: and his uncle's as bad.

LADY SNEERWELL. Nay, but we should make allowance; Sir Benjamin is a wit and a poet.

MARIA. For my part, I own, madam, wit loses its respect with me, when I see it in company with malice. What do you think, Mr. Surface?

JOSEPH. Certainly, madam; to smile at the jest which plants a thorn in another's breast is to become a principal in the mischief.

LADY SNEERWELL. Psha! there's no possibility of being witty without a little ill-nature: the malice of a good thing is the barb that makes it stick. What's your opinion, Mr. Surface?

JOSEPH. To be sure, madam; that conversation, where the spirit of raillery is suppressed, will ever appear tedious and insipid.

MARIA. Well, I'll not debate how far scandal may be allowable; but in a man, I am sure, it is always contemptible. We have pride, envy, rivalship, and a thousand motives to depreciate each other; but the male slanderer must have the cowardice of a woman before he can traduce one. [*Re-enter* SERVANT.]

SERVANT. Madam, Mrs. Candour is below, and, if your ladyship's at leisure, will leave her carriage.

LADY SNEERWELL. Beg her to walk in.— [*Exit* SERVANT.] Now, Maria, here is a character to your taste; for, though Mrs. Candour is a little talkative, everybody knows her to be the best-natured and best sort of woman.

MARIA. Yes, with a very gross affectation of good nature and benevolence, she does more mischief than the direct malice of old Crabtree.

JOSEPH. I'faith that's true, Lady Sneerwell: whenever I hear the current running against the characters of my friends, I never think them in such danger as when Candour undertakes their defence.

LADY SNEERWELL. Hush!—here she is!

[*Enter* MRS. CANDOUR.]

MRS. CANDOUR. My dear Lady Sneerwell, how have you been this century?—Mr. Surface, what news do you hear?—though indeed it is no matter, for I think one hears nothing else but scandal.

JOSEPH. Just so, indeed, ma'am.

MRS. CANDOUR. Oh, Maria! child,—what, is the whole affair off between you and Charles? His extravagance, I presume—the town talks of nothing else.

MARIA. I am very sorry, ma'am, the town has so little to do.

MRS. CANDOUR. True, true, child: but there's no stopping people's tongues. I own I was hurt to hear it, as I indeed was to learn, from the same quarter, that your guardian, Sir Peter, and Lady Teazle have not agreed lately as well as could be wished.

MARIA. 'Tis strangely impertinent for people to busy themselves so.

MRS. CANDOUR. Very true, child; but what's to be done? People will talk—there's no preventing it. Why, it was but yesterday I was told that Miss Gadabout had eloped with Sir Filagree Flirt. But, Lord! there's no minding what one hears; though, to be sure, I had this from very good authority.

MARIA. Such reports are highly scandalous.

MRS. CANDOUR. So they are, child—shameful, shameful! But the world is so censorious, no character escapes. Lord, now who would have suspected your friend, Miss Prim, of an indiscretion? Yet such is the ill-nature of people, that they say her uncle stopped her last week, just as she was stepping into the York mail with her dancing-master.

MARIA. I'll answer for't there are no grounds for that report.

MRS. CANDOUR. Ah, no foundation in the world, I dare swear: no more, probably, than the story circulated last month, of Mrs. Festino's affair with Colonel Cassino—though, to be sure, that matter was never rightly cleared up.

JOSEPH. The license of invention some people take is monstrous indeed.

MARIA. 'Tis so; but, in my opinion, those who report such things are equally culpable.

MRS. CANDOUR. To be sure they are; tale-bearers are as bad as the tale-makers—'tis an old observation, and a very true one: but what's to be done, as I said before? how will you prevent people from talking? Today, Mrs. Clackitt assured me, Mr. and Mrs. Honeymoon were at last become mere man and wife, like the rest of their acquaintance. She likewise hinted that a certain widow, in the next street, had got rid of her dropsy and recovered her shape in a most surprising manner. And at the same time Miss Tattle, who was by, affirmed, that Lord Buffalo had discovered his lady at a house of no extraordinary fame; and that Sir Harry Bouquet and Tom Saunter were to measure swords on a similar provocation. But, Lord, do you think I would report these things? No, no! tale-bearers, as I said before, are just as bad as the tale-makers.

JOSEPH. Ah! Mrs. Candour, if everybody had your forbearance and good nature!

MRS. CANDOUR. I confess, Mr. Surface, I cannot bear to hear people attacked behind their backs; and when ugly circumstances come out against our acquaintance I own I always love to think the best. By-the-by, I hope 'tis not true that your brother is absolutely ruined?

JOSEPH. I am afraid his circumstances are very bad indeed, ma'am.

MRS. CANDOUR. Ah!—I heard so—but you must tell him to keep up his spirits; everybody almost is in the same way: Lord Spindle, Sir Thomas Splint, Captain Quinze, and Mr.

Nickit—all up,[1] I hear, within this week; so, if Charles is undone, he'll find half his acquaintance ruined too, and that, you know, is a consolation.

JOSEPH. Doubtless, ma'am—a very great one. [*Re-enter* SERVANT.]

SERVANT. Mr. Crabtree and Sir Benjamin Backbite. [*Exit.*]

LADY SNEERWELL. So, Maria, you see your lover pursues you; positively you shan't escape. [*Enter* CRABTREE *and* SIR BENJAMIN BACKBITE.]

CRABTREE. Lady Sneerwell, I kiss your hand. Mrs. Candour, I don't believe you are acquainted with my nephew, Sir Benjamin Backbite? Egad, ma'am, he has a pretty wit, and is a pretty poet too. Isn't he, Lady Sneerwell?

SIR BENJAMIN. Oh, fie, uncle!

CRABTREE. Nay, egad it's true: I back him at a rebus or a charade against the best rhymer in the kingdom. Has your ladyship heard the epigram he wrote last week on Lady Frizzle's feather catching fire?—Do, Benjamin, repeat it, or the charade you made last night extempore at Mrs. Drowzie's conversazione. Come now; your first is the name of a fish, your second a great naval commander, and—

SIR BENJAMIN. Uncle, now—pr'ythee—

CRABTREE. I'faith, ma'am, 'twould surprise you to hear how ready he is at all these sort of things.

LADY SNEERWELL. I wonder, Sir Benjamin, you never publish anything.

SIR BENJAMIN. To say truth, ma'am, 'tis very vulgar to print; and, as my little productions are mostly satires and lampoons on particular people, I find they circulate more by giving copies in confidence to the friends of the parties. However, I have some elegies, which, when favoured with this lady's smiles, I mean to give the public. [*Pointing to* MARIA.]

CRABTREE. [*To* MARIA.] 'Fore heaven, ma'am, they'll immortalize you—you will be handed down to posterity, like Petrarch's Laura, or Waller's Sacharissa.

SIR BENJAMIN. [*To* MARIA.] Yes, madam, I think you will like them, when you shall see them on a beautiful quarto page, where a neat rivulet of text shall meander through a meadow of margin. 'Fore Gad, they will be the most elegant things of their kind!

CRABTREE. But, ladies, that's true—have you heard the news?

MRS. CANDOUR. What, sir, do you mean the report of—

CRABTREE. No, ma'am, that's not it.— Miss Nicely is going to be married to her own footman.

MRS. CANDOUR. Impossible!

CRABTREE. Ask Sir Benjamin.

SIR BENJAMIN. 'Tis very true, ma'am: everything is fixed, and the wedding liveries bespoke.

CRABTREE. Yes—and they do say there were pressing reasons for it.

LADY SNEERWELL. Why, I have heard something of this before.

MRS. CANDOUR. It can't be—and I wonder any one should believe such a story of so prudent a lady as Miss Nicely.

SIR BENJAMIN. O Lud! ma'am, that's the very reason 'twas believed at once. She has always been so cautious and so reserved, that everybody was sure there was some reason for it at bottom.

MRS. CANDOUR. Why, to be sure, a tale of scandal is as fatal to the credit of a prudent lady of her stamp as a fever is generally to those of the strongest constitutions. But there is a sort of puny sickly reputation, that is always ailing, yet will outlive the robuster characters of a hundred prudes.

SIR BENJAMIN. True, madam, there are valetudinarians in reputation as well as constitution, who, being conscious of their weak part, avoid the last breath of air, and supply their want of stamina by care and circumspection.

MRS. CANDOUR. Well, but this may be all a mistake. You know, Sir Benjamin, very trifling circumstances often give rise to the most injurious tales.

CRABTREE. That they do, I'll be sworn, ma'am. Did you ever hear how Miss Piper came to lose her lover and her character last summer at Tunbridge?—Sir Benjamin, you remember it?

SIR BENJAMIN. Oh, to be sure!—the most whimsical circumstance.

LADY SNEERWELL. How was it, pray?

CRABTREE. Why, one evening, at Mrs. Ponto's assembly, the conversation happened to turn on the breeding Nova Scotia sheep in this country. Says a young lady in company, I have known instances of it; for Miss Letitia Piper, a first cousin of mine, had a Nova Scotia sheep that produced her twins. "What!" cries the Lady Dowager Dundizzy (who you know is as deaf as a post), "has Miss Piper had twins?" This mistake, as you may imagine, threw the whole company into a fit of laughter. However, 'twas the next morning everywhere reported, and in a few days believed by the whole town, that Miss Letitia Piper had actually been brought to bed of a fine boy and girl: and in less than a week there were some people who could name the father, and the farm-house where the babies were put to nurse.

LADY SNEERWELL. Strange, indeed!

CRABTREE. Matter of fact, I assure you. O Lud! Mr. Surface, pray is it true that your uncle, Sir Oliver, is coming home?

JOSEPH. Not that I know of, indeed, sir.

CRABTREE. He has been in the East Indies a long time. You can scarcely remember him, I believe? Sad comfort, whenever he returns, to hear how your brother has gone on!

JOSEPH. Charles has been imprudent, sir, to be sure; but I hope no busy people have already prejudiced Sir Oliver against him. He may reform.

SIR BENJAMIN. To be sure he may; for my part I never believed him to be so utterly void of principle as people say; and though he has lost all his friends, I am told nobody is better spoken of by the Jews.[2]

CRABTREE. That's true, egad, nephew. If the old Jewry was a ward, I believe Charles would be an alderman: no man more popular there, 'fore Gad! I hear he pays as many annuities as the Irish tontine,[3] and that, whenever he is sick, they have prayers for the recovery of his health in all the synagogues.

SIR BENJAMIN. Yet no man lives in greater splendour. They tell me,

when he entertains his friends he will sit down to dinner with a dozen of his own securities; have a score of tradesmen in the antechamber, and an officer behind every guest's chair.

JOSEPH. This may be entertainment to you, gentlemen, but you pay very little regard to the feelings of a brother.

MARIA. [*Aside.*] Their malice is intolerable!—[*Aloud.*] Lady Sneerwell, I must wish you a good morning: I'm not very well. [*Exit.*]

MRS. CANDOUR. O dear! she changes colour very much.

LADY SNEERWELL. Do, Mrs. Candour, follow her; she may want your assistance.

MRS. CANDOUR. That I will, with all my soul, ma'am.—Poor dear girl, who knows what her situation may be! [*Exit.*]

LADY SNEERWELL. 'Twas nothing but that she could not bear to hear Charles reflected on, notwithstanding their difference.

SIR BENJAMIN. The young lady's *penchant* is obvious.

CRABTREE. But, Benjamin, you must not give up the pursuit for that: follow her, and put her into good humour. Repeat her some of your own verses. Come, I'll assist you.

SIR BENJAMIN. Mr. Surface, I did not mean to hurt you; but depend on't your brother is utterly undone.

CRABTREE. O Lud, ay! undone as ever man was—can't raise a guinea.

SIR BENJAMIN. And everything sold, I'm told, that was movable.

CRABTREE. I have seen one that was at his house. Not a thing left but some empty bottles that were overlooked, and the family pictures, which I believe are framed in the wainscots.

SIR BENJAMIN. And I'm very sorry also to hear some bad stories against him. [*Going.*]

CRABTREE. Oh, he has done many mean things, that's certain.

SIR BENJAMIN. But, however, as he's your brother—[*Going.*]

CRABTREE. We'll tell you all another opportunity. [*Exeunt* CRABTREE *and* SIR BENJAMIN.]

LADY SNEERWELL. Ha, ha! 'tis very hard

for them to leave a subject they have not quite run down.

JOSEPH. And I believe the abuse was no more acceptable to your ladyship than to Maria.

LADY SNEERWELL. I doubt[4] her affections are further engaged than we imagine. But the family are to be here this evening, so you may as well dine where you are, and we shall have an opportunity of observing further; in the meantime, I'll go and plot mischief, and you shall study sentiment. [*Exeunt.*]

Scene 2

A room in SIR PETER TEAZLE's *house. Enter* SIR PETER TEAZLE.

SIR PETER. When an old bachelor marries a young wife, what is he to expect? 'Tis now six months since Lady Teazle made me the happiest of men—and I have been the most miserable dog ever since! We tift a little going to church, and fairly quarrelled before the bells had done ringing. I was more than once nearly choked with gall during the honeymoon, and had lost all comfort in life before my friends had done wishing me joy. Yet I chose with caution—a girl bred wholly in the country, who never knew luxury beyond one silk gown, nor dissipation above the annual gala of a race ball. Yet she now plays her part in all the extravagant fopperies of fashion and the town, with as ready a grace as if she never had seen a bush or a grass-plot out of Grosvenor Square! I am sneered at by all my acquaintance, and paragraphed in the newspapers. She dissipates my fortune, and contradicts all my humours; yet the worst of it is, I doubt I love her, or I should never bear all this. However, I'll never be weak enough to own it. [*Enter* ROWLEY.]

ROWLEY. Oh! Sir Peter, your servant: how is it with you, sir?

SIR PETER. Very bad, Master Rowley, very bad. I meet with nothing but crosses and vexations.

ROWLEY. What can have happened since yesterday?

SIR PETER. A good question to a married man!

ROWLEY. Nay, I'm sure, Sir Peter, your lady can't be the cause of your uneasiness.

SIR PETER. Why, has anybody told you she was dead?

ROWLEY. Come, come, Sir Peter, you love her, notwithstanding your tempers don't exactly agree.

SIR PETER. But the fault is entirely hers, Master Rowley. I am myself, the sweetest-tempered man alive, and hate a teasing temper; and so I tell her a hundred times a day.

ROWLEY. Indeed!

SIR PETER. Ay; and what is very extraordinary, in all our disputes she is always in the wrong! But Lady Sneerwell, and the set she meets at her house, encourage the perverseness of her disposition. Then, to complete my vexation, Maria, my ward, whom I ought to have the power of a father over, is determined to turn rebel too, and absolutely refuses the man whom I have long resolved on for her husband; meaning, I suppose, to bestow herself on his profligate brother.

ROWLEY. You know, Sir Peter, I have always taken the liberty to differ with you on the subject of these two young gentlemen. I only wish you may not be deceived in your opinion of the elder. For Charles, my life on't! he will retrieve his errors yet. Their worthy father, once my honoured master, was, at his years, nearly as wild a spark; yet, when he died, he did not leave a more benevolent heart to lament his loss.

SIR PETER. You are wrong, Master Rowley. On their father's death, you know, I acted as a kind of guardian to them both, till their uncle Sir Oliver's liberality gave them an early independence: of course, no person could have more opportunities of judging of their hearts, and I was never mistaken in my life. Joseph is indeed a model for the young men of the age. He is a man of sentiment, and acts up to the sentiments he professes; but, for the other, take my word for't, if he had any grain of virtue by descent, he has dissipated it with the rest of his inheritance. Ah! my old friend, Sir Oliver, will be deeply mortified when he finds how part of his bounty has been misapplied.

ROWLEY. I am sorry to find you so violent against the young man, because this may be the most critical period of his fortune. I came hither with news that will surprise you.

SIR PETER. What! let me hear.

ROWLEY. Sir Oliver is arrived, and at this moment in town.

SIR PETER. How! you astonish me! I thought you did not expect him this month.

ROWLEY. I did not: but his passage has been remarkably quick.

SIR PETER. Egad, I shall rejoice to see my old friend. 'Tis sixteen years since we met. We have had many a day together: but does he still enjoin us not to inform his nephews of his arrival?

ROWLEY. Most strictly. He means, before it is known, to make some trial of their dispositions.

SIR PETER. Ah! There needs no art to discover their merits—however, he shall have his way; but, pray, does he know I am married?

ROWLEY. Yes, and will soon wish you joy.

SIR PETER. What, as we drink health to a friend in consumption! Ah, Oliver will laugh at me. We used to rail at matrimony together, but he has been steady to his text. Well, he must be soon at my house, though—I'll instantly give orders for his reception. But, Master Rowley, don't drop a word that Lady Teazle and I ever disagree.

ROWLEY. By no means.

SIR PETER. For I should never be able to stand Noll's jokes; so I'll have him think, Lord forgive me! that we are a very happy couple.

ROWLEY. I understand you:—but then you must be very careful not to differ while he is in the house with you.

SIR PETER. Egad, and so we must—and that's impossible. Ah! Master Rowley, when an old bachelor marries a young wife, he deserves—no—the

crime carries its punishment along with it. [*Exeunt.*]

Act 2

Scene 1

A room in SIR PETER TEAZLE's *house. Enter* SIR PETER *and* LADY TEAZLE.

SIR PETER. Lady Teazle, Lady Teazle, I'll not bear it!

LADY TEAZLE. Sir Peter, Sir Peter, you may bear it or not, as you please; but I ought to have my own way in everything, and what's more, I will too. What though I was educated in the country, I know very well that women of fashion in London are accountable to nobody after they are married.

SIR PETER. Very well, ma'am, very well; so a husband is to have no influence, no authority?

LADY TEAZLE. Authority! No, to be sure:—if you wanted authority over me, you should have adopted me, and not married me: I am sure you were old enough.

SIR PETER. Old enough!—ay, there it is! Well, well, Lady Teazle, though my life may be made unhappy by your temper, I'll not be ruined by your extravagance!

LADY TEAZLE. My extravagance! I'm sure I'm not more extravagant than a woman of fashion ought to be.

SIR PETER. No, no, madam, you shall throw away no more sums on such unmeaning luxury. 'Slife! to spend as much to furnish your dressing-room with flowers in winter as would suffice to turn the Pantheon[5] into a greenhouse, and give a *fête champêtre*[6] at Christmas.

LADY TEAZLE. And am I to blame, Sir Peter, because flowers are dear in cold weather? You should find fault with the climate, and not with me. For my part, I'm sure I wish it was spring all the year round, and that roses grew under our feet!

SIR PETER. Oons! madam—if you had been born to this, I shouldn't wonder at your talking thus; but you forget what your situation was when I married you.

LADY TEAZLE. No, no, I don't; 'twas a very disagreeable one, or I should never have married you.

SIR PETER. Yes, yes, madam, you were then in somewhat a humbler style—the daughter of a plain country squire. Recollect, Lady Teazle, when I saw you first sitting at your tambour,[7] in a pretty figured linen gown, with a bunch of keys at your side, your hair combed smooth over a roll, and your apartment hung round with fruits in worsted, of your own working.

LADY TEAZLE. Oh, yes! I remember it very well, and a curious life I led. My daily occupation to inspect the dairy, superintend the poultry, make extracts from the family receipt-book, and comb my aunt Deborah's lapdog.

SIR PETER. Yes, yes, ma'am, 'twas so indeed.

LADY TEAZLE. And then, you know, my evening amusements! To draw patterns for ruffles, which I had not the materials to make up; to play Pope Joan[8] with the Curate; to read a sermon to my aunt; or to be stuck down to an old spinet to strum my father to sleep after a fox-chase.

SIR PETER. I am glad you have so good a memory. Yes, madam, these were the recreations I took you from; but now you must have your coach—*vis-à-vis*[9]—and three powdered footmen before your chair; and, in the summer, a pair of white cats[10] to draw you to Kensington Gardens. No recollection, I suppose, when you were content to ride double, behind the butler, on a docked[11] coach-horse?

LADY TEAZLE. No—I swear I never did that; I deny the butler and the coach-horse.

SIR PETER. This, madam, was your situation; and what have I done for you? I have made you a woman of fashion, of fortune, of rank—in short, I have made you my wife.

LADY TEAZLE. Well, then, and there is but one thing more you can make me to add to the obligation, that is—

SIR PETER. My widow, I suppose?

LADY TEAZLE. Hem! hem!

SIR PETER. I thank you, madam—but don't flatter yourself; for, though your ill-conduct may disturb my peace of mind, it shall never break my heart, I promise you: however, I am equally obliged to you for the hint.

LADY TEAZLE. Then why will you endeavour to make yourself so disagreeable to me, and thwart me in every little elegant expense.

SIR PETER. 'Slife, madam, I say, had you any of these little elegant expenses when you married me?

LADY TEAZLE. Lud, Sir Peter! would you have me be out of the fashion?

SIR PETER. The fashion, indeed! what had you to do with the fashion before you married me?

LADY TEAZLE. For my part, I should think you would like to have your wife thought a woman of taste.

SIR PETER. Ay—there again—taste! Zounds! madam, you had no taste when you married me!

LADY TEAZLE. That's very true, indeed, Sir Peter! and, after having married you, I should never pretend to taste again, I allow. But now, Sir Peter, since we have finished our daily jangle, I presume I may go to my engagement at Lady Sneerwell's?

SIR PETER. Ay, there's another precious circumstance—a charming set of acquaintance you have made there!

LADY TEAZLE. Nay, Sir Peter, they are all people of rank and fortune, and remarkably tenacious of reputation.

SIR PETER. Yes, egad, they are tenacious of reputation with a vengeance; for they don't choose anybody should have a character but themselves! Such a crew! Ah! many a wretch has rid on a hurdle[12] who has done less mischief than these utterers of forged tales, coiners of scandal, and clippers of reputation.

LADY TEAZLE. What, would you restrain the freedom of speech?

SIR PETER. Ah! they have made you just as bad as any one of the society.

LADY TEAZLE. Why, I believe I do bear a

part with a tolerable grace. But I vow I bear no malice against the people I abuse: when I say an ill-natured thing, 'tis out of pure good humour; and I take it for granted they deal exactly in the same manner with me. But, Sir Peter, you know you promised to come to Lady Sneerwell's too.

SIR PETER. Well, well, I'll call in just to look after my own character.

LADY TEAZLE. Then, indeed, you must make haste after me or you'll be too late. So good-bye to ye. [*Exit.*]

SIR PETER. So—I have gained much by my intended expostulation! Yet with what a charming air she contradicts everything I say, and how pleasantly she shows her contempt for my authority! Well, though I can't make her love me, there is great satisfaction in quarrelling with her; and I think she never appears to such advantage as when she is doing everything in her power to plague me. [*Exit.*]

Scene 2

A room in LADY SNEERWELL'*s house.* LADY SNEERWELL, MRS. CANDOUR, CRABTREE, SIR BENJAMIN BACKBITE, *and* JOSEPH SURFACE, *discovered.*

LADY SNEERWELL. Nay, positively, we will hear it.

JOSEPH. Yes, yes, the epigram by all means.

SIR BENJAMIN. O plague on't, uncle! 'tis mere nonsense.

CRABTREE. No, no; 'fore Gad, very clever for an extempore!

SIR BENJAMIN. But, ladies, you should be acquainted with the circumstance. You must know, that one day last week, as Lady Betty Curricle was taking the dust in Hyde Park, in a sort of duodecimo phaeton,[13] she desired me to write some verses on her ponies; upon which, I took out my pocket-book, and in one moment produced the following:—

Sure never were seen two such beautiful ponies;
Other horses are clowns, but these macaronies:
To give them this title I am sure can't

be wrong.
Their legs are so slim, and their tails are so long.

CRABTREE. There, ladies, done in the smack of a whip, and on horseback too.

JOSEPH. A very Phœbus, mounted—indeed, Sir Benjamin!

SIR BENJAMIN. Oh dear, sir!—trifles—trifles.— [*Enter* LADY TEAZLE *and* MARIA.]

MRS. CANDOUR. I must have a copy.

LADY SNEERWELL. Lady Teazle, I hope we shall see Sir Peter?

LADY TEAZLE. I believe he'll wait on your ladyship presently.

LADY SNEERWELL. Maria, my love, you look grave. Come, you shall sit down to piquet with Mr. Surface.

MARIA. I take very little pleasure in cards—however, I'll do as your ladyship pleases.

LADY TEAZLE. [*Aside.*] I am surprised Mr. Surface should sit down with her; I thought he would have embraced this opportunity of speaking to me before Sir Peter came.

MRS. CANDOUR. Now, I'll die; but you are so scandalous, I'll forswear your society.

LADY TEAZLE. What's the matter, Mrs. Candour?

MRS. CANDOUR. They'll not allow our friend Miss Vermillion to be handsome.

LADY SNEERWELL. Oh, surely she is a pretty woman.

CRABTREE. I am very glad you think so, ma'am.

MRS. CANDOUR. She has a charming fresh colour.

LADY TEAZLE. Yes, when it is fresh put on.

MRS. CANDOUR. Oh, fie! I'll swear her color is natural: I have seen it come and go!

LADY TEAZLE. I dare swear you have, ma'am: it goes off at night, and comes again in the morning.

SIR BENJAMIN. True, ma'am, it not only comes and goes; but, what's more, egad, her maid can fetch and carry it!

MRS. CANDOUR. Ha! ha! ha! how I hate to hear you talk so! But surely, now, her sister is, or was, very handsome.

CRABTREE. Who? Mrs. Evergreen? O Lord! she's six-and-fifty if she's an hour!

MRS. CANDOUR. Now positively you wrong her; fifty-two or fifty-three is the utmost—and I don't think she looks more.

SIR BENJAMIN. Ah! there's no judging by her looks, unless one could see her face.

LADY SNEERWELL. Well, well, if Mrs. Evergreen does take some pains to repair the ravages of time, you must allow she effects it with great ingenuity; and surely that's better than the careless manner in which the widow Ochre caulks her wrinkles.

SIR BENJAMIN. Nay, now, Lady Sneerwell, you are severe upon the widow. Come, come, 'tis not that she paints so ill—but, when she has finished her face, she joins it on so badly to her neck, that she looks like a mended statue, in which the connoisseur may see at once that the head's modern, though the trunk's antique!

CRABTREE. Ha! ha! ha! Well said, nephew!

MRS. CANDOUR. Ha! ha! ha! Well, you make me laugh; but I vow I hate you for it. What do you think of Miss Simper?

SIR BENJAMIN. Why, she has very pretty teeth.

LADY TEAZLE. Yes; and on that account, when she is neither speaking nor laughing (which very seldom happens), she never absolutely shuts her mouth, but leave it always on ajar, as it were—thus. [Shows her teeth.]

MRS. CANDOUR. How can you be so ill-natured?

LADY TEAZLE. Nay, I allow even that's better than the pains Mrs. Prime takes to conceal her losses in front. She draws her mouth till it positively resembles the aperture of a poor's-box, and all her words appear to slide out edge-wise, as it were—thus: *How do you do, madam? Yes, madam.*

LADY SNEERWELL. Very well, Lady Teazle; I see you can be a little severe.

LADY TEAZLE. In defense of a friend it is but justice. But here comes Sir Peter to spoil our pleasantry. [Enter SIR PETER.]

SIR PETER. Ladies, your most obedient—[Aside.] Mercy on me, here is the whole set! a character dead at every word, I suppose.

MRS. CANDOUR. I am rejoiced you are come, Sir Peter. They have been so censorious—and Lady Teazle as bad as any one.

SIR PETER. That must be very distressing to you, Mrs. Candour, I dare swear.

MRS. CANDOUR. Oh, they will allow good qualities to nobody; not even good nature to our friend Mrs. Pursy.

LADY TEAZLE. What, the fat dowager who was at Mrs. Quadrille's last night?

MRS. CANDOUR. Nay, her bulk is her misfortune; and, when she takes so much pains to get rid of it, you ought not to reflect on her.

LADY SNEERWELL. That's very true, indeed.

LADY TEAZLE. Yes, I know she almost lives on acids and small whey; laces herself by pulleys; and often, in the hottest noon in summer, you may see her on a little squat pony, with her hair plaited up behind like a drummer's and puffing round the Ring on a full trot.

MRS. CANDOUR. I thank you, Lady Teazle, for defending her.

SIR PETER. Yes, a good defence, truly.

MRS. CANDOUR. Truly, Lady Teazle is as censorious as Miss Sallow.

CRABTREE. Yes, and she is a curious being to pretend to be censorious—an awkward gawky, without any one good point under heaven.

MRS. CANDOUR. Positively you shall not be so very severe. Miss Sallow is a near relation of mine by marriage, and, as for her person, great allowance is to be made; for, let me tell you, a woman labours under many disadvantages who tries to pass for a girl of six-and-thirty.

LADY SNEERWELL. Though, surely, she is handsome still—and for the weakness in her eyes, considering how much she reads by candle-light, it is not to be wondered at.

MRS. CANDOUR. True; and then as to her manner, upon my word I think it is particularly graceful, considering she never had the least education; for you know her mother was a Welsh milliner, and her father a sugar-baker at Bristol.

SIR BENJAMIN. Ah! you are both of you too good-natured!

SIR PETER. [*Aside.*] Yes, damned good-natured! This their own relation!

MRS. CANDOUR. For my part, I own I cannot bear to hear a friend ill-spoken of.

SIR PETER. No, to be sure.

SIR BENJAMIN. Oh! you are of a moral turn. Mrs. Candour and I can sit for an hour and hear Lady Stucco talk sentiment.

LADY TEAZLE. Nay, I vow Lady Stucco is very well with the dessert after dinner; for she's just like the French fruit one cracks for mottoes—made up of paint and proverb.

MRS. CANDOUR. Well, I will never join in ridiculing a friend; and so I constantly tell my cousin Ogle, and you all know what pretensions she has to be critical on beauty.

CRABTREE. Oh, to be sure! she has herself the oddest countenance that ever was seen; 'tis a collection of features from all the different countries of the globe.

SIR BENJAMIN. So she has, indeed—an Irish front—

CRABTREE. Caledonian locks—

SIR BENJAMIN. Dutch nose—

CRABTREE. Austrian lips—

SIR BENJAMIN. Complexion of a Spaniard—

CRABTREE. And teeth *à la Chinoise*—

SIR BENJAMIN. In short, her face resembles a table d'hôte at Spa—where no two guests are of a nation—

CRABTREE. Or a congress at the close of a general war—wherein all the members, even to her eyes, appear to have a different interest, and her nose and her chin are the only parties likely to join issue.

MRS. CANDOUR. Ha! ha! ha!

SIR PETER. [*Aside.*] Mercy on my life!—a person they dine with twice a week!

LADY SNEERWELL. Go—go—you are a couple of provoking toads.

MRS. CANDOUR. Nay, but I vow you shall not carry the laugh off so—for give

me leave to say, that Mrs. Ogle—

SIR PETER. Madam, madam, I beg your pardon—there's no stopping these good gentlemen's tongues. But when I tell you, Mrs. Candour, that the lady they are abusing is a particular friend of mine, I hope you'll not take her part.

LADY SNEERWELL. Ha! ha! ha! well said, Sir Peter! but you are a cruel creature—too phlegmatic yourself for a jest, and too peevish to allow wit in others.

SIR PETER. Ah, madam, true wit is more nearly allied to good nature than your ladyship is aware of.

LADY TEAZLE. True, Sir Peter: I believe they are so near akin that they can never be united.

SIR BENJAMIN. Or rather, madam, I suppose them man and wife, because one seldom sees them together.

LADY TEAZLE. But Sir Peter is such an enemy to scandal, I believe he would have it put down by parliament.

SIR PETER. 'Fore heaven, madam, if they were to consider the sporting with reputation of as much importance as poaching on manors, and pass an act for the preservation of fame, I believe many would thank them for the bill.

LADY SNEERWELL. O Lud! Sir Peter; would you deprive us of our privileges!

SIR PETER. Ay, madam; and then no person should be permitted to kill characters and run down reputations, but qualified old maids and disappointed widows.

LADY SNEERWELL. Go, you monster!

MRS. CANDOUR. But, surely, you would not be quite so severe on those who only report what they hear?

SIR PETER. Yes, madam, I would have law merchant[14] for them too; and in all cases of slander currency, whenever the drawer of the lie was not to be found, the injured parties should have a right to come on any of the indorsers.

CRABTREE. Well, for my part, I believe there never was a scandalous tale without some foundation.

LADY SNEERWELL. Come, ladies, shall we sit down to cards in the next room?

[*Enter* SERVANT, *who whispers* SIR PE-TER.]

SIR PETER. I'll be with them directly.—[*Exit* SERVANT. *Aside.*] I'll get away unperceived.

LADY SNEERWELL. Sir Peter, you are not going to leave us?

SIR PETER. You ladyship must excuse me; I'm called away by particular business. But I leave my character behind me. [*Exit.*]

SIR BENJAMIN. Well—certainly, Lady Teazle, that lord of yours is a strange being: I could tell you some stories of him would make you laugh heartily if he were not your husband.

LADY TEAZLE. Oh, pray don't mind that; come, do let's hear them. [*Exeunt all but* JOSEPH SURFACE *and* MARIA.]

JOSEPH. Maria, I see you have no satisfaction in this society.

MARIA. How is it possible I should? If to raise malicious smiles at the infirmities or misfortunes of those who have never injured us be the province of wit or humour, Heaven grant me a double portion of dulness!

JOSEPH. Yet they appear more ill-natured than they are; they have no malice at heart.

MARIA. Then is their conduct still more contemptible; for, in my opinion, nothing could excuse the intemperance of their tongues but a natural and uncontrollable bitterness of mind.

JOSEPH. Undoubtedly, madam; and it has always been a sentiment of mine, that to propagate a malicious truth wantonly is more despicable than to falsify from revenge. But can you, Maria, feel thus for others, and be unkind to me alone? Is hope to be denied the tenderest passion?

MARIA. Why will you distress me by renewing this subject?

JOSEPH. Ah, Maria! you would not treat me thus, and oppose your guardian, Sir Peter's will, but that I see that profligate Charles is still a favoured rival.

MARIA. Ungenerously urged! But, whatever my sentiments are for that unfortunate young man, be assured I shall not feel more bound to give

him up, because his distresses have lost him the regard even of a brother.

JOSEPH. Nay, but, Maria, do not leave me with a frown; by all that's honest, I swear—[*Kneels. Re-enter* LADY TEAZLE *behind.*] [*Aside.*] Gad's life, here's Lady Teazle.[*Aloud to* MARIA.] You must not-no, you shall not—for, though I have the greatest regard for Lady Teazle—

MARIA. Lady Teazle!

JOSEPH. Yet were Sir Peter to suspect—

LADY TEAZLE. [*Coming forward.*] What is this, pray? Do you take her for me?—Child, you are wanted in the next room.— [*Exit* MARIA.] What is all this, pray?

JOSEPH. Oh, the most unlucky circumstance in nature! Maria has somehow suspected the tender concern I have for your happiness, and threatened to acquaint Sir Peter with her suspicions, and I was just endeavouring to reason with her when you came in.

LADY TEAZLE. Indeed! but you seemed to adopt a very tender mode of reasoning—do you usually argue on your knees?

JOSEPH. Oh, she's a child, and I thought a little bombast—but, Lady Teazle, when are you to give me your judgment on my library, as you promised?

LADY TEAZLE. No, no; I begin to think it would be imprudent, and you know I admit you as a lover no farther than fashion requires.

JOSEPH.—True—a mere Platonic cicisbeo,[15] what every wife is entitled to.

LADY TEAZLE. Certainly, one must not be out of the fashion. However, I have so many of my country prejudices left, that, though Sir Peter's ill humour may vex me ever so, it never shall provoke me to—

JOSEPH. The only revenge in your power. Well, I applaud your moderation.

LADY TEAZLE. Go—you are an insinuating wretch! But we shall be missed—let us join the company.

JOSEPH. But we had best not return together.

LADY TEAZLE. Well, don't stay; for Maria

shan't come to hear any more of your reasoning, I promise you. [*Exit.*]

JOSEPH. A curious dilemma, truly, my politics have run me into! I wanted, at first, only to ingratiate myself with Lady Teazle, that she might not be my enemy with Maria; and I have, I don't know how, become her serious lover. Sincerely I begin to wish I had never made such a point of gaining so very good a character, for it has led me into so many cursed rogueries that I doubt I shall be exposed at last. [*Exit.*]

Scene 3

A room in SIR PETER TEAZLE's *house. Enter* SIR OLIVER SURFACE *and* ROWLEY.

SIR OLIVER. Ha! ha! ha! so my old friend is married, hey?—a young wife out of the country. Ha! ha! ha! that he should have stood bluff[16] to old bachelor so long, and sink into a husband at last!

ROWLEY. But you must not rally him on the subject, Sir Oliver; 'tis a tender point, I assure you, though he has been married only seven months.

SIR OLIVER. Then he has been just half a year on the stool of repentance!— Poor Peter! But you say he has entirely given up Charles—never sees him, hey?

ROWLEY. His prejudice against him is astonishing, and I am sure greatly increased by a jealousy of him with Lady Teazle, which he has industriously been led into by a scandalous society in the neighbourhood, who have contributed not a little to Charles's ill name. Whereas the truth is, I believe, if the lady is partial to either of them, his brother is the favourite.

SIR OLIVER. Ay, I know there are a set of malicious, prating, prudent gossips, both male and female, who murder characters to kill time, and will rob a young fellow of his good name before he has years to know the value of it. But I am not to be prejudiced against my nephew by such, I promise you! No, no; if Charles has done nothing false or mean, I shall compound for his extravagance.

ROWLEY. Then, my life on't, you will reclaim him. Ah, sir, it gives me new life to find that your heart is not turned against him, and that the son of my good old master has one friend, however, left.

SIR OLIVER. What! shall I forget, Master Rowley, when I was at his years myself? Egad, my brother and I were neither of us very prudent youths; and yet, I believe, you have not seen many better men than your old master was?

ROWLEY. Sir, 'tis this reflection gives me assurance that Charles may yet be a credit to his family. But here comes Sir Peter.

SIR OLIVER. Egad, so he does! Mercy on me, he's greatly altered, and seems to have a settled married look! One may read husband in his face at this distance! [*Enter* SIR PETER TEAZLE.]

SIR PETER. Ha! Sir Oliver—my old friend! Welcome to England a thousand times!

SIR OLIVER. Thank you, thank you, Sir Peter! and i'faith I am glad to find you well, believe me!

SIR PETER. Oh! 'tis a long time since we met—fifteen years, I doubt, Sir Oliver, and many a cross accident in the time.

SIR OLIVER. Ay, I have had my share. But, what! I find you are married, hey, my old boy? Well, well, it can't be helped; and so—I wish you joy with all my heart!

SIR PETER. Thank you, thank you, Sir Oliver.—Yes, I have entered into— the happy state; but we'll not talk of that now.

SIR OLIVER. True, true, Sir Peter; old friends should not begin on grievances at first meeting. No, no, no.

ROWLEY. [*Aside to* SIR OLIVER.] Take care, pray, sir.

SIR OLIVER. Well, so one of my nephews is a wild rogue, hey?

SIR PETER. Wild! Ah! my old friend, I grieve for your disappointment there; he's a lost young man, indeed. However, his brother will make you amends; Joseph is, indeed, what a youth should be—everybody in the world speaks well of him.

SIR OLIVER. I am sorry to hear it; he has too good a character to be an honest fellow. Everybody speaks well of him! Psha! then he has bowed as low to knaves and fools as to the honest dignity of genius and virtue.

SIR PETER. What, Sir Oliver! do you blame him for not making enemies?

SIR OLIVER. Yes, if he has merit enough to deserve them.

SIR PETER. Well, well—you'll be convinced when you know him. 'Tis edification to hear him converse; he professes the noblest sentiments.

SIR OLIVER. Oh, plague of his sentiments! If he salutes me with a scrap of morality in his mouth, I shall be sick directly. But, however, don't mistake me, Sir Peter; I don't mean to defend Charles's errors: but, before I form my judgment of either of them, I intend to make a trial of their hearts; and my friend Rowley and I have planned something for the purpose.

ROWLEY. And Sir Peter shall own for once he has been mistaken.

SIR PETER. Oh, my life on Joseph's honour!

SIR OLIVER. Well—come, give us a bottle of good wine, and we'll drink the lads' health, and tell you our scheme.

SIR PETER. *Allons,* then!

SIR OLIVER. And don't, Sir Peter, be so severe against your old friend's son. Odds my life! I am not sorry that he has run out of the course a little: for my part, I hate to see prudence clinging to the green suckers of youth; 'tis like ivy round a sapling, and spoils the growth of the tree. [*Exeunt.*]

Act 3

Scene 1

A room in SIR PETER TEAZLE'*s house. Enter* SIR PETER TEAZLE, SIR OLIVER SURFACE, *and* ROWLEY.

SIR PETER. Well, then, we will see this fellow first, and have our wine afterwards. But how is this, Master Rowley? I don't see the jet[17] of your scheme.

ROWLEY. Why, sir, this Mr. Stanley, whom I was speaking of, is nearly related to them by their mother. He was once a merchant in Dublin, but has been ruined by a series of undeserved misfortunes. He has applied, by letter, since his confinement, both to Mr. Surface and Charles: from the former he has received nothing but evasive promises of future service, while Charles has done all that his extravagance has left him power to do; and he is, at this time, endeavouring to raise a sum of money, part of which, in the midst of his own distresses, I know he intends for the service of poor Stanley.

SIR OLIVER. Ah, he is my brother's son.

SIR PETER. Well, but how is Sir Oliver personally to—

ROWLEY. Why, sir, I will inform Charles and his brother that Stanley has obtained permission to apply personally to his friends; and, as they have neither of them ever seen him, let Sir Oliver assume his character, and he will have a fair opportunity of judging, at least, of the benevolence of their dispositions: and believe me, sir, you will find in the youngest brother one who, in the midst of folly and dissipation, has still, as our immortal bard expresses it,—

"a heart to pity, and a hand Open as day, for melting charity."[18]

SIR PETER. Psha! What signifies his having an open hand or purse either, when he has nothing left to give? Well, well, make the trial, if you please. But where is the fellow whom you brought for Sir Oliver to examine, relative to Charles's affairs?

ROWLEY. Below, waiting his commands, and no one can give him better intelligence.—This, Sir Oliver, is a friendly Jew, who, to do him justice, has done everything in his power to bring your nephew to a proper sense of his extravagance.

SIR PETER. Pray let us have him in.

ROWLEY. [*Calls to* SERVANT.] Desire Mr. Moses to walk upstairs.

SIR PETER. But, pray, why should you suppose he will speak the truth?

ROWLEY. Oh, I have convinced him that he has no chance of recovering certain sums advanced to Charles but through the bounty of Sir Oliver, who he knows is arrived; so that you may depend on his fidelity to his own interests. I have also another evidence in my power, one Snake, whom I have detected in a matter little short of forgery, and shall shortly produce to remove some of your prejudices, Sir Peter, relative to Charles and Lady Teazle.

SIR PETER. I have heard too much on that subject.

ROWLEY. Here comes the honest Israelite. [*Enter* MOSES.] This is Sir Oliver.

SIR OLIVER. Sir, I understand you have lately had great dealings with my nephew Charles.

MOSES. Yes, Sir Oliver, I have done all I could for him; but he was ruined before he came to me for assistance.

SIR OLIVER. That was unlucky, truly; for you have had no opportunity of showing your talents.

MOSES. None at all; I hadn't the pleasure of knowing his distresses till he was some thousands worse than nothing.

SIR OLIVER. Unfortunate, indeed! But I suppose you have done all in your power for him, honest Moses?

MOSES. Yes, he knows that. This very evening I was to have brought him a gentleman from the city, who does not know him, and will, I believe, advance him some money.

SIR PETER. What, one Charles has never had money from before?

MOSES. Yes, Mr. Premium, of Crutched Friars, formerly a broker.

SIR PETER. Egad, Sir Oliver, a thought strikes me!—Charles, you say, does not know Mr. Premium?

MOSES. Not at all.

SIR PETER. Now then, Sir Oliver, you may have a better opportunity of satisfying yourself than by an old romancing tale of a poor relation: go with my friend Moses, and represent Premium, and then, I'll answer for it, you'll see your nephew in all his glory.

SIR OLIVER. Egad, I like this idea better than the other, and I may visit Joseph afterwards as old Stanley.

SIR PETER. True—so you may.

ROWLEY. Well, this is taking Charles rather at a disadvantage, to be sure. However, Moses, you understand Sir Peter, and will be faithful.

MOSES. You may depend upon me.— [*Looks at his watch.*] This is near the time I was to have gone.

SIR OLIVER. I'll accompany you as soon as you please, Moses—But hold! I have forgot one thing—how the plague shall I be able to pass for a Jew?

MOSES. There's no need—the principal is Christian.

SIR OLIVER. Is he? I'm very sorry to hear it. But, then again, an't I rather too smartly dressed to look like a moneylender?

SIR PETER. Not at all; 'twould not be out of character, if you went in your carriage—would it, Moses?

MOSES. Not in the least.

SIR OLIVER. Well, but how must I talk? there's certainly some cant of usury and mode of treating that I ought to know.

SIR PETER. Oh, there's not much to learn. The great point, as I take it, is to be exorbitant enough in your demands. Hey, Moses?

MOSES. Yes, that's a very great point.

SIR OLIVER. I'll answer for't I'll not be wanting in that. I'll ask him eight or ten percent on the loan, at least.

MOSES. If you ask him no more than that, you'll be discovered immediately.

SIR OLIVER. Hey! what, the plague! how much then?

MOSES. That depends upon the circumstances. If he appears not very anxious for the supply, you should require only forty or fifty percent.; but if you find him in great distress, and want the moneys very bad, you may ask double.

SIR PETER. A good honest trade you're learning, Sir Oliver!

SIR OLIVER. Truly I think so—and not

unprofitable.

MOSES. Then, you know, you haven't the moneys yourself, but are forced to borrow them for him of a friend.

SIR OLIVER. Oh! I borrow it of a friend, do I?

MOSES. And your friend is an unconscionable dog: but you can't help that.

SIR OLIVER. My friend is an unconscionable dog, is he?

MOSES. Yes, and he himself has not the moneys by him, but is forced to sell stocks at a great loss.

SIR OLIVER. He is forced to sell stocks at a great loss, is he? Well, that's very kind of him.

SIR PETER. I'faith, Sir Oliver—Mr. Premium, I mean—you'll soon be master of the trade. But, Moses! would not you have him run out a little against the annuity bill?[19] That would be in character, I should think.

MOSES. Very much.

ROWLEY. And lament that a young man now must be at years of discretiion before he is suffered to ruin himself?

MOSES. Ay, great pity!

SIR PETER. And abuse the public for allowing merit to an act whose only object is to snatch misfortune and imprudence from the rapacious grip of usury, and give the minor a chance of inheriting his estate without being undone by coming into possession.

SIR OLIVER. So, so—Moses shall give me further instructions as we go together.

SIR PETER. You will not have much time, for your nephew lives hard by.

SIR OLIVER. Oh, never fear! my tutor appears so able, that though Charles lived in the next street, it must be my own fault if I am not a complete rogue before I turn the corner. [Exit with MOSES.]

SIR PETER. So, now, I think Sir Oliver will be convinced: you are partial, Rowley, and would have prepared Charles for the other plot.

ROWLEY. No, upon my word, Sir Peter.

SIR PETER. Well, go bring me this Snake, and I'll hear what he has to say presently. I see Maria, and want to speak with her.—[Exit ROWLEY.] I should be glad to be convinced my suspicions of Lady Teazle and Charles were unjust. I have never yet opened my mind on this subject to my friend Joseph—I am determined I will do it—he will give me his opinion sincerely. [Enter MARIA.] So, child, has Mr. Surface returned with you?

MARIA. No, sir; he was engaged.

SIR PETER. Well, Maria, do you not reflect, the more you converse with that amiable young man, what return his partiality for you deserves?

MARIA. Indeed, Sir Peter, your frequent importunity on this subject distresses me extremely—you compel me to declare, that I know no man who has ever paid me a particular attention whom I would not prefer to Mr Surface.

SIR PETER. So—here's perverseness! No, no, Maria, 'tis Charles only whom you would prefer. 'Tis evident his vices and follies have won your heart.

MARIA. This is unkind, sir. You know I have obeyed you in neither seeing nor corresponding with him: I have heard enough to convince me that he is unworthy my regard. Yet I cannot think it culpable, if, while my understanding severely condemns his vices, my heart suggests pity for his distresses.

SIR PETER. Well, well, pity him as much as you please; but give your heart and hand to a worthier object.

MARIA. Never to his brother!

SIR PETER. Go, perverse and obstinate! But take care, madam; you have never yet known what the authority of a guardian is: don't compel me to inform you of it.

MARIA. I can only say, you shall not have just reason. 'Tis true, by my father's will, I am for a short period bound to regard you as his substitute; but must cease to think you so, when you would compel me to be miserable. [Exit.]

SIR PETER. Was ever man so crossed as I am, everything conspiring to fret me! I had not been involved in matrimony a fortnight, before her father, a hale and hearty man, died, on purpose, I believe, for the pleasure of plaguing me with the care of his daughter.—[LADY TEAZLE *sings with-out.*] But here comes my helpmate! She appears in great good humour. How happy I should be if I could tease her into loving me, though but a little! [*Enter* LADY TEAZLE.]

LADY TEAZLE. Lud! Sir Peter, I hope you haven't been quarrelling with Maria? It is not using me well to be ill humoured when I am not by.

SIR PETER. Ah, Lady Teazle, you might have the power to make me good humoured at all times.

LADY TEAZLE. I am sure I wish I had; for I want you to be in a charming sweet temper at this moment. Do be good humoured now, and let me have two hundred pounds, will you?

SIR PETER. Two hundred pounds; what, an't I to be in a good humour without paying for it! But speak to me thus, and i'faith there's nothing I could refuse you. You shall have it; but seal me a bond for the repayment.

LADY TEAZLE. Oh, no—there—my note of hand will do as well. [*Offering her hand.*]

SIR PETER. And you shall no longer reproach me with not giving you an independent settlement. I mean shortly to surprise you; but shall we always live thus, hey?

LADY TEAZLE. If you please, I'm sure I don't care how soon we leave off quarrelling, provided you'll own you were tired first.

SIR PETER. Well—then let our future contest be, who shall be most oblig-ing.

LADY TEAZLE. I assure you, Sir Peter, good nature becomes you. You look now as you did before we were mar-ried, when you used to walk with me under the elms, and tell me stories of what a gallant you were in your youth, and chuck me under the chin, you would; and ask me if I thought I could love an old fellow, who would deny me nothing—didn't you?

SIR PETER. Yes, yes, and you were as kind and attentive—

LADY TEAZLE. Ay, so I was, and would always take your part, when my ac-quaintance used to abuse you, and turn you into ridicule.

SIR PETER. Indeed!

LADY TEAZLE. Ay, and when my cousin Sophy has called you a stiff, peevish old bachelor, and laughed at me for thinking of marrying one who might be my father, I have always defended you, and said, I didn't think you so ugly by any means, and that you'd make a very good sort of a husband.

SIR PETER. And you prophesied right; and we shall now be the happiest couple—

LADY TEAZLE. And never differ again?

SIR PETER. No, never—though at the same time, indeed, my dear Lady Teazle, you must watch your temper very seriously; for in all our little quarrels, my dear, if you recollect, my love, you always began first.

LADY TEAZLE. I beg your pardon, my dear Sir Peter: indeed, you always gave the provocation.

SIR PETER. Now, see, my angel! take care—contradicting isn't the way to keep friends.

LADY TEAZLE. Then, don't you begin it, my love!

SIR PETER. There, now! you—you are going on. You don't perceive, my life, that you are just doing the very thing which you know always makes me angry.

LADY TEAZLE. Nay, you know if you will be angry without any reason, my dear—

SIR PETER. There! now you want to quarrel again.

LADY TEAZLE. No, I'm sure I don't: but, if you will be so peevish—

SIR PETER. There now! who begins first?

LADY TEAZLE. Why, you, to be sure. I said nothing—but there's no bearing your temper.

SIR PETER. No, no, madam: the fault's in your own temper.

LADY TEAZLE. Ay, you are just what my cousin Sophy said you would be.

SIR PETER. Your cousin Sophy is a for-ward, impertinent gipsy.

LADY TEAZLE. You are a great bear, I am sure, to abuse my relations.

SIR PETER. Now may all the plagues of marriage be doubled on me, if ever I try to be friends with you any more!

LADY TEAZLE. So much the better.

SIR PETER. No, no, madam: 'tis evident

you never cared a pin for me, and I
was a madman to marry you—a pert,
rural coquette, that had refused half
the honest 'squires in the neighbourhood!

LADY TEAZLE. And I am sure I was a
fool to marry you—an old dangling
bachelor, who was single at fifty, only
because he never could meet with
any one who would have him.

SIR PETER. Ay, ay, madam; but you were
pleased enough to listen to me: you
never had such an offer before.

LADY TEAZLE. No! didn't I refuse Sir
Tivy Terrier, who everybody said
would have been a better match? for
his estate is just as good as yours, and
he has broke his neck since we have
been married.

SIR PETER. I have done with you,
madam! You are an unfeeling, ungrateful—but there's an end of
everything. I believe you capable of
everything that is bad. Yes, madam, I
now believe the reports relative to
you and Charles, madam. Yes,
madam, you and Charles are, not
without grounds—

LADY TEAZLE. Take care, Sir Peter! you
had better not insinuate any such
thing! I'll not be suspected without
cause, I promise you.

SIR PETER. Very well, madam! very well!
a separate maintenance as soon as
you please. Yes, madam, or a divorce!
I'll make an example of myself for
the benefit of all old bachelors. Let
us separate, madam.

LADY TEAZLE. Agreed! agreed! And
now, my dear Sir Peter, we are of a
mind once more, we may be the
happiest couple, and never differ
again, you know: ha! ha! ha! Well,
you are going to be in a passion, I
see, and I shall only interrupt you—
so bye! bye! [Exit.]

SIR PETER. Plages and tortures! can't I
make her angry either! Oh, I am the
most miserable fellow! But I'll not
bear her presuming to keep her temper: no! she may break my heart, but
she shan't keep her temper. [Exit.]

Scene 2

A room in CHARLES SURFACE'*s house. Enter*
TRIP, MOSES, *and* SIR OLIVER SURFACE.

TRIP. Here, Master Moses! If you'll stay
a moment; I'll try whether—what's
the gentleman's name?

SIR OLIVER. [Aside to MOSES.] Mr.
Moses, what is my name?

MOSES. Mr. Premium.

TRIP. Premium—very well. [*Exit, taking
snuff.*]

SIR OLIVER. To judge by the servants,
one wouldn't believe the master was
ruined. But what!—sure, this was my
brother's house?

MOSES. Yes, sir; Mr. Charles bought it
of Mr. Joseph, with the furniture,
pictures, &c., just as the old gentleman left it. Sir Peter thought it a
piece of extravagance in him.

SIR OLIVER. In my mind, the other's
economy in selling it to him was
more reprehensible by half. [*Re-enter*
TRIP.]

TRIP. My master says you must wait,
gentlemen: he has company, and
can't speak with you yet.

SIR OLIVER. If he knew who it was
wanted to see him, perhaps he would
not send such a message?

TRIP. Yes, yes, sir; he knows you are
here—I did not forget little Premium: no, no, no.

SIR OLIVER. Very well; and I pray, sir,
what may be your name?

TRIP. Trip, sir; my name is Trip, at your
service.

SIR OLIVER. Well, then, Mr. Trip, you
have a pleasant sort of place here, I
guess?

TRIP. Why, yes—here are three or four
of us pass our time agreeably
enough; but then our wages are
sometimes a little in arrear—and not
very great either—but fifty pounds a
year, and find our own bags and
bouquets.[20]

SIR OLIVER. [*Aside.*] Bags and bouquets!
halters and bastinadoes!

TRIP. And *à propos,* Moses, have you
been able to get me that little bill
discounted?

SIR OLIVER. [*Aside.*] Wants to raise
money, too!—mercy on me! Has his
distresses too, I warrant, like a lord,
and affects creditors and duns.

MOSES. 'Twas not to be done, indeed,
Mr. Trip.

TRIP. Good lack, you surprise me! My
friend Brush has indorsed it, and I

thought when he put his name at the back of a bill 'twas the same as cash.

MOSES. No, 'twouldn't do.

TRIP. A small sum—but twenty pounds. Hark'ee, Moses, do you think you couldn't get it me by way of annuity?

SIR OLIVER. [*Aside.*] An annuity! ha! ha! a footman raise money by way of annuity! Well done, luxury, egad!

MOSES. Well, but you must insure your place.

TRIP. Oh, with all my heart! I'll insure my place, and my life too, if you please.

SIR OLIVER. [*Aside.*] It's more than I would your neck.

MOSES. But is there nothing you could deposit?

TRIP. Why, nothing capital of my master's wardrobe has dropped lately; but I could give you a mortgage on some of his winter clothes, with equity of redemption before November—or you shall have the reversion of the French velvet, or a post-obit on the blue and silver;—these, I should think, Moses, with a few pair of point ruffles, as a collateral security—hey, my little fellow?

MOSES. Well, well. [*Bell rings.*]

TRIP. Egad, I heard the bell! I believe, gentlemen, I can now introduce you. Don't forget the annuity, little Moses! This way, gentlemen, I'll insure my place, you know.

SIR OLIVER. [*Aside.*] If the man be a shadow of the master, this is the temple of dissipation indeed! [*Exeunt.*]

Scene 3

Another room in the same. CHARLES SURFACE, SIR HARRY BUMPER, CARELESS, *and* GENTLEMEN, *discovered drinking.*

CHARLES. 'Fore heaven, 'tis true!—there's the great degeneracy of the age. Many of our acquaintance have taste, spirit, and politeness; but plague on't they won't drink.

CARELESS. It is so, indeed, Charles! they give in to all the substantial luxuries of the table, and abstain from nothing but wine and wit. Oh, certainly society suffers by it intolerably! for now, instead of the social spirit of

railery that used to mantle over a glass of bright Burgundy, their conversation is become just like the spawater they drink, which has all the pertness and flatulency of champagne, without its spirit or flavour.

FIRST GENTLEMAN. But what are they to do who love play better than wine?

CARELESS. True! there's Sir Harry diets himself for gaming, and is now under a hazard regimen.

CHARLES. Then he'll have the worst of it. What! you wouldn't train a horse for the course by keeping him from corn? For my part, egad, I'm never so successful as when I am a little merry: let me throw on a bottle of champagne, and I never lose—at least I never feel my losses, which is exactly the same thing.

SECOND GENTLEMAN. Ay, that I believe.

CHARLES. And, then, what man can pretend to be a believer in love, who is an abjurer of wine? 'Tis the test by which the lover knows his own heart. Fill a dozen bumpers to a dozen beauties, and she that floats at the top is the maid that has bewitched you.

CARELESS. Now then, Charles, be honest, and give us your real favourite.

CHARLES. Why, I have withheld her only in compassion to you. If I toast her, you must give a round of her peers, which is impossible—on earth.

CARELESS. Oh, then we'll find some canonised vestals or heathen goddesses that will do, I warrant!

CHARLES. Here then, bumpers, you rouges! Bumpers! Maria! Maria—

SIR HARRY. Maria who?

CHARLES. Oh, damn the surname!—'tis too formal to be registered in Love's calendar—but now, Sir Harry, beware, we must have beauty superlative.

CARELESS. Nay, never study, Sir Harry: we'll stand to the toast, though your mistress should want an eye, and you know you have a song will excuse you.

SIR HARRY. Egad, so I have! and I'll give him the song instead of the lady. [*Sings.*]

Here's to the maiden of bashful fifteen;
Here's to the widow of fifty;

Here's to the flaunting extravagant
quean,
    And here's to the housewife
    that's thrifty.
Chorus. Let the toast pass,—
    Drink to the lass,
I'll warrant she'll prove an excuse for
a glass.

    Here's to the charmer whose dim-
    ples we prize;
    Now to the maid who has none,
    sir;
    Here's to the girl with a pair of
    blue eyes,
    And here's to the nymph with
    but one, sir.

Chorus. Let the toast pass,—
    Drink to the lass,
I'll warrant she'll prove an excuse for
a glass.

    Here's to the maid with a bosom of
    snow:
    Now to her that's as brown as a
    berry:
    Here's to the wife with a face full
    of woe,
    And now to the damsel that's
    merry.

Chorus. Let the toast pass,—
    Drink to the lass,
I'll warrant she'll prove an excuse for
a glass.

    For let 'em be clumsy, or let 'em be
    slim,
    Young or ancient, I care not a
    feather;
    So fill a pint bumper quite up to
    the brim,
    So fill up your glasses, nay, fill to
    the brim,
    And let us e'en toast them to-
    gether.

Chorus. Let the toast pass—
    Drink to the lass,
I'll warrant she'll prove an excuse for
a glass.

ALL. Bravo! Bravo! [*Enter* TRIP, *and whispers to* CHARLES SURFACE.]
CHARLES. Gentlemen, you must excuse
me a little.—Careless take the chair,
will you?
CARELESS. Nay, pr'ythee, Charles, what

now? This is one of your peerless
beauties, I suppose, dropped in by
chance?
CHARLES. No, faith! To tell you the
truth, 'tis a Jew and a broker, who
are come by appointment.
CARELESS. Oh, damn it! let's have the
Jew in.
FIRST GENTLEMAN. Ay, and the broker
too, by all means.
SECOND GENTLEMAN. Yes, yes the Jew
and the broker.
CHARLES. Egad, with all my heart!—
Trip, bid the gentlemen walk in.—
[*Exit* TRIP.] Though there's one of
them a stranger, I can tell you.
CARELESS. Charles, let us give them
some generous burgundy, and perhaps they'll grow conscientious.
CHARLES. Oh, hang'em, no! wine does
but draw forth a man's natural
qualities; and to make them drink
would only be to whet their knavery.
[*Re enter* TRIP, *with* SIR OLIVER SURFACE
and MOSES.]
CHARLES. So, honest Moses; walk in,
pray, Mr Premium—that's the gentleman's name, isn't it, Moses?
MOSES. Yes, sir.
CHARLES. Set chairs, Trip.—Sit down,
Mr. Premium.—Glasses, Trip.—[TRIP
gives chairs and glasses, and exit.] Sit
down, Moses.—Come, Mr. Premium,
I'll give you a sentiment; here's *Success to usury!*—Moses, fill the
gentleman a bumper.
MOSES. Success to usury! [*Drinks.*]
CARELESS. Right, Moses—usury is pru-
dence and industry, and deserves to
succeed.
SIR OLIVER. Then here's—All the success it deserves! [*Drinks.*]
CARELESS. No, no, that won't do! Mr.
Premium, you have demurred at the
toast, and must drink it in a pint
bumper.
FIRST GENTLEMAN. A pint bumper, at
least.
MOSES. Oh, pray, sir, consider—Mr.
Premium's a gentleman.
CARELESS. And therefore loves good
wine.
SECOND GENTLEMAN. Give Moses a quart
glass—this is mutiny, and a high con-
tempt for the chair.
CARELESS. Here, now for't! I'll see jus-

tice done, to the last drop of my bottle.

SIR OLIVER. Nay, pray, gentlemen—I did not expect this usage.

CHARLES. No, hang it, you shan't; Mr. Premium's a stranger.

SIR OLIVER. [*Aside.*] Odd! I wish I was well out of their company.

CARELESS. Plague on'em then! if they won't drink, we'll not sit down with them. Come, Harry, the dice are in the next room.—Charles, you'll join us when you have finished your business with the gentlemen?

CHARLES. I will! I will!—[*Exeunt* SIR HARRY BUMPER *and* GENTLEMEN; CARELESS *following.*] Careless.

CARELESS. [*Returning.*] Well!

CHARLES. Perhaps I may want you.

CARELESS. Oh, you know I am always ready: word, note, or bond, 'tis all the same to me. [*Exit.*]

MOSES. Sir, this is Mr. Premium, a gentleman of the strictest honour and secrecy; and always performs what he undertakes. Mr. Premium, this is—

CHARLES. Psha! have done. Sir, my friend Moses is a very honest fellow, but a little slow at expression: he'll be an hour giving us our titles. Mr. Premium, the plain state of the matter is this: I am an extravagant young fellow who wants to borrow money; you I take to be a prudent old fellow, who has got money to lend. I am blockhead enough to give fifty percent sooner than not have it! and you, I presume, are rogue enough to take a hundred if you can get it. Now, sir, you see we are acquainted at once, and may proceed to business without further ceremony.

SIR OLIVER. Exceeding frank, upon my word. I see, sir, you are not a man of many compliments.

CHARLES. Oh, no sir! plain dealing business I always think best.

SIR OLIVER. Sir, I like you the better for it. However, you are mistaken in one thing; I have no money to lend, but I believe I could procure some of a friend; but then he's an unconscionable dog. Isn't he, Moses? And must sell stock to accommodate you. Mustn't he, Moses?

MOSES. Yes, indeed! You know I always speak the truth, and scorn to tell a lie!

CHARLES. Right. People that speak truth generally do. But these are trifles, Mr. Premium. What! I know money isn't to be bought without paying for't!

SIR OLIVER. Well, but what security could you give? You have no land, I suppose?

CHARLES. Not a mole-hill, nor a twig, but what's in the bough-pots[21] out of the window!

SIR OLIVER. Nor any stock, I presume?

CHARLES. Nothing but livestock—and that's only a few pointers and ponies. But pray, Mr. Premium, are you acquainted at all with any of my connections?

SIR OLIVER. Why, to say the truth, I am.

CHARLES. Then you must know that I have a devilish rich uncle in the East Indies, Sir Oliver Surface, from whom I have the greatest expectations?

SIR OLIVER. That you have a wealthy uncle, I have heard; but how your expectations will turn out is more, I believe, than you can tell.

CHARLES. Oh, no!—there can be no doubt. They tell me I'm a prodigious favourite, and that he talks of leaving me everything.

SIR OLIVER. Indeed! this is the first I've heard of it.

CHARLES. Yes, yes, 'tis just so. Moses knows 'tis true; don't you, Moses?

MOSES. Oh, yes! I'll swear to't.

SIR OLIVER. [*Aside.*] Egad, they'll persuade me presently I'm at Bengal.

CHARLES. Now I propose, Mr. Premium, if it's agreeable to you, a post-obit on Sir Oliver's life: though at the same time the old fellow has been so liberal to me, that I give you my word, I should be very sorry to hear that anything had happened to him.

SIR OLIVER. Not more than I should, I assure you. But the bond you mention happens to be just the worst security you could offer me—for I might live to a hundred and never see the principal.

CHARLES. Oh, yes, you would! the moment Sir Oliver dies, you know, you would come on me for the money.

SIR OLIVER. Then I believe I should be the most unwelcome dun you ever had in your life.

CHARLES. What! I suppose you're afraid that Sir Oliver is too good a life?

SIR OLIVER. No, indeed I am not; though I have heard he is as hale and healthy as any man of his years in Christendom.

CHARLES. There again, now, you are misinformed. No, no, the climate has hurt him considerably, por uncle Oliver. Yes, yes, he breaks apace, I'm told—and is so much altered lately that his nearest relations would not know him.

SIR OLIVER. No! Ha! ha! ha! so much altered lately that his nearest relations would not know him! Ha! ha! ha! egad—ha! ha! ha!

CHARLES. Ha! ha!—you're glad to hear that, little Premium?

SIR OLIVER. No, no, I'm not.

CHARLES. Yes, yes, you are—ha! ha! ha!—you know that mends your chance.

SIR OLIVER. But I'm told Sir Oliver is coming over; nay, some say he has actually arrived.

CHARLES. Psha! sure I must know better than you whether he's come or not. No, no, rely on't he's at this moment at Calcutta. Isn't he, Moses?

MOSES. Oh, yes, certainly.

SIR OLIVER. Very true, as you say, you must know better than I, though I have it from pretty good authority. Haven't I, Moses?

MOSES. Yes, most undoubted!

SIR OLIVER. But, sir, as I understand you want a few hundreds immediately, is there nothing you could dispose of?

CHARLES. How do you mean?

SIR OLIVER. For instance, now, I have heard that your father left behind him a great quantity of massy old plate.

CHARLES. O Lud, that's gone long ago. Moses can tell you how better than I can.

SIR OLIVER. [Aside.] Good lack! all the family race-cups and corporation-bowls!—[Aloud.] Then it was also supposed that his library was one of the most valuable and compact.

CHARLES. Yes, yes, so it was—vastly too much so for a private gentleman. For my part, I was always of a communicative disposition, so I thought it a shame to keep so much knowledge to myself.

SIR OLIVER. [Aside.] Mercy upon me! learning that had run in the family like an heirloom!—[Aloud.] Pray, what has become of the books?

CHARLES. You must inquire of the auctioneer, Master Premium, for I don't believe even Moses can direct you.

MOSES. I know nothing of books.

SIR OLIVER. So, so, nothing of the family property left, I suppose?

CHARLES. Not much, indeed; unless you have a mind to the family pictures. I have got a room full of ancestors above: and if you have a taste for old paintings, egad, you shall have 'em a bargain!

SIR OLIVER. Hey! what the devil! sure, you wouldn't sell your forefathers, would you?

CHARLES. Every man of them, to the best bidder.

SIR OLIVER. What! your great-uncles and aunts?

CHARLES. Ay, and my great-grand-fathers and grandmothers too.

SIR OLIVER. [Aside.] Now I give him up!—[Aloud.] What the plague, have you no bowels for your own kindred? Odd's life! do you take me for Shylock in the play, that you would raise money of me on your own flesh and blood?

CHARLES. Nay, my little broker, don't be angry: what need you care, if you have your money's worth?

SIR OLIVER. Well, I'll be the purchaser: I think I can dispose of the family canvas.—[Aside.] Oh, I'll never forgive him this! never! [Re-enter CARELESS.]

CARELESS. Come, Charles, what keeps you?

CHARLES. I can't come yet. I'faith, we are going to have a sale above stairs, here's little Premium will buy all my ancestors!

CARELESS. Oh, burn your ancestors!

CHARLES. No, he may do that afterwards, if he pleases. Stay, Careless, we want you: egad, you shall be auctioneer—so come along with us.

CARELESS. Oh, have with you, if that's the case. I can handle a hammer as well as a dice box; Going! going!

SIR OLIVER. [*Aside.*] Oh, the profligates!

CHARLES. Come, Moses, you shall be appraiser, if we want one. Gad's life, little Premium, you don't seem to like the business?

SIR OLIVER. Oh, yes, I do, vastly! Ha! ha! ha! yes, yes, I think it a rare joke to sell one's family by auction—ha! ha!—[*Aside.*] Oh, the prodigal!

CHARLES. To be sure! when a man wants money, where the plague should he get assistance, if he can't make free with his own relations? [*Exeunt.*]

SIR OLIVER. I'll never forgive him; never! never!

Act 4

Scene 1

A picture room in CHARLES SURFACE's *house. Enter* CHARLES SURFACE, SIR OLIVER SURFACE, MOSES, *and* CARELESS.

CHARLES. Walk in, gentlemen, pray walk in;—here they are, the family of the Surfaces, up to the Conquest.

SIR OLIVER. And, in my opinion, a goodly collection.

CHARLES. Ay, ay, these are done in the true spirit of portrait-painting; no *volontière grace* or expression. Not like the works of your modern Raphaels, who give you the strongest resemblance, yet contrive to make your portrait independent of you; so that you may sink the original and not hurt the picture. No, no; the merit of these is the inveterate likeness—all stiff and awkward as the originals, and like nothing in human nature besides.

SIR OLIVER. Ah! we shall never see such figures of men again.

CHARLES. I hope not. Well, you see, Master Premium, what a domestic character I am; here I sit of an evening surrounded by my family. But come, get to your pulpit, Mr. Auctioneer; here's an old gouty chair of my grandfather's will answer the purpose.

CARELESS. Ay, ay, this will do. But, Charles, I haven't a hammer; and what's an auctioneer without his hammer?

CHARLES. Egad, that's true. What parchment have we here? Oh, our genealogy in full. [*Taking pedigree down.*] Here, Careless, you shall have no common bit of mahogany, here's the family tree for you, you rogue! This shall be your hammer, and now you may knock down my ancestors with their own pedigree.

SIR OLIVER. [*Aside.*] What an unnatural rogue!—an *ex post facto* parricide!

CARELESS. Yes, yes, here's a list of your generation indeed;—faith, Charles, this is the most convenient thing you could have found for the business, for 'twill not only serve as a hammer, but a catalogue into the bargain. Come, begin—A-going, a-going!

CHARLES. Bravo, Careless! Well, here's my great uncle, Sir Richard Ravelin, a marvellous good general in his day, I assure you. He served in all the Duke of Marlborough's wars, and got that cut over his eye at the battle of Malplaquet. What say you, Mr. Premium? look at him—there's a hero! not cut out of his feathers as your modern clipped captains are, but enveloped in wig and regimentals, as a general should be. What do you bid?

SIR OLIVER. [*Aside to* MOSES.] Bid him speak.

MOSES. Mr. Premium would have you speak.

CHARLES. Why, then, he shall have him for ten pounds, and I'm sure that's not dear for a staff-officer.

SIR OLIVER. [*Aside.*] Heaven deliver me! his famous uncle Richard for ten pounds!—[*Aloud.*] Very well, sir, I take him at that.

CHARLES. Careless, knock down my uncle Richard!—Here, now, is a maiden sister of his, my great-aunt Deborah, done by Kneller, in his best manner, and esteemed a very formidable likeness. There she is, you see, a shepherdess feeding her flock. You shall have her for five pounds ten—the sheep are worth the money.

SIR OLIVER. [*Aside.*] Ah! poor Deborah! a woman who set such a value on herself!—[*Aloud.*] Five pounds ten—she's mine.

CHARLES. Knock down my aunt Deborah! Here, now, are two that were a sort of cousins of theirs.—You see, Moses, these pictures were done some time ago, when beaux wore wigs, and the ladies their own hair.

SIR OLIVER. Yes, truly, head-dresses appear to have been a little lower in those days.

CHARLES. Well, take that couple for the same.

MOSES. 'Tis a good bargain.

CHARLES. Careless!—This, now, is a grandfather of my mother's, a learned judge, well known on the western circuit.—What do you rate him at, Moses?

MOSES. Four guineas.

CHARLES. Four guineas! Gad's life, you don't bid me the price of his wig.—Mr. Premium, you have more respect for the woolsack;[22] do let us knock his lordship down at fifteen.

SIR OLIVER. By all means.

CARELESS. Gone.

CHARLES. And there are two brothers of his, William and Walter Blunt, Esquires, both members of Parliament, and noted speakers; and, what's very extraordinary, I believe, this is the first time they were ever bought or sold.

SIR OLIVER. That is very extraordinary, indeed! I'll take them at your own price, for the honour of Parliament.

CARELESS. Well said, little Premium! I'll knock them down at forty.

CHARLES. Here's a jolly fellow—I don't know what relation, but he was mayor of Norwich: take him at eight pounds.

SIR OLIVER. No, no; six will do for the mayor.

CHARLES. Come, make it guineas, and I'll throw you the two aldermen

there into the bargain.

SIR OLIVER. They're mine.

CHARLES. Careless, knock down the mayor and aldermen. But, plague on't! we shall be all day retailing in this manner; do let us deal whosesale: what say you, little Premium? Give me three hundred pounds for the rest of the family in the lump.

CARELESS. Ay ay, that wil be the best way.

SIR OLIVER. Well, well, anything to accommodate you; they are mine. But there is one portrait which you have always passed over.

CARELESS. What, that ill-looking little fellow over the settee?

SIR OLIVER. Yes, sir, I mean that; though I don't think him so ill-looking a little fellow, by any means.

CHARLES. What, that? Oh; that's my uncle Oliver! 'Twas done before he went to India.

CARELESS. Your uncle Oliver! Gad, then you'll never be friends, Charles. That, now, to me, is as stern a looking rogue as ever I saw; an unforgiving eye, and a damned disinheriting countenance! an inveterate knave, depend on't. Don't you think so, little Premium?

SIR OLIVER. Upon my soul, sir, I do not; I think it is as honest a looking face as any in the room, dead or alive. But I suppose uncle Oliver goes with the rest of the lumber?

CHARLES. No, hang it! I'll not part with poor Noll. The old fellow has been very good to me, and, egad, I'll keep his picture while I've a room to put it in.

SIR OLIVER. [*Aside.*] The rogue's my nephew after all!—[*Aloud.*] But, sir, I have somehow taken a fancy to that picture.

CHARLES. I'm sorry for't, for you certainly will not have it. Oons, haven't you got enough of them?

SIR OLIVER. [*Aside.*] I forgive him everything!—[*Aloud.*] But, sir, when I take a whim in my head, I don't value money. I'll give you as much for that as for all the rest.

CHARLES. Don't tease me, master bro-

ker; I tell you I'll not part with it,
and there's an end of it.

SIR OLIVER. [*Aside.*] How like his father
the dog is.—[*Aloud.*] Well, well, I have
done.—[*Aside.*] I did not perceive it
before, but I think I never saw such a
striking resemblance.—[*Aloud.*] Here
is a draught for your sum.

CHARLES. Why, 'tis for eight hundred
pounds!

SIR OLIVER. You will not let Sir Oliver
go?

CHARLES. Zounds! no! I tell you, once
more.

SIR OLIVER. Then never mind the difference, we'll balance that another
time. But give me your hand on the
bargain; you are an honest fellow,
Charles—I beg pardon, sir, for being
so free.—Come, Moses.

CHARLES. Egad, this is a whimsical old
fellow!—But hark'ee, Premium,
you'll prepare lodgings for these
gentlemen.

SIR OLIVER. Yes, yes, I'll send for them
in a day or two.

CHARLES. But hold; do now send a
genteel conveyance for them, for, I
assure you, they were most of them
used to ride in their own carriages.

SIR OLIVER. I will, I will—for all but
Oliver.

CHARLES. Ay, all but the little nabob.

SIR OLIVER. You're fixed on that?

CHARLES. Peremptorily.

SIR OLIVER. [*Aside.*] A dear extravagant
rogue!—[*Aloud.*] Good day!—Come,
Moses.—[*Aside.*] Let me hear now
who dares call him profligate! [*Exit
with* MOSES.]

CARELESS. Why, this is the oddest genius
of the sort I ever met with!

CHARLES. Egad, he's the prince of bro-
kers, I think. I wonder how the devil
Moses got acquainted with so honest
a fellow.—Ha! here's Rowley.—Do,
Careless, say I'll join the company in
a few moments.

CARELESS. I will—but don't let that old
blockhead persuade you to squander
any of that money on old musty
debts, or any such nonsense; for
tradesmen, Charles, are the most exorbitant fellows.

CHARLES. Very true, and paying them is

only encouraging them.

CARELESS. Nothing else.

CHARLES. Ay, ay, never fear.—[*Exit*
CARELESS.] So! this was an odd old
fellow, indeed. Let me see, two-thirds
of these five hundred and thirty odd
pounds are mine by right. 'Fore
Heaven! I find one's ancestors are
more valuable relations than I took
them for!—Ladies and gentlemen,
your most obedient and very grateful
servant. [*Bows ceremoniously to the pictures. Enter* ROWLEY.] Ha! old Rowley!
egad, you are just come in time to
take leave of your old acquaintance.

ROWLEY. Yes, I heard they were a-going.
But I wonder you can have such
spirits under so many distresses.

CHARLES. Why, there's the point! my
distresses are so many, that I can't
afford to part with my spirits; but I
shall be rich and splenetic, all in
good time. However, I suppose you
are surprised that I am not more
sorrowful at parting with so many
near relations; to be sure, 'tis very
affecting; but you see they never
move a muscle, so why should I?

ROWLEY. There's no making you serious
a moment.

CHARLES. Yes, faith, I am so now. Here,
my honest Rowley, here, get me this
changed directly, and take a hundred
pounds of it immediately to old
Stanley.

ROWLEY. A hundred pounds! Consider
only—

CHARLES. Gad's life, don't talk about it!
poor Stanley's wants are pressing,
and, if you don't make haste, we shall
have some one call that has a better
right to the money.

ROWLEY. Ah! there's the point! I never
will cease dunning you with the old
proverb—

CHARLES. *Be just before you're generous.*—
Why, so I would if I could; but Jus-
tice is an old hobbling beldame, and
I can't get her to keep pace with
Generosity, for the soul of me.

ROWLEY. Yet, Charles, believe me, one
hour's reflection—

CHARLES. Ay, ay, it's very true; but,
hark'ee, Rowley, while I have, by
Heaven I'll give; so, damn your econ-

omy! and now for hazard. [*Exeunt.*]

Scene 2

Another room in the same. Enter SIR
OLIVER SURFACE *and* MOSES.

MOSES. Well, sir, I think, as Sir Peter
said, you have seen Mr. Charles in
high glory; 'tis great pity he's so extravagant.

SIR OLIVER. True, but he would not sell
my picture.

MOSES. And loves wine and women so
much.

SIR OLIVER. But he would not sell my
picture.

MOSES. And games so deep.

SIR OLIVER. But he would not sell my
picture. Oh, here's Rowley. [*Enter*
ROWLEY.]

ROWLEY. So, Sir Oliver, I find you have
made a purchase—.

SIR OLIVER. Yes, yes, our young rake has
parted with his ancestors like old tapestry.

ROWLEY. And here has he commis-
sioned me to re-deliver you part of
the purchase-money—I mean,
though, in your necessitous character
of old Stanley.

MOSES. Ah! there is the pity of all: he is
so damned charitable.

ROWLEY. And I left a hosier and two
tailors in the hall, who, I'm sure,
won't be paid, and this hundred
would satisfy them.

SIR OLIVER. Well, well, I'll pay his debts,
and his benevolence too. But now I
am no more a broker, and you shall
introduce me to the elder brother as
old Stanley.

ROWLEY. Not yet awhile; Sir Peter, I
know, means to call there about this
time. [*Enter* TRIP.]

TRIP. Oh, gentlemen, I beg pardon for
not showing you out; this way—
Moses, a word. [*Exit with* MOSES.]

SIR OLIVER. There's a fellow for you!
Would you believe it, that puppy intercepted the Jew on our coming,
and wanted to raise money before he
got to his master!

ROWLEY. Indeed.

SIR OLIVER. Yes, they are now planning

an annuity business. Ah, Master
Rowley, in my days servants were
content with the follies of their masters, when they were worn a little
threadbare; but now they have their
vices, like their birthday clothes, with
the gloss on. [*Exeunt.*]

Scene 3

A library *in* JOSEPH SURFACE's *house. Enter*
JOSEPH SURFACE *and* SERVANT.

JOSEPH. No letter from Lady Teazle?

SERVANT. No, sir.

JOSEPH. [*Aside.*] I am surprised she has
not sent, if she is prevented from
coming. Sir Peter certainly does not
suspect me. Yet I wish I may not lose
the heiress, through the scrape I
have drawn myself into with the wife;
however, Charles's imprudence and
bad character are great points in my
favour. [*Knocking without.*]

SERVANT. Sir, I believe that must be
Lady Teazle.

JOSEPH. Hold! See whether it is or not,
before you go to the door: I have a
particular message for you if it
should be my brother.

SERVANT. 'Tis her ladyship, sir; she always leaves the chair at the milliner's
in the next street.

JOSEPH. Stay, stay: draw that screen before the window—that will do;—my
opposite neighbour is a maiden lady
of so curious a temper.—[SERVANT
draws the screen, and exit.] I have a
difficult hand to play in this affair.
Lady Teazle has lately suspected my
views on Maria; but she must by no
means be let into that secret,—at
least, till I have her more in my
power.

[*Enter Lady Teazle.*]

LADY TEAZLE. What sentiment in soliloquy now? Have you been very
impatient? O Lud! don't pretend to
look grave. I vow I couldn't come
before.

JOSEPH. O madam, punctuality is a species of constancy very unfashionable
in a lady of quality. [*Places chairs, and
sits after* LADY TEAZLE *is seated.*]

LADY TEAZLE. Upon my word, you

ought to pity me. Do you know Sir Peter is grown so ill-natured to me of late, and so jealous of Charles too—that's the best of the story, isn't it?

JOSEPH. [*Aside.*] I am glad my scandalous friends keep that up.

LADY TEAZLE. I am sure I wish he would let Maria marry him, and then perhaps he would be convinced; don't you, Mr. Surface?

JOSEPH. [*Aside.*] Indeed I do not.—[*Aloud*] Oh, certainly I do! for then my dear Lady Teazle would also be convinced how wrong her suspicions were of my having any design on the silly girl.

LADY TEAZLE. Well, well, I'm inclined to believe you. But isn't it provoking, to have the most ill-natured things said at one? And there's my friend Lady Sneerwell has circulated I don't know how many scandalous tales of me, and all without any foundation, too; that's what vexes me.

JOSEPH. Ay, madam, to be sure, that is the provoking circumstance—without foundation; yes, yes, there's the mortification, indeed; for, when a scandalous story is believed against one, there certainly is no comfort like the consciousness of having deserved it.

LADY TEAZLE. No, to be sure, then I'd forgive their malice; but to attack me, who am really innocent, and who never say an ill-natured thing of anybody—that is, of any friend; and then Sir Peter, too, to have him so peevish, and so suspicious, when I know the integrity of my own heart—indeed 'tis monstrous!

JOSEPH. But, my dear Lady Teazle, 'tis your own fault if you suffer it. When a husband entertains a groundless suspicion of his wife, and withdraws his confidence from her, the original compact is broken, and she owes it to the honour of her sex to endeavour to outwit him.

LADY TEAZLE. Indeed! So that, if he suspects me without cause, it follows, that the best way of curing his jealousy is to give him reason for't?

JOSEPH. Undoubtedly—for your husband should never be deceived in you: and in that case it becomes you to be frail in compliment to his discernment.

LADY TEAZLE. To be sure, what you say is very reasonable, and when the consciousness of my innocence—

JOSEPH. Ah, my dear madam, there is the great mistake; 'tis this very conscious innocence that is of the greatest prejudice to you. What is it makes you negligent of forms, and careless to the world's opinion? why, the consciousness of your own innocence. What makes you thoughtless in your conduct, and apt to run into a thousand little imprudences? why, the consciousness of your own innocence. What makes you impatient of Sir Peter's temper, and outrageous at his suspicions? why, the consciousness of your innocence.

LADY TEAZLE. 'Tis very true!

JOSEPH. Now, my dear Lady Teazle, if you would but once make a trifling *faux pas,* you can't conceive how cautious you would grow, and how ready to humor and agree with your husband.

LADY TEAZLE. Do you think so?

JOSEPH. Oh, I'm sure on't; and then you would find all scandal would cease at once, for—in short, your character at present is like a person in a plethora, absolutely dying from too much health.

LADY TEAZLE. So, so; then I perceive your prescription is, that I must sin in my own defence, and part with my virtue to preserve my reputation?

JOSEPH. Exactly so, upon my credit, ma'am.

LADY TEAZLE. Well, certainly this is the oddest doctrine, and the newest receipt for avoiding calumny?

JOSEPH. An infallible one, believe me. Prudence, like experience, must be paid for.

LADY TEAZLE. Why, if my understanding were once convinced—

JOSEPH. Oh, certainly, madam, your understanding should be convinced. Yes, yes—Heaven forbid I should persuade you to do anything you thought wrong. No, no, I have too much honour to desire it.

LADY TEAZLE. Don't you think we may as well leave honour out of the argument? [*Rises.*]

JOSEPH. Ah, the ill effects of your country education, I see, still remain with you.

LADY TEAZLE. I doubt they do, indeed; and I will fairly own to you, that if I could be persuaded to do wrong, it would be by Sir Peter's ill-usage sooner than your honourable logic, after all.

JOSEPH. Then, by this hand, which is unworthy of—[*Taking her hand. Reenter* SERVANT.] 'Sdeath, you blockhead—what do you want?

SERVANT. I beg your pardon, sir, but I thought you would not choose Sir Peter to come up without announcing him.

JOSEPH. Sir Peter!—Oons—the devil!

LADY TEAZLE. Sir Peter! O Lud! I'm ruined! I'm ruined!

SERVANT. Sir, 'twasn't I let him in.

LADY TEAZLE. Oh! I'm quite undone! What will become of me? Now, Mr. Logic—Oh! mercy, sir, he's on the stairs—I'll get behind here—and if ever I'm so imprudent again—[*goes behind the screen.*]

JOSEPH. Give me that book. [*Sits down.* SERVANT *pretends to adjust his chair.*] [*Enter* SIR PETER TEAZLE.]

SIR PETER. Ay, ever improving himself. Mr. Surface. Mr. Surface— [*pats* JOSEPH *on the shoulder.*]

JOSEPH. Oh, my dear Sir Peter, I beg your pardon. [*Gaping, throws away the book.*] I have been dozing over a stupid book. Well, I am much obliged to you for this call. You haven't been here, I believe, since I fitted up this room. Books, you know, are the only things I am a coxcomb in.

SIR PETER. 'Tis very neat indeed. Well, well, that's proper; and you can make even your screen a source of knowledge—hung, I perceive, with maps.

JOSEPH. Oh, yes, I find great use in that screen.

SIR PETER. I dare say you must, certainly, when you want to find anything in a hurry.

JOSEPH. [*Aside.*] Ay, or to hide anything in a hurry either.

SIR PETER. Well, I have a little private business—

JOSEPH. [*To* SERVANT.] You need not stay.

SERVANT. No sir. [*Exit.*]

JOSEPH. Here's a chair, Sir Peter—I beg—

SIR PETER. Well, now we are alone, there is a subject, my dear friend, on which I wish to unburden my mind on you—a point of the greatest moment to my peace; in short, my good friend, Lady Teazle's conduct of late has made me very unhappy.

JOSEPH. Indeed! I am very sorry to hear it.

SIR PETER. Yes, 'tis but too plain she has not the least regard for me; but, what's worse, I have pretty good authority to suppose she has formed an attachment to another.

JOSEPH. Indeed! you astonish me!

SIR PETER. Yes! and, between ourselves, I think I've discovered the person.

JOSEPH. How! you alarm me exceedingly.

SIR PETER. Ay, my dear friend, I knew you would sympathize with me!

JOSEPH. Yes, believe me, Sir Peter, such a discovery would hurt me just as much as it would you.

SIR PETER. I am convinced of it. Ah! it is a happiness to have a friend whom we can trust even with one's family secrets. But have you no guess who I mean?

JOSEPH. I haven't the most distant idea. It can't be Sir Benjamin Backbite!

SIR PETER. Oh, no! what say you to Charles?

JOSEPH. My brother! impossible!

SIR PETER. Oh, my dear friend, the goodness of your own heart misleads you. You judge of others by yourself.

JOSEPH. Certainly, Sir Peter, the heart that is conscious of its own integrity is ever slow to credit another's treachery.

SIR PETER. True; but your brother has no sentiment—you never hear him talk so.

JOSEPH. Yet I can't but think Lady Teazle herself has too much principle.

SIR PETER. Ay; but what is principle against the flattery of a handsome, lively young fellow?

JOSEPH. That's very true.

SIR PETER. And then, you know, the difference of our ages makes it very improbable that she should have any great affection for me; and if she were to be frail, and I were to make it public, why the town would only laugh at me, the foolish old bachelor, who had married a girl.

JOSEPH. That's true, to be sure—they would laugh.

SIR PETER. Laugh! ay, and make ballads, and paragraphs, and the devil knows what of me.

JOSEPH. No, you must never make it public.

SIR PETER. But then again—that the nephew of my old friend, Sir Oliver, should be the person to attempt such a wrong, hurts me more nearly.

JOSEPH. Ay, there's the point. When ingratitude barbs the dart of injury, the wound has double danger in it.

SIR PETER. Ay—I, that was, in a manner, left his guardian: in whose house, he had been so often entertained; who never in my life denied him—my advice!

JOSEPH. Oh, 'tis not to be credited! There may be a man capable of such baseness, to be sure; but, for my part, till you can give me positive proofs, I cannot but doubt it. However, if it should be proved on him, he is no longer a brother of mine—I disclaim kindred with him: for the man who can break the laws of hospitality, and tempt the wife of his friend, deserves to be branded as the pest of society.

SIR PETER. What a difference there is between you! What noble sentiments!

JOSEPH. Yet I cannot suspect Lady Teazle's honour.

SIR PETER. I am sure I wish to think well of her, and to remove all ground of quarrel between us. She has lately reproached me more than once with having made no settlement on her; and, in our last quarrel, she almost hinted that she should not break heart if I was dead. Now, as we seem to differ in our ideas of expense, I have resolved she shall have her own way, and be her own mistress in that respect for the future; and, if I were to die, she will find I have not been inattentive to her interest while living. Here, my friend, are the drafts of two deeds, which I wish to have

your opinion on. By one, she will enjoy eight hundred a year independent while I live; and, by the other, the bulk of my fortune at my death.

JOSEPH. This conduct, Sir Peter, is indeed truly generous.— [*Aside.*] I wish it may not corrupt my pupil.

SIR PETER. Yes, I am determined she shall have no cause to complain, though I would not have her acquainted with the latter instance of my affection yet awhile.

JOSEPH. [*Aside.*] Nor I, if I could help it.

SIR PETER. And now, my dear friend, if you please, we will talk over the situation of your hopes with Maria.

JOSEPH. [*Softly.*] Oh, no, Sir Peter; another time, if you please.

SIR PETER. I am sensibly chagrined at the little progress you seem to make in her affections.

JOSEPH. [*Softly.*] I beg you will not mention it. What are my disappointments when your happiness is in debate!— [*Aside.*] 'Sdeath, I shall be ruined every way!

SIR PETER. And though you are averse to my acquainting Lady Teazle with your passion, I'm sure she's not your enemy in the affair.

JOSEPH. Pray, Sir Peter, now oblige me. I am really too much affected by the subject we have been speaking of to bestow a thought on my own concerns. The man who is entrusted with his friend's distresses can never—[*Re-enter* SERVANT.] Well, sir?

SERVANT. Your brother, sir, is speaking to a gentleman in the street, and says he knows you are within.

JOSEPH. 'Sdeath, blockhead, I'm not within—I'm out for the day.

SIR PETER. Stay—hold—a thought has struck me:—you shall be at home.

JOSEPH. Well, well, let him up.—[*Exit* SERVANT. *Aside.*] He'll interrupt Sir Peter, however.

SIR PETER. Now, my good friend, oblige me, I entreat you. Before Charles comes, let me conceal myself somewhere, then do you tax him on the point we have been talking, and his answer may satisfy me at once.

JOSEPH. Oh, fie, Sir Peter! would you have me join in so mean a trick?—to trepan my brother too?

SIR PETER. Nay, you tell me you are sure

he is innocent; if so, you do him the greatest service by giving him an opportunity to clear himself, and you will set my heart at rest. Come, you shall not refuse me: [*Going up.*] here, behind the screen will be—Hey! what the devil! there seems to be one listener here already—I'll swear I saw a petticoat!

JOSEPH. Ha! ha! ha! Well, this is ridiculous enough. I'll tell you, Sir Peter, though I hold a man of intrigue to be a most despicable character, yet you know, it does not follow that one is to be an absolute Joseph[23] either! Hark'ee, 'tis a little French milliner, a silly rogue that plagues me; and having some character to lose, on your coming, sir, she ran behind the screen.

SIR PETER. Ah, a rogue—But, egad, she has overheard all I have been saying of my wife.

JOSEPH. Oh, 'twill never go any farther, you may depend upon it!

SIR PETER. No, then, faith, let her hear it out.—Here's a closet will do as well.

JOSEPH. Well, go in there.

SIR PETER. [*Goes into the closet.*] Sly rogue! sly rogue!

JOSEPH. A narrow escape, indeed! and a curious situation I'm in, to part man and wife in this manner.

LADY TEAZLE. [*Peeping.*] Couldn't I steal off?

JOSEPH. Keep close, my angel!

SIR PETER. [*Peeping.*] Joseph, tax him home.

JOSEPH. Back, my dear friend!

LADY TEAZLE. [*Peeping.*] Couldn't you lock Sir Peter in?

JOSEPH. Be still, my life!

SIR PETER. [*Peeping.*] You're sure the little milliner won't blab?

JOSEPH. In, in, my dear Sir Peter!—'Fore Gad, I wish I had a key to the door. [*Enter* CHARLES SURFACE.]

CHARLES. Holla! brother, what has been the matter? Your fellow would not let me up at first. What! have you had a Jew or a wench with you?

JOSEPH. Neither, brother, I assure you.

CHARLES. But what has made Sir Peter steal off? I thought he had been with you.

JOSEPH. He was, brother; but, hearing you were coming, he did not choose to stay.

CHARLES. What! was the old gentleman afraid I wanted to borrow money of him!

JOSEPH. No, sir: but I am sorry to find, Charles, you have lately given that worthy man grounds for great uneasiness.

CHARLES. Yes, they tell me I do that to a great many worthy men. But how so, pray?

JOSEPH. To be plain with you, brother, he thinks you are endeavouring to gain Lady Teazle's affections from him.

CHARLES. Who, I? O Lud! not I, upon my word.—Ha! ha! ha! ha! so the old fellow has found out that he has got a young wife, has he?—or, what is worse, Lady Teazle has found out she has an old husband?

JOSEPH. This is no subject to jest on, brother. He who can laugh—

CHARLES. True, true, as you were going to say—then, seriously, I never had the least idea of what you charge me with, upon my honour.

JOSEPH. Well, it will give Sir Peter great satisfaction to hear this. [*Raising his voice.*]

CHARLES. To be sure, I once thought the lady seemed to have taken a fancy to me; but, upon my soul, I never gave her the least encouragement. Besides, you know my attachment to Maria.

JOSEPH. But sure, brother, even if Lady Teazle had betrayed the fondest partiality for you—

CHARLES. Why, look'ee, Joseph, I hope I shall never deliberately do a dishonourable action; but if a pretty woman was purposely to throw herself in my way—and that pretty woman married to a man old enough to be her father—

JOSEPH. Well!

CHARLES. Why, I believe I should be obliged to borrow a little of your morality, that's all. But, brother, do you know now that you surprise me exceedingly, by naming me with Lady Teazle; for i'faith, I always understood you were her favourite.

JOSEPH. Oh, for shame, Charles! This retort is foolish.

CHARLES. Nay, I swear I have seen you exchange such significant glances—

JOSEPH. Nay, nay, sir, this is no jest.

CHARLES. Egad, I'm serious! Don't you remember one day, when I called here—

JOSEPH. Nay, pr'ythee, Charles—

CHARLES. And found you together—

JOSEPH. Zounds, sir, I insist—

CHARLES. And another time, when your servant—

JOSEPH. Brother, brother, a word with you!—[*Aside*.]. Gad, I must stop him.

CHARLES. Informed, I say, that—

JOSEPH. Hush! I beg your pardon, but Sir Peter has overheard all we have been saying. I knew you would clear yourself, or I should not have consented.

CHARLES. How, Sir Peter! Where is he?

JOSEPH. Softly, there! [*Points to the closet.*]

CHARLES. Oh, 'fore Heaven, I'll have him out. Sir Peter, come forth!

JOSEPH. No, no—

CHARLES. I say, Sir Peter, come into court.—[*Pulls in* SIR PETER.] What! my old guardian!—What!—turn inquisitor, and take evidence, incog.? Oh, fie! Oh, fie!

SIR PETER. Give me your hand, Charles—I believe I have suspected you wrongfully; but you mustn't be angry with Joseph—'twas my plan!

CHARLES. Indeed!

SIR PETER. But I acquit you. I promise you I don't think near so ill of you as I did. What I have heard has given me great satisfaction.

CHARLES. Egad, then, 'twas lucky you didn't hear any more. Wasn't it, Joseph?

SIR PETER. Ah! you would have retorted on him.

CHARLES. Ah, ay, that was a joke.

SIR PETER. Yes, yes, I know his honour too well.

CHARLES. But you might as well have suspected him as me in this matter, for all that. Mightn't he, Joseph?

SIR PETER. Well, well, I believe you.

JOSEPH. [*Aside*.] Would they were both out of the room!

SIR PETER. And in future, perhaps, we may not be such strangers. [*Re-enter* SERVANT *and whispers to* JOSEPH SURFACE.]

SERVANT. Lady Sneerwell is below, and says she will come up.

JOSEPH. Gentlemen, I beg pardon—I must wait on you downstairs; here's a person come on particular business.

CHARLES. Well, you can see him in another room. Sir Peter and I have not met a long time, and I have something to say to him.

JOSEPH. [*Aside*.] They must not be left together.—[*Aloud*.] I'll send Lady Sneerwell away, and return directly.—[*Aside to* SIR PETER.] Sir Peter, not a word of the French milliner.

SIR PETER. [*Aside to* JOSEPH SURFACE.] I! not for the world!—[*Exit* JOSEPH SURFACE.] Ah, Charles, if you associated more with your brother, one might indeed hope for your reformation. He is a man of sentiment. Well, there is nothing in the world so noble as a man of sentiment.

CHARLES. Psha! he is too moral by half; and so apprehensive of his good name, as he calls it, that I suppose he would as soon let a priest into his house as a wench.

SIR PETER. No, no,—come, come,—you wrong him. No, no, Joseph is no rake, but he is no such saint either, in that respect.—[*Aside*.] I have a great mind to tell him—we should have such a laugh at Joseph.

CHARLES. Oh, hang him! he's a very anchorite, a young hermit!

SIR PETER. Hark'ee—you must not abuse him: he may chance to hear of it again, I promise you.

CHARLES. Why, you won't tell him?

SIR PETER. No—but—this way.—[*Aside*.] Egad, I'll tell him. [*Aloud*.] Hark'ee, have you a mind to have a good laugh at Joseph?

CHARLES. I should like it of all things.

SIR PETER. Then, i'faith, we will! I'll be quit with him for discovering me. He had a girl with him when I called. [*Whispers*.]

CHARLES. What! Joseph? you jest.

SIR PETER. Hush!—a little French milliner—and the best of the jest is—she's in the room now.

CHARLES. The devil she is!

SIR PETER. Hush! I tell you. [*Points to the screen.*]

CHARLES. Behind the screen! Odds life, let's unveil her!

SIR PETER. No, no, he's coming:—you shan't, indeed!

CHARLES. Oh, egad, we'll have a peep at the little milliner!

SIR PETER. Not for the world!—Joseph will never forgive me.

CHARLES. I'll stand by you—

SIR PETER. Odds, here he is! [CHARLES SURFACE *throws down the screen. Re-enter* JOSEPH SURACE.]

CHARLES. Lady Teazle, by all that's wonderful!

SIR PETER. Lady Teazle, by all that's damnable!

CHARLES. Sir Peter, this is one of the smartest French milliners I ever saw. Egad, you seem all to have been diverting yourselves here at hide and seek, and I don't see who is out of the secret. Shall I beg your ladyship to inform me? Not a word!—Brother, will you be pleased to explain this matter? What! is Morality dumb too?—Sir Peter, though I found you in the dark, perhaps you are not so now! All mute! Well—though I can make nothing of the affair, I suppose you perfectly understand one another; so I'll leave you to yourselves.—[*Going.*] Brother, I'm sorry to find you have given that worthy man grounds for so much uneasiness.—Sir Peter! there's nothing in the world so noble as a man of sentiment! [*Exit.*]

JOSEPH. Sir Peter—notwithstanding—I confess—that appearances are against me—if you will afford me your patience—I make no doubt—but I shall explain everything to your satisfaction.

SIR PETER. If you please, sir.

JOSEPH. The fact is, sir, that Lady Teazle, knowing my pretensions to your ward Maria—I say, sir, Lady Teazle, being apprehensive of the jealousy of your temper—and knowing my friendship to the family—she, sir, I say—called here—in order that—I might explain these pretensions—but on your coming—being apprehen-

sive—as I said—of your jealousy—she withdrew—and this, you may depend on it, is the whole truth of the matter.

SIR PETER. A very clear account, upon my word; and I dare swear the lady will vouch for every article of it.

LADY TEAZLE. For not one word of it, Sir Peter!

SIR PETER. How! don't you think it worth while to agree in the lie?

LADY TEAZLE. There is not one syllable of truth in what that gentleman has told you.

SIR PETER. I believe you, upon my soul, ma'am!

JOSEPH. [*Aside to* LADY TEAZLE.] 'Sdeath, madam, will you betray me?

LADY TEAZLE. Good Mr. Hypocrite, by your leave, I'll speak for myself.

SIR PETER. Ay, let her alone, sir; you'll find she'll make out a better story than you, without prompting.

LADY TEAZLE. Hear me, Sir Peter!—I came here on no matter relating to your ward, and even ignorant of this gentleman's pretensions to her. But I came, seduced by his insidious arguments, at least to listen to his pretended passion, if not to sacrifice your honour to his baseness.

SIR PETER. Now, I believe, the truth is coming, indeed!

JOSEPH. The woman's mad!

LADY TEAZLE. No, sir; she has recovered her senses, and your own arts have furnished her with the means.—Sir Peter, I do not expect you to credit me—but the tenderness you expressed for me, when I am sure you could not think I was a witness to it, has penetrated so to my heart, that had I left the place without the shame of this discovery, my future life should have spoken the sincerity of my gratitude. As for that smooth-tongued hypocrite, who would have seduced the wife of his too credulous friend, while he affected honourable addresses to his ward—I behold him now in a light so truly despicable, that I shall never again respect myself for having listened to him. [*Exit.*]

JOSEPH. Notwithstanding all this, Sir Peter, Heaven knows—

SIR PETER. That you are a villain! and so I leave you to your conscience.

JOSEPH. You are too rash, Sir Peter; you shall hear me. The man who shuts out conviction by refusing to—[*Exeunt* SIR PETER *and* JOSEPH SURFACE, *talking.*]

Act 5

Scene 1

The library in JOSEPH SURFACE's *house. Enter* JOSEPH SURFACE *and* SERVANT.

JOSEPH. Mr. Stanley! and why should you think I would see him? you must know he comes to ask something.

SERVANT. Sir, I should not have let him in, but that Mr. Rowley came to the door with him.

JOSEPH. Psha! blockhead! to suppose that I should now be in a temper to receive visits from poor relations!— Well, why don't you show the fellow up?

SERVANT. I will, sir.—Why, sir, it was not my fault that Sir Peter discovered my lady—

JOSEPH. Go, fool!—[*Exit* SERVANT.] Sure Fortune never played a man of my policy such a trick before! My character with Sir Peter, my hopes with Maria, destroyed in a moment! I'm in a rare humour to listen to other people's distresses! I shan't be able to bestow even a benevolent sentiment on Stanley.—So! here he comes, and Rowley with him. I must try to recover myself, and put a little charity into my face, however. [*Exit. Enter* SIR OLIVER SURFACE *and* ROWLEY.]

SIR OLIVER. What! does he avoid us? That was he, was it not?

ROWLEY. It was, sir. But I doubt you are come a little too abruptly. His nerves are so weak, that the sight of a poor relation may be too much for him. I should have gone first to break it to him.

SIR OLIVER. Oh, plague of his nerves! Yet this is he whom Sir Peter extols as a man of the most benevolent way of thinking!

ROWLEY. As to his way of thinking, I cannot pretend to decide; for, to do him justice, he appears to have as much speculative benevolence as any private gentleman in the kingdom, though he is seldom so sensual as to indulge himself in the exercise of it.

SIR OLIVER. Yet he has a string of charitable sentiments at his fingers' ends.

ROWLEY. Or, rather, at his tongue's end, Sir Oliver; for I believe there is no sentiment he has such faith in as that *Charity begins at home.*

SIR OLIVER. And his, I presume, is of that domestic sort which never stirs abroad at all.

ROWLEY. I doubt you'll find it so;—but he's coming. I mustn't seem to interrupt you; and you know, immediately as you leave him, I come in to announce your arrival in your real character.

SIR OLIVER. True; and afterwards you'll meet me at Sir Peter's.

ROWLEY. Without losing a moment. [*Exit.*]

SIR OLIVER. I don't like the complaisance of his features. [*Re-enter* JOSEPH SURFACE.]

JOSEPH. Sir, I beg you ten thousand pardons for keeping you a moment waiting.—Mr. Stanley, I presume.

SIR OLIVER. At your service.

JOSEPH. Sir, I beg you will do me the honour to sit down—I entreat you, sir.

SIR OLIVER. Dear sir—there's no occasion.—[*Aside.*] Too civil by half!

JOSEPH. I have not the pleasure of knowing you, Mr. Stanley; but I am extremely happy to see you look so well. You were nearly related to my mother, I think, Mr. Stanley?

SIR OLIVER. I was, sir; so nearly that my present poverty, I fear, may do discredit to her wealthy children, else I should not have presumed to trouble you.

JOSEPH. Dear sir, there needs no apology: he that is in distress, though a stranger, has a right to claim kindred with the wealthy. I am sure I wish I was one of that class, and had it in my power to offer you even a small relief.

SIR OLIVER. If your uncle, Sir Oliver, were here, I should have a friend.

JOSEPH. I wish he was, sir, with all my heart: you should not want an advocate with him, believe me, sir.

SIR OLIVER. I should not need one—my distresses would recommend me. But I imagined his bounty would enable you to become the agent of his charity.

JOSEPH. My dear sir, you were strangely misinformed. Sir Oliver is a worthy man, a very worthy man; but avarice, Mr. Stanley, is the vice of age. I will tell you, my good sir, in confidence, what he has done for me has been a mere nothing; though people, I know, have thought otherwise, and, for my part, I never chose to contradict the report.

SIR OLIVER. What! has he never transmitted you bullion—rupees—pagodas?[24]

JOSEPH. Oh, dear sir, nothing of the kind! No, no; a few presents now and then—china, shawls, congou tea, avadavats,[25] and Indian crackers[26]—little more, believe me.

SIR OLIVER. [Aside.] Here's gratitude for twelve thousand pounds!—Avadavats and Indian crackers!

JOSEPH. Then, my dear sir, you have heard, I doubt not, of the extravagance of my brother; there are very few would credit what I have done for that unfortunate young man.

SIR OLIVER. [Aside.] Not I, for one!

JOSEPH. The sums I have lent him! Indeed I have been exceedingly to blame; it was an amiable weakness; however, I don't pretend to defend it—and now I feel it doubly culpable, since it has deprived me of the pleasure of serving you, Mr. Stanley, as my heart dictates.

SIR OLIVER. [Aside.] Dissembler!—[Aloud.] Then, sir, you can't assist me?

JOSEPH. At present, it grieves me to say, I cannot; but, whenever I have the ability, you may depend upon hearing from me.

SIR OLIVER. I am extremely sorry—

JOSEPH. Not more than I, believe me; to pity, without the power to relieve, is still more painful than to ask and be denied.

SIR OLIVER. Kind sir, your most obedient humble servant.

JOSEPH. You leave me deeply affected, Mr. Stanley.—[Calls to SERVANT.] William, be ready to open the door.

SIR OLIVER. O, dear sir, no ceremony.

JOSEPH. Your very obedient.

SIR OLIVER. Your most obsequious.

JOSEPH. You may depend upon hearing from me, whenever I can be of service.

SIR OLIVER. Sweet sir, you are too good.

JOSEPH. In the meantime I wish you health and spirits.

SIR OLIVER. Your ever grateful and perpetual humble servant.

JOSEPH. Sir, yours as sincerely.

SIR OLIVER. Charles!—you are my heir. [Exit.]

JOSEPH. This is one bad effect of a good character; it invites application from the unfortunate, and there needs no small degree of address to gain the reputation of benevolence without incurring the expense. The silver ore of pure charity is an expensive article in the catalogue of a man's good qualities; whereas the sentimental French plate I use instead of it makes just as good a show, and pays no tax. [Re-enter ROWLEY.]

ROWLEY. Mr. Surface, your servant: I was apprehensive of interrupting you, though my business demands immediate attention, as this note will inform you.

JOSEPH. Always happy to see Mr. Rowley.—[Aside. Reads the letter.] Sir Oliver Surface!—My uncle arrived!

ROWLEY. He is, indeed: we have just parted—quite well, after a speedy voyage, and impatient to embrace his worthy nephew.

JOSEPH. I am astonished!—[Calls to SERVANT.] William! stop Mr. Stanley, if he's not gone.

ROWLEY. Oh! he's out of reach, I believe.

JOSEPH. Why did you not let me know this when you came in together?

ROWLEY. I thought you had particular business. But I must be gone to inform your brother, and appoint him here to meet your uncle. He will be with you in a quarter of an hour.

JOSEPH. So he says. Well, I am strangely overjoyed at his coming.—[*Aside.*] Never, to be sure, was anything so damned unlucky!

ROWLEY. You will be delighted to see how well he looks.

JOSEPH. Oh! I'm overjoyed to hear it.—[*Aside.*]—Just at this time!

ROWLEY. I'll tell him how impatiently you expect him.

JOSEPH. Do, do; pray give my best duty and affection. Indeed, I cannot express the sensations I feel at the thought of seeing him.—[*Exit* ROWLEY.] Certainly his coming just at this time is the cruellest piece of ill fortune. [*Exit.*]

Scene 2

A room in SIR PETER TEAZLE's *house. Enter* MRS. CANDOUR *and* MAID.

MAID. Indeed, ma'am, my lady will see nobody at present.

MRS. CANDOUR. Did you tell her it was her friend Mrs. Candour?

MAID. Yes, ma'am; but she begs you will excuse her.

MRS. CANDOUR. Do go again; I shall be glad to see her, if it be only for a moment, for I am sure she must be in great distress.—[*Exit* MAID.] Dear heart, how provoking! I'm not mistress of half the circumstances! We shall have the whole affair in the newspapers, with the names of the parties at length, before I have dropped the story at a dozen houses. [*Enter* SIR BENJAMIN BACKBITE.] Oh, dear Sir Benjamin! you have heard, I suppose—

SIR BENJAMIN. Of Lady Teazle and Mr. Surface—

MRS. CANDOUR. And Sir Peter's discovery—

SIR BENJAMIN. Oh, the strangest piece of business, to be sure!

MRS. CANDOUR. Well, I never was so surprised in my life. I am so sorry for all parties, indeed.

SIR BENJAMIN. Now, I don't pity Sir Peter at all: he was so extravagantly partial to Mr. Surface.

MRS. CANDOUR. Mr. Surface! Why, 'twas with Charles Lady Teazle was detected.

SIR BENJAMIN. No, no, I tell you: Mr. Surface is the gallant.

MRS. CANDOUR. No such thing! Charles is the man. 'Twas Mr. Surface brought Sir Peter on purpose to discover them.

SIR BENJAMIN. I tell you I had it from one—

MRS. CANDOUR. And I have it from one—

SIR BENJAMIN. Who had it from one, who had it—

MRS. CANDOUR. From one immediately—But here comes Lady Sneerwell; perhaps she knows the whole affair. [*Enter* LADY SNEERWELL.]

LADY SNEERWELL. So, my dear Mrs. Candour, here's a sad affair of our friend Lady Teazle!

MRS. CANDOUR. Ay, my dear friend, who would have thought—

LADY SNEERWELL. Well, there is no trusting to appearances; though indeed, she was always too lively for me.

MRS. CANDOUR. To be sure, her manners were a little too free; but then she was so young!

LADY SNEERWELL. And had, indeed, some good qualities.

MRS. CANDOUR. So she had, indeed. But have you heard the particulars?

LADY SNEERWELL. No; but everybody says that Mr. Surface—

SIR BENJAMIN. Ay, there; I told you Mr. Surface was the man.

MRS. CANDOUR. No, no: indeed the assignation was with Charles.

LADY SNEERWELL. With Charles! You alarm me, Mrs. Candour.

MRS. CANDOUR. Yes, yes: he was the lover. Mr. Surface, to do him justice, was only the informer.

SIR BENJAMIN. Well, I'll not dispute with you, Mrs. Candour; but, be it which it may, I hope that Sir Peter's wound will not—

MRS. CANDOUR. Sir Peter's wound! Oh, mercy! I didn't hear a word of their fighting.

LADY SNEERWELL. Nor I, a syllable.

SIR BENJAMIN. No! what, no mention of the duel?

MRS. CANDOUR. Not a word.

SIR BENJAMIN. Oh, yes: they fought before they left the room.

LADY SNEERWELL. Pray let us hear.

MRS. CANDOUR. Ay, do oblige us with the duel.

SIR BENJAMIN. *"Sir,"* says Sir Peter, immediately after the discovery, *"you are a most ungrateful fellow."*

MRS. CANDOUR. Ay, to Charles—

SIR BENJAMIN. No, no—to Mr. Surface—*"a most ungrateful fellow; and old as I am, sir,"* says he, *"I insist on immediate satisfaction."*

MRS. CANDOUR. Ay, that must have been to Charles; for 'tis very unlikely Mr. Surface should fight in his own house.

SIR BENJAMIN. 'Gad's life, ma'am, not at all—*"giving me immediate satisfaction."*—On this, ma'am, Lady Teazle, seeing Sir Peter in such danger, ran out of the room in strong hysterics, and Charles after her, calling out for hartshorn[27] and water; then, madam, they began to fight with swords—[*Enter* CRABTREE.]

CRABTREE. With pistols, nephew—pistols! I have it from undoubted authority.

MRS. CANDOUR. Oh, Mr. Crabtree, then it is all true!

CRABTREE. Too true, indeed, madam, and Sir Peter is dangerously wounded—

SIR BENJAMIN. By a thrust in second[28] quite through his life side—

CRABTREE. By a bullet lodged in the thorax.

MRS. CANDOUR. Mercy on me! Poor Sir Peter!

CRABTREE. Yes, madam; though Charles would have avoided the matter, if he could.

MRS. CANDOUR. I knew Charles was the person.

SIR BENJAMIN. My uncle, I see, knows nothing of the matter.

CRABTREE. But Sir Peter taxed him with the basest ingratitude—

SIR BENJAMIN. That I told you, you know—

CRABTREE. Do, nephew, let me speak!—and insisted on immediate—

SIR BENJAMIN. Just as I said—

CRABTREE. Odds life, nephew, allow others to know something too! A pair of pistols lay on the bureau (for Mr.

Surface, it seems, had come home the night before late from Salthill, where he had been to see the Montem[29] with a friend, who has a son at Eton), so, unluckily, the pistols were left charged.

SIR BENJAMIN. I heard nothing of this.

CRABTREE. Sir Peter forced Charles to take one, and they fired, it seems, pretty nearly together. Charles's shot took effect, as I tell you, and Sir Peter's missed; but, what is very extraordinary, the ball struck against a little bronze Shakespeare that stood over the fireplace, grazed out of the window at a right angle, and wounded the postman, who was just coming to the door with a double letter[30] from Northamptonshire.

SIR BENJAMIN. My uncle's account is more circumstantial, I confess; but I believe mine is the true one for all that.

LADY SNEERWELL. [*Aside.*] I am more interested in this affair than they imagine, and must have better information. [*Exit.*]

SIR BENJAMIN. Ah! Lady Sneerwell's alarm is very easily accounted for.

CRABTREE. Yes, yes, they certainly do say—but that's neither here nor there.

MRS. CANDOUR. But, pray, where is Sir Peter at present?

CRABTREE. Oh! they brought him home, and he is now in the house, though the servants are ordered to deny him.

MRS. CANDOUR. I believe so, and Lady Teazle, I suppose, attending him.

CRABTREE. Yes, yes; and I saw one of the faculty[31] enter just before me.

SIR BENJAMIN. Hey! who comes here?

CRABTREE. Oh, this is he: the physician, depend on't.

MRS. CANDOUR. Oh, certainly! it must be the physician; and now we shall know. [*Enter* SIR OLIVER SURFACE.]

CRABTREE. Well, doctor, what hopes?

MRS. CANDOUR. Ay, doctor, how's your patient?

SIR BENJAMIN. Now, doctor, isn't it a wound with a small-sword?

CRABTREE. A bullet lodged in the thorax, for a hundred!

SIR OLIVER. Doctor! a wound with a

small-sword! and a bullet in the thorax?—Oons! are you mad, good people?

SIR BENJAMIN. Perhaps, sir, you are not a doctor?

SIR OLIVER. Truly, I am to thank you for my degree, if I am.

CRABTREE. Only a friend of Sir Peter's, then, I presume. But, sir, you must have heard of his accident?

SIR OLIVER. Not a word!

CRABTREE. Not of his being dangerously wounded?

SIR OLIVER. The devil he is!

SIR BENJAMIN. Run through the body—

CRABTREE. Shot in the breast—

SIR BENJAMIN. By one Mr. Surface—

CRABTREE. Ay, the younger.

SIR OLIVER. Hey! what the plague! you seem to differ strangely in your accounts: however, you agree that Sir Peter is dangerously wounded.

SIR BENJAMIN. Oh, yes, we agree in that.

CRABTREE. Yes, yes, I believe there can be no doubt in that.

SIR OLIVER. Then , upon my word, for a person in that situation, he is the most imprudent man alive; for here he comes, walking as if nothing at all was the matter. [*Enter* SIR PETER TEAZLE.] Odds heart, Sir Peter! you are come in good time, I promise you; for we had just given you over!

SIR BENJAMIN. [*Aside to* CRABTREE.] Egad, uncle, this is the most sudden recovery!

SIR OLIVER. Why, man! what do you do out of bed with a small-sword through your body, and a bullet lodged in you thorax?

SIR PETER.A small-sword and a bullet?

SIR OLIVER. Ay; these gentlemen would have killed you without law or physic, and wanted to dub me a doctor, to make me an accomplice.

SIR PETER.Why, what is all this?

SIR BENJAMIN. We rejoice, Sir Peter, that the story of the duel is not true, and are sincerely sorry for your other misfortune.

SIR PETER. [*Aside.*] So, so; all over the town already.

CRABTREE. Though, Sir Peter, you were certainly vastly to blame to marry at your years.

SIR PETER. Sir, what business is that of yours?

MRS. CANDOUR. Though, indeed, as Sir Peter made so good a husband, he's very much to be pitied.

SIR PETER. Plague on your pity, ma'am! I desire none of it.

SIR BENJAMIN. However, Sir Peter, you must not mind the laughing and jests you will meet with on the occasion.

SIR PETER. Sir, sir! I desire to be master in my own house.

CRABTREE. 'Tis no uncommon case, that's one comfort.

SIR PETER. I insist on being left to myself: without ceremony, I insist on your leaving my house directly!

MRS. CANDOUR. Well, well, we are going; and depend on't, we'll make the best report of it we can. [*Exit.*]

SIR PETER. Leave my house!

CRABTREE. And tell how hardly you've been treated. [*Exit.*]

SIR PETER. Leave my house!

SIR BENJAMIN. And how patiently you bear it. [*Exit.*]

SIR PETER. Fiends! vipers! furies! Oh! that their own venom would choke them!

SIR OLIVER. They are very provoking indeed, Sir Peter. [*Enter* ROWLEY.]

ROWLEY. I heard high words: what has ruffled you, sir?

SIR PETER. Psha! what signifies asking? Do I ever pass a day without my vexations?

ROWLEY. Well, I'm not inquisitive.

SIR OLIVER. Well, Sir Peter, I have seen both my nephews in the manner we proposed.

SIR PETER. A precious couple they are!

ROWLEY. Yes, and Sir Oliver is convinced that your judgment was right, Sir Peter.

SIR OLIVER. Yes, I find Joseph is indeed the man, after all.

ROWLEY. Ay, as Sir Peter says, he is a man of sentiment.

SIR OLIVER. And acts up to the sentiments he professes.

ROWLEY. It certainly is edification to hear him talk.

SIR OLIVER. Oh, he's a model for the young men of the age! But how's this, Sir Peter? you don't join us in your friend Joseph's praise, as I expected.

SIR PETER. Sir Oliver, we live in a damned wicked world, and the fewer we praise the better.

ROWLEY. What! do you say so, Sir Peter, who were never mistaken in your life?

SIR PETER. Psha! plague on you both! I see by your sneering you have heard the whole affair. I shall go mad among you!

ROWLEY. Then, to fret you no longer, Sir Peter, we are indeed acquainted with it all. I met Lady Teazle coming from Mr. Surface's so humbled, that she deigned to request me to be her advocate with you.

SIR PETER. And does Sir Oliver know all this?

SIR OLIVER. Every circumstance.

SIR PETER. What, of the closet and the screen, hey?

SIR OLIVER. Yes, yes, and the little French milliner. Oh, I have been vastly diverted with the story! ha! ha! ha!

SIR PETER. 'Twas very pleasant.

SIR OLIVER. I never laughed more in my life, I assure you: ha! ha! ha!

SIR PETER. Oh, vastly diverting! ha! ha! ha!

ROWLEY. To be sure, Joseph with his sentiments! ha! ha! ha!

SIR PETER. Yes, his sentiments! ha! ha! ha! Hypocritical villain!

SIR OLIVER. Ay, and that rogue Charles to pull Sir Peter out of the closet: ha! ha! ha!

SIR PETER. Ha! ha! 'twas devilish entertaining, to be sure!

SIR OLIVER. Ha! ha! ha! Egad, Sir Peter, I should like to have seen your face when the screen was thrown down: ha! ha!

SIR PETER. Yes, my face when the screen was thrown down: ha! ha! ha! Oh, I must never show my head again!

SIR OLIVER. But come, come, it isn't fair to laugh at you neither, my old friend; though, upon my soul, I can't help it.

SIR PETER. Oh, pray don't restrain your mirth on my account: it does not hurt me at all! I laugh at the whole affair myself. Yes, yes, I think being a standing jest for all one's acquaintance a very happy situation. Oh, yes, and then of a morning to read the paragraphs about Mr. S——, Lady ——, and Sir P——, will be so entertaining!

ROWLEY. Without affectation, Sir Peter, you may despise the ridicule of fools. But I see Lady Teazle going towards the next room; I am sure you must desire a reconciliation as earnestly as she does.

SIR OLIVER. Perhaps my being here prevents her coming to you. Well, I'll leave honest Rowley to mediate between you; but he must bring you all presently to Mr. Surface's, where I am now returning, if not to reclaim a libertine, at least to expose hypocrisy.

SIR PETER. Ah, I'll be present at your discovering yourself there with all my heart; though 'tis a vile unlucky place for discoveries.

ROWLEY. We'll follow. [*Exit* SIR OLIVER SURFACE.]

SIR PETER. She is not coming here, you see, Rowley.

ROWLEY. No, but she has left the door of that room open, you perceive. See, she is in tears.

SIR PETER. Certainly a little mortification appears very becoming in a wife. Don't you think it will do her good to let her pine a little?

ROWLEY. Oh, this is ungenerous in you!

SIR PETER. Well, I know not what to think. You remember the letter I found of hers evidently intended for Charles!

ROWLEY. A mere forgery, Sir Peter! laid in your way on purpose. This is one of the points which I intend Snake shall give you conviction of.

SIR PETER. I wish I were once satisfied of that. She looks this way. What a remarkably elegant turn of the head she has. Rowley, I'll go to her.

ROWLEY. Certainly.

SIR PETER. Though, when it is known that we are reconciled, people will laugh at me ten times more.

ROWLEY. Let them laugh, and retort their malice only by showing them you are happy in spite of it.

SIR PETER. I'faith, so I will! and, if I'm not mistaken, we may yet be the happiest couple in the country.

ROWLEY. Nay, Sir Peter, he who once

lays aside suspicion—

SIR PETER. Hold, Master Rowley! if you have any regard for me, never let me hear you utter anything like a sentiment: I have had enough of them to serve me the rest of my life. [*Exeunt.*]

Scene 3

The library in JOSEPH SURFACE's *house.* *Enter* JOSEPH SURFACE *and* LADY SNEERWELL.

LADY SNEERWELL. Impossible! Will not Sir Peter immediately be reconciled to Charles, and of course no longer oppose his union with Maria? The thought is distraction to me.

JOSEPH. Can passion furnish a remedy?

LADY SNEERWELL. No, nor cunning either. Oh, I was a fool, an idiot, to league with such a blunderer!

JOSEPH. Surely, Lady Sneerwell, I am the greatest sufferer; yet you see I bear the accident with calmness.

LADY SNEERWELL. Because the disappointment doesn't reach your heart; your interest only attached you to Maria. Had you felt for her what I have for that ungrateful libertine, neither your temper nor hypocrisy could prevent your showing the sharpness of your vexation.

JOSEPH. But why should your reproaches fall on me for this disappointment?

LADY SNEERWELL. Are you not the cause of it? Had you not a sufficient field for your roguery in imposing upon Sir Peter, and supplanting your brother, but you must endeavour to seduce his wife? I hate such an avarice of crimes; 'tis an unfair monopoly, and never prospers.

JOSEPH. Well, I admit I have been to blame. I confess I deviated from the direct road of wrong, but I don't think we're so totally defeated either.

LADY SNEERWELL. No!

JOSEPH. You tell me you have made a trial of Snake since we met, and that you still believe him faithful to us?

LADY SNEERWELL. I do believe so.

JOSEPH. And that he has undertaken, should it be necessary, to swear and prove, that Charles is at this time

contracted by vows and honour to your ladyship, which some of his former letters to you will serve to support?

LADY SNEERWELL. This, indeed, might have assisted.

JOSEPH. Come, come; it is not too late yet.—[*Knocking at the door.*] But hark! this is probably my uncle, Sir Oliver: retire to that room; we'll consult further when he's gone.

LADY SNEERWELL. Well, but if he should find you out too.

JOSEPH. Oh, I have no fear of that. Sir Peter will hold his tongue for his own credit's sake—and you may depend on it I shall soon discover Sir Oliver's weak side!

LADY SNEERWELL. I have no diffidence of your abilities! only be constant to one roguery at a time.

JOSEPH. I will, I will!—[*Exit* LADY SNEERWELL.] So! 'tis confounded hard, after such bad fortune, to be baited by one's confederate in evil. Well, at all events, my character is so much better than Charles's, that I certainly—hey!—what—this is not Sir Oliver, but old Stanley again. Plague on't that he should return to tease me just now! I shall have Sir Oliver come and find him here—and—[*Enter* SIR OLIVER SURFACE.] Gad's life, Mr. Stanley, why have you come back to plague me at this time? You must not stay now, upon my word.

SIR OLIVER. Sir, I hear your uncle Oliver is expected here, and though he has been so penurious to you, I'll try what he'll do for me.

JOSEPH. Sir, 'tis impossible for you to stay now, so I must beg—Come any other time, and I promise you, you shall be assisted.

SIR OLIVER. No: Sir Oliver and I must be acquainted.

JOSEPH. Zounds, sir! then I insist on your quitting the room directly.

SIR OLIVER. Nay, sir—

JOSEPH. Sir, I insist on't!—Here, William! show this gentleman out. Since you compel me, sir, not one moment—this is such insolence. [*Going to push him out. Enter* CHARLES SURFACE.]

CHARLES. Heyday! what's the matter

now? What the devil have you got hold of my little broker here? Zounds, brother, don't hurt little Premium. What's the matter, my little fellow?

JOSEPH. So! he has been with you, too, has he?

CHARLES. To be sure he has. Why, he's as honest a little—Be sure, Joseph, you have not been borrowing money too, have you?

JOSEPH. Borrowing! no! But, brother, you know we expect Sir Oliver here every—

CHARLES. O Gad, that's true! Noll mustn't find the little broker here, to be sure.

JOSEPH. Yet, Mr. Stanley insists—

CHARLES. Stanley! why his name's Premium.

JOSEPH. No, sir, Stanley.

CHARLES. No, no, Premium.

JOSEPH. Well, no matter which—but—

CHARLES. Ay, ay, Stanley or Premium, 'tis the same thing, as you say; for I suppose he goes by half a hundred names, besides A. B. at the coffee-house. [Knocking.]

JOSEPH. 'Sdeath! here's Sir Oliver at the door. Now I beg, Mr. Stanley—

CHARLES. Ay, ay, and I beg, Mr. Premium—

SIR OLIVER. Gentlemen—

JOSEPH. Sir, by heaven you shall go!

CHARLES. Ay, out with him, certainly.

SIR OLIVER. This violence—

JOSEPH. Sir, —tis your own fault.

CHARLES. Out with him, to be sure.

[Both forcing SIR OLIVER out. Enter SIR PETER and LADY TEAZLE, MARIA, and ROWLEY.]

SIR PETER. My old friend, Sir Oliver— hey! What in the name of wonder!— here are dutiful nephews—assault their uncle at his first visit!

LADY TEAZLE. Indeed, Sir Oliver, 'twas well we came in to rescue you.

ROWLEY. Truly it was; for I perceive, Sir Oliver, the character of old Stanley was no protection to you.

SIR OLIVER. Nor of Premium either: the necessities of the former could not extort a shilling from that benevolent gentleman; and with the other I stood a chance of faring worse than my ancestors, and being knocked

down without being bid for.

JOSEPH. Charles!

CHARLES. Joseph!

JOSEPH. 'Tis now complete!

CHARLES. Very.

SIR OLIVER. Sir Peter, my friend, and Rowley too—look on that elder nephew of mine. You know what he has already received from my bounty; and you also know how gladly I would have regarded half my fortune as held in trust for him? judge, then, my disappointment in discovering him to be destitute of truth, charity, and gratitude!

SIR PETER. Sir Oliver, I should be more surprised at this declaration, if I had not myself found him to be mean, treacherous, and hypocritical.

LADY TEAZLE. And if the gentleman pleads not guilty to these, pray let him call me to his character.

SIR PETER. Then, I believe, we need add no more: if he knows himself, he will consider it as the most perfect punishment that he is known to the world.

CHARLES. [Aside.] If they talk this way to Honesty, what will they say to me, by-and-by? [SIR PETER, LADY TEAZLE, and MARIA retire.]

SIR OLIVER. As for that prodigal, his brother, there—

CHARLES. [Aside.] Ay, now comes my turn: the damned family pictures will ruin me!

JOSEPH. Sir Oliver—uncle, will you hon-our me with a hearing?

CHARLES. [Aside.] Now, if Joseph would make one of his long speeches, I might recollect myself a little.

SIR OLIVER. [To JOSEPH SURFACE.] I sup-pose you would undertake to justify yourself?

JOSEPH. I trust I could.

SIR OLIVER. [To CHARLES SURFACE.] Well, sir!—and you could justify yourself too, I suppose?

CHARLES. Not that I know of, Sir Oliver.

SIR OLIVER. What!—Little Premium has been let too much into the secret, I suppose?

CHARLES. True, sir; but they were fam-ily secrets, and should not be mentioned again, you know.

ROWLEY. Come, Sir Oliver, I know you

cannot speak of Charles's follies with anger.

SIR OLIVER. Odd's heart, no more I can; nor with gravity either. Sir Peter, do you know the rogue bargained with me for all his ancestors; sold me judges and generals by the foot, and maiden aunts as cheap as broken china.

CHARLES. To be sure, Sir Oliver, I did make a little free with the family canvas, that's the truth on't. My ancestors may rise in judgment against me, there's no denying it; but believe me sincere when I tell you—and upon my soul I would not say so if I was not—that if I do not appear mortified at the exposure of my follies, it is because I feel at this moment the warmest satisfaction at seeing you, my liberal benefactor.

SIR OLIVER. Charles, I believe you. Give me your hand again: the ill-looking little fellow over the settee has made your peace.

CHARLES. Then, sir, my gratitude to the original is still increased.

LADY TEAZLE. [*Advancing.*] Yet, I believe, Sir Oliver, here is one whom Charles is still more anxious to be reconciled to. [*Pointing to* MARIA.]

SIR OLIVER. Oh, I have heard of his attachment there; and, with the young lady's pardon, if I construe right—that blush—

SIR PETER. Well, child, speak your sentiments.

MARIA. Sir, I have little to say, but that I shall rejoice to hear that he is happy; for me, whatever claim I had to his attention, I willingly resign to one who has a better title.

CHARLES. How, Maria!

SIR PETER. Heyday! what's the mystery now? While he appeared an incorrigible rake, you would give your hand to no one else; and now that he is likely to reform I'll warrant you won't have him.

MARIA. His own heart and Lady Sneerwell know the cause.

CHARLES. Lady Sneerwell!

JOSEPH. Brother, it is with great concern I am obliged to speak on this point, but my regard to justice compels me, and Lady Sneerwell's injuries can no longer be concealed. [*Opens the door. Enter* LADY SNEERWELL.]

SIR PETER. So! another French milliner! Egad, he has one in every room in the house, I suppose!

LADY SNEERWELL. Ungrateful Charles! Well may you be surprised, and feel for the indelicate situation your perfidy has forced me into.

CHARLES. Pray, uncle, is this another plot of yours? For, as I have life, I don't understand it.

JOSEPH. I believe, sir, there is but the evidence of one person more necessary to make it extremely clear.

SIR PETER. And that person, I imagine, is Mr. Snake.—Rowley, you were perfectly right to bring him with us, and pray let him appear.

ROWLEY. Walk in, Mr. Snake. [*Enter* SNAKE.] I thought his testimony might be wanted; however, it happens unluckily, that he comes to confront Lady Sneerwell, not to support her.

LADY SNEERWELL. A villain! Treacherous to me at last! Speak, fellow, have you too conspired against me?

SNAKE. I beg your ladyship ten thousand pardons: you paid me extremely liberally for the lie in question; but I unfortunately have been offered double to speak the truth.

LADY SNEERWELL. The torments of shame and disappointment on you all! [*Going.*]

LADY TEAZLE. Hold, Lady Sneerwell—before you go, let me thank you for the trouble you and that gentleman have taken, in writing letters from me to Charles, and answering them yourself; and let me also request you to make my respects to the scandalous college, of which you are president, and inform them, that Lady Teazle, licentiate, begs leave to return the diploma they granted her, as she leaves off practice, and kills characters no longer.

LADY SNEERWELL. You too, madam!—provoking—insolent! May your husband live these fifty years! [*Exit.*]

SIR PETER. Oons! what a fury!

LADY TEAZLE. A malicious creature, indeed!

SIR PETER. What! not for her last wish?

LADY TEAZLE. Oh, no!

SIR OLIVER. Well, sir, and what have you to say now?

JOSEPH. Sir, I am so confounded, to find that Lady Sneerwell could be guilty of suborning Mr. Snake in this manner, to impose on us all, that I know not what to say: however, lest her revengeful spirit should prompt her to injure my brother, I had certainly better follow her directly. [*Exit.*]

SIR PETER. Moral to the last drop!

SIR OLIVER. Ay, and marry her, Joseph, if you can. Oil and vinegar!—egad, you'll do very well together.

ROWLEY. I believe we have no more occasion for Mr. Snake at present?

SNAKE. Before I go, I beg pardon once for all, for whatever uneasiness I have been the humble instrument of causing to the parties present.

SIR PETER. Well, well, you have made atonement by a good deed at last.

SNAKE. But I must request of the company, that it shall never be known.

SIR PETER. Hey! what the plague! are you ashamed of having done a right thing once in your life?

SNAKE. Ah, sir, consider—I live by the badness of my character; and, if it were once known that I had been betrayed into an honest action, I should lose every friend I have in the world.

SIR OLIVER. Well, well—we'll not traduce you by saying anything in your praise, never fear. [*Exit* SNAKE.]

SIR PETER. There's a precious rogue!

LADY TEAZLE. See, Sir Oliver, there needs no persuasion now to reconcile your nephew and Maria.

SIR OLIVER. Ay, ay, that's as it should be, and, egad, we'll have the wedding tomorrow morning.

CHARLES. Thank you, dear uncle.

SIR PETER. What, you rogue! don't you ask the girl's consent first?

CHARLES. Oh, I have done that a long time—a minute ago—and she has looked yes.

MARIA. For shame, Charles!—I protest, Sir Peter, there has not been a word—

SIR OLIVER. Well, then, the fewer the better: may your love for each other never know abatement.

SIR PETER. And may you live as happily together as Lady Teazle and I intend to do!

CHARLES. Rowley, my old friend, I am sure you congratulate me; and I suspect that I owe you much.

SIR OLIVER. You do, indeed, Charles.

ROWLEY. If my efforts to serve you had not succeeded you would have been in my debt for the attempt—but deserve to be happy—and you overrepay me.

SIR PETER. Ay, honest Rowley always said you would reform.

CHARLES. Why as to reforming, Sir Peter, I'll make no promises, and that I take to be a proof that I intend to set about it. But here shall be my monitor—my gentle guide.—Ah! can I leave the virtuous path those eyes illumine?

Though thou, dear maid, shouldst wave by thy beauty's sway,
Thou still must rule, because I will obey:
An humble fugitive from Folly view,
No sanctuary near but Love and you:
[*To the audience.*]
You can, indeed, each anxious fear remove,
For even Scandal dies, if you approve.

[*Exeunt omnes.*]

1. Arrested for debt.
2. I.e., among the moneylenders.
3. An insurance lottery.
4. Used throughout the play in its older sense of "suspect."
5. A popular concert hall.
6. An outdoor party.
7. Embroidery frame.
8. A card game.
9. The particular kind of coach in which the passengers sit facing each other.
10. Ponies.
11. Having its tail clipped.
12. A cart on which prisoners were dragged through the streets to execution.
13. Very small carriage.
14. Commercial law.
15. The lover of a married woman.

16. Firm.
17. Point.
18. Cf. *2 Henry IV*, 4.4.31–32.
19. An act then under consideration that would protect minors in certain business transactions.
20. Footman's trappings.
21. Flower pots.
22. A symbol of the legal profession.
23. Cf. Genesis 39.
24. Indian coins.
25. Indian songbirds.
26. Firecrackers.
27. Smelling salts.
28. A parrying position in fencing.
29. A traditional ceremony performed by the schoolboys at Eton.
30. Heavy enough to require double postage.
31. Medical profession.

Figaro's Marriage

Beaumarchais

Pierre-Augustin Caron, who added to his name the phrase "de Beaumarchais" after an estate owned by his first wife, led so varied and adventurous a life that he had only a little time to spare for playwriting. He was born in Paris, the son of a watchmaker, on January 24, 1732. After a rudimentary education, he was apprenticed to his father and, at the age of nineteen, invented an escapement mechanism that is still used in modern watches. Another watchmaker stole the idea, and young Caron filed an action against him that was not only successful, but that brought the young inventor to the attention of the court and led to his appointment as watchmaker to Louis XV. In 1756 he married the wealthy widow of a court official, but she died only ten months later. Beaumarchais was appointed teacher of the harp to the daughters of Louis XV in 1759 and obtained a patent of nobility in 1760. Through his court connections, he was able to amass considerable wealth, and he spent more than a year on business in Spain from 1764 to 1766.

It was after his Spanish sojourn that Beaumarchais began his playwriting career. He had already published a number of pamphlets and polemics defending his viewpoints in the legal conflicts in which he seemed perpetually involved, but on January 29, 1767, his first play, *Eugénie*, opened at the Comédie-Française. It was a bourgeois domestic drama of the type whose popularity was sweeping Europe, but it was only moderately successful. His second play, *Les deux amis*, was of the same type; it opened on January 13, 1770, and was a flop. In the meantime, he had been working on a comedy which became *The Barber of Seville*, but its production was delayed for several years because of a complex legal quarrel that led to Beaumarchais' imprisonment. Through a series of published pamphlets Beaumarchais won a moral victory in the case, but both he and his opponents were legally declared disgraced. To regain his honor, Beaumarchais became a secret agent for the king (first Louis XV and later Louis XVI) in London, Germany, and Vienna. Upon his return, *The Barber of Seville* finally was produced by the Comédie-Française, opening on February 23, 1775.

It was a great hit, and Beaumarchais set to work almost at once on a sequel entitled *Figaro's Marriage*. Once again he was delayed, however. His continued activities as a secret agent in London brought him into contact with representatives of the American colonies, and he became one of France's most ardent and active supporters of American independence. He persuaded the French government to support the Americans, and personally poured a good share of his own fortune into arms and supplies for the colonies. (Later, impoverished, he was to seek repayment from the then-established United States government, but it never materialized in his lifetime.) When the script of *Figaro's Marriage* was completed, Beaumarchais ran into further delays with the official censors, for the portrayal of a nobleman outwitted by a servant and the spirit of freedom and resistance to authority inherent in the play were viewed as seditious. Louis XVI, upon hearing it read aloud, is reported to have said, "The Bastille would have to be destroyed

256

before it could be performed." Only five years after the play finally opened on April 27, 1784, that is exactly what the citizens of Paris did.

The revolutionary spirit in the air made Beaumarchais seem more radical than in fact he was. He was imprisoned again briefly, became involved in a series of legal disputes, married for the second time in 1768 (his wife died within two years and their infant son shortly thereafter), and married for the third time in 1786. He wrote an opera, *Tarare*, that was produced in 1787; another domestic drama, *A Mother's Guilt* (1792), continued the stories of the characters made so popular in his two comedies. But neither of these works was particularly successful, and in the meantime Beaumarchais found himself again in prison and this time in danger of the guillotine under the new revolutionary government. He escaped into exile, and was imprisoned for debt in London by a friend who was trying to prevent him from risking his life by returning to Paris. Although he undertook several missions for the revolutionary government out of devotion to his country, he could not safely return to Paris until 1796, at which time he found his wife and daughter living in poverty in the ruins of his Paris mansion. Beaumarchais was still trying to recoup his fortunes when he died in Paris on the night of May 17, 1799.

Beaumarchais' reputation as a playwright rests entirely on *The Barber of Seville* and *Figaro's Marriage;* that reputation was further enhanced by Rossini's operatic version of the former (1816) and Mozart's version of the latter (1786). The earlier play is a frothy but thoroughly entertaining piece in which Count Almaviva woos Rosine, the ward of Dr. Bartholo, who, although older than she, intends to wed her himself and thus claim her inheritance. Almaviva meets quite by accident his former servant, Figaro, who has led a picaresque existence as writer, barber (surgeon), and vagabond since leaving Almaviva's employ. With Figaro's inventive help, Almaviva outwits Bartholo and his music teacher accomplice, Basil, and marries Rosine. The play is utterly without thematic content, and even the plot, though somewhat complicated, is really little more than an excuse for extended exchanges of comic dialogue rather than a carefully articulated structure. The characters, however, are so totally endearing that the French public took them to their hearts, and Figaro, especially, became one of the supremely successful variations on the stock comic servant in all dramatic literature. Many saw in Figaro Beaumarchais himself, and perhaps it was this connection as much as anything that caused the author so much difficulty when he brought back the same characters in the sequel.

In contrast with the usual diminution of merit in theatrical sequels, *Figaro's Marriage* is much the better of Beaumarchais's two comedies. While retaining the madcap comic motif of the first play, Beaumarchais has deepened and broadened his characters in the second, giving them complete biographical backgrounds and more complex motives from which to react. Furthermore, he has introduced thematic issues like freedom, justice, and oppression of the common people by the nobility that, however unremarkable they may seem today, were to brand Beaumarchais a rabid revolutionary in Louis XVI's France. In thus enriching the play, he also lengthened it to one of the longest stage works in French literature, but its approximately three and one-half hours' running time has not dampened the enthusiasm of theater audiences for it. It has continued to enjoy frequent productions to the present day.

The plot structure of *Figaro's Marriage* still leaves something to be desired. Although nominally observing the unities of time and place, it preserves little of the compact neoclassic form that had gained so tight a hold over French drama in the seventeenth century and was still staunchly defended by the critics in the eighteenth and early nineteenth. Here, the action sprawls over five acts, usually by the expedient of presenting a new impediment to Figaro's happiness each time it appears that he has successfully removed the last. When five acts have been filled, Figaro's final trick is resolved in such a way that everyone is left happy. Nor can the rich texture of interconnected incident typical of Shakespeare or the romanticists be said to redeem Beaumarchais's play; here, one complication simply leads to another until the play is full. Within the usual limits of comedy, the story is believable enough;

such unexplained coincidences as exist are unlikely to bother a theater audience whose attentions are elsewhere. Still, the rather ungainly nature of this play's plot can hardly be described as among its stronger features.

In *Figaro's Marriage*, even more than in *The Barber of Seville*, it is the characters that give the play its great theatrical richness. Figaro, already a loveable rogue in his earlier incarnation, here is a mature philosopher as well, comically duped at times but still clever, sensible, and balanced in his approach to the vicissitudes of life. His famous soliloquy in act 5 lacks the purely theatrical impact of a Shakespearean soliloquy, but is marvelously revealing of Figaro's thought processes as well as of Beaumarchais's thematic notions. Count Almaviva has lost some of the dashing quality he enjoyed as the young hero of the earlier play and has become corrupted in the thoughtless pursuit of pleasure. Withal, he remains noble and spirited, and an interesting challenge for a good actor—as Beaumarchais points out in his introductory note. Rosine and Suzanne are both completely delightful women; Suzanne is the more lighthearted and playful as befits her youth and her station in life, but both women are honest, chaste, sincere workers for the general good, which is nowhere clearer than in their relationship to Cherubino. Cherubino is perhaps the most delicate comic portrait of the lot. He does not appear in *The Barber of Seville*, but Beaumarchais has greatly enriched the present play with the presence of one so sensitive yet foolish, just emerging from childhood and vulnerable to any hurt, yet zestful and committed to the ideals that he can perceive. Beaumarchais's interesting suggestion that this role must be played by a girl is not, it should be noticed, based on sexual titilation or cuteness, but on his conviction that no male actor available was "sufficiently educated to feel the subtleties of the part." Bartholo and Basil have much less to do than they did in *The Barber of Seville* and thus are little more developed, but new characters Marceline and Bridlegoose are especially rich caricatures, and the other characters, even in the smallest roles, are interesting and challenging. Beaumarchais is one of the finest creators of characters ever to write for the stage, for not only are his two or three leading roles supremely interesting, but every role in the play is suitably motivated, complex, and comically challenging.

Beaumarchais's own life was so full of adventure that he had but little time to write for the theater. Evidently he lived, to a remarkably full exstent, the picaresque qualities that he captured so vividly in Figaro. His devotion to other ideals prevented him from creating more than the two comic masterpieces on which his reputation now rests. In common with most of the major eighteenth-century European playwrights, Beaumarchais dabbled brilliantly in the theater but had a breadth of other interests that the theater alone could not satisfy. Although he came to the theater more or less by accident, it is a pity that he did not take up permanent abode there.

N.B. All footnotes are by the translator. Portions of the character descriptions were taken by the translator from *The Barber of Seville*.

Figaro's Marriage or One Mad Day

English Version by Jacques Barzun

Characters and Costuming

Count Almaviva (Governor of Andalusia)
must be played with nobility of mien,
but also with lightness and ease. The
corruption of his heart must not
diminish the perfect good form of
his manners. In keeping with the
morals *of those days*, the great
regarded the conquest of women as a
frolic. This role is an uncomfortable
one in that its grandeur is invariably
brought down and sacrificed to the
other characters. But in the hands of
a good actor, the role can bring out
all the others and insure the success
of the piece.
In the first and second acts the
Count wears a hunting costume in
the old Spanish style with half-length
boots. In the remaining acts he wears
a more gorgeous version of the same
costume.

Countess Almaviva, who is moved by two
opposite feelings, must show only a
restrained tenderness and a
moderate anger. Nothing must lower
in the spectator's eyes her virtuous
and lovable character. This role is
one of the most difficult in the play.
The Countess's costume in the first,
second, third, and fourth acts
consists of a comfortable housecoat
of straight and simple lines. She
wears no ornament on her head. She
is supposed to be indisposed and
keeping to her room. In the fifth act
she wears Suzanne's clothes and the
high headdress that goes with them.

*Figaro (valet to the Count and Steward of
the castle).* The actor who plays this
role cannot be too strongly urged to
study and make prevail at all times

the true spirit of the character. If the
actor finds in the part nothing but
argumentativeness spiced with gaiety
and wit; or even worse, if he allows
himself any burlesquing, he will
debase a role with which the greatest
comedian can do himself honor by
seizing upon its many nuances and
sustaining the highest possibilities of
its conception.
Figaro's clothes are the same as in
The Barber of Seville, that is, the suit of
a Spanish major-domo. On his hair
he wears a net; his hat is white and
has a colored ribbon around the
crown. A silk scarf is loosely tied
around his neck. His vest and
breeches are of satin with buttons
and buttonholes finished in silver.
His silk sash is very broad, his garters
tied with cord and tassels which hang
down on the leg. His coat must be of
a color contrasting with the vest, but
the lapels match the latter. White
stockings and gray shoes.

*Suzanne (chief chambermaid to the
Countess).* A clever girl, full of wit and
laughter, but displaying nothing of
the impudent frivolity of our
corruptive chambermaids. In her
role, though it is nearly the longest in
the play, there is not a word that is
not inspired by goodness and
devotion to her duty. The only
trickery she allows herself is in behalf
of her mistress, who relies on
Suzanne's attachment and who has
herself none but honorable thoughts.
Suzanne's costume in the first four
acts in a tight bodice with flounced
skirt, elegant though modeled on the
peasant style. Her hat is a high toque

(later called in France *à la Suzanne*). In the festivities of act 4, the Count places on her head a white toque adorned with a long veil, tall feathers, and ribbons. In act 5 she wears the Countess's housecoat and nothing on her head.

Marceline (housekeeper of the castle) is an intelligent woman with lively instincts whose experiences and mistakes have amended her character. If the actress who plays the role can rise with a certian judicious pride to the high morality that follows the recognition scene in act 3, it will add greatly to the interest of the play.
Her costume is that of the Spanish duenna, modest in color, a black bonnet on the head.

Antonio (a gardener, uncle of Suzanne and father of Fanchette) must display only a half-tipsy condition, which gradually wears off, so that by act 5 it is almost unnoticeable.
His clothes are those of a Spanish peasant; the sleeves hang down behind; a hat and white shoes.

Fanchette (the daughter of Antonio) is a girl of twelve and very naïve. Her costume has a tight-fitting bodice, peasant style, brown with silver buttons. The skirt is of contrasting color. She wears a black toque with feathers. The other girls in the wedding party are dressed like her.

Cherubino (chief page to the Count). This role cannot be properly played except by a young and very pretty woman. There is no young man on our stage who is sufficiently educated to feel the subtleties of the part. Excessively shy before the Countess, he is elsewhere a charmingly naughty boy. A vague restless desire is at the root of his character. He is rushing headlong through adolescence, but aimlessly and without worldly knowledge; he is the plaything of each passing event. In short, he is probably what every mother would like her son to be, even when she knows she will suffer for it.
In the first and second acts, Cherubino's costume is the rich court

dress of a Spanish page, white trimmed with silver lace. He wears a light blue cloak off the shoulder and a hat with large plumes. In act 4, he wears the bodice, skirt, and toque of the peasant girls; in act 5, an officer's uniform, a sword, and a cockade.

Bartholo (a doctor from Seville). His character and costume are the same as in *The Barber of Seville,* that is, a short black gown, buttoned up to the neck, and a large wig. The collar and cuffs are turned back and the belt is black. Outdoors he wears a long scarlet coat. In the present play, his role is secondary.

Basil (the Countess's music master). Also secondary, Basil's character and costume are the same as in *The Barber,* which is to say: a black hat with hanging brim, a gown like a cassock, and a long coat without turned-up collar or cuffs.

Don Guzman Bridlegoose (associate justice of the district). He must have the open and easy self-assurance of an animal that has overcome its shyness. His stammer is only an additional charm, scarcely noticeable though it is. The performer would make a grave mistake to stress the ludicrous in this part, for the principle of it is the natural contrast between the solemnity of his office and the absurdity of his person. Therefore the less the actor burlesques the man, the more truly will the character appear and the actor's talent shine. The costume is the robe of a Spanish judge, but less full than that of our state's attorneys—it is almost a cassock. He wears a great wig and a neckband Spanish style, and he carries a long white wand.

Doublefist (clerk and secretary to Bridlegoose). He is dressed like the justice, but carries a shorter wand.

The Beadle, of Alguazil, wears a coat and carries at his side a sword with a leather guard, but without a leather belt. Not boots but shoes, which are black. A white curly wig and a short white wand.

Sunstruck (a young shepherd) wears peasant clothes, sleeves hanging down, bright colored coat, white hat.

A young shepherdess—dressed like Fanchette.

Peter (the count's postilion). Short belted coat over a vest, a courier's boots, hat and whip, a net over his hair.

Walk-on parts (valets and peasants). Some in judge's costume, others dressed as peasants, the rest in livery.

Act 1

The scene is a half-furnished room. An invalid chair is in the middle. FIGARO *is measuring the floor with a yardstick.* SUZANNE, *in front of a mirror, is fixing in her hair the sprig of orange blossoms commonly called "the bride's bonnet."*

FIGARO. Nineteen feet by twenty-six.

SUZANNE. Look, Figaro—my bonnet. Do you like it better now?

FIGARO. [*Taking both her hands in his.*] Infinitely better, my sweet. My, what that bunch of flowers—so pretty, so virginal, so suited to the head of a lovely girl—does to a lover on the morning of his wedding!

SUZANNE. [*Leaving.*] What are you measuring there, my lad?

FIGARO. I am finding out, dear Suzy, whether the beautiful big bed that his lordship is giving us will fit into this room.

SUZANNE. *This* room?

FIGARO. He's letting us have it.

SUZANNE. But I don't want it.

FIGARO. Why not?

SUZANNE. I don't want it.

FIGARO. But tell me why.

SUZANNE. I don't like it.

FIGARO. You might give a reason.

SUZANNE. And supposing I don't?

FIGARO. Women! As soon as they have us tied down—

SUZANNE. To give a reason would imply that I might be unreasonable. Are you with me or against me?

FIGARO. You are turning down the most convenient room in the castle. It connects with both suites. At night, if my lady is unwell and wants you, she rings—and crack! there you are in two hops. Is it something that my lord requires? A tinkle from his side, and zing! I am at the ready in three strides.

SUZANNE. Right enough! But when he's tinkled in the morning and given you a good long errand, zing! in three strides he is at my door, and crack! in two hops he—

FIGARO. What do you mean by those words?

SUZANNE. You'd better listen to me carefully.

FIGARO. What the devil is going on?

SUZANNE. What is going on is that his lordship Count Almaviva is tired of pursuing the beauties of the neighborhood and is heading for home—not to *his* wife, you understand, but to yours. *She* is the one he has his eye on, and he hopes this apartment will favor his plans. And that is what the faithful Basil, the trusted agent of the Count's pleasures, and my noble singing master as well, tells me every day during my lesson.

FIGARO. Basil, my boy, if ever the application of green birch to an ailing back has helped to correct curvature of the spine, I will—

SUZANNE. So in your innocence you thought that this dowry the Count is giving me was for your beaux yeux and your high merit?

FIGARO. I've done enough to hope it was.

SUZANNE. How stupid bright people are!

FIGARO. So they say.

SUZANNE. But *they* won't believe it!

FIGARO. *They* are wrong.

SUZANNE. Get it into your head that the dowry is to get from me, privately, a certain privilege which formerly was the right of the lord of the manor—you know what a grievous right it was.[1]

FIGARO. I know it so well that if the Count had not abolished its shameful exercise when he himself was married, I should never have planned to marry you on his lands.

SUZANNE. He abolished it right enough, but he has had second thoughts. And he's thinking your fiancée is the one to restore it to him.

FIGARO. [*Rubbing his forehead.*] My head grows mushy with surprise and my sprouting forehead—²

SUZANNE. Please don't rub it.

FIGARO. What's the harm?

SUZANNE. If you brought on a little pimple, superstitious people might—

FIGARO. You're laughing at me, you slut. Now if I could think of some way to catch out this professional deceiver, turn the tables on him and pocket his money—

SUZANNE. Plotting and pocketing— you're in your element.

FIGARO. It certainly isn't shame that holds me back.

SUZANNE. Fear, then?

FIGARO. It's no great feat to start on a dangerous undertaking; the thing is to succeed and avoid trouble. Any knavish fool can go into a man's house at night, enjoy his wife, and get a beating for his pains—nothing is easier. But—[*A bell rings.*]

SUZANNE. My lady is awake. She wanted me to be sure and be the first to talk to her this morning about the wedding.

FIGARO. Some more goings on?

SUZANNE. The almanac says it brings good luck to forsaken wives. Goodby, Fi-fi-garo darling; think about ways and means.

FIGARO. To prime my brains give a little kiss.

SUZANNE. To a lover, today? No, sir! What would my husband say tomorrow? [FIGARO *kisses her.*]

SUZANNE. Now, now!

FIGARO. You don't know how much I love you.

SUZANNE. [*Adjusting her dress.*] When will you learn not to bore me with it from morning till night?

FIGARO. [*As if telling a secret.*] Why, when I can prove it to you from night till morning. [*The bell rings again.*]

SUZANNE. [*Blowing him a kiss from the door.*] There's your kiss, sir, I have nothing else of yours to return.

FIGARO. [*Running after her.*] But you didn't receive mine across the void like this. [*Exit* SUZANNE.]

FIGARO. [*Alone.*] What a ravishing girl! Always gay, laughing, full of sap, wit, love, joy—and how well behaved! [*He walks about briskly, rubbing his hands.*] Ah, my lord, my dear lord! You want to give me—something to remember? I was wondering, too, why I am first made Steward, and then supposed to become part of the embassy and serve as King's Messenger. Now I understand, Your Excellency: three promotions at one stroke—you as envoy plenipotentiary; myself as political lightning rod; and Suzy as lady in residence, as private ambassadress—and then, Sir Messenger, be off! While I gallop in one direction, you will drive my girl a long way in the other. While I wade through mud and break my neck for the glory of your family, you will collaborate in the increase of mine. What sweet reciprocity! But, my lord, there is excess in this. To carry on in London the business at once of the King your master and of your humble servant, to represent in a foreign court both him and me—that is too much by half, much too much. As for you, Basil, my pretty scoundrel, I will teach you to limp with the halt and the lame. I will—no! We must play up to both of them if we are to knock their heads together. Now, Figaro, concentrate on today. First, move ahead the time for the wedding, so as to make sure the knot is tied; then distract old Marceline, who is too fond of you; pick up whatever money and gifts there may be; mislead the Count and his little appetites; give a sound drubbing to Mister Basil, and—well, well, well, here is the fat doctor! The party is complete. [*Enter* BARTHOLO *and* MARCELINE.] Good morning, dear doctor of my heart. Is it my wedding with Suzy that brings you to the house?

BARTHOLO. [*Disdainful.*] Not at all, my dear sir.

FIGARO. It would indeed be a generous act.

BARTHOLO. Exactly, and therefore inconceivably stupid.

FIGARO. It was my bad luck that I had to thwart your designs.[3]

BARTHOLO. Haven't you anything else to say?

FIGARO. Perhaps your mule hasn't been looked after?[3]

BARTHOLO. [*Furious.*] Confounded babbler, leave us alone!

FIGARO. You are angry, Doctor? Yours is a cruel profession: no more kindness to animals than if they were men. Farewell, Marceline, are you still thinking of suing me at law? "Though thou love not, must thou therefore hate?"[4] I put it to the doctor.

BARTHOLO. What is all this about?

FIGARO. [*Leaving.*] She will tell you. [*Exit.*]

BARTHOLO. [*Looking at the departing* FIGARO.] That fellow never improves. If someone doesn't flog him alive he will die inside the skin of the most conceited ass I know.

MARCELINE. [*Attracting his attention.*] Well, here you are at last, Doctor Ubiquitous, you—always so grave and respectable that one could die waiting for your help, just as some time back someone got married despite your efforts.[3]

BARTHOLO. And you—always bitter and provoking. But why am I needed here so urgently? Has the Count met with an accident?

MARCELINE. No, Doctor.

BARTHOLO. And Rosine, his conspiring countess, could she be—God be praised—ailing?

MARCELINE. She is pining away.

BARTHOLO. What about?

MARCELINE. Her husband neglects her.

BARTHOLO. [*With great satisfaction.*] Ah, worthy husband, my avenger!

MARCELINE. It is hard to make out the Count: at once jealous and a philanderer.

BARTHOLO. A philanderer from boredom and jealous from vanity—it's clear as day.

MARCELINE. Today, for example, he is marrying off our Suzanne to Figaro, on whom he lavishes gifts in honor of this union . . .

BARTHOLO. Which His Excellency has made necessary?

MARCELINE. Not quite; but which His Excellency would like to celebrate in secret with the bride . . .

BARTHOLO. Of Mister Figaro? That's an arrangement the latter is surely willing to enter into.

MARCELINE. Basil is sure it is not so.

BARTHOLO. That other lout lives here too? It's a regular den. What does he do?

MARCELINE. All the evil he can. The worst is the hopeless passion he has so long nursed for me.

BARTHOLO. In your place I should have disposed of that for good.

MARCELINE. How?

BARTHOLO. By marrying him.

MARCELINE. Tiresome, brutish wit! Why don't you dispose of mine in the same way? You're in honor-bound: remember all your promises—and also our little Emmanuel, offspring of a forgotten love, who was to lead us to the altar.

BARTHOLO. Was it to listen to this rigmarole that you had me come from Seville? . . . What is this fit of marrying you've suddenly fallen into?

MARCELINE. We'll say no more about it. But at least help me marry someone else.

BARTHOLO. Gladly. But what mortal, bereft of heaven and women's favors, would . . .

MARCELINE. Now, who *could* it be, Doctor, but the gay, handsome, lovable Figaro!

BARTHOLO. That good-for-nothing?

MARCELINE. Never cross, always good-humored, always ready to enjoy the passing moment, worrying as little about the future as about the past—attractive, generous, oh generous! . . .

BARTHOLO. . . . . as a scamp . . .

MARCELINE. . . . . as a lord. Delightful, in short. But he is a monster too.

BARTHOLO. What about his Suzanne?

MARCELINE. She'd never get him, clever as she is, if you would help me, dear Doctor, and hold him to a promissory note of his that I have.

BARTHOLO. On his wedding day?

MARCELINE. Weddings have gone farther than this and been broken off. If I didn't mind giving away a feminine secret—

BARTHOLO. There aren't any secrets for a physician.

MARCELINE. You know very well I have no secrets from you. Well, our sex is ardent but shy. A certain attraction may draw us toward pleasure, yet the most adventurous woman will say to herself—"be beautiful if you can, sensible if you will, but stay respectable: you must!" Now since every woman knows what reputation is worth, we can scare off Suzanne by threatening to expose the offers that are being made to her.

BARTHOLO. What will that accomplish?

MARCELINE. Just this: ashamed and apprehensive, she will keep on refusing the Count. He, from spite, will support my opposition to her marriage, and hence mine will become a certainty.

BARTHOLO. She's right, by God! It's an excellent trick to marry off my old housekeeper to the scoundrel who pinched my young protégée . . .

MARCELINE. [*Quickly.*] . . . the man who plans to serve his pleasure and disappoint my hopes . . .

BARTHOLO. . . . . the man who once upon a time swindled me out of a hundred pounds that I haven't forgotten.

MARCELINE. Ah, what bliss!—

BARTHOLO. To punish a swindler!—

MARCELINE. To marry him, Doctor, to marry him! [*Enter* SUZANNE.]

SUZANNE. [*Holding a bonnet with large ribbons and a woman's dress over her arm.*] To marry? To marry whom? My Figaro?

MARCELINE. [*Sourly.*] Why not? Aren't you thinking of it yourself?

BARTHOLO. [*Laughing.*] An angry woman's typical argument! We were speaking, Suzanne my dear, of his happiness in possessing you.

MARCELINE. To say nothing of the my lord besides.

SUZANNE. [*With a curtsy.*] Your servant, madam. There is always a touch of gall in your remarks.

MARCELINE. [*Curtsying.*] Your servant as well, madam. Where is the gall? Isn't it justice that a freehanded nobleman should share a little in the good things he procures for his people?

SUZANNE. He procures?

MARCELINE. Yes, madam.

SUZANNE. Fortunately, your jealousy is as well known as your claims on Figaro are slight.

MARCELINE. They could have been strengthened by the same means that you chose to use.

SUZANNE. But those means, madam, are open only to learned ladies.

MARCELINE. And this poor child is all innocence—like an old judge!

BARTHOLO. [*Pulling* MARCELINE *away.*] Good-by, little bride of Figaro!

MARCELINE. [*Curtsying.*] Also promised to the Count.

SUZANNE. [*Curtsying.*] She gives you best regards, madam.

MARCELINE. [*Curtsying.*] Will she also love me a little, madam?

SUZANNE. [*Curtsying.*] As to that, pray have no fears.

MARCELINE. [*Curtsying.*] Madam is as kind as she is pretty.

SUZANNE. [*Curtsying.*] Enough, perhaps, to disconcert madam.

MARCELINE. [*Curtsying.*] And above all, respectable.

SUZANNE. [*Curtsying.*] That's a monopoly of dowagers.

MARCELINE. [*Outraged.*] Dowagers, dowagers!

BARTHOLO. [*Interrupting her.*] Marceline!

MARCELINE. Let's go, Doctor, or I shan't be able to restrain myself. Good-by, madam. [*She curtsies. Exeunt.*]

SUZANNE. Go, madam; go, pedant. I am as little afraid of your plots as I am of your insults. Look at the old sibyl! Because she has a little learning and used it to torment my lady in her youth, she wants to rule the castle. [*Throws the dress from her arm to a chair.*] I've forgotten what I came for. [*Enter* CHERUBINO.]

CHERUBINO. [*Running in.*] Suzy, I've been waiting two hours to catch you alone. I'm miserable: you're getting married and I'm going away.

SUZANNE. How does my getting married cause the departure of his lordship's favorite page?

CHERUBINO. [*Piteously.*] Suzanne: he's dismissed me!

SUZANNE. [*Mimicking him.*] Cherubino: what nonsense!

CHERUBINO. He found me yesterday at your cousin's, at Fanchette's. I was rehearsing her ingénue part in tonight's show and he flew into a rage on seeing me. "Get out," he said, "You little—" I don't dare repeat the bad word he used. "Get out! Tonight is your last night in this house!" If my lady, my dear godmother, doesn't calm him down about this, it's all over with me, Suzy; I'll never lay eyes on you again.

SUZANNE. On *me?* It's my turn, is it? So you don't go sighing around my lady any more?

CHERUBINO. Oh, Suzy. She is beautiful, majestic, but so—imposing!

SUZANNE. That is to say, I am not and you can take liberties.

CHERUBINO. You're mean! You know perfectly well I never dare take anything. How lucky you are, seeing her all the time, talking to her, dressing her in the morning, undressing her at night, unpinning each pin—Oh, Suzy, I'd give anything—What's that in your hand?

SUZANNE. [*Mockingly.*] It's the blissful bonnet and the fortunate ribbon which enclose, at night, the hair of your beautiful godmother . . .

CHERUBINO. Her ribbon—at night! Give it to me, be a dear, my love.

SUZANNE. [*Pulling it away.*] Not so fast. "His love!" What familiarity! If you weren't just a whippersnapper— [CHERUBINO *seizes the ribbon.*] Oh, the ribbon!

CHERUBINO. [*Going behind and around the invalid chair.*] You can say you mislaid it, ruined it, lost it. Say anything like.

SUZANNE. [*Chases after him around the chair.*] I promise you that in three or four years you will be the biggest little miscreant on earth! Give me back that ribbon. [*She snatches at it.*]

CHERUBINO. [*Drawing a paper from his pocket.*] Let me, do let me have it, Suzy. I'll give you my song here, and while the memory of my beautiful mistress will sadden all my days, the thought of you will bring me the only ray of joy that could lighten my heart.

SUZANNE. [*Tears the song out of his grasp.*]

"Lighten his heart!" The little scoundrel! Do you think you are talking to your Fanchette? My lord finds you with her; you breathe vows in secret to my lady; and on top of that you make me declarations to my face!

CHERUBINO. [*Excited.*] It's true, on my honor! I don't know who I am or what I'm doing, but just lately, at the mere sight of a woman I've felt my breath come in gasps and my heart beat fast. The words "love" and "bliss" arouse and upset me. In short, the need to say to someone "I love you" has become so compelling that I say it to myself when I cross the park, I say it to our lady and to you, to the clouds and the wind that carries my useless words away. Yesterday I ran into Marceline—

SUZANNE. [*Laughing.*] Ahahaha!

CHERUBINO. Why not? She's a woman! She a maid! A maid! A woman! Oh, what sweet words are those—and how interesting!

SUZANNE. He is losing his mind.

CHERUBINO. Fanchette is very sweet: at least she listens to me and you don't.

SUZANNE. What a pity! Let us listen to the gentleman. [*She snatches again at the ribbon.*]

CHERUBINO. [*Turns and runs.*] Not on your life! No one can take it, you see, except with *my* life. But if the price does not suit you, I'll increase it by a thousand kisses. [*He starts chasing her around the chair.*]

SUZANNE. [*Turning on him as she flees.*] A thousand slaps in the face if you come near me. I'll complain to my lady, and far from interceding for you I'll go to my lord and say: "Send back that petty thief to his parents. He is a good-for-nothing who puts on airs about being in love with Madam, and on the rebound tries to kiss me."

CHERUBINO. [*Sees the* COUNT *entering and hides behind the armchair.*] That's the end of me!

SUZANNE. Coward! [*Intercepts the* COUNT *and helps to conceal the* PAGE.]

COUNT. [Coming forward.] You are upset, Suzette, you were talking to yourself. Your little heart seems to me full of agitation—understandably enough on a day like this.

SUZANNE. [*Embarrassed.*] My lord, what do you want with me? If someone saw us . . .

COUNT. I should hate to be surprised here. But you know the interest I take in you. Basil must have told you I love you. I have only a moment to tell you so myself. Listen—[*He sits in the armchair.*]

SUZANNE. I will not listen.

COUNT. [*Taking her hand.*] Just one word. You know the King has made me ambassador to London. I am taking Figaro with me, giving him an excellent post. Now since it is a wife's duty to follow her husband—

SUZANNE. Oh, if I had the courage to speak—

COUNT. [*Drawing her to him.*] Don't hesitate, speak, my dear. Assume a privilege which you may use with me for life.

SUZANNE. [*Frightened.*] I don't want to, my lord, I don't want to. Please leave me.

COUNT. But first tell me.

SUZANNE. [*Angrily.*] I don't know what I was saying.

COUNT. Something about a wife's duty.

SUZANNE. Very well. When you, my lord, eloped with your lady from the Doctor's house and married her for love, and when in her honor you abolished that dreadful right of the lord of the manor—

COUNT. Which annoyed the girls so much, no doubt! Look, Suzette, it was a charming right and if you'll come and prattle with me about it this evening in the garden, I'll rate that little favor so high—

BASIL. [*Speaking from without.*] My lord isn't in his room.

COUNT. [*Rising.*] Whose voice is that?

SUZANNE. This is dreadful!

COUNT. Go out so that nobody comes in.

SUZANNE. [*Upset.*] And leave you here?

BASIL. [*From outside.*] His lordship was with my lady, then he left; I'll go look for him.

COUNT. No spot where I can hide. Yes, behind that chair. It's not very good but—send him packing. [SUZANNE *bars his way; he gently pushes her; she*

retreats and thus comes between him and the PAGE. *But while the* COUNT *stoops and takes* CHERUBINO's *place, the latter throws himself kneeling on the seat and clings to the cushions.* SUZANNE *picks up the dress she formerly carried, drapes it over the* PAGE, *and takes her stand in front of the chair.*]

BASIL. [*Entering.*] Did you by any chance see the Count, miss?

SUZANNE. [*Brusquely.*] How could I? Please go.

BASIL. [*Coming nearer.*] If you only think a little you will see there was nothing surprising about my question. Figaro is looking for him.

SUZANNE. So he's looking for the man who is his worst enemy after yourself.

COUNT. [*Aside.*] Let's see how he takes my part.

BASIL. Is it being a man's enemy to wish his wife well?

SUZANNE. Not in your book of rules, you vile corrupter.

BASIL. What does anyone ask of you that you aren't going to bestow on another? Thanks to a lovely ceremony, the things that were forbidden yesterday will be required tomorrow.

SUZANNE. Disgusting wretch!

BASIL. Marriage being the most comic of all serious things, I had thought—

SUZANNE. [*Outraged.*] Contemptible thought! Who gave you leave to come in here!

BASIL. There, there, naughty girl. God grant you peace! You'll do just as you like. But don't go thinking that I regard Mister Figaro as an impediment to my lord—and if it weren't for the little page . . .

SUZANNE. [*Shyly.*] Don Cherubino?

BASIL. [*Mimicking her.*] *Cherubino di amore*, yes. He's always buzzing about you and this morning again was at this door when I left you: say it isn't true.

SUZANNE. What lies! Slanderer! Go away!

BASIL. A slanderer because I see things as they are. Isn't it also for you the page has a song he carries mysteriously about him?

SUZANNE. [*Angrily.*] For me indeed!

BASIL. Unless he made it up for her

ladyship. Truth to tell, when he serves at table, they say that he cannot take his eyes off her. But let him look out: my lord is a brute upon that point.

SUZANNE. [*Outraged.*] And you are a scoundrel, going about spreading gossip and ruining a wretched child who is already in disgrace with his master.

BASIL. Did I make it up? I say these things becasue everybody says them.

COUNT. [*Rising.*] Who, everybody?

SUZANNE. Heavens!

BASIL. Ha ha!

COUNT. Run along, Basil, and see that the boy is sent away.

BASIL. I am truly sorry that I came in here.

SUZANNE. [*Upset.*] Oh dear, oh dear!

COUNT. She is faint, help her into the chair.

SUZANNE. [*Fending him off energetically.*] I don't want to sit. To walk in here without leave is an outrage.

COUNT. But there are two of us with you, my dear. There's not the slightest danger.

BASIL. For my part, I deeply regret having made light of the page—since you overheard me. I was using it to ascertain her feelings, because essentially—

COUNT. Fifty pounds, a horse, and back to his parents.

BASIL. My lord, it was frivolous gossip.

COUNT. A young libertine whom I found only yesterday with the gardener's daughter.

BASIL. With Fanchette?

COUNT. In her room.

SUZANNE. [*Outraged.*] Where my lord had business also?

COUNT. [*Cheerfully.*] That's an idea!

BASIL. It is of good omen.

COUNT. [*Still cheerful.*] Of course not. I was looking for your uncle Antonio, my drunken gardener, to give him some instructions. I knock. No one opens for quite a while. Your little cousin looks embarrassed. I grow suspicious while I talk to her and as I do so I cast an eye about. Behind the door there was a curtain of sorts, a wardrobe, something for old clothes. Without seeming to, I gently, slowly

lift the curtain . . . [*He illustrates by lifting the dress off the armchair.*] And I see . . . [*He catches sight of* CHERUBINO.] . . . I say!

BASIL. Ha ha!

COUNT. This is as good as before.

BASIL. It's better.

COUNT. [*To* SUZANNE.] Congratulations, dear lady: hardly engaged to be married and yet able to manage such tricks! Was it to entertain my page that you wished to be alone? As for you sir, whose behavior never varies, the only lack of respect for your godmother you had so far overlooked was to pay your addresses to her maid, who is the bride of your friend. But I will not allow Figaro, a man I love and esteem, to be the victim of this deception. Was he with you, Basil?

SUZANNE. [*Indignant.*] There is no deception and no victim. [*Pointing.*] He was here while you were talking to me.

COUNT. [*Carried away.*] I hope you lie when you say so. His worst enemy could wish him nothing worse.

SUZANNE. He was asking me to beseech my lady to obtain his pardon from you. Your coming in upset him so much that he hid in the chair.

COUNT. [*Angrily.*] Infernal cleverness! But I sat in that chair the moment I arrived.

CHERUBINO. Alas, my lord, I was shaking in my shoes behind it.

COUNT Another trick! I stood there myself just now.

CHERUBINO. Forgive me, but that is when I came around and crouched inside.

COUNT. This young snake in the grass must be a—poisonous adder: he heard what we said?

CHERUBINO. On the contrary, my lord, I did my best to hear nothing at all.

COUNT. O treachery! [*To* SUZANNE.] You shan't marry Figaro!

BASIL. Moderation, if you please: someone's coming.

COUNT. [*Pulling* CHERUBINO *out of the armchair and setting him on his feet.*] He would stay there in front of the whole world! [*Enter* FIGARO, *the* COUNTESS, FANCHETTE, *with several footmen and country people dressed in white.*]

FIGARO. [*Holding a woman's hat covered with white feathers and ribbons and speaking to the* COUNTESS.] Only you, my lady, can obtain this favor for us.

COUNTESS. You hear him, Count? They imagine that I wield an influence I do not in fact possess. Still, as their request is not unreasonable—

COUNT. [*Embarrassed.*] It would indeed have to be very much so—

FIGARO. [*Speaking low to* SUZANNE.] Back up my attempt—

SUZANNE. [*The same to* FIGARO.] Which won't help any.

FIGARO. [*In low voice.*] Never mind, do it.

COUNT. [*To* FIGARO.] What is it you want?

FIGARO. My lord, your vassals, who are deeply touched by the abolition of a certain regrettable right that you gave up out of love for my lady—

COUNT. Well, the right is abolished; what are you getting at?

FIGARO. Only that it is high time the virtue of so good a master should be manifest. I myself stand to gain so much from it today that I want to be the first to glorify it at our wedding.

COUNT. [*Still more embarrassed.*] You can't be serious. The abolition of a shameful right is only the payment of a debt to decency. A Spaniard may want to conquer beauty by devotion, but to be the first to exact the sweetest of rewards as if it were a servile due—why, that's the tyrannical violence of a Vandal, not the acknowledged right of a Castilian noblemen!

FIGARO. [*Holding* SUZANNE's *hand.*] Then deign that this young creature, whose honor has been preserved by your noble reason, receive from your hand the virgin's coif of white feathers and ribbons as a symbol of the purity of your intentions. Have this ceremony become a custom at all weddings and let an appropriate chorus be sung each time to commemorate the event.

COUNT. [*Embarrassed.*] If I did not know that to be a lover, a poet, and a musician excused every kind of folly—

FIGARO. Join with me, my friends.

ALL. [*Together.*]My lord! My lord!

SUZANNE. [*To the* COUNT.] Why brush aside an honor you so much deserve?

COUNT. [*Aside.*] Deceitful wench!

FIGARO. Look at her, my lord: no prettier face will ever signalize the extent of your sacrifice.

SUZANNE. Leave my face out of it and let us only praise his virtue.

COUNT. [*Aside.*] The whole thing is a plot.

COUNTESS. I too join with them, Count, knowing as I do that this ceremony, ever to be cherished, owes its being to the gracious love you used to have for me.

COUNT. Which I still have, madam, and because of which I now yield.

ALL. [*Together.*] Bravo!

COUNT. [*Aside.*] I've been had. [*Aloud.*] In order to give the ceremony yet more splendor, I should like to see it postponed till somewhat later. [*Aside.*] Quick, let us get hold of Marceline!

FIGARO. [*To* CHERUBINO.] What about you, my lad, you don't applaud?

SUZANNE. He is in despair; his lordship is sending him home.

COUNTESS. Ah, my lord, I ask for his pardon.

COUNT. He doesn't deserve it.

COUNTESS. The poor boy is so young.

COUNT. Not so young as you think.

CHERUBINO. [*Trembling.*] Clemency is not the lordly right you gave up when you married my lady.

COUNTESS. He only gave up the one that afflicted you all.

SUZANNE. If my lord had abandoned the right to pardon, it would surely be the first right he would want to restore in secret.

COUNT. [*Embarrassed.*] Oh, quite.

COUNTESS. So what need to restore it?

CHERUBINO. [*To the* COUNT.] I was giddy in my actions, my lord, that is true. But there never was the least impropriety in my words.

COUNT. [*Embarrassed.*] All right, that's enough.

FIGARO. What does he mean?

COUNT. [*Sharply.*] Enough, enough! Everybody wants him pardoned: I so order it. I'll do more: I'll give him a company in my regiment.

ALL. [*Together.*] Bravo!

COUNT. But on one condition—that he leave at once to join up in Catalonia.

FIGARO. Oh, my lord, make it tomorrow.

COUNT. I have given an order.

CHERUBINO. And I obey.

COUNT. Salute your godmother and entreat her protection. [CHERUBINO *kneels on one knee before the* COUNTESS, *unable to utter a word.*]

COUNTESS. [*Much moved.*] Since you cannot stay even for today, young man, go. New duties call you: fulfill them worthily. Honor your benefactor. Remember this house where your youth was so leniently treated. Be upright, obedient, and brave. We shall all share in the pleasure of your success. [CHERUBINO *gets up and goes back to where he stood before.*]

COUNT. You seem deeply moved, madam.

COUNTESS. I do not apologize for it. Who knows what fate is in store for a child thrown into such a dangerous career? He is related to my family, as well as being my godson.

COUNT. [*Aside.*] Basil was evidently right. [*Aloud.*] Young man, give a kiss to Suzanne, for the last time.

FIGARO. Why the last, my lord? He'll come and spend the winter with us. Give me a kiss too, captain. [*They embrace.*] Good-by, Cherubino. You are going to lead a very different life, my child. Thus: no more hanging about the women's quarters the livelong day, no more sweet drinks and pastries, no more blindman's buff and spinning the bottle. Just veteran soldiers, by God, weather-beaten and dressed in rags, a huge musket that weighs a ton—Right . . . turn! Left . . . turn! Forward! march! To glory—and don't you go stumbling on the way—unless a well-placed shot—

SUZANNE. Horror! Be quiet!

COUNTESS. What a send-off!

COUNT. Where can Marceline be? Isn't it odd that she isn't with the rest of you?

FANCHETTE. My lord, she went walking to town, by the lane along the farm.

COUNT. And she is coming back?

BASIL. When it may please God.

FIGARO. May it please Him never to please . . .

FANCHETTE. The gentleman doctor was giving her his arm.

COUNT. [*Quickly.*] The doctor is here?

BASIL. She fastened upon him at once . . .

COUNT. [*Aside.*] He could not come at a better time.

FANCHETTE. She was all excited. She spoke very loud and paced back and forth and stopped and did like this with her arms. And the gentleman doctor, he did like this with his hand, to calm her down. She mentioned my cousin Figaro.

COUNT. [*Taking her chin in his hand.*] Cousin . . . yet to be.

FANCHETTE. [*Pointing to* CHERUBINO.] My lord, have you forgiven us for yesterday?

COUNT. [*Interrupting.*] Good day, good day, my dear.

FIGARO. It's her confounded love that keeps her obsessed.[5] She would have spoiled our party.

COUNT. [*Aside.*] She will spoil it yet, I promise you. [*Aloud.*] Come, madam, let us go in. Basil, please stop in to see me.

SUZANNE. [*To* FIGARO.] You'll be joining me, sonny?

FIGARO. [*In low voice to* SUZANNE.] Wasn't he properly stuck?

SUZANNE. [*Low.*] Delightful character![6] [*Exeunt all but* FIGARO, CHERUBINO, *and* BASIL.]

FIGARO. By the way, you fellows: the new ceremony having been adopted, the show tonight becomes a sequel to it and we mustn't forget our lines. Let's not be like those players who never act so poorly as on the night when the critics are wide awake. We haven't any tomorrow to recoup ourselves, so let's learn our parts today.

BASIL. [*Maliciously.*] Mine is more difficult than you think.

FIGARO. [*In pantomime, unseen by* BASIL, *pretends to give him a beating.*] But you don't suspect the ovation you will get.

CHERUBINO. Dear friend, you forget that I am leaving—

FIGARO. —when you would like to stay.

CHERUBINO. Oh, if I only could!

FIGARO. Then we must have a scheme. Not a murmur against your leaving. Traveling cloak on your shoulders. Make a show of packing, your horse at the gates, a brief gallop as far as the farm and come back on foot by the back way. My lord will think you gone: just keep out of his sight. I undertake to calm him down after the wedding party.

CHERUINO. But Fanchette does not know her part.

BASIL. What the dickens were you teaching her this last week when you've hardly been away from her?

FIGARO. You have nothing to do today— for heaven's sake coach her in her lines.

BASIL. Be careful, young man, be careful! Her father is suspicious; the girl has been slapped and hasn't learned her lines—Cherubino, Cherubino, she will be sorry—the pot that goes once too often to the well . . .

FIGARO. Ah, there's our curmudgeon with his old proverbs. Tell us, you old pedant, what the wisdom of nations has to say about the pot that goes to the well.

BASIL. It gets filled.

FIGARO. [*Leaving.*] Not so dumb as I thought.

Act 2

A magnificent bedroom with a large bed in an alcove and a platform in front. The main door is upstage to the right, the dressing-room door downstage to the left. A third door, at the back, leads to the women's quarters. The window is on the opposite side. SUZANNE *and the* COUNTESS *enter, right.*

COUNTESS. [*Throws herself into a wing chair.*] Shut the door, Suzanne, and tell me everything in detail.

SUZANNE. I do not mean to hold anything back, my lady.

COUNTESS. And so he wanted to seduce you?

SUZANNE. Certainly not! My lord does not take that much trouble with servants: he wanted to buy me.

COUNTESS. And the little page was there all the while?

SUZANNE. Yes, that is to say, he was hidden behind the big armchair. He had come to ask me to intercede with you for his pardon.

COUNTESS. Why not come to me direct? Do you suppose I would have refused him, Suzy?

SUZANNE. That's what I told him, but his sadness at leaving, especially at leaving you— "Ah, Suzy," he said, "how noble and beautiful she is, but how imposing!"

COUNTESS. Do I really look that way, Suzy, I who have always stood up for him?

SUZANNE. Then he saw the ribbon of your nightdress which I had in my hand and he jumped and grabbed it.

COUNTESS. [*Smiling.*] My ribbon? What a child!

SUZANNE. I tried to take it from him, madam, but he was like a wild beast, his eyes shone: "You'll get it only with my life," he said, and his voice cracked.

COUNTESS. [*Dreamily.*] And then, Suzy?

SUZANNE. Well, madam, how can one put a stop to it? The little devil! "My godmother," he says, and "I wish I could," says he. And just because he wouldn't even dare kiss the hem of your gown, my lady, he always wants to be kissing me in earnest.

COUNTESS. [*Still dreaming.*] Enough . . . enough nonsense. At last, then, my husband came to the point and told you . . .

SUZANNE. . . . . that if I refused to listen to him, he would use his influence in behalf of Marceline.

COUNTESS. [*Rising, pacing, and fanning herself vigorously.*] He does not love me at all any more.

SUZANNE. Why then is he so jealous?

COUNTESS. Like every husband, my dear—it is pride. Ah, I loved him too much. I wearied him with my caresses, bored him with my love. That is my chief wrong in relation to him.

But I do not intend that his charming thoughts should bring you harm; you shall marry Figaro. He alone can help us: is he going to join us?

SUZANNE. As soon as the hunt is on its way.

COUNTESS. [*Using her fan again.*] Open the window on the garden a bit. It's exceedingly warm in here.

SUZANNE. That is because my lady has been talking and walking so actively. [*She opens the window at the back.*]

COUNTESS. [*Absent-mindedly.*] In avoiding me of set purpose . . . men are creatures full of guilt.

SUZANNE. [*Shouting from the window.*] There is my lord riding through the big field. Peter is with him and one, two, three, four—setters.

COUNTESS. That gives us plenty of time. [*She sits.*] Someone is knocking, Suzy.

SUZANNE. [*Runs singing to the door.*] Why, it's my Figaro, it's my Figaro! [*Enter* FIGARO.]

SUZANNE. Dear friend, come in. My lady can hardly wait.

FIGARO. And what about you, little Sue? Her ladyship must not take on so. After all, what is all the fuss about?— A trifle. My lord Count finds our young lady charming and would like to make her his mistress—perfectly natural.

SUZANNE. Natural?

FIGARO. Then he appointed me King's Messenger and my Suzy—er—attachée to the embassy. No mental confusion there.

SUZANNE. Are you through?

FIGARO. And because Suzanne, my bride, declines the post and privileges, he wants to promote the plans of Marceline. Could anything be more simple? To seek revenge on those who thwart our purpose by interfering with theirs is what everybody does, it's what we ourselves are about to do. And that, so to speak, is that.

COUNTESS. Figaro, how can you joke about a project that will rob us all of happiness?

FIGARO. Who says it will, my lady?

SUZANNE. Instead of sharing our grief, you—

FIGARO. Isn't it enough that I am busy about it? No, no, let us be as methodical as he, and cool his desire for our belongings by arousing in him an apprehension for his own.

COUNTESS. A good idea, but how?

FIGARO. It is all done, madam. A piece of false information about you—

COUNTESS. About me! You are out of your mind!

FIGARO. No: it is he who must be driven out of his.

COUNTESS. A man as jealous as he—

FIGARO. So much the better. To make the most out of people like him, all you have to do is to whip up their blood—a device all women use. As soon as a man of his type is red-hot with passion, the most trifling subterfuge enables one to lead him by the nose into the nearest fishpond. I have used Basil to deliver an anonymous note which informs his lordship that tonight a gallant will try to approach you during the ball.

COUNTESS. You play fast and loose with the truth about a woman of honor?

FIGARO. There are but few I would have dared to risk it with, madam, for fear of stating no more than the facts.

COUNTESS. So now you'll expect me to thank you!

FIGARO. Honestly, isn't it delightful to have cut out his work for him so that he will be prowling around his lady and swearing under his breath during the time that he counted on for dallying with mine? Already he is bewildered: will he gallop over this one, shall he mount guard over that one? [*At the window.*] In his disturbed state of mind—look, look, how he races across the meadow after a poor hare who can't help himself! The hour of the wedding hastens on, but he won't be able to decide against it: he will never dare oppose it to my lady's face.

SUZANNE. No, but Marceline, that *grande dame*, will not hesitate to dare.

FIGARO. Ah! That doesn't worry me. Just let my lord know that you will meet him at dusk in the garden.

SUZANNE. So that's your great device— to rely on him?

FIGARO. See here: people who don't

want to do anything about anything
never achieve anything and aren't
good for anything. That's my last
word.

SUZANNE. A pleasant one!

COUNTESS. And so is her question: you
really would let her meet him in the
garden?

FIGARO. Not at all. I'll arrange for
someone to put on one of Suzy's
dresses. Taken in the act, how can he
get out of it?

SUZANNE. Who will wear my dress?

FIGARO. Cherubino.

COUNTESS. He's gone.

FIGARO. Not as far as I'm concerned.
Will the ladies allow me?

SUZANNE. One can always trust this fellow to hatch a scheme.

FIGARO. A scheme! Two, three, or four
at once, well scrambled and working
from both ends against the middle: I
was born to be a courtier.

SUZANNE. They say it's a difficult profession.

FIGARO. Accept, take, and ask—that's
the secret in three words.

COUNTESS. He has so much self-con-
fidence it rubs off on me!

FIGARO. That was my idea.

SUZANNE. You were saying?

FIGARO. That during the Count's absence I will send you Cherubino.
Dress him up and do his hair and I'll
conceal and indoctrinate him. After
which, my lord, how you will dance!
[*Exit.*]

COUNTESS. [*Holding her box of patches.*]
Heavens, Suzy, I look a sight, and
this young man is coming in!

SUZANNE. Don't you want him to get
over it?

COUNTESS. [*Gazing in the mirror.*] I?
You'll see how I'm going to scold
him!

SUZANNE. Let's get him to sing his romance. [*She lays it on the* COUNTESS's
lap]

COUNTESS. But really my hair is in a
state—

SUZANNE. I'll just roll up these two
curls; they will help your ladyship to
scold him.

COUNTESS. [*Returning to reality.*] What
are you saying, missy?

SUZANNE. Come in, officer. We are visi-

ble. [*Enter* CHERUBINO.]

CHERUBINO. [*Trembling.*] Oh how that
title distresses me, madam. It tells me
I must leave a place . . . a godmother
. . . so good to me.

SUZANNE. And so beautiful.

CHERUBINO. [*With a sigh.*] Oh, yes.

SUZANNE. [*Mimicking him.*] "Oh, yes."
The nice young man, with his long,
hypocritical lashes. Come, bluebird,
sing us a song for my lady.

COUNTESS. [*Unfolding the paper.*] Whose
is it?

SUZANNE. See the guilty blush: it's a foot
deep on his face.

CHERUBINO. Is it forbidden to—cher-
ish?

SUZANNE. [*Shaking her fist in his face.*] I
am going to tell on you, ne'er-do-
well!

COUNTESS. Enough. Does he sing?

CHERUBINO. Please, madam, I am shaking all over.

SUZANNE. [*Laughing and mimicking.*]
Nya, nya, nya, nya, nya, nya, nya. As
soon as madam wishes. These modest
authors! I'll accompany him.

COUNTESS. Take my guitar. [*Seated, she
holds the paper to follow the words.*
SUZANNE, *behind her armchair, begins
the introduction, reading the notes over
her mistress's head. The* PAGE *stands in
front, his eyes lowered. The scene dupli-
cates the beautiful print made from
Vanloo's painting entitled "Conversation
in Spain."*]

(*To the tune of "Malbrouck"*)[7]
My weary steed astride
(*Oh my heart, oh my heart, it is breaking*)
Uncaring where, I ride
The solitary plain.

Uncaring where I ride,
No squire is at my side,
(*Oh my heart, oh my heart, it is breaking*)
For my godmother I pine,
And weep for her in vain.

For her I weep in vain,
And as the fates decree,
I carve upon a tree
(*Oh my heart, oh my heart, it is breaking*)
The letters of her name—
The King that moment came.

The King that moment came,
His bishops and his peers.

"Sweet page," spoke up the Queen,
(Oh my heart, oh my heart, it is breaking)
" 'Tis sore distress, I ween,
"That draws from you these tears.

"What draws from you these tears,
"Declare to us, poor lad."
"My lady Queen, my lord,"
(Oh my heart, oh my heart, it is breaking)
"A godmother I had,
"Whom always I adored—

"Whom always I adored
"And I'll die dreaming of."
"Sweet page," the Queen implored,
(Oh my heart, oh my heart, it is breaking)
"That godmother you love,
"Pray let me take her place.

"Yes, let me take her place,
"And give you, page of mine,
"A maiden fair of face
(Oh my heart, oh my heart, it is breaking)
"A captain's daughter true,
"To whom I'll marry you."

" 'To whom I'll marry you!'
"Those words I must deny
"And for one favor sue:
(Oh my heart, oh my heart, it is breaking)
"To let me live in grief,
"And from my grieving die."

COUNTESS. It is full of naïve simplicity, and even of true sentiment.

SUZANNE. [*Laying the guitar on a chair.*] Oh, as far as sentiment goes, this young man is—But say, officer, have you been told that to enliven this evening's party we need to know whether one of my gowns will more or less fit you?

COUNTESS. I'm afraid it won't.

SUZANNE. [*Comparing their statures.*] He's about my size. Let's take off the coat. [*She takes if off him.*]

COUNTESS. What if someone comes in?

SUZANNE. We're not doing anything wrong. I'll shut the door. [*She runs.*] But it's the hair I want to see.

COUNTESS. In my dressing room, one of my wrappers. [SUZANNE *goes into the dressing room.*]

COUNTESS. Until the ball opens, the Count will not know that you are still in the castle. We shall tell him afterward that the time required to prepare your commission gave us the idea of—

CHERUBINO. [*Showing her the paper.*] Unfortunately, madam, my commission is here, signed. Basil gave it to me from my lord.

COUNTESS. Already! Not a minute lost. [*She reads.*] In such a hurry that he forgot to affix the seal. [*She hands it back.*]

SUZANNE. [*Carrying also a wide-brimmed hat.*] The seal to what?

COUNTESS. His commission.

SUZANNE. Already?

COUNTESS. That's what I was saying. Is that the wrapper?

SUZANNE. [*Seated near the* COUNTESS.] The handsomest of all. [*She sings with pins in her mouth.*]

Turn your head, oh Johnny my dear,
Turn, my handsome cavalier.
[CHERUBINO *kneels beside her to have his hair dressed.*]

Madam, he is sweet!

COUNTESS. Pull his collar more like a woman.

SUZANNE. There—look at that ragamuffin, what a pretty girl he makes. I'm jealous. [*She takes his chin in her hand.*] Will you please not be so pretty as you are?

COUNTESS. Silly girl! You must turn back the cuff so that the undersleeve shows up better. [*She lifts the sleeve.*] What has he put on his arm?—A ribbon!

SUZANNE. *Your* ribbon. I am glad madam saw it. I warned him I would tell on him. I swear, if my lord had not come in, I would have got the ribbon back. I'm almost as strong as he is.

COUNTESS. I see blood. [*She takes off the ribbon.*]

CHERUBINO. [*Shamefaced.*] This morning, when I knew I had to leave, I was adjusting the snaffle on my horse. He tossed his head and the boss on the bit scratched my arm.

COUNTESS. But why put a ribbon—

SUZANNE. A *stolen* ribbon at that! Just imagine what the baffle—the snaffle—the raffle—I can't keep these things straight—look at that white skin! It's a woman's arm, whiter than mine, see? [*She compares.*]

COUNTESS. [*Freezingly.*] Kindly get me some court plaster from my dressing table. [SUZANNE *gives* CHERUBINO *a shove; he falls forward on his hands. She goes into the dressing room. The* COUNTESS *remains silent a moment, her eyes on the ribbon.* CHERUBINO *gazes at her intently.*] As to my ribbon, sir—it's the color I find most becoming to me—I was very much annoyed to be without it.

SUZANNE. [*Returning.*] The bandage for his arm. [*She gives the* COUNTESS *the plaster and a pair of scissors.*]

COUNTESS. When you go for your dress, bring back the ribbon from some other bonnet. [SUZANNE *leaves by the center door, taking the* PAGE's *coat with her.*]

CHERUBINO. [*Eyes lowered.*] The ribbon you're taking from me would have cured me in no time.

COUNTESS. Owing to what specific virtue? [*Pointing to the plaster.*] That is so much better.

CHERUBINO. [*Hesitating.*] When a ribbon . . . has bound the head . . . or touched the skin . . . of a person . . .

COUNTESS. [*Breaking in.*] . . . . of a stranger, it cures wounds? That is news to me. I will test it by keeping the one you put around your arm. At the first scratch—on one of my maids—I shall try it out.

CHERUBINO. [*Deeply moved.*] You are keeping it—but I'm leaving!

COUNTESS. But not forever.

CHERUBINO. I'm so unhappy!

COUNTESS. [*Moved.*] Now he is weeping. It's Figaro's fault for prophesying—

CHERUBINO. Oh, how I wish the time had come that he spoke about! If I were sure of dying at once, perhaps my lips would dare—

COUNTESS. [*Interrupts by wiping his eyes with her handkerchief.*] Be quiet, child, be quiet. There isn't a grain of sense in what you're saying. [*A knock at the door; she raises her voice.*] Who is it?

COUNT. [*Outside.*] Why are you locked in?

COUNTESS. [*Upset.*] It's my husband. Heavens! . . . [*To* CHERUBINO, *who has also got up.*] You, without your coat, your collar open and your arms bare—alone with me—the general

disarray—the anonymous letter he received, his jealousy—

COUNT. [*Outside.*] You won't open?

COUNTESS. The fact is . . . I am alone.

COUNT. Alone? With whom are you talking, then?

COUNTESS. [*Fumbling.*] With you, I should think.

CHERUBINO. [*Aside.*] After those scenes of yesterday and this morning he would kill me on the spot. [*He runs into the dressing room and shuts the door.*]

COUNTESS. [*Removes the key and opens the other door to admit the* COUNT.] What a dreadful mistake!

COUNT. [*Somewhat severe.*] You are not in the habit of shutting yourself up.

COUNTESS. [*Upset.*] I was trying on— yes—odds and ends—with Suzanne. She went for a minute to her room.

COUNT. You look and sound quite strange.

COUNTESS. It's not surprising, not surprising at all, I assure you. We were speaking about you. She just left, as I said—

COUNT. You were speaking about me? Well, here I am. I've come back much disturbed. On setting out, I was handed a note—though I take no stock in it—it upset me.

COUNTESS. How so, what note, sir?

COUNT. You must admit, madam, that you or I must be surrounded by people who are—uncommonly wicked. Someone informs me that a person, whom I falsely suppose to be absent, will attempt to approach you.

COUNTESS. Whoever this rash being may be, he will have to make his way to this very spot, for I do not intend to stir for the rest of the day.

COUNT. What about tonight, for Suzanne's wedding?

COUNTESS. Not on any account; I am quite indisposed.

COUNT. Fortunately the doctor is here. [*The* PAGE *overturns a chair in the dressing room.*] What noise was that?

COUNTESS. [*Distraught.*] Noise?

COUNT. Someone in there upset a piece of furniture.

COUNTESS. I—I heard nothing.

COUNT. You must be powerfully preoccupied.

COUNTESS. Preoccupied? What about?

COUNT. Madam: there is someone in that dressing room!

COUNTESS. Indeed, who could there be, sir?

COUNT. It is for me to ask that question: I have just arrived.

COUNTESS. It must be Suzanne putting things away.

COUNT. You told me she had gone to her room.

COUNTESS. Gone there—or here—I don't know which.

COUNT. If it is Suzanne, why your evident distress?

COUNTESS. Distress—over my maid?

COUNT. Over your maid it may be, but distress without a doubt.

COUNTESS. Without a doubt, sir, that girl concerns and occupies your mind much more than I.

COUNT. She concerns me so much that I want to see her at once.

COUNTESS. I readily believe that this is what you often want. But your ill-founded suspicions—[SUZANNE *enters at the back, unseen, with clothes in her arms.*]

COUNT. If so, they will be easily dispelled. [*He speaks through the dressing-room door.*] Come out, Suzanne, I order you to. [SUZANNE *stops near the alcove at the back.*]

COUNTESS. She is almost naked, sir. How can you intrude in this way on women in their apartments? She was trying on some old things I am giving her on the occasion of her wedding. She fled when she heard you.

COUNT. If she is afraid to show herself, she can at least speak. [*He turns again to the closed door.*] Answer me, Suzanne: are you in the dressing room? [SUZANNE, *still at the back of the alcove, hides behind the bed.*]

COUNTESS. [*Quickly, to the closed door.*] Suzy, I forbid you to answer. [*To the* COUNT.] No one has ever carried tyranny so far!

COUNT. [*Turning again.*] If she won't speak, dressed or undressed I shall see her.

COUNTESS. [*Intercepting him.*] Anywhere else I can't prevent you, but I trust that in my own room—

COUNT. And I trust that in one minute I shall know who this mysterious Suzanne is. I can see it is useless to ask you for the key, but it is not hard to break down this trumpery door. Ho, there, anybody!

COUNTESS. You would bring in your people, create a public scandal—all on the strength of a vague suspicion! We'll be the talk of the castle.

COUNT. An excellent point, madam, I can do without help. This instant I go to my room and return with what I need. [*He starts to go and turns back.*] But in order that everything shall remain as it is, will you kindly accompany me, quietly and decently—since scandal displeases you so? My simple request will surely not be denied?

COUNTESS. [*Upset.*] Sir, who would dream of crossing you?

COUNT. Oh, I was forgetting: the door which leads to your maids' quarters. I must also shut it so that you may be fully vindicated. [*He shuts the center door and takes the key.*]

COUNTESS. [*Aside.*] Oh, what a fateful whim!

COUNT. [*Returning.*] Now that this chamber is sealed, I beg you to accept my arm. [*He raises his voice.*] As for the Suzanne in the dressing room, she will have the goodness to await my return. The least of the evils that may befall her then is—

COUNTESS. Really, sir, this is the most odious performance—[*The* COUNT *leads her out and locks the door.*]

SUZANNE. [*Runs from the alcove to the dressing-room door and speaks through the keyhole.*] Open up, Cherubino, open, quick, it's Suzanne, open and hurry out.

CHERUBINO. [*Coming out.*] Oh, Suzy, what a dreadful mess!

SUZANNE. Go, go, you haven't a minute to lose.

CHERUBINO. [*Frightened.*] How can I get out?

SUZANNE. Don't ask me, just go.

CHERUBINO. But I can't if I'm locked in.

SUZANNE. After this afternoon's encounter he would break you, and she and I would be doomed. Go tell Figaro—

CHERUBINO. Maybe the window over the garden isn't too high up. [*He runs to see.*]

SUZANNE. [*Frightened.*] A whole story—you can't do it! Oh, my poor lady! And my marriage, dear God!

CHERUBINO. [*Coming back.*] It overlooks the melon patch. All it would spoil is a couple of beds.

SUZANNE. [*Holding him back and crying out.*] You will kill yourself!

CHERUBINO. [*Excited.*] I'd throw myself into an open furnace—I would, Suzy—rather than cause her harm. And a kiss from you will bring me luck. [*Kisses her, runs toward the window, and leaps out.*]

SUZANNE. [*Again cries out; then, overcome, falls into a chair, finally drags herself to the window and comes back.*] He's off and away, the young devil! As light on his feet as he's pretty to look at. He'll have all the women he wants, I bet. Now to take his place, quick! [*Goes into the dressing room.*] From here on, my lord, you can tear down the wall if it gives you pleasure, you don't get a word out of me. [*Shuts the door. The* COUNT *and* COUNTESS *return. He holds a pair of pliers which he soon throws upon a chair.*]

COUNT. Everything is as I left it. Madam, if you compel me to break down that door you must think of the consequences: once again, will you open it yourself?

COUNTESS. But sir, what singular ill-temper can so destroy considerateness between husband and wife? If it were love that possessed you to the point of causing this fury, I could excuse it, however demented. The motive could make me forget the offense. But how can mere vanity move a well-bred man to such excesses?

COUNT. Love or vanity, you open that door or I do it on the spot.

COUNTESS. [*Before the door.*] My lord, please desist! Can you think me capable of forgetting what I owe to my self-respect?

COUNT. Put it any way you like, madam, I mean to see who is in that dressing room.

COUNTESS. [*Frightened.*] Very well, you shall see. But first listen to me quietly.

COUNT. So it isn't Suzanne?

COUNTESS. [*Embarrassed.*] At least it isn't a person . . . about whom you should have any . . . we were bent on a practical joke . . . quite harmless, really, for this evening . . . and I swear to you . . .

COUNT. You swear to me—what?

COUNTESS. That neither he nor I meant to offend you.

COUNT. He—it is a man, then?

COUNTESS. A child, dear sir.

COUNT. And who, pray tell?

COUNTESS. I hardly dare give his name.

COUNT. [*Furious.*] I'll kill him!

COUNTESS. Merciful powers!

COUNT. Speak up!

COUNTESS. The young . . . Cherubino.

COUNT. That impudent whelp! That explains my suspicions—and the anonymous note.

COUNTESS. [*Her hands joined in prayer.*] Oh, sir, do not allow yourself to suppose—

COUNT. [*Stamping his foot and speaking aside.*] That accursèd page turns up whereever I go. [*Aloud.*] Come, madam, now that I know everything, open up. You would not have been so moved saying good-by to him this morning, you would not have used such elaborate lies in your tale of Suzanne, and he would not have hidden so quickly and so long, unless misconduct and guilt were the reason.

COUNTESS. He was afraid of irritating you by showing himself.

COUNT. [*Beside himself, shouting at the dressing-room door.*] Come out of there, you little scrub!

COUNTESS. [*Seizing the* COUNT *with both arms and thrusting him aside.*] My dear sir, my dear sir, your anger makes me afraid for him. Don't, I beg, trust your own suspicions, which are unjust, and don't let his disheveled state—

COUNT. Disheveled!

COUNTESS. Alas, you will see—one of my bonnets on his head, without his coat, his neckband open and arms bare, ready to dress up as a woman. He was going to try to—

COUNT. And you wanted to stay all day in your room! Worthless woman! You shall keep to your room—I shall see to it—and for a long time! But first I must kick out that insolent stripling that I may never come upon him again.

COUNTESS. [*On her knees, arms uplifted.*] Count, you must spare a mere child. I shall never forgive myself for being the cause of—

COUNT. Your fears deepen his guilt.

COUNTESS. He is not guilty—he was leaving. It is I who had him fetched.

COUNT. [*In anger.*] Get up. Remove yourself—shameless woman, to dare entreat me in behalf of another.

COUNTESS. Very well. I will remove myself, I will get up and give you the key to the door, but in the name of your love—

COUNT. My love, hypocrite!

COUNTESS. [*Gets up and gives him the key.*] Promise that you will let the child go harmless—and may you vent your fury on me later if I do not convince you that—

COUNT. [*Taking the key.*] I'm no longer listening.

COUNTESS. [*Throws herself into an armchair, her handkerchief over her face.*] God, oh God, he will be killed!

COUNT. [*Opens the door.*] You!

SUZANNE. [*Comes out laughing.*] "I will kill him—I will kill him!" Why *don't* you kill him, your villainous page?

COUNT. [*Aside.*] Lord! What a lesson! [*Looking at the* COUNTESS, *who is stupefied.*] And you pretend to be surprised, too? But perhaps Suzanne wasn't alone. [*He goes in.*]

SUZANNE. [*Going to* COUNTESS] Recover yourself, madam, he's nowhere near—he jumped. [*Gesture.*]

COUNTESS. Oh, Suzy, I am all in.

COUNT. [*Emerges, vexed and silent.*] There's no one else and this time I was wrong. Madam, you are a good actress—

SUZANNE. What about me, my lord? [COUNTESS *holds her handkerchief to her mouth and says nothing, to regain her composure.*]

COUNT. [*Approaching.*] And so, madam, you were joking?

COUNTESS. [*Recovering.*] And why not, sir?

COUNT. An absurd practical joke, and

for what reason, tell me?

COUNTESS. Does your outrageous behavior deserve consideration?

COUNT. Do you call outrageous what relates to honor?

COUNTESS. [*Gradually herself again.*] Did I join my life to yours only to be a perpetual victim of your neglect and your jealousy, two things which only you can reconcile?

COUNT. Ah, madam, you spare me nothing—

SUZANNE. She did! My lady had only to let you call the servants—

COUNT. You are right and I abase myself. Forgive me. I am discomfited.

SUZANNE. And deserve to be, you must admit.

COUNT. But why wouldn't you come out when I called to you?

SUZANNE. I was putting on some clothes as well as I could, with a multitude of pins: my lady's forbidding me to stir was for a good reason.

COUNT. Instead of reminding me of my error, help me to soothe her.

COUNTESS. No, my lord, an offense such as this is not to be palliated. I am about to retire to a convent. It is high time I did.

COUNT. Shall you be without regrets?

SUZANNE. For my part, I am sure the day you leave will be the beginning of endless grief.

COUNTESS. Even if it is, Suzy, I'd rather miss him than basely forgive him. He has wounded me too deeply.

COUNT. Rosine!

COUNTESS. I am Rosine no longer, the Rosine you so tenaciously pursued. I am the poor Countess Almaviva, the sad forsaken wife you no longer love.

SUZANNE. Oh, madam!

COUNT. [*Suppliant.*] For charity's sake!

COUNTESS. When have you ever shown me any?

COUNT. But that anonymous letter—it curdled my blood.

COUNTESS. I did not agree to its being written.

COUNT. You knew about it?

COUNTESS. It was that harebrained Figaro—

COUNT. He was party to it?

COUNTESS. —who gave it to Basil—

COUNT. —who told me he had it from a

peasant. Oh, sinister singing-master, two-faced underling: you shall pay for everybody's crimes!

COUNTESS. How like a man! You beg for yourself a forgiveness you deny to others. Let me tell you: if ever I consent to pardon you for the error you committed on the strength of that note, I shall demand that the amnesty be general.

COUNT. With all my heart, Countess. But how can I ever make up for so humiliating a blunder?

COUNTESS. [*Rising.*] It humiliated us both.

COUNT. No, no, only myself, believe me. But I am still amazed at the ease with which you women take on the proper look and tone of each circumstance. You were flushed, crying, your face was working—I assure you, you still look undone.

COUNTESS. [*Trying to smile.*] I was flushing with resentment against your suspiciousness. But men are not delicate enough creatures to distinguish between the indignation of an honorable person suffering outrage and the confusion produced by a justified accusation.

COUNT. [*Smiling.*] What about the disheveled page, coatless and half naked?

COUNTESS. [*Pointing to* SUZANNE.] There he is. Aren't you glad to have caught this one instead of the other? Generally speaking, you do not hate to catch this one.

COUNT. [*Laughing.*] And your entreaties and simulated tears?

COUNTESS. You make me laugh and I do not feel like it.

COUNT. We men think we are practiced in the art of politics, but we are children. It is you, you madam, whom the King should appoint ambassador to London! Your sex must have made a deep study of the art of controlling the countenance to succeed as you did today.

COUNTESS. We are forced into it—and always by men.

SUZANNE. But put us on parole and you will see what honorable beings we are.

COUNTESS. Enough for the moment, Count. Possibly I went too far, but my leniency in so grave a case must be matched by yours.

COUNT. Do say again that you forgive me.

COUNTESS. Have I said it at all, Suzy?

SUZANNE. I did not hear it, madam.

COUNT. Well then, let the words slip out.

COUNTESS. You think you deserve it, you ungrateful man?

COUNT. I do, I do—because I repent.

SUZANNE. To suspect a man in my lady's dressing room!

COUNT. She has already punished me so severely!

SUZANNE. Not to believe her when she says it is her chambermaid!

COUNT. Rosine, are you unrelenting?

COUNTESS. Oh, Suzy, how weak I am! What a poor example I give you! [*Holding out her hand to the* COUNT.] No one will ever believe again in a woman's anger.

SUZANNE. It's all right, madam. One always comes to this with men. [*The* COUNT *ardently kisses his wife's hand.*]

FIGARO. [*Enters, breathless.*] I heard that madam was seriously unwell. I've been running. I see there is no truth in the report.

COUNT. [*Dryly.*] You are most attentive.

FIGARO. It is my duty. But since there is nothing in it, my lord, let me say that all your younger vassals of either sex are downstairs with their violins and pipes, awaiting the moment when you will allow me to bring my bride, so that they may accompany—

COUNT. And who will look after the Countess indoors?

FIGARO. Look after her—but she's not ill?

COUNT. No, but there is a mysterious stranger who will try to approach her.

FIGARO. What stranger?

COUNT. The man in the note that you gave to Basil.

FIGARO. Who said I gave him a note?

COUNT. Even if I hadn't been told, rascal, I could read it in your lying face.

FIGARO. Then it's my face deceiving you, not I.

SUZANNE. Figaro, my poor darling, don't waste your eloquence in defeat: we told his lordship everything.

FIGARO. Told what? You treat me as if I were Basil!

SUZANNE. Told him you had written a note to make my lord believe that when he came in here he would find the young page in the dressing room where I shut myself up.

COUNT. What have you to say to that?

COUNTESS. There's no further need to conceal anything, Figaro, the joke is over.

FIGARO. [*Trying to guess.*] The joke is over?

COUNT. Yes, over, consummated: what do you say to that?

FIGARO. Consummated? I say that—that I wish I could say the same about my marriage. You have only to give the word—

COUNT. You admit the anonymous note?

FIGARO. Since my lady wants it so, and Suzanne wants it so, and you want it so, I can't help wanting it too. But if I were you, my lord, really, I wouldn't believe a word of anything we are telling you.

COUNT. You're always telling lies and always in the teeth of evidence; it's beginning to get on my nerves.

COUNTESS. [*Laughing.*] The poor fellow! Why should you expect, sir, that he would tell the truth even once?

FIGARO. [*Low, to* SUZANNE.] I've warned him of the danger ahead—that's all a gentleman can do.

SUZANNE. [*Low.*] Did you see the page?

FIGARO. [*Low.*] Yes, all rumpled.

SUZANNE. [*Low.*] Oh, wretched!

COUNTESS. Look, my dear Count, they long to be united. Their impatience is understandable: let us go and celebrate the wedding.

COUNT. [*Aside.*] But Marceline . . . where is Marceline? [*Aloud.*] I'd like a moment to dress.

COUNTESS. To be with our own people? You see what I have on. [*Enter* ANTONIO.]

ANTONIO. [*Half tipsy, holding a pot of partly crushed flowers.*] My lord, my lord!

COUNT. What do you want with me, Antonio?

ANTONIO. I wish you'd have the windows over my beds fitted with bars.

They throw every kind of thing out of those windows, a while back they threw out a man.

COUNT. Out of these windows?

ANTONIO. Just look at my gillyflowers!

SUZANNE. [*Low, to* FIGARO.] Look out, Figaro, on your toes!

FIGARO. My lord, he gets drunk every day from the crack of dawn.

ANTONIO. You're wrong—with me there's always a little left over from the day before. But that's how people judge you—in the dark.

COUNT. [*Breathing fire.*] The man, the man, where is he?

ANTONIO. Where he is?

COUNT. Yes, where?

ANTONIO. That's what *I* say. I want to have him found. I'm your servant. There's only me takes real care of your garden. Man falls on it—you can't help . . . appreciating . . . my reputation is . . . uprooted.

SUZANNE. [*Low, to* FIGARO.] Change the subject, quick!

FIGARO. Won't you ever give up drinking?

ANTONIO. If I didn't drink I'd go out of my mind.

COUNTESS. But to drink as you do, without thirst . . .

ANTONIO. To drink without thirst and make love at any time, my lady, 'swhat distinguishes us from the other animals.

COUNT. [*Fiercely.*] Answer me or I'll have you thrown on the parish.

ANTONIO. I wouldn't go.

COUNT. What's that?

ANTONIO. [*Touching his forehead.*] If *that* isn't enough to make you keep a good servant, on my side I'm not so dumb as to get rid of a good master.

COUNT. [*Shaking him violently.*] You say they threw a man out the window.

ANTONIO. Yes, excellency, just a while back, in a white vest, and he picked himself up and ran away.

COUNT. [*Impatient.*] And then?

ANTONIO. I tried to run after him, but I bumped into the fence so hard my finger . . . [*He shows which.*] . . . is still numb. It can't move hand or foot of itself.

COUNT. But you'd recognize the man?

ANTONIO. That I could if I had seen

him, as you might say.

SUZANNE. [*Low, to* FIGARO.] He never saw him.

FIGARO. What a pother about a pot! How long do you mean to carry on about your bluebells, you old watering jug? No use asking, my lord, it was I who jumped down.

COUNT. You? Why?

ANTONIO. "How long I carry on," eh? Why, you must have grown since I saw you jump, 'case you were smaller and thinner at the time.

FIGARO. Naturally: when one jumps one gathers oneself together.

ANTONIO. Methought 'twas rather the whippersnapper I saw—the page.

COUNT. Cherubino, you mean?

FIGARO. Of course, having come back—he and his horse—from the gates of Seville, where he probably is now.

ANTONIO. I didn't say that, I didn't say that! I didn't see a horse jump, or I'd say so.

COUNT. Oh, to be patient!

FIGARO. I was in the women's quarters in my white vest—terribly hot day. I was waiting there for Suzanette, when suddenly I heard your voice, my lord, and a great noise going on. I don't know why, I was seized with fear—perhaps about the anonymous note. . . To make a clean breast of it, I lost my head and jumped down on the flowers, spraining my ankle for my pains. [*He rubs his foot.*]

ANTONIO. As it's you, then I've got to give you back this bit of paper that fell out of your vest when you landed.

COUNT. [*Snatching it.*] Give it to me. [*He unfolds the paper and folds it again.*]

FIGARO. [*Aside.*] This is the end.

COUNT. [*To* FIGARO.] Your great fright has surely not made you forget the contents of this paper, nor how it got into your pocket?

FIGARO. [*Embarrassed, looks into all his pockets, bringing out letters and papers.*] Oh, certainly not—but I carry so many about me—every one has to be answered. [*He looks at a paper.*] This, for instance, what's—? Ah, yes, a letter from Marceline, four pages, a beautiful letter. Could that other one be the petition from that poacher

who is in prison? No—here it is. I also had a list of the furniture in the pavilion, in my other pocket—[*The* COUNT *reopens the paper in his hand.*]

COUNTESS. [*Low, to* SUZANNE.] Heavens, Suzy, it's the officer's commission.

SUZANNE. [*Low, to* FIGARO.] We're undone; it's the commission!

COUNT. [*Folding the paper.*] Well, resourceful sir, you can't guess?

ANTONIO. [*Going toward* FIGARO.] My lord says as how can't you guess?

FIGARO. [*Pushing him away.*] Hence, varlet, and don't speak into my nose!

COUNT. You cannot recall for me what the paper might be?

FIGARO. Ah, ah, ah! I have it! The poor boy! It must be Cherubino's commission, which the dear child showed me and I forgot to give back. What a scatterbrain I am! But how can he manage without his commission? We must go after him—

COUNT. Why should he have given it to you?

FIGARO. [*Embarrassed.*] He wanted—something done to it.

COUNT. [*Looks at paper.*] There's nothing needs doing.

COUNTESS. [*Low, to* SUZANNE.] The seal.

SUZANNE. [*Low, to* FIGARO.] The seal's not on it.

COUNT. [*To* FIGARO.] You have nothing to say?

FIGARO. Yes, the fact is . . . something *is* missing. He says it is customary.

COUNT. Customary? What is customary?

FIGARO. To affix the seal showing your coat of arms. But perhaps it isn't worth the trouble.

COUNT. [*Reopens the paper and crumples it up angrily.*] Confound it! My fate decrees that I'm to be kept in the dark. [*Aside.*] This—this Figaro is the mastermind, and I—I should keep from striking back! [*He starts to stalk out.*]

FIGARO. [*Stopping him.*] You're not going without giving the word about my wedding? [*Enter* BASIL, BARTHOLO, MARCELINE, *and* SUNSTRUCK.]

MARCELINE. [*To the* COUNT.] Don't give the word, my lord. Before you do him a favor, you must do me justice. He has obligations toward me.

COUNT. [*Aside.*] My revenge at last!

FIGARO. Obligations? Of what sort?

Please explain.

MARCELINE. Of course I shall explain, false knave! [COUNTESS *sits in an arm-chair,* SUZANNE *behind her.*]

COUNT. What is it you are referring to, Marceline?

MARCELINE. A promise of marriage.

FIGARO. A promissory note for money I borrowed, nothing more.

MARCELINE. [*To* COUNT.] But with the forfeit of marrying me. You are a great lord, the highest judge in the province . . .

COUNT. Come to the assizes. I will give everybody justice.

BASIL. [*Pointing to* MARCELINE.] In that case, your worship will permit me to put in evidence my claims on Marceline?

COUNT. [*Aside.*] This is the scoundrel of the anonymous note.

FIGARO. As mad as she is—birds of a feather!

COUNT. [*To* BASIL, *angrily.*] Your claims, your claims! What right have you to speak up in my presence, master fool?

ANTONIO. [*Striking his fist into the palm of his other hand.*] Got him the first time: it sure is his right name!

COUNT. Marceline, everything is re-cessed until the public hearing of your plea, which shall take place in the large reception room. You, wise Basil, as my faithful and reliable agent, shall go into town and sum-mon the bench.

BASIL. For her case?

COUNT. And bring along the peasant who gave you the note.

BASIL. How should I know him?

COUNT. You object?

BASIL. I did not enter your service to run errands.

COUNT. What's that?

BASIL. A talented performer on the parish organ, I teach my lady the keyboard, coach her women in sing-ing and your pages on the mandolin. But my chief employment is to enter-tain your company on the guitar, when it pleases you to command me.

SUNSTRUCK. [*Coming forward.*] I'll go, your lordsy, if they's what you want.

COUNT. What is your name and your employment?

SUNSTRUCK. My name is Sunstruck, good lordsy. I watch the goats, and bin asked in for the fireworks. It's holiday today for all us herds. But I know where's the roaring big trial-shop in town.

COUNT. Your gumption pleases me, go do my errand. As for you . . . [*To* BASIL.] . . . go along with this gen-tleman, singing and playing the guitar to entertain him on the way, for he is of my company.

SUNSTRUCK. [*Elated.*] I—I'm of the— [SUZANNE *calms him down by pointing to the* COUNTESS.]

BASIL. [*Taken aback.*] Go along with Sun-struck while playing the guitar?

COUNT. It is your profession: off you go, or you're dismissed. [*Exit.*]

BASIL. [*To himself.*] I'm certainly not going to fight the iron pot, I who am—

FIGARO. —already cracked.

BASIL. [*Aside.*] Instead of furthering their wedding, I am going to insure Marceline's and mine. [*To* FIGARO.] Don't sign anything, I warn you, un-til I come back. [*He picks up his guitar from a chair at the back.*]

FIGARO. [*Following him.*] Sign anything? Don't worry! I shan't, even if you never come back. But you don't seem in the mood for song. Would you like me to begin? Come on, a smile, and the high *la-mi-la* for my bride. [*He walks backward and dances the following seguidilla.* BASIL *accompanies him and everyone joins in.*]

ALL. [Together.]

Better than riches, I love
  The goodness of
  My Suzanne,
Zann, zann, zann,
Zann, zann, zann,
Zann, zann, zann.
Always on her I'll depend
  And madly end
  As I began
Gan, gan, gan,
Gan, gan, gan,
Gan, gan, gan.
          [*Exeunt singing and dancing.*]

COUNTESS. [*In the wing chair.*] You see, Suzanne, the ordeal I had to go through, thanks to your wild friend's anonymous note?

SUZANNE. Oh, madam, if you could have seen your face when I came out of the dressing room—you lost all your color, but only for an instant, then you grew red—oh so red!

COUNTESS. And he jumped out of the window?

SUZANNE. Without a moment's hesitation, the dear child—light as a bird.

COUNTESS. That deplorable gardener! The whole thing made me so dizzy I couldn't keep two ideas together in my mind.

SUZANNE. Not at all, my lady, on the contrary. I saw at once what facility the habit of high society confers on respectable ladies who have to tell lies.

COUNTESS. Do you think the Count was taken in? What if he finds the poor child in the castle?

SUZANNE. I'm going to make sure he is well hidden.

COUNTESS. He must go away. After what happened, you can imagine I'm not tempted to send him into the garden dressed like you.

SUZANNE. And I shan't go either, so once again my wedding is—

COUNTESS. Wait! What if in your place, or another's—why shouldn't *I* go?

SUZANNE. You, madam?

COUNTESS. No one could be reprimanded—and the Count couldn't explain the facts away. First to have punished his jealousy, and then to demonstrate his infidelity—it would be. . . ! Come, our luck in the first adventure encourages me to try a second. Let him know quickly that you will go into the garden. But be sure no one knows—

SUZANNE. Not Figaro?

COUNTESS. No, no. He would want to contribute ideas . . . Fetch me my stick and my velvet mask. I'll go out on the terrace and daydream.

[SUZANNE *goes into the dressing room.*]

COUNTESS. My scheme is surely brash enough. [*She turns around.*] Ah, my ribbon, my pretty ribbon, I had forgotten you. [*She takes it, sits, and rolls it up.*] Henceforth you will be with me always, you will remind me of the scene in which that poor boy . . . Oh,

Count, what have you done! And what am *I* doing right now? [SUZANNE *re-enters; the* COUNTESS *furtively slips the ribbon into her bosom.*]

SUZANNE. Here is the stick and your mask.

COUNTESS. Remember, I forbid you to say one word to Figaro.

SUZANNE. [*Joyful.*] Your plan is delightful, my lady. I've been thinking about it. It brings everything together, concludes everything, embraces everything. Whatever comes of it, my marriage is now assured. [*She kisses the* COUNTESS' *hand. Exeunt.*]

During the intermission, the courtroom is prepared. Two setees are brought in for counsel, one on each side of the stage, but allowing free passage behind. In the center, toward the back, a raised platform with two steps, on which is put the COUNT's *chair of state. The* CLERK's *table and his stool are to one side downstage; seats for* BRIDLEGOOSE *and the other judges are placed alongside the* COUNT's *platform.*

Act 3

A room in the castle, known as the throne room and used as a reception room. To one side a canopy over a monumental chair, and on the wall, a portrait of the King. The COUNT *with* PETER, *who is wearing coat and boots and is holding a sealed package.*

COUNT. [*Speaking fast.*] It's clearly understood?

PETER. Yes, Your Excellency. [*Exit.*]

COUNT. [*Shouting.*] Peter!

PETER. [*Returning.*] Excellency?

COUNT. No one saw you?

PETER. Not a soul.

COUNT. Take the arab.

PETER. He's at the garden gate saddled and ready.

COUNT. Straight to Seville without a stop.

PETER. It's only ten miles and a fair road.

COUNT. As soon as you arrive, find out if the page is there.

PETER. At the house?

COUNT. Yes, and how long he's been there.

PETER. I understand.

COUNT. Give him his commission and come back as fast as you can.

PETER. What if he isn't there?

COUNT. Come back even faster. Tell me at once. Quick, be off! [*Exit* PETER.]

COUNT. [*Pacing and meditating.*] It was clumsy of me to send Basil away . . . Anger is a bad counselor . . . That note he gave me telling of an attempt to approach the Countess . . . The chambermaid locked in that room when I came back . . . Her mistress making believe she was a prey to terror, or really terrified . . . A man jumps out of the window and the other, later, owns up to it, or pretends it was he. There is a link missing. Something devious is going on. A certain license among my vassals—what can it matter? But the Countess, if some upstart dared! . . . My mind wanders. Truly, when anger rules, the most controlled imagination runs wild, as in a dream. She was laughing—I heard her smothered giggles, their ill-concealed amusement. But she has self-respect . . . and my honor—in whose keeping is it? As to the other affair, where do I stand? Did that rascally Suzanne give me away? . . . seeing it isn't *her* secret yet. Why am I so bent on having her? A dozen times, I've thought of giving her up. The results of indecision are certainly strange: if I wanted her without hesitation, I shouldn't feel nearly so much desire. Figaro is behind time as usual: I must deftly plumb his thoughts. [FIGARO *enters upstage and stops.*] At any rate I must find out from his replies to what I shall put to him casually whether or not he knows I'm in love with Suzanne.

FIGARO. [*Aside.*] Here it comes.

COUNT. That is, if she has dropped a hint.

FIGARO. [*Aside.*] I guessed it, I guess.

COUNT. Next, I marry him off to the old girl . . .

FIGARO. [*Aside.*] Mister Basil's belovèd?

COUNT. And then see what I can do with the young one.

FIGARO. [*Aside.*] With my wife, if you please.

COUNT. [*Turning around.*] Eh, what? Who is it?

FIGARO. Me, at your service.

COUNT. What were you saying?

FIGARO. I haven't breathed a word.

COUNT. "My wife, if you please."

FIGARO. Oh, that!—That is the conclusion of a reply I was making: "Go and tell my wife, if you please."

COUNT. [*Pacing.*] His wife! I am curious to know what business can detain your lordship when I have you called.

FIGARO. [*Pretending to adjust his clothing.*] I'd got dirty falling on that flower bed, so I changed.

COUNT. Does it take an hour?

FIGARO. It takes the time it takes.

COUNT. The servants here need longer to dress than the masters.

FIGARO. That's because they have no valets to help them.

COUNT. I didn't quite understand what compelled you a moment ago to risk your life for nothing by jumping—

FIGARO. Risk my life! One would suppose I had leaped into a bottomless pit!

COUNT. Don't try to put me off the point by pretending you missed it yourself, you devious lackey. You understand very well that it isn't the danger to your life that concerns me, but your motives.

FIGARO. On the strength of a false alarm you come rushing in furiously, overturning everything like a mountain torrent. You're looking for a man: you have to find one or you will break down the doors and splinter the walls! I happen to be in your way—how am I to know that in your wrath—

COUNT. You could have escaped by the stairs—

FIGARO. And you'd catch me in the hall.

COUNT. [*Angry.*] In the hall! [*Aside.*] I'm getting the worst of it and no nearer finding out what I am after.

FIGARO. [*Aside.*] Let us see his game and match him trick for trick.

COUNT. [*Softening his tone.*] That isn't what I wanted to tell you. Let's drop the subject. I thought—as a matter of fact, I did think of taking you with me to London, as King's Messenger, but on second thoughts—

FIGARO. Your lordship has changed his mind?

COUNT. In the first place you don't know English.

FIGARO. I know "God damn!"

COUNT. I don't follow you.

FIGARO. I say that I know "God damn!"

COUNT. What about it?

FIGARO. I mean, English is a wonderful language—it takes but a few words to cover a lot of ground. With "God damn," in English, a man need lack for nothing. Do you want to sink your teeth into a nice juicy fowl? Go into a tavern and make this gesture [*Turning a spit.*] and say "God damn!" The waiter brings you a joint of salt beef with no bread—it's marvelous! Do you want a good glass of burgundy or claret—just do this [*Drawing a cork.*] "God damn!" and they bring you a foaming tankard of beer—it's perfectly wonderful! Should you meet one of those attractive ladies who go trotting about with their elbows pulled back and their hips swinging a bit, just put your four fingers delicately on your lips— "God damn!"—and you get slapped as by a stevedore. That proves they get your meaning. The English people, it is true, use a word or two more, here and there in conversation, but it is clear that "God damn" is the core of the language— so if your only reason for leaving me behind in Spain is—

COUNT. [*Aside.*] He wants to go to London: she hasn't told him.

FIGARO. [*Aside.*] He thinks I know nothing. Let's encourage his delusion.

COUNT. What motive did the Countess have for playing that trick on me?

FIGARO. Really, my lord, you know the reason better than I.

COUNT. I anticipate all her wishes and smother her with gifts.

FIGARO. You give but you aren't faithful: would anyone be grateful for luxuries who is starved of necessities?

COUNT. You used to tell me everything.

FIGARO. And now I keep nothing from you.

COUNT. How much did the Countess give you for being in league with her?

FIGARO. How much did you give me to extricate her from Bartholo's hands?[8] Look here, my lord, it's best not to humiliate a man who serves you well, for fear he may turn into a nasty underling.

COUNT. Why is there something shady about everything you do?

FIGARO. Things always look bad when someone is bent on finding fault.

COUNT. You have a hateful reputation!

FIGARO. Maybe it's undeserved: how many noblemen can say as much?

COUNT. Time and again I've seen you on the path to fame and fortune— you always go astray.

FIGARO. What do you expect? The mob is all around, pushing, struggling, crowding, using their elbows, knocking you down. Survives who can; the rest are crushed. And so my mind's made up: I'm through.

COUNT. Through with success? [*Aside.*] That's news.

FIGARO. [*Aside.*] My turn now. [*Aloud.*] Your Excellency favored me with the stewardship of the castle: my lot is a happy one. True, I shan't be King's Messenger and be the first to hear interesting news; but by way of compensation, I'll enjoy wedded bliss here in the heart of Andalusia.

COUNT. Why not take your wife to London?

FIGARO. I'd have to leave her so often I'd soon find marriage a bore.

COUNT. With your brains and character, you could make your way in the administration.

FIGARO. Make your way with brains? You must think mine are addled: be dull and obsequious if you want to succeed.

COUNT. All you'd have to do is to learn statecraft under me.

FIGARO. I know all about it.

COUNT. As you do English—the basic tongue?

FIGARO. Yes—and it's nothing to boast about. Only pretend not to know what you do know and vice versa; understand what's unintelligible and fail to take in what is clear; above all, put forth more strength than you possess; make a secret, often, of what no one is hiding; shut yourself up and trim goose quills so as to seem deep when you are only, as they say, a stuffed shirt; play a part well or ill, send out spies and hire informers, tamper with seals and intercept letters, and try to make ignoble tricks look noble in the light of important ends—that's all of statecraft or God strike me dead!

COUNT. But that's mere intrigue you're describing.

FIGARO. Statecraft, intrigue—as you like. To me, they're kith and kin, and the world is welcome to them. "I'd rather have my own best girl," as the man told the king in the ballad.[9]

COUNT. [*Aside.*] He wants to stay. I see. . . . Suzanne gave me away.

FIGARO. [*Aside.*] I've scored and paid him back in his own coin.

COUNT. And so you hope to win your case against Marceline?

FIGARO. Do you impute it to me as a crime that I refuse an old maid when Your Excellency feels free to snatch all the young ones?

COUNT. [*Bantering.*] On the bench the judge will put self aside and heed nothing but the law.

FIGARO. The law! Lenient to the great, harsh to the humble.

COUNT. Do you think I am joking?

FIGARO. Who knows, my lord? But *"Tempo è galant 'uomo,"* as the Italian proverb says. Time always tells the truth—that's how I'll learn what good or ill is to befall me.

COUNT. [*Aside.*] I can see she's told him everything; he's got to marry the duenna.

FIGARO. [*Aside.*] He thinks he has me fooled. Actually, what has he found out?

FOOTMAN. [*Announcing.*] Don Guzman Bridlegoose.[10]

COUNT. Bridlegoose?

FIGARO. Of course, the associate justice, your understudy and right-hand man.

COUNT. Let him wait. [*Exit* FOOTMAN.]

FIGARO. [*Waiting a moment longer while the* COUNT *is abstracted.*] What else did your lordship require?

COUNT. [*Wide awake.*] I? I was saying this room should be prepared for the public hearing.

FIGARO. It's all set: the big chair for you, pretty good chairs for the justices, the clerk's stool, benches for the lawyers, the foreground for the quality and the rest of the floor for the groundlings. I shall dismiss the cleaning women. [*Exit.*]

COUNT. [*To himself.*] That upstart is becoming a nuisance. When he argues he gets the best of me. He presses in and corners you. Oh, fox and vixen! You have combined to take me in. Well, be friends, be lovers, be what you will—I don't care. But when it comes to marrying—

SUZANNE. [*Breathless.*] My lord, forgive me, my lord.

COUNT. [*Crossly.*] What is it, miss?

SUZANNE. You are angry?

COUNT. I take it there is something you want?

SUZANNE. [*Shyly.*] It's because my lady has the vapors. I ran to ask you to lend us your bottle of ether. I'll bring it back immediately.

COUNT. [*Giving it to her.*] Never mind. Keep it for yourself: you'll soon need it.

SUZANNE. Do women of my sort have vapors too? Isn't it a class disease, which is caught only in boudoirs?

COUNT. Well, a girl who is in love and engaged and who loses her intended—

SUZANNE. But if he pays Marceline out of the dowry you promised me—

COUNT. *I* promised you?

SUZANNE. [*Lowering her eyes.*] Sir, I believe I heard you say so.

COUNT. You did, but only if on your side you were willing to listen to me.

SUZANNE. [*Eyes still lowered.*] Isn't it my duty to listen to you?

COUNT. Then, cruel girl, why didn't you tell me sooner?

SUZANNE. It's never too late to tell the

truth.

COUNT. You'll come into the garden tonight?

SUZANNE. As if I didn't go walking there every evening.

COUNT. This morning you behaved very harshly to me.

SUZANNE. This morning, yes, with the page behind the armchair.

COUNT. You are right. I forgot. But why your stubbornness before, when Basil spoke to you on my behalf?

SUZANNE. Why should someone like Basil—

COUNT. You are *always* right. Still, there is a certain Figaro to whom I think you have told everything.

SUZANNE. To be sure: I tell him everything . . . except what need never be told.

COUNT. [*Laughing.*] You darling! You promise, then? If you break your word—let's be clear about it, sweetheart—no dowry, no marriage.

SUZANNE. [*Curtsying.*] By the same token, my lord, no marriage, no right of the lord of the manor.

COUNT. Where does she learn this repartee? I swear, I'm crazy about her—but your mistress is waiting for the ether.

SUZANNE. [*Laughing and giving back the bottle.*] How could I have talked to you without a pretext?

COUNT. [*Trying to kiss her.*] Lovely creature!

SUZANNE. [*Starts to run off.*] People are coming.

COUNT. [*Aside.*] She is mine! [*He runs off.*]

SUZANNE. Quick, now, to report to my lady.

FIGARO. [*Entering from upstage right.*] Suzanne, Suzanne, where are you off to in such a hurry after leaving my lord?

SUZANNE. You can go to court now, you've just won your suit. [*Running offstage.*]

FIGARO. [*Following.*] See here—[*Exit.*]

COUNT. [*Returning.*] "You've just won your suit!" So I was pitching headlong into a trap! O my dear damnable schemers, you will rue the day! . . . a sound, solid decision from the bench . . . of course, he might

pay off the duenna . . . but what with? If he should pay . . . Ah, ah, I have the proud Antonio, whose worthy ambition looks down on Figaro as rootless and unworthy of his niece. By nursing this *idée fixe*—and why not? In the field of intrigue one must cultivate everything, even the vanity of fools. [*He starts to call.*] Anto—[*He sees* MARCELINE *and* OTHERS, *exit. Enter* MARCELINE, BARTHOLO, *and* BRIDLEGOOSE.]

MARCELINE. [*To* BRIDLEGOOSE.] Sir, pray listen to my case.

BRIDLEGOOSE. [*Gowned and stammering slightly.*] Very well, let us s-s-speak of it verbally.

BARTHOLO. It's a promise of marriage—

MARCELINE. Linked with a loan of money.

BRIDLEGOOSE. I und-derstand, et cetera and the rest.

MARCELINE. No, sir, no et cetera.

BRIDLEGOOSE. I und-derstand: you have the money?

MARCELINE. No, sir, it was I who lent it.

BRIDLEGOOSE. I quite und-derstand: you want the money back.

MARCELINE. No, sir, I want him to marry me.

BRIDLEGOOSE. I told you I und-derstood. But he—does he want to m-marry you?

MARCELINE. No sir, that is the point of the case.

BRIDLEGOOSE. Do you mean to imply that I do not und-derstand the case?

MARCELINE. No, sir. [*To* BARTHOLO.] What a spot we're in! [*To* BRIDLEGOOSE.] You say you are going to decide the case?

BRIDLEGOOSE. Why else would I have bought my j-judgeship?

MARCELINE. [*Sighing.*] It seems to me a great wrong to sell them.

BRIDLEGOOSE. True, it would be better to g-give them to us for n-nothing. Whom are you suing? [*Enter* FIGARO, *rubbing his hands.*]

MARCELINE. [*Pointing.*] That unscrupulous man!

FIGARO. [*Cheerfully, to* MARCELINE.] Perhaps I'm in your way? My lord will be back in a moment, Your Worship.

BRIDLEGOOSE. I've seen that fellow somewhere.

FIGARO. In the house of your lady wife, at Seville, and in her service, counselor.

BRIDLEGOOSE. In what year?

FIGARO. A little less than a year before the birth of your younger son, who is a very pretty child if I do say so myself.

BRIDLEGOOSE. Yes, he is the b-best looking of them all. They tell me here that you are up to your old tricks.

FIGARO. You flatter me, sir. It's only a trifle.

BRIDLEGOOSE. A promise of marriage! What a booby it is!

FIGARO. Sir!

BRIDLEGOOSE. Have you seen my secretary, a very nice chap?

FIGARO. You mean Doublefist, the clerk?

BRIDLEGOOSE. Yes, I do. He feeds in two places, too.

FIGARO. Feeds! I'll swear he wolfs: Yes indeed, I saw him about the writ, and then again about the supplement to the writ, as is customary.

BRIDLEGOOSE. Forms must be observed.

FIGARO. Unquestionably. Just as the cause of the suit belongs to the parties, so the forms are the property of the court.

BRIDLEGOOSE. The lad is not so stupid as I thought at first. Well, friend, since you know so much, we'll t-take care of you in court.

FIGARO. Sir, I rely on your sense of equity even though you are one of our justices.

BRIDLEGOOSE. What? . . . It's true I am a j-justice. But what if you owe and don't pay?

FIGARO. Surely you can see it comes out exactly as if I didn't owe.

BRIDLEGOOSE. No d-doubt . . . what? What? What did he say? [*Enter the* COUNT *and a* BEADLE, *who walks ahead of him shouting for silence.*]

COUNT. Gown and bands in this place, Master Bridlegoose? For a hearing in camera, ordinary clothes are good enough.

BRIDLEGOOSE. 'Tis you are good enough, my lord. But I never go out ung-gowned, don't you see, it is a matter of f-form. A man will laugh at a judge in a short coat but tremble at the sight of an attorney in a g-gown, thanks to the f-form, the f-form.

COUNT. Let the court convene.

BEADLE. [*Croaking as he opens the doors.*] The court! the court! [*Enter* ANTONIO, *the* COUNT's *servants and his tenants, men and women, who are dressed for the wedding. The* COUNT *sits in the big chair,* BRIDLEGOOSE *to one side, the clerk* DOUBLEFIST *on his stool. The justices and counsel on the benches,* MARCELINE *next to* BARTHOLO, FIGARO *on another bench, the servants and tenants behind them.*]

BRIDLEGOOSE. [*To* DOUBLEFIST.] Doublefist, call up the cases.

DOUBLEFIST. [*Reading from a paper.*] The noble, high, and puisant Don Pedro George, Hidalgo and Baron de los Altos y Montes Fieros y otros montes v. Alonzo Calderón, a young playwright, in the matter of a stillborn play, which each disowns and attributes to the other.

COUNT. They are both right. With a view to insuring public attention if they write another work together, it is ordered that the nobleman shall contribute his name and the poet his talent. Case dismissed.

DOUBLEFIST. [*From another paper.*] Andrea Petrucchio, farmer, *v.* the tax collector, in the matter of an arbitrary foreclosure.

COUNT. Not within my jurisdiction. I shall serve my vassals best by sponsoring them at the King's court. Next.

DOUBLEFIST. [*Reading a third paper.* BARTHOLO *and* FIGARO *rise.*] Barbara Hagar Rahab Magdelene Nicola Marceline Greenleaf, spinster of age . . . [MARCELINE *rises and bows.*] . . . *v.* Figaro, first name missing—

FIGARO. Anonymous.

BRIDLEGOOSE. Anonymous? What patron s-saint is that?

FIGARO. Mine.

DOUBLEFIST. [*Writing.*] . . . *versus* "Anonymous Figaro." Profession?

FIGARO. Gentleman.

COUNT. You, a gentleman? [DOUBLEFIST *is still writing.*]

FIGARO. God willing, I should have been the son of a prince.

COUNT. [*To* DOUBLEFIST.] Go on.

BEADLE. [*Croaking.*] Silence in court!

DOUBLEFIST. [*Reading.*] . . . in the matter of a dispute about the marriage of the said Figaro to the said Greenleaf, the learned Dr. Bartholo appearing for the plaintiff and the said Figaro for himself—provided the court allows it against the tenor of custom and the rules of the bench.

FIGARO. Custom, Mister Doublefist, is often mere corruption. A party to a suit always knows his case better than some barrister who sweats without conviction and shouts his head off about everything he knows, except the facts, and who does not mind ruining the suitor, boring the court, and putting the jury to sleep. And afterward he is as puffed up as if he had written Cicero's orations. I can put my case in two words. Gentlemen—

DOUBLEFIST. Those you've uttered so far are wasted, for you are not the plaintiff. You can only defend. Come forward, Doctor, and read into the evidence the promise of marriage.

FIGARO. Yes, the promise.

BARTHOLO. [*Putting on his glasses.*] It is explicit.

BRIDLEGOOSE. We have to see.

DOUBLEFIST. Gentlemen, please be quiet.

BEADLE. [*Croaking.*] Silence in court!

BARTHOLO. "I, the undersigned, acknowledge, having received from the Damozel, et cetera, Marceline Greenleaf, of the manor of Aguas-Frescas, the sum of two thousand piastres, which sum I shall repay on her demand and in the said manor,—er—and shall marry her as a token of gratitude, et cetera, signed: Figaro—er—just Figaro." My client asks for the payment of the note and the execution of the promise, with costs. [*Pleading.*] Gentlemen! Never was a more moving request brought to the bar of a court. Since the case of Alexander the Great, who promised marriage to the beautiful Thalestris—

COUNT. [*Interrupting.*] Before you go farther, counsel, is the genuineness of the document stipulated?

BRIDLEGOOSE. [*To* FIGARO.] What do you say to the f-f-facts just read into the evidence?

FIGARO. I say there is malice, error, or inadvertence in the manner in which the document was read. For the statement does not say: "Which sum I shall repay *and* I shall marry her"; it says: "Which sum I shall repay *or* I shall marry her," which is very different.

COUNT. Does the document say *and* or does it say *or?*

BARTHOLO. It says *and.*

FIGARO. It says *or.*

BRIDLEGOOSE. Doublefist, you read it.

DOUBLEFIST. [*Taking the paper.*] That's always wise, because the parties twist things as they read. Er—er—er— "Damozel—er—Greenleaf—er—Ha! Which sum I shall repay on her demand, and in the said manor,—er— shall marry—and . . . or . . ." there's *and* after demand and *o r* at the end of man*or*, but after that it's hard to make out—there is a blot.

BRIDLEGOOSE. A b-blot? Ah, I und-derstand!

BARTHOLO. [*Pleading again.*] I submit, my lord and gentlemen, that the decisive word is the copulative conjunction *and* which links the correlative members of the sentence: "I shall pay the Damozel, et cetera, *and* I shall marry her."

FIGARO. [*In the same tone.*] And I maintain that it is the alternative conjunction *or*, which separates the said members: "I shall pay the damsel *or* I shall marry her." To his pedantry I oppose my superpedantry: if he drops into Latin, I come up with Greek and exterminate him.

COUNT. How am I to adjudicate such a question?

BARTHOLO. To settle it and no longer quibble over a syllable, we stipulate the absence of the second *and* after *manor.*

FIGARO. I ask for an affidavit to that effect.

BARTHOLO. We stand by our stipulation. But it affords no escape for the guilty, for let us examine the document with the stipulation in mind: "Which sum I shall repay on demand and in the said manor shall marry her . . ." It is as if one said: "I shall have myself bled in this room—and in this bed will remain until I feel better." Or again: "He will take a dose of calomel tonight—and in the morning will experience the good effect." Thus, my lord and gentlemen, "He will repay on demand—and in the said manor will marry. . . ."

FIGARO. Nothing of the kind! There is a word under the blot and it is *or*, as thus: "Either illness carries you off, OR your physician will see to it." That is irrefutable. Another example: "Either you write wretched stuff, OR all the fools will mark you down." Does Dr. Bartholo think that I have forgotten my grammar? "I shall repay, on her demand and in the said manor COMMA or I shall marry her."

BARTHOLO. [*Quickly.*] There's no comma.

FIGARO. [*Just as quickly.*] There is. It goes: "COMMA, or I shall marry her."

BARTHOLO. [*Glancing at the paper.*] It's without a comma.

FIGARO. It was there, my lord and gentlemen, before the blot. Besides, does a man who marries have to pay the debt as well?

BARTHOLO. [*Instantly.*] Yes, because we marry under a separate property agreement.

FIGARO. [*Just as fast.*] If marriage does not cancel the debt, we insist on the separation of persons *and* property! [*The judges rise and confer.*]

BARTHOLO. A rewarding cancellation!

DOUBLEFIST. Silence, gentlemen!

BEADLE. [*Croaking.*] Silence in court!

BARTHOLO. Scoundrels of this stripe call it paying their debts!

FIGARO. Are you speaking now on your own behalf?

BARTHOLO. I am defending this lady.

FIGARO. You may go on raving, but please stop casting aspersions. When the law, fearing the passions of the interested parties, allowed the intervention of counsel, it did not mean to permit these termperate defenders to become privileged slanderers. That would have been to degrade the noblest of institutions. [*The judges are still conferring.*]

ANTONIO. [*To* MARCELINE, *and pointing to the judges.*] Why must they palaverate so long?

MARCELINE. They got at the chief justice, he is getting around the other one, and I am about to lose the case.

BARTHOLO. [*Somberly.*] I am afraid so.

FIGARO. [*Gaily.*] Cheer up, Marceline!

DOUBLEFIST. [*Jumping up and addressing* MARCELINE.] That's too much! I denounce you, and for the honor of the court I ask that before the other case is settled you be tried for contempt!

COUNT. [*Sitting down.*] No, master clerk. I shall not judge in my own case for an insult to my person. No Spanish judge will have to blush for such an abuse of power, worthy only of an oriental despot. We commit enough wrongs as it is. I am now going to correct one of these by stating the reasons for my decision. Any judge who rules and gives no reason is an enemy of the law. What does the plaintiff ask? Marriage failing payment. Both together would be contradictory.

DOUBLEFIST. Silence, gentlemen!

BEADLE. [*Croaking.*] Silence in court!

COUNT. What does the defendant rejoin? That he wants to retain possession of his person. Permission is granted.

FIGARO. I've won!

COUNT. But since the text says: Which sum I shall repay on the first demand *or* I shall marry, etc., the court orders the defendant to pay the plaintiff two thousand piastres *or* to marry her within the day. [*Rises.*]

FIGARO. [*Petrified.*] I've lost!

ANTONIO. [*Delighted.*] A magnificent decision!

FIGARO. How, magnificent?

ANTONIO. On account of how you aren't no longer my nephew-in-law, thank the Lord!

BEADLE. [*Croaking.*] Move along, gem'mun. [*Exeunt.*]

ANTONIO. I'm off to tell all about it to my niece.

MARCELINE. [*Sitting down.*] Now I can breathe freely.

FIGARO. But I am suffocating.

COUNT. [*Aside.*] And I am avenged; it's very soothing.

FIGARO. [*Aside.*] Where's Basil, who was

supposed to prevent Marceline's marriage—he's back in good time, I don't think! [*To the* COUNT, *on his way out.*] Leaving us, my lord?

COUNT. There's nothing more to judge.

FIGARO. [*Looking at* BRIDLEGOOSE.] If it weren't for that fathead—

BRIDLEGOOSE. Me, a fathead?

FIGARO. Who can doubt it? And I shan't marry her: I am a gentleman after all. [*The* COUNT *stops.*]

BARTHOLO. You will marry her.

FIGARO. Without my noble progenitors' consent?

BARTHOLO. Give us their name, exhibit them.

FIGARO. Give me a little time. I must be close to finding them, I've been looking for fifteen years.

BARTHOLO. Conceited ass! A foundling!

FIGARO. Not found, Doctor, lost, or rather, stolen.

COUNT. [*Returning.*] Stolen, lost— where's the proof? Otherwise he'll cry out that he's being cheated.

FIGARO. My lord, even if the lace on my baby clothes, and the embroidered coverlet, and the gold and jewels I wore when the brigands snatched me, did not suffice to prove my high birth, the care that had been taken to put distinctive marks on me would show that I was a valuable offspring. I have hieroglyphics on my arm . . . [*He starts to roll up his right sleeve.*]

MARCELINE. [*Rising quickly.*] You have a mark like a spatula on your right arm?

FIGARO. How do you know I have?

MARCELINE. Good God, it's he!

FIGARO. Of course it's me.

BARTHOLO. [*To* MARCELINE.] Who?

MARCELINE. [*Quickly.*] It's Emmanuel!

BARTHOLO. [*To* FIGARO.] You were kidnaped by gypsies?

FIGARO. [*Excited.*] Near a castle, yes. My good Doctor, if you restore me to my noble family, set a high price on your services. Gold and treasure are trifles to my illustrious parents.

BARTHOLO. [*Pointing to* MARCELINE.] There is your mother.

FIGARO. Foster mother?

BARTHOLO. Your own mother.

COUNT. His mother?

FIGARO. Explain.

MARCELINE. [*Pointing to* BARTHOLO.] There is your father.

FIGARO. [*In distress.*] Ah, oh, woe is me!

MARCELINE. Didn't the voice of nature tell you so again and again?

FIGARO. Not once.

COUNT. [*Aside.*] His mother!

BRIDLEGOOSE. One thing is c-c-clear: he won't marry her.[11]

COUNT. Stupid turn of events—most annoying!

BRIDLEGOOSE. [*To* FIGARO.] And your nobility? Your castle? You would hoodwink the law with false pretenses?

FIGARO. The law! It nearly made me commit a prize blunder, the law did—on top of the fact that for those accursed hundred pounds,[12] many is the time I almost beat up this gentleman who turns out to be my father. But since heaven has saved my virtue from these temptations, Father of mine, please accept my apologies . . . And you, Mother mine, fold me in your arms—as maternally as you can. [MARCELINE *clasps him about the neck.*]

SUZANNE. [*Running with a purse in her hand.*] My lord, stop everything! Do not marry them: I've come to pay this lady with the dowry madam has given me.

COUNT. [*Aside.*] The devil take the Countess! It is as if everything conspired . . . [*Exit.*]

ANTONIO. [*Seeing* FIGARO *embracing his mother, addresses* SUZANNE.] Payment, eh? I see, I see.

SUZANNE. [*Turning her back.*] I've seen enough; let's go, Uncle.

FIGARO. Please don't! What is it you've seen enough?

SUZANNE. My weakness of mind and your lack of integrity—

FIGARO. Neither of them a fact.

SUZANNE. [*Angrily.*] . . . and your willingness to marry her and caress her.

FIGARO. [*Gaily.*] I caress but don't marry. [SUZANNE *tries to leave;* FIGARO *prevents her;* SUZANNE *slaps him.*]

SUZANNE. You are impertinent and rude, let me go!

FIGARO. [*To the company.*] That's love for you! Before you go, though, I beg you take a good look at the dear woman in front of you.

SUZANNE. I'm looking.

FIGARO. How does she strike you?

SUZANNE. Horrible!

FIGARO. Long live jealousy! No half measures about it.

MARCELINE. [*Arms open to* SUZANNE.] Come kiss your mother, my pretty Suzanette. The naughty boy who is tormenting you is my son.

SUZANNE. [*Running to her.*] You—his mother! [*They stay clasped in each other's arms.*]

ANTONIO. It must have just happened.

FIGARO. No, only just disclosed.

MARCELINE. [*With fervor.*] My heart was right to be so strongly drawn to him, though mistaking its reason. Blood was speaking to me.

FIGARO. And good sense to me, which worked like instinct to make me refuse you. For I was far from hating you, witness the money . . .

MARCELINE. [*Handing him a paper.*] The money is yours: take back your note. It is your dowry.

SUZANNE. [*Throwing the purse to him.*] And take this too!

FIGARO. Many thanks!

MARCELINE. [*Excited.*] I was unfortunate as a girl, and just now was about to become the most wretched of wives; I am now the happiest of mothers. Come kiss me, children: all my feelings of love are centered upon you. I am as happy as anyone can be and—oh, children, how I am going to love you!

FIGARO. [*Moved and speaking with vehemence.*] Please stop, dearest Mother, or you will see my eyes dissolve away in the first tears I have ever shed. They are tears of joy—but what a fool I am: I nearly felt ashamed of myself as I felt the drops on my hands. [*He shows his hands, fingers outspread.*] I stupidly tried to hold them back. Away, false shame! I want to laugh and cry all at once. What I now feel does not come to man twice in a lifetime. [*He kisses his mother to one side of him,* SUZANNE *on the other.*]

MARCELINE. Oh, my dear!

SUZANNE. My very dear!

BRIDLEGOOSE. [*Wiping his eyes.*] It seems I am a f-fool also!

FIGARO. [*Excited.*] Grief! I can now defy you: afflict me if you can, between these two women I love.

ANTONIO. [*To* FIGARO.] Not so many pretty speeches, if you please. Apropos of marriage, in good families, that of the parents is supposed to precede. Do your parents ask each other's hand?

BARTHOLO. May my hand rot and fall off if I ever offer it to the mother of such a character!

ANTONIO. [*To* BARTHOLO.] In other words you're nothing but an unnatural father? [*To* FIGARO.] In that case, Lothario, the bargain's off.

SUZANNE. Oh, Uncle!

ANTONIO. D'you think I'll give my sister's child to this here who's no one's child?

BRIDLEGOOSE. How do you make that out, idiot? Everyone is somebody's child!

ANTONIO. Yah, yah: he shan't have her nohow. [*Exit.*]

BARTHOLO. [*To* FIGARO.] Better look for somebody to adopt you. [*He tries to go, but* MARCELINE *seizes him around the middle and pulls him back.*]

MARCELINE. One moment, Doctor, don't go.

FIGARO. [*Aside.*] It's incredible but all the fools in Andalusia are rabid against my poor desire to get married.

SUZANNE. [*To* BARTHOLO.] Dear little Father, he is your son.

MARCELINE. He has wit, talent, and presence.

FIGARO. And he never cost you a penny.

BARTHOLO. What about the hundred pounds he robbed me of?

MARCELINE. [*Cuddling him.*] We'll take such good care of you, Papa![13]

SUZANNE. [*Cuddling.*] We'll love you so much, dear little Papa!

BARTHOLO. [*Yielding.*] "Papa, Papa, dear Papa—" Now I'm going to be as big a fool as this gentleman . . . [*Pointing to* BRIDLEGOOSE.] I'm being led like a child. [MARCELINE *and* SUZANNE *kiss him.*] Now, now, I haven't said yes. [*Turning around.*] What's become of his lordship?

FIGARO. Let's join him, quick, and force a decision from him. If he were to think up some new scheme, we'd have to start all over again.

ALL. [*Together.*] Let's go, let's go! [*They drag* BARTHOLO *outside.*]

BRIDLEGOOSE. [*Left alone.*] "As big a fool as this gentleman." A man can say that sort of thing about himself, but . . . they're not at all p-polite in this p-place. [*Exit.*]

Act 4

A large room with candelabra all lighted, floral decorations, and other ornaments indicative of preparations for a party. Downstage right stands a table and on it a writing case. Behind the table is an armchair.

FIGARO. [*Hugging* SUZANNE.] Well, love, are you happy? She got round the doctor, didn't she, my silver-tongued mother? Despite his distaste he is marrying her, and your curmudgeon of an uncle can't help himself. That leaves only my lord in a rage; for after all, our marriage is the upshot of theirs. What a happy ending! Aren't you inclined to laugh?

SUZANNE. I never knew anything so odd.

FIGARO. Say rather so jolly. All we wanted was a dowry, squeezed out of His Excellency. Now we have two which owe nothing to him. A relentless rival was hounding you and I was bedeviled by a fury. That trouble has for us both taken the form of a loving mother. Yesterday I was, so to speak, alone in the world; today I have all my relatives complete about me. True, they're not so resplendent as if I had designed them myself, but good enough for us who haven't the ambition to be rich.

SUZANNE. And yet none of the things that you had planned and expected came through.

FIGARO. Chance did a better job, my sweet. That's the way of the world. You toil, you scheme, you make pro-

jects, all in your own corner; Fortune works in another. From the insatiable conqueror who would like to swallow the globe to the peaceable blind man led by his dog, all human beings are the playthings of fate. Indeed, the blind man is often better served by his dog, less deceived in his opinions, than some other self-blinded man with his retinue. As for that delightful blind fellow called Love . . . [*He again embraces her tenderly.*]

SUZANNE. He's the only one I care about.

FIGARO. Well then, let me be the serviceable dog in folly's employ, who makes it his job to lead him to your charming little door. And there we'll be cozy for the rest of our lives.

SUZANNE. [*Laughing.*] Love and you?

FIGARO. I and Love.

SUZANNE. And you won't look for other lodgings?

FIGARO. If you catch me at it, I'm willing to have a hundred million philanderers—

SUZANNE. You're going to say more than you mean: tell me the honest truth.

FIGARO. My truest truth?

SUZANNE. Shame on you, rascal! Is there more than one?

FIGARO. I should say so! Ever since it has been observed that with the passage of time old follies turn into wisdom, and that early little lies, even though poorly planted, bloom into great big truths—ever since then, there have been endless species of truths. There are those one dare not utter, for not every truth is fit to say; there are those one flaunts without putting faith in them, for not every truth is fit to believe. And then there are the passionate promises, the parental threats, the resolutions of drinkers, the assurances of office holders, the "positively final offers" of businessmen—there's no end to them. Only my love for my Suzy is true coin.

SUZANNE. I love your gaiety because it is wild. It shows you are happy. But let's talk about meeting the Count in the garden.

FIGARO. Far better never speak of that again. It nearly cost me my Sue.

SUZANNE. You don't want me to go through with it?

FIGARO. If you love me, Suzy, give me your word on this. Let him eat his heart out—it'll be his punishment.

SUZANNE. I found it harder at first to agree to it than now to give it up—I'll never mention it again.

FIGARO. That's your truest truth?

SUZANNE. I'm not like you learned people. I have only one truth.

FIGARO. And you'll love me a little?

SUZANNE. Much.

FIGARO. That isn't much.

SUZANNE. What do you mean?

FIGARO. Why, in love, don't you see, too much is barely enough.

SUZANNE. Your subtleties are beyond me, but I intend to love only my husband.

FIGARO. Stick to it and you will represent a remarkable exception to the rule. [*Starts to kiss her. Enter* COUNTESS.]

COUNTESS. I was just saying: wherever they happen to be, you may be sure they're together. I really think, Figaro, that each time you indulge in a tête-à-tête you are living off the future, drawing on wedded bliss, and robbing yourself. People look for you and get impatient.

FIGARO. You are right, madam. I was forgetting myself. I will show them my excuse. [*He tries to take* SUZANNE *with him.*]

COUNTESS. [*Holding her back.*] She'll follow later. [*Exit* FIGARO. *To* SUZANNE.] Have you what's needed to change clothes with me?

SUZANNE. Nothing is needed, madam. The assignation is off.

COUNTESS. You have changed your mind?

SUZANNE. It's Figaro—

COUNTESS. You are deceiving me.

SUZANNE. God is my witness!

COUNTESS. Figaro is not a man to let a dowry slip from his grasp.

SUZANNE. Oh, madam, what can you be thinking?

COUNTESS. Why, that in concert with the Count, you are now sorry you made me privy to his plans. I can read you like a book. Leave me to myself. [*She starts to leave.*]

SUZANNE. [*On her knees.*] In the name of heaven which is our hope, you cannot know the wrong you do me. When you have been so endlessly good to me, after the dowry you've given me, how could I—

COUNTESS. [*Lifting her up.*] But—of course! I must have been out of my mind. Since you are changing places with me, dear heart, you won't be going into the garden. You'll be keeping your word to your husband and helping me recapture mine.

SUZANNE. Oh, how you upset me!

COUNTESS. I've been terribly scatterbrained. [*Kisses* SUZANNE *on the forehead.*] Where is the meeting place?

SUZANNE. [*Kisses the* COUNTESS's *hand.*] All I heard was "garden."

COUNTESS. [*Motioning* SUZANNE *to the table.*] Take that pen and we will name a spot.

SUZANNE. I, write to him?

COUNTESS. You must.

SUZANNE. But at least, madam, you—

COUNTESS. I'll take the responsibility for everything. [SUZANNE *sits at the table.*]

COUNTESS. [*Dictating*] "A new song to the tune of: 'How lovely under the elms at night, How lovely . . .'"

SUZANNE. [*Writing.*] "'. . . under the elms.'" Yes, nothing else?

COUNTESS. Have you the slightest fear that he won't understand?

SUZANNE. You're right. [*She folds the note.*] What sort of seal?

COUNTESS. A pin, quick—it will serve to reply with. Write on the back: "Please return the seal."

SUZANNE. [*Laughing.*] Ho! the seal! This seal, my lady, is a funnier joke than the one on the officer's commission.

COUNTESS. [*In painful recollection.*] Oh!

SUZANNE. [*Looking on her person.*] I haven't a pin on me.

COUNTESS. [*Unpinning her coat collar.*] Take this. [*The* PAGE's *ribbon falls from her bosom.*] Oh, my ribbon!

SUZANNE. [*Picking it up.*] Ah, the little thief's property . . . and you were cruel enough to—

COUNTESS. Could I let him wear it on his arm? A fine spectacle! Give it back to me.

SUZANNE. Your ladyship cannot wear it:

it is spotted with the young man's blood.

COUNTESS. It will be just right for Fanchette . . . when she next brings me flowers. [*Enter a young shepherdess,* CHERUBINO *dressed as a girl,* FANCHETTE *and other girls dressed like her and carrying bouquets.*]

FANCHETTE. My lady, these girls from the village bring you flowers.

COUNTESS. [*Quickly hides the ribbon again.*] They are delightful. It grieves me, dears, not to know you all by name. [*Pointing to* CHERUBINO.] But who is this lovely child who seems so shy?

SHEPHERDESS. A cousin of mine, ma'am, come to visit for the wedding.

COUNTESS. So pretty! Since I can't wear all twenty of your posies, I'll honor the stranger. [*She takes* CHERUBINO's *bouquet and kisses him on the forehead.*] She's blushing. Suzy, don't you think she looks like someone we know?

SUZANNE. So much so I can hardly tell them apart.

CHERUBINO. [*Aside, both hands on his heart.*] Oh, that kiss went right through me!

ANTONIO. [*Entering with the* COUNT.] And I tell you he's here somewhere. They dressed him at my daughter's, all the clothes are still around, and here's his regulation hat, which I picked out of the lot. [*Steps forward, scans the girls' faces, and recognizes* CHERUBINO, *whose female bonnet he pulls off. As* CHERUBINO's *long hair falls in ringlets,* ANTONIO *tosses the military hat on top.*] By gum, there's your officer!

COUNTESS. [*Stepping back.*] Heavens!

SUZANNE. The rapscallion!

ANTONIO. I was telling you upstairs it was him.

COUNT. [*Angry.*] Well, madam?

COUNTESS. Well, sir, you find me as surprised as you and equally angry.

COUNT. It may be, but what about this morning?

COUNTESS. I should be guilty indeed if I kept up the deception any longer. He had dropped in to see me, and it was then we undertook the practical joke which these children have completed. You discovered Suzanne and me dressing him up. You are so quick to anger that he ran away, I lost my good judgment, and general dismay did the rest.

COUNT. [*Disgruntled.*] Why haven't you left?

CHERUBINO. [*Flinging off the hat.*] My lord—

COUNT. I shall punish you for disobeying.

FANCHETTE. [*Thoughtlessly.*] Oh, my lord, please listen to me: every time you come by and kiss me you always say: "Fanchette, dear, if you will love me, I'll give you anything you want."

COUNT. [*Flushing.*] I have said that?

FANCHETTE. Yes, my lord. Well, instead of punishing Cherubino, give him to me for a husband, and then I'll love you madly.

COUNT. [*Aside.*] Diddled by a page!

COUNTESS. Count, it is your turn now. This child's naïve confession, as innocent as mine, bears witness to a double truth, which is that when I cause you anguish it is always unintentionally, whereas you do your utmost to increase and justify my own.

ANTONIO. You too, my lord? By gum, I'm going to get after that chit as I did after her mother, now gathered. . . . Not that it's of consequence, but as my lady knows, these little girls when they group up. . . .

COUNT. [*Discomfited, aside.*] There is an evil genius in this place who turns everything against me.

FIGARO. [*Entering.*] My lord, if you detain the young ladies, the party can't begin, or the dance either.

COUNT. You want to dance? Have you forgotten how you fell this morning and sprained your right foot?

FIGARO. [*Swinging his leg.*] It's still a trifle sore, but it's nothing. [*To the girls.*] Come along, darlings, come.

COUNT. [*Turning* FIGARO *about.*] You were lucky the flower bed was soft earth.

FIGARO. Very lucky—otherwise . . .

ANTONIO. [*Twists him the other way.*] Besides he "gathered himself together" as he fell all the way to the bottom.

FIGARO. A really clever man would have stopped halfway down. [*To the girls.*]

Are you coming, ladies?

ANTONIO. [*Twisting* FIGARO *again.*] All the while the little page was galloping on his horse toward Seville.

FIGARO. Galloping, or maybe sauntering.

COUNT. [*Twists* FIGARO *the other way.*] And his commission was in your pocket.

FIGARO. [*Somewhat surprised.*] Undoubtedly, but why this examination? [*To the girls.*] Now come on, girls!

ANTONIO. [*Pulling* CHERUBINO *by the arm.*] Here's one who says my future nephew is a liar.

FIGARO. [*Taken aback.*] Cherubino! [*Aside.*] Blast the little braggart!

ANTONIO. Have you got it now?

FIGARO. Got it, got it! . . . By the by, what's his story?

COUNT. [*Dryly.*] Hardly a story; he says it was he who jumped into the gillyflowers.

FIGARO. [*Abstracted.*] Hm, if he says so . . . it may well be. I don't argue about what I don't know.

COUNT. So both you and he . . .

FIGARO. Why not? The jumping fever is catching—just think of sheep over a fence.[14] And when my lord is angry, anyone would prefer to risk his neck—

COUNT. Now really, two by two?

FIGARO. We'd have done it by the dozen—and why should you care, my lord, seeing no one was hurt? [*To the girls.*] I say, are you coming in or aren't you?

COUNT. [*Outraged.*] Is it a farce we're playing together, you and I? [*Music begins offstage.*]

FIGARO. There's the opening march. Fall in, my beauties, fall in. Here, Suzanne, give me your arm. [*Exeunt except* CHERUBINO, *who stays behind, his head hung down.*]

COUNT. [*Gazing at* FIGARO'*s back.*] Did you ever see greater nerve? [*To* CHERUBINO.] As for you, sly boots who now pretend to be ashamed, go dress yourself properly and let me not see your face for the rest of the evening.

COUNTESS. He will be terribly bored.

CHERUBINO. [*Thoughtless.*] Bored? I carry on my brow enough happiness to outweigh a hundred years in jail!

[*He puts on his hat and leaves. The* COUNTESS *fans herself violently.*]

COUNT. What is so happy about his brow?

COUNTESS. [*Embarrassed.*]His first military hat, I suppose. With children any novelty is like a toy. [*She starts to leave.*]

COUNT. You won't stay, Countess?

COUNTESS. I told you I did not feel well.

COUNT. One moment more for the sake of your protégée—or I'll think you are cross.

COUNTESS. Here come the two wedding processions. Let us sit and receive them.

COUNT. [*Aside.*] The wedding! . . . Well, what can't be cured must be endured. [COUNT *and* COUNTESS *sit to one side of the room. Enter the processions to a march based on the Folies d'Espagne:[15] A Gamekeeper, a musket on his shoulder. The mayor, the aldermen,* BRIDLEGOOSE. *Peasants and their women in party dress. Two young girls carrying the virgin's bonnet. Two others in white veils. Two others, wearing gloves and a corsage at the waist.* ANTONIO *holding* SUZANNE'*s hand to give her away to* FIGARO. *Other girls with other types of bonnets and veils.* MARCELINE *wearing a white veil and bonnet similar to the first.* FIGARO *holding* MARCELINE'*s hand to give her away to: The doctor, who brings up the rear of the procession, wearing a large boutonniere. The girls, as they pass in front of the* COUNT, *deliver to his footmen the paraphernalia for* SUZANNE *and* MARCELINE. *The peasants, men and women, in two lines, dance the fandango to an accompaniment of castanets. Then the orchestra plays the introduction of the duet, during which* ANTONIO *takes* SUZANNE *to the* COUNT. *She kneels before him, he puts the virgin's bonnet on her head, and gives her a bouquet. During this ceremony the girls sing the following duet:*]

Sing, young bride, the grateful benefaction!
Your master has his selfish lust displaced:
He gives up pleasure for a noble action,
And to your husband hands you pure and chaste.

As the duet concludes, SUZANNE, *still kneeling, tugs at the* COUNT'*s cloak and shows him the note she has for him. She then puts her hand to her hair and he takes the note while seeming to adjust her bonnet. He puts the note inside his coat, the duet ends,* SUZANNE *rises and makes a low curtsy.* FIGARO *receives* SUZANNE *from the hand of the* COUNT *and steps back with her to the other end of the room, near* MARCELINE. *There is meanwhile a reprise of the fandango. The* COUNT, *being in a hurry to read his note, comes downstage and pulls the paper from his pocket. The pin evidently pricks him, for he shakes his finger, squeezes it, and licks it. He looks at the folded paper and speaks.*]

COUNT. The devil take all women! They stick pins into everything. [*He throws the pin on the ground, reads the note, and kisses it. While he and* FIGARO *speak, the orchestra plays pianissimo.* FIGARO, *who has seen the byplay, speaks to* SUZANNE *and his mother.*]

FIGARO. It must be a billet-doux some little wench slipped into his hand as she walked by. It was sealed with a pin which impudently pricked him. [*The dance resumes. The* COUNT *turns the note over and sees the request to return the pin. He looks for it on the ground, finds it, and sticks it in his sleeve.*]

FIGARO. [*To* SUZANNE *and* MARCELINE.] From the beloved any object is dear, so he's retrieved the pin. What a harlequin he is! [*Meanwhile,* SUZANNE *and the* COUNTESS *have been exchanging signals. The dance concludes and the introduction of the duet is played again.* FIGARO *takes* MARCELINE *to the* COUNT, *and the ceremony repeats. But just as the* COUNT *lifts the bonnet and as the duet strikes up, the proceedings are interrupted by a great noise at the door.*]

FOOTMAN. Keep back, keep back, gentlemen, you can't all get in together. Help here! The guards! [*Guards step quickly toward the door.*]

COUNT. [*Rising.*] What is the matter there?

FOOTMAN. My lord, it is Mister Basil, who is followed by the whole township because he sings as he walks.

COUNT. Admit him alone.

COUNTESS. Please command me to withdraw.

COUNT. I shan't forget your obliging me.

COUNTESS. Suzanne! . . . [*To the* COUNT.] She will be back at once. [*Aside to* SUZANNE.] Let's go change our clothes. [*Exeunt.*]

MARCELINE. He never shows up but to do harm.

FIGARO. You see if I don't change his tune. [*Enter* BASIL, *guitar in hand, followed by* SUNSTRUCK.]

BASIL. [*Sings to the music of the final song of the play.*]

Faithful, tender, loving hearts
Who condemn love's wanderings
Do not launch your angry darts:
It is not a crime to change,
For if Cupid carries wings
It must be to flit and range!
It must be to flit and range!

FIGARO. [*Going toward* BASIL.] Yes, that's the reason precisely why Love has wings on his back. Friend, what do you mean by your song?

BASIL. [*Pointing to* SUNSTRUCK.] I mean that after showing submissiveness to my lord and entertaining this gentleman, who is of my lord's company, I want to claim my lord's justice.

SUNSTRUCK. Pah, your lordsy, he didn't entertain me at all—he just had fits of yodeling!

COUNT. What is it you want, Basil?

BASIL. That which already beongs to me, my lord—the hand of Marceline.

FIGARO. [*Drawing near.*] How long has it been since you saw the face of a lunatic?

BASIL. My good sir, I see one right now.

FIGARO. Since you use my eyes as a mirror, study the effect therein of the prophecy I am about to make: if you so much as seem to gravitate toward madame—

BARTHOLO. [*Laughing.*] But why? Let him speak.

BRIDLEGOOSE. [*Coming forward.*] Is it n-necessary for two old f-friends . . .

FIGARO. He and I friends?

BASIL. Absurd!

FIGARO. [*Setting a rapid pace for the ensuing dialogue.*] Friends because he writes the dullest church music?

BASIL. While he writes newspaper

verse?

FIGARO. A tavern musician!

BASIL. A penny-a-liner!

FIGARO. An oratorio-monger!

BASIL. A diplomatic nag!

COUNT. [*Seated.*] Vulgarians both!

BASIL. He's failed me at every turn.

FIGARO. That's an idea I wish were true.

BASIL. He goes round calling me an ass.

FIGARO. Don't mistake me for public opinion.

BASIL. Whereas there's hardly a talented singer I haven't trained.

FIGARO. Strained!

BASIL. He persists!

FIGARO. And why shouldn't I, if I speak the truth? Are you a prince that you should be flattered? Learn to live with the truth, faker! It's certain no liar could make much of you. Perhaps you're afraid the truth will come out of our mouths? If so, why did you interrupt our nuptials?

BASIL. [*To* MARCELINE.] Did you or did you not promise me that if you weren't provided for within four years, you would give me your hand?

MARCELINE. Under what condition did I promise this?

BASIL. That if you found your lost child, I would adopt him out of kindness to you.

ALL. [*Together.*] He's been found!

BASIL. All right, I'm ready.

ALL. [*Together, pointing to* FIGARO.] There he is!

BASIL. [*Shrinking back.*] Get thee behind me!

BRIDLEGOOSE. That means you g-give up his d-dear mother?

BASIL. What could be worse than to be thought the father of such a fellow?

FIGARO. Why, to be thought your son! You're pulling my leg!

BASIL. [*Pointing to* FIGARO.] The moment this character is somebody in this house, I want everyone to know that I am nobody. [*Exit.*]

BARTHOLO. [*Laughing.*] Hahahaha!

FIGARO. [*Leaping with joy.*] At last, at last, I'll have my bride!

COUNT. [*Aside.*] And I my mistress. [*He rises.*]

BRIDLEGOOSE. [*To* MARCELINE.] With everybody s-satisfied.

COUNT. Let the two marriage contracts

be drawn up. I shall sign them.

ALL. [*Together.*] Bravo!

COUNT. I need time to myself. [*He starts to leave with the others.*]

SUNSTRUCK. [*To* FIGARO.] Now I'm going to set up the fireworks under the elms as I was told.

COUNT. [*Coming back.*] What idiot gave you that order?

FIGARO. What's wrong with it?

COUNT. Why, the Countess is indisposed. How can she see the display from indoors unless it's on the terrace, below her room?

FIGARO. You heard him, Sunstruck? On the terrace.

COUNT. Under the elms, the idea! [*Leaving, aside.*] They were going to set fire to my tête-à-tête.

FIGARO. What considerateness for his wife! [*Starts to leave.*]

MARCELINE. [*Stopping him.*] A word with you, my son. I owe you an apology. Mistaken feeling for you made me unjust to your wife: I thought her in league with the Count, even though Basil had told me she always rejected his advances.

FIGARO. You don't know your son if you think that female whims and wiles can shake him. I challenge the cleverest to upset me.

MARCELINE. It's nice to feel that way, at any rate, because jealousy—

FIGARO. Is but a stupid child of pride, or else it's a madman's disease. I assure you, Mother, on this point I'm a philosopher—unshakable. So if Suzanne ever deceives me, I forgive her in advance, for she will have worked hard and long to do it. [*He turns and sees* FANCHETTE, *who is looking everywhere for someone.*]

FIGARO. So-o, little cousin! Getting an earful?

FANCHETTE. Oh, no! I was brought up to think it's not nice.

FIGARO. True enough, but since it's useful, it's often considered worth the trouble.

FANCHETTE. I was finding out if somebody was here.

FIGARO. So young and so full of guile! You know perfectly well he can't be here.

FANCHETTE. Who's that?

FIGARO. Cherubino.

FANCHETTE. It isn't he I'm after. I know where *he* is. It's cousin Sue.

FIGARO. And what do you want with her?

FANCHETTE. I can tell *you*, because you're my cousin now. It's about a pin I'm supposed to give her.

FIGARO. [*Startled.*] A pin? A pin did you say? And from whom, you little hussy? At your age you're already in the business of—[*He catches himself and goes on gently.*] You're already pretty good at whatever you do, Fanchette; and my pretty cousin is so obliging that—

FANCHETTE. What did I do to make you cross with me? I'm going . . .

FIGARO. Don't. I was only teasing. I'll tell you: that pin of yours is one that my lord told you to give to Suzanne. It's the one that fastened the paper he had in his hand: you see I know what I'm talking about.

FANCHETTE. Why ask me if you know?

FIGARO. [*Fumbling.*] Oh . . . because it's fun to know how his lordship went about sending you on your errand.

FANCHETTE. [*With naïveté.*] Well, he did it almost as you say: "Here, Fanchette," he said, "give back this pin to your beautiful cousin; just tell her it's the seal for the big elms."

FIGARO. "The big—"?

FANCHETTE. "—elms." Oh, yes, and he added: "Be sure no one sees you."

FIGARO. Well, cousin, you must do as you're told and it's lucky no one *has* seen you. Run your pretty errand and don't tell Suzanne a word more than his lordship told you.

FANCHETTE. Why should I say more, cousin? He takes me for a child. [*She goes out, skipping.*]

FIGARO. Well, Mother?

MARCELINE. Well, my son?

FIGARO. [*Choking.*] That cursèd clown! Really some things are too much!

MARCELINE. Some things? What things?

FIGARO. [*Hands on his breast.*] What I've just learned, Mother, weighs on me like lead—here.

MARCELINE. [*Laughing.*] It would seem that your assured countenance of a while ago was only an inflated bag of wind—a pin has made it collapse.

FIGARO. [*Furious.*] But that pin, Mother, that pin was the one he picked up!

MARCELINE. [*Recalling his words.*] "As for jealousy, I am a philosopher—unshakable: if Suzanne deceives me, I forgive her . . ."

FIGARO. Oh, Mother, a man speaks as he feels at the time. Let the coolest judge on the bench plead his own case and see how he explains the law. I understand now why he was so annoyed about the fireworks. As for my darling and her subtlety with pins, she hasn't got where she thinks she is, elms or no elms. It's true my marriage is enough to warrant my anger, but it isn't enough to keep me from dropping one wife and wedding another.

MARCELINE. A splendid conclusion! Let's wreck everything on a mere suspicion. How do you know it's you she's deceiving and not the Count? Have you studied her thoroughly that you condemn her without appeal? Do you know for a fact that she is going under those trees, or what her intentions are, or what she will say and do if she goes there? I thought you had more judgment!

FIGARO. [*Kissing her hand.*] A mother is always right, Mother, and you are right, entirely right! But make allowance, dear Mamma, for natural impulse. One feels better after giving way to it. Now let us weigh before accusing and acting. I know where the assignation is to be. Farewell, Mother. [*Exit.*]

MARCELINE. Farewell. And I too know where it is. Now that I've stopped him, I'd better look after Suzanne— or rather, give her warning. She is such a pretty creature! I must say, when our own interest does not divide us, we women are all inclined to make common cause in defense of our downtrodden sex against this proud, terrifying [*Laughing.*] and somewhat slow-witted masculine sex. [*Exit.*]

Act 5

A stand of elms in the park. Two pavilions, kiosks, or garden temples occupy respectively the right and left middle ground. Behind is a clearing hung with decorations; in front a lawn with seats. The scene is dark.

FANCHETTE. [*Alone and carrying in one hand two small cakes and an orange; in the other, a lighted paper lantern.*] He said the pavilion on the left. It must be this one. But what if my fine fellow doesn't show up? They wouldn't even give me an orange and two cookies, those kitchen people. "But for whom, miss?" "Why, sir, it's for somebody." "We thought as much, miss." Supposing the worst— just because my lord doesn't want to set eyes on him, that's no reason he should starve. All the same, it cost me a big kiss on the cheek. Who knows, maybe he'll pay me back for it in kind. [*She catches sight of* FIGARO, *who comes forward to identify her. She cries out.*] Ah! . . . [*Runs away and enters pavilion at left.*]

FIGARO. [*In a large cloak, alone at first.*] It's Fanchette! [*He scans the others as they arrive and speaks roughly to them.*] Good day, gentlemen, good evening. Are you all here?

BASIL. All those you asked to come.

FIGARO. What time is it, about?

ANTONIO. [*Nose in the air.*] The moon should be up.

BARTHOLO. What black arts are you getting ready for? He looks like a conspirator.

FIGARO. Isn't it for a wedding that you're gathered at the castle?

BRIDLEGOOSE. C-certainly.

ANTONIO. We were going over yonder, in the park, and wait for the signal to start the festivities.

FIGARO. You shan't go a step farther. It's here, under the elms, that we're going to celebrate the faithful bride I am marrying and the faithful lord who has reassigned her to himself.

BASIL. [*Recalling the day's events.*]Ah, yes. I know all about it. Let's remove ourselves, if you please. It's a matter of a rendezvous. I'll tell you about it later.

BRIDLEGOOSE. [*To* FIGARO.] We'll c-come back.

FIGARO. When you hear me call, don't fail to appear. You can curse me if I don't provide you with a fine spectacle.

BARTHOLO. Remember that a wise man does not start a quarrel with the great and powerful.

FIGARO. I'll remember.

BARTHOLO. They begin with a score of forty-love against us, thanks to their rank.

FIGARO. To say nothing of their capacity for hard work, which you're forgetting. But remember also that once a man is known to be scared, he's at the mercy of every scoundrel.

BARTHOLO. Well said.

FIGARO. And among my names is Greenleaf, from my mother's side.

BARTHOLO. He is full of the devil.

BRIDLEGOOSE. He y-y-is.

BASIL. [*Aside.*] The Count and Suzanne planned this without me—I'm rather glad of this ambush.

FIGARO. [*To the* FOOTMEN.] You fellows do as I told you—light up all around here, or in the name of Death, which I'd like to throttle, when I grab the arm of one of you—[*He grabs* SUNSTRUCK.]

SUNSTRUCK. [*Goes off crying.*] Ah, oh, ah, perish the brute!

BASIL. [*Leaving.*] God give you joy, young newlywed!

FIGARO. [*Pacing up and down alone in the dark and speaking in somber tones.*] Oh, woman, woman, woman! weak and deceitful creature! No animal on earth can go against instinct; is it yours to deceive? After refusing me stubbornly when I begged her in front of her mistress—in the very instant of plighting her troth to me, in the middle of the ceremony—He was laughing as he read, the traitor! And I, like a poor booby . . . No, my lord Count, you shan't have her, you shan't! Because you are a great lord you think you are a great genius. Nobility, wealth, honors, emoluments—it all makes a man so proud! What have you done to earn so many advantages? You took the trouble to be born, nothing more. Apart from that, you're a rather common type. Whereas I—by God!—lost in the nameless crowd, I had to exert more strategy and skill merely to survive than has been spent for a hundred years in governing the Spanish Empire. . . . And you want to tangle with me! Someone's coming—it is she—no, it's nobody. The night is dark as pitch and here am I plying the silly trade of husband, even though I'm only half of one. [*He sits on a bench.*] Can anything be stranger than my career? The son of God knows whom, stolen by bandits and reared in their ways, I become disgusted and try to lead an honest life. Everywhere I am repulsed. I learn chemistry, pharmacy, surgery, yet the whole influence of a great lord hardly succeeds in securing me the practice of a veterinary. Tired of pestering sick animals, hoping in fact to do just the opposite, I go headlong for the stage. Far better have hung a millstone around my neck! I write a play satirizing life in the harem: being a Spanish author I thought I could make fun of Mohammed without fear. At once, an emissary from God knows where complains that my verses offend the Sublime Porte, Persia, part of the Indian peninsula, all of Egypt, the kingdoms of Barca, Tripoli, Tunis, Algiers, and Morocco—and there goes my play up the spout, to please the Mohammedan princes, not one of whom (I believe) can read, and all of whom brand us on the shoulder and call us Christian dogs. Whoever fails to degrade the mind avenges himself by insulting it. My cheeks were growing hollow, my lodging was unpaid, I could see from afar the threatening bailiff with a pen stuck in his wig, so I shudder and exert myself afresh. A public debate starts up about the nature of wealth, and since one needn't own something in order to argue about it, being in fact penniless, I write on the value of money and interest. Immediately, I find myself inside a coach looking at the drawbridge of a prison and leaving hope and freedom behind. [*He gets up.*] How I should like to hold in the hollow of my hand one of these potentates who last four days in office and are so ready to ordain punishments! When a healthy fall from grace had sobered his pride, I'd let him know that printed nonsense is dangerous only in countries where its free circulation is hampered; that without the right to criticize, praise and approval are worthless, and that only petty men fear petty writings. [*Sits down.*] One day, tired of feeding an obscure guest, they threw me out into the street, and since a man must eat even when out of jail, I sharpen my quill once more and ask people what is in the news. I am told that during my retreat at public expense, free trade and a free press have been established in Madrid, so that, provided I do not write about the government, or about religion, or politics, or morals, or those in power, or public bodies, or the Opera, or the other state theaters, or about anybody who is active in anything, I can print whatever I want with perfect freedom under the supervision of two or three censors. To take advantage of such sweet liberty, I let it be known that I am starting a periodical, and to make sure that I am not treading on anybody's heels, I call it *The Useless Journal.* Mercy! No sooner done than I see a thousand poor devils of subsidized hacks in arms against me. I am put down and once again unemployed. Despair nearly had me by the throat when someone thought of me for a vacant place. Unfortunately I was qualified for it. They needed an accountant and put in a dancer. The only way out was to turn thief. I set up as croupier of a gambling den. Ah, then, my dears, I was in the swim! I dine out and people known as respectable courteously open their houses to me, keeping for themselves only three-quarters of the take. I could have recouped all my losses—I had even begun to understand that to grow rich, know-how is better than knowledge, but since everyone around me was robbing the till while requiring that I stay honest, I went under for the third time. I'd had enough and meant to break with the world—five fathoms of water would suffice, and nearly did, when my guardian angel recalled me to my original trade. I take up my razors and lancet and leave glory to the fools who feed on its aroma. With it also, I leave behind dishonor, which is too heavy a load for a pedestrian. Hiking from town to town, shaving as I go, I live at last a life without care. But a great lord passing through Seville recognizes me. I get him married off, and as a reward for my helping him secure a wife, he now wants to intercept mine. Thereupon, storms and intrigues. I am on the edge of an abyss, nearly wedded to my own mother, when lo! my relatives materialize, Indian file. [*He gets up and grows vehement.*] Follows a regular scrimmage—"It's he, it's you, it's I. No, it isn't, not I." Well, who then? [*He falls back into the seat.*] What an incredible series of events! How did it happen to me? Why these things and not others? Who drew them down on my head? Forcibly set on the road of life, not knowing where it leads, and bound to leave it against my will, I've tried to keep it as rosy as my natural cheerfulness permits. Here again I say *my* cheerfulness without knowing if it belongs to me any more than those other things; nor do I know who this *I* may be with which I am so concerned—it's first a shapeless collection of unknown parts, then a helpless puny thing, then a lively little animal, then a young man thirsting for pleasure, with a full capacity to enjoy and ready to use any shifts to live—master here and valet there, at the whim of fortune; ambitious from vanity, industrious from need—and lazy . . . with delight! An orator in tight spots, a poet for relaxation, a musician from time to time, a lover in hot fits: I have seen everything, done everything, worn out everything. At last my illusion is shattered and I'm now

wholly disabused . . . blasé. . . . Oh, Suzy! Suzy! my Suzy, what torments you are putting me through! I hear footsteps . . . someone's coming . . . This is the crisis. [*He retires into the downstage wing on his right. Enter the* COUNTESS *dressed as* SUZANNE, SUZANNE *dressed as the* COUNTESS, *and* MARCELINE.]

SUZANNE. [*Speaking low to the* COUNTESS.] Yes, Marceline said Figaro would be here.

MARCELINE. And so he is; be quiet.

SUZANNE. I see; the one's eavesdropping, the other's coming to fetch me—let the show begin.

MARCELINE. I don't want to miss a word; I'm going to hide in the pavilion. [*Enters the same pavilion as* FANCHETTE.]

COUNTESS. [*Aloud.*] You're trembling, madam: are you cold?

SUZANNE. [*Aloud.*] The evening is damp, I am going in.

COUNTESS. [*Aloud.*] If my lady does not need me, I should like to take the air while under the trees.

SUZANNE. —[*Aloud.*] Take the air! Catch your death, you mean.

COUNTESS. I'm used to it.

FIGARO. [*Aside.*] Her death, my eye! [SUZANNE *retreats to a spot near the wings, on the opposite side from* FIGARO.]

CHERUBINO. [*Dressed as an officer, comes on singing the words of his song.*] "Tra-la-la-la-la, / A godmother I had, / Whom always I adored!"

COUNTESS. [*Aside.*] The little page!

CHERUBINO. People are walking about. I must take to my refuge, where Fanchette is—oh, it's a woman!

COUNTESS. Oh, mercy!

CHERUBINO. [*Stooping and peering.*] Am I mistaken? That hat I see with feathers outlined against the sky looks to me like Suzy.

COUNTESS. Oh, if the Count were to appear! [*The* COUNT *enters from the back.*]

CHERUBINO. [*Goes up to* COUNTESS *and takes her hand; she pulls away.*] I'm right, it's that adorable girl named Sue! How could I mistake this soft hand, or that slight trembling . . . or the beating of my own heart! [*He tries to put the* COUNTESS' *hand against his heart.*]

COUNTESS. [*Whispering.*] Go away!

CHERUBINO. Could it be that you took pity on my lot and came here when I have been hiding since afternoon?

COUNTESS. Figaro is coming.

COUNT. [*Stepping forward, aside.*] Isn't that Suzanne I see?

CHERUBINO. [*To* COUNTESS.] I'm not afraid of Figaro and it's not him you're waiting for.

COUNTESS. Who then?

COUNT. [*Aside.*] Somebody is with her.

CHERUBINO. It's my lord, hussy, who asked you out here this morning when I hid behind the chair.

COUNT. [*Aside, furious.*] It's that infernal page again!

FIGARO. [*Aside.*] And they say it isn't nice to eavesdrop!

SUZANNE. [*Aside.*] The little chatterbox!

COUNTESS. [*To* CHERUBINO.] Do me the kindness to go away.

CHERUBINO. Not without a reward for my compliance.

COUNTESS. [*Frightened.*] You claim—?

CHERUBINO. [*With heat.*] Twenty kisses on your account first; then a hundred for your fair mistress.

COUNTESS. You would not dare!

CHERUBINO. Yes, I would! You're taking her place with my lord, I take this with you. The one who gets left is Figaro.

FIGARO. [*Aside.*] The rapscallion!

SUZANNE. [*Aside.*] Brash as a little page!

[CHERUBINO *tries to kiss the* COUNTESS; *the* COUNT *comes between them and receives the kiss.*]

COUNTESS. [*Retreating.*] Dear God!

FIGARO. [*Aside, hearing the sound of the kiss.*]It's a pretty baggage I'm marrying! [*Listens intently.*]

CHERUBINO. [*Feeling the* COUNT'*s clothes; aside.*] It's my lord! [*He flees into the pavilion where* FANCHETTE *and* MARCELINE *are hiding.*]

FIGARO. [*Approaching.*] I'm going to—

COUNT. [*Thinking the* PAGE *still there.*] Since you don't repeat the kiss . . . [*Lashes out with his hand.*]

FIGARO. [*Coming within range, gets the slap.*] Ow!

COUNT. That's one paid off, anyhow.

FIGARO. [*Retreating and rubbing his cheek.*] This eavesdropping business isn't all pure gain.

SUZANNE. [*Laughing.*] Hahahaha!

COUNT. [*To* COUNTESS, *whom he mistakes for* SUZANNE.] That page is beyond belief—he gets slapped full in the face and goes off laughing.

FIGARO. [*Aside.*] He should be grieving for me!

COUNT. And he's intolerable: I can't take a step—But let's forget the puzzle or it will spoil the delight I feel in finding you here.

COUNTESS. [*Imitating* SUZANNE'*s voice.*] Were you expecting me?

COUNT. What do you think, after your clever note? [*He takes her hand.*] You're trembling.

COUNTESS. I've been frightened.

COUNT. It wasn't to deprive you of a kiss that I took his. [*Kisses her on the forehead.*]

COUNTESS. Such liberties!

FIGARO. [*Aside.*] The trollop!

SUZANNE. [*Aside.*] The darling!

COUNT. [*Takes* COUNTESS' *hand.*] How fine and soft your skin is! Your hand is more lovely than the Countess's.

COUNTESS. [*Aside.*] What preconception will do!

COUNT. And this little arm, how firm and round . . . these pretty fingers full of grace and mischief!

COUNTESS. [*Speaking like* SUZANNE.] And what of love. . . ?

COUNT. Love . . . is the fiction of the heart. Its history is pleasure, and hence you find me at your feet.

COUNTESS. You do not love her any more?

COUNT. I love her very much, but three years make marriage so respectable.

COUNTESS. What did you want from her?

COUNT. [*Caressing her.*] What I find in you, my sweet.

COUNTESS. But tell me what . . .

COUNT. I don't know . . . less sameness, perhaps; more spice in your manner—something, I don't know what, which makes for charm, it's because you deny me sometimes, I don't know. Our wives think they can't do better than to love us. They take this for granted and love us and love us—if they love us—and they are so compliant and constant, always and without stint, that suddenly one day one finds satiety where one looked for happiness.

COUNTESS. [*Aside.*] What a lesson to me!

COUNT. To tell the truth, Suzy, I have often thought that when we seek elsewhere the pleasure we miss in them, it is because they make no effort to sustain our interest, to renew their attractions in love, to resurrect (so to speak) the delight of possession by affording that of variety.

COUNTESS. [*Vexed.*] And so theirs is the whole responsibility?

COUNT. [*Laughing.*] And the man has none, you mean? Well, can we change nature? Our task is to obtain . . .

COUNTESS. Yes, and theirs—?

COUNT. Is to . . . retain . . . That's generally overlooked.

COUNTESS. Not by me.

COUNT. Nor me.

FIGARO. [*Aside.*] Nor me.

SUZANNE. [*Aside.*] Nor me.

COUNT. [*Taking* COUNTESS' *hand again.*] There's an echo hereabouts; let's lower our voices. You for one needn't worry about holding a man! Love has fashioned you so fair and sprightly. Add a touch of caprice and you would be the most titillating mistress. [*Kissing her forehead.*] My Suzy, a Castilian has nothing but his word of honor. I give you the ransom I promised, to redeem that old claim I no longer have upon the sweet concession you are about to make me.

COUNTESS. [*Curtsying.*] Your Suzanne accepts everything.

FIGARO. [*Aside.*] They don't exist more wanton than that.

SUZANNE. [*Aside.*] It means good money in our pockets.

COUNT. [*Aside.*] She's mercenary—all the better!

COUNTESS. [*Turning toward the back.*] I see torches.

COUNT. That's for your wedding. Let's go into the pavilion until they're by.

COUNTESS. Without a light?

COUNT. [*Pulling her gently.*] Why a light? We don't intend to read.

FIGARO. [*Aside.*] She's going in, the drab! I thought so. [*He steps forward.*]

COUNT. [*Turning around, in a voice of command.*] Who's wandering around there?

FIGARO. [*Angry.*] Nobody's wandering; I'm coming on purpose!

COUNT. [*To* COUNTESS.] It's Figaro. [*He runs away.*]

COUNTESS. I'll follow you. [*She enters the pavilion on the right while the* COUNT *hides in the wood at the back.*]

FIGARO. [*Trying to find them both.*] I don't hear anything. They must have gone in. So here we are. [*In a changed voice.*] Oh, you clumsy husbands who hire spies and toy with suspicion for months without confirming it, why not take your cue from me? I shadow my wife from the beginning, the first day. I listen secretly, and in a twinkling I know everything: it's enchanting—no doubts left, all is known. [*Pacing briskly.*] Lucky that it doesn't bother me and that I'm no longer upset by her treachery. I've got them at last.

SUZANNE. [*Creeping up behind him; aside.*] You're going to pay for those fine suspicions! [*Imitating the* COUNTESS.] Who goes there?

FIGARO. [*Wildly.*] "Who goes there?" A man who thinks the plague should have taken—

SUZANNE. Why, it's Figaro!

FIGARO. [*Quickly.*] My lady Countess!

SUZANNE. Speak low!

FIGARO. [*Quickly.*] Ah, madam, how fortunate that you should have come. Where do you think my lord may be?

SUZANNE. What does an ungrateful husband matter to me? Tell me rather—

FIGARO. [*Speaking still more rapidly.*] And Suzanne, my bride, where do you imagine she might be?

SUZANNE. *Please* lower your voice!

FIGARO. Suzanne, my Suzy whom everybody thought so virtuous, who acted so modest! Well, they're locked up in there. I'm going to call out.

SUZANNE. [*Putting her hand on his mouth and forgetting to disguise her voice.*] Don't call out!

FIGARO. [*Aside.*] *This* is Suzy! Damn!

SUZANNE. [*Imitating the* COUNTESS.] You seem upset.

FIGARO. [*Aside.*] The minx! Trying to catch me!

SUZANNE. We must avenge ourselves, Figaro.

FIGARO. Do you feel a pressing need of it?

SUZANNE. Am I not a woman? Men, though, have better means.

FIGARO. [*Confiding.*] Madam, your presence is as necessary as mine. And women's means . . . are the best.

SUZANNE. [*Aside.*] I'd like to slap the lout!

FIGARO. [*Aside.*] Wouldn't it be fun if even before we're married . . .

SUZANNE. But what kind of revenge is it that lacks the spice of love?

FIGARO. If you see no signs of love, you may be sure I am only restrained by deference.

SUZANNE. [*Nettled.*] I can't tell whether you mean that honestly, but you certainly don't say it gracefully.

FIGARO. [*With comical fervor, kneeling.*] Oh, madam, I worship you. But consider the time, the place, the circumstance, and let your anger supply the fire which my entreaty lacks.

SUZANNE. [*Aside.*] My hand is itching.

FIGARO. [*Aside.*] My heart is beating.

SUZANNE. But sir, have you reflected?

FIGARO. Oh, yes, madam, yes indeed, I have reflected.

SUZANNE. In anger and in love—

FIGARO. Delay is fatal, I know. Your hand, madam.

SUZANNE. [*In her own voice and slapping him.*] Here it is.

FIGARO. Lucifer, what a fist!

SUZANNE. What fist—is this the one? [*Slaps him again.*]

FIGARO. Now, what the devil? Are you playing windmill?

SUZANNE. [*Slapping him with each phrase.*] "Ah, Lucifer, Suzanne!" Take *that* for your suspicion, and *that* for your revenge, and *that* for your schemes, and your insults, and your double-dealing. Then you can say as you did this morning! "That's love for you!"

FIGARO. [*Laughing as he gets up.*] By all the saints, it is!—pure love! What happiness, what bliss! Thrice-blessed Figaro. Hit me, beloved, again and again. Only, when you're through painting me black and blue, Suzy, look kindly upon the luckiest man

ever beaten by a woman.

SUZANNE. The luckiest, you scoundrel? As if you weren't busy seducing the Countess with your pretty turns of phrase, to the point where I was forgetting myself and yielding in her place!

FIGARO. As if I had mistaken the sound of your lovely voice!

SUZANNE. [*Laughing.*] You recognized me, did you? I'll take my toll for that too.

FIGARO. Just like a woman to beat a body and bear a grudge besides. But tell me by what good fortune I find you here when I thought you there. And these clothes, which fooled me at first, and now prove you innocent . . .

SUZANNE. *You* are the innocent, to walk into a trap laid for someone else. Is it our fault if in trying to catch a fox we catch two?

FIGARO. Who's catching the other?

SUZANNE. His wife.

FIGARO. His wife?

SUZANNE. His wife.

FIGARO. [*Wildly.*] Ah, Figaro, go hang yourself on the nearest tree. You never guessed! His wife! Oh, clever, clever, clever women. So all those resounding kisses . . .

SUZANNE. Fell on my lady.

FIGARO. And the one from the page?

SUZANNE. On my lord.

FIGARO. And this morning, behind the chair?

SUZANNE. On nobody.

FIGARO. Are you sure?

SUZANNE. [*Laughing.*] Figaro! You know how fists fly about at dusk!

FIGARO. [*Seizes her hand and kisses it.*] Yours are jewels to me. But the Count's in my face was fair enough.

SUZANNE. Come, proud one, abase yourself.

FIGARO. [*Acting as he speaks.*] Fair enough: on my knees, bowed low, prone and flat on the ground.

SUZANNE. [*Laughing.*] The poor Count! What trouble he's gone to . . .

FIGARO. [*Rising and kneeling.*] . . . to seduce his wife.

COUNT. [*Entering from the back and going straight to the pavilion on the right; aside.*] I can't find her in the wood;

perhaps she's stepped in here.

SUZANNE. [*Whispering to* FIGARO.] There he goes.

COUNT. [*At the open door of the pavilion.*] Suzanne, are you there?

FIGARO. [*Low.*] He's looking for her. I thought . . .

SUZANNE. [*Low.*] He never recognized her.

FIGARO. Let's finish him off, shall we? [*Kisses her hand noisily.*]

COUNT. [*Turning around.*] A man kneeling before the Countess . . . And I'm unarmed. [*He comes forward.*]

FIGARO. [*Rising and disguising his voice.*] Forgive me, madam, if I did not realize that this meeting place would be in the path of the festivities.

COUNT. [*Aside.*] That's the man of this morning in the dressing room. [*He strikes his forehead.*]

FIGARO. But such a silly interference shan't postpone our pleasure.

COUNT. [*Aside.*] Death and damnation!

FIGARO. [*Leading* SUZANNE *to the pavilion; aside.*] He's cursing. [*Aloud.*] Let us hasten, madam, and repair the misfortune we suffered earlier when I jumped out of the window.

COUNT. [*Aside.*] Now I see it all!

SUZANNE. [*Near the pavilion on the left.*] Before we go in, make sure nobody is following. [*He kisses her forehead.*]

COUNT. [*Shouting.*] Revenge! [SUZANNE *flees into the pavilion where* MARCELINE, FANCHETTE, *and* CHERUBINO *already are. The* COUNT *seizes* FIGARO *by the arm.*]

FIGARO. [*Pretending great fright.*] It's the master!

COUNT. Ah, villain, it's you! Ho, somebody, come at once! [*Enter* PETER, *booted and spurred.*]

PETER. So there you are, my lord, at last.

COUNT. Good! Are you alone, Peter?

PETER. Back from Seville, hell for leather.

COUNT. Come close to me and shout very loud.

PETER. [*At the top of his lungs.*] No more page in Seville than on the back of my hand—and that's a fact!

COUNT. [*Pushing him away.*] Stupid oaf!

PETER. Your lordship said I must shout aloud.

COUNT. [*Holding* FIGARO.] It was to call for help. Ho, there, somebody! Whoever hears me, come quick!

PETER. Figaro's here with me: what are you afraid of? [*Enter* BRIDLEGOOSE, BARTHOLO, BASIL, ANTONIO, *and* SUNSTRUCK, *followed by the wedding party carrying torches.*]

BARTHOLO. [*To* FIGARO.] You see: we came as soon as we heard you.

COUNT. [*Pointing to the pavilion on the left.*] Peter, guard that door. [PETER *goes.*]

BASIL. [*Low, to* FIGARO.] You caught him with Suzanne?

COUNT. [*Pointing to* FIGARO.] You, vassals, surround this man and answer for him with your lives.

BASIL. Oh, oh!

COUNT. [*Angry.*] Be quiet. [*To* FIGARO, *freezingly.*] Sir Knight, will you answer a few questions?

FIGARO. [*Coolly.*] Who indeed could give me leave not to? You have command of everybody here except yourself.

COUNT. [*Mastering his fury.*] Except myself?

ANTONIO. That's the way we talk!

COUNT. [*Giving way to his anger.*] If anything could make me angrier, it's the air of calmness he puts on.

FIGARO. Are we like soldiers, killing and being killed for reasons they know nothing of? For my part, I always like to know what I'm angry about.

COUNT. [*Beside himself.*] Murder! [*Controlling himself.*] Man of gentle birth who pretend not to know my reasons, would you at least do us the favor of telling us what lady you have brought into this pavilion?

FIGARO. [*Mischievously pointing to the other.*] Into that one?

COUNT. [*Quickly.*] Into this.

FIGARO. [*Coldly.*] That's different. It's a young lady who honors me with her favors.

BASIL. [*Surprised.*] Oh?

COUNT. [*Quickly.*] You heard him, gentlemen?

BARTHOLO. [*Surprised.*] We heard him.

COUNT. And this young person is otherwise unattached?

FIGARO. [*Coldly.*] I know that a great lord paid her some attention for a while. But whether it be that he neglected her or that she likes me better, I am the one preferred.

COUNT. [*Quickly.*] The one pref—[*Restraining himself.*] At least he is candid. What he has just admitted, I myself have seen and heard, gentlemen, from the mouth of his accomplice. I give you my word on it.

BRIDLEGOOSE. [*Petrified.*] His accomplice!

COUNT. [*In a fury.*] Now, when dishonor is public, so must be the revenge! [*He goes into the pavilion.*]

ANTONIO. He's right.

BRIDLEGOOSE. [*To* FIGARO.] Who took who-o-o's wife?

FIGARO. [*Laughing.*] No one had that special satisfaction.

COUNT. [*Speaking from inside the pavilion and tugging at someone not yet identifiable.*] It is no use, madam, the hour has struck and you are doomed. [*He comes out and turns to the rest without looking.*] How fortunate that there lives no pledge of our hateful union—!

FIGARO. [*Calling out.*] Cherubino!

COUNT. The page!

BASIL. Haha!

COUNT. Always the damned page! What were you doing in that room?

CHERUBINO. [*Shyly.*] I was hiding, as you ordered me to do.

PETER. What use was it to nearly kill a horse!

COUNT. Go in there, Antonio, and bring before her judge the criminal who has dishonored me.

BRIDLEGOOSE. Is it my lady that you are l-looking for?

ANTONIO. 'Tis Providence, by gum, for your carryings-on all over the countryside.

COUNT. [*Furious.*] Get in there! [ANTONIO *goes in.*]

COUNT. You shall see, gentlemen, that the page was not alone.

CHERUBINO. [*Shyly.*] It would have been hard on me if a gentle soul had not sweetened the bitter pill.

ANTONIO. [*Pulling out someone not recognizable at first.*] Come, my lady, don't make me coax you, everybody knows you went in.

FIGARO. [*Calling out.*] My little cousin!

BASIL. Haha!

COUNT. Fanchette!

ANTONIO. [*Turns around.*] By jiminy 'twas right smart, my lord, to pick on me to show the company it's my daughter caused all the randan, now wasn't it?

COUNT. [*Indignant.*] Who could suppose she was in there? [*He tries to go in.*]

BARTHOLO. [*Interposing.*] Allow me, my lord. All this is far too upsetting for you; but perhaps I can deal with it in cold blood. [*He goes in.*]

BRIDLEGOOSE. It's certainly too confusing for me.

BARTHOLO. [*Speaking from inside and coming out.*] Do not be afraid, madam, no one will hurt you, I promise you. [*He turns around and cries out.*] Marceline!

BASIL. Haha!

FIGARO. [*Laughing.*] A madhouse! My mother in it too!

ANTONIO. The jades are playing who can be the worst.

COUNT. [*Outraged.*] What is that to me? It's the Countess . . . [SUZANNE *comes out, her face behind a fan.*] Ah, there she is at last, gentlemen. [*He takes her violently by the arm.*] What does such an odious woman deserve, gentlemen—? [SUZANNE *falls on her knees, bowing her head.*]

COUNT. Never, never! [FIGARO *kneels next to her.*]

COUNT. [*Louder.*] Never! [MARCELINE *kneels beside the others.*]

COUNT. [*Still louder.*] Never, never! [*They all kneel.*]

COUNT. [*Beside himself.*] Never, not if there were a hundred of you!

COUNTESS. [*Coming out of the other pavilion.*] At least, I can make one more. [*She kneels.*]

COUNT. [*Looking alternately at* SUZANNE *and the* COUNTESS.] What do I see?

BRIDLEGOOSE. [*Laughing.*] What d'you kn-n-know, it's my lady!

COUNT. [*Trying to lift her up.*] It was you, Countess? [*In a supplicating tone.*] Only the most generous forgiveness. . .

COUNTESS. [*Laughing.*] In my place, you would say "Never, never!" whereas I, for the third time today, forgive you unconditionally. [*She gets up.*]

SUZANNE. [*Getting up.*] And so do I.

MARCELINE. [*Getting up.*] And I.

FIGARO. [*Getting up.*] And I. There's an echo hereabouts. [*All get up.*]

COUNT. An echo! I tried to outsmart them and they fooled me like a child.

COUNTESS. [*Laughing.*] Don't act as if you were sorry, my lord.

FIGARO. [*Brushing off his knees with his hat.*] A day like today is ideal training for an ambassador.

COUNT. [*To* SUZANNE.] That note sealed with a pin? . . .

SUZANNE. Madam dictated it.

COUNT. The answer is overdue. [*He kisses the* COUNTESS's *hand.*]

COUNTESS. Each will regain his own. [*She gives the purse to* FIGARO *and the diamond to* SUZANNE.]

SUZANNE. [*To* FIGARO.] Still another dowry!

FIGARO. [*Striking the purse.*] That makes three. But this one took some contriving.

SUZANNE. Like our marriage.

SUNSTRUCK. What about the bride's garter? Can I have it?

COUNTESS. [*Taking out the ribbon from her bosom.*] The garter? It was in her clothes. Here you are. [*She throws the ribbon; the boys try to scramble for it.*]

CHERUBINO. [*Swiftly picking it up.*] Try and get it!

COUNT. [*Laughing.*] Since you're so touchy a gentleman, what made you laugh so hard when I boxed your ear?

CHERUBINO. [*Taking a step backward and half drawing his sword.*] My ear, colonel?

FIGARO. [*Comically angry.*] He got it on my cheek, as always happens when lords mete out justice.

COUNT. [*Laughing.*] On your cheek, ha, ha, ha, isn't that good, what do you say, dear Countess?

COUNTESS. [*Abstracted and returning to reality.*] Indeed, dear Count, I do—for life, unswervingly: I swear it.

COUNT. [*Slapping* BRIDLEGOOSE *on the shoulder.*] And you, Bridlegoose, let us have your opinion.

BRIDLEGOOSE. On what has taken p-place, my lord? Well, my opinion is that I d-don't know what to think, and that's my op-pinion.

ALL. [*Together*] A very sound judgment!

FIGARO. I was poor and despised. When I showed a little cleverness, hatred dogged me. Now with a pretty girl and some money . . .

BARTHOLO. [*Laughing.*] Everybody will crowd around you!

FIGARO. Do you think so?

BARTHOLO. I know my kind.

FIGARO. [*Bowing to the spectators.*] Aside from my wife and my goods, you are welcome to all I have.

[*The orchestra plays the introduction to the entertainment.*]

BASIL

Triple dowry, handsome wife—
To a husband, what largesse!
'Gainst a lord or beardless page
Only fools feel jealous rage.
Let the Latin proverb bless
Man's incalculable life:

FIGARO. Don't I know that proverb! [*Sings.*] "Happy those of noble birth!"

BASIL. No you *don't* know it [*Sings.*] "Happy those who own the earth!"

SUZANNE.

Let a man his wife betray
He is boastful, all are gay;
Let his wife indulge her whim
She is punished, unlike him.
If you ask why this is so,
'Tis the stronger's wicked law.

MARCELINE.

Every man his mother knows,
Her who gives sweet life to him.
But beyond this all is dim—
How explain love's secret lure?

FIGARO. [*Breaking in.*]

Secret, though the end disclose
That the offspring of a boor
May turn out a gentleman.

FIGARO.

By the accident of birth,
One is shepherd, t'other king.
Chance made lord and underling,
Only genius threads the maze:
Twenty kings are fed on praise
Who in death are common earth,
While Voltaire immortal stays.

CHERUBINO.

Flighty sex we all adore,
You who torment all our days,
Everyone complains of you;
In the end we kneel and sue.
To the pit thus players do:
Such a one professes scorn
Who would crawl to earn your bays.

FIGARO.

Jack McJohn, the jealous lout,
Hoped to have both wife and peace;
Hired a dog to roam about
In the garden, fierce and free;
Barks as claimed in guaranty:
All are bitten by the beast,
Save the lover from whom leased.

COUNTESS.

There's a wife who's proudly prude
Though she loves her husband not;
There's another, nearly lewd,
Swears she loveth none but he;
Now the worthiest is she,
Never swearing this or that,
Who but strives for honesty.

COUNT.

Any woman far from Court
Who believes in duty strict
In romance falls somewhat short.
I prefer the derelict:
Like a piece of currency,
Stamped with one man's effigy,
She can serve the needs of all.

SUZANNE.

If there should a moral lurk
In this mad yet cheerful work,
For the sake of gaiety,
Pray accept it as a whole.
Thus does Nature, sensibly,
Using pleasures we pursue,
Lead us gently to her goal.

BRIDLEGOOSE.

Now dear sirs, the c-comic art,
Which you shortly mean to j-judge,
Apes the life of all of you
Sitting there and taking part.

When annoyed you bear a g-grudge
But although you grumble l-long,
All our d-doings end in song.

1. This supposed right to enjoy the bride on the wedding night of any vassal is without foundation in law or history, but was widely believed by the anti-medieval writers.

2. The play contains several allusions to the horns of the cuckold, expressed by references to his forehead.

3. An allusion to the events of *The Barber of Seville,* in which Figaro helped the Count to marry Rosine, the ward of Bartholo, who had himself planned to marry her. Rosine is now Countess Almaviva.

4. A line from Voltaire's *Nanine.*

5. This remark refers to Marceline, not to Fanchette.

6. She means Figaro.

7. As in Beaumarchais, the verses do not everywhere fit the tune accurately. But his ballad, being an early (though feeble) attempt to imitate folk poetry, deserves to be translated as closely as possible.

8. The implied answer is: "Nothing." The allusion is to the plot for freeing Rosine in *The Barber of Seville.*

9. *J'aime mieux ma mie, o gué,* a song of the time of Henry IV which is quoted in Moliére's *Misanthrope.*

10. The don's first name is an allusion to the judge whom Beaumarchais fought and satirized in the course of his protracted lawsuit. Bridlegoose is from Rabelais, though Beaumarchais modestly changed the name to "Bridlegosling" to suggest his descent.

11. At this point occurs a declamatory passage of about two pages on society's unjust treatment of women. It was omitted in the original production and has not been played since, although Beaumarchais printed it in his Preface.

12. An allusion to Figaro's successful swindle of Bartholo in *The Barber of Seville.*

13. Accent on the second syllable, as in Mamma later.

14. In the original Beaumarchais refers to the sheep in Rabelais which Panurge induced to jump overboard by throwing over the first one.

15. Presumed to be an old Spanish dance, but known to us only through a theme in ¾ time called Follia in Corelli's Solos, op. 5, and used also by Vivaldi and others. *Folies* here does not imply folly but foliape, as in *Folies Bergère.*